D1124532

NEGRO ORATORS
AND
THEIR ORATIONS

BY

CARTER G. WOODSON, Ph.D.

EDITOR OF THE JOURNAL OF NEGRO HISTORY, AUTHOR OF A CENTURY OF NEGRO MIGRATION, THE EDUCATION OF THE NEGRO PRIOR TO 1861, THE HISTORY OF THE NEGRO CHURCH, THE NEGRO IN OUR HISTORY, FREE NEGRO HEADS OF FAMILIES OF THE UNITED STATES IN 1830, AND THE MIND OF THE NEGRO AS REFLECTED IN LETTERS WRITTEN DURING THE CRISIS, 1800-1860

NEW YORK / RUSSELL & RUSSELL

FIRST PUBLISHED IN 1925 BY THE ASSOCIATION
FOR THE STUDY OF NEGRO LIFE AND HISTORY
REISSUED, 1969, BY RUSSELL & RUSSELL
A DIVISION OF ATHENEUM PUBLISHERS, INC.
BY ARRANGEMENT WITH THE ASSOCIATION FOR THE STUDY
OF NEGRO LIFE AND HISTORY, INC.
L. C. CATALOG CARD NO: 69-14223
PRINTED IN THE UNITED STATES OF AMERICA

To

THE CHERISHED MEMORY OF

MY SISTER

SUSIE WOODSON

CONTENTS

FOREWORD

These orations were to be edited by another writer, but because of his many duties he had to abandon the task after having collected a number of the important discourses. The original plan was for a much smaller work than this, consisting of a few select orations of literary worth. In the hands of the new editor, however, the plan was changed so as to include orations of all sorts, in fact, practically all of the extant speeches of consequence delivered by Negroes of the United States.

A short sketch of the orator appears with his oration and the occasion of the delivery is also given. The source of the oration as originally recorded is accounted for in the introductory paragraph, the footnote, or in the title of the address.

In reprinting these orations the editor has endeavored to present them here as nearly as possible in their original form. No effort has been made to improve the English. Published in this form, then, these orations will be of value not only to persons studying the development of the Negro in his use of a modern idiom but also in the study of the history of the race. It is in this spirit that these messages are again given to the public.

C. G. Woodson.

Washington, D. C.
September, 1925.

NEGRO ORATORS AND THEIR ORATIONS

CHAPTER I

INTRODUCTION

Oratory has always been fascinating to the majority of men. It is somewhat so today in spite of its declining influence. Doubtless for this reason Tacitus called it the master of arts. Beecher, similarly impressed with its worth, said that oratory is "the consecration of the whole man to the noblest purpose to which one can address himself—the education and inspiration of his fellowmen."

In definitely depicting oral expression writers have been equally as laudatory. Pascal considered eloquence the painting of thoughts. "Eloquence," says Colton, "is the language of nature and cannot be learned in the schools." Emerson styled it "the power to translate a truth into language." Having in mind polished speech, Bryant defined eloquence as the poetry of prose.

Oratory in the broad sense requires no other equipment than fluency of speech and self-confidence. This gift, according to La Bruyère, may be exhibited in conversations and in all kinds of writing. "It is rarely found when looked for," says this author, "and sometimes is discovered where it is least expected." For ages past, therefore, it has been considered a natural gift known among even the most uncivilized people. One does not have to be educated then to become an orator, for in most cases delivery counts more than the information given. As Lord Rosebery has said, "few speeches which have produced an electrical effect on an audience can bear the colorless photography of a printed record."

The importance of delivery has often been emphasized as the essential in oratory. When Demosthenes was asked what is the first part of oratory, he answered, "Action," and what is the second part, he replied, "Action," and what is the third part, he still answered, "Action." From Coriolanus we learn also that eloquence is action. Pliny, the Younger, said: "We are much more affected by the words which we hear, for though what you read in books may be more pointed, yet there is something in the voice, the look, the carriage, and even the gesture of the speaker, that makes a deeper impression on the mind." According to Goethe, it is delivery that "makes the orator's success." R. C. Ringwalt says: "The art of the actor and reader is joined with that of the man of letters, the philosopher, and statesman in producing the great orator."

Many writers in this field, however, insist that the orator must have more than fluency of speech, grace in gesture, and self-confidence. The higher type of oratory found in the masterpieces, they say, shows superior power of thought, logical consistency in reasoning, quickness and brilliancy of conception, and abundance of knowledge. The orator, too, must so arrange his facts as to regard the three distinct elements of an oration: the introduction, the discussion, and the conclusion. He must observe the laws of clearness, elegance, concreteness, grace, simplicity, sequence, and unity.

Such drawing of hard and fast lines, however, eliminates the real orator. An orator does not need to conform to all of the requirements of rhetoric and logic. It will be fortunate for him if he can do so; but to carry his point it may be necessary for him to ignore some of these very requirements. It must be borne in mind that the oration is the outgrowth of a conflict between the real and the ideal; it is a "manifestation of man's idealizing tendency—the desire to make existing institutions harmonize with the ideal."

To do this rhetoricians say the orator must follow three thought processes, the thesis, the antithesis, and the synthesis. The thesis is the position, or proposition which he advances; the antithesis, the position or proposition which he opposes; and the synthesis, the presentation of facts in support of his position. Certainly in meeting these requirements the orator may be governed by the principles of rhetoric and logic, but in carrying his point the ethics of his profession permits him to violate them. According to Quintilian, the orator should not only instruct but he should move and he should delight.

The orator, it must be understood, is essentially a partisan. His aims are conviction and persuasion. If he cannot do the one, he will resort to the other. Aristotle says that oratory is the faculty of finding all the means of persuasion on any subject. Cicero says it is "the art of persuasion," and Macaulay asserts that "the object of oratory alone is not truth, but persuasion." Goethe says that "oral delivery aims at persuasion, at making the listener believe he is convinced. Few persons are capable of being convinced; the majority allow themselves to be persuaded."

The orator may appeal to emotions—self-interest, prejudice, anger, fear, honor, duty, love, and the like. E. G. Parker says that "the capital of the orator is in the bank of the highest sentimentalities and the purest enthusiasms." William Pitt, the Younger, learned that "it is with eloquence as with a flame; it requires fuel to feed it, motion to excite it, and it brightens as it burns." La Rochefoucauld says, "that the passions are the only orators that always persuade: they are, as it were, a natural art, the rules of which are infallible; and the simplest man with passion is more persuasive than the most eloquent without it." Carlyle observed that "the orator persuades and carries all with him, he knows not how; the rhetorician can prove that he ought to have persuaded and carried all with him." The helplessness of man under the influence of the orator is set forth in these words of Tennyson: "Charm us, orator, till the lion looks no larger than the cat."

Some orators have been produced largely by training. Brougham and Jeffrey practiced speaking in the Speculative Society of the University of Edinburgh, Canning engaged in extemporaneous speaking at Eton, Curran declaimed daily before a mirror, Chatham studied Latin and Greek models, Macaulay attended the Cambridge Union, Lord Mansfield and Fox studied ancient orators, Palmerston attended a debating society of the University of Cambridge, and Gladstone became a famous debater in the Oxford Union. Thus equipped, most of these men spoke in words of beauty and precision. Unlike the extemporaneous speaker, these men were never guilty of departing from accurate thinking and clear statement. Their orations even today, therefore, are regarded as examples of literary excellence. Yet history will show that most of their elegant speeches did not have as much of an electrifying effect as those of illiterate men who in their own way have swayed the masses.

The requirements are often outlined as many. Considering it critically, the judge of oratory requires two essential elements, matter and manner. Senator Hoar believed that the orator must be a master of the great things which interest mankind. What he says ought to have as permanent a place in literature as the highest poetry. He must be able to play at will on the mighty organ, his audience, of which human souls are keys. He must have knowledge, wit, wisdom, fancy, imagination, courage, nobleness, sincerity, grace, a heart of fire. He must himself respond to every emotion as an Æolian harp to the breeze. . . . He must have the quality which Burke manifested when Warren Hastings said, "I felt as I listened to him as if I were the most culpable being on earth"; and which made Philip say of Demosthenes, "Had I been there, he would have persuaded me to take up arms against myself."

Such orations, as selected masterpieces will show, moreover, have not always come from the functionaries of governments. The so-called representatives of the people who enjoy long service in deliberative bodies are generally the servants of the factions or parties by which they are elected. While parties advocate principles to obtain the support of voters, they seldom carry them out when elected. Natural oratory has sprung spontaneously from the breast of patriots inspired to rally the people against the established order of things when they finally decide that it is no longer better to bear the ills they have than to fly to those they know not of. In this class belongs Brutus in the effort to save the Roman republic, Patrick Henry in the cause of American independence, and Frederick Douglass in the abolition of slavery.

Some writers are of the opinion that these natural orators would have done their task better if they had been men of better training and of legislative experience. Others contend that if such orators had been otherwise developed in that conventional atmosphere, they would not have heard the call of divinity and would not have responded with the nobleness of soul.

Judged from the critical point of view, the Negro orator might be expected to lack most of the essentials. Yet, for various reasons, this would not hold. In the first place, the Negro in his sequestered sphere is much better informed, much more capable than the white man who passes him by supposes. When fortune suddenly brings the Negro spokesman before the public eye, then, the so-called superior group is surprised at such knowledge as well as at the manner in which it is presented. Such was the case when Frederick Douglass finally got a chance to speak for the slave and men shouted, "What have we listened to? A thing or a man? We have heard a man!" Booker T.

Washington in his speech at the Atlanta Exposition in 1895 showed such knowledge of the solution of a problem which had long baffled the skill of the white man that he thereafter passed into history as one of the greatest orators of his time.

Classification on the basis of values set forth on the printed page, then, would do injustice to scores of Negro orators who without literary equipment often moved multitudes. Many of their speeches are extant but when we examine their woof and texture they make such an unfavorable impression that we wonder how they could have moved the people. But this can be explained only by the unusually effective manner in which most Negro orators delivered their eloquent appeals. It can be said of them that they had

> "An eye that tears can on a sudden fill
> And lips that smile before the tears are gone."

Their tones were beautiful, and their gestures natural. They could suit the word to the action and the action to the word. Using skillfully the eye and voice, they reached the souls of man. Unable to hear these orations, however, the public is thus deprived of the ideal method of studying them. They must, therefore, be judged not so much by their style as by the effect which they produced on their hearers. As this varies according to the taste, experience and environment of the hearers, an absolute standard in regard to their oratory, then, is impossible.

Some have not considered oratory itself an important acquisition. Goethe says: "He who has reason and good sense at his command needs few of the arts of the orator. With little art, clear wit and sense suggest their own delivery." Disraeli believed "eloquence is the child of knowledge. When the mind is full, like a wholesome river, it is also clear." Boileau thought that "whatever we conceive well we express freely, and words flow with ease." Cicero said that "he is an eloquent man who can treat humble subjects with delicacy, lofty things impressively, and moderate things temperately." Carlyle underrated it thus with the advice "not to speak your opinion well, but to have a good and just opinion worth speaking."

True oratory, then, has regard to truth and justice. There must be some lofty purpose in the eloquent appeal which will stand the test of time on the printed page. Pascal had this in mind when he said that "true eloquence scorns eloquence." Plato said that "he who would be a good orator ought to be just, and skilled in the knowledge of things just." Marlowe thought that "love always makes those eloquent that have it. The heart must glow before the tongue can gild." Another believed that "it is the heart which inspires eloquence." "In eloquence," says Emerson, "the great triumphs of the art are when the orator is lifted above himself; when consciously he makes himself the mere tongue of the occasion and the hour, and says what cannot but be said." "There is no true orator who is not a hero."

Oratory, according to most people of our day, however, is a lost art. In the ancient world it was the means by which the multitude was moved. All of a statesman's constituents could be easily reached in the forum or the market place. Government, restricted as it was to the few, concerned only the upper strata, which in the ancient republics and kingdoms never numbered more than a few thousand. In the increase of the governing body and thinking classes it became more difficult to reach the electorate. Newspapers, the printed journal, and the like, therefore, have been depended upon to inform the public as to what its spokesmen say about the affairs of state. Yet these very agencies of the printed page have become the means by which the public has had its attention attracted so much to the library, the theater, the opera, and other social centers, that they have tended to diminish rather than increase the influence of the orator.

Changes in the aspirations of the people have also contributed to the decline of the orator. In the ancient world, men were struggling to attain lofty ideals. To secure aristocracy the so-called best people had to overthrow despots, and to relieve themselves of an aristocracy degenerated into an oligarchy, other elements of the social order had to supplant this form of government with a democracy of classes. Then came the Christian religion as another factor emphasizing toleration to the extent of endeavoring to make democracy universal. To reach such objectives eloquent spokesmen held up for emulation those personages and situations which exhibited love for humanity and martyrdom in the cause of the truth. In fact, men of that time aspired to be saints and sages, whereas in our day of materialism most persons would consider it a calamity to be suddenly transformed into either.

Not being an empty sort of stilted performance, then, oratory has always had behind it certain great motives by which men have been impelled to act. Liberty, broadly interpreted, may be considered the mainspring of oratory. Demosthenes, Pericles, Alcibiades, and Cleon spoke for the independence of Greece; Cicero for the Roman republic; Mirabeau for the rights of the third estate; Burke and Chatham for the liberties of the colonies; Otis and Henry for American independence; Webster for the Union; and Garrison, Sumner and Lincoln for freedom. Most of these men, moreover, had high moral qualities or successfully voiced the sentiments of such constituents. They spoke for the preservation of some right then enjoyed, for the extension of some privilege desired, or for precaution against some dreaded evil which might prove disastrous to the body politic. They spoke at the opportune moment of the impending danger, which supplied the great occasion which every great oration requires.

Orations have been variously classified, but writers in this field have been unable to improve on the classification made by Aristotle. Having observed that audiences are either judges of things lying in the past or of things lying in the future, or pose as critics, he asserted that there are but three kinds of speeches—judicial, deliberative, and epideictic. Since Aristotle's day Christianity has added pulpit oratory as a fourth class, in which the Negro seems destined to excel all others.

By judicial oratory Aristotle meant forensic debate, resorted to among the ancients in the effort to obtain and defend personal rights in the courts. In those days when such privileges were withheld or begrudgingly granted this form of oratory was the most common and the most popular. In this style Cicero spoke for Milo and Archias, and Lord Brougham for Queen Caroline.

By deliberative oratory Aristotle meant speeches before legislative bodies or any assembly of persons whom the speaker endeavors to induce to accept or reject some espoused policy. Such were most orations of Demosthenes and Cicero, of Elliot, Pym and Cromwell, and of Charles Sumner and Abraham Lincoln.

By epideictic oratory Aristotle meant occasional or rather demonstrative speeches to present themes which appeal to the taste and cultivation of audiences. The ancients spoke in such style when praising or censuring persons. In this mood the orator aims not to convince so much as to please his hearers. Yet in the eulogy, the invective, the lecture, the commemorative address, the commencement oration, the after-dinner speech—all which fall in this class—the speaker may convince as well as please.

Pulpit oratory, the fourth class, belongs to modern times. It finds no models in the ancient orator. It has been the means by which the doctrine of the Christian church has been popularized and by which its sway has extended throughout the modern world. As such orators appeared

Chrysostom in the Middle Ages, and Savonarola, Luther, Calvin, and Knox as the leaders of the Reformation.

It might seem to the reader that because of social proscription the Negro has been eliminated from some of the oratory of our day. This, however, is not exactly the case. It is true that in contact with the white man justice is administered by a so-called superior class, and the Negro has not figured extensively in forensic discussion before courts. In pleading the cause of his oppressed people, however, he has appeared as their advocate before assemblies which have influenced governments. With the exception of the experience in Liberia, Haiti, and the South during the Reconstruction, the Negro has not often figured in the deliberations of legislative bodies, but the opportunities so far afforded him have been well used in demonstrating his capacity for this style of oratory.

In the occasional or demonstrative address there are few who do not concede the Negro equal honor with the best on the platform. Furthermore, while the pulpit among the majority of whites has become merely a social agency as a result of their substituting the worship of race superiority for that of God, among the Negroes it has become an electrifying force by which the Negro preacher has surpassed all ministers of his time in expounding the very principles of Jesus, which the large majority of these "chosen people of God" have long since repudiated.

Since deliberative oratory as a popular attraction has long since ceased, the forensic as it peculiarly concerns the courts is the only form of oratory in which the Negro does not figure among the world's greatest orators. The large number of the Negro youth now qualifying at the bar assures an increase of the ranks of those who will doubtless leave masterpieces of eloquence inspired by the cries of a people long outraged by agents of injustice in a world of race hate and religious prejudice. Sojourner Truth, Charles Lenox Remond, Lunsford Lane and Frederick

Douglass figured in the physical emancipation of the bondmen, but these later champions are endeavoring to make a case for their liberation from peonage, their deliverance from caste, and their full incorporation into the body politic.

The Negro orators of the Reconstruction did not develop in the direction of the forensic. The Civil War resulted in the enlargement of the domain of the liberty of the Negro. For a time he had everything he wanted. Their oratory, therefore, was deliberative, speeches delivered in such bodies as the State legislatures and the Congress of the United States. B. K. Bruce's discourse in the Senate on the Indian question and R. B. Elliot's speech in the House on the Civil Rights Bill are examples of such eloquence. When the undoing of the Reconstruction brought the Negro again under the domination of the white man in the South, the Negro orator sometimes resorted to the forensic but he was better prepared for the invective, in which he finally indulged as he saw his race illegally deprived of its rights. This form of public address continued and is popular today among Negroes complaining of their woes. After the Reconstruction there came the optimistic Negro orator who had little to say about the rights of the race and emphasized the necessity for making the most of an undesirable situation by practical educational and economic efficiency. The best representative of this class was Booker T. Washington.

Since the program thus presented did not at once materially advance the Negro on the way toward the attainment of his civic rights, there developed a number of orators promoting agitative organizations. They fearlessly denounced Booker T. Washington and his program and proclaimed war on the strongholds of aristocracy and caste. At first their efforts were largely fiery speeches delivered sporadically at centers where persons whom they desired to reach seldom heard them. Later, however, their work has been more systematized and their method of attack has tended to become more of an argumentative appeal to reason. As such, these Negro orators have furnished the only humanizing theme which has stimulated eloquence during the last generation. The whites of our day are little concerned about human rights. They are becoming rapidly involved in the covetous life and death struggle between capital and labor, between those that have and those that have not, a thing lacking the higher motives by which men are ennobled. During the World War, Woodrow Wilson made a strenuous effort to popularize the idea of "making the world safe for democracy," but the hypocrisy of this pronunciamento doubtless contributed to the collapse of the program. Men had to be converted to support the movement, and the war all but suddenly so ended as to leave more wounds than it healed. As the treaty of peace and the rehabilitation consequent thereupon so worked out as to make the world economically safe for the conquering few, there arose among the discordant elements a number of bold spokesmen who have easily caught the ear of the multitude in advocating a radical reconstruction of the social order. Among such orators have appeared a few Negroes.

Radicals among Negroes have appeared before, but not in the advocacy of socialism or communism. In presenting their case, moreover, these progressive spokesmen have not merely exhibited the fire of the Negro enraged because of the loss of civic rights. These new orators are well informed in the doctrines of the socialist and can, therefore, show how human rights are largely determined by the economic rights which individuals enjoy. They argue that as long as Negroes are economically enslaved along with the poor whites in no better circumstances, the tenure of all human rights is precarious. These orators are endeavoring to unite the Negroes and poor whites to make common cause against their foes.

CHAPTER II

THE FIRST PROTEST

HISTORIANS commonly mention the Germantown Quaker Memorial against slavery in 1688 as the first protest against the institution in the Western Hemisphere. Others refer to that of Alfonso Sandoval [1] in Havana as the first of such an expression of liberal sentiment. The first protest of the sort, however, came from the free Negro himself. Many Negroes were never slaves. All of those imported in 1619 were first indentured servants, many of whom obtained their freedom at the expiration of a term of service, while others were debased to the status of slaves. However, they were unwillingly slaves. In many cases, therefore, the bondmen obtained their freedom by manumission for meritorious service or purchased themselves. In their freedom these more fortunate members of the race never forgot their brethren in bondage. They themselves as successful members of the community were walking evidence against the institution, and they never failed to attack it whenever the opportunity presented itself.

Their protest at first was not heard because it required time for such freedmen to acquire the means of expressing their thought forcefully. During the last quarter of the eighteenth century, however, the struggle for the rights of man did so much for the amelioration of the lower strata of society that the Negro himself profited by the new liberalism. Availing themselves of the opportunities offered for education, many of these Negroes learned to write and speak intelligently. In spite of their training, in spite of their vocation, in spite of their connections, they almost

[1] Bourne, *Spain in America*, 241.

invariably drifted into antislavery discussion, just as most intelligent Negroes of today write and speak of the wrongs of the race. As free speech was not then exactly established as the right of all men, these men had to write and speak under assumed names. These two extracts which here follow are cases in evidence. They are speeches made by aggrieved Negroes who sought a larger audience by publishing them as essays and letters in magazines.

NEGRO SLAVERY[1]

By "Othello"

Amidst the infinite variety of moral and political subjects proper for public commendation, it is truly surprising that one of the most important and affecting should be so generally neglected. An encroachment on the smallest civil or political privilege shall fan the enthusiastic flames of liberty till it shall extend over vast and distant regions, and violently agitate a whole continent. But the cause of humanity shall be basely violated, justice shall be wounded to the heart, and national honor deeply and lastingly polluted, and not a breath or murmur shall arise to disturb the prevailing quiescence or to rouse the feelings of indignation against such general, extensive, and complicated iniquity.—To what cause are we to impute this frigid silence—this torpid indifference—this cold inanimated conduct of the otherwise warm and generous Americans? Why do they remain inactive amidst the groans of injured humanity, the shrill and distressing complaints of expiring justice and the keen remorse of polluted integrity?—Why do they not rise up to assert the cause of God and the world, to drive the fiend Injustice into remote and distant regions, and to exterminate oppression from the face of the fair fields of America?

When the united colonies revolted from Great Britain, they did it upon this principle, "that all men are by nature and of right ought to be free."—After a long, successful, and glorious struggle for liberty, during which they manifested the firmest attachment to the rights of mankind, can they so soon forget the principles

[1] "Othello," the author, was identified as a Negro by Abbé Grégoire in his *De la Litterature des Nègres*.

that then governed their determinations? Can Americans, after the noble contempt they expressed for tyrants, meanly descend to take up the scourge? Blush, ye revolted colonies, for having apostatized from your own principles!

Slavery, in whatever point of light it is considered, is repugnant to the feelings of nature, and inconsistent with the original rights of man. It ought, therefore, to be stigmatized for being unnatural; and detested for being unjust. 'Tis an outrage to Providence and an affront offered to divine Majesty, who Has given to man His own peculiar image.—That the Americans, after considering the subject in this light—after making the most manly of all possible exertions in defense of liberty—after publishing to the world the principle upon which they contended, viz., "that all men are by nature and of right ought to be free," should still retain in subjection a numerous tribe of the human race merely for their own private use and emolument, is, of all things, the strongest inconsistency, the deepest reflection on our conduct, and the most abandoned apostasy that ever took place since the Almighty fiat spoke into existence this habitable world. So flagitious a violation can never escape the notice of a just Creator, whose vengeance may be now on the wing, to disseminate and hurl the arrows of destruction.

In what light can the people of Europe consider America after the strange inconsistency of her conduct? Will they not consider her as an abandoned and deceitful country? In the hour of calamity she petitioned heaven to be propitious to her cause. Her prayers were heard. Heaven pitied her distress, smiled on her virtuous exertions, and vanquished all her afflictions. The ungrateful creature forgets this timely assistance—no longer remembers her own sorrows—but basely commences oppression in her turn.—Beware, America! pause—and consider the difference between the mild effulgence of approving Providence and the angry countenance of incensed divinity!

The importation of slaves into America ought to be a subject of the deepest regret to every benevolent and thinking mind.—And one of the greatest defects in the federal system is the liberty it allows on this head. Venerable in everything else, it is injudicious here; and it is to be much deplored that a system of so much political perfection should be stained with anything that does an outrage to human nature. As a door, however, is open to amendment, for the sake of distressed humanity, of injured national reputation, and the glory of doing so benevolent a thing, I hope some wise and virtuous patriot will advocate the measure, and introduce an alteration in that pernicious part of the government.[1] —So far from encouraging the importation of slaves, and countenancing that vile traffic in human flesh, the members of the late Constitutional Convention should have seized the happy opportunity of prohibiting forever this cruel species of reprobated villainy. —That they did not do so will forever diminish the luster of their other proceedings, so highly extolled and so justly distinguished for their intrinsic value.—Let us for a moment contrast the sentiments and actions of the Europeans on this subject with those of our own countrymen. In France the warmest and most animated exertions are making, in order to introduce the entire abolition of the slave trade; and in England many of the first characters of the country advocate the same measure with an enthusiastic philanthropy. The Prime Minister himself is at the head of that society,[2] and nothing can equal the ardor of their endeavors but the glorious goodness of the cause.[3]—Will the Americans allow the people of England to get the start of them in acts of humanity? Forbid it, shame!

The practice of stealing or bartering for human flesh is pregnant with the most glaring turpitude, and the blackest barbarity of disposition.—For can any one say that this is doing as he would be done by? Will such a practice stand the scrutiny of this great rule of moral government? Who can, without the complicated emotions of anger and impatience, suppose himself in the predica-

[1] The reference here is to the Convention of 1787, which framed the Constitution of the United States. The slavery question came up in that body but it was not permitted to divide the delegates to the extent of diverting attention from the important thing for which the Convention was called, namely, to "form a more perfect Union." Some delegates took high ground in denouncing slavery as inconsistent with liberty, but their attack on the institution was mild when compared with the bolder protests against the system registered by some of the fathers of the Revolution. To placate South Carolina and Georgia, the Convention finally incorporated provisions for the return of fugitive slaves, and deferred the prohibition of the slave trade until 1808.

[2] The author has in mind here the culmination of the efforts of Granville Sharp and Thomas Clarkson, in 1787, when they could count upon the sympathy and coöperation of Pitt, who was friendly toward William Wilberforce, then doing everything possible to force through Parliament a measure to abolish the slave trade. A group of liberal Frenchmen of the same type were directing the attention of their country also to this evil.

[3] In England these efforts led to the organization of the Society for the Abolition of the Slave Trade, and in France to the formation of the Society of the Friends of the Blacks, supported by Brissot, Clavière, Mirabeau, Condorcet, and Grégoire.

ment of a slave? Who can bear the thought of his relatives being torn from him by a savage enemy; carried to distant regions of the habitable globe, never more to return; and treated there as the unhappy Africans are in this country? Who can support the reflection of his father—his mother—his sister—or his wife—perhaps his children—being barbarously snatched away by a foreign invader, without the prospect of ever beholding them again? Who can reflect upon their being afterwards publicly exposed to sale—obliged to labor with unwearied assiduity—and because all things are not possible to be performed by persons so unaccustomed to robust exercise, scourged with all the rage and anger of malignity until their unhappy carcasses are covered with ghastly wounds and frightful contusions? Who can reflect on these things when applying the case to himself without being chilled with horror at circumstances so extremely shocking?—Yet hideous as this concise and imperfect description is of the sufferings sustained by many of our slaves, it is nevertheless true; and so far from being exaggerated, falls infinitely short of a thousand circumstances of distress, which have been recounted by different writers on the subject and which contribute to make their situation in this life the most absolutely wretched and completely miserable that can possibly be conceived. —In many places in America the slaves are treated with every circumstance of rigorous inhumanity, accumulated hardship, and enormous cruelty.—Yet when we take them from Africa we deprive them of a country which God hath given them for their own, as free as we are, and as capable of enjoying that blessing. Like pirates we go to commit devastation on the coast of an innocent country, and among a people who never did us wrong.

An insatiable, avaricious desire to accumulate riches, coöperating with a spirit of luxury and injustice, seems to be the leading cause of this peculiarly degrading and ignominious practice. Being once accustomed to subsist without labor, we become soft and voluptuous; and rather than afterwards forego the gratification of our habitual indolence and ease, we countenance the infamous violation, and sacrifice at the shrine of cruelty, all the finer feelings of elevated humanity.

Considering things in this view, there surely can be nothing more justly reprehensible or disgusting than the extravagant finery of many country people's daughters. It hath not been at all uncommon to observe as much gauze, lace, and other trappings on one of those country maidens as hath employed two or three of her father's slaves for twelve months afterwards to raise tobacco to pay for. It is an ungrateful reflection that all this frippery and affected finery can only be supported by the sweat of another person's brow, and consequently only by lawful rapine and injustice. If these young females could devote as much time from their amusements as would be necessary for reflection; or was there any person of humanity at hand who could inculcate the indecency of this kind of extravagance, I am persuaded that they have hearts good enough to reject with disdain the momentary pleasure of making a figure in behalf of the rational and lasting delight of contributing by their forbearance to the happiness of many thousand individuals.

In Maryland, where slaves are treated with as much lenity as perhaps they are anywhere, their situation is to the last degree ineligible. They live in wretched cots that scarcely secure them from the inclemency of the weather, sleep in the ashes or on straw, wear the coarsest clothing, and subsist on the most ordinary food that the country produces. In all things they are subject to their master's absolute command, and, of course, have no will of their own. Thus circumstanced, they are subject to great brutality, and are often treated with it. In particular instances they may be better provided for in this state, but this suffices for a general description. But in the Carolinas and the island of Jamaica the cruelties that have been wantonly exercised on those miserable creatures are without a precedent in any other part of the world. If those who have written on the subject may be believed, it is not uncommon there to tie a slave up and whip him to death.

On all occasions impartiality in the distribution of justice should be observed. The little State of Rhode Island has been reprobated by other States for refusing to enter into measures respecting a new general government; and so far it is admitted that she is culpable.[1] But if she is worthy of blame in this respect, she is entitled to the highest admiration for the philanthropy, justice, and humanity she hath displayed respecting the subject I am treat-

[1] Rhode Island, like North Carolina, had failed to ratify the Constitution of the United States, although it had been put into execution by virtue of that provision in the ratifying clause to the effect that the consent of nine states would be sufficient.

ing on. She hath passed an act prohibiting the importation of slaves into that State, and forbidding her citizens to engage in the iniquitous traffic. So striking a proof of her strong attachment to the rights of humanity will rescue her name from oblivion and bid her live in the good opinion of distant and unborn generations.

Slavery unquestionably should be abolished, particularly in this country; because it is inconsistent with the declared principles of the American Revolution. The sooner, therefore, we set about it the better. Either we should set our slaves at liberty immediately and colonize them in the western territory,[1] or we should immediately take measures for the gradual abolition of it, so that it may become a known and fixed point that ultimately universal liberty in these United States shall triumph.—This is the least we can do in order to evince our sense of the irreparable outrages we have committed, to wipe off the odium we have incurred, and to give mankind a confidence again in the justice, liberality, and honor of our national proceedings.

It would not be difficult to show, were it necessary, that America would soon become a richer and more happy country provided the step was adopted. That corrosive anguish of persevering in anything improper, which now embitters the enjoyments of life, would vanish as the mist of a foggy morn doth before the rising sun; and we should find as great a disparity between our present situation, and that which would succeed to it, as subsists between a cloudy winter and a radiant spring.—Besides, our lands would not be then cut down for the support of a numerous train of useless inhabitants—useless, I mean, to themselves, and effectually to us by encouraging sloth and voluptuousness among our young farmers and planters, who might otherwise know how to take care of their money as well as how to dissipate it.—In all other respects, I conceive them to be as valuable as we are—as capable of worthy purposes, and to possess the same dignity that we do, in the estimation of Providence; although we consider the value of their work apart, for which we are dependent on them, we generally consider them as good for nothing, and accordingly treat them with greatest neglect.

[1] During the first forty years of the republic there was much talk about colonizing the Negroes in the West. Granville Sharp, Anthony Benezet, Thomas Brannagan and Thomas Jefferson had this idea.

But be it remembered that this cause is the cause of heaven; and that the father of them as well as of us will not fail, at a future settlement, to adjust the account between us with a dreadful attention to justice.

Upon no better principle do we plunder the coasts of Africa and bring away its wretched inhabitants as slaves than that by which the greater fish swallows up the lesser. Superior power seems only to produce superior brutality; and that weakness and imbecility, which ought to engage our protection and interest the feelings of social benevolence in behalf of the defenseless, seems only to provoke us to acts of illiberal outrage and unmanly violence.

The practice which has been followed by the English nation since the establishment of the slave trade—I mean that of stirring up the natives of Africa against each other with a view of purchasing the prisoners mutually taken in battle—must strike the humane mind with sentiments of the deepest abhorrence, and confer on that people a reproach as lasting as time itself. It is surprising that the eastern world did not unite to discourage a custom so diabolical in its tendency, and to exterminate a species of oppression which humbles the dignity of all mankind. But this torpid inattention can only be accounted for by adverting to the savage disposition of the times which countenanced cruelties unheard of at this enlightened period. What rudeness of demeanor and brutality of manner, which had been introduced into Europe by those swarms of barbarians that overwhelmed it from the North, had hardly begun to dissipate before the enlivening sun of civilization, when this infernal practice first sprang up into existence! Before this distinguished era of refined barbarity the sons of Africa were in possession of all the mild enjoyments of peace—all the pleasing delights of uninterrupted harmony—and all the diffusive blessings of profound tranquillity. Boundless must be the punishment which irritated Providence will inflict on those whose wanton cruelty has prompted them to destroy this fair arrangement of nature—this flowery prospect of human felicity. Engulfed in the dark abyss of never-ending misery, they shall in bitterness atone for the stab thus given to human nature, and in anguish unutterable expiate crimes for which nothing less than eternal sufferings can make adequate retribution! Equally iniquitous is the practice of robbing that country of its inhabitants; and equally tremendous will be the punishment. The voice of injured thousands who have been violently torn from their native country and carried to distant and inhospitable climes—the bitter lamentations of the wretched, helpless female—the cruel, agonizing sensations of the husband, the father and the friend—will ascend to the throne of Omnipotence, and, from the elevated heights of heaven, cause him, with the whole force of Almighty vengeance, to hurl the guilty perpetrators of those inhuman beings down the steep precipice of inevitable ruin into the bottomless gulf of final, irretrievable and endless destruction!

Ye sons of America, forbear!—Consider the dire consequences that will attend the prosecution, against which the all-powerful God of nature holds up his hands and loudly proclaims, desist!

In the insolence of self-consequence we are accustomed to esteem ourselves and the Christian powers of Europe the only civilized people on the globe; the rest, without distinction, we presumptuously denominate barbarians. But, when the practices above mentioned come to be deliberately considered—when added to these we take a view of the proceedings of the English in the East Indies, under the direction of the late Lord Clive, and remember what happened in the streets of Bengal and Calcutta—when we likewise reflect on our American mode of driving, butchering and exterminating the poor defenseless Indians, the native and lawful proprietors of the soil—we shall acknowledge, if we possess the smallest degree of candor, that the appellation of barbarian does not belong to them alone. While we continue those practices the term Christian will only be a burlesque expression signifying more than that it ironically denominates the rudest sect of barbarians that ever disgraced the hand of their Creator. We have the precepts of the gospel for the government of our moral deportment, in violation of which those outrageous wrongs are committed; but they have no such meliorating influence among them, and only adhere to the simple dictates of reason and natural religion, which they never violate.

Might not the inhabitants of Africa, with still greater justice on their side than we have on ours, cross the Atlantic, seize our citizens, carry them into Africa, and make slaves of them, provided they were able to do it? But should this really be the case, every corner of the globe would reverberate with the sound of African oppression, so loud would be their complaint and so "feeling our appeal" to the inhabitants of the world at large. We should represent them as a lawless, piratical set of unprincipled robbers, plunderers and villains, who basely prostituted the superior power and information which God had given them for worthy purposes to the vilest of all ends. We should not hesitate to say that they made use of those advantages only to infringe upon every dictate of justice, to trample under foot every suggestion of principle, and to spurn with contempt every right of humanity.

The Algerines are reprobated all the world over for their unlawful depredations, and stigmatized as pirates for their unreasonable exactions from foreign nations. But the Algerines are no greater pirates than the Americans; nor are they a race more destructive to the happiness of mankind. The depredations of the latter on the coast of Africa, and upon the Indian's territory, make the truth of this assertion manifest. The piratical depredations of the Algerines appear to be a judgment from heaven upon the nations to punish their perfidy and atrocious violations of justice; and never did any people more justly merit the scourge than Americans, on whom it seems to fall with peculiar and reiterated violence. When they yoke our citizens to the plow, and compel them to labor in that degraded manner, they only retaliate on us for similar barbarities. For Algiers is a part of the same country whose helpless inhabitants we are accustomed to carry away. But the English and Americans cautiously avoid engaging with a warlike people whom they fear to attack in a manner so base and unworthy; whilst the Algerines, more generous and courageous plunderers, are not afraid to make war on brave and well-disciplined enemies who are capable of making a gallant resistance.

Whoever examines into the conditions of the slaves in America will find them in a state of the most uncultivated rudeness. Not instructed in any kind of learning, they are grossly ignorant of all refinement, and have little else about them belonging to the nature of civilized man than mere form. They are strangers to almost every idea that doth not relate to their labor or their food, and though possessed naturally of strong sagacity and lively parts are, in all respects, in a state of most deplorable brutality.—This is owing to the iron hand of oppression, which ever crushes the bud of genius and binds up in chains every expansion of the human mind.—Such is their extreme ignorance that they are utterly unacquainted with the laws of the world—the injunctions of religion—their own natural rights, and the forms, ceremonies and privileges of marriage originally established by the Divinity. Accordingly they live in open violation of the precepts of Christianity and with as little formality or restrictions as the brutes of the field unite for the purposes of procreation. Yet this is a civilized country and a most enlightened period of the world! The resplendent glory of the gospel is at hand to conduct us in safety through the labyrinths of life. Science hath grown up to maturity, and is discovered to possess not only all the properties of solidity of strength, but likewise every ornament of elegance and every embellishment of fancy. Philosophy hath here attained the most exalted height of elevation, and the art of government hath received such refinements among us as hath equally astonished our friends, our enemies and ourselves. In fine, no annals are more brilliant than those of America; nor do any more luxuriantly abound with examples of exalted heroism, refined policy, and sympathetic humanity. Yet now the prospect begins to change, and all the splendor of this august assemblage will soon be overcast by sudden and impenetrable clouds, and American greatness be obliterated and swallowed up by one enormity. Slavery diffuses the gloom, and casts around us the deepest shade of approaching darkness. No longer shall the United States of America be famed for liberty. Oppression pervades their bowels; and while they exhibit a fair exterior to the other parts of the world, they are nothing more than "painted sepulchers," containing within them nought but rottenness and corruption.

Ye voluptuous, ye opulent and great, who hold in subjection such numbers of your fellow creatures, and suffer these things to happen—beware! Reflect on this lamentable change that may, at a future period, take place against you. Arraigned before the Almighty Sovereign of the universe, how will you answer the charge of such complicated enormity? The presence of these slaves, who have been lost for want of your instruction and by means of your oppression, shall make you dart deeper into the flames to avoid their just reproaches, and seek out for an asylum in the hidden corners of perdition.

Our slaves unquestionably have the strongest of all claims upon us for protection and support, we having compelled them to involuntary servitude and deprived them of every means of protecting or supporting themselves. The injustice of our conduct, and barbarity of our neglect, when this reflection is allowed to predominate, becomes so glaringly conspicuous as even to excite against ourselves the strongest emotion of detestation and abhorrence.

To whom are the wretched sons of Africa to apply for redress if their cruel master treats them with unkindness? To whom will they resort for protection if he is base enough to refuse it to them? The law is not their friend—alas! too many statutes are enacted against them. The world is not their friend—the iniquity is too general and extensive. No one who hath slaves of his own will protect those of another, less the practice should be retorted. Thus when their masters abandon them, their situation is destitute and forlorn, and God is their only friend!

Let us imitate the conduct of a neighboring State and immediately take measures, at least, for the gradual abolition of slavery.[1] Justice demands it of us, and we ought not to hesitate in obeying its inviolable mandates.—All the feelings of pity, compassion, affection, and benevolence—all the emotions of tenderness, humanity, philanthropy, and goodness—all the sentiments of mercy, probity, honor, and integrity, unite to solicit for their emancipation. Immortal will be the glory of accomplishing their liberation; and eternal the disgrace of keeping them in chains.

But if the State of Pennsylvania is to be applauded for her conduct, that of South Carolina can never be too strongly execrated.[2] The legislature of that State, at no very remote period, brought in a bill for prohibiting the use of letters to their slaves and forbidding them the privilege of being taught to read!—This was a deliberate attempt to enslave the minds of those unfortunate objects, whose persons they already held in arbitrary subjection—detestable deviation from the becoming rectitude of man.

One more peculiarly distressing circumstance remains to be recounted before I take my final leave of the subject.—In the ordinary course of the business of the country the punishment of

[1] The writer refers here to the acts of Pennsylvania, providing for the abolition of slavery by a gradual process.

[2] In 1740 South Carolina enacted a law prohibiting any one from teaching a slave to read or employing one in "any manner of writing," Georgia enacted the same law in 1770. Further provisions to this effect were later incorporated into the laws of these States.

relatives frequently happens on the same farm, and in view of each other.—The father often sees his beloved son—the son his venerable sire—the mother her much-loved daughter—the daughter her affectionate parent—the husband the wife of his bosom, and she the husband of her affection, cruelly bound up without delicacy or mercy and punished with all extremity of incensed rage and all the rigor of unrelenting severity, whilst these unfortunate wretches dare not even interpose in each other's behalf. Let us reverse the case and suppose it ours—all is silent horror![1]

SLAVERY

By a Free Negro

I am one of that unfortunate race of men who are distinguished from the rest of the human species by a black skin and woolly hair—disadvantages of very little moment in themselves, but which prove to us a source of greatest misery, because there are men who will not be persuaded that it is possible for a human soul to be lodged within a sable body.[2] The West Indian planters could not, if they thought us men, so wantonly spill our blood; nor could the natives of this land of liberty, deeming us of the same species with themselves, submit to be instrumental in enslaving us, or think us proper subjects of a sordid commerce. Yet, strong as the prejudices against us are, it will not, I hope on this side of the Atlantic, be considered as a crime for a poor African not to confess himself a being of an inferior order to those who happen to be of a different color from himself, or be thought very presumptuous in one who is but a Negro to offer to the happy subjects of this free government some reflection upon the wretched condition of his countrymen. They will not, I trust, think worse of my brethren for being discontented with so hard a lot as that of slavery, nor disown me for their fellow-creature merely because I deeply feel the unmerited sufferings which my countrymen endure.

It is neither the vanity of being an author, nor a sudden and capricious gust of humanity, which has prompted this present design. It has long been conceived and long been the principal

[1] *American Museum,* IV, 412-415, 509-512 (1788).

[2] This Negro was doubtless a native of the West Indies, but he so admirably expressed the sentiment of the bondmen and their friends on the American continent that this production was published and extensively read here in liberal circles.

subject of my thoughts. Ever since an indulgent master rewarded my youthful services with freedom and supplied me at a very early age with the means of acquiring knowledge, I have labored to understand the true principles on which the liberties of mankind are founded, and to possess myself of the language of this country in order to plead the cause of those who were once my fellow slaves, and if possible to make my freedom, in some degree, the instrument of their deliverance.

The first thing, then, which seems necessary in order to remove those prejudices which are so unjustly entertained against us is to prove that we are men—a truth which is difficult of proof only because it is difficult to imagine by what argument it can be combated. Can it be contended that a difference of color alone can constitute a difference of species?—If not, in what single circumstance are we different from the rest of mankind? What variety is there in our organization? What inferiority of art in the fashioning of our bodies? What imperfection in the faculties of our minds? —Has not a Negro eyes? has not a Negro hands, organs, dimensions, senses, affections, passions?—fed with the same food; hurt with the same weapons; subject to the same diseases; healed by the same means; warmed and cooled by the same summer and winter as a white man? If you prick us, do we not bleed? If you poison us, do we not die? Are we not exposed to all the same wants? Do we not feel all the same sentiments—are we not capable of all the same exertions—and are we not entitled to all the same rights as other men? [1]

Yes—and it is said we are men, it is true; but that we are men addicted to more and worse vices than those of any other complexion; and such is the innate perverseness of our minds that nature seems to have marked us out for slavery.—Such is the apology perpetually made for our masters and the justification offered for that universal proscription under which we labor.

But I supplicate our enemies to be, though for the first time, just in their proceedings toward us, and to establish the fact before they attempt to draw any conclusions from it. Nor let them imagine that this can be done by merely asserting that such is our universal character. It is the character, I grant, that our inhuman masters

[1] This Negro had evidently studied literature extensively. Here one observes the influence of Shakespeare.

have agreed to give us and which they have so industriously and too successfully propagated in order to palliate their own guilt by blackening the helpless victims of it and to disguise their own cruelty under the semblance of justice. Let the natural depravity of our character be proved—not by appealing to declamatory invectives and interest representations, but by showing that a greater proportion of crimes have been committed by the wronged slaves of the plantation than by the luxurious inhabitants of Europe, who are happily strangers to those aggravated provocations by which our passions are every day irritated and incensed. Show us that, of the multitude of Negroes who have within a few years transported themselves to this country,[1] and who are abandoned to themselves; who are corrupted by example, prompted by penury, and instigated by the memory of their wrongs to the commission of crimes—show us, I say (and the demonstration, if it be possible, cannot be difficult), that a greater proportion of these than of white men have fallen under the animadversions of justice and have been sacrificed to your laws. Though avarice may slander and insult our misery, and though poets heighten the horror of their fables by representing us as monsters of vice—that fact is that, if treated like other men, and admitted to a participation of their rights, we should differ from them in nothing, perhaps, but in our possessing stronger passions, nicer sensibility, and more enthusiastic virtue.

Before so harsh a decision was pronounced upon our nature, we might have expected—if sad experience had not taught us to expect nothing but injustice from our adversaries—that some pains would have been taken to ascertain what our nature is; and that we should have been considered as we are found in our native woods and not as we now are—altered and perverted by an inhuman political institution. But instead of this, we are examined, not by philosophers, but by interested traders; not as nature formed us, but as man has depraved us—and from such an inquiry, prosecuted under such circumstances, the perverseness of our dispositions is said to be established. Cruel that you are! you make us slaves; you implant in our minds all the vices which are in some degree inseparable from that condition; and you then impiously impute to nature, and to God, the origin of those vices, to which you alone

[1] This letter was originally published in England, where the number of Negroes had considerably increased after the war in America.

have given birth; and punish in us the crimes of which you are yourselves the authors.

The condition of the slave is in nothing more deplorable than in its being so unfavorable to the practice of every virtue. The surest foundation of virtue is love of our fellow-creatures; and that affection takes its birth in the social relations of men to one another. But to a slave these are all denied. He never pays or receives the grateful duties of a son—he never knows or experiences the fond solicitude of a father—the tender names of husband, of brother, and of friend, are to him unknown. He has no country to defend and bleed for—he can relieve no sufferings—for he looks around in vain to find a being more wretched than himself. He can indulge no generous sentiment—for he sees himself every hour treated with contempt and ridiculed, and distinguished from irrational brutes by nothing but the severity of punishment. Would it be surprising if a slave, laboring under all these disadvantages—oppressed, insulted, scorned, trampled on—should come at last to despise himself—to believe the calumnies of his oppressors—and to persuade himself that it would be against his nature to cherish any honorable sentiment or to attempt any virtuous action? Before you boast of your superiority over us, place some of your own color (if you have the heart to do it) in the same situation with us and see whether they have such innate virtue, and such unconquerable vigor of mind, as to be capable of surmounting such multiplied difficulties, and of keeping their minds free from the infection of every vice, even under the oppressive yoke of such a servitude.

But, not satisfied with denying us that indulgence, to which the misery of our condition gives us so just a claim, our enemies have laid down other and stricter rules of morality to judge our actions by than those by which the conduct of all other men is tried. Habits, which in all human beings except ourselves are thought innocent, are, in us, deemed criminal—and actions, which are even laudable in white men, become enormous crimes in Negroes. In proportion to our weakness, the strictness of censure is increased upon us; and as resources are withheld from us, our duties are multiplied. The terror of punishment is perpetually before our eyes; but we know not how to avert, what rules to act by, or what guides to follow. We have written laws, indeed, composed in a language we do not understand and never promulgated: but what avail written laws, when the supreme law, with us, is the capricious will of our overseers? To obey the dictates of our own hearts, and to yield to the strong propensities of nature, is often to incur severe punishment; and by emulating examples which we find applauded and revered among Europeans, we risk inflaming the wildest wrath of our inhuman tyrants.

To judge of the truth of these assertions, consult even those milder and subordinate rules for our conduct, the various codes of your West India laws—those laws which allow us to be men, whenever they consider us as victims of their vengeance, but treat us only like a species of living property, as often as we are to be the objects of their protection—those laws by which (it may be truly said) that we are bound to suffer and be miserable under pain of death. To resent an injury received from a white man, though of the lowest rank, and to dare to strike him, though upon the strongest and grossest provocation, is an enormous crime. To attempt to escape from the cruelties exercised upon us by flight is punished with mutilation, and sometimes with death. To take arms against masters, whose cruelties no submission can mitigate, no patience exhaust, and from whom no other means of deliverance are left, is the most atrocious of all crimes, and is punished by a gradual death, lengthened out by torments so exquisite that none but those who have been long familiarized with West Indian barbarity can hear the bare recital of them without horror. And yet I learn from writers, whom the Europeans hold in the highest esteem, that treason is a crime which cannot be committed by a slave against his master; that a slave stands in no civil relation towards his master, and owes him no allegiance; that master and slave are in a state of war; and if the slave take up arms for his deliverance, he acts not only justifiably but in obedience to a natural duty, the duty of self-preservation. I read in authors whom I find venerated by our oppressors, that to deliver one's self and one's countrymen from tyranny is an act of the sublimest heroism. I hear Europeans exalted as the martyrs of public liberty, the saviors of their country, and the deliverers of mankind—I see other memories honored with statues, and their names immortalized in poetry—and yet when a generous Negro is animated by the same passion which ennobled them—when he feels the wrongs of his countrymen as deeply, and attempts to avenge them as boldly—

I see him treated by those same Europeans as the most execrable of mankind, and led out, amidst curses and insults, to undergo a painful, gradual and ignominious death. And thus the same Briton, who applauds his own ancestors for attempting to throw off the easy yoke imposed on them by the Romans, punishes us, as detested parricides, for seeking to get free from the cruelest of all tyrannies, and yielding to the irresistible eloquence of an African Galgacus or Boadicea.

Are then the reason and morality, for which Europeans so highly value themselves, of a nature so variable and fluctuating as to change with the complexion of those to whom they are applied?—Do rights of nature cease to be such when a Negro is to enjoy them?—Or does patriotism in the heart of an African rankle into treason? [1]

[1] *American Museum*, V, 77 *et seq.* (1789).

CHAPTER III

MORE FORCEFUL ATTACKS

A NEW epoch was reached in the history of the Negro in the United States, however, meaning more free speech for the race. Within a generation after the rights of man movement of the American Revolution the South tended to become reactionary, whereas the Northern States had either abolished slavery instantly or were doing so by gradual means. While the Negro could say very little about his condition in the South, he had a better audience among active groups of his own people in the North, although most whites there, influenced also by the reaction, tried to evade the disturbing discussion. There always was some antislavery sentiment in the North, but the radical abolition movement of the thirties and forties had not then developed. In the working out of this more vigorous program the Negro as an orator took an active part. Among the Negroes who thus spoke for the race were George Liele, Andrew Bryan, Richard Allen, Absalom Jones, James Varick, and Lemuel Haynes. While we have numerous religious discourses of these leaders of the church justifying the religious independence of the Negro, we have few expressions of their thought on social and political matters during the reaction.

The Negro, however, finally had an occasion for expressing his emotion as a result of the partial victory of the legal prohibition of the slave trade by Congress in 1808. On account of economic pressure and the change of the attitude of the South toward the institution as a result of the industrial revolution which made slavery apparently profitable, the trade was not abolished until the Civil War;

but believing that federal functionaries would live up to their oath of executing the laws of the United States, the Negro acclaimed with great joy what they considered the dawn of a new day.

On January 1, 1808, the day when prohibition of the traffic was supposed to go into effect, Peter Williams, Jr., a son of one of the founders of the A. M. E. Zion Church by the same name, and for years the rector of St. Philips Episcopal Church of New York City, delivered there the following address, expressing the sentiments of the Negroes at that time:[2]

ORATION ON THE ABOLITION OF THE SLAVE TRADE[1]

By Peter Williams[2]

Fathers, Brethren, and Fellow Citizens: At this auspicious moment I felicitate you on the abolition of the Slave Trade. This inhuman branch of commerce which, for some centuries past, has been carried on to a considerable extent, is, by the singular interposition of Divine Providence, this day extinguished. An event so important, so pregnant with happy consequences, must be extremely consonant to every philanthropic heart.

But to us, Africans and descendants of Africans, this period is deeply interesting. We have felt, sensibly felt, the sad effects of this abominable traffic. It has made, if not ourselves, our forefathers and kinsmen its unhappy victims; and pronounced on them, and their posterity, the sentence of perpetual slavery. But benevo-

[1] Peter Williams, Jr., was the son of Peter Williams, one of the founders of the African Methodist Episcopal Zion Church, in New York City. The son, however, became an Episcopalian, was educated for the ministry, and inducted into the services of that denomination at St. Phillip's Church in New York City. In this important position, he rendered not only the services expected of a minister, but endeavored to improve the life of the Negroes in whatever way they could be reached through the ministrations of the church.

He was a hospitable and generous man, well trained and interested in the education of the Negroes. With so many interests, he was naturally drawn into the discussion of the Negro question which, during his day, was very intense because of the difference in points of view as to whether colonization was the best remedy, or whether anything could be gained by the anti-slavery movement. He continued as an influential factor among the Negroes until his death in 1849.

[2] *An Oration on the Abolition of the Slave Trade, delivered in the African Church in the City of New York, Jan. 1, 1808,* by Peter Williams.

lent men have voluntarily stepped forward to obviate the consequences of this injustice and barbarity. They have striven, assiduously, to restore our natural rights; to guaranty them from fresh innovations; to furnish us with necessary information; and to stop the source from whence our evils have flowed.

The fruits of these laudable endeavors have long been visible; each moment they appear more conspicuous; and this day has produced an event which shall ever be memorable and glorious in the annals of history. We are now assembled to celebrate this momentous era; to recognize the beneficial influences of humane exertions; and by suitable demonstrations of joy, thanksgiving, and gratitude, to return to our heavenly Father, and to our earthly benefactors, our sincere acknowledgments.

Review, for a moment, my brethren, the history of the Slave Trade. Engendered in the foul recesses of the sordid mind, the unnatural monster inflicted gross evils on the human race. Its baneful footsteps are marked with blood; its infectious breath spreads war and desolation; and its train is composed of the complicated miseries of cruel and unceasing bondage.

Before the enterprising spirit of European genius explored the western coast of Africa, the state of our forefathers was a state of simplicity, innocence, and contentment. Unskilled in the arts of dissimulation, their bosoms were the seats of confidence; and their lips were the organs of truth. Strangers to the refinements of civilized society, they followed with implicit obedience the (simple) dictates of nature. Peculiarly observant of hospitality, they offered a place of refreshment to the weary, and an asylum to the unfortunate. Ardent in their affections, their minds were susceptible of the warmest emotions of love, friendship, and gratitude.

Although unacquainted with the diversified luxuries and amusements of civilized nations, they enjoyed some singular advantages from the bountiful hand of nature and from their own innocent and amiable manners, which rendered them a happy people. But, alas! this delightful picture has long since vanished; the angel of bliss has deserted their dwelling; and the demon of indescribable misery has rioted, uncontrolled, on the fair fields of our ancestors. After Columbus unfolded to civilized man the vast treasures of this western world, the desire of gain, which had chiefly induced the first colonists of America to cross the waters of the Atlantic, surpassing the bounds of reasonable acquisition, violated the sacred injunctions of the gospel, frustrated the designs of the pious and humane, and, enslaving the harmless aborigines, compelled them to drudge in the mines.

The severities of this employment was so insupportable to men who were unaccustomed to fatigue that, according to Robertson's "History of America," upwards of nine hundred thousand were destroyed in the space of fifteen years on the island of Hispaniola. A consumption so rapid must, in a short period, have deprived them of the instruments of labor, had not the same genius which first produced it found out another method to obtain them. This was no other than the importation of slaves from the coast of Africa.

The Genoese made the first regular importation, in the year 1517, by virtue of a patent granted by Charles of Austria to a Flemish favorite; since which, this commerce has increased to an astonishing and almost incredible degree.

After the manner of ancient piracy, descents were first made on the African coast; the towns bordering on the ocean were surprised, and a number of the inhabitants carried into slavery.

Alarmed at these depredations, the natives fled to the interior, and there united to secure themselves from the common foe. But the subtle invaders were not easily deterred from their purpose. Their experience, corroborated by historical testimony, convinced them that this spirit of unity would baffle every violent attempt; and that the most powerful method to dissolve it would be to diffuse in them the same avaricious disposition which they themselves possessed; and to afford them the means of gratifying it, by ruining each other. Fatal engine: fatal thou hast proved to man in all ages: where the greatest violence has proved ineffectual, their undermining principles have wrought destruction. By thy deadly power, the strong Grecian arm, which bid the world defiance, fell nerveless; by thy potent attacks, the solid pillars of Roman grandeur shook to their base; and, oh! Africans! by this parent of the Slave Trade, this grandsire of misery, the mortal blow was struck which crushed the peace and happiness of our country. Affairs now assumed a different aspect; the appearances of war were changed into the most amicable pretensions; presents apparently inestimable were made; and all the bewitching and alluring wiles of the seducer were practiced. The harmless African, taught to believe a friendly countenance, the sure token of a corresponding heart, soon disbanded his fears and evinced a favorable disposition towards his flattering enemies.

Thus the foe, obtaining an intercourse by a dazzling display of European finery, bewildered their simple understandings and corrupted their morals. Mutual agreements were then made; the Europeans were to supply the Africans with those gaudy trifles which so strongly affected them; and the Africans in return were to grant the Europeans their prisoners of war and convicts as slaves. These stipulations, naturally tending to delude the mind, answered the twofold purpose of enlarging their criminal code and of exciting incessant war at the same time that it furnished a specious pretext for the prosecution of this inhuman traffic. Bad as this may appear, had it prescribed the bounds of injustice, millions of unhappy victims might have still been spared. But, extending widely beyond measure and without control, large additions of slaves were made by kidnaping and the most unpalliated seizures.

Trace the past scenes of Africa and you will manifestly perceive these flagrant violations of human rights. The prince who once delighted in the happiness of his people, who felt himself bound by a sacred contract to defend their persons and property, was turned into their tyrant and scourge: he, who once strove to preserve peace and good understanding with the different nations, who never unsheathed his sword but in the cause of justice, at the signal of a slave ship assembled his warriors and rushed furiously upon his unsuspecting friends. What a scene does that town now present, which a few moments past was the abode of tranquillity. At the approach of the foe, alarm and confusion pervade every part; horror and dismay are depicted on every countenance; the aged chief, starting from his couch, calls forth his men to repulse the hostile invader: all ages obey the summons; feeble youth and decrepit age join the standard; while the foe, to effect his purpose, fires the town.

Now, with unimaginable terror the battle commences: hear now the shrieks of the women, the cries of the children, the shouts of the warriors, and the groans of the dying. See with what desperation the inhabitants fight in defense of their darling joys. But, alas! overpowered by a superior foe, their force is broken; their ablest warriors fall; and the wretched remnant are taken captives.

Where are now those pleasant dwellings, where peace and harmony reigned incessant? where those beautiful fields, whose smiling crops and enchanting verdure enlivened the heart of every beholder? Alas! those tenements are now enveloped in destructive flames; those fair fields are now bedewed with blood and covered with mangled carcasses. Where are now those sounds of mirth and gladness, which loudly rang throughout the village? where those darling youth, those venerable aged, who mutually animated the festive throng? Alas! those exhilarating peals are now changed into the dismal groans of inconceivable distress; the survivors of those happy people are now carried into cruel captivity. Ah! driven from their native soil, they cast their languishing eyes behind, and with aching hearts bid adieu to every prospect of joy and comfort.

A spectacle so truly distressing is sufficient to blow into a blaze the most latent spark of humanity; but, the adamantine heart of avarice, dead to every sensation of pity, regards not the voice of the sufferers, but hastily drives them to market for sale.

Oh, Africa, Africa! to what horrid inhumanities have thy shores been witness; thy shores, which were once the garden of the world, the seal of almost paradisaical joys, have been transformed into regions of woe; thy sons, who were once the happiest of mortals, are reduced to slavery, and bound in weighty shackles, now fill the trader's ship. But, though defeated in the contest for liberty, their magnanimous souls scorn the gross indignity, and choose death in preference to slavery. Painful; ah! painful, must be that existence which the rational mind can deliberately doom to self-destruction. Thus the poor Africans, robbed of every joy, while they see not the saddened hearts, sink into the abyss of consummate misery. Their lives, embittered by reflection, anticipation, and present sorrows, they feel burthensome; and death (whose dreary mansions appal the stoutest hearts) they view as their only shelter.

You, my brethren, beloved Africans, who had passed the days of infancy when you left your country, you best can tell the aggravated sufferings of our unfortunate race; your memories can bring to view these scenes of bitter grief. What, my brethren, when dragged from your native land on board the slave ship, what was the anguish which you saw, which you felt? what the pain, what the dreadful forebodings which filled your throbbing bosoms?

But you, my brethren, descendants of African forefathers, I call upon you to view a scene of unfathomable distress. Let your imagination carry you back to former days. Behold a vessel, bearing our forefathers and brethren from the place of their nativity to a distant and inhospitable clime; behold their dejected countenances, their streaming eyes, their fettered limbs; hear them, with piercing cries, and pitiful moans, deploring their wretched fate. After their arrival in port, see them separated without regard to the ties of blood or friendship: husband from wife; parent from child; brother from sister; friend from friend. See the parting tear rolling down their fallen cheeks; hear the parting sigh die on their quivering lips.

But let us no longer pursue a theme of boundless affliction. An enchanting sound now demands your attention. Hail! hail! glorious day, whose resplendent rising disperseth the clouds which have hovered with destruction over the land of Africa, and illumines it by the most brilliant rays of future prosperity. Rejoice, oh! Africans! No longer shall tyranny, war, and injustice, with irresistible sway, desolate your native country; no longer shall torrents of human blood deluge its delightful plains; no longer shall it witness your countrymen wielding among each other the instruments of death; nor the insidious kidnapper, darting from his midnight haunt, on the feeble and unprotected; no longer shall its shores resound with the awful howlings of infatuated warriors, the deathlike groans of vanquished innocents, nor the clanking fetters of woe-doomed captives. Rejoice, oh, ye descendants of Africans! No longer shall the United States of America, nor the extensive colonies of Great Britain, admit the degrading commerce of the human species; no longer shall they swell the tide of African misery by the importation of slaves. Rejoice, my brethren, that the channels are obstructed through which slavery, and its direful concomitants, have been entailed on the African race. But let incessant strains of gratitude be mingled with your expressions of joy. Through the infinite mercy of the great Jehovah, this day announces the abolition of the Slave Trade. Let, therefore, the heart that is warmed by the smallest drop of African blood glow in grateful transports, and cause the lofty arches of the sky to reverberate eternal praise to his boundless goodness.

Oh, God! we thank Thee, that thou didst condescend to listen to the cries of Africa's wretched sons, and that Thou didst interfere in their behalf. At Thy call humanity sprang forth and espoused the cause of the oppressed; one hand she employed in drawing from their vitals the deadly arrows of injustice; and the other in holding a shield, to defend them from fresh assaults; and at that illustrious moment, when the sons of '76 pronounced these United States free and independent; when the spirit of patriotism erected a temple sacred to liberty; when the inspired voice of Americans first uttered those noble sentiments, "We hold these truths to be self-evident, that all men are created equal; that they are endowed by their Creator with certain unalienable rights; among which are life, liberty, and the pursuit of happiness"; and when the bleeding African, lifting his fetters, exclaimed, "Am I not a man and a brother"; then, with redoubled efforts, the angel of humanity strove to restore to the African race the inherent rights of man.

To the instruments of divine goodness, those benovolent men who voluntarily obeyed the dictates of humanity, we owe much. Surrounded with innumerable difficulties, their undaunted spirits dared to oppose a powerful host of interested men. Heedless to the voice of fame, their independent souls dared to oppose the strong gales of popular prejudice. Actuated by principles of genuine philanthropy, they dared to despise the emoluments of ill-gotten wealth, and to sacrifice much of their temporal interests at the shrine of benevolence.

As an American, I glory in informing you that Columbia boasts the first men who distinguished themselves eminently in the vindication of our rights and the improvement of our state.

Conscious that slavery was unfavorable to the benign influences of Christianity, the pious Woolman loudly declaimed against it; and, although destitute of fortune, he resolved to spare neither time nor pains to check its progress. With this view he traveled over several parts of North America on foot and exhorted his brethren, of the denomination of Friends, to abjure the iniquitous custom. These, convinced by the cogency of his arguments, denied the privileges of their society to the slaveholder, and zealously engaged in destroying the aggravated evil. Thus, through the beneficial labors of this pattern of piety and brotherly kindness, commenced a work which has since been promoted by the humane of every denomination. His memory ought therefore to be deeply engraven on the tablets of our hearts; and ought ever to inspire us with the most ardent esteem.

Nor less to be prized are the useful exertions of Anthony Benezet. This inestimable person, sensible of the equality of mankind, rose superior to the illiberal opinions of the age; and, disallowing an inferiority in the African genius, established the first school to cultivate our understandings and to better our condition.

Thus, by enlightening the mind and implanting the seeds of virtue, he banished, in a degree, the mists of prejudice, and laid the foundations of our future happiness. Let, therefore, a due sense of his meritorious actions ever create in us a deep reverence of his beloved name. Justice to the occasion, as well as his merits, forbid me to pass in silence over the name of the honorable William Wilberforce. Possessing talents capable of adorning the greatest subjects, his comprehensive mind found none more worthy his constant attention than the abolition of the Slave Trade. For this he soared to the zenith of his towering eloquence, and for this he struggled with perpetual ardor. Thus, anxious in defense of our rights, he pledged himself never to desert the cause; and, by his repeated and strenuous exertions, he finally obtained the desirable end. His extensive services have, therefore, entitled him to a large share of our affections, and to a lasting tribute of our unfeigned thanks.

But think not, my brethren, that I pretend to enumerate the persons who have proved our strenuous advocates, or that I have portrayed the merits of those I have mentioned. No, I have given but a few specimens of a countless number, and no more than the rude outlines of the beneficence of these. Perhaps there never existed a human institution which has displayed more intrinsic merit than the societies for the abolition of slavery.

Reared on the pure basis of philanthropy, they extend to different quarters of the globe, and comprise a considerable number of humane and respectable men. These, greatly impressed with the importance of the work, entered into it with such disinterestedness, engagedness, and prudence, as does honor to their wisdom and virtue. To effect the purposes of these societies no legal means were left untried which afforded the smallest prospects of success. Books were disseminated, and discourses delivered, wherein every argument was employed which the penetrating mind could adduce from religion, justice or reason, to prove the turpitude of slavery, and numerous instances related calculated to awaken sentiments of compassion. To further their charitable intentions, applications were constantly made to different bodies of legislature, and every concession improved to our best possible advantage. Taught by preceding occurrences, that the waves of oppression are ever ready to overwhelm the defenseless, they became the vigilant guardians of all our reinstated joys. Sensible that the inexperienced mind is greatly exposed to the allurements of vice, they cautioned us, by the most salutary precepts and virtuous examples against its fatal encroachments; and the better to establish us in the paths of rectitude they instituted schools to instruct us in the knowledge of letters and the principles of virtue.

By these and similar methods, with divine assistance they assailed the dark dungeon of slavery; shattered its rugged wall, and enlarging thousands of the captives, bestowed on them the blessings of civil society. Yes, my brethren, through their efficiency, numbers of us now enjoy the invaluable gem of liberty; numbers have been secured from a relapse into bondage, and numbers have attained a useful education.

I need not, my brethren, take a further view of our present circumstances, to convince you of the providential benefits which we have derived from our patrons; for if you take a retrospect of the past situation of Africans, and descendants of Africans, in this and other countries, to your observation our advancements must be obvious. From these considerations, added to the happy event which we now celebrate, let us ever entertain the profoundest veneration for our munificent benefactors, and return to them from the altars of our hearts the fragrant incense of incessant gratitude. But let not, my brethren, our demonstrations of gratitude be confined to the mere expressions of our lips.

The active part which the friends of humanity have taken to ameliorate our sufferings has rendered them, in a measure, the pledges of our integrity. You must be well aware that notwithstanding their endeavors, they have yet remaining, from interest.

and prejudice, a number of opposers. These, carefully watching for every opportunity to injure the cause, will not fail to augment the smallest defects in our lives and conversation; and reproach our benefactors with them as the fruits of their actions.

Let us, therefore, by a steady and upright deportment, by a strict obedience and respect to the laws of the land, form an invulnerable bulwark against the shafts of malice. Thus, evincing to the world that our garments are unpolluted by the stains of ingratitude, we shall reap increasing advantages from the favors conferred; the spirits of our departed ancestors shall smile with complacency on the change of our state; and posterity shall exult in the pleasing remembrance.

May the time speedily commence when Ethiopia shall stretch forth her hands; when the sun of liberty shall beam resplendent on the whole African race; and its genial influences promote the luxuriant growth of knowledge and virtue.

Although enjoying some free speech in the non-slaveholding States, the Negro found that he was not removed from the inconveniences of his race resulting from the reaction of the industrial revolution. The very effort of the Negro to migrate from the South, where he was oppressed, to the North, where he would have more liberty, tended a hundred years ago, as it does today, to make the race problem national rather than sectional. As soon as these migrants to the North increased to the extent that they were unable to find employment and consequently became a public charge, an effort was made to restrict the movement. Upon hearing that there had been offered in the legislature of Pennsylvania a bill to prevent the coming of free people of color into that State, one of their number, over the signature of a MAN OF COLOR, addressed a series of letters to the public.

This writer has been identified as James Forten,[1] of

[1] James Forten developed in Philadelphia. There he accumulated a considerable fortune out of his new device which he perfected for handling sales. His manufacturing

Philadelphia. Along with Robert Purvis [1] and Russell Perrott of the same city, Forten constituted the backbone of resistance to encroachments on the rights of the free people of color in that commonwealth. Like his predecessors, the writer was forcibly expressing this thought wherever he had an opportunity and was seeking a larger audience by giving the public the benefit of knowing what he had already said on various occasions in his own group. His thought thus expressed in 1813 here follows:

A LATE BILL BEFORE THE SENATE OF PENNSYLVANIA

By James Forten

We hold this truth to be self-evident, that God created all men equal, is one of the most prominent features in the Declaration of Independence, and in that glorious fabric of collected wisdom, our noble Constitution. This idea embraces the Indian and the European, the savage and the Saint, the Peruvian and the Laplander, the white man and the African, and whatever measures are adopted subversive of this inestimable privilege, are in direct violation of the letter and spirit of our Constitution, and become subject to the animadversion of all, particularly those who are deeply interested in the measure.

business was widely known. Like Robert Purvis, he joined others in the attack on colonization, believing that the Negro had as much right to remain in this country as any other group of persons. In his attack, he was both logical and forceful, and he fearlessly belabored the advocates of colonization in spite of the fact that such a position was not popular in Philadelphia during these years because of its close commercial connection with the South.

[1] Robert Purvis was born in Charleston, South Carolina. However, he was educated in New England, where he early embraced the principles of freedom as advocated by William Lloyd Garrison. To these principles he adhered throughout life, although he was a man of means and could have easily lived in some part of the world where the influence of slavery could not handicap a person of color. He gave of his abundant means, made personal sacrifices, and ran the risk of losing his life in doing what he could to aid the slave.

In personal appearance, Robert Purvis was practically white. He could have easily denied connection with the Negro race, and lived as a white man, a thing which he would never do. He was "a man of fine manners, of a cultivated mind, a reflective imagination, and eloquent speech."

During his career as a worker for the uplift of the Negroes, he lived in and about Philadelphia. There he passed as a man of unblemished character, blameless life, an ardent friend, and a dangerous foe of slavery.

These thoughts were suggested by the promulgation of a late bill, before the Senate of Pennsylvania, to prevent the emigration of people of color into this state. It was not passed into a law at this session, and must in consequence lay over until the next, before when we sincerely hope, the white men, whom we should look upon as our protectors, will have become convinced of the inhumanity and impolicy of such a measure, and forbear to deprive us of those inestimable treasures, liberty and independence. This is almost the only state in the Union wherein the African race have justly boasted of rational liberty and the protection of the laws, and shall it now be said they have been deprived of that liberty, and publicly exposed for sale to the highest bidder? Shall colonial inhumanity that has marked many of us with shameful stripes, become the practice of the people of Pennsylvania, while Mercy stands weeping at the miserable spectacle? People of Pennsylvania, descendants of the immortal Penn, doom us not to the unhappy fate of thousands of our countrymen in the Southern States and the West Indies; despise the traffic in blood, and the blessing of the African will forever be around you. Many of us are men of property, for the security of which we have hitherto looked to the laws of our blessed state, but should this become a law, our property is jeopardized, since the same power which can expose to sale an unfortunate fellow creature, can wrest from him those estates, which years of honest industry have accumulated. Where shall the poor African look for protection, should the people of Pennsylvania consent to oppress him? We grant there are a number of worthless men belonging to our color, but there are laws of sufficient rigor for their punishment, if properly and duly enforced. We wish not to screen the guilty from punishment, but with the guilty do not permit the innocent to suffer. If there are worthless men, there are also men of merit among the African race, who are useful members of Society. The truth of this let their benevolent institutions and the numbers clothed and fed by them witness. Punish the guilty man of color to the utmost limit of the laws, but sell him not to slavery! If he is in danger of becoming a public charge, prevent him! If he is too indolent to labor for his own subsistence, compel him to do so; but sell him not to slavery. By selling him you do not make him better, but commit a wrong, without benefiting the object of it or society at large.

Many of our ancestors were brought here more than one hundred years ago; many of our fathers, many of ourselves, have fought and bled for the independence of our country. Do not then expose us to sale. Let not the spirit of the father behold the son robbed of that liberty which he died to establish, but let the motto of our legislature be: "The law knows no distinction."

* * * * * * * * *

Those patriotic citizens, who, after resting from the toils of an arduous war, which achieved our independence and laid the foundation of the only reasonable republic upon earth, associated together, and for the protection of those inestimable rights for the establishment of which they had exhausted their blood and treasure, framed the Constitution of Pennsylvania, have by the ninth article declared, that "All men are born equally free and independent, and have certain inherent and indefeasible rights, among which are those of enjoying life and liberty." Under the restraint of wise and well administered laws, we cordially unite in the above glorious sentiment, but by the bill upon which we have been remarking, it appears as if the committee who drew it up mistook the sentiment expressed in this article, and do not consider us as men, or that those enlightened statesmen who formed the constitution upon the basis of experience, intended to exclude us from its blessings and protection. If the former, why are we not to be considered as men? Has the God who made the white man and the black left any record declaring us a different species? Are we not sustained by the same power, supported by the same food, hurt by the same wounds, wounded by the same wrongs, pleased with the same delights, and propagated by the same means? And should we not then enjoy the same liberty, and be protected by the same laws? We wish not to legislate, for our means of information and the acquisition of knowledge are, in the nature of things, so circumscribed, that we must consider ourselves incompetent to the task; but let us, in legislation, be considered as men. It cannot be that the authors of our Constitution intended to exclude us from its benefits, for just emerging from unjust and cruel emancipation, their souls were too much affected with their own deprivations to commence the reign of terror over others. They knew we were deeper skinned than they were, but they acknowledged us as men, and found that many an honest heart beat beneath a dusky bosom.

They felt that they had no more authority to enslave us, than England had to tyrannize over them. They were convinced that if amenable to the same laws in our actions we should be protected by the same laws in our rights and privileges. Actuated by these sentiments they adopted the glorious fabric of our liberties, and declaring "all men" free, they did not particularize white and black, because they never supposed it would be made a question whether *we were men or not.* Sacred be the ashes, and deathless be the memory of those heroes who are dead; and revered be the persons and the characters of those who still exist and lift the thunders of admonition against the traffic in blood. And here my brethren in color, let the tear of gratitude and the sigh of regret break forth for that great and good man, who lately fell a victim to the promiscuous fury of death, in whom you have lost a zealous friend, a powerful, an herculean advocate; a sincere adviser, and one who spent many an hour of his life to break your fetters, and ameliorate your condition—I mean the ever to be lamented Dr. Benjamin Rush.

It seems almost incredible that the advocates of liberty should conceive the idea of selling a fellow creature to slavery. It is like the heroes of the French Revolution, who cried *"Vive la Republique,"* while the decapitated Nun was precipitated into the general reservoir of death, and the palpitating embryo decorated the point of the bayonet. Ye, who should be our protectors, do not destroy.—We will cheerfully submit to the laws, and aid in bringing offenders against them of every color to justice; but do not let the laws operate so severely, so degradingly, so unjustly against us alone.

Let us put a case, in which the law in question operates peculiarly hard and unjust.—I have a brother, perhaps, who resides in a distant part of the Union, and after a separation of years, actuated by the same fraternal affection which beats in the bosom of a white man, he comes to visit me. Unless that brother be registered in twenty-four hours after, and be able to produce a certificate to that effect, he is liable, according to the second and third sections of the bill, to a fine of twenty dollars, to arrest, imprisonment and sale. Let the unprejudiced mind ponder upon this, and then pronounce it the justifiable act of a free people, if he can. To this we trust our cause, without fear of the issue. The unprejudiced must pronounce any act tending to deprive a free man of his right, freedom and immunities, as not only cruel in the extreme, but decidedly unconstitutional both as regards the letter and spirit of that glorious instrument. The same power which protects the white man, should protect the black.

The evils arising from the bill before our Legislature, so fatal to the rights of freemen, and so characteristic of European despotism, are so numerous, that to consider them all would extend these numbers further than time or my talent will permit me to carry them. The concluding paragraph of my last utterance, states a case of peculiar hardship, arising from the second section of this bill, upon which I cannot refrain from making a few more remarks. The man of color receiving as a visitor any other person of color, is bound to turn informer, and rudely report to the Register, that a friend and brother has come to visit him for a few days, whose name he must take within twenty-four hours, or forfeit a sum which the iron hand of the law is authorized to rend from him, partly for the benefit of the Register. Who is this Register? A man, and exercising an office, where ten dollars is the fee for each delinquent, will probably be a cruel man and find delinquents where they really do not exist. The poor black is left to the merciless gripe of an avaricious Register, without an appeal, in the event, from his tyranny or oppression! O miserable race, born to the same hopes, created with the same feeling, and destined for the same goal, you are reduced by your fellow creatures below the brute. The dog is protected and pampered at the board of his master, while the poor African and his descendant, whether a Saint or a felon, is branded with infamy, registered as a slave, and we may expect shortly to find a law to prevent their increase, by taxing them according to numbers, and authorizing the Constables to seize and confine every one who dare to walk the streets without a collar on his neck!—What have the people of color been guilty of, that they more than others, should be compelled to register their houses, lands, servants and *children?* Yes, ye rulers of the black man's destiny, reflect upon this: our *children* must be registered, and bear about them a certificate, or be subject to imprisonment and fine. You, who are perusing this effusion of feeling, are you a parent? Have you children around whom your affections are bound, by those delightful bonds which none but a parent can know? Are they the delight of your prosperity, and the solace of your afflictions? If all this be true, to you we submit our cause. The parent's feeling cannot err. By your verdict will we stand or fall —by your verdict, live slaves or freemen. It is said that the bill does not extend to children, but the words of the bill are, "Whether as an *inmate, visitor, hireling, or tenant, in his or her house or room.*" Whether this does not embrace every soul that can be in a house, the reader is left to judge; and whether the father should be bound to register his child, even within the twenty-four hours after it is brought into the world, let the father's feelings determine. This is the fact, and our children sent on our lawful business, not having sense enough to understand the meaning of such proceedings, must show their certificate of registry or be borne to prison. The bill specifies neither age nor sex—designates neither the honest man or the vagabond—but like the fretted porcupine, his quills aim its deadly shafts promiscuously at all.

For the honor and dignity of our native state, we wish not to see this bill pass into a law, as well as for its degrading tendency towards us; for although oppressed by those to whom we look for protection, our grievances are light compared with the load of reproach that must be heaped upon our commonwealth. The story will fly from the north to the south, and the advocates of slavery, the traders in human blood, will smile contemptuously at the once boasted moderation and humanity of Pennsylvania! What! That place, whose institutions for the prevention of slavery, are the admiration of surrounding states and of Europe, becomes the advocate of mancipation and wrong, and the oppressor of the free and innocent!—Tell it not in Gath! publish it not in the streets of Askelon! lest the daughters of the Philistines rejoice! lest the children of the uncircumcised triumph!

It is to be hoped that in our Legislature there is patriotism, humanity, and mercy sufficient to crush this attempt upon the civil liberty of freemen, and to prove that the enlightened body who have hitherto guarded their fellow creatures, without regard to the color of the skin, will still stretch forth the wings of protection to that race, whose persons have been the scorn, and whose calamities have been the jest of the world for ages. We trust the time is at hand when this obnoxious Bill will receive its death warrant, and freedom still remain to cheer the bosom of a man of color.

* * * * * * * * *

I proceed again to the consideration of the bill of *unalienable* rights belonging to black men, the passage of which will only tend to show that the advocates of emancipation can enact laws more degrading to the free man, and more injurious to his feelings, than all the tyranny of slavery, or the shackles of infatuated despotism. And let me here remark, that this unfortunate race of humanity, although protected by our laws, are already subject to the fury and caprice of a certain set of men, who regard neither humanity, law nor privilege. They are already considered as a different species, and little above the brute creation. They are thought to be objects fit for nothing else than lordly men to vent the effervescence of their spleen upon, and to tyrannize over, like the bearded Mussulman over his horde of slaves. Nay, the Mussulman thinks more of his horse than the generality of people do of the despised black!—Are not men of color sufficiently degraded? Why then increase their degradation? It is a well known fact, that black people, upon certain days of public jubilee, dare not be seen after twelve o'clock in the day, upon the field to enjoy the times; for no sooner do the fumes of that potent devil, Liquor, mount into the brain, than the poor black is assailed like the destroying Hyena or the avaricious Wolf! I allude particularly to the *Fourth of July!*—Is it not wonderful, that the day set apart for the festival of liberty, should be abused by the advocates of freedom, in endeavouring to sully what they profess to adore. If men, though they know that the law protects all, will dare, in defiance of law, to execute their hatred upon the defenceless black, will they not by the passage of this bill, believe him still more a mark for their venom and spleen?—Will they not believe him completely deserted by authority, and subject to every outrage brutality can inflict—too surely they will, and the poor wretch will turn his eyes around to look in vain for protection. Pause, ye rulers of a free people, before you give us over to despair and violation—we implore you, for the sake of humanity, to snatch us from the pinnacle of ruin, from that gulf, which will swallow our rights, as fellow creatures; our privileges, as citizens; and our liberties, as men!

There are men among us of reputation and property, as good

citizens as any men can be, and who, for their property, pay as heavy taxes as any citizens are compelled to pay. All taxes, except personal, fall upon them, and still even they are not exempted from this degrading bill. The villainous part of the community, of all colors, we wish to see punished and retrieved as much as any people can. Enact laws to punish them severely, but do not let them operate against the innocent as well as the guilty. Can there be any generosity in this? Can there be any semblance of justice, or of that enlightened conduct which is ever the boasted pole star of freedom? By no means. This bill is nothing but the *ignus fatuus* of mistaken policy!

* * * * * * * * *

By the third section of this bill, which is its peculiar hardship, the police officers are authorized to apprehend any black, whether a vagrant or a man of reputable character, who cannot produce a certificate that he has been registered. He is to be arrayed before a justice, who is thereupon to commit him to prison!—The jailor is to advertise a Freeman, and at the expiration of six months, if no owner appear for this degraded black, he is to be *exposed to sale,* and if not sold to be confined at hard labor for seven years!! —Man of feeling, read this!—No matter who, no matter where. The constable, whose antipathy generally against the black is very great, will take every opportunity of hurting his feelings!—Perhaps he sees him at a distance, and having a mind to raise the boys in hue and cry against him, exclaims, "Halloa! Stop the Negro!" The boys, delighting in the sport, immediately begin to hunt him, and immediately from a hundred tongues is heard the cry—*"Hoa, Negro, where is your Certificate!"*—Can anything be conceived more degrading to humanity! Can anything be done more shocking to the principles of civil liberty! A person arriving from another state, ignorant of the existence of such a law, may fall a victim to its cruel oppression. But he is to be advertised, and if no owner appear—how can an owner appear for a man who is free and belongs to no one!—if no owner appear, he is exposed for sale!—Oh, inhuman spectacle: found in no unjust act, convicted of no crime, he is barbarously sold, like the produce of the soil, to the highest bidder, or what is still worse, for no crimes, without the inestimable privilege of a trial by his peers, doomed to the dreary walls of a prison for the term of seven tedious years!—My

God, what a situation is his! Search the legends of tyranny and find no precedent. No example can be found in all the reigns of violence and oppression, which have marked the lapse of time. It stands alone. It has been left for Pennsylvania to raise her ponderous arm against the liberties of the black, whose greatest boast has been that he resided in a state where civil liberty, and sacred justice were administered alike to all.—What must be his reflection now, that the asylum he had left from mancipation has been destroyed, and that he is left to suffer, like Daniel of old, with no one but his God to help him! Where is the bosom that does not heave a sigh for his fall, unless it be callous to every sentiment of humanity and mercy?

The fifth section of this bill is also peculiarly hard, inasmuch as it prevents freemen from living where they please.—Pennsylvania has always been a refuge from slavery, and to this state the Southern black, when freed, has flown for safety. Why does he this! When masters in many of the Southern states, which they frequently do, free a particular black, unless the black leaves the state in so many hours, any person resident of the said state, can have him arrested and again sold to slavery:—The hunted black is obliged to flee, or remain and be again a slave. I have known persons of this description sold three times after being first emancipated. Where shall he go? Shut every state against him, and, like Pharaoh's kine, drive him into the sea.—Is there no spot on earth that will protect him! Against their inclination, his ancestors were forced from their homes by traders in human flesh, and even under such circumstances the wretched offspring are denied the protection you afford to brutes.

It is in vain that we are forming societies of different kinds to ameliorate the conditions of our unfortunate brethren, to correct their morals and to render them not only honest but useful members to society. All our efforts by this bill are despised, and we are doomed to feel the lash of oppression:—As well may we be outlawed, as well may the glorious privileges of the Gospel be denied us, and all endeavours used to cut us off from happiness hereafter as well as here!—The case is similar, and I am much deceived if this bill does not destroy the morals it is intended to produce.

I have done. My feelings are acute, and I have ventured to express them without intending either accusation or insult to any one. An appeal to the heart is my intention, and if I have failed, it is my great misfortune not to have had a power of eloquence sufficient to convince. But I trust the eloquence of nature will succeed, and that the law-givers of this happy Commonwealth will yet remain the Blacks' friend, and the advocates of Freemen.

Following this same method of an address to the public expressive of sentiments which they as leaders of the race were setting forth on the rostrum, James Forten as chairman and Russell Perrott as secretary of a large indignation meeting of the people of color in Philadelphia, held on August 10, 1817, proclaimed the following sentiments. The cause of this assembly was the effort of certain white elements in the country to deport the free people of color and such slaves as might be emancipated. This had culminated in the organization of the American Colonization Society in 1816. This organization became unusually popular, although it meant all things to all men. It pleased the Southern slaveholder desiring to remove the free Negroes who might interfere with the permanence of slavery; it met the requirements of the gradual emancipationists; and it proved acceptable to the few philanthropists actually interested in seeing the Negro establish himself in the land of his fathers. As agents of this society touring the country in its behalf were warmly welcomed with this new solution of the race problem, the Negroes of the North became fearful that they might be expatriated. This fear was further intensified by efforts of Negroes at servile insurrection, like that of Gabriel in Richmond, in 1800, Denmark Vesey in Charleston in 1822, and Nat Turner in Southampton County, Virginia, in 1831. The opinion among the whites thereafter was that the free Negroes had to leave this country immediately, regardless of their attachment to their respective communities. This address not only shows what the Negroes were thinking, but what they were saying whenever they had an opportunity to speak on African Colonization.

AN ADDRESS TO THE HUMANE AND BENEVOLENT INHABITANTS OF THE CITY AND COUNTY OF PHILADELPHIA[1]

BY JAMES FORTEN AND RUSSELL PERROTT

The free people of colour, assembled together, under circumstances of deep interest to their happiness and welfare, humbly and respectfully lay before you this expression of their feelings and apprehensions.

Relieved from the miseries of slavery, many of us by your aid, possessing the benefits which industry and integrity in this prosperous country assure to all its inhabitants, enjoying the rich blessings of religion, by opportunities of worshiping the only true God, under the light of Christianity, each of us according to his understanding; and having afforded to us and to our children the means of education and improvement; we have no wish to separate from our present homes, for any purpose whatever. Contented with our present situation and condition we are not desirous of increasing their prosperity, but by honest efforts and by the use of those opportunities for their improvement, which the constitution and laws allow to all. It is therefore with painful solicitude, and sorrowing regret, we have seen a plan for colonizing the free people of colour of the United States on the coast of Africa, brought forward under the auspices and sanction of gentlemen whose names give value to all they recommend, and who certainly are among the wisest, the best, and the most benevolent of men, in this great nation.

If the plan of colonizing is intended for our benefit and those who now promote it, will never seek our injury; we humbly and respectfully urge that it is not asked for by us; nor will it be required by any circumstances, in our present or future condition; as long as we shall be permitted to share the protection of the excellent laws, and just government which we now enjoy, in common with every individual of the community.

We therefore, a portion of those, who are objects of this plan, and among those whose happiness, with that of others of our colour, it is intended to promote, with humble and grateful acknowledgments to those who have devised it, renounce, and disclaim every

[1] From pages 69 to 72 of Vol. I-IV of Minutes of the Proceedings of a Special Meeting of the Fifteenth American Convention, etc.

connection with it, and respectfully but firmly declare our determination not to participate in any part of it.

If this plan of colonization now proposed is intended to provide a refuge and a dwelling for a portion of our brethren, who are now held in slavery in the south, we have other and stronger objections to it, and we entreat your consideration of them.

The ultimate and final abolition of slavery in the United States is, under the guidance and protection of a just God, progressing. Every year witnesses the release of numbers of the victims of oppression, and affords new and safe assurances that the freedom of all will in the end be accomplished. As they are thus, by degrees relieved from bondage, our brethren have opportunities for instruction and improvement; and thus they become in some measure fitted for their liberty.—Every year, many of us have restored to us by the gradual, but certain march of the cause of abolition—parents, from whom we have been long separated—wives and children, whom we had left in servitude—and brothers, in blood as well as in early sufferings, from whom we had been long parted.

But if the emancipations of our kindred shall, when the plan of colonization shall go into effect, be attended with transportation to a distant land, and shall be granted on no other condition; the consolation for our past sufferings and of those of our colour, who are in slavery, which have hitherto been, and under the present situation of things, would continue to be afforded to us and to them, will cease for ever. The cords, which now connect them with us will be stretched by the distance to which their ends will be carried until they break; and all the sources of happiness, which affection and connection, and blood bestow, will be ours or theirs no more.

Nor do we view the colonization of those who may become emancipated by its operation among our southern brethren, as capable of producing their happiness. Unprepared by education, and a knowledge of the truths of our blessed religion, for their new situation, those who will thus become colonists will themselves be surrounded by every suffering which can afflict the members of the human family.

Without arts, without habits of industry, and unaccustomed to provide by their own exertions and foresight for their wants, the colony will soon become the abode of every vice and the home of every misery. Soon will the light of Christianity, which now dawns among that section of our species, be shut out by the clouds of ignorance, and their day of life be closed, without the illuminations of the Gospel.

To those of our brethren who shall be left behind, there will be assured perpetual slavery and augmented sufferings.—Diminished in numbers the slave population of the southern states, which by its magnitude alarms its proprietors, will be easily secured. Those among their bondmen, who feel that they should be free, by rights which all mankind have from God and from nature, and who thus may become dangerous to the quiet of their masters, will be sent to the colony; and the tame and submissive will be retained, and subjected to increased rigour. Year after year will witness these means to assure safety and submission among their slaves; and the southern masters will colonize only those whom it may be dangerous to keep among them. The bondage of a large portion of our brethren will thus be rendered perpetual.

Should the anticipations of misery and want among the colonists, which with great deference we have submitted to your better judgment, be realized; to emancipate and transport to the colony, will be held forth by slave-holders as the worst and heaviest of punishments, and they will be threatened and successfully used to enforce increased submission to their wishes and subjection to their commands.

Nor ought the sufferings and sorrows, which must be produced by an exercise of the right to transport and colonize such only of their slaves as may be selected by the slave-holders escape the attention and consideration of those whom with all humility we now address. Parents will be torn from their children—husbands from their wives—brothers from brothers—and all the heart-rending agonies which were endured by our forefathers when they were dragged into bondage from Africa will be again renewed, and with increased anguish. The shores of America will like the sands of Africa be watered by the tears of those who will be left behind. Those who shall be carried away will roam childless, widowed, and alone, over the burning plains of Guinea.

Disclaiming, as we emphatically do, a wish or desire to interpose our opinions and feelings between all plans of colonization, and the judgment of those whose wisdom as far exceeds ours, as their situations are exalted above ours; *We humbly*, respectfully, and fervently entreat and beseech your disapprobation of the plan of colonization now offered by "the American society for colonizing the free people of colour of the United States."—Here, in the city of Philadelphia, where the voice of the suffering sons of Africa was first heard; where was first commenced the work of abolition, on which Heaven hath smiled, for it could have had success only from the Great Maker; let not a purpose be assisted which will stay the cause of the entire abolition of slavery in the United States, and which may defeat it altogether; which proffers to those who do not ask for them what it calls benefits, but which they consider injuries; and which must insure to the multitudes whose prayers can only reach you through us, *misery, and sufferings, and perpetual slavery.*

Throughout the period one finds that now and then other Negroes fearlessly spoke out on questions of importance to their race. One of the avenues through which they expressed themselves was the periodical convocation of the antislavery group. As the abolitionists were always interested in hearing the horrors of slavery portrayed by the Negroes themselves, those who early developed the power of intelligent expression were welcomed to the antislavery platform. On December 11, 1818, then, Prince Saunders submitted to the American Convention of Abolition Societies the following address voicing his sentiments which he had often expressed in the same language in speaking to his own people and their friends. His interest here was in the maintenance of the independence of Haiti, which had not been generally recognized by European countries and was not recognized by the United States until the Civil War. There was some apprehension that France might reëstablish its control over that island. Interested in the natives of Haiti, and thinking, too, that many free Negroes of the United States would settle there, Prince Saunders urged that this land be kept open to serve as such an asylum.

PROMOTING THE ABOLITION OF SLAVERY, AND IMPROVING THE CONDITION OF THE AFRICAN RACE

By Prince Saunders

Respected Gentlemen and Friends: At a period so momentous as the present, when the friends of abolition and emancipation, as well as those whom observation and experience might teach us to beware to whom we should apply the endearing appellations, are professedly concerned for the establishment of an Asylum for those Free Persons of Colour, who may be disposed to remove to it, and for such persons as shall hereafter be emancipated from slavery, a careful examination of this subject is imposed upon us.

So large a number of abolitionists, convened from different sections of the country, is at all times and under any circumstances, an interesting spectacle to the eye of the philanthropist, how doubly delightful then is it, to me, whose interests and feelings so largely partake in the object you have in view, to behold this convention engaged in solemn deliberation upon those subjects employed to promote the improvement of the condition of the African race.

It was in this city and its vicinity, that the eccentric, the humane, the pious, and the practically philanthropic Lay, was the first who laboured to draw aside that thick, and then impenetrable veil, with which prejudice and avarice had obscured the enormities of the slave-trade; being seemingly conscious that it was only necessary that its iniquitous and barbarous character should be discovered and known in order to effect its condemnation and abolition, by every community of practical Christians.

This commonwealth was, also, the scene of a great portion of the benevolent exertions of that early and zealous advocate for the injured descendants of Africa, the candid and upright Sandiford.

Philadelphia had the honour and the happiness of being for years adorned and illumined by the beneficent light of the precepts and example of that distinguished philanthropist, the late venerable and excellent Benezet. Those rays of the light of truth and justice, which had beamed upon his own mind and heart, and which he communicated to the public through the medium of the press, in this country, were sent across the Atlantic; and Anthony Benezet's historical account of Guinea seems to have done much towards interesting the mind of the celebrated Thomas Clarkson, upon the great subject of the abolition. This city and its neighbourhood were the region, which was enlightened by the residence and labours of that illustrious pattern of practical beneficence, the pious and humane Woolman.

Among other distinguished abolitionists, who were contemporaries with Woolman and Benezet,[1] the late Warner Mifflin, of Kent county in Delaware, stands preëminently conspicuous. So deeply did he become impressed with a sense of the injustice, and the inhumanity of holding slaves, that he fixed upon a day for the emancipation of thirty-seven persons of colour, who were received from his father. On that interesting occasion it appears that he called them into his chamber, one after the other, and that the following is the substance of the conversation which took place between him and one of them: "Well, my friend James, how old art thou?" "My master," said he, "I am twenty-nine years and a half old." The master replied, "Thou shouldst have been free at twenty-one years of age, as our white brethren are. Religion and humanity enjoin it upon me this day to give thee thy liberty, and justice commands me to pay thee for eight and a half years' services: which, at £21 5s. per year, including thy food and raiment, makes the sum of £95 12s. 6d. which I owe thee." Would that every slaveholder would "go and do likewise."

The names of Pemberton, Wistar, and Rush, who have been successively called to preside over the interests of the Abolition Society,[2] in this city, will be cherished in affectionate remembrance, in conjunction with those of many other eminently distinguished abolitionists, in different parts of the United States, who have also passed the bourn of that more elevated scene of human destiny, where the wicked cease from troubling and oppressing their fellow beings, and where the weary have entered upon an interminable state of rest, felicity and immortal peace, in those bright mansions, which the King of Glory has gone to prepare for the reception of all those who have, with religious fidelity and care, assiduously

[1] Woolman and Benezet were Quaker abolitionists as were most of the anti-slavery people of that day. Benezet was a French Huguenot, but on coming to this country he found common anti-slavery ground with that society and joined them to promote the emancipation and education of Negroes.

[2] The Pennsylvania Abolition Society herein referred to was one of the first and most effective agencies promoting freedom in this country.

cherished and cultivated that celestial principle, which the inspiration of the Almighty hath lighted up in the soul of every individual; and which, when duly nurtured and improved, must inevitably bring forth the fruits of those beneficent, philanthropic, humane, benevolent and pious affections, which constitute that pure and elevated charity and love, which fulfill all the laws of Christian purity and human excellence.

To those who have thus laboured to discipline their minds and hearts, and to bring them into an entire subjection and imitation of the great example of excellence, by religiously considering the wrongs endured by those persecuted and afflicted children of sorrow, whose liberty has been cloven down by the artifice, intrigue, violence or oppressive cruelty, of the stronger portion of mankind; to such as have so believed, and practiced, are the thoughts of an immortality beaming with the lustre of a faith so strong, and a hope so clear and transporting, peculiarly interesting.

To those excellent men who have exemplified the dignity of human nature by their labour of practical piety and goodness, while sojourning in this state of discipline and probation, by becoming the protectors of the friendless, among all the various descriptions of their brethren of mankind; to them belongs the happiness of looking forward with delightful anticipation to that animating period, when the great and excellent benefactors of the human race shall shine as the stars, for ever and ever, for the illumination of that eternal city, which hath foundation, whose maker and builder is God Almighty, in the heavens.

Many of the most distinguished and enlightened individuals in different regions, and among various nations, are habitual in their labours to unbind the chains of unjust captivity and servitude; and to set the innocent victims of avarice and cupidity upon the broad basis of the enjoyment of those inalienable rights,[1] which the universal Parent has entrusted to the care of every individual among his intelligent, and accountable children.

And if those who consider the poor, in the ordinary concerns of charity and pious almsgiving, are authorized to look for the favour of Providence; with how much more full an assurance may those

[1] Here the speaker shows the influence of the American Revolution. Many Negroes discussed the rights of man as the fathers of the republic had during that crisis, the former, however, insisting on such rights for the Negroes.

who have delivered their fellow beings from the inhuman grasp of the unprincipled kidnapper, or saved them from dragging out a miserable existence, amidst the thraldoms of the most abject slavery; with what confident expectation of becoming the recipients of that inconceivably glorious recompense of reward, which God has prepared for those who love and obey Him (and keep His commandments), may such persons anticipate the period when Christ shall reappear, to make up his jewels.

Among the various projects or plans which have been devised or suggested, in relation to emigration, there are none which appear to many persons to wear so much the appearance of feasibility, and ultimate successful and practical operation, as the luxuriant, beautiful and extensive island of Hayti.

The French claims we all know are merely nominal, and may easily be for ever silenced in the contemplated pacification, as without doubt, may all the political connections of Spain. In this great island there seems to be some foundation for the hopes of those who are to emigrate to rest upon; as there are already governments established there, which, although they may be arbitrary, and somewhat allied to military despotism in their present features and character, they are still susceptible of being improved, whenever a tranquillized state of society and their stability and independence as a nation, shall authorize it.

Assembled as this Convention is, for the promotion and extension of its beneficent and humane views and principles, I would respectfully beg leave to lay before it a few remarks upon the character, condition and wants of the afflicted and divided people of Hayti, as they, and that island, may be connected with plans for the emigration of the free people of colour of the United States.

God in the mysterious operation of His providence has seen fit to permit the most astonishing changes to transpire upon that naturally beautiful (and as to soil and productions), astonishingly luxuriant island.

The abominable principles, both of action and belief, which pervaded France during the long series of vicissitudes which until recently she has experienced, extended to Hayti, or St. Domingo; and have undoubtedly had an extensive influence upon the character, sentiments, and feelings of all descriptions of its present inhabitants.

This magnificent and extensive island which has by travellers and historians been often denominated the "paradise of the New World," seems from its situation, extent, climate, and fertility peculiarly suited to become an object of interest and attention to the many distinguished and enlightened philanthropists whom God has been graciously pleased to inspire with a zeal for the promotion of the best interests of the descendants, of Africa. The recent proceedings in several of the slave states towards the free population of colour in those states seem to render it highly probable that that oppressed class of the community will soon be obliged to flee to the free states for protection. If the two rival governments of Hayti were consolidated into one well balanced pacific power, there are many hundreds of the free people in the New England and middle states, who would be glad to repair there immediately to settle. And believing that the period has arrived, when many zealous friends to abolition and emancipation are of opinion that it is time for them to act in relation to an asylum for such persons as shall be emancipated from slavery or for such portion of the free coloured population at present existing in the United States as shall feel disposed to emigrate from this country, are among the considerations which have induced me to lay this subject before the Convention.

The present spirit of rivalry which exists between the two chiefs in the French part of the island, and the consequent belligerent aspect and character of the country, may at first sight appear somewhat discouraging to the beneficent views and labours of the friends of peace; but these I am inclined to think are by no means to be considered as insurmountable barriers against the benevolent exertions of those Christian philanthropists whose sincere and hearty desire it is to reunite and pacify them.

There seems to be no probability of their ever being reconciled to each other without the philanthropic interposition and mediation of those who have the welfare of the African race at heart. And where in the whole circle of practical Christian philanthropy and active beneficence is there so ample a field for the exertion of those heaven-born virtues as in that hitherto distracted region? In those unhappy divisions which exist in Hayti is strikingly exemplified the saying which is written in the sacred oracles, "that when men forsake the true worship and service of the only true God, and bow down to images of silver, and gold, and four-footed beasts and creeping things, and become contentious with each other," says the inspired writer, "in such a state of things trust ye not a friend, put ye not confidence in a guide; keep the doors of thy mouth from her that lieth in thy bosom; for there the son dishonoureth the father, and the daughter riseth up against her mother, the daughter-in-law against her mother-in-law, and a man's enemies shall be those of his own house."

Had the venerable prophet in the foregoing predictions alluded expressly and entirely to the actual moral, political, and above all, to the religious character and condition of the Haytians, he could scarcely have given a more correct description of it.

For there is scarcely a family whose members are not separated from each other. In many instances the husband is with Henry, and the wife and children with Boyer, and there are other instances in which the heads of the family are with Boyer, and the other members with Henry.[1]

Let it be distinctly remembered that these divided and distressed individuals are not permitted to hold any intercourse with each other; so that it is only when some very extraordinary occurrence transpires, that persons in the different sections of the country receive any kind of information from their nearest relatives and friends.

"Blessed are the peace-makers" is the language of that celestial law-giver, who taught as never man taught; and His religion uniformly assures the obedient recipients of His spirit that they shall be rewarded according to the extent, fidelity and sincerity of their works of piety and beneficence.

And if, according to the magnitude of the object in all its political, benevolent, humane and Christian relations, the quantum of recompense is to be awarded and apprised to the just, to how large a share of the benediction of our blessed Saviour to the promoters of peace, shall those be authorized to expect, who may be made the instruments of the pacification and reunion of the Haytian people? Surely the blessings of thousands who are, as it were, ready to perish, must inevitably come upon them.

When I reflect that it was in this city that the first abolition soci-

[1] Revolutions in Haiti were frequent, but this was the case in most Latin-American countries.

ety that was formed in the world was established, I am strongly encouraged to hope that here also there may originate a plan which shall be the means of restoring many of our fellow beings to the embraces of their families and friends, and place that whole country upon the basis of unanimity and perpetual peace.

If the American Convention should in their wisdom think it expedient to adopt measures for attempting to affect a pacification of the Haytians, it is most heartily believed that their benevolent views would be hailed and concurred in with alacrity and delight by the English philanthropists.

It is, moreover, believed that a concern so stupendous in its relations, and bearing upon the cause of universal abolition and emancipation, and to the consequent improvement and elevation of the African race, would tend to awaken an active and a universally deep and active interest in the minds of that numerous host of abolitionists in Great Britain, whom we trust have the best interests of the descendants of Africa deeply at heart. Among those distinguished and illustrious philanthropists are the following gentlemen:

Thomas Clarkson, Esq., W. Wilberforce, Esq. M. P., William Smith, Esq. M. P., William Allen, Esq., Z. M'Caulay, Esq., Sir Samuel Romilly, Mr. Vansittart, Lord Teignmouth, Sir Joseph Banks, the Marquis of Downshire, the Bishops of Gloucester, Norwich, London, Salisbury, and Bristol; James Stephens, Esq., William Roscoe, Esq., the Messrs. Babington, Harrison, etc.

The author of these remarks is personally acquainted with most of the above mentioned gentlemen and has been assured by many of them that they have considered it as one of their highest honours, as well as its constituting a great portion of pleasing reflection to them, that they have, under Providence, been permitted to aid in effecting the abolition of slavery, and that they were ever ready to unite in any object which might serve to advance the great cause of African improvement and happiness.

It is undoubtedly well known to the Convention that their Britannic Majesties, the Prince Regent, and, in fact, all the members of the illustrious house of Brunswick (with one solitary exception), have been zealous in the great cause of African emancipation, some of whom have particularly distinguished themselves in parliamentary debates upon the subject of universal abolition.

The Duke of Gloucester is to be numbered among the foremost and most zealous friends to the African cause in the whole united kingdom. His Royal Highness was called to the presidential chair at the first regular meeting of the African institution;[1] and has been indefatigable in his endeavours to promote the interests of an establishment which is designed to remunerate Africa for the evils they as a nation have inflicted on her, by now diffusing along her desolated and benighted shores the blessings of legitimate commerce, and all the cheering lights of civilization and instruction in morality and religion.

Prince Saunders, however, had no intention of leaving the impression that the only relief for the slave was through such an asylum as Haiti. To counteract the influence of the promoters of the deportation of the Negroes to Africa, many of their leaders advocated colonization in some country in the Western Hemisphere. In this way Negroes were settled in Canada and a few sent to Trinidad. Texas and several of the West Indies, moreover, were mentioned as inviting fields and some effort was made to determine the possibilities of such lands. Saunders, like most Negroes, however, undismayed by the reaction, hoped for a brighter day. The abolition of slavery in New York in 1827 justified such expectation.

This thought is well expressed below in the oration of N. Paul, delivered in Albany on the fifth of July, 1827. This oration deserves mention among the great utterances of truth so near to the hearts of the people for whom the minister spoke. Throughout this address the speaker plays the rôle of the prophet. Slavery is considered a terrible institution. It is inconsistent with moral law. God has not ordained that it shall continue. It must go. If it does not, he will doubt God himself.

[1] This was a well organized body, about which much was said at that time. Organized for the general uplift of the Africans, the management of it did something for the amelioration of the blacks in various British colonies, especially in Sierra Leone.

THE ABOLITION OF SLAVERY[1]

By N. Paul

Through the long lapse of ages it has been common for nations to record whatever was peculiar or interesting in the course of their history. Thus when Heaven, provoked by the iniquities of man, has visited the earth with the pestilence which moves in darkness or destruction, that wasteth at noonday, and has swept from existence, by thousands, its numerous inhabitants, or when the milder terms of mercy have been dispensed in rich abundance, and the goodness of God has crowned the efforts of any people with peace and prosperity; they have been placed upon their annals, and handed down to future ages, both for their amusement and profit. And as the nations which have already passed away have been careful to select the most important events, peculiar to themselves, and have recorded them for the good of the people that should succeed them, so will we place it upon our history; and we will tell the good story to our children and to our children's children, down to the latest posterity, that on the Fourth Day of July, in the year of our Lord 1827, slavery was abolished in the state of New York.

Seldom, if ever, was there an occasion which required a public acknowledgment, or that deserved to be retained with gratitude of heart to the all-wise disposer of events, more than the present on which we have assembled.

It is not the mere gratification of the pride of the heart, or any vain ambitious notion, that has influenced us to make our appearance in the public streets of our city or to assemble in the sanctuary of the Most High this morning; but we have met to offer our tribute of thanksgiving and praise to almighty God for His goodness; to retrace the acts and express our gratitude to our public benefactors, and to stimulate each other to the performance of every good and virtuous act, which now does, or hereafter may devolve as a duty upon us, as freemen and citizens, in common with the rest of the community.

And if ever it were necessary for me to offer an apology to an

[1] *An Address Delivered on the Celebration of the Abolition of Slavery in the State of New York, July 5, 1827*, by Nathaniel Paul, Pastor of African Baptist Society, Albany, New York. See *Freedom's Journal*, Aug. 10, 1837.

audience for my absolute inability to perform a task assigned me, I feel that the present is the period. However, relying for support on the hand of Him who has said, "I will never leave nor forsake," and confiding in your charity for every necessary allowance, I venture to engage in the arduous undertaking.

In contemplating the subject before us, in connection with the means by which so glorious an event has been accomplished, we find much which requires our deep humiliation and our most exalted praises. We are permitted to behold one of the most pernicious and abominable of all enterprises, in which the depravity of human nature ever led man to engage, entirely eradicated. The power of the tyrant is subdued, the heart of the oppressed is cheered, liberty is proclaimed to the captive, and the opening of the prison to those who were bound, and he who had long been the miserable victim of cruelty and degradation, is elevated to the common rank in which our benevolent Creator first designed that man should move,—all of which have been effected by means the most simple, yet perfectly efficient. Not by those fearful judgments of the almighty, which have so often fallen upon the different parts of the earth, which have overturned nations and kingdoms, scattered thrones and scepters, nor is the glory of the achievement tarnished with the horrors of the field of battle. We hear not the cries of the widow and the fatherless; nor are our hearts affected with the sight of garments rolled in blood; but all has been done by the diffusion and influence of the pure, yet powerful principles of benevolence, before which the pitiful impotency of tyranny and oppression is scattered and dispersed, like the chaff before the rage of the whirlwind.

I will not, on this occasion, attempt fully to detail the abominable traffic to which we have already alluded. Slavery, with its concomitants and consequences, in the best attire in which it can possibly be presented, is but a hateful monster, the very demon of avarice and oppression, from its first introduction to the present time; it has been among all nations the scourge of heaven, and the curse of the earth. It is so contrary to the laws which the God of nature has laid down as the rule of action by which the conduct of man is to be regulated towards his fellow man, which binds him to love his neighbor as himself, that it ever has, and ever will meet the decided disapprobation of heaven.

In whatever form we behold it, its visage is satanic, its origin the very offspring of hell, and in all cases its effects are grievous.

On the shores of Africa, the horror of the scene commences; here, the merciless tyrant, divested of everything human except the form, begins the action. The laws of God and the tears of the oppressed are alike disregarded; and with more than savage barbarity, husbands and wives, parents and children are parted to meet no more: and, if not doomed to an untimely death, while on the passage, yet are they for life consigned to a captivity still more terrible; a captivity, at the very thought of which, every heart, not already biassed with unhallowed prejudices, or callous to every tender impression, pauses and revolts; exposed to the caprice of those whose tender mercies are cruel; unprotected by the laws of the land, and doomed to drag out miserable existence, without the remotest shadow of a hope of deliverance, until the king of terrors shall have executed his office, and consigned them to the kinder slumbers of death. But its pernicious tendency may be traced still farther: not only are its effects of the most disastrous character, in relation to the slave, but it extends its influence to the slaveholder; and in many instances it is hard to say which is most wretched, the slave or the master.

After the fall of man, it would seem that God, foreseeing that pride and arrogance would be the necessary consequences of the apostacy, and that man would seek to usurp undue authority over his fellow, wisely ordained that he should obtain his bread by the sweat of his brow; but contrary to this sacred mandate of heaven, slavery has been introduced, supporting the one in all the absurd luxuries of life, at the expense of the liberty and independence of the other. Point me to any section of the earth where slavery, to any considerable extent exists, and I will point you to a people whose morals are corrupted; and when pride, vanity and profusion are permitted to range unrestrained in all their desolating effects, and thereby idleness and luxury are promoted, under the influence of which, man, becoming insensible of his duty to his God and his fellow creature; and indulging in all the pride and vanity of his own heart, says to his soul, thou hast much goods laid up for many years. But while thus sporting, can it be done with impunity? Has conscience ceased to be active? Are there no forebodings of a future day of punishment, and of meeting the merited avenger? Can he retire after the business of the day and repose in safety? Let the guards around his mansion, the barred doors of his sleeping room, and the loaded instruments of death beneath his pillow, answer the question.—And if this were all, it would become us, perhaps, to cease to murmur, and bow in silent submission to that providence which had ordained this present state of existence, to be but a life of degradation and suffering.

Since affliction is but the common lot of men, this life, at best, is but a vapor that ariseth and soon passeth away. "Man," said the inspired sage, "that is born of a woman, is of few days and full of trouble"; and in a certain sense, it is not material what our present situation may be, for short is the period that humbles all to the dust, and places the monarch and the beggar, the slave and the master, upon equal thrones. But although this life is short, and attended with one entire scene of anxious perplexity, and few and evil are the days of our pilgrimage; yet man is advancing to another state of existence, bounded only by the vast duration of eternity in which happiness or misery await us all. The great author of our existence has marked out the way that leads to the glories of the upper world, and through the redemption which is in Christ Jesus, salvation is offered to all. But slavery forbids even the approach of mercy; it stands as a barrier in the way to ward off the influence of divine grace; it shuts up the avenues of the soul, and prevents its receiving divine instruction; and scarcely does it permit its miserable captives to know that there is a God, a Heaven or a Hell!

Its more than detestable picture has been attempted to be portrayed by the learned and the wise, but all have fallen short, and acknowledged their inadequacy to the task, and have been compelled to submit, by merely giving an imperfect shadow of its reality. Even the immortal Wilberforce, a name that can never die while Africa lives, after exerting his ingenuity, and exhausting the strength of his masterly mind, resigns the effort, and calmly submits by saying, "Never was there, indeed, a system so replete with wickedness and cruelty to whatever part of it we turn our eyes; we could find no comfort, no satisfaction, no relief. It was the gracious ordinance of Providence, both in the natural and moral world, that good should often arise out of evil. Hurricanes clear the air; and the propagation of truth was promoted by persecution, pride, vanity, and profusion contributed often, in their remoter consequences, to the happiness of mankind. In common, what was in itself evil and vicious, was permitted to carry along with it some circumstances of palliation. The Arab was hospitable, the robber brave; we did not necessarily find cruelty associated with fraud or meanness with injustice. But here the case was far otherwise. It was the prerogative of this detestable traffic to separate from evil its concomitant good, and to reconcile discordant mischief. It robbed war of its generosity, it deprived peace of its security. We saw in it the vices of polished society, without its knowledge or its comforts, and the evils of barbarism without its simplicity; no age, no sex, no rank, no condition, was exempt from the fatal influence of this wide-wasting calamity. Thus it attained to the fullest measure of its pure, unmixed, unsophisticated wickedness; and scorning all competition or comparison, it stood without a rival in the secure and undisputed possession of its detestable preëminence.''

Such were the views which this truly great and good man, together with his fellow philanthropists, took of this subject, and such are the strong terms in which he has seen fit to express his utter abhorrence of its origin and effects. Thus have we hinted at some of the miseries connected with slavery. And while I turn my thoughts back and survey what is past, I see our forefathers seized by the hand of the rude ruffian, and torn from their native homes and all that they held dear or sacred. I follow them down the lonesome way, until I see each safely placed on board the gloomy slave ship; I hear the passive groan, and the clanking of the chains which bind them. I see the tears which follow each other in quick succession adown the dusky cheek.

I view them casting the last and longing look towards the land which gave them birth, until at length the ponderous anchor is weighed, and the canvas spread to catch the favored breeze; I view them wafted onward until they arrive at the destined port; I behold those who have been so unfortunate as to survive the passage, emerging from their loathsome prison, and landing amidst the noisy rattling of the massy fetters which confine them; I see the crowd of traffickers in human flesh gathering, each anxious to seize the favored opportunity of enriching himself with their toils, their tears and their blood. I view them doomed to the most abject state of degraded misery, and exposed to suffer all that unrestrained tyranny can inflict, or that human nature is capable of sustaining.

Tell me, ye mighty waters, why did ye sustain the ponderous load of misery? Or speak, ye winds, and say why it was that ye executed your office to waft them onward to the still more dismal state; and ye proud waves, why did you refuse to lend your aid and to have overwhelmed them with your billows? Then should they have slept sweetly in the bosom of the great deep, and so have been hid from sorrow. And, oh thou immaculate God, be not angry with us, while we come into this thy sanctuary, and make the bold inquiry in this thy holy temple, why it was that thou didst look on with the calm indifference of an unconcerned spectator, when thy holy law was violated, thy divine authority despised and a portion of thine own creatures reduced to a state of mere vassalage and misery? Hark! while he answers from on high: hear Him proclaiming from the skies—Be still, and know that I am God! Clouds and darkness are round about me; yet righteousness and judgment are the habitation of my throne. I do my will and pleasure in the heavens above, and in the earth beneath; it is my sovereign prerogative to bring good out of evil, and cause the wrath of man to praise me, and the remainder of that wrath I will restrain.

Strange, indeed, is the idea that such a system, fraught with such consummate wickedness, should ever have found a place in this the otherwise happiest of all countries—a country, the very soil of which is said to be consecrated to liberty, and its fruits the equal rights of man. But strange as the idea may seem, or paradoxical as it may appear to those acquainted with the constitution of the government, or who have read the bold declaration of this nation's independence; yet it is a fact that can neither be denied or controverted, that in the United States of America, at the expiration of fifty years after its becoming a free and independent nation, there are no less than fifteen hundred thousand human beings still in a state of unconditional vassalage.

Yet America is first in the profession of the love of liberty, and loudest in proclaiming liberal sentiments towards all other nations, and feels herself insulted, to be branded with anything bearing the appearance of tyranny or oppression. Such are the palpable inconsistencies that abound among us and such is the medley of contradictions which stain the national character, and renders the American republic a byword, even among despotic nations. But while we pause and wonder at the contradictory sentiments held forth by the nation, and contrast its profession and practice, we are happy to have it in our power to render an apology for the existence of the evil, and to offer an excuse for the framers of the constitution. It was before the sons of Columbia felt the yoke of their oppressors, and rose in their strength to put it off that this land became contaminated with slavery. Had this not been the case, led by the spirit of pure republicanism that then possessed the souls of those patriots who were struggling for liberty, this soil would have been sufficiently guarded against its intrusion, and the people of these United States to this day would have been strangers to so great a curse. It was by the permission of the British parliament that the human species first became an article of merchandise among them, and as they were accessory to its introduction, it well becomes them to be first, as a nation, in arresting its progress and effecting its expulsion. It was the immortal Clarkson, a name that will be associated with all that is sublime in mercy, until the final consummation of all things, who first looking abroad, beheld the sufferings of Africa, and looking at home, he saw his country stained with her blood. He threw aside the vestments of the priesthood, and consecrated himself to the holy purpose of rescuing a continent from rapine and murder, and of erasing this one sin from the book of his nation's iniquities. Many were the difficulties to be encountered, many were the hardships to be endured, many were the persecutions to be met with; formidable, indeed, was the opposing party. The sensibility of the slave merchants and planters was raised to the highest pitch of resentment. Influenced by the love of money, every scheme was devised, every measure was adopted, every plan was executed that might throw the least barrier in the way of the holy cause of the abolition of this traffic. The consequences of such a measure were placed in the most appalling light that ingenious falsehood could invent; the destruction of commerce, the ruin of the merchants, the rebellion of the slaves, the massacre of the planters, were all artfully and fancifully pictured and reduced to a certainty in the minds of many of the members of Parliament and a large proportion of the community. But the cause of justice and humanity were not to be deserted by him and his fellow philanthropists on account of difficulties. We have seen them for twenty years persevering against all opposition and surmounting every obstacle they found in their way. Nor did they relax aught of their exertions until the cries of the oppressed having roused the sensibility of the nation, the island empress rose in her strength and said to this foul traffic, "Thus far thou hast gone, but thou shalt go no farther." Happy for us, my brethren, that the principles of benevolence were not exclusively confined to the isle of Great Britain. There have lived, and there still do live, men in this country who are patriots and philanthropists, not merely in name, but in heart and practice; men whose compassions have long since led them to pity the poor and despised sons of Africa. They have heard their groans, and have seen their blood, and have looked with an holy indignation upon the oppressor; nor was there anything except the power to have crushed the tyrant and liberated the captive. Through their instrumentality, the blessings of freedom have long since been enjoyed by all classes of people throughout New England, and through their influence, under the Almighty, we are enabled to recognize the fourth day of the present month as the day in which the cause of justice and humanity have triumphed over tyranny and oppression, and slavery is forever banished from the State of New York.

Among the many who have vindicated the cause of the oppressed, within the limits of this State, we are proud to mention the names of Eddy and Murray, of Jay and Tompkins, who, together with their fellow philanthropists, embarked in the holy cause of emancipation with a zeal which well expressed the sentiments of their hearts. They proved themselves to be inflexible against scorn, persecution, and contempt; and although all did not live to see the conflict ended, yet their survivors never relaxed their exertions until the glorious year of 1817, when, by the wise and patriotic legislature of this State, a law was passed for its final extirpation. We will mourn for those who are gone, we will honor those who survive, until time extinguishes the lamp of their existence. When dead, they shall still live in our memory; we will follow them to their tombs, we will wet their graves with our tears; and upon the heart of every descendant of Africa their deeds shall be written, and their names shall vibrate sweetly from ear to ear, down to the latest posterity. From what has already taken place, we look forward with pleasing anticipation to that period when it shall no longer be said that in a land of freemen there are men in bondage, but when this foul stain will be entirely erased and this worst of evils will be forever done away. The progress of emancipation, though slow, is nevertheless certain. It is certain, because that God who has made of one blood all nations of men, and who is said to be no respecter of persons, has so decreed; I therefore have no hesitation in declaring from this sacred place that not only throughout the United States of America, but throughout every part of the habitable world where slavery exists, it will be abolished. However great may be the opposition of those who are supported by the traffic, yet slavery will cease. The lordly planter who has his thousands in bondage may stretch himself upon his couch of ivory and sneer at the exertions which are made by the humane and benevolent, or he may take his stand upon the floor of Congress and mock the pitiful generosity of the East or West for daring to meddle with the subject and attempting to expose its injustice; he may threaten to resist all efforts for a general or a partial emancipation even to a dissolution of the Union. But still I declare that slavery will be extinct; a universal and not a partial emancipation must take place; nor is the period far distant. The indefatigable exertions of the philanthropists in England to have it abolished in their West India Islands, the recent revolutions in South America, the catastrophe and exchange of power in the Isle of Hayti, the restless disposition of both master and slave in the Southern States, the Constitution of our government, the effects of literary and moral instruction, the generous feelings of the pious and benevolent, the influence and spread of the holy religion of the cross of Christ, and the irrevocable decrees of Almighty God, all combine their efforts, and with united voice declare that the power of tyranny must be subdued, the captive must be liberated, the oppressed go free, and slavery must revert back to its original chaos of darkness, and be forever annihilated from the earth. Did I believe that it would always continue, and that man to the end of time would be permitted with impunity to usurp the same undue authority over his fellow, I would disallow any allegiance or obligation I was under to my fellow creatures, or any submission that I owed to the laws of my country; I would deny the superintending power of divine Providence in the affairs of this life; I would ridicule the religion of the Savior of the world, and treat as the worst of men the ministers of the everlasting gospel; I would consider my Bible as a book of false and delusive fables, and commit it to the flames; nay, I would still go farther; I would at once confess myself an atheist, and deny the existence of a holy God.

But slavery will cease, and the equal rights of man will be universally acknowledged. Nor is its tardy progress any argument against its final accomplishment. But do I hear it loudly responded —this is but a mere wild fanaticism, or at best but the misguided conjecture of an untutored descendant of Africa. Be it so. I confess my ignorance, and bow with due deference to my superiors in understanding; but if in this case I err, the error is not peculiar to myself; if I wander, I wander in a region of light from whose political hemisphere the sun of liberty pours forth his refulgent rays, around which dazzle the starlike countenances of Clarkson, Wilberforce, Pitt, Fox and Grenville, Washington, Adams, Jefferson, Hancock and Franklin;[1] if I err, it is their sentiments that have caused me to stray. For these are the doctrines which they taught while with us; nor can we reasonably expect that since they have entered the unbounded space of eternity, and have learned more familiarly the perfections of that God who governs all things that their sentiments have altered. Could they now come forth among us, they would tell that what they have learned in the world of spirits has served only to confirm what they taught while here; they would tell us that all things are rolling on according to the sovereign appointment of the eternal Jehovah, who will overturn and overturn until he whose right it is to reign shall come and the period will be ushered in; when the inhabitants of the earth will learn by experience what they are now slow to believe—that our God is a God of justice and no respecter of persons. But while, on the one hand, we look back and rejoice at what has already taken place, and, on the other, we look forward with pleasure to that period when men will be respected according to their characters, and not according to their complexion, and when their vices alone will render them contemptible; while we rejoice at the thought of this land's becoming a land of freemen, we pause, we reflect. What,

[1] During the struggle for the rights of man all of these distinguished gentlemen had, in one way or another, expressed themselves as being opposed to slavery.

we would ask, is liberty without virtue? It tends to lasciviousness; and what is freedom but a curse, and even destruction, to the profligate? Not more desolating in its effects is the mountain torrent, breaking from its lofty confines and rushing with vast impetuosity upon the plains beneath, marring as it advances all that is lovely in the works of nature and of art, than the votaries of vice and immorality, when permitted to range unrestrained. Brethren, we have been called into liberty; only let us use that liberty as not abusing it. This day commences a new era in our history; new scenes, new prospects open before us, and it follows as a necessary consequence that new duties devolve upon us; duties, which if properly attended to, cannot fail to improve our moral condition and elevate us to a rank of respectable standing with the community; or if neglected, we fall at once into the abyss of contemptible wretchedness. It is righteousness alone that exalteth a nation, and sin is a reproach to any people. "Our liberties," says Mr. Jefferson, "are the gift of God, and they are not to be violated but with his wrath."[1] Nations and individuals have been blest of the Almighty in proportion to the manner in which they have appreciated the mercies conferred upon them; an abuse of His goodness has always incurred His righteous frown, while a right improvement of his beneficence has secured and perpetuated His gracious smiles; an abuse of His goodness has caused those fearful judgments which have destroyed cities, demolished thrones, overturned empires, and humbled to the dust the proudest and most exalted of nations. As a confirmation of which the ruinous heaps of Egypt, Tyre, Babylon, and Jerusalem stand as everlasting monuments. If we would then answer the great design of our creation, and glorify the God who has made us; if we would avert the judgment of Heaven; if we would honor our public benefactors; if we would counteract the designs of our enemies; if we would have our own blessings perpetuated, and secure the happiness of our children and our children's children, let each come forward and act well his part, in whatever circle he may move, or in whatever station he may fill; let the fear of God and the good of our fellowmen be the governing principles of the heart. We do well to remember, that every act of ours is more or less connected with the general cause of the

[1] Jefferson said so much against slavery that he would have been known as an abolitionist had be lived as late as 1840.

people of color, and with the general cause of emancipation. Our conduct has an important bearing, not only on those who are yet in bondage in this country, but its influence is extended to the isles of India, and to every part of the world where the abomination of slavery is known. Let us then relieve ourselves from the odious stigma which some have long since cast upon us, that we were incapacitated by the God of nature for the enjoyment of the rights of freemen, and convince them and the world that although our complexion may differ, yet we have hearts susceptible of feeling, judgment capable of discerning, and prudence sufficient to manage our affairs with discretion, and by example prove ourselves worthy the blessings we enjoy. That it is the duty of all rational creatures to consult the interest of their species is a fact against which there can be no reasonable objection. It is recorded to the honor of Titus, who perhaps was the most benevolent of all the Roman emperors, on recollecting one evening that he had done nothing the day preceding beneficial to mankind, the monarch exclaimed, "I have lost a day." The wide field of usefulness is now open before us, and we are called upon by every consideration of duty which we owe to our God, to ourselves, to our children, and to our fellow-creatures generally, to enter with a fixed determination to act well our part, and labor to promote the happiness and welfare of all.

There remains much to be done, and there is much to encourage us to action. The foundation for literary, moral and religious improvement, we trust, is already laid in the formation of the public and private schools for the instruction of our children, together with the churches of different denominations already established. From these institutions we are encouraged to expect the happiest results; and while many of us are passing down the declivity of life, and fast hastening to the grave, how animating the thought that the rising generation is advancing under more favorable auspices than we were permitted to enjoy, soon to fill the places we now occupy; and in relation to them vast is the responsibility that rests upon us; much of their future usefulness depends upon the discharge of the duties we owe them. They are advancing, not to fill the place of slaves, but of freemen; and in order to fill such a station with honor to themselves, and with good to the public, how necessary their education, how important the moral and religious cultivation of their minds! Blessed be God, we live in a day that our fathers desired to see, but died without the sight: a day in which science, like the sun of the firmament, rising, darting as he advances his beams to every quarter of the globe. The mists and darkness scatter at his approach, and all nations and people are blessed with his rays; so the glorious light of science is spreading from east to west, and Afric's sons are catching the glance of its beams as it passes; its enlightening rays scatter the mists of moral darkness and ignorance which have but too long overshadowed their minds; it enlightens the understanding, directs the thoughts of the heart, and is calculated to influence the soul to the performance of every good and virtuous act. The God of Nature has endowed our children with intellectual powers surpassed by none; nor is there anything wanting but their careful cultivation in order to fit them for stations the most honorable, sacred, or useful. And may we not, without becoming vain in our imaginations, indulge the pleasing anticipation that within the little circle of those connected with our families there may hereafter be found the scholar, the statesman, or the herald of the cross of Christ. Is it too much to say, that among that little number there shall yet be one found like to the wise legislator of Israel, who shall take his brethren by the hand and lead them forth from worse than Egyptian bondage to the happy Canaan of civil and religious liberty; or one whose devotedness towards the cause of God, and whose zeal for the salvation of Africa, shall cause him to leave the land which gave him birth, and cross the Atlantic, eager to plant the standard of the cross upon every hill of that vast continent, that has hitherto ignobly submitted to the baleful crescent, or crouched under the iron bondage of the vilest superstition. Our prospects brighten as we pursue the subject, and we are encouraged to look forward to that period when the moral desert of Africa shall submit to cultivation, and verdant groves and fertile valleys, watered by the streams of Siloia, shall meet the eye that has long surveyed only the widespread desolations of slavery, despotism, and death. How changed shall then be the aspect of the moral and political world! Africa, elevated to more than her original dignity, and redressed for the many aggravated and complicated wrongs she has sustained, with her emancipated sons, shall take her place among the other nations of the earth. The iron manacles of slavery shall give place to the still stronger bonds of brotherly love and affection, and justice and equity shall be the governing principles that shall regulate the conduct of men of every nation. Influenced by such motives, encouraged by such prospects, let us enter the field with a fixed determination to live and to die in the holy cause.

With the injection of the colonization movement into the race problem in the United States by the organization of a society for the purpose in 1816, the antislavery speakers were compelled to fight with a two-edged sword. They had to combat not only the arguments of those who opposed slavery, but of those who had once given the antislavery movement impetus but were then interested in the emancipation only on the condition that the slaves thus liberated should be removed from the country. The increasing race prejudice thereby resulting from the effort to make this strictly a white man's country tended to deprive the people of color in the North of the rights which they had enjoyed. Peter Williams, referred to above, admirably expressed this very thought in this Fourth of July address delivered at St. Philips Church, New York City, in 1830, for the benefit of the Wilberforce Settlement in Upper Canada. He held the colonization movement responsible for the Negro's loss of civil and social privileges.

SLAVERY AND COLONIZATION[1]

By Peter Williams

On this day the fathers of this nation declared, "We hold these truths to be self-evident, that all men are created equal, that they are endowed by their Creator with certain unalienable rights, among which are life, liberty, and the pursuit of happiness."

These truly noble sentiments have secured to their author a deathless fame. The sages and patriots of the Revolution subscribed them with enthusiasm and "pledged their lives, their fortunes, and their sacred honour" in their support.

[1] A Discourse delivered by Peter Williams at St. Phillip's Church, July 4, 1830, *passim*.

The result has been the freedom and happiness of millions, by whom the annual returns of this day are celebrated with the loudest and most lively expressions of joy.

But although this anniversary affords occasion of rejoicing to the mass of the people of the United States, there is a class, a numerous class, consisting of nearly three millions, who participate but little in its joys, and are deprived of their unalienable rights by the very men who so loudly rejoice in the declaration that "all men are born free and equal."

The festivities of this day serve but to impress upon the minds of reflecting men of colour a deeper sense of the cruelty, the injustice, and oppression, of which they have been the victims. While others rejoice in their deliverance from a foreign yoke, they mourn that a yoke a thousandfold more grievous is fastened upon them. Alas, they are slaves in the midst of freedom; they are slaves to those who boast that freedom is the unalienable right of all; and the clanking of their fetters, and the voice of their wrongs, make a horrid discord in the songs of freedom which resound through the land.

No people in the world profess so high a respect for liberty and equality as the people of the United States, and yet no people hold so many slaves, or make such great distinctions between man and man.

From various causes (among which we cheerfully admit a sense of justice to have held no inconsiderable rank) the work of emancipation has within a few years been rapidly advancing in a number of States. The State we live in, since the 4th of July, 1827, has been able to boast that she has no slaves, and other States where there still are slaves appear disposed to follow her example.

These things furnish us with cause of gratitude to God, and encourage us to hope that the time will speedily arrive when slavery will be universally abolished. Brethren, what a bright prospect would there be before us in this land had we no prejudices to contend against after being made free.

But, alas! the freedom to which we have attained is defective. Freedom and equality have been "put asunder." The rights of men are decided by the colour of their skin; and there is as much difference made between the rights of a free white man and a free coloured man as there is between a free coloured man and a slave.

Though delivered from the fetters of slavery, we are oppressed by an unreasonable, unrighteous, and cruel prejudice, which aims at nothing less than the forcing away of all the free coloured people of the United States to the distant shores of Africa. Far be it from me to impeach the motives of every member of the African Colonization Society. The civilizing and Christianizing of that vast continent, and the extirpation of the abominable traffic in slaves (which notwithstanding all the laws passed for its suppression is still carried on in all its horrors), are no doubt the principal motives which induce many to give it their support.

But there are those, and those who are most active and most influential in its cause, who hesitate not to say that they wish to rid the country of the free coloured population, and there is sufficient reason to believe, that with many, this is the principal motive for supporting that society; and that whether Africa is civilized or not, and whether the Slave Trade be suppressed or not, they would wish to see the free coloured people removed from this country to Africa.

Africa could certainly be brought into a state of civil and religious improvement without sending all the free people of colour in the United States there.

A few well-qualified missionaries, properly fitted out and supported, would do more for the instruction and improvement of the natives of that country than a host of colonists, the greater part of whom would need to be instructed themselves, and all of whom for a long period would find enough to do to provide for themselves instead of instructing the natives.

How inconsistent are those who say that Africa will be benefited by the removal of the free people of colour of the United States there, while they say they are the *most vile and degraded* people in the world. If we are as vile and degraded as they represent us, and they wish the Africans to be rendered a virtuous, enlightened and happy people, they should not *think* of sending *us* among them, lest we should make them worse instead of better.

The colonies planted by white men on the shores of America, so far from benefiting the aborigines, corrupted their morals, and caused their ruin; and yet those who say *we* are the most vile people in the world would send us to Africa to improve the character and condition of the natives. Such arguments would not be listened to for a moment were not the minds of the community strangely warped by prejudice.

Those who wish that that vast continent should be *compensated* for the injuries done it, by sending thither the light of the gospel and the arts of civilized life, should aid in sending and supporting well-qualified missionaries, who should be wholly devoted to the work of instruction, instead of sending colonists who would be apt to turn the ignorance of the natives to their own advantage, and do them more harm than good.

Much has also been said by Colonizationists about improving the character and condition of the people of colour of this country by sending them to Africa. This is more inconsistent still. We are to be improved by being sent far from civilized society. This is a novel mode of improvement. What is there in the burning sun, the arid plains, and barbarous customs of Africa, that is so peculiarly favourable to our improvement? What hinders our improving here, where schools and colleges abound, where the gospel is preached at every corner, and where all the arts and sciences are verging fast to perfection? Nothing, nothing but prejudice. It requires no large expenditures, no hazardous enterprises to raise the people of colour in the United States to as highly improved a state as any class of the community. All that is necessary is that those who profess to be anxious for it should lay aside their prejudices and act towards them as they do by others.

We are NATIVES of this country, we ask only to be treated as well as FOREIGNERS. Not a few of our fathers suffered and bled to purchase its independence; we ask only to be treated as well as those who fought against it. We have toiled to cultivate it, and to raise it to its present prosperous condition; we ask only to share equal privileges with those who come from distant lands, to enjoy the fruits of our labour. Let these moderate requests be granted, and we need not go to Africa nor anywhere else to be improved and happy. We cannot but doubt the purity of the motives of those persons who deny us these requests, and would send us to Africa to gain what they might give us at home.

But they say the prejudices of the country against us are invincible; and as they cannot be conquered, it is better that we should be removed beyond their influence. This plea should never proceed from the lips of any man who professes to believe that a just God rules in the heavens.

The African Colonization Society is a numerous and influential body. Would they lay aside their *own* prejudices, much of the burden would be at once removed; and their example (especially if they were as anxious to have *justice done us here* as to send us to Africa) would have such an influence upon the community at large as would soon cause prejudice to hide its deformed head.

But, alas! the course which they have pursued has an opposite tendency. By the *scandalous misrepresentations* which they are continually giving of our character and conduct we have sustained much injury, and have reason to apprehend much more.

Without any charge of crime we have been denied all access to places to which we formerly had the most free intercourse; the coloured citizens of other places, on leaving their homes, have been denied the privilege of returning; and others have been absolutely driven out.

Has the Colonization Society had no effect in producing these barbarous measures?

They profess to have no other object in view than the colonizing of the free people of colour on the coast of Africa, with their *own consent;* but if our homes are made so uncomfortable that we cannot continue in them, or, if like our brethren of Ohio and New Orleans, we are driven from them, and no other door is open to receive us but Africa, our removal there will be anything but voluntary.

It is very certain that very few free people of colour *wish* to go to that *land.* The Colonization Society *know* this, and yet they do certainly calculate that in time they will have us all removed there.

How can this be effected but by making our situation worse here, and closing every other door against us?

God in His good providence has opened for such of us as may choose to leave these States an asylum in the neighbouring British Province of Canada.

There is a large tract of land on the borders of Lake Huron, containing a million of acres, which is offered to our people at $1.50 per acre. It lies between the 42nd and 44th degrees of north latitude. The climate is represented as differing but little from this; the soil as good as any in the world; well timbered and watered. The laws are good, and the same for the coloured man as the white man. A powerful sympathy prevails there in our behalf, instead of the prejudice which here oppresses us; and everything encourages the hope, that by prudence and industry we may rise to as prosperous and happy a condition as any people under the sun.

To secure this land as a settlement for our people it is necessary that a payment of $6,000 be made on or before the 10th of November next.

This sum it is proposed to lay out in the purchase of 4,000 acres, and when paid will secure the keeping of the remainder in reserve for coloured emigrants ten years. The land so purchased is to be sold out by agents, or trustees to emigrants, and the moneys received in return to be appropriated to a second purchase, which is to be sold as at first, and the returns again laid out in land, until the whole tract is in their possession; and then the capital so employed is to be expended on objects of general utility.

The persons who have bargained for the land have found it necessary to apply to the citizens of the United States to aid them by their donations in raising the amount necessary to make their first purchase, and also to aid a number of emigrants who were driven away in a cruel manner, and in a destitute condition from Cincinnati, to seek a home where they might, and who have selected the Huron tract as their future abode.

Each of these particulars present powerful claims to your liberality. "Cast thy bread upon the waters," says the wise man in the text, "and thou shalt find it after many days. Give a portion to seven and also to eight, for thou knowest not what evil shall be upon the earth." Oh! truly we "know not what evil shall be upon the earth."

When we look at the course of events, relative to our people in this country, we find reason to conclude that it is proper we should provide a convenient asylum to which we and our children may flee in case we should be so oppressed as to find it necessary to leave our present homes. The opinion is daily gaining ground, and has been often openly expressed, that it would be a great blessing to the country if all its free coloured population could be removed to Africa. As this opinion advances, recourse will naturally be had to such measures as will make us feel it necessary to go. Its operation has been already much felt in various States.

The coloured population of Cincinnati were an orderly, industrious and thriving people, but the white citizens, having determined to force them out, first entered into a combination that they would give none of them employment; and finally resorted to violent measures to compel them to go. Should the anxiety to get rid of us increase, have we not reason to fear that some such courses may be pursued in other places.

Satan is an inventive genius. He often appears under the garb of an angel of light, and makes religion and patriotism his plea for the execution of his designs. Our Lord foretold His disciples that "the time cometh, when whosoever killeth you, will think that he doeth God service." Brethren, the time is already come when *many* think that whosoever causeth us to remove from our native home does service to his country and to God.

Ah! to many in other places beside Cincinnati and New Orleans the sight of *free* men of colour is so unwelcome that we know not what they may think themselves justifiable in doing to get rid of them. Will it not then be wise for us to provide ourselves with a convenient asylum in time. We have now a fair opportunity of doing so; but if we neglect it, it may be occupied by others, and I know of none likely to be offered which promises so many advantages. Indeed, I feel warranted in saying, that if they are not speedily secured, attempts will be made to prevent our securing them hereafter, and that propositions have *actually* been made, by influential men, to purchase them, in order that the coloured people may not get them in their possession.

It is true that Africa and Hayti, and perhaps some other countries, will still afford us a place of refuge, yet it will not certainly be amiss to have Canada also at our choice. Some may prefer going there to any other place. But suppose we should never stand in need of such an asylum (and some think that our having provided it will make it less necessary, an effect we should all rejoice in, as we have no wish to go if we can stay in comfort); suppose we should never stand in need of such an asylum, still the amount required to secure it is so small that we can never regret parting with it for such an object. What is $6,000 to be raised by the coloured people throughout the United States? How few are so poor that they cannot give a few shillings without missing it? Let it have the amount which is usually spent by our people in this city on the Fourth of July in celebrating the national independence, and it will make up a very considerable part of it.

I have been informed that at the suggestion of one of our coloured clergymen the members of one of the societies who intended to dine together to-morrow have agreed to give the money which would have been paid for dinner tickets to this object. This is truly patriotic. I would say to each of you, brethren "go and do likewise." Give what you would probably expend in celebrating the Fourth of July to the colony of your brethren in Canada; and on the birthday of American freedom secure the establishment of a colony in which you and your children may rise to respectability and happiness. Give it, and you will be no poorer than if you gave it not; and you will secure a place of refuge to yourselves in case of need. "Give a portion to seven and also to eight, for thou knowest not what evil shall be upon the earth."

You are strongly urged to liberality on this occasion by a regard to your future welfare. No scheme for our colonization that has ever yet been attempted has so few objections, or promises so many advantages; but if you withhold your aid until every imaginable objection is removed, you will never effect any object beneficial to yourselves or to your brethren.

Brethren, it is no time to cavil, but to help. If you mean to help the colony, help now. The amount of the first purchase must be paid by the 10th of November, or not at all. Brethren, this scheme of colonization opens to us a brighter door of hope than was ever opened to us before, and has a peculiar claim upon our patronage, because it has originated among our own people. It is not of the devising of the white men, nor of foreigners, but of our own kindred and household. If it succeeds, ours will be the credit. If it succeeds not, ours will be the fault. I am happy, however, to find that it meets the approbation of most, if not of all, of those wise and good men who have for many years been our most zealous and faithful friends, and it evidently appears to be specially favoured by Providence. But the occasion has not only an appeal to your interest, but to your charity.

Your brethren exiled from Cincinnati for no crime but because God was pleased to clothe them with a darker skin than their neighbours cry to you from the wilderness for help. They ask you for bread, for clothing, and other necessaries to sustain them, their wives and their little ones, until by their industry they can provide themselves the means of support. It is true, there are some among them that are able to help themselves; but for these we do not plead. Those who can help themselves, will; but as the ablest have been sufferers in the sacrifice of their property, and the expenses and dangers of their forced and hurried removal, they are not able to assist their destitute brethren.

Indeed, most of the wealthy men of colour in Cincinnati arranged so as to remain until they could have a chance of disposing of their property to advantage; but the poor were compelled to fly without delay, and consequently need assistance. Brethren, can you deny it to them? I know you too well to harbour such a thought. It is only necessary to state to you their case to draw forth your liberality. Think then what these poor people must have suffered in being driven with their wives and their little ones from their comfortable homes late in autumn to take up their residence in a wide and desolate wilderness. Oh, *last* winter must have been to them a terrible one indeed! We hope that they, by their own efforts, will be better prepared for the next; but they must yet stand in need of help. They have the rude forest to subdue, houses to build, food to provide. They are the pioneers for the establishment of a colony, which may be a happy home for thousands and tens of thousands of our oppressed race. Oh, think of the situation of these, your brethren, whom the hand of oppression has driven into exile, and whom the providence of God has perhaps doomed, like Joseph, to suffering, that at some future day *much people may be saved alive*. Think of them, and give to their relief as your hearts may dictate. "Cast thy bread upon the waters," etc.

With a thought very much like that of Peter Williams in the preceding oration, the Rev. Theodore S. Wright[1]

[1] Theodore S. Wright served for a number of years as a minister in New York City. He enjoyed the unique reputation of claiming Princeton Seminary as his alma mater. He served in that city as a predecessor of Rev. Henry Highland Garnet at the Shiloh Presbyterian Church. There he came into contact with the opponents of colonization and the abolitionists. At the various anti-slavery meetings, he was called upon to express himself on the important question of emancipation. As this subject was so near to his heart, he, a man of literary attainment, usually expressed himself with clearness and force. He,

delivered an address before the Convention of the New York State Antislavery Society, September 20, 1837. This discourse is informing in that it reviews the development of the antislavery sentiment and the beginning of the reaction which culminated in the promulgation of the principles of expatriation. While expressive of such thought, then, the discourse is at the same time a review of history by one of the most prominent Negroes of that time. During these years colonization was the all-absorbing topic among the people of color and their friends; and the question of their amelioration could not be mentioned without also rising up in the form of colonization, as the orator here eloquently shows.

THE PROGRESS OF THE ANTISLAVERY CAUSE[1]

By Theodore S. Wright

Mr. President: All who have heard the report which has been presented are satisfied it needs no eulogy. It supports itself. But, sir, I would deem it a privilege to throw out a few thoughts upon it—thoughts which arise on beholding this audience. My mind is involuntarily led back a few years to the period prior to the commencement of this great moral effort for the removal of the giant sin of oppression from our land. It is well known to every individual who is at all acquainted with the history of slavery in this land, that the convention of 1776, when the foundations of our government were laid, proclaimed to the world the inalienable rights of man; and they supposed that the great principles of liberty would work the destruction of slavery throughout this land. This remark is sustained by an examination of the document then framed, and by the fact that the term "slavery" is not even named. The opinion that slavery would be abolished—indeed, that it had already received a death-blow, was cherished by all the reform-

therefore, became associated with the most prominent reformers of his time and deserves to be ranked among those who made the sacrifice of denouncing a once popular institution, a thing which often worked economic loss and personal danger.

[1] *Address of the Rev. Theodore S. Wright before the Convention of the New York State Antislavery Society, on the Acceptance of the Annual Report, held at Utica, Sept. 20, 1837.* See *Colored American,* July 8 and Oct. 14, 1837.

ers.—This spirit actuated Woolman, Penn, Edwards, Jefferson, and Benezet, and it worked out the entire emancipation of the North.—But it is well known that about 1817 a different drift was given—a new channel was opened for the benevolence which was working so well. The principle of expatriation, like a great sponge, went around in church and state, among men of all classes, and sponged up all the benevolent feelings which were then prevalent, and which promised so much for the emancipation of the enslaved and down-trodden millions of our land. That, sir, we call the dark period.—Oh, sir! if my father who sits beside me were to rise up and tell you how he felt and how men of his age felt, and how I felt (though a boy at that time), sir, it would be seen to have been a dark period. Why, sir, the heavens gathered blackness, and there was nothing cheering in our prospects. A spirit was abroad, which said "this is not your country and home," a spirit which would take us away from our firesides, tear the freeman away from his oppressed brother.—This spirit was tearing the free father away from his children, separating husband and wife, sundering those cords of consanguinity which bind the free with the slave. This scheme was as popular as it possibly could be. The slaveholder and the pro-slavery man, the man of expanded views, the man who loved the poor and oppressed of every hue and of every clime, all united in this feeling and principle of expatriation. But, sir, there were hundreds of thousands of men in the land who never could sympathize in this feeling; I mean those who were to be removed. The people of color were broken-hearted; they knew, sir, there were physical impossibilities to their removal. They knew, sir, that nature, reason, justice and inclination forbade the idea of their removing; and hence in 1817, the people of color in Philadelphia, with James Forten at their head—(and I envy them the honor they had in the work in which they were engaged), in an assembly of three thousand, before high heaven, in the Presence of Almighty God, and in the midst of a persecuting nation, resolved that they never would leave the land. They resolved to cling to their oppressed brethren. They felt that every ennobling spirit forbade their leaving them. They resolved to remain here, come what would, persecution or death. They determined to grapple themselves to their enslaved brethren as with hooks of steel. My father, at Schenectady, under great anxiety, took a journey to Philadelphia to investigate the subject. This was the spirit which prevailed among the people of color, and it extended to every considerable place in the North and as far South as Washington and Baltimore. They lifted up their voice and said, this is my country, here I was born, here I have toiled and suffered, and here will I die. Sir, it was a dark period. Although they were unanimous, and expressed their opinions, they could not gain access to the public mind: for the press would not communicate the facts in the case—it was silent. In the city of New York, after a large meeting, where protests were drawn up against the system of colonization, there was not a single public journal in the city, secular or religious, which would publish the views of the people of color on the subject.

Sir, despair brooded over our minds. It seemed as though everything was against us. We saw philanthropists, for instance, such men as Rev. Dr. Cox, swept away by the waves of expatriation. Other men, such as our President before us, who were engaged in schemes of benevolence in behalf of the people here, abandoning those schemes. It was a general opinion that it would do no good to elevate the people of color here. Our hearts broke. We saw that colonization never could be carried out, for the annual increase of the people of color was 70,000. We used to meet together and talk and weep and what to do we knew not. We saw indications that coercive measures would be resorted to. Immediately after the insurrection in Virginia, under Nat Turner, we saw colonization spreading all over the land; and it was popular to say the people of color must be removed. The press came out against us, and we trembled. Maryland passed laws to force out the colored people. It was deemed proper to make them go, whether they would or not. Then we despaired. Ah, Mr. President, that was a dark and gloomy period. The united views and intentions of the people of color were made known, and the nation awoke as from slumber. The *Freedom's Journal*, edited by Rev. Sam'l E. Cornish, announced the facts in the case, our entire opposition. Sir, it came like a clap of thunder! I recollect at Princeton, where I was then studying, Dr. Miller came out with his letter, disapproving of the editor's views, and all the faculty and the students gave up the paper. Benj. Lundy of Baltimore nobly lifted up his voice. But he did not feel the vileness of colonization. A young man, for making certain expositions touching slavery, was incarcerated in a dungeon, where truth took a lodgment in his heart, where he avowed eternal hatred to slavery, and where before high heaven, in the secrecy of his dungeon, with the chains upon him, he resolved to devote his life to the cause of emancipation. . . . And when the President of the American Anti-slavery Society stepped forward and paid the fine, we were crying for help—we were remonstrating. We had no other means but to stand up as men and protest. We declared this is our country and our home; here are the graves of our fathers. But none came to the rescue.

At that dark moment we heard a voice—it was the voice of Garrison, speaking in trumpet tones! It was like the voice of an angel of mercy! Hope, hope then cheered our path. The signs of the times began to indicate brighter days. He thundered, and next we hear of a Jocelyn of New Haven, an Arthur Tappan at his side, pleading for the rights of the Colored American. He stood up in New Haven amid commotion and persecution like a rock amid the dashing waves. Ought I not this afternoon to call upon my soul, and may I not ask you to call upon *your souls* to bless the Lord for His unspeakable goodness in bringing about the present state of things? What gratitude is called for on our part, when we contrast the state of things developed in your report with the dark period when we could number the abolitionists, when they were few and far between? Now a thousand societies exist, and there are hundreds of thousands of members. Praise God and persevere in this great work. Should we not be encouraged? We have everything to hope for, and nothing to fear. God is at the helm. The Bible is your platform—the Holy Spirit will aid you. We have everything necessary pledged, because God is with us. Hath he not said—"Break every yoke, undo the heavy burdens, and let the oppressed go free"?—"Remember them that are in bonds, as bound with them"? Why do I see so many who minister at the sacred altar—so many who have everything to lose and nothing to gain, personally, by identifying themselves with this cause? Nothing but the spirit of Almighty God brought these men here.

This cause, noble though persecuted, has a lodgment in the piety of our countrymen, and never can be expatriated. How manifest has been the progress of this cause! Why, sir, three years ago, nothing was more opprobrious than to be called an "abolitionist" or "antislavery man"!

Now you would be considered as uncharitable towards proslavery men, whether editors of newspapers, presidents of colleges or theological seminaries, if you advance the idea that they are not abolitionists or antislavery men. Three years ago, when a man professed to be an abolitionist, we knew where he was. He was an individual who recognized the identity of the human family. Now a man may call himself an abolitionist and we know not where to find him. Your tests are taken away. A rush is made into the abolition ranks. Free discussion, petition Anti-Texas, and political favor converts are multiplying. Many throw themselves in, without understanding the breadth and depth of the principles of emancipation. I fear not the annexation of Texas. I fear not all the machinations, calumny and opposition of slaveholders, when contrasted with the annexation of men whose hearts have not been deeply imbued with these high and holy principles. Why, sir, unless men come out and take their stand on the principle of recognizing man as man, I tremble for the ark, and I fear our society will become like the expatriation society; everybody an abolitionist. These points which have lain in the dark must be brought out to view. The identity of the human family, the principle of recognizing all men as brethren—that is the doctrine, that is the point which touches the quick of the community. It is an easy thing to ask about the vileness of slavery at the South, but to call the dark man a brother, heartily to embrace the doctrine advanced in the second article of the constitution, to treat all men according to their moral worth, to treat the man of color in all circumstances as a man and brother—that is the test.

Every man who comes into this society ought to be catechized. It should be ascertained whether he looks upon man as man, all of one blood and one family. A healthful atmosphere must be created, in which the slave may live when rescued from the horrors of slavery. I am sensible I am detaining you, but I feel that this is an important point. I am alarmed sometimes when I look at the constitutions of our societies. I am afraid that brethren sometimes endeavor so to form the constitutions of societies that they will be popular. I have seen constitutions of abolition societies, where nothing was said about the improvement of the man of color! They have overlooked the giant sin of prejudice. They have passed by this foul monster, which is at once the parent and offspring of slavery. Whilst you are thinking about the annexation of Texas—whilst you are discussing the great principles involved in this noble cause, remember this prejudice must be killed or slavery will never be abolished. Abolitionists must annihilate in their own bosoms the cord of caste. We must be consistent—recognize the colored man in every respect as a man and brother. In doing this we shall have to encounter scorn; we shall have to breast the storm.—This society would do well to spend a whole day in thinking about it and praying over it. Every abolitionist would do well to spend a day in fasting and prayer over it and in looking at his own heart. Far be it from me to condemn abolitionists. I rejoice and bless God for this first institution which has combined its energies for the overthrow of this heaven-daring —this soul-crushing prejudice.

The successors of Penn, Franklin and Woolman have shown themselves the friends of the colored race. They have done more in this cause than any other church and they are still doing great things both in Europe and America. I was taught in childhood to remember the man of the broad-brimmed hat and drab-colored coat and venerate him. No class have testified more to the truth on this subject. They lifted up their voices against slavery and the slave-trade. But, ah! with but here and there a noble exception, they go but halfway.—When they come to the grand doctrine, to lay the ax right down at the root of the tree, and destroy the very spirit of slavery—there they are defective. Their doctrine is to set the slave free, and let him take care of himself. Hence, we hear nothing about their being brought into the Friends' Church, or of their being viewed and treated according to their moral worth. Our hearts have recently been gladdened by an address of the Annual Meeting of the Friends' Society in the city of New York, in which they insist upon the doctrine of immediate emancipation. But that very good man who signed the document as the organ of that society within the past year, received a man of color, a Presbyterian minister, into his house, gave him his meals alone in the kitchen, and did not introduce him to his family. That shows how men can testify against slavery at the South, and not assail it at the North, where it is tangible. Here is something for abolitionists to do. What can the friends of emancipation effect while the spirit of slavery is so fearfully prevalent. Let every man take his stand, burn out this prejudice, live it down, talk it down, everywhere consider the colored man as a man, in the church, the stage, the steamboat, the public house, in all places, and the death-blow to slavery will be struck.

Theodore S. Wright, feeling this proscription in the State of New York, availed himself of the opportunity to express himself on *Race Prejudice Against the Colored Man* before the New York Antislavery Society Sept. 20, 1837, speaking to the following resolution:

Resolved, that the prejudice peculiar to our country, which subjects our colored brethren to a degrading distinction in our worship, assemblies and schools, which withholds from them that kind and courteous treatment to which as well as other citizens, they have a right, at public houses, on board steamboats, in stages, and in places of public concourse, is the spirit of slavery, is nefarious and wicked and should be practically reprobated and discountenanced.

This was the situation in New York and Pennsylvania; and, in fact, race prejudice, as the author points out, was increasing throughout the land. With this thought in mind, the reader will appreciate the words which follow:

PREJUDICE AGAINST THE COLORED MAN [1]

By Theodore S. Wright

Mr. President, with much feeling do I rise to address the society on this resolution, and I should hardly have been induced to have done it had I not been requested. I confess I am personally interested in this resolution. But were it not for the fact that none can feel the lash but those who have it upon them, that none know where the chain galls but those who wear it, I would not address you.

[1] This speech appears in a small volume bearing this title.

This is a serious business, sir. The prejudice which exists against the colored man, the free man is like the atmosphere, everywhere felt by him. It is true that in these United States and in this State, there are men, like myself, colored with the skin like my own, who are not subjected to the lash, who are not liable to have their wives and their infants torn from them; from whose hand the Bible is not taken. It is true that we may walk abroad; we may enjoy our domestic comforts, our families; retire to the closet; visit the sanctuary, and may be permitted to urge on our children and our neighbors in well doing. But sir, still we are slaves—everywhere we feel the chain galling us. It is by that prejudice which the resolution condemns, the spirit of slavery, the law which has been enacted here, by a corrupt public sentiment, through the influence of slavery which treats moral agents different from the rule of God, which treats them irrespective of their morals or intellectual cultivation. This spirit is withering all our hopes, and ofttimes causes the colored parent as he looks upon his child, to wish he had never been born. Often is the heart of the colored mother, as she presses her child to her bosom, filled with sorrow to think that, by reason of this prejudice, it is cut off from all hopes of usefulness in this land. Sir, this prejudice is wicked.

If the nation and church understood this matter, I would not speak a word about that killing influence that destroys the colored man's reputation. This influence cuts us off from everything; it follows us up from childhood to manhood; it excludes us from all stations of profit, usefulness and honor; takes away from us all motive for pressing forward in enterprises, useful and important to the world and to ourselves.

In the first place, it cuts us off from the advantages of the mechanic arts almost entirely. A colored man can hardly learn a trade, and if he does it is difficult for him to find any one who will employ him to work at that trade, in any part of the State. In most of our large cities there are associations of mechanics who legislate out of their society colored men. And in many cases where our young men have learned trades, they have had to come to low employments for want of encouragement in those trades.

It must be a matter of rejoicing to know that in this vicinity colored fathers and mothers have the privileges of education. It must be a matter of rejoicing that in this vicinity colored parents can have their children trained up in schools.—At present, we find the colleges barred against them.

I will say nothing about the inconvenience which I have experienced myself, and which every man of color experiences, though made in the image of God. I will say nothing about the inconvenience of traveling; how we are frowned upon and despised. No matter how we may demean ourselves, we find embarrassments everywhere.

But sir, this prejudice goes farther. It debars men from heaven. While sir, slavery cuts off the colored portion of the community from religious privileges, men are made infidels. What, they demand, is your Christianity? How do you regard your brethren? How do you treat them at the Lord's table? Where is your consistency in talking about the heathen, traversing the ocean to circulate the Bible everywhere, while you frown upon them at the door? These things meet us and weigh down our spirits.

And, sir, the constitution of society, molded by this prejudice, destroys souls. I have known extensively, that in revivals which have been blessed and enjoyed in this part of the country, the colored population were overlooked. I recollect an instance. The Lord God was pouring out His Spirit. He was entering every house, and sinners were converted. I asked, Where is the colored man? where is my brother? where is my sister? who is feeling for him or her? who is weeping for them? who is endeavoring to pull them out of the fire? No reply was made.—I was asked to go round with one of the elders and visit them. We went and they humbled themselves. The Church commenced efficient efforts, and God blessed them as soon as they began to act for these people as though they had souls.

And sir, the manner in which our churches are regulated destroys souls. Whilst the church is thrown open to everybody, and one says come, come in and share the blessings of the sanctuary, this is the gate of heaven—he says to the colored man, *be careful where you take your stand.* I know an efficient church in this State, where a respectable colored man went to the house of God, and was going to take a seat in the gallery, and one of the officers contended with him, and said, "you cannot go there, sir."

In one place the people had come together to the house of the Lord. The sermon was preached—the emblems were about to be administered—and all at once the person who managed the church thought the value of the pews would be diminished if the colored people sat in them. They objected to their sitting there, and the colored people left and went into the gallery, and that, too, when they were thinking of handling the memorials of the broken body and shed blood of the Savior! And, sir, this prejudice follows the colored man everywhere, and depresses his spirits.

Thanks be to God, there is a buoyant principle which elevates the poor down-trodden colored man above all this:—It is that there is society which regards man according to his worth; it is the fact, that when he looks up to Heaven he knows that God treats him like a moral agent, irrespective of caste or the circumstances in which he may be placed. Amid the embarrassments which he has to meet, and the scorn and contempt that is heaped upon him, he is cheered by the hope that he will be disenthralled, and soon, like a bird set forth from its cage, wing his flight to Jesus, where he can be happy, and look down with pity on the man who despises the poor slave for being what God made him, and who despises him because he is identified with the poor slave. Blessed be God for the principles of the Gospel. Were it not for these, and for the fact that a better day is dawning, I would not wish to live.—Blessed be God for the antislavery movement. Blessed be God that there is a war waging with slavery, that the granite rock is about to be rolled from its base. But as long as the colored man is to be looked upon as an inferior caste, so long will they disregard his cries, his groans, his shrieks.

I rejoice, sir, in this Society; and I deem the day when I joined this Society as one of the proudest days of my life. And I know I can die better, in more peace to-day, to know there are men who will plead the cause of my children.

Let me, through you, sir, request this delegation to take hold of this subject. This will silence the slaveholder, when he says where is your love for the slave? Where is your love for the colored man who is crushed at your feet? Talking to us about emancipating our slaves when you are enslaving them by your feelings, and doing more violence to them by your prejudice, than we are to our slaves by our treatment. They call on us to evince our love for the slave, by treating man as man, the colored man as a man, according to his worth.

CHAPTER IV

FURTHER EFFORTS FOR A HEARING

The migration of the Negroes to the North developed in the minds of the white people of that section not only the purpose to restrict the movement, but to make it impossible for Negroes to be comfortable thereafter in the free States. Local governments devised special regulations and States enacted laws depriving the free people of color of the rights which they had theretofore enjoyed. This, of course, did not pass without eloquent protests from the Negroes thereby proscribed. When it was proposed in the legislature of Pennsylvania to disfranchise the free people of color they held numerous indignation meetings, where their orators expressed themselves on the injustice of this new attack. We are unable to find in the records a copy of the speeches thus delivered, but the thought and even the words of their orators appear in the sentiments set forth in the following appeal of 1838:

APPEAL OF FORTY THOUSAND CITIZENS THREATENED WITH DISFRANCHISEMENT TO THE PEOPLE OF PENNSYLVANIA [1]

By Robert Purvis, *Chairman*

Fellow Citizens: We appeal to you from the decision of the "Reform Convention," which has stripped us of a right peaceably enjoyed during forty-seven years under the Constitution of this commonwealth. We honor Pennsylvania and her noble institutions too much to part with our birthright, as her free citizens, without a struggle. To all her citizens the right of suffrage is

[1] This appeal appears in a small volume bearing this title.

valuable in proportion as she is free; but surely there are none who can so ill afford to spare it as ourselves.

Was it the intention of the people of this commonwealth that the Convention to which the Constitution was committed for revision and amendment should tear up and cast away its first principles? Was it made the business of the Convention to deny "that all men are born equally free," by making political rights depend upon the skin in which a man is born, or to divide what our fathers bled to unite, to wit, TAXATION and REPRESENTATION? We will not allow ourselves for one moment to suppose that the majority of the people of Pennsylvania are not too respectful of the rights and too liberal towards the feelings of others, as well as too much enlightened to their own interests, to deprive of the right of suffrage a single individual who may safely be trusted with it. And we cannot believe that you have found among those who bear the burdens of taxation any who have proved, by their abuse of the right, that it is not safe in their hands. This is a question, fellow citizens, in which we plead your cause as well as our own. It is the safeguard of the strongest that he lives under a government which is obliged to respect the voice of the weakest. When you have taken from an individual his right to vote, you have made the government, in regard to him, a mere despotism to all. To your women and children, their inability to vote at the polls may be no evil, because they are united by consanguinity and affection with those who can do it. To foreigners and paupers the want of the right may be tolerable, because a little time or labor will make it theirs. They are candidates for the privilege and hence substantially enjoy its benefits. But when a distinct class of the community, already sufficiently the objects of prejudice, are wholly, and for ever, disfranchised and excluded, to the remotest posterity, from the possibility of a voice in regard to the laws under which they are to live—it is the same thing as if their abode were transferred to the dominions of the Russian Autocrat, or of the Grand Turk. They have lost their check upon oppression, their wherewith to buy friends, their panoply of manhood; in short, they are thrown upon the mercy of a despotic majority. Like every other despot, this despot majority will believe in the mildness of its own sway; but who will the more willingly submit to it for that?

To us our right under the Constitution has been more precious, and our deprivation of it will be the more grievous, because our expatriation has come to be a darling project with many of our fellow citizens. Our abhorrence of a scheme which comes to us in the guise of Christian benevolence, and asks us to suffer ourselves to be transplanted to a distant and barbarous land, because we are a "nuisance" in this, is not more deep and thorough than it is reasonable. We love our native country, much as it has wronged us; and in the peaceable exercise of our inalienable rights, we cling to it. The immortal Franklin and his fellow laborers in the cause of humanity have bound us to our homes here with chains of gratitude. We are PENNSYLVANIANS, and we hope to see the day when Pennsylvania will have reason to be proud of us, as we believe she has now none to be ashamed. Will you starve our patriotism? Will you cast our hearts out of the treasury of the commonwealth? Do you count our enmity better than our friendship?

* * * * * * * * *

Are we then presumptuous in the hope that this grave sentence will be as incapable of resurrection fifty years hence, as is that which the Chief Justice assures us was pronounced "about the year 1795"? No. The blessings of the broad and impartial charter of Pennsylvania rights can no more be wrested from us by legal subtlety than the beams of our common sun or the breathing of our common air.

What have we done to forfeit the inestimable benefits of this charter? Why should tax-paying colored men, any more than other taxpayers, be deprived of the right of voting for their representatives? It was said in the Convention that this government belongs to the whites. We have already shown this to be false as to the past. Those who established our present government designed it equally for all. It is for you to decide whether it shall be confined to the European complexion in future. Why should you exclude us from a fair participation in the benefits of the republic? Have we oppressed the whites? Have we used our right to the injury of any class? Have we disgraced it by receiving bribes? Where are the charges written down, and who will swear to them? We challenge investigation. We put it to the conscience of every Pennsylvanian, whether there is, or ever has been, in the commonwealth, either a political party or religious sect which has less deserved than ourselves to be thus disfranchised. As to the charge of idleness, we fling it back indignantly. Whose brows have sweat for our livelihood but our own? As to vice, if it disqualifies us for civil liberty, why not apply the same rule to the whites, so far as they are vicious? Will you punish the innocent for the crimes of the guilty? The execution of the laws is in the hands of the whites. If we are bad citizens let them apply the proper remedies. We do not ask the right of suffrage for the inmates of our jails and penitentiaries, but for those who honestly and industriously contribute to bear the burdens of the State. As to inferiority to the whites, if indeed we are guilty of it, either by nature or education, we trust our enjoyment of the rights of freemen will on that account be considered the less dangerous. If we are incompetent to fill the offices of State, it will be the fault of the whites only if we are suffered to disgrace them. We are in too feeble a minority to cherish a mischievous ambition. Fair protection is all that we aspire to.

* * * * * * * * *

Our fathers shared with yours the trials and perils of the wilderness. Among the facts which illustrate this, it is well known that the founder of your capital, from whom it bears the name of Harrisburg, was rescued by a colored man from a party of Indians, who had captured, and bound him to the stake for execution. In gratitude for this act he invited colored persons to settle in his town, and offered them land on favorable terms. When our common country has been invaded by a foreign foe, colored men have hazarded their lives in its defense. Our fathers fought by the side of yours in the struggle which made us an independent republic.

* * * * * * * * *

Are we to be thus looked to for help in the "hour of danger," but trampled under foot in the time of peace? In which of the battles of the revolution did not our fathers fight as bravely as yours for American liberty? Was it that their children might be disfranchised and loaded with insult that they endured the famine of Valley Forge and horrors of the Jersey Prison Ship? Nay, among those from whom you are asked to wrench the birthright of CIVIL LIBERTY are those who themselves shed their blood on the snows of Jersey, and faced British bayonets in the most desperate hour of the revolution.

* * * * * * * * *

Are we to be disfranchised, lest the purity of the white blood should be sullied by an intermixture with ours? It seems to us that our white brethren might well enough reserve their fear till we seek such alliance with them. We ask no social favors. We would not willingly darken the doors of those to whom the complexion and features which our Maker has given us are disagreeable. The territories of the commonwealth are sufficiently ample to afford us a home without doing violence to the delicate nerves of our white brethren for centuries to come. Besides, we are not intruders here, nor were our ancestors. Surely you ought to bear as unrepiningly the evil consequences of your fathers' guilt, as we those of our fathers' misfortune. Proscription and disfranchisement are the last things in the world to alleviate these evil consequences. Nothing, as shameful experience has already proved, can so powerfully promote the evil which you profess to deprecate, as the degradation of our race by the oppressive rule of yours. Give us that fair and honorable ground which self-respect requires to stand on, and the dreaded amalgamation, if it take place at all, shall be by your own fault, as indeed it always has been. We dare not give full vent to the indignation we feel on this point, but we will not attempt wholly to conceal it. We ask a voice in the disposition of those public resources which we ourselves have helped to earn; we claim a right to be heard, according to our numbers, in regard to all those great public measures which involve our lives and fortunes, as well as those of our fellow citizens; we assert our right to vote at the polls as a shield against that strange species of benevolence which seeks legislative aid to banish us—and we are told that our white fellow citizens cannot submit to an intermixture of the races! Then let the indentures, title-deeds, contracts, notes of hand, and all other evidences of bargain, in which colored men have been treated as men, be torn and scattered on the winds. Consistency is a jewel. Let no white man hereafter ask his colored neighbor's consent when he wants his property or his labor, lest he should endanger the Anglo-Saxon purity of his descendants. Why should not the same principle hold good between neighbor and neighbor, which is deemed necessary, as a fundamental principle, in the Constitution itself? Why should you be ashamed to act in private business as the Reform Convention would have you act in the capacity of a commonwealth? But, no! we do not believe our fellow citizens, while with good faith they hold themselves bound by their contracts with us, and while they feel bound to deal with us only by fair contract, will ratify the arbitrary principle of the Convention, how much so ever they may prefer the complexion in which their Maker has pleased to clothe themselves.

We would not misrepresent the motives of the Convention, but we are constrained to believe that they have laid our rights a sacrifice on the altar of slavery. We do not believe our disfranchisement would have been proposed, but for the desire which is felt by political aspirants to gain the favor of the slaveholding States. This is not the first time that northern statesmen have "bowed the knee to the dark spirit of slavery," but it is the first time that they have bowed so low! Is Pennsylvania, which abolished slavery in 1780, and enfranchised her tax-paying colored citizens in 1790, now, in 1838, to get upon her knees and repent of her humanity, to gratify those who disgrace the very name of American liberty, by holding our brethren as goods and chattels? We freely acknowledge our brotherhood to the slave, and our interest in his welfare. Is this a crime for which we should be ignominiously punished? The very fact that we are deeply interested for our kindred in bonds shows that we are the right sort of stuff to make good citizens of. Were we not so, we should better deserve a lodging in your penitentiaries than a franchise at your polls. Doubtless it will be well pleasing to the slaveholders of the South to see us degraded. They regard our freedom from chains as a dangerous example, much more our political freedom. They see in everything which fortifies our rights an obstacle to the recovery of their fugitive property. Will Pennsylvania go backwards toward slavery, for the better safety of southern slave property? Be assured the South will never be satisfied till the old "Keystone" has returned to the point from which she started in 1780. And since the number of colored men in the commonwealth is so inconsiderable, the safety may require still more. It may demand that a portion of the white taxpayers should be unmanned and turned into chattels—we mean those whose hands are hardened by daily toil. Fellow citizens, will you take the first step towards reimposing the chains which have now rusted for more than fifty years? Need we inform you that every colored man in Pennsylvania is exposed to be arrested as a fugitive from slavery, and that it depends not upon the verdict of a jury of his peers, but upon the decision of a judge on summary process whether or not he shall be dragged into southern bondage? The Constitution of the United States provides that "no person shall be deprived of life, liberty, or property, without due process of law"—by which is certainly meant a TRIAL BY JURY. Yet the act of Congress of 1793, for the recovery of fugitive slaves, authorizes the claimant to seize his victim without a warrant from any magistrate, and allows him to drag him before "any magistrate of a county, city, or town corporate, where such seizure has been made," and upon proving, by "oral testimony or affidavit," to the satisfaction of such magistrate that the man is his slave, gives him a right to take him into everlasting bondage. Thus may a free-born citizen of Pennsylvania be arrested, tried without counsel, jury, or power to call witness, condemned by a single man, and carried across Mason and Dixon's line, within the compass of a single day. An act of this commonwealth passed in 1820 and enlarged and reënacted in 1825, it is true, puts some restraint upon the power of the claimant under the act of Congress; but it still leaves the case to the decision of a single judge, without the privilege of a jury! What unspeakably aggravates our loss of the right of suffrage at this moment is that, while the increased activity of the slave-catchers enhances our danger, the Reform Convention has refused to amend the Constitution so as to protect our liberty by a jury trial! We entreat you to make our case your own—imagine your own wives and children to be trembling at the approach of every stranger, lest their husbands and fathers should be dragged into a slavery worse than Algerine—worse than death! Fellow citizens, if there is one of us who has abused the right of suffrage, let him be tried and punished according to law. But in the name of humanity, in the name of justice, in the name of the God you profess to worship, who has no respect of persons, do not turn into gall and wormwood the friendship we bear to yourselves by ratifying a Constitution which tears from us a privilege dearly earned and inestimably prized. We lay hold of the principles which Pennsylvania asserted in the hour which tried men's souls—which BENJAMIN FRANKLIN and his eight colleagues, in the name of the commonwealth, pledged their lives, their fortunes, and their sacred honor to sustain. We take our stand upon that solemn declaration, that to protect inalienable rights "governments are instituted among men, deriving their JUST POWERS from the CONSENT of the governed," and proclaim that a government which tears away from us and our posterity the very power of CONSENT is a tyrannical usurpation which we will never cease to oppose. We have seen with amazement and grief the apathy of white Pennsylvanians while the "Reform Convention" has been perpetrating this outrage upon the good old principles of Pennsylvania freedom. But however others may forsake these principles, we promise to maintain them on Pennsylvania soil to the last man. If this disfranchisement is designed to uproot us, it shall fail. Pennsylvania's fields, valleys, mountains and rivers; her canals, railroads, forests and mines; her domestic altars and her public, religious and benevolent institutions; her Penn and Franklin, her Rush, Rawle, Wistar and Vaux; her consecrated past and her brilliant future are as dear to us as they can be to you. Firm upon our old Pennsylvania BILL OF RIGHTS, and trusting in a God of Truth and Justice, we lay our claim before you, with the warning that no amendments of the present Constitution can compensate for the loss of its foundation principle of equal rights, nor for the conversion into enemies of 40,000 friends.

While it may seem paradoxical it is nevertheless true that these very Negroes who were foremost in the attack on slavery were at the same time advocates of peace. It will be remembered that one of the first suggestions from an American for the abolition of war came from Benjamin Banneker, a Negro astronomer and mathematician, who in a memorial to the country, idealized the arts of peace and recommended that there be added to the President's cabinet a secretary of peace, whose function would be to devise measures for the prevention of international strife. The Negro antislavery leaders, influenced by the Quakers, never advocated war as a means to destroy the institution. They always fell back on moral suasion in carrying out the doctrine of non-resistance to offensive aggression.

One of the most outspoken advocates of this doctrine was William Whipper[1] of Columbia, Pennsylvania, noted for years as an antislavery worker and as an agent of the underground railroad. He was speaking to the resolution that the practice of non-resistance to physical aggression is not only consistent with reason, but the surest method of obtaining a speedy triumph of the principles of universal peace. His address follows:

NON-RESISTANCE TO OFFENSIVE AGGRESSION[2]

By William Whipper

Mr. President: The above resolution presupposes that if there were no God to guide and govern the destinies of man on this planet, no Bible to light his path through the wilds of sin, darkness and error, and no religion to give him a glorious and lasting consolation while traversing the gloomy vale of despondency, and to light up his soul anew with fresh influence from the fountain of Divine grace—that mankind might enjoy an exalted state of civilization, peace and quietude in their social, civil and international relations, far beyond that which Christians now enjoy, guarded and protected by the great Author of all good and the doctrines of the Prince of Peace.

But, sir, while I am assuming the position that the cause of peace

[1] William Whipper was of Columbia, Pennsylvania. Early in life he engaged in the lumber trade in that town, where he secured a competency. In his business relations with all, he left a good impression of the Negro's ability, honesty, and gentlemanly deportment.

Although engaged in business, he devoted much of his time to the development of his mind. He could, therefore, serve as one of the editors of the *National Reformer*, a monthly magazine published by the American Moral Reform Society. In this position, he wrote editorials in chaste and plain language, but bold and outspoken in the advocacy of truth. He promoted the anti-slavery cause, and was one of the chief agents of the Underground Railroad.

A contemporary says that Mr. Whipper was "a mulatto of fine personal appearance, above the middle size, stoops a little—that bend of the shoulders that marks the student. . . . He is social and genial, and very interesting and entertaining in conversation." Mr. Whipper frequently resided in Philadelphia, where he was highly respected by all classes and loved particularly by his own race.

[2] *Colored American*, Sept. 9, 16, 23, 30, 1837.

amongst mankind may be promoted without the scriptures, I would not, for a single moment, sanction the often made assertion that the doctrines of the holy scriptures justify war—for they are in my humble opinion its greatest enemy. And I further believe that as soon as they become fully understood and practically adopted, wars and strifes will cease. I believe that every argument urged in favor of what is termed a "just and necessary war," or physical self-defense, is at enmity with the letter and spirit of the scriptures, and when they emanate from its professed advocates should be repudiated, as inimical to the principles they profess, and a reproach to Christianity itself.

I have said this much in favor of the influence of the scriptures on the subject of peace. It is neither my intention nor my province, under the present resolution, to give proofs for my belief by quotations from holy writ. That portion of the discussion I shall leave to the minister of the altar, and the learned and biblical theologian. Though I may make a few incidental quotations hereafter, I shall now pass on for a few brief moments to the resolution under consideration, viz.:

The resolution asserts that the practice of non-resistance to physical aggression is consistent with reason. A very distinguished man asserts "that reason is that distinguishing characteristic that separates man from the brute creation," and that this power was bestowed upon him by his Maker, that he might be capable of subduing all subordinate intelligence to his will. It is this power when exerted in its full force that enables him to conquer the animals of the forest, and which makes him lord of creation. There is a right and a wrong method of reasoning. The latter is governed by our animal impulses and wicked desires, without regard to the end to be attained. The former fixes its premises, in great fundamental and unalterable truths—surveys the magnitude of the objects and the difficulties to be surmounted, and calls to its aid the resources of enlightened wisdom as a landmark by which to conduct its operations.

It is self-evident that when the greatest difficulties surround us, we should summon our noblest powers. "Man is a being formed for action as well as contemplation"; for this purpose there are interwoven in his constitution powers, instincts, feelings and affections which have a reference to his improvement in virtue, and which excite him to promote the happiness of others. When we behold them by their noble sentiments exhibiting sublime virtues and performing illustrious actions, we ascribe the same to the goodness of their hearts, their great reasoning powers and intellectual abilities. For were it not for these high human endowments, we should never behold men in seasons of calamity, displaying tranquillity and fortitude in the midst of difficulties and dangers, enduring poverty and distress with a noble heroism, suffering injuries and affronts with patience and serenity—stifling resentment when they have it in their power to inflict vengeance—displaying kindness and generosity towards enemies and slanderers—submitting to pain and disgrace in order to promote the prosperity of their friends and relatives, or the great interests of the human race.

Such acts may be considered by persons of influence and rank as the offspring of pusillanimity, because they themselves are either incapable of conceiving the purity of the motives from which they emanate, or are too deeply engulfed in the ruder passions of our nature, to allow them to bestow a just tribute to the efforts of enlightened reason.

It is happy for us to contemplate that every age, both of the pagan and the Christian world, has been blessed, that they always have fastened their attention on the noblest gifts of our nature, and that they now still shine as ornaments to the human race, connecting the interests of one generation with that of another. Rollin, in speaking of Aristides the Just, says "that an extraordinary greatness of soul made him superior to every passion. Interest, pleasure, resentment and jealousy were extinguished in him by the love of virtue and his country," and just in proportion as we cultivate our intellectual faculties, we shall strengthen our reasoning powers, and be prepared to become his imitators.

Our country and the world have become the munificent patron of many powerful, existing evils, that have spread their devastating influence over the best interests of the human race. One of which is the adopting of the savage custom of wars and fighting as a redress for grievances, instead of some means more consistent with reason and civilization.

The great law of love forbids our doing aught against the interests of our fellow men. It is altogether inconsistent with reason and common sense for persons when they deem themselves insulted by the vulgar aspersions of others, to maltreat their bodies for the acts of their minds. Yet how frequently do we observe those that are blessed by nature and education (and if they would but aspire to acts that bear a parallel to their dignified minds, they would shine as illustrious stars in the created throngs), that degrade themselves by practicing this barbarous custom, suited only to tyrants —because in this they may be justly ranked with the untutored savages or the animals of the forest that are impelled only by instinct.

Another fatal error arises from the belief that the only method of maintaining peace is always to be ready for war. The spirit of war can never be destroyed by all the butcheries and persecutions the human mind can invent. The history of all the "bloody tragedies" by which the earth has been drenched by human blood, cannot be justified in the conclusion, for it is the spirit of conquest that feeds it—Thomas Dick, after collecting the general statistics of those that have perished by the all-desolating pestilence of war, says "it will not be overrating the destruction of human life if we affirm that one-tenth of the human race has been destroyed by the ravages of war"—and if this estimate be admitted, it will follow that more than fourteen thousand millions of beings have been slaughtered in war since the beginning of the world, which is about eighteen times the number of its present inhabitants. This calculation proceeds from a geographical estimate "that since the Mosaic creation one hundred and forty-five thousand millions of beings have existed."

But, sir, it is not my intention to give a dissertation on the subject of national wars, although it appropriately belongs to my subject. I decline it only for the simple reason that it would be inapplicable to us as a people, while we may be more profitably employed in inveighing against the same evil as practiced by ourselves, although it exists under another form, but equally obnoxious to the principles of reason and Christianity. My reason for referring to national wars was to exhibit by plain demonstration that the war principle, which is the production of human passions, has never been, nor can ever be, conquered by its own elements. Hence, if we ever expect the word of prophecy to be fulfilled—"when the swords shall be turned into plowshares, and the spears into pruning hooks, and that the nations of the earth shall learn war no more," we must seek the destruction of the principle that animates, quickens and feeds it, by the elevation of another more powerful and omnipotent and preservative; or mankind will continue, age after age, to march on in their mad career, until the mighty current of time will doubtless sweep thousands of millions more into endless perdition, beyond the reach of mercy and the hope of future bliss. Thus the very bones, sinews, muscles and immortal mind, that God, in his infinite mercy has bestowed on man, that he might work out his own glory and extend the principles of "righteousness, justice, peace on earth and good-will to their fellow men," are constantly employed in protracting the period when the glorious millennium shall illumine our world, "and righteousness cover the earth as the water of the great deep."

Now let us solemnly ask ourselves is it reasonable, that for the real or supposed injuries that have been inflicted on mankind from the beginning to the present day, that the attempted redress of the same should have cost so much misery, pain, sweat, blood and tears and treasure? Most certainly not; since the very means used has measurably entailed the evil a thousandfold on coming generations. If man's superiority over the brute creation consists only in his reasoning powers and rationality of mind, his various methods of practicing violence towards his fellow-creatures has in many cases placed him on a level with, and sometimes below, many species of the quadruped race. We search in vain amongst the animal race to find a parallel for their cruelties to each other on their own species that is faithfully recorded in the history of wars and bloodshed, that have devoured empires, desolated kingdoms, overthrown governments and well-nigh aimed at the total annihilation of the human race. There are many species of animals that are so amiable in their disposition to each other that they might well be considered an eminent pattern for mankind in their present rude condition. The sheep, the ox, the horse and many other animals exist in a state of comparative quietude, both among themselves and the other races of animals when compared with man. And if it were possible for them to know the will of their Author, and enjoy that communion with the Creator of all worlds, all men and all animals, they might justly be entitled to a distinction above all other species of creation that had made greater departures from the will of the divine government.

It is evidently necessary that man should at all times bear in mind his origin and his end. That it is not because he was born a ruler, and superior to all other orders of creation that he continually reigns above them—it is because he has made a right use of the powers that God has given him of rising in the scale of existence. The rich bequest of Heaven to man was a natural body, a reasonable soul, and an immortal mind. With these he is rendered capable through the wisdom of Providence of ascending to the throne of angels, or descending to the abyss of devils. Hence there seems to be a relation between man and the animal creation, that subsists, neither in their origin nor their end, but satisfactorily exhibits that man may exist in a state of purity, as far *superior* to theirs as future happiness is to this world, and as far *inferior* as we are distant from future misery.

There is scarcely a single fact more worthy of indelible record than the utter inefficiency of human punishments to cure human evils. The history of wars exhibits a hopeless, as well as a fatal lesson, to all such enterprises. All the associated powers of human governments have been placed in requisition to quell and subdue the spirit of passion, without improving the condition of the human family. Human bodies have been lacerated with whips and scourges—prisons and penitentiaries have been erected for the immolation of human victims—the gibbet and halter have performed their office—while the increase of crime has kept pace with the genius of punishments, and the whole march of mind seems to have been employed in evading penal enactments and inventing new methods of destroying the blessings of the social state, not recognized by human codes.

If mankind ever expects to enjoy a state of peace and quietude, it must at all times be ready to sacrifice on the altar of principle the rude passions that animate them. This they can only perform by exerting their reasoning powers. If there be those that desire to overlook the offenses of others, and rise above those inflictions that are the offspring of passion, they must seek for protection in something *higher* than human power. They must place their faith in Him who is able to protect them from danger, or they will soon fall a prey to the wicked artifices of their wicked enemies.

Human passion is the hallucination of a distempered mind. It renders the subject of it like a ship upon the ocean without ballast or cargo, always in danger of being wrecked by every breeze. Phrenologically speaking, a mind that is subject to the fluctuating whims of passion is without the organ of order, "which is nature's first law." Our reasoning powers ought to be the helm that should guide us through the shoals and quicksands of life.

I am aware that there are those who consider the non-resistance wholly impracticable. But I trust that but few such can be found that have adopted the injunction of the Messiah for their guide and future hope, for He commands us to "love our enemies, bless them that curse you, pray for them that despitefully use you, and persecute you." These words were peculiarly applicable at the period they were uttered, and had a direct reference to the wars and strifes that then convulsed the world, and they are equally applicable at this moment. If the Christian church had at her beginning made herself the enemy of war, the evil would doubtless have been abolished throughout Christendom. The Christians of the present day do not seem to regard the principles of peace as binding, or they are unwilling to become subject to the Divine government. Human governments then, as well as now, were too feeble to stay the ravages of passion and crime, and hence there was an evident necessity for the imperious command, "Whomsoever shall smite thee on thy right cheek, turn unto him the other also."

And now, Mr. President, I rest my argument on the ground that whatever is *Scriptural* is *right,* and that whatever is right is reasonable, and from this invulnerable position I mean not to stray for the sake of any expediency whatever. The doctrine evidently taught by the Scriptural quotation evidently instructs us that resistance to physical aggression is wholly unnecessary as well as unrighteous, and subjects the transgressor to the penalty due from a willful departure from the moral and Divine law. Therefore every act of disobedience to the commands of Christian duty, in relation to our fellowmen may fairly be deemed unreasonable, as it is at enmity with our true interests and the welfare of human society. We are further instructed to turn away from the evil one, rather than waste our strength, influence and passions in a conflict that must in the end prove very injurious to both.

But someone perhaps is ready to raise an objection against this method of brooking the insults of others, and believe it right to refer to the maxim "that self-defense is the first law of nature." I will readily agree that it is the unbounded duty of every individual to defend himself against both the vulgar and false aspersions of a wicked world. But then I contend that his weapons should be his reasoning powers. That since a kind Providence has bestowed on him the power of speech and the ability to reason, he degrades his Creator by engulfing himself in the turmoils of passion and physical conflict. A mode of warfare practiced by barbarous tribes in their native forests and suited only to those animals that are alone endowed with the powers of instinct. Nor is it possible to suppose that men can pursue such a course without first parting with their reason. We often see men, while under the reigning influence of passion, as fit subjects for the lunatic asylum as any that are confined in the lunatic asylum on account of insanity.

In every possible and impartial view we take of the subject we find that physical conflict militates against the interest of the parties in collision. If I, in conflict with mine enemy, overcome him by my superior physical powers, or my skill in battle, I neither wholly subdue him, nor convince him of the justice of my cause. His spirit becomes still more enraged and he will seek retaliation and conquest on some future occasion that may seem to him more propitious. If I intimidate him I have made him a slave, while I reign a despot, and our relation will continue unnatural, as well as dangerous to each other, until our friendship has become fully restored. And what has been gained by this barbarous method of warfare when both parties become losers thereby? Yet this single case illustrates the value of all personal conflicts.

But let us pursue this subject in a more dignified view. I mean as it respects the moral and Divine government. Is it possible that any Christian man or woman that will flog and maltreat their fellow beings can be in *earnest* when they with apparent devotion ask their heavenly Father to "forgive their trespasses as they forgive others"? Surely they must be asking God to punish them—or when they say "lead us not into temptation, but deliver us from evil," do they mean that they should run headlong into both, with all their infuriated madness? Certainly not. Who would not be more willing to apply to them insincerity of motive, and that they knew not what they were doing, rather than suppose that intelligent minds would be capable of such gross inconsistency? Would it not prove infinitely better in times of trials and difficulties, to leave the tempter and temptation behind and pursue our course onward? But, says the objector, there will be no safety nor security in this method from the insults of the vulgar and the brutal attacks of the assassin. I am inclined to believe to the contrary, and will be borne out in that belief by the evidence of those that have pursued this Christian course of conduct.

A writer under the signature of Philopacificus, while "taking a solemn view of the custom of war," says, "There are two sets of professed Christians in this country, which, as sects, are peculiar in their opinions respecting the lawfulness of war, and the right of repelling injury by violence." These are the Quakers and Shakers. They are remarkably pacific. Now we ask, does it appear from experience that their forbearing spirit brings on them a greater portion of injury and insults than what is experienced by people of other sects? Is not the reverse of this true, in fact? There may indeed be some such instances of gross depravity as a person taking advantage of their pacific character, to do them an injury with the hope of impunity. But in general it is believed their pacific principles and spirit command the esteem even of the vicious and operate as a shield from insult and abuse.

The question may be brought home to every society. How seldom do children of a mild and forbearing temper experience insults or injury, compared with the waspish, who will sting if they are touched? The same inquiry may be made in respect to persons of these opposite descriptions of every age, and in every situation of life, and the result will prove favorable to the point in question.

When William Penn took the government of Pennsylvania, he distinctly avowed to the Indians his forbearing and pacific principles, and his benevolent wishes for uninterrupted peace with them. On these principles the government was administered while it remained in the hands of the Quakers. This was an illustrious example of government on religious principles, worthy of imitation by all the nations of the earth.

I am happy to state that there are various incidents related by travelers, both among the native Africans and Indians, where lives have been saved by the presentation of a pacific attitude, when they would have otherwise fallen a prey to savage barbarity.

It has been my purpose to exhibit reason as a great safeguard, at all times capable of dethroning passion and alleviating our condition in periods of the greatest trouble and difficulty, and of being a powerful handmaid in achieving a triumph of the principles of universal peace. I have also thus far treated the subject as a grand fundamental principle, universal in its nature, and binding alike on every member of the human family. But if there be a single class of people in these United States on which these duties are more imperative and binding than another, that class is the colored population of this country, both free and enslaved. Situated as we are, among a people that recognize the lawfulness of slavery, and more of whom sympathize with the oppressor than the oppressed, it requires us to pursue our course calmly onward, with much self-denial, patience and perseverance.

We must be prepared at all times to meet the scoffs and scorns of the vulgar and indecent—the contemptible frowns of haughty tyrants and the blighting mildew of a popular and sinful prejudice. If amidst these difficulties we can but possess our souls in patience we shall finally triumph over our enemies. But among the various duties that devolve on us, not the least is that which relates to ourselves. We must learn on all occasions to rebuke the spirit of violence, both in sentiment and practice. God has said, "Vengeance is mine, and I will repay it." The laws of the land guarantee the protection of our persons from personal violence, and whoever for any cause inflicts a single blow on a fellow being violates the laws of God and of his country and has no just claim to being regarded as a Christian or a good citizen.

As a people we have suffered much from the pestilential influence of mob violence that has spread its devastating influence over our country. And it is to me no matter of astonishment that they continue to exist. They do but put in practice a common everyday theory that pervades every neighborhood, and almost every family, viz.: That it is right under certain circumstances to violate all law, both civil and national, and abuse, kick and cuff your fellowman when they deem that he has offended or insulted the community in which he resides.

Whenever the passions of individuals rise above all laws, human and divine, then they are in the first stages of anarchy, and then every act prosecuted under the influence of this spirit necessarily extends itself beyond the boundary of our laws. The act of the multitude is carried out on the principle of combination, which is the grand lever by which machinery as well as man is impelled in this fruitful age. There is no difference in principle between the acts of a few individuals and those of a thousand while actuated by the spirit of passion, dethroning reason, the laws of our country and the liberty of man. Hence every individual that either aids or abets an act of personal violence towards the humblest individual is guilty of sustaining the detestable practice of mobocratic violence. Yet such is the general spirit that pervades our common country, and receives its sanction from places of high honor and trust, that it is patriotism to disregard the laws. It is but reasonable to suppose that individuals, guided by views and motives, will on some occasions concentrate their power and carry on their operation on a large scale. Unless the hearts and reasoning powers of man become improved, it is impossible for the most sagacious mind to augur the consequences. The spirit of passion has become so implanted in human bosoms that the laws of our country give countenance to the same by exhibiting lenity for those who are under its influence.

This is doubtless a great error in legislation, because it not only presupposes the irrationality of man, but gives him a plea of innocence in behalf of his idiotism. The only sure method of conquering these evils is to commend a reform in ourselves, and then the spirit of passion will soon be destroyed in individuals, and communities, and governments, and then the ground-work will be fully laid for a speedy triumph of the principles of universal peace.

The love of power is one of the greatest human infirmities, and with it comes the usurping influence of despotism, the mother of slavery. Show me any country or people where despotism reigns triumphant, and I will exhibit to your view the spirit of slavery, whether the same be incorporated in the government or not. It is this demonlike spirit of passion that sends forth its poignant influence over professedly civilized nations, as well as the more barbarous tribes. Its effects on human interest is the same, whether it emanates from the subjugator of Poland—the throne of Britain—the torrid zone of the South, or the genial clime of Pennsylvania; from the white, the red, or the black man—whether he be of European or African descent—or the native Indian that resides in the wilds of the forest, their combined action is at war with the principles of peace and the liberty of the world.

How different is the exercise of this love of power when exercised by man, or enforced by human governments, to the exercise of Him who holds all "power over the heavens, earth, and seas, and all that in them is." With God, all is order—with man, all confusion. The planets perform their annual revolutions—the tides ebb and flow—the seas obey His command—the whole government of universal worlds are sustained by His wisdom and power—each invariably performing the course marked out by their great Author, because they are impelled by His love. But with man, governments are impelled by the law of force; hence despotism becomes an ingredient in all human governments.

The power of reason is the noblest gift of Heaven to man, because it assimilates man to his Maker. And were he to improve his mind by cultivating his reasoning powers, his acts of life would bear the impress of the Deity indelibly stamped upon them. If human governments bore any direct resemblance to the government of God they would be mild in their operation, and the principles of universal peace would become implanted in every mind. Wars, fighting, and strifes would cease—there would be a signal triumph of truth over error—the principles of peace, justice, righteousness, and universal love would guide and direct mankind onward in that sublime path marked out by the great Prince of Peace.

And now, my friends, let us cease to be guided by the influence of a wild and beguiling passion—the wicked and foolish fantasies of pride, folly and lustful ambition—the alluring and detestable examples of despotism and governments—the sickly sensibility of those who from false notions of honor attempt to promote the ends of justice by placing "righteousness under their feet," and are at all times ready to imbue their hands in a fellow creature's blood for the purpose of satisfying their voracious appetites for crime, murder and revenge. I say from them let us turn away, for a terrible retaliation must shortly await them, even in this life. The moral power of this nation and the world is fast wakening from the sleep of ages, and wielding a swift besom that will sweep from the face of the earth error and iniquity with the power of a whirlwind. But a few years ago and dueling was considered necessary to personal honor, and the professional Christian, or the most upright citizen, might barter away the lives and happiness of a nation with his guilty traffic in ardent spirits with impunity. But now a regenerated public sentiment not only repudiates their conduct, but consigns them with "body and soul murderers." Though the right to be free has been deemed inalienable by this nation from a period antecedent to the Declaration of American Independence, yet a mental fog hovered over this nation on the subject of slavery that had well-nigh sealed her doom were it not that in the Providence of God a few noble spirits arise in the might of moral power to her rescue. They girded on the power of truth for their shield and the principles of peace for their buckler, and thus boldly pierced through the incrustations of a false and fatal philosophy, and from the *incision* sprang forth the light of glorious liberty, disseminating its delectable rays over the dark chasms of slavery and lighting up the vision of a ruined world. And the effect has been to awaken the nation to her duty with regard to the rights of man—to render slaveholders despicable and guilty of robbery and murder—and in many places those that profess Christianity have been unchurched, denied the privilege of Christian fellowship. And the same moral power is now awakening in the cause of peace, and will bring disgrace and dishonor on all who engage in wars and fighting.

The period is fast approaching when church, as at present constituted, must undergo one of the severest contests she has met with since her foundation, because in so many cases she has refused to sustain her own principles. The moral warfare that is now commenced will not cease if the issue should be a dissolution of both church and state. The time has already come when those believe that intemperance, slavery, war, and fighting are sinful, and it will soon arrive when those who practice either their rights to enjoy Christian fellowship will be questioned.

And now, Mr. President, I shall give a few practical illustrations, and then I shall have done. It appears by history that there have been many faithful advocates of peace since the apostolic age, but none have ever given a more powerful impetus to the cause of peace than the modern abolitionists. They have been beaten and stoned, mobbed and persecuted from city to city, and never returned evil for evil, but submissively, as a sheep brought before the shearer, have they endured scoffings and scourges for the cause's sake while they prayed for their persecutors. And how miraculously they have been preserved in the midst of a thousand dangers from without and within. Up to the present moment not the life of a single individual has been sacrificed on the altar of popular fury. Had they set out in this glorious undertaking of freeing 2,500,000 human beings with the war-cry of "liberty or death," they would have been long since demolished, or a civil war would have ensued; thus would have dyed the national soil with human blood. And now let me ask you, was not their method of attacking the system of human slavery the most reasonable? And would not their policy have been correct, even if we were to lay aside their Christian motives? Their weapons were reason and moral truth, and on them they desired to stand or fall—and so it will be in all causes that are sustained from just and Christian principles, they will ultimately triumph. Now let us suppose for a single moment what would have been our case if they had started on the principle that "resistance to tyrants is obedience to God"?—what would have been our condition, together with that of the slave population? Why, we should have doubtless perished by the sword, or been praying for the destruction of our enemies, and probably engaged in the same bloody warfare.

And now we are indebted to the modern abolitionists more than to any other class of men for the instructions we have received from the dissemination of their principles, or we would not at this moment be associated here to advocate the cause of moral reform—of temperance, education, peace and universal liberty. Therefore let us, like them, obliterate from our minds the idea of revenge, and from our hearts all wicked intentions towards each other and the world, and we shall be able through the blessing of Almighty God to do much to establish the principles of universal peace. Let us not think the world has no regard for our efforts—they are looking forward to them with intense interest and anxiety. The enemies of the abolitionists are exhibiting a regard for the power of their principles that they are unwilling to acknowledge, although it is everywhere known over the country that abolitionists "will not fight," yet they distrust their own strength so much that they frequently muster a whole neighborhood of from 50 to 300 men, with sticks, stones, rotten eggs and bowie knives, to mob and beat a single individual, probably in his " 'teens," whose heart's law is nonresistance. There is another way in which they do us honor —they admit the right of all people to fight for their liberty but colored people and abolitionists—plainly inferring that they are too good for the performance of such un-Christian acts—and lastly, while we endeavor to control our own passions and keep them in subjection, let us be mindful of the weakness of others; and for acts of wickedness committed against us let us reciprocate in the spirit of kindness. If they continue their injustice towards us, let us always decide that their reasoning powers are defective, and that it is with men as the laws of mechanics—large bodies move slowly, while smaller ones are easily propelled with swift velocity. In every case of passion that presents itself the subject is one of pity rather than derision, and in his cooler moments let us earnestly advise him to improve his understanding by cultivating his intellectual powers, and thus exhibit his close alliance with God, who is the author of all wisdom, peace, justice, righteousness, and truth. And in conclusion, let it always be our aim to live in a spirit of unity with each other, supporting one common cause by spreading our influence for the good of mankind, with the hope that the period will ultimately arise when the principles of universal peace will triumph throughout the world.

The Negro felt, however, that his case in this country was not hopeless. As they were encouraged in 1808 by the act of Congress prohibiting slave trade, they were similarly exultant on learning that the British and French were actually abolishing slavery and the slave trade in their colonies. The British act of emancipation was passed in 1833, and by gradual methods through a system of apprenticeship the institution was actually abolished by 1838. Hoping to encourage the Negroes in bondage in the United States and at the same time pour out the feelings of a glad heart, James McCune Smith [1] delivered this address, speaking to the following resolution:

[1] James McCune Smith was distinguished as a graduate of medicine in the University of Glasgow and a successful practitioner in the city of New York. He was also noted for

Resolved, That we contemplate with heartfelt satisfaction the noble efforts of the Abolitionists of Britain and France for the total cessation of *Slavery* and its concomitant—*the Slave Trade;* and pledge to them our coöperation until by the blessing of God both these cruel customs shall wholly cease.

THE ABOLITION OF SLAVERY AND THE SLAVE TRADE IN THE FRENCH AND BRITISH COLONIES[1]

By James McCune Smith

Mr. President, Ladies and Gentlemen: I rise to offer a resolution expressive of our high satisfaction in the noble efforts of the abolitionists of Great Britain and France, who, although they are separated from us by the width of an ocean, and by distinct political institutions, are nevertheless united with us in sentiment and exertion in the sacred cause of immediate and universal emancipation.

With these two nations we are connected by ties of the closest amity, and enjoy greater reciprocal influence than with any others upon the globe. To these nations our struggle for independence gave the first impulse to the path of liberty, which, if they have trod with slower, they have trod with more consistent steps than we: for every step they have advanced, each measure they have gained, has been an advantage not only to themselves, but to all who are dependent on them. And whenever the people of Great Britain or of France have obtained any portion of civil liberty, their first exercise of it has been to extend the precious boon to their fellow subjects, held in the galling chains of West Indian slavery.

In the last century, the first Convention elected by the French people immediately abolished slavery in two French colonies: and in the present, the passing of the British Reform Bill has rapidly

his business ability, as evidenced by his accumulation of some property and the establishment of two drug stores in New York.

Dr. Smith was of mixed breed, of about equal proportion of Caucasian and African blood. In stature he was somewhat thick and corpulent. He had a fine head with a broad and lofty brow, full face, firm mouth, and dazzling eyes. As an educated man given to writing, he was easily drawn into the discussion on the race question, which his knowledge of history, science, and literature enabled him to treat in a scholarly way. He was also an eloquent speaker who always made himself clear and talked to the point.

[1] *Colored American,* June 9, 1838.

been followed by the abolition of British West Indian slavery. France, indeed, set the first, the most glorious example, because liberty was conferred without stint or restriction, without any lengthened delay to sicken hope, or purgatorial state to blast expectation; it was sudden and entire; the man who until yesterday had toiled in the field, and had known no other incentive to labor than the cart-whip, was to-day raised to the dignity and privileges of a citizen of the republic; the woman who until yesterday had sobbed over her youngling and besought the grave to snatch it from the horror of existence, to-day held it towards the skies and shrieked, "He is free!"

This example has proved most instructive, for when France again bent her neck to the iron yoke of a ruthless tyrant, and suffered her sons to be slaughtered at the altar of ambitious despotism, the men whom she had so suddenly liberated showed themselves worthy of their freedom; for, against the veterans of Europe's conqueror, against an armament sent out by the empire which overwhelmed Napoleon, amidst the loathing and scorn of a neighboring republic, and the cold and bitter neglect of all nations, they have maintained their freedom until now, when generous and consistent France, inspired with the genius of modern abolitionism, by acknowledging the independence of Hayti, completes the triumph which revolutionary France began. France, then, has been the first to grant immediate and entire emancipation, and the first to acknowledge the right and capacity of a community of freedmen to rank among the nations of the earth. And although she (France) still holds 260,000 slaves in some of her dependencies, yet recent movements nearly akin to her pristine efforts promise these a speedy liberation.

* * * * * * * * *

Sir, this transaction is one of the most cheering that has occurred in the history of abolitionism. For we here find a legislative body, without any recurrence to the primary assemblies of the people, without being urged by petitions or bound by pledges, without being incited by the tales of horror that always accompany slavery—for it is a remarkable fact that the slaves of Catholics are better fed and better treated than those of Protestants: I say we find a legislative body without any of the ordinary inducements, at the first discussion of the subject, not only adopting the measure proposed by the most sanguine of the abolitionists, but actually desirous of advancing still further. This was a manifestation of principle at which we may blush as Americans, but rejoice as men: and unwilling as I am to utter any remark, or draw any comparison reflecting even the slightest discredit on

"My own, my native land,"

yet there is something in the facts which, however humbling, may yet prove instructive. The very year that witnessed in our Hall of Representatives the appalling spectacle of a venerable man hooted and howled at when he sought even the right to petition in behalf of the slave, the same year beheld the legislature of king-ridden, priest-ridden, and as some say, infidel France, cheering on an abolitionist in his measures for emancipation.

Mr. President, if we next turn our eyes toward Great Britain, on whose dominions the sun never sets, whilst they extend through every clime, we find her the neighbor of almost every nation, and therefore capable of influencing all: and this influence is regulated by those sound principles for which she is so justly distinguished, which are her shelter in the hour of danger and her glory in the day of prosperity. Sound as these principles are on all other questions, they are preëminently so on that question which we are this day met to forward. For if, unwittingly, the British people became deeply imbued in the blood guiltiness of slavery and the slave trade, yet as soon as they became aware of the enormity of the crime and possessed the power to remove it, they made signal and instantaneous atonement by the immediate emancipation of their 800,000 slaves. And this great movement was distinguished by none of the bitterness of a political contest, none of the selfishness of a political victory. And when the battle was over and the victory won, the men who had gained it—the dissenters of England and Scotland—still heard the clank of chains, the groans of men and the wails of women held in slavery by other nations. They heard these sounds and they felt the principles by which they had recently been stirred still glow within them and expand their benevolence beyond the limits of a single empire: they felt the force of that sentiment uttered nearly a thousand years ago by an African slave, *"Homo sum humani nil alienum ama puto."*

They felt that their country was the world, their countrymen mankind, and were urged by motives that they could not resist to make the attempt to disenthrall all their countrymen: and they bound themselves by solemn compact to begin a moral agitation that shall not cease until the last fetter shall fall from the last slave upon our earth.

They formed the British Society for the immediate and universal emancipation of slaves, and the consequent destruction of the slave trade throughout the world.

Sir, what are the means by which they hope to obtain so glorious a result? The means are simple, but with God's blessing they will prove efficient. With the Bible in their hands, and its precepts for their guide, they are determined calmly, but earnestly and incessantly, to remonstrate with all slaveholders, and to beseech them to liberate their slaves.

* * * * * * * * *

Although at the present time their efforts are devoted to another and more appropriate object, the entire abolition of slavery, which yet lingers in their colonies under the name of apprenticeship, yet as soon as they have abolished the apprenticeship system—and they will do so, even if it be but one hour sooner than its appointed expiration, yet they will obtain that hour, in order that the principles of immediate emancipation may, in their colonies, vanquish the chicanery of slavery in its very metamorphosis—then, sir, with the renewed zeal, the additional experience, and the force of the complete example which this victory will give them, they will bring all their energies to bear upon slavery as it exists in these States.

We may rejoice then, sir, in the present efforts of the British abolitionists on account of the principle for which they are made. It is a struggle for immediate instead of gradual emancipation.

Should the apprenticeship, which works so badly, be permitted to continue until 1840, the evils which have resulted, and the insurrections which might arise from it, would be, to the slaveholder, an argument against emancipation in any form, and to many friends of liberty an argument for very gradual emancipation. The position in which the British abolitionists are now placed must convince slaveholders that they must grant, and abolitionists that they must obtain immediate emancipation, else they will be forced to "fight their battles o'er again."

We may rejoice in these efforts on account of the renewed zeal which they will infuse into the abolition party of Great Britain.

One moral victory gained raises the mind to an eminence whence it perceives others that must be achieved, and inspires it with new energies for the struggle. Each step advanced has increased their zeal and enlarged their views.

The flame of abolitionism is no longer confined to the dissenters of Great Britain; it has even penetrated within the walls of the church established by law; and bishops of the Church of England have at length discovered that the advocacy of the cause of God's suffering poor is not inconsistent with apostolic order. Men of every rank and of every sect are gathering around the standard of abolition, the great principle from which the anxiety grows—that of loving all men—is, imperceptibly to themselves, diffusing its healing influence over the hostile parties for once united; dissenter and churchman, Protestant and Papist, standing on the broad platform of humanity and covered with the mantle of charity, are beginning to love one another whilst united to manifest their common love towards the crushed and bleeding slave.

And when the apprenticeship is abolished, this mass of mind, animated by the principle which now unites it, and in the exercise of the same, will devote its entire energies to the emancipation of our slaves. And the Christians of Great Britain will call upon those of these states, in one long and loud and incessant series of remonstrances, entreating them to follow the British example.

Sir, I admire this method of remonstrance. Judging from those we have already received, they seem to be of the right tone, and calculated to effect much good. I deem the method of remonstrance right because it is warranted by the usages of nations in the past and at the present time. In our own time one government has freely remonstrated with another on the destruction of the African slave trade: why, then, may not one people—who are the source of all governmental power—remonstrate with another for the abolition of slavery! The people of these United States, at least that very large and respectable portion of them which constitutes the American Temperance Society, have remonstrated with the British people on the sin of intemperance; have not the people of Great Britain an equal right to remonstrate with us on the equally heinous sin of slavery? But, sir, not only has remonstrance

—in other words, moral interference—been sanctioned by common usage and our own practice, but British interference in our slave question has actually been solicited, and solicited, too, by all the good and the great of our land, who are at this moment receiving pecuniary assistance from a few of the British people for the abolition of American slavery by means of colonization. Can the good and the great complain then if other British subjects, once solicited by the same agent, see fit to strive for the self-same object by remonstrating with the slaveholder on the justice, safety and expediency of immediate emancipation?

But, sir, common usage may be wrong, the Temperance and even the Colonization Society may be wrong in sanctioning national interference in national sins. I still plead for the right of remonstrance on higher grounds than common usage, or the sanction of moral reforming associations. Christians are governed by the laws peculiar to the commonwealth of Christ, and which are independent of mere human laws imposed by human communities; the citizens of the Church Catholic of the Redeemer may be spread through many climes and subject to various forms of political government, but no difference in clime, no diversity in form of political creed can break the links which makes them fellow-citizens in Christ, or free them from obedience to the precepts of the Saviour. One of these precepts is, that they may rebuke one another in love: and another is, that they may exhort each other to "good works." Reposing on these precepts and obedient to them, the Christians of Britain have a right to call upon the Christians of these United States to desist from the sin of slaveholding.

CHAPTER V

THE ORATORY OF THE CRISIS

NEARER the middle of the nineteenth century Negro oratory developed into a more serious attack on the institution of slavery. The growth of antislavery societies in the North gave additional opportunities for the expression of such sentiment. A number of Negroes employed as antislavery lecturers, moreover, developed into the most forceful orators of that day. Among these appeared Negroes who, as fugitive slaves, accompanied abolitionists from place to place to give their own personal experiences in bondage. Some of these undergoing training at the same time learned to address audiences intelligently. So did Lunsford Lane, from North Carolina, and Williams Wells Brown, from Missouri. Others like Sojourner Truth could move multitudes even with their untutored language.

The most famous of the Negro antislavery orators, however, were Charles Lenox Remond, Samuel Ringold Ward, Henry Highland Garnet, Martin R. Delany, Charles B. Ray, and Frederick Douglass. Remond and Douglass devoted practically all of their time to the work of stirring up the people. The others had various interests. A few of the speeches of Remond are available, and most of those of Douglass may be easily obtained. Of the others little eloquence has been preserved. The reason is probably that with the exception of Ward, whom Douglass considered one of the most eloquent men of his time, most of these orators were overshadowed first by Remond and then by Douglass. In giving publicity to the utterances of these men the abolition press brought forward what it considered the most eloquent. Furthermore, some of these men, like Ward, were so gifted with oral expression that they did not need to reduce their thought to written form; and, as in the case of most orators, even if they had, their words in cold type would not have made as favorable an impression as they did when spoken.

On account of the unusual career of Frederick Douglass, Charles Lenox Remond has been all but forgotten as an antislavery orator. Remond, however, the precursor of Douglass, was easily the most famous Negro in the United States prior to the rise of the latter. Remond, to start with, was a free man of color able to maintain himself comfortably. He lived in Salem, Massachusetts, where he was born. He was "small in stature, of spare make, neat wiry build, genteel appearance, and pleasant voice." He had fundamental education and developed into an acceptable speaker. He was one of the seventeen members of the first antislavery society formed in America. In 1838 he became a lecturer of the American Antislavery Society and toured Massachusetts, Rhode Island, and Maine, in company with Ichabod Codding. He became so popular in antislavery circles that during the early forties he was generally sought whenever the Negro's opinion on slavery was desired on the platform. The abolition papers gave him honorable mention and the proslavery press expressed fear that he would harm its cause. And well might the defenders of slavery have this attitude, for he fearlessly belabored the enemies of liberty.

Developing more force in the presentation of the case of the slave, Remond was encouraged to go to Great Britain to arouse interest there in the cause of freedom. There he addressed numerous audiences and left the impression of an eloquent man of earnestness of purpose and forcefulness of character. Returning home he was loudly acclaimed as the most noted Negro at that time. One of his most successful efforts was the following speech, delivered before the British and Foreign Antislavery Society in July, 1841, on rising to second a resolution:

SLAVERY AS IT CONCERNS THE BRITISH

By Charles Lenox Remond [1]

In the few remarks which I propose to offer on this occasion, I shall confine myself to the merits of the resolution. I approve of it throughout, and I hope you will do the same. The friends of the colored man in America have been wont to despond; for never, while Great Britain pursues the course she does at the present time, can they hope to carry their cause to a successful termination. It is in vain to attempt the annihilation of American slavery while that system receives the encouragement now afforded to it in this country. [Hear! hear!] I know that the question is a difficult and a troublesome one; but, inasmuch as the antislavery party of Great Britain have been the chosen instruments of the Almighty for carrying out the great doctrine of human rights, I hope they will continue to stimulate their friends in America. If ever there was a class of the fellow inhabitants of any portion of the civilized world which deserved the coöperation of philanthropic minds in this country, it is their fellow abolitionists, comparatively few in number, in the United States. [Loud cheers.]

I was one of seventeen members of the first Antislavery Society formed in America. From that time to the present I have been acquainted with all their movements, and they have had to make larger sacrifices, and to undergo deeper sufferings, than any other class of men in the world who have associated for so noble and good an object. [Loud cheers.] The foreign slave trade, to say nothing of the domestic slave trade in my own country, never flourished to such an extent as at the present moment; and we cannot hope to lessen it while it continues to be so lucrative, arising from the consumption of slave-grown cotton in this country. I cannot but regret whenever attempts are made to call away the minds of persons met for the discussion of this great question. [Cheers.] When the British and Foreign Antislavery Society cannot stand on its own merits, then let it fall. [Hear! hear!]

[1] *Liberator,* July 9, 1841.

I need not refer to the thousands of colored people who have been driven to a premature grave by the impetus which Great Britain still gives to slavery. The system which we wish to see destroyed rolls on unheeded by recreant Americans, and, for having spoken the truth, the whole truth, and nothing but the truth, I have been stigmatized as a traitor to my country. Sooner than approve of the system of slavery in the United States, if I must take the alternative of being the oppressed slave or the oppressor, give me the condition of the former. [Loud cheers.] Give me the chance, if I may so express it, of being the poor slave, rather than the oppressor, when they shall meet at the bar of God, and there shall be no question of bank or antibank, tariff or antitariff. I trust that the day is not far distant when, in my own beloved country, as well as yours, mankind shall be considered great only as they are good. [Cheers.]

At the present day, in the United States, men, women and children are enslaved for the complexion they wear. If a man there has one drop of African blood flowing in his veins, it not only dooms him to be an outlaw, but exposes him to seizure as a slave. But, if the growth of cotton in the East Indies be taken up as it ought by the British public, slavery will become the great question of the day in America, and it will soon be terminated. [Cheers.] Liberty has a name in my country, but in practice it is completely dead. [Cheers.] I hope the meeting will bear with me while I read one or two extracts confirmatory of the remarks I have made. I will refer to a source which has had a powerful action on a great and influential part of the District of Columbia. If a colored man goes to Columbia to attend the funeral of a deceased relative, he is liable to be seized, bound, and detained, till he proves his freedom. [Hear! hear!] He must prove it while immured within the bolts and bars of a dungeon, otherwise he is sold as a slave. [Hear! hear!] There are two young men being flogged as slaves whose father receives a pension for his services in the Revolutionary War. [Hear! hear!]

The extract to which I refer is taken from the Natchez *Free Trader,* which, in copying an account of the great meeting in Manchester, England, with reference to the growth of cotton in India, says:

"It may be remembered that when Capt. Baylis, of the British East India forces, came to this city, in the early part of last summer, for the purpose of getting men acquainted with the process of raising cotton to accompany him to India, the *Free Trader* was the first journal to expose and denounce his plan, as a dangerous scheme to undermine the prosperity of the American planters, and ruin the sale of their great staple. In no measured terms of rebuke, the *Free Trader* denounced both those wealthy and influential planters in Adams county who lent themselves to aid Capt. Baylis in his designs, and those nine young men from the States of Mississippi and Louisiana who sold themselves to the ancient and inveterate enemy of their native land; but, at that time, the acting editor of that journal knew not the whole enormity of the insidious scheme. Little, perhaps, thought those young planters and overseers, when they consented to go to India, that they were to be used as tools in the unholy hands of the abolitionists! [Hear! hear!]

"Of the startling fact that the East India cotton growing Project is but a powerful organization designed to overthrow the system of domestic slavery in the American States, we have now the most ample evidence. This evidence we hasten to present to our readers; it is vitally important to the South, and merits all the attention which it will surely receive. . . .

"The attitude of the South in sustaining the patriarchal institutions of slavery at this moment is full of interest. England is arraying its vast moral, commercial, and political power against us. The ocean queen is about to work her thirty millions of slaves and serfs in the jungles and on the plains of India, for the express purpose of rendering the labor of three millions of black slaves in America unproductive and of no value. This will be done. There is no vacillation or weakness of purpose in the English character. [Cheers.] All India will, in a year or two, teem like a vast beehive with the cotton enterprise, cheered on by the fratricide abolitionists and mock philanthropists of the Northern States. Meanwhile, O'Connell, the Irish agitator, is invoked to agitate his countrymen against slavery on this side of the water, while, both in Ireland and England, his roaring voice is perpetually lifted up in abuse of the noble-hearted, the independent, and the fearless Southern planters, as well as the American character at large.

The Kirk of Scotland thunders her anathemas against the American Presbyterians, because they will not excommunicate slave-holding church members. The Wesleyans and the Quakers are perpetually using clerical influence against the rights and peace of our social institutions. The royal consort of the Queen of England is not ashamed to preside over the opening of a meeting, vauntingly called the 'World's Convention,' the chief business of which was to abuse American institutions—where Birney, once a slaveholder, and the Negro Remond, side by side on the same platform with the highest Bishops of the Church of England, and with O'Connell, lifted up their voices, traitors as they are against their own native land; all joining in full cry against a domestic institution which has come down unbroken from the 'world's grey fathers,' the holy patriarchs, with whom angels walked and talked." [Laughter, and very loud cheers.]

I have only to add, that, if speaking before so large an audience as this on behalf of freedom constitutes me a traitor, I am proud of the appellation. [Cheers.] I expect to return to my native country soon, and I have said nothing here which I shall not say there, and which I have not already said there again and again. [Loud cheers.] I have been in danger of my life on more occasions than one, and before slavery is abolished it is probable that I shall again. I believe that there will be more martyrs to the great cause of emancipation than one. Let slavery in America be abolished, and it will then be a happy country, and England will receive the gratitude of the colored man for the efforts she has made. [Loud cheers.]

In the following address Remond made a still more eloquent appeal, speaking before the Hibernian Antislavery Society on November 19, 1841. It is remarkable that he was so warmly received here, just as Frederick Douglass was by the Irish some time thereafter, when in a few years the Irish immigrants and the Negroes by competition in menial service in the Northern States were to become estranged to the extent that the former would practically wage war upon the latter. This speech, however, showed such exact knowledge of slavery in all of its international bearings that it is little wonder that the orator made a favorable impression.

SLAVERY AND THE IRISH [1]

By Charles Lenox Remond

In rising to make some remarks on the great cause which has brought us together, I wish to preface them with one request: it is, that those by whom I am surrounded will do me the favor of listening to me as attentively and as noiselessly as they may—partly in consideration of my own health, and partly for their own sake. [Hear.] If I rise for one thing more than another, on the present occasion, it is to utter a few sentiments which are founded on the truth, and nothing but the truth, and such being the broad and immutable principle on which are grounded the doctrines I would propound, and the facts to which I would direct attention, I trust that you will not consider that anything which may fall from me is meant to be directed to any one sect or portion of the oppressed, but that my words are designed to have a general and unbounded application to all who suffer under persecution or sorrow, under the bondage of the enthraller. [Cheers.]

There is not a single individual, of all who surround me in this assembly, who may not have it in his power to promote and forward the glorious cause, to the advocacy of which I have devoted myself; nor is there one, the effect and benefit of whose exertions in behalf of the unhappy slave will not be felt and appreciated even in the remote land from which I have traveled hither. It is not the lack of friends, nor of means, nor of publications devoted to our interests, which prevents our progressing as rapidly in this holy work as we would wish to progress; but I know from long experience that there is wanting, on the part of the people of Ireland, England, and Scotland, a strong and thorough conviction of the service and benefit which each individual man may, in his own person, render to the cause of liberty, by his own adhesion to our ranks. [Hear! hear!]

I mean not to deny that in your enlightened and intellectual

[1] *Liberator*, Nov. 19, 1841.

land, my friends, there are many wise and good men who sympathize most cordially with us, and whose hearts bleed as they think of the heartless cruelty by which the slave is victimized; but keenly though they feel his wrongs, and deeply though they regret his sorrows, they are deterred from taking an active part in the efforts now making to restore him to the life of liberty, from the mistaken and most infatuated idea, that their assistance and co-operation could be but of little service. This is a fatal error, and one against which I cannot too emphatically forewarn you. [Hear! and cheers.]

It is the proud prerogative of all men—even of the most lowly and unobtrusive—to conduce in their own persons to the furtherance of the sacred cause of liberty and tolerance. Nor is it in words only that we should testify our love of freedom, and detestation of oppression. It is very easy to come here and pass resolutions laudatory of the one, and condemnatory of the other; but little advance will be made towards freedom's goal, by our resolving, unless we take care that the tone, tenor, and practice of our lives shall keep pace with our professions. How fondly do I hope that all in this meeting—yea more, in this city, and even throughout the wide extent of your country—may be induced to regard the subject in this light, and to model the practice of their lives accordingly!

I stand here to advocate a cause which, above all others, should be, and ever has been, dear to the Irish heart—the cause of liberty. Nor do I pretend to ask from any Irishman that which I would not always most willingly and delightfully concede to him, if the occasion should ever arise. [Loud cheers.] The request which I would make of you is the request of suffering humanity—the observations I would direct to you are the observations of justice and of truth; and, such being the case, surely there is no Irishman, worthy the name, who will consider that my request is unreasonable, or my observations ill-timed or out of place. The request which I now make, and have often made, is, that those who hear me will forget complexion, and that when the hateful truth is naked to their ears, that slavery exists in America, they will be inclined to consider the subject not as one of color, but of kind—not as one, the merits of which are to be decided by the hue of the skin, but rather one the test whereof should be the nature and character of the being who is enslaved. Enough! he is a man, and so are ye. [Cheers.]

Our love of freedom, our execration of tyrants and tyranny, are founded not merely upon our own individual principles, but also upon a grand and heavenly principle which we draw from the source whence all we have of noble and of good is derived—the source of holy writ. This is the principle which sways the mind of the society which I represent—such, too, I feel assured is the principle of the society I address; and while we can, with truth, make such an averment, there is not a slaveholder in America—there is not a slaveholder in Cuba—there is not a slaveholder in India, but must admit our principle to be good. They acknowledge that principle in their words, but act in defiance of it by their promotion of slavery. We, too, recognize the same heavenly principle, but be it ours to act in accordance with it, by loathing, contemning, and trampling under foot the unholy cause of bondage, meet it where we may.

Many there are, I grieve to say, who are deterred from the consideration of this subject through a vain and silly thought that the question is an elaborate and complicated one, and that in the discussion of it they would become bewildered and mentally blinded, as it were. 'Tis false, most corruptly false, to say so. There is no complication in the matter. The road lies before us, clear, straight, and unwarped as is the path of truth and justice. The question is resolved into two words only—liberty or slavery? And all men who acknowledge and reverence the one as pure and holy, and who loathe and execrate the other as hateful and infamous, ought to come forward and speak the sentiments of their hearts.

These are the few things I had intended to give utterance to as prefatory to the facts I will briefly lay before you in seconding the resolution commended to my charge—after which I will take occasion to make another motion in connexion with that brought forward by my friend Allen.

The question now before us—namely, that of slavery as it exists in the United States—is probably of greater moment and importance than that of the same evil as it may exist in any other land. This I say, not merely because there are in the United States a vast number of slaves, but also because I know that there are very many countries which, in this as in other respects, take their cue (so to use the word) from America; and of this I feel assured, that while the eyes of the whole world are directed to my own guilty country, the fingers of the wise and of the good in all lands are also pointed ignominiously at that glorious charter which she pretends to have adopted as the rule of her life, but which, day by day, desecrates and dishonors—therefore it is that I consider the behavior of America on the slavery question is looked upon with greater attention, and she exercises in this respect a more paramount influence by her example than does any other country. [Hear! hear!]

I know that in the pictures which I have drawn of the atrocities to which America is witness, and in the descriptions I have given of the horrors of the slave trade in that country, I am said to have been too severe and rather exaggerated. This, too, was said of the first man who ever mooted the question; but in my own case, as in his, my own breast tells me the charge is unfounded, and the accusation will only have the effect of making me more zealous and energetic in the vindication of truth and humanity. [Cheers.]

Some there are who are prevented from joining in the great struggle wherein we are engaged from a false and corrupt pride, for they consider (or feign to consider) that the vindication of the slaves' rights is an undignified employment; but I tell them it is an employment more dignified, more noble, more exalted than any other whatsoever in which man can be engaged. [Cheers.] It is not because the slave is a poor man, nor an ignorant man, nor a lowly man, that I profess myself his friend—it is because he is a despised man, an outraged man, a trampled man, a brutified man—one who, being a man as the best of you are men, is yet herded with the things that crawl and the beasts that grovel. [Loud cheers.] It is because I know that He who has promulgated to us all truth—who is Himself the fountain of justice—the source of truth—the perfection of loveliness—has announced from the hill of Sinai, that man cannot attempt the bondage of his fellowman without being guilty of a deadly crime. [Loud cheering.]

I mean not to draw an afflicting picture of the tortures to which the slave is subjected in the United States, and thus, by harrowing your feeling, enlist your sympathies. Sufficient to say he is a man. You are yourselves of his nature, feelings, and character—in his sufferings you are tortured—in his indignities you are insulted.

[Hear! hear! and cheers.] What care I how a man is murdered?—whether he be drowned, strangled, shot, stabbed, or beheaded, is to me indifferent. I only know that he is murdered, and it little boots to him or me whether the wretch be prostrated dead upon the plain in a moment of time—or whether he is murdered piecemeal in being condemned to a hateful, lingering existence, from which man would be relieved by death, and whereof the only solace is the hope of the grave. [Great applause.]

It has been said that for slavery as it exists in British India there is "Balm in Gilead," and it is with pleasure I assent to the proposition. [Hear! hear!] You have learned from my friend, Mr. Allen, how you in this country are situated with respect to British India. He has described to you in vivid and forcible language the position and capabilities of this latter country, and he has proved in the clearest manner how incalculable are the benefits which the people of Ireland, England, and Scotland have it in their power to confer not merely on those who suffer beneath the yoke of bondage in that fine colony, but even upon themselves, at home, by resolving on having recourse to the fertility of the British Indian soil, and the ingenuity of its population, for those tropical products which are now derived from other climes. [Hear! hear!]

Such, my friends, being the case, I ask you, are we looking for more than we ought to expect from the honor, virtue, and magnanimity of the British people, in expressing a strong and fervent hope that when they shall have considered the horrible nature and fatal tendency of slavery, they will unite as one man in adopting a measure which will at once promote their own interests, and exterminate that inhuman mode of traffic which pours forth human blood like mountain streams, and the continuing of which gives a death-stab to the high renown and glory of England? If you will not consent to do this, you avow yourselves part and parcel of that class of men who whirl the whip and bear the branding-iron. Ah! believe me, my friends, it is a noble work, that in which we are now engaged. [Hear! hear!] No reproaches of conscience—no inward chidings—no sighing after lost time can embitter the remembrance of this evening's proceedings; and I hope that, if the clock chimes ten ere we shall have concluded, there is none amongst us who will regret that we have devoted so much of our time to a noble task, the aim and object whereof is to raise the lowly, to exalt the afflicted, and strike the ignoble fetter from the dusky limbs of our fellowmen.

My bosom swells with pride and pleasure when I reflect that I am standing before Irishmen—men who in the year 1841 have the name of philanthropists. [Hear! hear! and loud cheers.] Be it yours, my friends, to retain the lofty title, conditioned as you are as to your political influences, rather than having the name of republicans and democrats, to nurture slavery, and to countenance oppression. [Loud cheers.] Give me a monarchy—give me an oligarchy—give me an autocracy—yea, or even give me a despotic and tyrannical government, if, despite the pride of place and the "proud man's contumely," I see the living spirit of liberty blowing bright and imperishable in the people's breast, rather than a republicanism whose watchwords are, "Equality to all, and mastery to none," but whose deeds belie their splendid promises, and whose actions are those of oppression and persecution. [Cheers.] "Despotism" is a fearful scourge; but there is no delusion in the word. "Despotism" is not a sound which wins softly but deceptively on the ear, lulling it to ruin: it closes no man's mouth—it steals not away the sense—it blinds not the victim: stern and detestable in itself, it falls strongly and detestably on the ear; but give it to me, with all its horrors, rather than that which is in itself, a lie—professing, indeed, to be all that is sweet and goodly, but doing such deeds as, to think of, makes men's blood to freeze. [Immense applause.]

Flattering though this applause cannot but prove to my feelings, I will, however, experience a sentiment of far greater rapture, if, in some six or eight months hence, when in my own country, I shall learn that the call which I this evening make upon you has been responded to, not in words merely, but in deeds: then, indeed, will I feel great delight in having visited your Hibernian country; for I will know that I stood before men who have not merely professed their love and devotion for liberty, but whose life and actions are testimonials of the sincerity of the words they have uttered in witness thereof. [Cheers.]

One word more with reference to British India. It has been my high privilege, for the last few years, to have been associated with George Thompson, the eloquent advocate of the slave in the West Indies. He has been successful in his noble enterprise as regards the West Indies; and never have I listened to him for half an hour upon this subject that I did not feel the truth of what Mr. Allen avers, that if Great Britain would strike the chains off the slaves in America and elsewhere, it must be by giving encouragement to India. In British India is to be found the instrument which will put to death American slavery. If British India may produce, in as great excellence and abundance, those things which are now imported from America at the expense of slave toil, why should not Britain give the preference to the former country? It is only consistent with her well-known love of liberty that she should do so. Look to the confessions of the slaveholders themselves, and you will find it there avowed that the people of England, Ireland, and Scotland, have this power vested in their own hands. Many worthy persons in my own country are deterred from giving their aid and co-operation to the antislavery cause, from an apprehension which, to my mind, is exceedingly silly and unfounded. [Hear!] Their objection to do so is, that they imagine the slaveholders have, in their own hands, the means of putting down all abolitionists, for that they (the slaveholders) have threatened that, in case an effort were made to emancipate the slaves they would dissolve the American Union. Very many good and well-intentioned men in America would have lent us their assistance long ago, were it not for this threat, that the slaveholders would dissolve the American Union. Now, if in this assertion there was or could be one iota of truth—the smallest particle of rationality—I would grant that the objection should have some weight; but the thing is preposterous; beyond all parallel. [Hear! hear!] Why, the very thought is absurdity. What does the American Union mean? Nothing more than this, that the twenty-six States of America are joined together in government and civil rights. The Union is but a parchment document, and as there is no hill so lofty that it may not be surmounted, no space of ocean so boundless that it may not be traversed, there is nothing more possible than that the Union might be dissolved. But is it probable? Suppose that the Union were dissolved to-morrow, by what power or agency, let me ask, would it be possible for the holders to retain their slaves greater in number than themselves? [Loud cries of "hear! hear!"] To whom should the slaveholders look for sympathy, co-operation, and support, in their endeavors to keep these wretches in bondage? Will they look to the free States? Certainly not, for the very deed of dissolution precludes the possibility of that. Will they look to Mexico? No; for the Mexicans regard them with an eye of the rankest jealousy. Will they look to Canada? The thought is absurd. Will they look to the West Indies? What! ask men who are themselves but just liberated to aid in forging chains for other wretches! Who will believe it? Spain is the only land to which they can turn their eyes; but Spain has her own foes to trouble her, and the demon of slavery lurks within her own confines. Where, then, will they look for sympathy, and whither will they fly for aid? [Hear!] Every door is shut against them. Ah, Sir, believe me, the moment when the American Union is dissolved, that instant the power of the slaveholder is prostrated in the dust. Hopeless, helpless, friendless, they become an isolated class of beings, having nothing to depend on but their own strength, and that is weakness indeed. Then will rouse the crushed worm, turning on its torturer, and, in the fierce indignation of outraged men, the slaves will demand the right of measuring arms with their masters. [Immense cheering.] (A voice from the gallery—"Heaven speed the day!")

I do not think I shall myself live to see that day, but that such would be the effect of a dissolution of the American Union I feel confidently assured. [Hear!] Where is the man, who, if asked to become a slave, would not hurl back the offer indignantly in the teeth of the oppressor?—Nay, where is the woman—where is the child? The slaves of the United States are men, women, and children; and that they are as worthy this appellation, nay, worthier, perhaps, than the denizens of more favored lands, is amply testified by their patient and enduring conduct under contumely and outrage, for they, like yourselves, have preferred rather to suffer wrong than to do wrong. [Loud cheers.] I care not, then, for the insolent threat of those contumacious masters, for if the slaveholders of our country were to dissolve the Union sometime next year—if it were to be dissolved at twelve o'clock in the day, it is my firm conviction that before one o'clock (and that is but a single hour) there could not be found a solitary slave throughout the wide dominion of our land. [Cheers.] To suppose, therefore, that the slaveholders are serious in their haughty threat, bears absurdity on its very front: they'll never do it. They would not be so foolish—so thoroughly destitute of common sense as to dissolve the American Union, because forsooth it might be forbidden them to expose their slaves for sale, whip them with thongs, or brand them with iron within the confines of the land.

Is there amongst yourselves, think you, a single man who would be so detestably cruel, so utterly heartless, as to brand his sheep, his oxen, or his horse? For the sake of human nature, I trust there is not one; yet in the guilty land from which I have travelled hither, you will find men calling themselves republicans and patriots, who, with professions of universal equality for ever in their mouths, and the words of liberty ever on their lips, can yet find in their hearts to stand unmoved and unaffected by, while the sleeve is turned up of the wretched helot's garment, and the noise of the red-hot iron, branding the word "slave" in the flesh of his fellow-man is hissing in his ears (sensation). I ask of you are you men? and, being men, will you acknowledge or endure such a system as this? [No, no.] Who is there that can visit the Egyptian Hall in London, and having seen there the picture of a slave-market, will not turn away in disgust and indignation, and vow himself from that moment out the inveterate and implacable enemy of that atrocious system which brings ruin, infamy, and disgrace on human nature, and which can have first originated only in motives unearthly and infernal? Look at this state of things, and, freemen as you are yourselves, say will you suffer your fellowmen thus to be trampled on, and insulted with impunity?—Forget the past, but dwell with minds, calm as the intensity of your honest indignation will suffer them to be calm, on the present condition of the slave, and prove that you are worthy of the freedom you yourselves enjoy by aiding to unshackle him. [Loud applause.] Only picture to your mind's eye one man presuming in the face of high heaven, and before the civilized world to spread such wild havoc among his fellowmen as that which I have seen spread by a single slaveholder! When I see a woman condemned to wear such a collar as it were cruelty to bind around the neck of a dog, working in that collar, eating in it, aye, even sleeping in it, for no other crime than merely that of having asked permission to visit her child in an adjoining plantation—when, I repeat, I look on sights like these, my frame shudders with disgust—my blood freezes, and my heart bursts with indignation as I exclaim, "If these things be the result of Christianity or of patriotism, may heaven deliver me from the influence of either!" [Loud cheers.] Such is the system which prevails in many districts of the United States—such the hateful system that I beg of you to aid me in destroying. Who, sir, that looks around and views such scenes as have met my eye full often, could believe that we have the authority of heaven itself for averring "that God has made of one blood the nations of men to dwell on all the face of the earth"? Yet, so it is. What I now demand of all Irishmen is, not merely that they should assent to the resolutions we may here propose, nor be content in merely promising that they will further my plans, but that their whole lives will be a system of unceasing warfare against the inhuman principles of slavery. And, in the name of truth and of justice—in the name of Him who is the God of truth and justice—in the name of dishonored humanity, and of the unhappy slave, whatever be the hue of the skin he wears, whether white or black, blue (if such might be) or red—I call upon you, Irishmen, to extend to the oppressed and enthralled man, under whatsoever sun he may be found, that aid and co-operation, that sympathy and affection, which you would wish, were you in similar circumstances, should be extended to yourselves. [Cheers.]

I regret not, my friends, having made allusion to the brandings and other inhuman cruelties practised by the slaveholders on their unhappy victims—for, as soon will I believe the school-boy's wild and idle tale of the phantom who affrighted him, as believe that anything I have uttered can shock the delicacy of any around me. The recital will, I know, have a salutary effect upon the well organised mind. It may shock the sensibility, but it will inspirit you the rather to use your best exertions to annihilate this cruel system. I mean not here to be understood as saying that every slaveholder in America brands his slaves—I care not, though there be but one branded slave, it is enough for me. That one, so disfigured and disgraced, is a man, and it behoves not those, who are of the same kind, to stand quiescently by, and suffer such an outrage on their fellowman. [Cheers.] Yet such an outrage is actually attempted under the American laws. Oh, let such laws be disowned and repudiated by all who love liberty and abhor oppression. Let Irishmen shun a land, however goodly, however fair, where deeds are done which call to heaven for vengeance—let them say to the Americans, "Long have we wished to visit your country; but never will we soil a foot by planting it on your shore until such enormities as now disfigure your national character shall have been done away with and atoned for.''—[Cheers.] Let them tear the flag of freedom down, which flaunts absurdly over a recreant land which has nurtured oppression and makes liberty a mockery, while she pretends to extol its sacred cause.

When Mr. O'Connell—and now, that I have mentioned his name, let me take occasion to say how deeply I venerate that good and mighty man, who has put himself forth the undaunted and fearless champion of liberty and the rights of man in every clime the sun adorns. [A peal of applause here burst from the whole assembly which almost made the walls to shake, and which continued for several minutes.] I could wish, my friends, that if you consider me worthy the honor of your approbation, you would do me the favor of applauding with somewhat more of discretion and good judgment. I was about to say something with reference to a man who is justly dear to all your hearts, but you interrupted me in the middle of my sentence, and I am not sure that I have not forgotten all that I intended to utter. [Laughter and cheers.]

When, not many months ago, Mr. O'Connell, in the discharge of his duty as a public man and the advocate of liberty, asserted in his place in the House of Commons that there were to be found in Virginia many men who were not merely slaveholders, but even slave-breeders, and furthermore, that the gentleman who discharged the office of American ambassador at the English court, was himself a slaveholder, this latter person, instead of disproving the averment, challenged Mr. O'Connell to fight a duel. [Laughter.] As soon as he did so, and that the fact of his being a slaveholder had become known, that instant all Ireland should have raised her voice against him, and he should have been politely requested to pack up and return to his own estates, for that Irishmen were not in the habit of being called out to fight for having told the truth. [Cheers and laughter.] What a pretty fellow was this to represent a great nation at the court of St. James's!—a man who felt himself so troubled and scandalized by the truth, that the fighting of a duel was the only device he could have recourse to for healing his wounded honor. Such a man was not fit to have had a local habitation amid a free people. He ought to have been ashamed to have visited free and happy England.

Can any more eloquent evidence be adduced of the state of things in my own guilty land than that which is comprised in this fact, that America despatches as her ambassador to the Court of St. James's, not the representative of human liberty—not a man whose life bore evidence of the zeal and faithfulness wherewith he obeyed the doctrines of republicanism, but a man who is himself actually one of the greatest slaveholders in the United States! Should the words which I now utter chance to reach the ears of Mr. Stevenson, it may be, perhaps, that he will challenge me, too, to fight a duel with him, but he should wait until I had learned the art of doing so first, and I fear that so long a postponement might be considered inconvenient. [Laughter.]

But perhaps I am wandering from my subject. I hold in my hand a resolution, which I will now read for you, and for which I am anxious for your assenting voices. It is this—

"That we receive in the fullest acceptation the Scripture declaration 'that God has made of one blood all nations of men to dwell on all the face of the earth': and that to attach any stamp of inferiority or degradation to any portion of the human family, however the Creator has dyed their skins of a deeper hue, is, in our deliberate opinion, at once wicked and anti-Christian."

(Mr. Remond continued at considerable length, and having animadverted in fluent and forcible language on the sinful and infamous prejudice against color, as also on the absurdity of the arguments used by certain of the slaveholders against the amalgamation of the white and negro populations, he concluded his eloquent appeal.)

And now my friends, in resuming my seat, I have nothing further to say unless it be to express my unfeigned gratitude, and that of the Antislavery Society, to the proprietor of this house, who, in the most generous manner, has laid it gratuitously at our disposal. [Cheers.] It is a new edifice, and if I were asked to what purpose a structure intended for the service of the Irish public should on the first night of its opening be devoted, I would unhesitatingly say that the project which would most ennoble it and that which would be dearest to the Irish heart, would be such an one as we who are here assembled within these walls are now engaged in—a project which derives its origin from the best and purest feelings of our nature, and whose object is none other than that holy and godlike one of elevating to the station and glorious dignity of a man, him who is degraded and dishonored almost beyond the level of the beast. If in the course of the remarks which I have this evening offered, I may have said anything in reference to my native country—America—which may perhaps be looked upon as severe and unmitigated in its tone—I regret that I cannot make amends—I grieve to think, not that I should have so spoken, but that I should have been compelled so to speak. [Hear! hear! and cheers.] I have testified only to that which I have seen—I have borne evidence solely to that which I have witnessed. With all her faults and all her follies, I cannot but regard my native land with feelings of the proudest affection, and I adopt with pleasure, as wholly consonant with my own sentiments, the beautiful lines of an American poet, once resident in England:

"I love thee—witness Heaven above
That I, that land—that people love;
And, rail thy slanders as they will,
Columbia, I will love thee still.
Nor love thee less when I do tell,
Of crimes which in thy bosom dwell.
Oh! that my weakest words might roll,
Like Heaven's own thunder through thy soul.
There is oppression in thy hand
A sin corrupting all the land;
There is within thy gates a pest,
Gold and a Babylonish vest,
Not hid in shame's concealing shade,
But broad against the sun displayed.
Repent thee, then, and quickly bring
Forth from the camp the accursed thing;
Consign it to remorseless fire,
Watch till the latest sparks expire—
Then, strew its ashes on the wind,
Nor leave an atom wreck behind.
Then shall thy wealth and power increase—
Then shall thy people dwell in peace,
On thee the Almighty's glory rest,
And all on earth in thee be blest!"

Having enjoyed liberty abroad, Remond returned to this country decidedly embittered against slavery. He could never be happy again in his status of social and political inferiority. He must now attack slavery and its incidents more fearlessly than ever. He therefore took up the fight against the customs and laws of discrimination in Massachusetts which made life there intolerable for a man of color determined to be free. He was, therefore, instrumental in effecting some change there, as is evidenced by the following speech before the Legislative Committee respecting the rights of colored citizens in traveling:

THE RIGHTS OF COLORED CITIZENS IN TRAVELING[1]

By Charles Lenox Remond

Before the Legislative Committee in the House of Representatives, respecting the rights of colored citizens in traveling, &c.

Mr. Chairman, and Gentlemen of the Committee: In rising at this time, and on this occasion, being the first person of color who has ever addressed either of the bodies assembling in this building, I should, perhaps, in the first place, observe that, in consequence of the many misconstructions of the principles and measures of which I am the humble advocate, I may in like manner be subject to similar misconceptions from the moment I open my lips in behalf of the prayer of the petitioners for whom I appear, and therefore feel I have the right at least to ask, at the hands of this intelligent Committee, an impartial hearing; and that whatever prejudices they may have imbibed, be eradicated from their minds, if such exist. I have, however, too much confidence in their intelligence, and too much faith in their determination to do their duty as the representatives of this Commonwealth, to presume they can be actuated by partial motives. Trusting, as I do, that the day is not distant, when, on all questions touching the rights of the citizens of this State, men shall be considered great only as they are good—and not that it shall be told, and painfully experienced, that,

[1] *Liberator*, Feb. 25, 1842.

in this country, this State, aye, this city, the Athens of America, the rights, privileges and immunities of its citizens are measured by complexion, or any other physical peculiarity or conformation, especially such as over which no man has any control. Complexion can in no sense be construed into crime, much less be rightfully made the criterion of rights. Should the people of color, through a revolution of Providence, become a majority, to the last I would oppose it upon the same principle; for, in either case, it would be equally reprehensible and unjustifiable—alike to be condemned and repudiated. It is JUSTICE I stand here to claim, and not FAVOR for either complexion.

And now, sir, I shall endeavor to confine my remarks to the same subject which has occupied the attention of the Committee thus far, and to stand upon the same principle which has been so ably and so eloquently maintained and established by my esteemed friend, Mr. Phillips.

Our right to citizenship in this State has been acknowledged and secured by the allowance of the elective franchise and consequent taxation; and I know of no good reason, if admitted in this instance, why it should be denied in any other.

With reference to the wrongs inflicted and injuries received on railroads, by persons of color, I need not say they do not end with the termination of the route, but, in effect, tend to discourage, disparage and depress this class of citizens. All hope of reward for upright conduct is cut off. Vice in them becomes a virtue. No distinction is made by the community in which we live. The most vicious is treated as well as the most respectable, both in public and private.

But it is said we all look alike. If this is true, it is not true that we all behave alike. There is a marked difference; and we claim a recognition of this difference.

In the present state of things, they find God's provisions interfered with in such a way, by these and kindred regulations, that virtue may not claim her divinely appointed rewards. Color is made to obscure the brightest endowments, to degrade the fairest character, and to check the highest and most praiseworthy aspirations. If the colored man is vicious, it makes but little difference; if besotted, it matters not; if vulgar, it is quite as well; and he finds himself as well treated, and received as readily into society, as those of an opposite character. Nay, the higher our aspirations, the loftier our purposes and pursuits, does this iniquitous principle of prejudice fasten upon us, and especial pains are taken to irritate, obstruct and injure. No reward of merit, no remuneration for services, no equivalent is rendered the deserving. And I submit, whether this unkind and unchristian policy is not well calculated to make every man disregardful of his conduct, and every woman unmindful of her reputation.

The grievances of which we complain, be assured, sir, are not imaginary, but real—not local, but universal—not occasional, but continual, every day matter of fact things—and have become, to the disgrace of our common country, matter of history.

Mr. Chairman, the treatment to which colored Americans are exposed in their own country finds a counterpart in no other; and I am free to declare that, in the course of nineteen months' traveling in England, Ireland, and Scotland, I was received, treated and recognized, in public and private society, without any regard to my complexion. From the moment I left the American packet ship in Liverpool, up to the moment I came in contact with it again, I was never reminded of my complexion; and all that know anything of my usage in the American ship, will testify that it was unfit for a brute, and none but one could inflict it. But how unlike that afforded in the British steamer *Columbia!* Owing to my limited resources, I took a steerage passage. On the first day out, the second officer came to inquire after my health; and finding me the only passenger in that part of the ship, ordered the steward to give me a berth in the second cabin; and from that hour until my stepping on shore at Boston, every politeness was shown me by the officers, and every kindness and attention by the stewards; and I feel under deep and lasting obligations to them, individually and collectively.

In no instance was I insulted or treated in any way distinct or dissimilar from other passengers or travellers, either in coaches, railroads, steampackets, or hotels; and if the feeling was entertained, in no case did I discover its existence.

I may with propriety here relate an accident, illustrative of the subject now under consideration. I took a passage ticket at the steampacket office in Glasgow, for Dublin; and on going into the cabin to retire, I found the berth I had engaged occupied by an

Irish gentleman and merchant. I enquired if he had not mistaken the number of his berth. He thought not. On comparing tickets, we saw that the clerk had given two tickets of the same number; and it appeared I had received mine first. The gentleman at once offered to vacate the berth, against which I remonstrated, and took my berth in an opposite stateroom. Here, sir, we discover treatment just, impartial, reasonable; and we ask nothing beside.

There is a marked difference between social and civil rights. It has been well and justly remarked, by my friend Mr. Phillips, that we all claim the privilege of selecting our society and associations; but, in civil rights, one man has not the prerogative to define rights for another. For instance, sir, in public conveyances, for the rich man to usurp the privileges to himself, to the injury of the poor man, would be submitted to in no well regulated society. And such is the position suffered by persons of color. On my arrival home from England, I went to the railway station, to go to Salem, being anxious to see my parents and sisters as soon as possible—asked for a ticket—paid 50 cents for it, and was pointed to the American designation car. Having previously received information of the regulations, I took my seat peaceably, believing it better to suffer wrong than do wrong. I felt then, as I felt on many occasions prior to leaving home, unwilling to descend so low as to bandy words with the superintendents, or contest my rights with conductors, or any others in the capacity of servants of any stage or steamboat company, or rail-road corporation; although I never, by any means, gave evidence that, by my submission, I intended to sanction usages which would derogate from uncivilized, much less long and loud professing and high pretending America.

Bear with me while I relate an additional occurrence. On the morning after my return home, I was obliged to go to Boston again, and on going to the Salem station I met two friends, who enquired if I had any objection to their taking seats with me. I answered, I should be most happy. They took their seats accordingly, and soon afterwards one of them remarked to me—"Charles, I don't know if they will allow us to ride with you." It was some time before I could understand what they meant, and, on doing so, I laughed—feeling it to be a climax to every absurdity I had heard attributed to Americans. To say nothing of the wrong done those friends, and the insult and indignity offered me by the appearance of the conductor, who ordered the friends from the car in a somewhat harsh manner—they immediately left the carriage.

On returning to Salem some few evenings afterwards, Mr. Chase, the superintendent on this road, made himself known to me by recalling bygone days and scenes, and then enquired if I was not glad to get home after so long an absence in Europe. I told him I was glad to see my parents and family again, and this was the only object I could have, unless he thought I should be glad to take a hermit's life in the great pasture; inasmuch as I never felt to loathe my American name so much as since my arrival. He wished to know my reasons for the remark. I immediately gave them, and wished to know of him, if, in the event of his having a brother with red hair, he should find himself separated while traveling because of this difference, he should deem it just. He could make no reply. I then wished to know if the principle was not the same; and if so, there was an insult implied by his question.

In conclusion, I challenged him as the instrument inflicting the manifold injuries upon all not colored like himself to the presentation of an instance in any other Christian or unchristian country, tolerating usages at once so disgraceful, unjust and inhuman. What if some few of the West or East India planters and merchants should visit our liberty-loving country, with their colored wives—how would he manage? Or, if R. M. Johnson, the gentleman who has been elevated to the second office in the gift of the people, should be travelling from Boston to Salem, if he was prepared to separate him from his wife or daughters. [Involuntary burst of applause, instantly restrained.]

Sir, it happens to be my lot to have a sister a few shades lighter than myself; and who knows, if this state of things is encouraged, whether I may not on some future occasion be mobbed in Washington Street, on the supposition of walking with a white young lady! [Suppressed indications of sympathy and applause.]

Gentlemen of the Committee, these distinctions react in all their wickedness—to say nothing of their concocted and systematized odiousness and absurdity—upon those who instituted them; and particularly so upon those who are illiberal and mean enough to practise them.

Mr. Chairman, if colored people have abused any rights granted them, or failed to exhibit due appreciation of favors bestowed, or shrunk from dangers or responsibility, let it be made to appear. Or if our country contains a population to compare with them in loyalty and patriotism, circumstances duly considered, I have it yet to learn. The history of our country must ever testify in their behalf. In view of these and many additional considerations, I unhesitatingly assert their claim, on the naked principle of merit, to every advantage set forth in the Constitution of this Commonwealth.

Finally, Mr. Chairman, there is in this and other States a large and growing colored population, whose residence in your midst has not been from choice (let this be understood and reflected upon), but by the force of circumstances over which they never had control. Upon the heads of their oppressors and calumniators be the censure and responsibility. If to ask at your hands redress for injuries, and protection in our rights and immunities, as citizens, is reasonable, and dictated alike by justice, humanity and religion, you will not reject, I trust, the prayer of your petitioners.

Before sitting down, I owe it to myself to remark, that I was not apprised of the wish of my friends to appear here until passing through Boston, a day or two since; and having been occupied with other matters, I have had no opportunity for preparation on this occasion. I feel much obliged to the Committee for their kind, patient, and attentive hearing. [Applause.]

Another radical Negro appeared on the horizon about this time. This was Henry Highland Garnet.[1] Like so many other antislavery orators, Garnet was a fugitive slave. In his free status in the North he had learned to detest the institution as the worst agency for evil imaginable.

[1] Henry Highland Garnet, scholar, lecturer, minister, was born a slave of William Spencer, December 23, 1815. He escaped with his parents in 1824 and settled in New Hope, Pennsylvania, where young Henry had his first schooling. Early in 1825 the family moved to New York City, took a new name, and established a home. The period from 1825 to 1840 Henry Highland Garnet devoted almost wholly to acquiring an education. He was at first a student under Charles C. Andrews. He, with Alexander Crummel, sought admission to an academy at Canaan, New Hampshire, but a mob frustrated the plan. He then attended Oneida Institute, from which he was graduated in 1840. Garnet settled in Troy, New York, and began his life work in the capacity of a teacher. He next studied theology and entered the ministry, serving congregations in New York and the District of Columbia. He served also as president of Avery College in Pittsburgh, where he succeeded as an educator. At the time of his death, in 1882, he was serving his country as Minister to Liberia.

He had from time to time denounced the institution before persons whom he endeavored to enlist in the antislavery cause, but this procedure did not lead to immediate results. At the national Convention of Colored Citizens held in Buffalo, New York, in 1843, therefore, he offered the following address to be sent broadcast to all the slaves of the United States. It was so radical that the Convention refused to adopt it. The effort, however, was not entirely lost. Six years later John Brown had it published at his own expense.

AN ADDRESS TO THE SLAVES OF THE UNITED STATES AMERICA[1]

By Henry Highland Garnet

Brethren and Fellow Citizens: Your brethren of the North, East, and West have been accustomed to meet together in National Conventions, to sympathize with each other, and to weep over your unhappy condition. In these meetings we have addressed all classes of the free, but we have never, until this time, sent a word of consolation and advice to you. We have been contented in sitting still and mourning over your sorrows, earnestly hoping that before this day your sacred liberties would have been restored. But, we have hoped in vain. Years have rolled on, and tens of thousands have been borne on streams of blood and tears to the shores of eternity. While you have been oppressed, we have also been partakers with you; nor can we be free while you are enslaved. We, therefore, write to you as being bound with you.

Many of you are bound to us, not only by the ties of a common humanity, but we are connected by the more tender relations of parents, wives, husbands, and sisters, and friends. As such we most affectionately address you.

Slavery has fixed a deep gulf between you and us, and while it shuts out from you the relief and consolation which your friends would willingly render, it afflicts and persecutes you with a fierceness which we might not expect to see in the fiends of hell. But still the Almighty Father of mercies has left to us a glimmering ray of hope, which shines out like a lone star in a cloudy sky.

[1] This address was published under this title.

Mankind are becoming wiser, and better—the oppressor's power is fading, and you, every day, are becoming better informed, and more numerous. Your grievances, brethren, are many. We shall not attempt, in this short address, to present to the world all the dark catalogue of the nation's sins, which have been committed upon an innocent people. Nor is it indeed necessary, for you feel them from day to day, and all the civilized world looks upon them with amazement.

Two hundred and twenty-seven years ago the first of our injured race were brought to the shores of America. They came not with glad spirits to select their homes in the New World. They came not with their own consent, to find an unmolested enjoyment of the blessings of this fruitful soil. The first dealings they had with men calling themselves Christians exhibited to them the worst features of corrupt and sordid hearts: and convinced them that no cruelty is too great, no villainy and no robbery too abhorrent for even enlightened men to perform, when influenced by avarice and lust. Neither did they come flying upon the wings of Liberty to a land of freedom. But they came with broken hearts, from their beloved native land, and were doomed to unrequited toil and deep degradation. Nor did the evil of their bondage end at their emancipation by death. Succeeding generations inherited their chains, and millions have come from eternity into time, and have returned again to the world of spirits, cursed and ruined by American slavery.

The propagators of the system, or their immediate successors, very soon discovered its growing evil, and its tremendous wickedness, and secret promises were made to destroy it. The gross inconsistency of a people holding slaves, who had themselves "ferried o'er the wave" for freedom's sake, was too apparent to be entirely overlooked. The voice of Freedom cried, "Emancipate your slaves." Humanity supplicated with tears for the deliverance of the children of Africa. Wisdom urged her solemn plea. The bleeding captive plead his innocence, and pointed to Christianity who stood weeping at the cross. Jehovah frowned upon the nefarious institution, and thunderbolts, red with vengeance, struggled to leap forth to blast the guilty wretches who maintained it. But all was vain. Slavery had stretched its dark wings of death over the land, the Church stood silently by—the priests prophesied falsely, and the people loved to have it so. Its throne is established, and now it reigns triumphant.

Nearly three millions of your fellow-citizens are prohibited by law and public opinion (which in this country is stronger than law) from reading the Book of Life. Your intellect has been destroyed as much as possible, and every ray of light they have attempted to shut out from your minds. The oppressors themselves have become involved in the ruin. They have become weak, sensual, and rapacious—they have cursed you—they have cursed themselves—they have cursed the earth which they have trod.

The colonies threw the blame upon England. They said that the mother country entailed the evil upon them, and they would rid themselves of it if they could. The world thought they were sincere, and the philanthropic pitied them. But time soon tested their sincerity. In a few years the colonists grew strong, and severed themselves from the British Government. Their independence was declared, and they took their station among the sovereign powers of the earth. The declaration was a glorious document. Sages admired it, and the patriotic of every nation reverenced the God-like sentiments which it contained. When the power of Government returned to their hands, did they emancipate the slaves? No; they rather added new links to our chains. Were they ignorant of the principles of Liberty? Certainly they were not. The sentiments of their revolutionary orators fell in burning eloquence upon their hearts, and with one voice they cried, LIBERTY OR DEATH. Oh, what a sentence was that! It ran from soul to soul like electric fire, and nerved the arms of thousands to fight in the holy cause of Freedom. Among the diversity of opinions that are entertained in regard to physical resistance, there are but a few found to gainsay the stern declaration. We are among those who do not.

SLAVERY! How much misery is comprehended in that single word. What mind is there that does not shrink from its direful effects? Unless the image of God be obliterated from the soul, all men cherish the love of liberty. The nice discerning political economist does not regard the sacred right more than the untutored African who roams in the wilds of Congo. Nor has the one more right to the full enjoyment of his freedom than the other. In every man's mind the good seeds of liberty are planted, and he who brings his fellow down so low, as to make him contented with a condition of slavery, commits the highest crime against God and man. Brethren, your oppressors aim to do this. They endeavor to make you as much like brutes as possible. When they have blinded the eyes of your mind—when they have embittered the sweet waters of life—when they have shut out the light which shines from the word of God—then, and not till then, has American slavery done its perfect work.

TO SUCH DEGRADATION IT IS SINFUL IN THE EXTREME FOR YOU TO MAKE VOLUNTARY SUBMISSION. The divine commandments you are in duty bound to reverence and obey. If you do not obey them, you will surely meet with the displeasure of the Almighty. He requires you to love Him supremely, and your neighbor as yourself—to keep the Sabbath day holy—to search the Scriptures—and bring up your children with respect for His laws, and to worship no other God but Him. But slavery sets all these at nought, and hurls defiance in the face of Jehovah. The forlorn condition in which you are placed does not destroy your obligation to God. You are not certain of heaven, because you allow yourselves to remain in a state of slavery, where you cannot obey the commandments of the Sovereign of the universe. If the ignorance of slavery is a passport to heaven, then it is a blessing, and no curse, and you should rather desire its perpetuity than its abolition. God will not receive slavery, nor ignorance, nor any other state of mind, for love and obedience to Him. Your condition does not absolve you from your moral obligation. The diabolical injustice by which your liberties are cloven down, NEITHER GOD NOR ANGELS, OR JUST MEN, COMMAND YOU TO SUFFER FOR A SINGLE MOMENT. THEREFORE IT IS YOUR SOLEMN AND IMPERATIVE DUTY TO USE EVERY MEANS, BOTH MORAL, INTELLECTUAL, AND PHYSICAL, THAT PROMISES SUCCESS. If a band of heathen men should attempt to enslave a race of Christians, and to place their children under the influence of some false religion, surely Heaven would frown upon the men who would not resist such aggression, even to death. If, on the other hand, a band of Christians should attempt to enslave a race of heathen men, and to entail slavery upon them, and to keep them in heathenism in the midst of Christianity, the God of heaven would smile upon every effort which the injured might make to disenthral themselves.

Brethren, it is as wrong for your lordly oppressors to keep you in slavery as it was for the man thief to steal our ancestors from the coast of Africa. You should therefore now use the same manner of resistance as would have been just in our ancestors when the bloody foot-prints of the first remorseless soul-thief was placed upon the shores of our fatherland. The humblest peasant is as free in the sight of God as the proudest monarch that ever swayed a sceptre. Liberty is a spirit sent out from God, and like its great Author, is no respecter of persons.

Brethren, the time has come when you must act for yourselves. It is an old and true saying that, "if hereditary bondmen would be free, they must themselves strike the blow." You can plead your own cause, and do the work of emancipation better than any others. The nations of the Old World are moving in the great cause of universal freedom, and some of them at least will, ere long, do you justice. The combined powers of Europe have placed their broad seal of disapprobation upon the African slave-trade. But in the slaveholding parts of the United States the trade is as brisk as ever. They buy and sell you as though you were brute beasts. The North has done much—her opinion of slavery in the abstract is known. But in regard to the South, we adopt the opinion of the *New York Evangelist*—"We have advanced so far, that the cause apparently waits for a more effectual door to be thrown open than has been yet." We are about to point you to that more effectual door. Look around you, and behold the bosoms of your loving wives heaving with untold agonies! Here the cries of your poor children! Remember the stripes your fathers bore. Think of the torture and disgrace of your noble mothers. Think of your wretched sisters, loving virtue and purity, as they are driven into concubinage and are exposed to the unbridled lusts of incarnate devils. Think of the undying glory that hangs around the ancient name of Africa—and forget not that you are native-born American citizens, and as such you are justly entitled to all the rights that are granted to the freest. Think how many tears you have poured out upon the soil which you have cultivated with unrequited toil and enriched with your blood; and then go to your lordly enslavers and tell them plainly, that you *are determined to be free.* Appeal to their sense of justice, and tell them that they have no more right to oppress you than you have to enslave them. Entreat them to remove the grievous burdens which they have imposed upon you, and to remunerate you for your labor. Promise them renewed diligence in the cultivation of the soil, if they will render to you an equivalent for your services. Point them to the increase of happiness and prosperity in the British West Indies since the Act of Emancipation. Tell them in language which they cannot misunderstand of the exceeding sinfulness of slavery, and of a future judgment, and of the righteous retributions of an indignant God. Inform them that all you desire is FREEDOM, and that nothing else will suffice. Do this, and forever after cease to toil for the heartless tyrants, who give you no other reward but stripes and abuse. If they then commence work of death, they, and not you, will be responsible for the consequences. You had far better all die—*die immediately,* than live slaves, and entail your wretchedness upon your posterity. If you would be free in this generation, here is your only hope. However much you and all of us may desire it, there is not much hope of redemption without the shedding of blood. If you must bleed, let it all come at once—rather *die freemen than live to be the slaves.* It is impossible, like the children of Israel, to make a grand exodus from the land of bondage. The Pharaohs are on both sides of the blood-red waters! You cannot move *en masse* to the dominions of the British Queen—nor can you pass through Florida and overrun Texas, and at last find peace in Mexico. The propagators of American slavery are spending their blood and treasure that they may plant the black flag in the heart of Mexico and riot in the halls of the Montezumas. In language of the Reverend Robert Hall, when addressing the volunteers of Bristol, who were rushing forth to repel the invasion of Napoleon, who threatened to lay waste the fair homes of England, "Religion is too much interested in your behalf not to shed over you her most gracious influences."

You will not be compelled to spend much time in order to become inured to hardships. From the first movement that you breathed the air of heaven, you have been accustomed to nothing else but hardships. The heroes of the American Revolution were never put upon harder fare than a peck of corn and few herrings per week. You have not become enervated by the luxuries of life. Your sternest energies have been beaten out upon the anvil of severe trial. Slavery has done this to make you subservient to its own purposes; but it has done more than this, it has prepared you for any emergency. If you receive good treatment, it is what you can hardly expect; if you meet with pain, sorrow, and even death, these are the common lot of the slaves.

Fellowmen! patient sufferers! behold your dearest rights crushed to the earth! See your sons murdered, and your wives, mothers and sisters doomed to prostitution. In the name of the merciful God, and by all that life is worth, let it no longer be a debatable question, whether it is better to choose *liberty* or *death.*

In 1822, Denmark Veazie, of South Carolina, formed a plan for the liberation of his fellowmen. In the whole history of human efforts to overthrow slavery, a more complicated and tremendous plan was never formed. He was betrayed by the treachery of his own people, and died a martyr to freedom. Many a brave hero fell, but history, faithful to her high trust, will transcribe his name on the same monument with Moses, Hampden, Tell, Bruce, and Wallace, Toussaint L'Ouverture, Lafayette, and Washington. That tremendous movement shook the whole empire of slavery. The guilty soul-thieves were overwhelmed with fear. It is a matter of fact that at this time, and in consequence of the threatened revolution, the slave States talked strongly of emancipation. But they blew but one blast of the trumpet of freedom, and then laid it aside. As these men became quiet, the slaveholders ceased to talk about emancipation: and now behold your condition to-day! Angels sigh over it, and humanity has long since exhausted her tears in weeping on your account!

The patriotic Nathaniel Turner followed Denmark Veazie. He was goaded to desperation by wrong and injustice. By despotism, his name has been recorded on the list of infamy, and future generations will remember him among the noble and brave.

Next arose the immortal Joseph Cinque, the hero of the Amistad. He was a native African, and by the help of God he emancipated a whole ship-load of his fellowmen on the high seas. And he now sings of liberty on the sunny hills of Africa and beneath his native palm-trees, where he hears the lion roar and feels himself as free as the king of the forest.

Next arose Madison Washington, that bright star of freedom, and took his station in the constellation of true heroism. He was a slave on board the brig *Creole,* of Richmond, bound to New Orleans, that great slave mart, with a hundred and four others. Nineteen struck for liberty or death. But one life was taken, and the whole were emancipated, and the vessel was carried into Nassau, New Providence.

Noble men! Those who have fallen in freedom's conflict, their memories will be cherished by the true-hearted and the God-fearing in all future generations; those who are living, their names are surrounded by a halo of glory.

Brethren, arise, arise! Strike for your lives and liberties. Now is the day and the hour. Let every slave throughout the land do this, and the days of slavery are numbered. You cannot be more oppressed than you have been—you cannot suffer greater cruelties than you have already. *Rather die freemen than live to be slaves.* Remember that you are FOUR MILLIONS!

It is in your power so to torment the God-cursed slaveholders that they will be glad to let you go free. If the scale was turned, and black men were the masters and white men the slaves, every destructive agent and element would be employed to lay the oppressor low. Danger and death would hang over their heads day and night. Yes, the tyrants would meet with plagues more terrible than those of Pharaoh. But you are a patient people. You act as though you were made for the special use of these devils. You act as though your daughters were born to pamper the lusts of your masters and overseers. And worse than all, you tamely submit while your lords tear your wives from your embraces and defile them before your eyes. In the name of God, we ask, are you men? Where is the blood of your fathers? Has it all run out of your veins? Awake, awake; millions of voices are calling you! Your dead fathers speak to you from their graves. Heaven, as with a voice of thunder, calls on you to arise from the dust.

Let your motto be resistance! *resistance!* RESISTANCE! No oppressed people have ever secured their liberty without resistance. What kind of resistance you had better make you must decide by the circumstances that surround you, and according to the suggestion of expediency. Brethren, adieu! Trust in the living God. Labor for the peace of the human race, and remember that you are FOUR MILLIONS!

At this time there appeared upon the platform another antislavery orator. He had escaped as a fugitive from

Maryland, where he had clandestinely learned to read. He had suddenly discovered his eloquence when called upon to address a meeting of the Antislavery Society in Nantucket in 1841, a few years after he had reached that free soil. This man was Frederick Douglass. His early speeches showed abundance of information, logical thinking, and forceful presentation. Telling so frequently his story of bondage, however, he soon disclosed his identity as a fugitive, and to escape from his would-be captors he transferred his operations to England for the time being. There, in Finsbury Chapel at Moorfields, he delivered one of his most famous speeches. This discourse shows originality of thought, beauty and force of expression, and impassioned eloquence.

RECEPTION SPEECH

At Finsbury Chapel, Moorfields, England, May 12, 1846 [1]

By Frederick Douglass

I feel exceedingly glad of the opportunity now afforded me of presenting the claims of my brethren in bonds in the United States to so many in London and from various parts of Britain who have assembled here on the present occasion. I have nothing to commend me to your consideration in the way of learning, nothing in the way of education, to entitle me to your attention; and you are aware that slavery is a very bad school for rearing teachers of morality and religion. Twenty-one years of my life have been spent in slavery—personal slavery—surrounded by degrading influences, such as can exist nowhere beyond the pale of slavery; and it will not be strange, if under such circumstances, I should betray, in what I have to say to you, a deficiency of that refinement which is seldom or ever found, except among persons that have experienced superior advantages to those which I have enjoyed. But I will take it for granted that you know something about the degrading influences of slavery, and that you will not expect great things from me this evening, but simply such facts as I may be able to

[1] Douglass, *My Bondage and Freedom*, Appendix.

advance immediately in connection with my own experience of slavery.

Now, what is this system of slavery? This is the subject of my lecture this evening—what is the character of this institution? I am about to answer this inquiry, what is American slavery? I do this the more readily, since I have found persons in this country who have identified the term slavery with that which I think it is not, and in some instances, I have feared, in so doing, have rather (unwittingly, I know) detracted much from the horror with which the term slavery is contemplated. It is common in this country to distinguish every bad thing by the name of slavery. Intemperance is slavery; to be deprived of the right to vote is slavery, says one; to have to work hard is slavery, says another; and I do not know but that if we should let them go on, they would say that to eat when we are hungry, to walk when we desire to have exercise, or to minister to our necessities, or have necessities at all, is slavery.

I do not wish for a moment to detract from the horror with which the evil of intemperance is contemplated—not at all; nor do I wish to throw the slightest obstruction in the way of any political freedom that any class of persons in this country may desire to obtain. But I am here to say that I think the term slavery is sometimes abused by identifying it with that which it is not. Slavery in the United States is the granting of that power by which one man exercises and enforces a right of property in the body and soul of another. The condition of a slave is simply that of the brute beast. He is a piece of property—a marketable commodity, in the language of the law, to be bought or sold at the will and caprice of the master who claims him to be his property; he is spoken of, thought of, and treated as property. His own good, his conscience, his intellect, his affections, are all set aside by the master. The will and the wishes of the master are the law of the slave. He is as much a piece of property as a horse. If he is fed, he is fed because he is property. If he is clothed, it is with a view to the increase of his value as property. Whatever of comfort is necessary to him for his body or soul that is inconsistent with his being property is carefully wrested from him, not only by public opinion, but by the law of the country. He is carefully deprived of everything that tends in the slightest degree to detract from his value as property. He is deprived of education. God has given him an intellect; the slaveholder declares it shall not be cultivated. If his moral perception leads him in a course contrary to his value as property, the slaveholder declares he shall not exercise it. The marriage institution cannot exist among slaves, and one-sixth of the population of democratic America is denied its privileges by the law of the land. What is to be thought of a nation boasting of its liberty, boasting of its humanity, boasting of its Christianity, boasting of its love of justice and purity, and yet having within its own borders three millions of persons denied by law the right of marriage?—what must be the condition of that people?

I need not lift up the veil by giving you any experience of my own. Every one that can put two ideas together must see the most fearful results from such a state of things as I have just mentioned. If any of these three millions find for themselves companions, and prove themselves honest, upright, virtuous persons to each other, yet in these cases—few as I am bound to confess they are—the virtuous live in constant apprehension of being torn asunder by the merciless men-stealers that claim them as their property. This is American slavery; no marriage—no education—the light of the gospel shut out from the dark mind of the bondman—and he forbidden by the law to learn to read. If a mother shall teach her children to read, the law in Louisiana proclaims that she may be hanged by the neck. If the father attempt to give his son a knowledge of letters, he may be punished by the whip in one instance, and in another be killed, at the discretion of the court. Three millions of people shut out from the light of knowledge! It is easy for you to conceive the evil that must result from such a state of things.

I now come to the physical evils of slavery. I do not wish to dwell at length upon these, but it seems right to speak of them, not so much to influence your minds on this question, as to let the slaveholders of America know that the curtain which conceals their crimes is being lifted abroad; that we are opening the dark cell, and leading the people into the horrible recesses of what they are pleased to call their domestic institution. We want them to know that a knowledge of their whippings, their scourgings, their brandings, their chainings, is not confined to their plantations, but that some Negro of theirs has broken loose from his chains—has burst through the dark incrustation of slavery, and is now exposing their deeds of deep damnation to the gaze of the Christian people of England.

The slaveholders resort to all kinds of cruelty. If I were disposed, I have matter enough to interest you on this question for five or six evenings, but I will not dwell at length upon these cruelties. Suffice it to say, that all the peculiar modes of torture that were resorted to in the West India islands are resorted to, I believe, even more frequently in the United States of America. Starvation, the bloody whip, the chain, the gag, the thumb-screw, cathauling, the cat-o'-nine-tails, the dungeon, the blood-hound, are all in requisition to keep the slave in his condition as a slave in the United States. If any one has a doubt upon this point, I would ask him to read the chapter on slavery in Dickens's Notes on America. If any man has a doubt upon it, I have here the "testimony of a thousand witnesses," which I can give at any length, all going to prove the truth of my statement. The blood-hound is regularly trained in the United States, and advertisements are to be found in the southern papers of the Union, from persons advertising themselves as blood-hound trainers, and offering to hunt down slaves at fifteen dollars a piece, recommending their hounds as the fleetest in the neighborhood, never known to fail. Advertisements are from time to time inserted, stating that slaves have escaped with iron collars about their necks, with bands of iron about their feet, marked with the lash, branded with red-hot irons, the initials of their master's name burned into their flesh; and the masters advertise the fact of their being thus branded with their own signature, thereby proving to the world that, however damning it may appear to non-slaveholders, such practices are not regarded discreditable among the slaveholders themselves. Why, I believe if a man should brand his horse in this country—burn the initials of his name into any of his cattle, and publish the ferocious deed here—that the united execrations of Christians in Britain would descend upon him. Yet, in the United States, human beings are thus branded. As Whittier says—

". . . Our countrymen in chains,
The whip on woman's shrinking flesh,
Our soil yet reddening with the stains
Caught from her scourgings warm and fresh."

The slave-dealer boldly publishes his infamous acts to the world. Of all things that have been said of slavery to which exception has been taken by slaveholders, this, the charge of cruelty, stands foremost, and yet there is no charge capable of clearer demonstration than that of the most barbarous inhumanity on the part of the slaveholders toward their slaves. And all this is necessary; it is necessary to resort to these cruelties, in order to make the slave a slave, and to keep him a slave. Why, my experience all goes to prove the truth of what you will call a marvelous proposition, that the better you treat a slave, the more you destroy his value as a slave, and enhance the probability of his eluding the grasp of the slaveholder; the more kindly you treat him, the more wretched you make him, while you keep him in the condition of a slave. My experience, I say, confirms the truth of this proposition. When I was treated exceedingly ill; when my back was being scourged daily; when I was whipped within an inch of my life—life was all I cared for. "Spare my life," was my continual prayer. When I was looking for the blow about to be inflicted upon my head, I was not thinking of my liberty; it was my life. But, as soon as the blow was not to be feared, then came the longing for liberty. If a slave has a bad master, his ambition is to get a better; when he gets a better, he aspires to have the best; and when he gets the best, he aspires to be his own master. But the slave must be brutalized to keep him as a slave. The slaveholder feels this necessity. I admit this necessity. If it be right to hold slaves at all, it is right to hold them in the only way in which they can be held; and this can be done only by shutting out the light of education from their minds, and brutalizing their persons.

The whip, the chain, the gag, the thumb-screw, the blood-hound, the stocks, and all the other bloody paraphernalia of the slave system are indispensably necessary to the relation of master and slave. The slave must be subjected to these, or he ceases to be a slave. Let him know that the whip is burned; that the fetters have been turned to some useful and profitable employment; that the chain is no longer for his limbs; that the blood-hound is no longer to be put upon his track; that his master's authority over him is no longer to be enforced by taking his life—and immediately he walks out from the house of bondage and asserts his freedom as a man. The slaveholder finds it necessary to have these implements to keep the slave in bondage; finds it necessary to be able to say, "Unless you do so and so; unless you do as I bid you—I will take away your life!"

Some of the most awful scenes of cruelty are constantly taking place in the middle states of the Union. We have in those states what are called the slave-breeding states. Allow me to speak plainly. Although it is harrowing to your feeling, it is necessary that the facts of the case should be stated. We have in the United States slave-breeding states. The very state from which the minister from our court to yours comes is one of these states—Maryland, where men, women, and children are reared for the market, just as horses, sheep, and swine are raised for the market. Slave-rearing is there looked upon as a legitimate trade; the law sanctions it, public opinion upholds it, the church does not condemn it. It goes on in all its bloody horrors, sustained by the auctioneer's block. If you would see the cruelties of this system, hear the following narrative. Not long since the following scene occurred. A slave-woman and a slave-man had united themselves as man and wife in the absence of any law to protect them as man and wife. They had lived together by the permission, not by right, of their master, and they had reared a family. The master found it expedient, and for his interest, to sell them. He did not ask them their wishes in regard to the matter at all; they were not consulted. The man and woman were brought to the auctioneer's block, under the sound of the hammer. The cry was raised, "Here goes; who bids cash?" Think of it—a man and wife to be sold! The woman was placed on the auctioneer's block; her limbs, as is customary, were brutally exposed to the purchasers, who examined her with all the freedom with which they would examine a horse. There stood the husband, powerless; no right to his wife; the master's right preeminent. She was sold. He was next brought to the auctioneer's block. His eyes followed his wife in the distance; and he looked beseechingly, imploringly, to the man that had bought his wife to buy him also. But he was at length bid off to another person. He was about to be separated forever from her whom he loved. No word of his, no work of his, could save him from this separation. He asked permission of his new master to go and take the hand of his wife at parting. It was denied him. In the agony of his soul he rushed from the man who had just bought him, that he might take a farewell of his wife; but his way was obstructed, he was struck over the head with a loaded whip, and was held for a moment; but his agony was too great. When he was let go, he fell a corpse at the feet of his master. His heart was broken. Such scenes are the every-day fruits of American slavery.

Some two years since, the Hon. Seth M. Gates, an antislavery gentleman of the state of New York, a representative in the congress of the United States, told me he saw with his own eyes the following circumstance. In the national District of Columbia, over which the star-spangled emblem is constantly waving, where orators are ever holding forth on the subject of American liberty, American democracy, American republicanism, there are two slave prisons. When going across a bridge, leading to one of these prisons, he saw a young woman run out, bare-footed and bare-headed, and with very little clothing on. She was running with all speed to the bridge he was approaching. His eye was fixed upon her, and he stopped to see what was the matter. He had not paused long before he saw three men run out after her. He now knew what the nature of the case was: a slave escaping from her chains—a young woman, a sister—escaping from the bondage in which she had been held. She made her way to the bridge, but had not reached it, ere from the Virginia side there came two slaveholders. As soon as they saw them, her pursuers called out, "Stop her!" True to their Virginian instincts, they came to the rescue of their brother kidnappers across the bridge. The poor girl now saw that there was no chance for her. It was a trying time. She knew if she went back, she must be a slave forever—she must be dragged down to the scenes of pollution which the slaveholders continually provide for most of the poor, sinking, wretched young women whom they call their property. She formed her resolution; and just as those who were about to take her were going to put hands upon her, to drag her back, she leaped over the balustrades of the bridge, and down she went to rise no more. She chose death, rather than to go back into the hands of those Christian slaveholders from whom she had escaped.

Can it be possible that such things as these exist in the United States? Are not these the exceptions? Are any such scenes as this general? Are not such deeds condemned by the law and denounced by public opinion? Let me read to you a few of the laws of the slaveholding states of America. I think no better exposure of slavery can be made than is made by the laws of the states in which slavery exists. I prefer reading the laws to making any statement in confirmation of what I have said myself; for the slaveholders cannot object to this testimony, since it is the calm, the cool, the deliberate enactment of their wisest heads, of their most clear-sighted, their own constituted representatives. "If more than seven slaves together are found in any road without a white person, twenty lashes a piece; for visiting a plantation without a written pass, ten lashes; for letting loose a boat from where it is made fast, thirty-nine lashes for the first offense; and for the second shall have cut off from his head one ear; for keeping or carrying a club, thirty-nine lashes; for having any article for sale, without a ticket from his master, ten lashes; for traveling in any other than the most usual and accustomed road, when going alone to any place, forty lashes; for traveling in the night without a pass, forty lashes."

I am afraid you do not understand the awful character of these lashes. You must bring it before your mind. A human being in a perfect state of nudity, tied hand and foot to a stake, and a strong man standing behind with a heavy whip, knotted at the end, each blow cutting into the flesh, and leaving the warm blood dripping to the feet; and for these trifles. For being found in another person's negro-quarters, forty lashes; for hunting with dogs in the woods, thirty lashes; for being on horseback without the written permission of his master, twenty-five lashes; for riding or going abroad in the night, or riding horses in the day time, without leave, a slave may be whipped, cropped, or branded in the cheek with the letter R, or otherwise punished, such punishment not extending to life, or so as to render him unfit for labor. The laws referred to may be found by consulting Brevard's Digest; Haywood's Manual; Virginia Revised Code; Prince's Digest; Missouri Laws; Mississippi Revised Code. A man, for going to visit his brethren, without the permission of his master—and in many instances he may not have that permission; his master, from caprice or other reasons, may not be willing to allow it—may be caught on his way, dragged to a post, the branding-iron heated, and the name of his master or the letter R branded into his cheek or on his forehead.

They treat slaves thus, on the principle that they must punish for light offenses in order to prevent the commission of larger ones.

I wish you to mark that in the single state of Virginia there are seventy-one crimes for which a colored man may be executed; while there are only three of these crimes which, when committed by a white man, will subject him to that punishment. There are many of these crimes which if the white man did not commit he would be regarded as a scoundrel and a coward. In the state of Maryland there is a law to this effect: that if a slave shall strike his master, he may be hanged, his head severed from his body, his body quartered, and his head and quarters set up in the most prominent places in the neighborhood. If a colored woman, in the defense of her own virtue, in defense of her own person, should shield herself from the brutal attacks of her tyrannical master, or make the slightest resistance, she may be killed on the spot. No law whatever will bring the guilty man to justice for the crime.

But you will ask me, can these things be possible in a land professing Christianity? Yes, they are so; and this is not the worst. No; a darker feature is yet to be presented than the mere existence of these facts. I have to inform you that the religion of the southern states, at this time, is the great supporter, the great sanctioner of the bloody atrocities to which I have referred. While America is printing tracts and Bibles; sending missionaries abroad to convert the heathen; expending her money in various ways for the promotion of the Gospel in foreign lands—the slave not only lies forgotten, uncared for, but is trampled under foot by the very churches of the land. What have we in America? Why, we have slavery made part of the religion of the land. Yes, the pulpit there stands up as the great defender of this cursed institution, as it is called. Ministers of religion come forward and torture the hallowed pages of inspired wisdom to sanction the bloody deed. They stand forth as the foremost, the strongest defenders of this "institution."

As a proof of this, I need not do more than state the general fact, that slavery has existed under the droppings of the sanctuary of the south for the last two hundred years, and there has not been any war between the religion and the slavery of the south. Whips, chains, gags, and thumb-screws have all lain under the droppings of the sanctuary, and instead of rusting from off the limbs of the bondman, those droppings have served to preserve them in all their strength. Instead of preaching the Gospel against this tyranny, rebuke, and wrong, ministers of religion have sought, by all and every means, to throw in the background whatever in the Bible could be construed into opposition to slavery, and to bring forward that which they could torture into its support.

This I conceive to be the darkest feature of slavery, and the most difficult to attack, because it is identified with religion, and exposes those who denounce it to the charge of infidelity. Yes, those with whom I have been laboring, namely, the old organization anti-slavery society of America, have been again and again stigmatized as infidels, and for what reason? Why, solely in consequence of the faithfulness of their attacks upon the slaveholding religion of the southern states, and the northern religion that sympathizes with it. I have found it difficult to speak on this matter without persons coming forward and saying, "Douglass, are you not afraid of injuring the cause of Christ? You do not desire to do so, we know; but are you not undermining religion?" This has been said to me again and again, even since I came to this country, but I cannot be induced to leave off these exposures. I love the religion of our blessed Savior. I love that religion that comes from above, in the "wisdom of God, which is first pure, then peaceable, gentle, and easy to be entreated, full of mercy and good fruits, without partiality and without hypocrisy." I love that religion that sends its votaries to bind up the wounds of him that has fallen among thieves. I love that religion that makes it the duty of its disciples to visit the fatherless and the widow in their affliction. I love that religion that is based upon the glorious principle, of love to God and love to man; which makes its followers do unto others as they themselves would be done by. If you demand liberty to yourself, it says, grant it to your neighbors. If you claim a right to think for yourself, it says, allow your neighbors the same right. If you claim to act for yourself, it says, allow your neighbors the same right. It is because I love this religion that I hate the slaveholding, the woman-whipping, the mind-darkening, the soul-destroying religion that exists in the southern states of America. It is because I regard the one as good, and pure, and holy, that I cannot but regard the other as bad, corrupt, and wicked. Loving the one I must hate the other; holding to the one I must reject the other.

I may be asked why I am so anxious to bring this subject before the British public—why I do not confine my efforts to the United States? My answer is, first, that slavery is the common enemy of mankind, and all mankind should be made acquainted with its abominable character. My next answer is, that the slave is a man, and, as such, is entitled to your sympathy as a brother. All the feelings, all the susceptibilities, all the capacities, which you have he has. He is a part of the human family. He has been the prey—the common prey—of christendom for the last three hundred years, and it is but right, it is but just, it is but proper, that his wrongs should be known throughout the world.

I have another reason for bringing this matter before the British public, and it is this: slavery is a system of wrong, so blinding to all around, so hardening to the heart, so corrupting to the morals, so deleterious to religion, so sapping to all the principles of justice in its immediate vicinity, that the community surrounding it lacks the moral stamina necessary to its removal. It is a system of such gigantic evil, so strong, so overwhelming in its power, that no one nation is equal to its removal. It requires the humanity of Christianity, the morality of the world to remove it. Hence, I call upon the people of Britain to look at this matter, and to exert the influence I am about to show they possess, for the removal of slavery from America. I can appeal to them, as strongly by their regard for the slaveholder as for the slave, to labor in this cause. I am here, because you have an influence on America that no other nation can have. You have been drawn together by the power of steam to a marvelous extent; the distance between London and Boston is now reduced to some twelve or fourteen days, so that the denunciations against slavery, uttered in London this week, may be heard in a fortnight in the streets of Boston, and reverberating amidst the hills of Massachusetts. There is nothing said here against slavery that will not be recorded in the United States.

I am here, also, because the slaveholders do not want me to be here; they would rather that I were not here. I have adopted a maxim laid down by Napoleon, never to occupy ground which the enemy would like me to occupy. The slaveholders would much rather have me, if I will denounce slavery, denounce it in the northern states, where their friends and supporters are, who will stand by and mob me for denouncing it. They feel something as the man felt, when he uttered his prayer, in which he made out a most horrible case for himself, and one of his neighbors touched him and said, "My friend, I always had the opinion of you that you have now expressed for yourself—that you are a very great sinner.'' Coming from himself, it was all very well, but coming from a stranger it was rather cutting.

The slaveholders felt that when slavery was denounced among themselves, it was not so bad; but let one of the slaves get loose, let him summon the people of Britain, and make known to them the conduct of the slaveholders toward their slaves, and it cuts them to the quick, and produces a sensation such as would be produced by nothing else. The power I exert now is something like the power that is exerted by the man at the end of the lever; my influence now is just in proportion to the distance that I am from the United States. My exposure of slavery abroad will tell more upon the hearts and consciences of slaveholders than if I was attacking them in America; for almost every paper that I now receive from the United States, comes teeming with statements about this fugitive negro, calling him a ''glib-tongued scoundrel,'' and saying that he is running out against the institutions and people of America.

I deny the charge that I am saying a word against the institutions of America, or the people, as such. What I have to say is against slavery and slaveholders. I feel at liberty to speak on this subject. I have on my back the marks of the lash; I have four sisters and one brother now under the galling chain. I feel it my duty to cry aloud and spare not. I am not averse to having the good opinion of my fellow-creatures. I am not averse to being kindly regarded by all men; but I am bound, even at the hazard of making a large class of religionists in this country hate me, oppose me, and malign me as they have done—I am bound by the prayers, and tears, and entreaties of three millions of kneeling bondsmen, to have no compromise with men who are in any shape or form connected with the slaveholders of America.

I expose slavery in this country, because to expose it is to kill it. Slavery is one of those monsters of darkness to whom the light of truth is death. Expose slavery, and it dies. Light is to slavery what the heat of the sun is to the root of a tree; it must die under it. All the slaveholder asks of me is silence. He does not ask me to go abroad and preach in favor of slavery; he does not ask any one to do that. He would not say that slavery is a good thing, but the best under the circumstances. The slaveholders want total darkness on the subject. They want the hatchway shut down, that the monster may crawl in his den of darkness, crushing human hopes, and happiness, destroying the bondman at will, and having no one to reprove or rebuke him. Slavery shrinks from the light; it hateth the light, neither cometh to the light, lest its deed should be reproved. To tear off the mask from this abominable system, to expose it to the light of heaven, aye, to the heat of the sun, that it may burn and wither it out of existence, is my object in coming to this country. I want the slaveholder surrounded, as by a wall of antislavery fire, so that he may see the condemnation of himself and his system glaring down in letters of light. I want him to feel that he has no sympathy in England, Scotland, or Ireland; that he has none in Canada, none in Mexico, none among the poor wild Indians; that the voice of the civilized, aye, and savage world, is against him. I would have condemnation blaze down upon him in every direction, till, stunned and overwhelmed with shame and confusion, he is compelled to let go the grasp he holds upon the persons of his victims, and restore them to their long-lost rights.

At Glasgow, Scotland, on the 29th of the same month, we hear from this orator again, delivering there a speech which dealt with the compromise of the Free Church on the question of slavery, and the hypocrisy of so-called Christianity. The speech itself, as reported, shows that he addressed a mixed audience of sympathizers and supporters, but he fearlessly maintained the position of exposing the inconsistencies of the hypocrites masquerading as the followers of Jesus.

SPEECH AT GLASGOW, SCOTLAND, MAY 29, 1846[1]

By Frederick Douglass

The abolitionists of the United States have been laboring, during the last fifteen years, to establish the conviction throughout that country that slavery is a sin, and ought to be treated as such by all professing Christians. This conviction they have written about,

[1] *Liberator*, May 29, 1846.

they have spoken about, they have published about—they have used all the ordinary facilities for forwarding this view of the question of slavery. Previous to that operation, slavery was not regarded as a sin. It was spoken of as an evil—in some cases it was spoken of as a wrong—in some cases it was spoken of as an excellent institution—and it was nowhere, or scarcely anywhere, counted as a sin, or treated as a sin, except by the Society of Friends, and by the Reformed Presbyterians, two small bodies of Christians in the United States. The abolitionists, for advocating or attempting to show that slaveholding is a sin, have been called incendiaries and madmen, and they have been treated as such—only much worse, in many instances; for they have been mobbed, beaten, pelted, and defamed in every possible way, because they disclaimed the idea that slavery is not a sin—a sin against God, a violation of the rights of man, a sin demanding immediate repentance on the part of the slaveholders, and demanding the immediate emancipation of the trampled and down-crushed slave. [Cheers.] They had made considerable progress in establishing this view of the case in the United States. They had succeeded in establishing, to a considerable extent, in the northern part of the United States, a deep conviction that to hold human beings in the condition of slavery is a sin, and ought to be treated as such, and that the slaveholder ought to be treated as a sinner. [Hear! and applause.] They had called upon the religious organizations of the land to treat slaveholding as sin. They had recommended that the slaveholder should receive the same treatment from the church that is meted out to the ordinary thief. They had demanded his exclusion from the churches, and some of the largest denominations in the country had separated at Mason and Dixon's line, dividing the free states from the slave states, solely on account of slaveholding, as those who hold antislavery views felt that they could not stand in fellowship with men who trade in the bodies and souls of their fellowmen. [Applause.] Indeed, the antislavery sentiment not to sit in communion with these men, and to warn the slaveholder not to come near nor partake of the emblems of Christ's body and blood, lest they eat and drink damnation to themselves, is become very prevalent in the free States. They demand of the slaveholder, first, to put away this evil—first, to wash his hands in innocency—first, to abandon his grasp on the throat of the slave; and until he was ready to do that, they can have nothing to do with him. All was going on gloriously—triumphantly; the moral and religious sentiment of the country was becoming concentrated against slavery, slaveholders and the abettors of slaveholders, when, at this period, the Free Church of Scotland sent a deputation to the United States, with a doctrine diametrically opposed to the abolitionists, taking up the ground that, instead of no fellowship they should fellowship the slaveholders. According to them, the slaveholding system is a sin, but not the slaveholder a sinner. They taught the doctrine that it was right for Christians to unite in Christian fellowship with slaveholders, and their influence has been highly detrimental to the anti-slavery cause in the United States. [Hear! hear!] All their reasonings and arguments, instead of being quoted on behalf of the abolition cause, are quoted on behalf of slavery. [Disapprobation.] The newspapers which came from the United States came laden with eulogies of Drs. Candish and Cunningham, and of the Free Church in general. While the slaveholders have long disconnected themselves with the Secession Church in this country, I do not say that the Secession Church has formally repudiated all alliance with them; but by the faithfulness of their remonstrances, by their denunciations of slavery, from time to time, and by their opinions and arguments being known of all men, the slaveholders have disconnected themselves with them. [Hear! hear! and applause.]

Now, we want to have the matter of the Free Church thoroughly sifted here to-night. We want to call attention to the deputation particularly which admitted the principle of holding fellowship with slaveholders—to fellowship slaveholders as the type and representatives of Jesus Christ on earth, and not only that, but to take their money to build churches, and pay their ministers. The Free Church sent a deputation to America. That deputation was met by the abolitionists of New York, and remonstrated with, and begged not to stain their cause by striking hands with man-stealers, and not to take the polluted gains of slavery to pay their ministers; but, by no means, to take the side of the oppressed. The deputation had an excellent opportunity of aiming an effectual blow at slavery; but they turned a deaf ear, and refused to listen to the friends of freedom. They turned a deaf ear to the groans of the oppressed slave—they neglected the entreaties of his friends—and they went into the slave States, not for the purpose of imparting knowledge to the slave, but to strike hands with the slaveholders, in order to get money to build Free Churches and pay Free Church ministers in Scotland. [Cries of "Shame!" and applause.] Now, I am here to charge that deputation with having gone into a country, where they saw three millions of human beings deprived of every right, stripped of every privilege, ranked with four-footed beasts and creeping things, with no power over their own bodies and souls, deprived of the privilege of learning to read the name of the God who made them, compelled to live in the grossest ignorance, herded together in a state of concubinage—without marriage, without God, and without hope;—they went into the midst of such a people—into the midst of those who held such a people—and never uttered a word of sympathy on behalf of the oppressed, or raised their voices against their oppressors!

We have been told, that that deputation went to the United States for the purpose of making the Christians of the United States acquainted with the position of the Free Church of Scotland; or, rather, to explain the nature of the struggles of the Free Church in behalf of religious freedom, and to preach the gospel. Now, I am here to say, that that deputation did not preach the gospel to the slave—that gospel which came from above—that gospel which is peaceable and pure, and easy to be entreated. Had they preached that God was the God of the poor slave, as well as of his rich master—had they raised their voices on behalf of that gospel—they would have been hung upon the first lamp-post. The slaveholders hate the gospel of the Lord Jesus Christ. There is nothing they hate so much. A man may go there, and preach certain doctrines connected with the gospel of Christ; but if ever he apply the principle of the love of God to man—to the slave as well as to the slaveholder—it will immediately appear how such a doctrine would be relished. But this is not all. Not only did the Free Church deputation not preach the gospel, or say a word on behalf of the slave, but they took care to preach such doctrines as would be palatable—as would be agreeably received—and as would bring them the slaveholders' money. [Cries of "Shame!" and applause.] They said, "We have only one object to accomplish"; and they justified themselves for not meddling with the sins with which they came into contact in America on the ground that they had one particular object to employ their attention. Was it to obey the voice of God? Was it to proclaim the terrors of the law against all iniquity? No. It was to get money to build Free Churches, and to pay Free Ministers. That was the object to be accomplished, and in following this course they acted more like thieves than like Christian ministers. [Applause.] I verily believe, that, had I been at the South, and had I been a slave, as I have been a slave—and I am a slave still by the laws of the United States—had I been there, and that deputation had come into my neighborhood, and my master had sold me on the auction block, and given the produce of my body and soul to them, they would have pocketed it, and brought it to Scotland to build their churches, and pay their ministers. [Cries of "No," "Yes, yes," and applause.] Why not? I am no better than the blackest slave in the Southern plantations. These men knew who were the persons they were going amongst. It may be said they were not bound to inquire as to where money comes from, when it is put into the treasury of the Lord. But in this case, there was no need for inquiry. They knew they were going to a class of people who were robbers—known stealers of men—for what is a thief? what is a robber? but he who appropriates to himself what belongs to another. The slaveholders do this continually. They publish their willingness to do so. They defend their right to do so, and the deputation knew they did this. They knew that the hat upon the head of the slaveholder, the coat upon his back, and the cash in his pocket, were the result of the unpaid toil of the fettered and bound slave; and yet, in view of this fact, they went amongst them. They went with a lighted candle in their hands. They were told what would be the consequence, but they went—purity gave way to temptation, and we see the result. The result is evil to Scotland, and evil to America, but more to the former than to the latter; for I think the Free Church has committed more sin in attempting to defend certain principles connected with this question than in accepting the money. They have had to upset all the first principles of Christianity in its defense. They have had to adopt the arguments of the Infidels of the Socialists, and others, by which to defend themselves, and have brought a foul blot upon Christianity. [Cheers, and slight sounds of disapprobation.]

Now, what are their arguments? Why is Dr. Chalmers speaking as he does of the slaveholders and slavery, and trying to make it appear that there is a distinction without a difference? This eminent Free Church leader says, "A distinction ought to be made between the character of a system and the character of persons whom circumstances have connected therewith. Nor would it be just," continues the Doctor, "to visit upon the person all the recoil and indignation which we feel toward the system itself." Here he lays down a principle by which to justify the present policy of the Free Church. This is the rock of their present position. They say, "Distinction ought to be made; for while slavery may be very bad, a sin and a crime, a violation of the law of God, and an outrage on the rights of man; yet, the slaveholder may be a good and excellent Christian, and that in him we may embrace a type and standing representative of Christ." While they would denounce theft, they would spare the thief; while they would denounce gambling, they would spare the gambler; while they would denounce the dice, they would spare the sharper; for a distinction should be made between the character of a system and the character of the men whom circumstances have connected therewith. [Cheers and laughter.] Dr. Chalmers and his Master are at odds. Christ says, "By their fruits shall they be known." Oh, no! says Dr. Chalmers, a distinction should be made between the fruits and character of a system! Oh, the artful dodger! [Great laughter.] Well may the thief be glad, the robber sing, and the adulterer clap his hands for joy. The character of adultery and the character of the adulterer—the character of slavery and the character of the slaveholder—are not the same. We may blame the system, therefore, but not the persons whom circumstances have connected therewith.

I would like to see the slaveholder made so by circumstances, and I should like to trace out the turn of circumstances which compelled him to be a slaveholder. I know what they say about this matter. They say the law compels a slaveholder to keep his slaves, but I utterly deny that any such law exists in the United States. There is no law to compel a man to keep his slaves, or to prevent them from being emancipated. There are three or four states where the master is not allowed to emancipate his slaves on the soil, but he can remove them to a free State, or, at all events, to Canada, where the British lion prowls upon three sides of us, and there they could be free. [Cheers.] The slaveholder who wishes to emancipate his slaves has but to say, "There is the north star—that is the road to Canada—I will never claim you"—and there will be but little doubt of their finding their way to freedom. There was not a single slaveholder in America but who, if he chose, could emancipate his slaves instantly; so all the argument on this basis falls to the ground, as the fact did not exist on which it is built. [Cheers.]

Slavery—I hold it to be an indisputable proposition—exists in the United States because it is respectable. The slaveholder is a respectable man in America. All the important offices in the Government and the Church are filled by slaveholders. Slaveholders are Doctors of Divinity; and men are sold to build churches, women to support missionaries, and children to send Bibles to the heathen. Revivals in religion and revivals in the slave trade go on at the same time. Now, what we want to do is to make slavery disrespectable. Whatever tends to make it respectable, tends to elevate the slaveholder; and whatever, therefore, proclaims the respectability of the slaveholders, or of slaveholding, tends to perpetuate the existence of this vile system. Now, I hold one of the most direct, one of the most powerful means of making him a respectable man, is to say that he is a Christian: for I hold that of all other men, a Christian is most entitled to my affection and regard. Well, the Free Church is now proclaiming that these men—all blood-besmeared as they are, with their stripes, gags and thumb-screws, and all the bloody paraphernalia of slaveholding, and who are depriving the slave of the right to learn to read the word of God—that these men are Christians, and ought to be in fellowship as such. [Cries of "No," and "Yes."] Does any one deny that the Free Church does this?

Mr. Pinkerton—You are libelling the Free Church.

Mr. Douglass—What! is this disputed? Will they not fellowship those who will not teach their slaves to read? I have to say, in answer, that there is not a slaveholder in the American Union who teaches his slaves to read, and I have to inform that individual, and the Free Church, and Scotland generally, that there are several States where it is punishable with death for the second offense to teach a slave his letters. [Great applause.] And further, said Mr. Douglass, I have to tell him there is yet to be the first petition to the legislature demanding a repeal of that law. If the Free

Church are to fellowship the slaveholders at all, they must fellowship them in their blood and their sins, just as they find them; and if they will not fellowship them, except they teach their slaves to read, then they will not fellowship them at all. It was necessary to keep the slaves in ignorance. If he were not kept in ignorance, where there are so many facilities for escape, he would not long remain a slave, and every means is resorted to to keep him ignorant. The sentiment is general that slaves should know nothing, but to do what is told them by their masters. But a short time ago there was a Sabbath school established in Richmond, Virginia, in which the slaves, it was supposed, were being educated. The story reached the north, and was some cause of gratification; but three weeks afterwards we found in the Richmond papers an article, inquiring into the character of that school, and demanding to know why a Sabbath school had been established in Virginia. Well, they gave an account of themselves, and what was it? In that Sabbath school nothing was taught but what would tend to make the slave a better servant than before it was established; and, in the second place, that there had not been, and there never would be, any book whatever. So they have schools there without books, and learn to read without letters. You will find Sabbath schools, therefore, in many parts of the country, but you will find these such as I have described. [Applause.]

On his return to the United States, Frederick Douglass easily increased in favor with the friends of freedom. Larger opportunities for hearing him were afforded, and he availed himself thereof. Probably the most eloquent expression of his thought, after his return from Europe, was his speech delivered in Faneuil Hall on June 8, 1849. He dealt with the illogical position of Henry Clay as a gradual emancipationist as expressed in his famous letter. Douglass showed that Clay could not have been interested in the actual emancipation of the race, inasmuch as the provisions set forth in this document could not be carried out. Douglass then combated the arguments of the Colonization Society of which Henry Clay was president. To this organization, the speaker traced the beginning of all of the social and civil evils from which the Negro then suffered in this country. It is interesting how the colonizationists at that time were saying then what so many people are today asserting, namely, that race prejudice can never be overcome because it is natural in that God implanted it. The conclusion, then, was that it could be removed only by removing the cause in deporting the Negroes to Africa or some other foreign land. This argument Douglass successfully refuted before this large audience in the following forceful address:

SPEECH IN FANEUIL HALL, JUNE 8, 1849 [1]

By Frederick Douglass

Mr. Chairman, Ladies and Gentlemen: I never rise to speak in Faneuil Hall without a deep sense of my want of ability to do justice to the subject upon which I undertake to speak. I can do a pretty good business, some have said, in the country school houses in Western New York and elsewhere; but when I come before the people of Boston in Faneuil Hall, I feel my exceeding weakness. I am all the more embarrassed this evening, because I have to speak to you in respect to a subject concerning which an apology seems to be demanded. I allude to the subject of the American Colonization Society—a subject which has had a large measure of anti-slavery attention, and been long since disposed of at the hands of Wm. Lloyd Garrison. The only apology that I can make for calling attention to it this evening is that it has had a sort of "revival" of late, through the agency of a man whom I presume a large portion of this audience esteem and admire. I allude to the Honorable Henry Clay of Kentucky. [Applause.] Though not a Yankee, you see I guessed correctly. I have presumed rightly that you esteem and admire that gentleman. Now, if you admire Mr. Clay, of course you would like to know all about him. You would like, of course, to hear whatever can be said of him, and said fairly, although a black man may presume to say it.

Mr. Clay has recently given to the world a letter, purporting to

[1] *Liberator*, June 8, 1849.

advocate the emancipation of the slaves of Kentucky. That letter has been extensively published in New England as well as other parts of the United States; and in almost every instance where a Whig paper has spoken of the letter it has done so in terms of high approval. The plan which Mr. Clay proposes is one which seems to meet almost the universal assent of the Whig party at the North; and many religious papers have copied the article, and spoken in terms of high commendation of the humanity, of the clear-sightedness and philanthropy of Henry Clay. Now, my friends, I am going to speak to you in a manner that, unless you allow your reason and not your prejudices to prevail, will provoke from you demonstrations of disapprobation. I beg of you, then, to hear me calmly—without prejudice or opposition. You, it must be remembered, have in your hands all power in this land. I stand here not only in a minority, but identified with a class whom everybody can insult with impunity. Surely, the ambition for superiority must be great indeed in honorable men to induce them to insult a poor black man, whom the basest fellow in the street can insult with impunity. Keep this in mind, and hear what I have to say with regard to Mr. Clay's letter, and his position as a slaveholder.

The letter of Mr. Clay commences in a manner that gives promise to the reader that he shall find it a consistent, straightforward antislavery document. It commences by refuting, with one or two strokes of the pen, the vast cart-loads of sophistry piled up by Mr. Calhoun and others in favor of perpetual slavery. He shows clearly that Mr. Calhoun's theory of slavery, if admitted to be sound, would enslave the whites as readily as it enslaves the blacks—this would follow necessarily. Glancing at the question of the natural inferiority of the colored man, he says: "Admitting a question he does not raise—admitting that the whites of this country are superior to the blacks, the fact devolves upon the former the duty of enlightening, instructing and improving the condition of the latter." These are noble sentiments, worthy of the heart and head of a great and good man. But how does Mr. Clay propose to carry out this plan? He goes on to state that, in carrying out his proposed plan of gradual emancipation, great care should be taken that the rights and interests of the slaveholder should not be jeopardized. He proceeds to state that the utmost caution and prudence should guide the hand that strikes down slavery in Kentucky. With reference to emancipation, he affirms that it should not commence until the year 1885. The plan is that all children born of slave parents in Kentucky after the year 1860 shall be free after arriving at the age of twenty-five. He sets, therefore, the day of emancipation beyond the average length of the slave's life, for a generation of slaves in the far South dies out in seven years. But how would he have these children of slave parents free? Not free to work for themselves—not free to live on the soil that they have cultivated with their own hard hands—that they have nourished with their best blood, and toiled over and beautified and adorned—but that then they shall be let out under an agent of the State for three long years, to raise one hundred and fifty dollars with which to pay the price of their own expatriation from their family and friends. [Voices—"Shame!"]

I hear the cry of shame—yes, it is a deep and damning shame. He declares in that letter that not only shall these emancipated slaves work three years, but that he, Mr. Clay, will oppose any measure for emancipation without the expatriation of the emancipated slaves. Just look at the peculiar operation of this plan. Let us suppose that it is adopted, and that in the year 1860 it commences. All children born of slave parents are to be free in the year 1888. It is well known that all persons in the South have contracted marriages long before this period, and have become parents, some having children from one to four years of age. Henry Clay's plan is that when these persons arrive at the age of twenty-eight, these parents shall be torn away from their tender children, and hurried off to Liberia or somewhere else; and that the children taken from these parents, before they have become acquainted with the paternal relation, shall remain another twenty-eight years; and when they have remained that period, and have contracted matrimonial alliances, and become fathers and mothers, they, too, shall be taken from their children, the slaveholders having kept them at work for twenty-eight years, and hurried off to Liberia.

But a darker, baser feature than all these appears in this letter of Mr. Clay. It is this: He speaks of the loss which the slaveholders will be called on to experience by the emancipation of his slaves. But he says that even this trifling expenditure may be prevented by leaving the slaveholder the right to sell—to mortgage—to transfer his slave property any time during the twenty-five years. Only look at Henry Clay's generosity to the slaveholders of Kentucky. He has twenty-five long years during which to watch the slave markets of New Orleans, of Memphis, of Vicksburg and other Southern cities, and to watch the prices of cotton and rice and tobacco on the other side of the Atlantic, and as the prices rise there in these articles, he may expect a corresponding rise in the price of flesh in the slave markets, and then he can sell his slaves to the best advantage. Thus it is that the glorious State of Kentucky shall be made free, and yet her purse be made the heavier in consequence of it. This is not a proposition for emancipation, but a proposition to Kentucky to sell off the slaves she holds in her possession, and throw them off into the far Southern States—and then hypocritically boast of being a free State, while almost every slave born upon her soil remains a slave. And this is the plan of the good Henry Clay, whom you esteem and admire so much. [Applause and hisses.] You that like to hiss, if you had the chain on your own limbs, and were pent up in Henry Clay's own quarter, and had free access to Henry Clay's own meal-tub, I think would soon change your tune. [Laughter.]

I want to say a word about the Colonization Society, of which Henry Clay is President. He is President of nothing else. [Laughter.] That Society is an old enemy of the colored people in this country. Almost every respectable man belongs to it, either by direct membership or by affinity. I meet with colonizationists everywhere; I met with a number of them the other day, on board the steamer *Alida,* going from Albany to New York. I wish to state my experience on board of that steamer, and as it is becoming a subject of newspaper remark, it may not be out of place to give my version of the story:—On Thursday last, I took my passage on board the steamer *Alida,* as I have stated, to go from Albany to New York. I happened to have, very contrary to American taste and American prejudices and customs, in my company, a couple of friends from England—persons who had not been ashamed—nor had they cause to be ashamed from any feeling that exists in that country against the colored man—of being found on equal social terms with him in the city of London. They happen now to be sojourning in this country; and as if unaware of the prejudice existing in this country, or, if aware, perfectly regardless of it, they accompanied me on the steamer, and shared, of course, my society, or permitted me to share theirs on the passage to New York. About noon, I went into the cabin, and inquired of one of the waiters if we could have dinner. The answer was, we could. They had on a sign on each side of the captain's office words to this effect: "Meals can be received in the cabin at any hour during the day, by application to the steward." I made the application, and expected, of course, that dinner would be forthcoming at the time appointed. The bell rung—and though I do not know as it was altogether wise and prudent, I took a lady on each arm—for my friends were white ladies, you must know—and moved forward to the cabin. The fact of their being white ladies will enable you more readily to understand the cause of the intensity of hate displayed towards me. I went below forgetting all about my complexion, the curl of my hair, or the flatness of my nose, only remembering I had two elbows and a stomach, and was exceedingly hungry. [Laughter.] I walked below, as I have said, and took my seat at the table, supposing that the table was the place where a man should eat.

I had been there but a few moments, before I observed a large number of American gentlemen rising up gradually—for we are gradualists in this country—and moving off to another table, on the other side. But feeling I was there on my own responsibility, and that those gentlemen could not eat dinner for me, and I must do it for myself, I preferred to sit still, unmoved by what was passing around me. I had been there but a few moments, when a white man—after the order of American white men—for I would say, for your consolation, that you are growing darker and darker every year—the steward came up to me in a very curious manner, and said, "Yer must get up from that table." [Laughter.] I demanded by what authority he ordered me from the table. "Well," said he, "yer know the rule?" "Sir," said I, "I know nothing of your rules. I know that the rule is, that the passengers can receive their meals at any hour of the day on applying to the steward." Says he, "Now, it is no use for yer to talk, yer must leave." [Laughter.] "But where is the rule?" "Well," said he, "yer cannot get dinner on any boat on this river." I told him I went up the river in the *Confidence,* and took dinner, and no remark had been made. "Well," said he, "what yer can do on the *Confidence,* yer can't do on the *Alida.* [Laughter.] Are yer a going to get up?" "No, sir," said I. "Well," says he, "I will have you up." So off he goes to the upper deck, and brings down the captain, mate, clerk, and two or three hands. I sat still during the time of his absence; but finding they were mustering pretty strong, and remembering I had but one coat, and not caring to have it torn, and feeling I had borne a sufficient testimony against their unrighteous treatment, I arose from the table, and walked to the other end of the cabin, in company with my friends. A scene then occurred which I shall never forget; not because of its impudence, but because of its malignity. A large number of American ladies and gentlemen, seated around the table on the other side of the cabin, the very moment we walked away, gave three cheers for the captain, and applauded in the most uproarious manner the steward, for having driven two ladies and one gentleman from the table, and deprived them of dinner.

Mr. Garrison—That is a fact for Europe.

Mr. Douglass—They drove us from the table, and gave three cheers for the captain for driving us away. I looked around on the audience there assembled, to see if I could detect one line of generous magnanimity on any face—any indignation manifested against the outrage that had been perpetrated upon me and my friends. But not a look, not a word, not the slightest expression of disapprobation in any part of the vessel. Now, I have traveled in England, Ireland, and Scotland—I mention this, not by way of boast, but because I want to contrast the freedom of our glorious country—and it is a glorious one, after all—with that of other countries through which I have traveled—by railroads, in highways and byways, steamboats, stagecoaches, and every imaginable kind of vehicle—I have stayed at some of the first hotels in London, Liverpool, Edinburgh, Glasgow, Dublin, and elsewhere—and I must say to you, good Americans, that I never, in any of those cities or towns, received the first mark, or heard the first word of disapprobation on account of the color of my skin. I may tell you that one of the ladies with me on the steamboat, though not a believer in the right of women to speak in public, was so excited and so indignant at the outrage perpetrated, that she went to the American captain and told him that she had heard much of the country, much of the gallantry of American gentlemen—that they would be willing to rise from their seats to allow a lady to be seated—and she was very happy in having the opportunity of witnessing a manifestation of American gallantry and American courtesy. I do think I saw one neck hang when this rebuke was administered. [Applause.]

Most of the passengers were of the baser sort, very much like some Western men—dark-complexioned, lean, lank, pinched up, about the ugliest set of men I ever saw in my life. [Laughter.] I went to the steward about two hours after they had cleared off the dinner table for those hungry, wolfish-looking people. [Laughter.] My dear friends, if you had seen them, you would have agreed with me. I then inquired of the steward if now, after this hungry multitude had been fed, we could have a cup of coffee and a biscuit. Said he—"Who are you? If you are the servant of those ladies, you shall have what you want." I thought that was kind, anyhow. "Yes," said I, "I am their most humble servant." [Great laughter.] "Well," said he, "what are you walking about on deck with them for, if you are their servant?" I told him they were very courteous to me—putting him off in that way. He then told me if I did not get out of the cabin, he would split my head open. He was rather a diminutive being, and would not have been a mouthful for anything like a Tom Hyer man. [Applause.] However, seeing his Anglo-Saxon blood was up, I thought I would move off; but tapping him on the shoulder, I told him I wanted to give him a piece of advice: "I am a passenger, you are a servant; and therefore you should always consult the wants of the passengers." [Laughter.] He finally told me he was ready to give me my dinner in the capacity of a servant, but not otherwise. This acknowledgment told the whole story of American prejudice. There were two or three slaveholders on board. One was a lady from New Orleans; rather a dark-looking person—for individuals from that quarter are dark, except the blacks, and they are getting lighter. [Laughter.] This woman was perfectly horrified with my appearance, and she said to gentlemen standing by, that she was really afraid to be near me, and that I would draw a bowie knife. Indeed, she had liked to have fainted. This woman, I learned from good authority, owned three hundred slaves in Louisiana; and yet she was afraid of a black man, and expected every moment I would attempt to commit violence on her. At the time she was affecting this horror of a Negro, she was being waited on at the table by colored men. It was, "Waiter, come here!" and "Waiter, go there!" and there they were actually, cutting up the meat, standing right over it, quite near those white persons who really shouted when I was driven out.

This tells the whole story. You have no prejudice against blacks—no more than against any other color—but it is against the black man appearing as the colored gentleman. He is then a contradiction of your theory of natural inferiority in the colored race. It was not in consequence of my complexion that I was driven out of the cabin, for I could have remained there as a servant; but being there as a gentleman, having paid my own passage, and being in company with intelligent, refined persons, was what awakened the hatred, and brought down upon me the insulting manifestations I have alluded to.

It is because the American Colonization Society cherishes and fosters this feeling of hatred against the black man, that I am opposed to it. And I am especially disposed to speak out my opposition to this colonization scheme to-night, because not only of the renewed interest excited in the colonization scheme by the efforts of Henry Clay and others, but because there is a lecturer in the shape of the Rev. Mr. Miller, of New Jersey, now in England, soliciting funds for our expatriation from this country, and going about trying to organize a society, and to create an impression in favor of removing us from this country. I would ask you, my friends, if this is not mean and impudent in the extreme, for one class of Americans to ask for the removal of another class? I feel, sir, I have as much right in this country as any other man. I feel that the black man in this land has as much right to stay in this land as the white man. Consider the matter in the light of possession in this country. Our connection with this country is contemporaneous with your own. From the beginning of the existence of this people, as a people, the colored man has had a place upon the American soil. To be sure, he was not driven from his home in pursuit of a greater liberty than he enjoyed at home, like the Pilgrim fathers; but in the same year that the Pilgrims were landing in this State, slaves were landing on the James River, in

Virginia. We feel on this score, then, that we have as much right here as any other class of people.

We have other claims to being regarded and treated as American citizens. Some of our number have fought and bled for this country, and we only ask to be treated as well as those who have fought against it. We are lovers of this country, and we only ask to be treated as well as the haters of it. We are not only told by Americans to go out of our native land to Africa, and there enjoy our freedom—for we must go there in order to enjoy it—but Irishmen newly landed on our soil, who know nothing of our institutions, nor of the history of our country, whose toil has not been mixed with the soil of the country as ours—have the audacity to propose our removal from this, the land of our birth. For my part, I mean, for one, to stay in this country; I have made up my mind to live among you. I had a kind offer, when I was in England, of a little house and lot, and the free use of it, on the banks of the river Eden. I could easily have stayed there, if I had sought for ease, undisturbed, unannoyed by American skin-aristocracy; for it is an aristocracy of skin [applause]—those passengers on board the *Alida* only got their dinners that day in virtue of color; if their skins had been of my color, they would have had to fast all day. Whatever denunciations England may be entitled to on account of her treatment of Ireland and her own poor, one thing can be said of her, that no man in that country, or in any of her dominions, is treated as less than a man on account of his complexion. I could have lived there; but when I remembered this prejudice against color, as it is called, and slavery, and saw the many wrongs inflicted on my people at the North that ought to be combated and put down, I felt a disposition to lay aside ease, to turn my back on the kind offer of my friends, and to return among you—deeming it more noble to suffer along with my colored brethren, and meet these prejudices, than to live at ease, undisturbed, on the other side of the Atlantic. [Applause.] I had rather be here now, encountering this feeling, bearing my testimony against it, setting it at defiance, than to remain in England undisturbed. I have made up my mind wherever I go, I shall go as a man, and not as a slave. When I go on board of your steamboats, I shall always aim to be courteous and mild in my deportment towards all with whom I come in contact, at the same time firmly and constantly endeavoring to assert my equal right as a man and a brother.

But the Colonization Society says this prejudice can never be overcome—that it is natural—God has implanted it. Some say so; others declare that it can only be removed by removing the cause, that is, by removing us to Liberia. I know this is false, from my own experience in this country. I remember that, but a few years ago, upon the railroads from New Bedford and Salem and in all parts of Massachusetts, a most unrighteous and proscriptive rule prevailed, by which colored men and women were subjected to all manner of indignity in the use of those conveyances. Antislavery men, however, lifted up their testimony against this principle from year to year; and from year to year, he whose name cannot be mentioned without receiving a round of applause, WENDELL PHILLIPS [applause] went abroad, exposing this proscription in the light of justice. What is the result? Not a single railroad can be found in any part of Massachusetts, where a colored man is treated and esteemed in any other light than that of a man and a traveller. Prejudice has given way and must give way. The fact that it is giving way proves that this prejudice is not invincible. The time was when it was expected that a colored man, when he entered a church in Boston, would go into the Jim Crow pew—and I believe such is the case now, to a large extent; but then there were those who would defend the custom. But you can scarcely get a defender of this proscription in New England now.

The history of the repeal of the intermarriage law shows that the prejudice against color is not invincible. The general manner in which white persons sit with colored persons shows plainly that the prejudice against color is not invincible. When I first came here, I felt the greatest possible diffidence of sitting with whites. I used to come up from the shipyard, where I worked, with my hands hardened with toil, rough and uncomely, and my movements awkward (for I was unacquainted with the rules of politeness), I would shrink back, and would not have taken my meals with the whites had they not pressed me to do so. Our president, in his earlier intercourse with me, taught me, by example, his abhorrence of this prejudice. He has, in my presence, stated to those who visited him, that if they did not like to sit at the table with me, they could have a separate one for themselves.

The time was, when I walked through the streets of Boston, I was liable to insult if in company with a white person. To-day I have passed in company with my white friends, leaning on their arm and they on mine, and yet the first word from any quarter on account of the color of my skin I have not heard. It is all false, this talk about the invincibility of prejudice against color. If any of you have it, and no doubt some of you have, I will tell you how to get rid of it. Commence to do something to elevate and improve and enlighten the colored man, and your prejudice will begin to vanish. The more you try to make a man of the black man, the more you will begin to think him a man.

Mr. Douglass here related an anecdote of his having once visited the town of Pittsfield, Massachusetts, for the purpose of lecturing. He was invited to the house of a friend, an antislavery man, who was filled with the prejudice against color. This man allowed him to walk to the place of the lecture without offering to take him into his carriage, and then left him, after the afternoon meeting to come home alone. While standing there, it began to rain, and the Hon. —— ——, a pro-slavery man, invited him into his house. The children, on seeing him enter, cried "nigger, nigger," and fled, and the whole family treated him with coldness. Determined to overcome it, he complained of a hoarseness, with which he was affected, and asked Mrs. —— if she would be kind enough to give him a glass of cold water, with a little sugar in it, to relieve his cold. Mrs. —— brought the articles, and Mr. Douglass thanked her, he said, with a swimming heart; and from that moment her coldness and formality were gone, and he was invited, whenever he visited Pittsfield again, to make his stay at their house.

Mr. Garrison desired to make a remark with reference to the exclamation of the children on the approach of Mr. Douglass, "There's a nigger in the house," and their precipitate flight. It was the same kind of feeling that was evinced on another occasion. When Mungo Park, the celebrated English traveler, visited Africa, he found himself, at a certain period, in a village where the inhabitants had never seen a white person before. On going into one of the huts, he greeted the children, who exhibited great trepidation, and ran out with all possible expedition, crying, "The devil! the devil!" [Great laughter.]

MR. DOUGLASS: It is a poor rule that won't work both ways. [Laughter and applause.] Most people think their Lord is like themselves. A certain very pious man was horribly shocked by hearing an abolitionist say that the Negro was made in the image of God. The Lord is in their image, they seem to think, and the devil in the image of the black man. [Laughter.]

I desire to bear my testimony, after hearing the eulogy pronounced by Mr. Garrison, with regard to our departed brother and co-laborer, John Murray, of Scotland. About three years ago I had the pleasure of bidding that noble man farewell on the shores of Scotland; and I remember well the deep interest he took in the antislavery questions of this country. His last battle in behalf of the slave was with the Free Church of Scotland; and while he lived, that Church, for its alliance with slaveholders—for receiving their money into its treasury, and extending to them its fellowship in return—obtained no repose. He bore a noble testimony against it; he had borne a noble testimony against slavery before. For the last twenty-eight years, John Murray stood up in Scotland, the firm, the untiring, the devoted friend of the slave. There are two or three colored persons, at least, now in this Hall, who have shared his generous hospitality, and received his hearty "God-speed" in their endeavors to break down slavery and prejudice against color in this country, by creating a public sentiment on that side of the Atlantic that should react in favor of human liberty here. I have no more to say respecting this good man; his consistent and irreproachable character is his best eulogy.

Some one has asked me to say a word about General Worth. I only know General Worth by his acts in Mexico and elsewhere, in the service of this slaveholding and slave-trading government. I know why that question is put: it is because one of your city papers, which does not rise to the dignity of being called a paper —a sheet of the basest sort—has said that my tongue ought to be cut out by its roots because, upon hearing of the death of that man, I made use of the remark—(it is not stated in what connection I made it, or where)—that another legalized murderer had gone to his account. I say so yet! [Loud cheering and some hisses.] I will not undertake to defend what I then said, or to show up his character or history. You know as well as I do, that Faneuil Hall has resounded with echoing applause of a denunciation of the Mexican war, as a murderous war—as a war against the free states —as a war against freedom, against the Negro, and against the interests of the workingmen of this country—and as a means of extending that great evil and damning curse, Negro slavery. [Immense applause.] Why may not the oppressed say, when an oppressor is dead, either by disease or by the hand of the foeman on the battlefield, that there is one the less of his oppressors left on earth? For my part, I would not care if, to-morrow, I should hear of the death of every man who engaged in that bloody war in Mexico, and that every man had met the fate he went there to perpetrate upon unoffending Mexicans. [Applause and hisses.]

A word more. There are three millions of slaves in this land, held by the United States Government, under the sanction of the American Constitution, with all the compromises and guaranties contained in that instrument in favor of the slave system. Among those guaranties and compromises is one by which you, the citizens of Boston, have sworn, before God, that three millions of slaves shall be slaves or die—that your swords and bayonets and arms shall, at any time at the bidding of the slaveholder, through the legal magistrate or governor of a slave State, be at his service in putting down the slaves. With eighteen millions of freemen standing upon the quivering hearts of three millions of slaves, my sympathies, of course, must be with the oppressed. I am among them, and you are treading them beneath your feet. The weight of your influence, numbers, political combinations and religious organizations, and the power of your arms, rest heavily upon them, and serve at this moment to keep them in their chains. When I consider their condition—the history of the American people—how they bared their bosoms to the storm of British artillery, in order to resist simply a three-penny tea tax, and to assert their independence of the mother country—I say, in view of these things, I should welcome the intelligence to-morrow, should it come, that the slaves had risen in the South, and that the sable arms which had been engaged in beautifying and adorning the South were engaged in spreading death and devastation there. [Marked sensation.] There is a state of war at the South at this moment. The slaveholder is waging a war of aggression on the oppressed. The slaves are now under his feet. Why, you welcomed the intelligence from France, that Louis Philippe had been barricaded in Paris—you threw up your caps in honor of the victory achieved by Republicanism over Royalty—you shouted aloud—"Long live the republic!"—and joined heartily in the watchword of "Liberty, Equality, Fraternity"—and should you not hail, with equal pleasure, the tidings from the South that the slaves had risen, and achieved for himself, against the iron-hearted slaveholder, what the republicans of France achieved against the royalists of France? [Great applause, and some hissing.]

CHAPTER VI

THE ORATORY OF DEFIANCE

Another impetus was given to the oral expression of the sentiment of Negroes when the infamous Fugitive Slave Law of 1850 was enacted. This unpopular measure was fearlessly attacked by all thinking Negroes throughout the North. They availed themselves of almost every occasion to express their disgust for such a low type of statesmanship as then dictated the policy of the United States.

These orations, however, assumed two forms. Along with the expression of their disapproval of the measure, men like Martin R. Delany and James Theodore Holly, evinced, also, their despair of rising to the status of the white man in the United States. Such persons, therefore, advocated colonization, not in Africa, but in foreign countries acceptable to the Negroes themselves. Most of those who actually sought foreign shores directed their steps toward Canada; but at first a few prospective colonists found Hayti, Trinidad, and Central America, also desirable.

The other type of orators, the more defiant of the two, were represented by Charles Lenox Remond and Samuel Ringgold Ward. These men were spurred on in their defiance by the drastic measures undertaken to reclaim fugitives in the North by slave-catchers, operating under the provisions of the recent law. For example, in the speech of Samuel Ringgold Ward which follows, he fearlessly criticized Mason of Virginia, the author of the measure, and denounced Daniel Webster because of his attempt to swallow this compromising act. Negroes and their friends, moreover, were openly urged to resist the execution of this Federal law.

SPEECH ON THE FUGITIVE SLAVE BILL [1]

BY SAMUEL R. WARD [2]

I am here to-night simply as a guest. You have met here to speak of the sentiments of a Senator of your State whose remarks you have the honor to repudiate. In the course of the remarks of the gentleman who preceded me, he has done us the favor to make honorable mention of a Senator of my own State—Wm. H. Seward. [Three hearty cheers were given for Senator Seward.]

I thank you for this manifestation of approbation of a man who has always stood head and shoulders above his party, and who has never receded from his position on the question of slavery. It was my happiness to receive a letter from him a few days since, in which he said he never would swerve from his position as the friend of freedom. [Applause.]

To be sure, I agree not with Senator Seward in politics, but when an individual stands up for the rights of men against slaveholders, I care not for party distinctions. He is my brother. [Loud cheers.]

We have here much of common cause and interest in this matter. That infamous bill of Mr. Mason, of Virginia, proves itself to be like all other propositions presented by Southern men. It finds just enough of Northern dough-faces who are willing to pledge

[1] *Liberator*, April 5, 1850.

[2] Samuel R. Ward was one of the most prominent Negroes of the critical period of our history, from 1830 to 1860. Impressed with the superior gifts of which he gave evidence at an early age, Gerrit Smith enabled him to secure a liberal education. Ward then entered upon the ministry in the Presbyterian Church. For several years he was settled over a white church at South Butler, New York, where, according to William Wells Brown, Ward "preached with great acceptance and was highly respected." Coming to the aid of his race during the trying days of the abolition agitation, Ward took the platform and from 1840 to the passage of the Fugitive Slave Law of 1850 preached or lectured in every church, hall, or schoolhouse in western and central New York. "Standing about six feet in height, possessing a strong voice, and energetic in his gestures, Ward," says his biographer, "always impressed his highly finished and logical speeches upon his hearers."

Ward became more of a platform orator than a preacher. His aim seemed to be not so much to preach the gospel of heaven as to preach the gospel of this world that men calling themselves Christians might learn to respect the natural and political rights of their fellows. In the interest of this cause he traveled through much of this country, visited England in 1852, and then went to Jamaica, where he finally resided until he died at an early age. Referring to the death of R. B. Elliot, Frederick Douglass, Ward's most famous contemporary, remarked: "I have known but one other black man to be compared with Elliot, and that was Samuel R. Ward, who, like Elliot, died in the midst of his years. The thought of both men makes me sad. We are not overrich with such men, and we may well mourn when one such has fallen."

themselves, if you will pardon the uncouth language of a backwoodsman, to lick up the spittle of the slavocrats, and swear it is delicious. [Applause.]

You of the old Bay State—a State to which many of us are accustomed to look as to our fatherland, just as well look back to England as our mother country—you have a Daniel who has deserted the cause of freedom. We, too, in New York, have a "Daniel who has come to judgment," only he don't come quite fast enough to the right kind of judgment. [Tremendous enthusiasm.] Daniel S. Dickinson represents some one, I suppose, in the State of New York; God knows, he doesn't represent me. I can pledge you that our Daniel will stand cheek by jowl with your Daniel. [Cheers.] He was never known to surrender slavery, but always to surrender liberty.

The bill of which you most justly complain, concerning the surrender of fugitive slaves, is to apply alike to your State and to our State, if it shall ever apply at all. But we have come here to make a common oath upon a common altar, that that bill shall never take effect. [Applause.] Honorable Senators may record their names in its behalf, and it may have the sanction of the House of Representatives; but we, the people, who are superior to both Houses and the Executive, too [hear! hear!], we, the people, will never be human bipeds, to howl upon the track of the fugitive slave, even though led by the corrupt Daniel of your State, or the degraded one of ours. [Cheers.]

Though there are many attempts to get up compromises—and there is no term which I detest more than this, it is always the term which makes right yield to wrong; it has always been accursed since Eve made the first compromise with the devil. [Repeated rounds of applause.] I was saying, sir, that it is somewhat singular, and yet historically true, that whensoever these compromises are proposed, there are men of the North who seem to foresee that Northern men, who think their constituency will not look into these matters, will seek to do more than the South demands. They seek to prove to Northern men that all is right and all is fair; and this is the game Webster is attempting to play.

"Oh," says Webster, "the will of God has fixed that matter, we will not re-enact the will of God." Sir, you remember the time in 1841, '42, '43 and '44, when it was said that Texas could never be annexed. The design of such dealing was that you should believe it, and then, when you thought yourselves secure, they would spring the trap upon you. And now it is their wish to seduce you into the belief that slavery never will go there, and then the slaveholders will drive slavery there as fast as possible. I think that this is the most contemptible proposition of the whole, except the support of that bill which would attempt to make the whole North the slave-catchers of the South.

You will remember that that bill of Mr. Mason says nothing about color. Mr. Phillips, a man whom I always loved [applause], a man who taught me my horn-book on this subject of slavery, when I was a poor boy, has referred to Marshfield. There is a man who sometimes lives in Marshfield, and who has the reputation of having an honorable dark skin. Who knows but that some postmaster may have to sit upon the very gentleman whose character you have been discussing to-night? [Hear! hear!] "What is sauce for the goose is sauce for the gander." [Laughter.] If this bill is to relieve grievances, why not make an application to the immortal Daniel of Marshfield? [Applause.] There is no such thing as complexion mentioned. It is not only true that the colored man of Massachusetts—it is not only true that the fifty thousand colored men of New York may be taken—though I pledge you there is one, whose name is Sam Ward, who will never be taken alive. [Tremendous applause.] Not only is it true that the fifty thousand black men in New York may be taken, but any one else also can be captured. My friend Theodore Parker alluded to Ellen Crafts. I had the pleasure of taking tea with her, and accompanied her here to-night. She is far whiter than many who come here slave-catching. This line of distinction is so nice that you cannot tell who is white or black. As Alexander Pope used to say, "White and black soften and blend in so many thousand ways, that it is neither white nor black." [Loud plaudits.]

This is the question, Whether a man has a right to himself and his children, his hopes and his happiness, for this world and the world to come. That is a question which, according to this bill, may be decided by any backwoods postmaster in this State or any other. Oh, this is a monstrous proposition; and I do thank God that if the Slave Power has such demands to make on us, that the proposition has come now—now, that the people know what is being done—now that the public mind is turned toward this subject—now that they are trying to find what is the truth on this subject.

Sir, what must be the moral influence of this speech of Mr. Webster on the minds of young men, lawyers and others, here in the North? They turn their eyes towards Daniel Webster as towards a superior mind, and a legal and constitutional oracle. If they shall catch the spirit of this speech, its influence upon them and upon following generations will be so deeply corrupting that it never can be wiped out or purged.

I am thankful that this, my first entrance into Boston, and my first introduction to Faneuil Hall, gives me the pleasure and privilege of uniting with you in uttering my humble voice against the two Daniels, and of declaring, in behalf of our people, that if the fugitive slave is traced to our part of New York State, he shall have the law of Almighty God to protect him, the law which says, "Thou shalt not return to the master the servant that is escaped unto thee, but he shall dwell with thee in thy gates, where it liketh him best." And if our postmasters cannot maintain their constitutional oaths, and cannot live without playing the pander to the slave-hunter, they need not live at all. Such crises as these leave us to the right of Revolution, and if need be, that right we will, at whatever cost, most sacredly maintain.[1]

Frederick Douglass, however, wiser in his generation than most of the leaders of his race, did not belong either to the extremely radical or to the safely conservative group of his race, and it hardly does him justice to say that he occupied the mean between the two extremes. About the middle of the century, he was becoming the most prominent figure of all Negroes in the United States, and consequently had the opportunity to express himself more frequently than most others of his race. He graphically portrayed the condition of the slave; he logically exposed the fallacy of the pro-slavery advocacy; he invariably inveighed against the cruel treatment of Negroes in the North; he persistently questioned the efficacy of a Christianity which, when it had

[1] The *Liberator*, April 5, 1850.

a revival of religion, experienced also a revival of the slave trade; he fearlessly denounced the protagonists of the slavocracy prostituting the government to the support of caste: but he never went to the extremes reached by his more emotional contemporaries.

His position, moreover, was very clear. He considered colonization, not only unwise, but impracticable. "Individuals migrate," he said, "but nations, never." Iniquitous legislation, he believed, should be questioned and opposed with all of the moral force and suasion of which man is capable, but open defiance to the law never appealed to him as feasible. He did not believe that the few persons then interested in the liberation of the slaves could do them very much good by arraying themselves against the Federal Government; and even if such a thing could be done, the Negro's position would hardly be improved by destroying the Government, but some amelioration might result by reforming it. His attitude and method of fighting within the ranks were well set forth in the following address:

SPEECH AT ROCHESTER, JULY 5, 1852

By Frederick Douglass

Mr. President, Friends and Fellow Citizens:

He who could address this audience without a quailing sensation, has stronger nerves than I have. I do not remember ever to have appeared as a speaker before any assembly more shrinkingly, nor with greater distrust of my ability, than I do this day. A feeling has crept over me quite unfavorable to the exercise of my limited powers of speech. The task before me is one which requires much previous thought and study for its proper performance. I know that apologies of this sort are generally considered flat and unmeaning. I trust, however, that mine will not be so considered. Should I seem at ease, my appearance would much misrepresent me. The little experience I have had in addressing public meetings, in country school houses, avails me nothing on the present occasion.

The papers and placards say that I am to deliver a Fourth of July Oration. This certainly sounds large, and out of the common way, for me. It is true that I have often had the privilege to speak in this beautiful Hall, and to address many who now honor me with their presence. But neither their familiar faces, nor the perfect gage I think I have of Corinthian Hall seems to free me from embarrassment.

The fact is, ladies and gentlemen, the distance between this platform and the slave plantation, from which I escaped, is considerable—and the difficulties to be overcome in getting from the latter to the former are by no means slight. That I am here to-day is, to me, a matter of astonishment as well as of gratitude. You will not, therefore, be surprised, if in what I have to say I evince no elaborate preparation, nor grace my speech with any high sounding exordium. With little experience and with less learning, I have been able to throw my thoughts hastily and imperfectly together; and trusting to your patient and generous indulgence, I will proceed to lay them before you.

This, for the purpose of this celebration, is the Fourth of July. It is the birthday of your National Independence, and of your political freedom. This, to you, is what the Passover was to the emancipated people of God. It carries your minds back to the day, and to the act of your great deliverance; and to the signs, and to the wonders, associated with that act, and that day. This celebration also marks the beginning of another year of your national life; and reminds you that the Republic of America is now 76 years old. I am glad, fellow-citizens, that your nation is so young. Seventy-six years, though a good old age for a man, is but a mere speck in the life of a nation. Three score years and ten is the allotted time for individual men; but nations number their years by thousands. According to this fact, you are, even now, only in the beginning of your national career, still lingering in the period of childhood. I repeat, I am glad this is so. There is hope in the thought, and hope is much needed, under the dark clouds which lower above the horizon. The eye of the reformer is met with angry flashes, portending disastrous times; but his heart may well beat lighter at the thought that America is young, and that she is still in the impressible stage of her existence. May he not hope that high lessons of wisdom, of justice and of truth, will yet give direction to her destiny? Were the nation older, the patriot's heart might be sadder, and the reformer's brow heavier. Its future might be shrouded in gloom, and the hope of its prophets go out in sorrow. There is consolation in the thought that America is young.—Great streams are not easily turned from channels, worn deep in the course of ages. They may sometimes rise in quiet and stately majesty, and inundate the land, refreshing and fertilizing the earth with their mysterious properties. They may also rise in wrath and fury, and bear away, on their angry waves, the accumulated wealth of years of toil and hardship. They, however, gradually flow back to the same old channel, and flow on as serenely as ever. But, while the river may not be turned aside, it may dry up, and leave nothing behind but the withered branch, and the unsightly rock, to howl in the abyss-sweeping wind, the sad tale of departed glory. As with rivers so with nations.

Fellow-citizens, I shall not presume to dwell at length on the associations that cluster about this day. The simple story of it is, that, 76 years ago, the people of this country were British subjects. The style and title of your "sovereign people" (in which you now glory) was not then born. You were under the British Crown. Your fathers esteemed the English Government as the home government; and England as the fatherland. This home government, you know, although a considerable distance from your home, did, in the exercise of its parental prerogatives, impose upon its colonial children, such restraints, burdens and limitations, as, in its mature judgment, it deemed wise, right and proper.

But your fathers, who had not adopted the fashionable idea of this day, of the infallibility of government, and the absolute character of its acts, presumed to differ from the home government in respect to the wisdom and the justice of some of those burdens and restraints. They went so far in their excitement as to pronounce the measures of government unjust, unreasonable, and oppressive, and altogether such as ought not to be quietly submitted to. I scarcely need say, fellow-citizens, that my opinion of those measures fully accord with that of your fathers. Such a declaration of agreement on my part would not be worth much to anybody. It would certainly prove nothing as to what part I might have taken had I lived during the great controversy of 1776. To say now that America was right, and England wrong, is exceedingly easy.

Everybody can say it; the dastard, not less than the noble brave, can flippantly discant on the tyranny of England towards the American Colonies. It is fashionable to do so; but there was a time when, to pronounce against England, and in favor of the cause of the colonies, tried men's souls. They who did so were accounted in their day plotters of mischief, agitators and rebels, dangerous men. To side with the right against the wrong, with the weak against the strong, and with the oppressed against the oppressor! here lies the merit, and the one which, of all others, seems unfashionable in our day. The cause of liberty may be stabbed by the men who glory in the deeds of your fathers. But, to proceed.

Feeling themselves harshly and unjustly treated, by the home government, your fathers, like men of honesty, and men of spirit, earnestly sought redress. They petitioned and remonstrated; they did so in a decorous, respectful, and loyal manner. Their conduct was wholly unexceptionable. This, however, did not answer the purpose. They saw themselves treated with sovereign indifference, coldness and scorn. Yet they persevered. They were not the men to look back.

As the sheet anchor takes a firmer hold, when the ship is tossed by the storm, so did the cause of your fathers grow stronger as it breasted the chilling blasts of kingly displeasure. The greatest and best of British statesmen admitted its justice, and the loftiest eloquence of the British Senate came to its support. But, with that blindness which seems to be the unvarying characteristic of tyrants, since Pharaoh and his hosts were drowned in the Red Sea, the British Government persisted in the exactions complained of.

The madness of this course, we believe, is admitted now, even by England; but we fear the lesson is wholly lost on our present rulers.

Oppression makes a wise man mad. Your fathers were wise men, and if they did not go mad, they became restive under this treatment. They felt themselves the victims of grievous wrongs, wholly incurable in their colonial capacity. With brave men there is always a remedy for oppression. Just here, the idea of a total separation of the colonies from the crown was born! It was a startling idea, much more so than we, at this distance of time, regard it. The timid and the prudent (as has been intimated) of that day were, of course, shocked and alarmed by it.

Such people lived then, had lived before, and will, probably, ever have a place on this planet; and their course, in respect to any great change (no matter how great the good to be attained, or the wrong to be redressed by it), may be calculated with as much precision as can be the course of the stars. They hate all changes, but silver, gold and copper change! Of this sort of change they are always strongly in favor.

These people were called Tories in the days of your fathers; and the appellation, probably, conveyed the same idea that is meant by a more modern, though a somewhat less euphonious term, which we often find in our papers, applied to some of our old politicians.

Their opposition to the then dangerous thought was earnest and powerful; but, amid all their terror and affrighted vociferations against it, the alarming and revolutionary idea moved on, and the country with it.

On the 2d of July, 1776, the old Continental Congress, to the dismay of the lovers of ease, and the worshippers of property, clothed that dreadful idea with all the authority of national sanction. They did so in the form of a resolution; and as we seldom hit upon resolutions, drawn up in our day, whose transparency is at all equal to this, it may refresh your minds and help my story if I read it.

Resolved, That these united colonies are, and of right, ought to be free and Independent States; that they are absolved from all allegiance to the British Crown; and that all political connection between them and the State of Great Britain is, and ought to be, dissolved.

Citizens, your fathers made good that resolution. They succeeded; and to-day you reap the fruits of their success. The freedom gained is yours; and you, therefore, may properly celebrate this anniversary. The 4th of July is the first great fact in your nation's history—the very ring-bolt in the chain of your yet undeveloped destiny.

Pride and patriotism, not less than gratitude, prompt you to celebrate and to hold it in perpetual remembrance. I have said that the Declaration of Independence is the RINGBOLT to the chain of your nation's destiny; so, indeed, I regard it. The principles contained in that instrument are saving principles. Stand by those principles, be true to them on all occasions, in all places, against all foes, and at whatever cost.

From the round top of your ship of state, dark and threatening clouds may be seen. Heavy billows, like mountains in the distance, disclose to the leeward huge forms of flinty rocks! That bolt drawn, that chain broken, and all is lost. Cling to this day —cling to it, and to its principles, with the grasp of a storm-tossed mariner to a spar at midnight.

The coming into being of a nation, in any circumstances, is an interesting event. But, besides general considerations, there were peculiar circumstances which make the advent of this republic an event of special attractiveness.

The whole scene, as I look back to it, was simple, dignified and sublime. The population of the country, at the time, stood at the insignificant number of three millions. The country was poor in the munitions of war. The population was weak and scattered, and the country a wilderness unsubdued. There were then no means of concert and combination, such as exist now. Neither steam nor lightning had then been reduced to order and discipline. From the Potomac to the Delaware was a journey of many days. Under these, and innumerable other disadvantages, your fathers declared for liberty and independence and triumphed.

Fellow Citizens, I am not wanting in respect for the fathers of this republic. The signers of the Declaration of Independence were brave men. They were great men, too—great enough to give frame to a great age. It does not often happen to a nation to raise, at one time, such a number of truly great men. The point from which I am compelled to view them is not, certainly, the most favorable; and yet I cannot contemplate their great deeds with less than admiration. They were statesmen, patriots and heroes, and for the good they did, and the principles they contended for, I will unite with you to honor their memory.

They loved their country better than their own private interests; and, though this is not the highest form of human excellence, all will concede that it is a rare virtue, and that when it is exhibited it ought to command respect. He who will, intelligently, lay down his life for his country is a man whom it is not in human nature to despise. Your fathers staked their lives, their fortunes, and their sacred honor, on the cause of their country. In their admiration of liberty, they lost sight of all other interests.

They were peace men; but they preferred revolution to peaceful submission to bondage. They were quiet men; but they did not shrink from agitating against oppression. They showed forbearance; but that they knew its limits. They believed in order; but not in the order of tyranny. With them, nothing was "settled" that was not right. With them, justice, liberty and humanity were "final"; not slavery and oppression. You may well cherish the memory of such men. They were great in their day and generation. Their solid manhood stands out the more as we contrast it with these degenerate times.

How circumspect, exact and proportionate were all their movements! How unlike the politicians of an hour! Their statesmanship looked beyond the passing moment, and stretched away in strength into the distant future. They seized upon eternal principles, and set a glorious example in their defence. Mark them! Fully appreciating the hardships to be encountered, firmly believing in the right of their cause, honorably inviting the scrutiny of an on-looking world, reverently appealing to heaven to attest their sincerity, soundly comprehending the solemn responsibility they were about to assume, wisely measuring the terrible odds against them, your fathers, the fathers of this republic, did, most deliberately, under the inspiration of a glorious patriotism, and with a sublime faith in the great principles of justice and freedom, lay deep, the corner-stone of the national super-structure, which has risen and still rises in grandeur around you.

Of this fundamental work, this day is the anniversary. Our eyes are met with demonstrations of joyous enthusiasm. Banners and pennants wave exultingly on the breeze. The din of business, too, is hushed. Even mammon seems to have quitted his grasp on this day. The ear-piercing fife and the stirring drum unite their accents with the ascending peal of a thousand church bells. Prayers are made, hymns are sung, and sermons are preached in honor of this day; while the quick martial tramp of a great and multitudinous nation, echoed back by all the hills, valleys and mountains of a vast continent, bespeak the occasion one of thrilling and universal interest—a nation's jubilee.

Friends and citizens, I need not enter further into the causes which led to this anniversary. Many of you understand them better than I do. You could instruct me in regard to them. That is a branch of knowledge in which you feel, perhaps, a much deeper interest than your speaker. The causes which led to the separation of the colonies from the British crown have never lacked for a tongue. They have all been taught in your common schools, narrated at your firesides, unfolded from your pulpits, and thundered from your legislative halls, and are as familiar to you as household words. They form the staple of your national poetry and eloquence.

I remember, also, that, as a people, Americans are remarkably familiar with all facts which make in their own favor. This is esteemed by some as a national trait—perhaps a national weakness. It is a fact, that whatever makes for the wealth or for the reputation of Americans and can be had cheap! will be found by Americans. I shall not be charged with slandering Americans if I say I think the American side of any question may be safely left in American hands.

I leave, therefore, the great deeds of your fathers to other gentlemen whose claim to have been regularly descended will be less likely to be disputed than mine!

My business, if I have any here to-day, is with the present. The accepted time with God and His cause is the ever-living now.

"Trust no future, however pleasant,
Let the dead past bury its dead;
Act, act in the living present,
Heart within, and God overhead."

We have to do with the past only as we can make it useful to the present and to the future. To all inspiring motives, to noble deeds which can be gained from the past, we are welcome. But now is the time, the important time. Your fathers have lived, died, and have done their work, and have done much of it well. You live and must die, and you must do your work. You have no right to enjoy a child's share in the labor of your fathers, unless your children are to be blest by your labors. You have no right to wear out and waste the hard-earned fame of your fathers to cover your indolence. Sydney Smith tells us that men seldom eulogize the wisdom and virtues of their fathers, but to excuse some folly or wickedness of their own. This truth is not a doubtful one. There are illustrations of it near and remote, ancient and modern. It was fashionable, hundreds of years ago, for the children of Jacob to boast, we have "Abraham to our father," when they had long lost Abraham's faith and spirit. That people contented themselves under the shadow of Abraham's great name, while they repudiated the deeds which made his name great. Need I remind you that a similar thing is being done all over this country to-day? Need I tell you that the Jews are not the only people who built the tombs of the prophets, and garnished the sepulchers of the righteous? Washington could not die till he had broken the chains of his slaves. Yet his monument is built up by the price of human blood, and the traders in the bodies and souls of men shout—"We have Washington to *our father.*"—Alas! that it should be so; yet so it is.

> "The evil that men do, lives after them,
> The good is oft interred with their bones."

Fellow-citizens, pardon me, allow me to ask, why am I called upon to speak here to-day? What have I, or those I represent, to do with your national independence? Are the great principles of political freedom and of natural justice, embodied in that Declaration of Independence, extended to us? and am I, therefore, called upon to bring our humble offering to the national altar, and to confess the benefits and express devout gratitude for the blessings resulting from your independence to us?

Would to God, both for your sakes and ours, that an affirmative answer could be truthfully returned to these questions! Then would my task be light, and my burden easy and delightful. For *who* is there so cold, that a nation's sympathy could not warm him? Who so obdurate and dead to the claims of gratitude, that would not thankfully acknowledge such priceless benefits? Who so stolid and selfish, that would not give his voice to swell the hallelujahs of a nation's jubilee, when the chains of servitude had been torn from his limbs? I am not that man. In a case like that, the dumb might eloquently speak, and the "lame man leap as an hart."

But such is not the state of the case. I say it with a sad sense of the disparity between us. I am not included within the pale of this glorious anniversary! Your high independence only reveals the immeasurable distance between us. The blessings in which you, this day, rejoice, are not enjoyed in common.—The rich inheritance of justice, liberty, prosperity and independence, bequeathed by your fathers, is shared by you, not by me. The sunlight that brought light and healing to you, has brought stripes and death to me. This Fourth July is *yours*, not *mine*. *You* may rejoice, *I* must mourn. To drag a man in fetters into the grand illuminated temple of liberty, and call upon him to join you in joyous anthems, were inhuman mockery and sacrilegious irony. Do you mean, citizens, to mock me, by asking me to speak to-day? If so, there is a parallel to your conduct. And let me warn you that it is dangerous to copy the example of a nation whose crimes, towering up to heaven, were thrown down by the breath of the Almighty, burying that nation in irrevocable ruin! I can to-day take up the plaintive lament of a peeled and woe-smitten people!

"By the rivers of Babylon, there we sat down. Yea! we wept when we remembered Zion. We hanged our harps upon the willows in the midst thereof. For there, they that carried us away captive, required of us a song; and they who wasted us required of us mirth, saying, Sing us one of the songs of Zion. How can we sing the Lord's song in a strange land? If I forget thee, O Jerusalem, let my right hand forget her cunning. If I do not remember thee, let my tongue cleave to the roof of my mouth."

Fellow-citizens, above your national, tumultuous joy, I hear the mournful wail of millions! whose chains, heavy and grievous yesterday, are, to-day, rendered more intolerable by the jubilee shouts that reach them. If I do forget, if I do not faithfully remember those bleeding children of sorrow this day, "may my right hand forget her cunning, and may my tongue cleave to the roof of my mouth!" To forget them, to pass lightly over their wrongs, and to chime in with the popular theme, would be treason most scandalous and shocking, and would make me a reproach before God and the world. My subject, then, fellow-citizens, is AMERICAN

SLAVERY. I shall see this day and its popular characteristics from the slave's point of view. Standing there identified with the American bondman, making his wrongs mine, I do not hesitate to declare, with all my soul, that the character and conduct of this nation never looked blacker to me than on this 4th of July! Whether we turn to the declarations of the past, or to the professions of the present, the conduct of the nation seems equally hideous and revolting. America is false to the past, false to the present, and solemnly binds herself to be false to the future. Standing with God and the crushed and bleeding slave on this occasion, I will, in the name of humanity which is outraged, in the name of liberty which is fettered, in the name of the constitution and the Bible which are disregarded and trampled upon, dare to call in question and to denounce, with all the emphasis I can command, everything that serves to perpetuate slavery—the great sin and shame of America! "I will not equivocate; I will not excuse"; I will use the severest language I can command; and yet not one word shall escape me that any man, whose judgment is not blinded by prejudice, or who is not at heart a slaveholder, shall not confess to be right and just.

But I fancy I hear some one of my audience say, "It is just in this circumstance that you and your brother abolitionists fail to make a favorable impression on the public mind. Would you argue more, and denounce less; would you persuade more, and rebuke less; your cause would be much more likely to succeed." But, I submit, where all is plain there is nothing to be argued. What point in the anti-slavery creed would you have me argue? On what branch of the subject do the people of this country need light? Must I undertake to prove that the slave is a man? That point is conceded already. Nobody doubts it. The slaveholders themselves acknowledge it in the enactment of laws for their government. They acknowledge it when they punish disobedience on the part of the slave. There are seventy-two crimes in the State of Virginia which, if committed by a black man (no matter how ignorant he be), subject him to the punishment of death; while only two of the same crimes will subject a white man to the like punishment. What is this but the acknowledgment that the slave is a moral, intellectual, and responsible being? The manhood of the slave is conceded. It is admitted in the fact that Southern statute books are covered with enactments forbidding, under severe fines and penalties, the teaching of the slave to read or to write. When you can point to any such laws in reference to the beasts of the field, then I may consent to argue the manhood of the slave. When the dogs in your streets, when the fowls of the air, when the cattle on your hills, when the fish of the sea, and the reptiles that crawl, shall be unable to distinguish the slave from a brute, *then* will I argue with you that the slave is a man!

For the present, it is enough to affirm the equal manhood of the Negro race. Is it not astonishing that, while we are ploughing, planting, and reaping, using all kinds of mechanical tools, erecting houses, constructing bridges, building ships, working in metals of brass, iron, copper, silver and gold; that, while we are reading, writing and ciphering, acting as clerks, merchants and secretaries, having among us lawyers, doctors, ministers, poets, authors, editors, orators and teachers; that, while we are engaged in all manner of enterprises common to other men, digging gold in California, capturing the whale in the Pacific, feeding sheep and cattle on the hill-side, living, moving, acting, thinking, planning, living in families as husbands, wives and children, and, above all, confessing and worshipping the Christian's God, and looking hopefully for life and immortality beyond the grave, we are called upon to prove that we are men!

Would you have me argue that man is entitled to liberty? that he is the rightful owner of his own body? You have already declared it. Must I argue the wrongfulness of slavery? Is that a question for Republicans? Is it to be settled by the rules of logic and argumentation, as a matter beset with great difficulty, involving a doubtful application of the principle of justice, hard to be understood? How should I look to-day, in the presence of Americans, dividing, and subdividing a discourse, to show that men have a natural right to freedom? speaking of it relatively and positively, negatively and affirmatively. To do so, would be to make myself ridiculous, and to offer an insult to your understanding.—There is not a man beneath the canopy of heaven that does not know that slavery is wrong *for him.*

What, am I to argue that it is wrong to make men brutes, to rob them of their liberty, to work them without wages, to keep them ignorant of their relations to their fellow men, to beat them with sticks, to flay their flesh with the lash, to load their limbs with irons, to hunt them with dogs, to sell them at auction, to sunder their families, to knock out their teeth, to burn their flesh, to starve them into obedience and submission to their masters? Must I argue that a system thus marked with blood, and stained with pollution, is *wrong?* No! I will not. I have better employment for my time and strength than such arguments would imply.

What, then, remains to be argued? Is it that slavery is not divine; that God did not establish it; that our doctors of divinity are mistaken? There is blasphemy in the thought. That which is inhuman, cannot be divine! *Who* can reason on such a proposition? They that can, may; I cannot. The time for such argument is passed.

At a time like this, scorching irony, not convincing argument, is needed. O! had I the ability, and could I reach the nation's ear, I would, to-day, pour out a fiery stream of biting ridicule, blasting reproach, withering sarcasm, and stern rebuke. For it is not light that is needed, but fire; it is not the gentle shower, but thunder. We need the storm, the whirlwind, and the earthquake. The feeling of the nation must be quickened; the conscience of the nation must be roused; the propriety of the nation must be startled; the hypocrisy of the nation must be exposed; and its crimes against God and man must be proclaimed and denounced.

What, to the American slave, is your 4th of July? I answer; a day that reveals to him, more than all other days in the year, the gross injustice and cruelty to which he is the constant victim. To him, your celebration is a sham; your boasted liberty, an unholy license; your national greatness, swelling vanity; your sounds of rejoicing are empty and heartless; your denunciation of tyrants, brass fronted impudence; your shouts of liberty and equality, hollow mockery; your prayers and hymns, your sermons and thanksgivings, with all your religious parade and solemnity, are, to Him, mere bombast, fraud, deception, impiety, and hypocrisy —a thin veil to cover up crimes which would disgrace a nation of savages. There is not a nation on the earth guilty of practices more shocking and bloody than are the people of the United States, at this very hour.

Go where you may, search where you will, roam through all the monarchies and despotisms of the Old World, travel through South America, search out every abuse, and when you have found the last, lay your facts by the side of the everyday practices of this nation, and you will say with me, that, for revolting barbarity and shameless hypocrisy, America reigns without a rival.

Take the American slave-trade, which we are told by the papers, is especially prosperous just now. Ex-Senator Benton tells us that the price of men was never higher than now. He mentions the fact to show that slavery is in no danger. This trade is one of the peculiarities of American institutions. It is carried on in all the large towns and cities in one-half of this confederacy; and millions are pocketed every year by dealers in this horrid traffic. In several states this trade is a chief source of wealth. It is called (in contradistinction to the foreign slave-trade) *"the internal slave-trade."* It is, probably, called so, too, in order to divert from it the horror with which the foreign slave-trade is contemplated. That trade has long since been denounced by this government as piracy. It has been denounced with burning words from the high places of the nation as an execrable traffic. To arrest it, to put an end to it, this nation keeps a squadron, at immense cost, on the coast of Africa. Everywhere, in this country, it is safe to speak of this foreign slave-trade as a most inhuman traffic, opposed alike to the laws of God and of man. The duty to extirpate and destroy it, is admitted even by our DOCTORS OF DIVINITY. In order to put an end to it, some of these last have consented that their colored brethren (nominally free) should leave this country, and establish themselves on the western coast of Africa! It is, however, a notable fact that, while so much execration is poured out by Americans upon all those engaged in the foreign slave-trade, the men engaged in the slave-trade between the states pass without condemnation, and their business is deemed honorable.

Behold the practical operation of this internal slave-trade, the American slave-trade, sustained by American politics and American religion. Here you will see men and women reared like swine for the market. You know what is a swine-drover? I will show you a man-drover. They inhabit all our Southern States. They perambulate the country, and crowd the highways of the nation, with droves of human stock. You will see one of these human flesh jobbers, armed with pistol, whip, and bowie-knife, driving a company of a hundred men, women, and children, from the Potomac to the slave market at New Orleans. These wretched people are to be sold singly, or in lots, to suit purchasers. They are food for the cotton-field and the deadly sugar-mill. Mark the sad procession, as it moves wearily along, and the inhuman wretch who drives them. Hear his savage yells and his blood-curdling oaths, as he hurries on his affrighted captives! There, see the old man with locks thinned and gray. Cast one glance, if you please, upon that young mother, whose shoulders are bare to the scorching sun, her briny tears falling on the brow of the babe in her arms. See, too, that girl of thirteen, weeping, *yes!* weeping, as she thinks of the mother from whom she has been torn! The drove moves tardily. Heat and sorrow have nearly consumed their strength; suddenly you hear a quick snap, like the discharge of a rifle; the fetters clank, and the chain rattles simultaneously; your ears are saluted with a scream, that seems to have torn its way to the centre of your soul! The crack you heard was the sound of the slave-whip; the scream you heard was from the woman you saw with the babe. Her speed had faltered under the weight of her child and her chains! that gash on her shoulder tells her to move on. Follow this drove to New Orleans. Attend the auction; see men examined like horses; see the forms of women rudely and brutally exposed to the shocking gaze of American slave-buyers. See this drove sold and separated forever; and never forget the deep, sad sobs that arose from that scattered multitude. Tell me, citizens, WHERE, under the sun, you can witness a spectacle more fiendish and shocking. Yet this is but a glance at the American slave-trade, as it exists, at this moment, in the ruling part of the United States.

I was born amid such sights and scenes. To me the American slave-trade is a terrible reality. When a child, my soul was often pierced with a sense of its horrors. I lived on Philpot Street, Fell's Point, Baltimore, and have watched from the wharves the slave ships in the Basin, anchored from the shore, with their cargoes of human flesh, waiting for favorable winds to waft them down the Chesapeake. There was, at that time, a grand slave mart kept at the head of Pratt Street, by Austin Woldfolk. His agents were sent into every town and county in Maryland, announcing their arrival, through the papers, and on flaming *"hand-bills,"* headed CASH FOR NEGROES. These men were generally well dressed men, and very captivating in their manners; ever ready to drink, to treat, and to gamble. The fate of many a slave has depended upon the turn of a single card; and many a child has been snatched from the arms of its mother by bargains arranged in a state of brutal drunkenness.

The flesh-mongers gather up their victims by dozens, and drive them, chained, to the general depot at Baltimore. When a sufficient number has been collected here, a ship is chartered for the purpose of conveying the forlorn crew to Mobile, or to New Orleans. From the slave prison to the ship, they are usually driven in the darkness of night; for since the anti-slavery agitation, a certain caution is observed.

In the deep, still darkness of midnight, I have been often aroused by the dead, heavy footsteps, and the piteous cries of the chained gangs that passed our door. The anguish of my boyish heart was intense; and I was often consoled, when speaking to my mistress in the morning, to hear her say that the custom was very wicked; that she hated to hear the rattle of the chains and the heart-rending cries. I was glad to find one who sympathized with me in my horror.

Fellow-citizens, this murderous traffic is, to-day, in active operation in this boasted republic. In the solitude of my spirit I see clouds of dust raised on the highways of the South; I see the bleeding footsteps; I hear the doleful wail of fettered humanity on the way to the slave-markets, where the victims are to be sold like *horses, sheep,* and *swine,* knocked off to the highest bidder. There I see the tenderest ties ruthlessly broken, to gratify the lust, caprice and rapacity of the buyers and sellers of men. My soul sickens at the sight.

"Is this the land your Fathers loved,
The freedom which they toiled to win?
Is this the earth whereon they moved?
Are these the graves they slumber in?"

But a still more inhuman, disgraceful, and scandalous state of things remains to be presented. By an act of the American Congress, not yet two years old, slavery has been nationalized in its most horrible and revolting form. By that act, Mason and Dixon's line has been obliterated; New York has become as Virginia; and the power to hold, hunt, and sell men, women and children, as slaves, remains no longer a mere state institution, but is now an institution of the whole United States. The power is co-extensive with the star-spangled banner, and American Christianity. Where these go, may also go the merciless slave-hunter. Where these are, man is not sacred. He is a bird for the sportsman's gun. By that most foul and fiendish of all human decrees, the liberty and person of every man are put in peril. Your broad republican domain is hunting ground for *men*. *Not* for thieves and robbers, enemies of society, merely, but for men guilty of no crime. Your law-makers have commanded all good citizens to engage in this hellish sport. Your President, your Secretary of State, your *lords, nobles*, and ecclesiastics enforce, as a duty you owe to your free and glorious country, and to your God, that you do this accursed thing. Not fewer than forty Americans have, within the past two years, been hunted down and, without a moment's warning, hurried away in chains, and consigned to slavery and excruciating torture. Some of these have had wives and children, dependent on them for bread; but of this, no account was made. The right of the hunter to his prey stands superior to the right of marriage, and to *all* rights in this republic, the rights of God included! For black men there is neither law nor justice, humanity nor religion. The Fugitive Slave *Law* makes MERCY TO THEM A CRIME; and bribes the judge who tries them. An American JUDGE GETS TEN DOLLARS FOR EVERY VICTIM HE CONSIGNS to slavery, and five, when he fails to do so. The oath of any two villains is sufficient, under this hell-black enactment, to send the most pious and exemplary black man into the remorseless jaws of slavery! His own testimony is nothing. He can bring no witnesses for himself. The minister of American justice is bound by the law to hear but *one* side; and *that* side is the side of the oppressor. Let this damning fact be perpetually told. Let it be thundered around the world that in tyrant-killing, king-hating, people-loving, democratic, Christian America the seats of justice are filled with judges who hold their offices under an open and palpable *bribe*, and are bound, in deciding the case of a man's liberty, *to hear only his accusers!*

In glaring violation of justice, in shameless disregard of the forms of administering law, in cunning arrangement to entrap the defenceless, and in diabolical intent this Fugitive Slave Law stands alone in the annals of tyrannical legislation. I doubt if there be another nation on the globe having the brass and the baseness to put such a law on the statute-book. If any man in this assembly thinks differently from me in this matter, and feels able to disprove my statements, I will gladly confront him at any suitable time and place he may select.

I take this law to be one of the grossest infringements of Christian Liberty, and, if the churches and ministers of our country were not stupidly blind, or most wickedly indifferent, they, too, would so regard it.

At the very moment that they are thanking God for the enjoyment of civil and religious liberty, and for the right to worship God according to the dictates of their own consciences, they are utterly silent in respect to a law which robs religion of its chief significance and makes it utterly worthless to a world lying in wickedness. Did this law concern the *"mint, anise, and cummin"*—abridge the right to sing psalms, to partake of the sacrament, or to engage in any of the ceremonies of religion, it would be smitten by the thunder of a thousand pulpits. A general shout would go up from the church demanding *repeal, repeal, instant repeal!*—And it would go hard with that politician who presumed to solicit the votes of the people without inscribing this motto on his banner. Further, if this demand were not complied with, another Scotland would be added to the history of religious liberty, and the stern old covenanters would be thrown into the shade. A John Knox would be seen at every church door and heard from every pulpit, and Fillmore would have no more quarter than was shown by Knox to the beautiful, but treacherous, Queen Mary of Scotland. The fact that the church of our country (with fractional exceptions) does not esteem "the Fugitive Slave Law" as a declaration of war against religious liberty, implies that that church regards religion simply as a form of worship, an empty ceremony, and *not* a vital principle, requiring active benevolence, justice, love, and good will towards man. It esteems sacrifice above mercy; psalm-singing above right doing; solemn meetings above practical righteousness. A worship that can be conducted by persons who refuse to give shelter to the houseless, to give bread to the hungry, clothing to the naked, and who enjoin obedience to a law forbidding these acts of mercy is a curse, not a blessing to mankind. The Bible addresses all such persons as "scribes, pharisees, hypocrites, who pay tithe of *mint, anise,* and *cummin,* and have omitted the weightier matters of the law, judgment, mercy, and faith."

But the church of this country is not only indifferent to the wrongs of the slave, it actually takes sides with the oppressors. It has made itself the bulwark of American slavery, and the shield of American slave-hunters. Many of its most eloquent Divines, who stand as the very lights of the church, have shamelessly given the sanction of religion and the Bible to the whole slave system. They have taught that man may, properly, be a slave; that the relation of master and slave is ordained of God; that to send back an escaped bondman to his master is clearly the duty of all the followers of the Lord Jesus Christ; and this horrible blasphemy is palmed off upon the world for Christianity.

For my part, I would say, welcome infidelity! welcome atheism! welcome anything! in preference to the gospel, *as preached by those Divines!* They convert the very name of religion into an engine of tyranny and barbarous cruelty, and serve to confirm more infidels, in this age, than all the infidel writings of Thomas Paine, Voltaire, and Bolingbroke put together have done! These ministers make religion a cold and flinty-hearted thing, having neither principles of right action nor bowels of compassion. They strip the love of God of its beauty and leave the throne of religion a huge, horrible, repulsive form. It is a religion for oppressors, tyrants, man-stealers, and *thugs.* It is not that "*pure and undefiled religion*" which is from above, and which is "*first pure, then peaceable, easy to be entreated,* full of mercy and good fruits, *without partiality, and without hypocrisy.*" But a religion which favors the rich against the poor; which exalts the proud above the humble; which divides mankind into two classes, tyrants and slaves; which says to the man in chains, *stay there;* and to the oppressor, *oppress on;* it is a religion which may be professed and enjoyed by all the robbers and enslavers of mankind; it makes God a respecter of persons, denies his fatherhood of the race, and tramples in the dust the great truth of the brotherhood of man. All this we affirm to be true of the popular church, and the popular worship of our land and nation—a religion, a church, and a worship which, on the authority of inspired wisdom, we pronounce to be an abomination in the sight of God. In the language of Isaiah, the American church might be well addressed, "Bring no more vain oblations; incense is an abomination unto me: the new moons and Sabbaths, the calling of assemblies, I cannot away with; it is iniquity, even the solemn meeting. Your new moons, and your appointed feasts my soul hateth. They are a trouble to me; I am weary to bear them; and when ye spread forth your hands I will hide mine eyes from you. Yea! when ye make many prayers, I will not hear. YOUR HANDS ARE FULL OF BLOOD; cease to do evil, learn to do well; seek judgment; relieve the oppressed; judge for the fatherless; plead for the widow."

The American church is guilty, when viewed in connection with what it is doing to uphold slavery; but it is superlatively guilty when viewed in its connection with its ability to abolish slavery.

The sin of which it is guilty is one of omission as well as of commission. Albert Barnes but uttered what the common sense of every man at all observant of the actual state of the case will receive as truth, when he declared that "There is no power out of the church that could sustain slavery an hour, if it were not sustained in it."

Let the religious press, the pulpit, the Sunday School, the conference meeting, the great ecclesiastical, missionary, Bible and tract associations of the land array their immense powers against slavery, and slave-holding; and the whole system of crime and blood would be scattered to the winds, and that they do not do this involves them in the most awful responsibility of which the mind can conceive.

In prosecuting the anti-slavery enterprise, we have been asked to spare the church, to spare the ministry; but *how*, we ask, could such a thing be done? We are met on the threshold of our efforts for the redemption of the slave, by the church and ministry of the country, in battle arrayed against us; and we are compelled to fight or flee. From *what* quarter, I beg to know, has proceeded a fire so deadly upon our ranks, during the last two years, as from the Northern pulpit? As the champions of oppressors, the chosen men of American theology have appeared—men honored for their so-called piety, and their real learning. The LORDS of

Buffalo, the SPRINGS of New York, the LATHROPS of Auburn, the COXES and SPENCERS of Brooklyn, the GANNETS and SHARPS of Boston, the DEWEYS of Washington, and other great religious lights of the land have, in utter denial of the authority of *Him* by whom they professed to be called to the ministry, deliberately taught us, against the example of the Hebrews, and against the remonstrance of the Apostles, *that we ought to obey man's law before the law of God.*

My spirit wearies of such blasphemy; and how such men can be supported, as the "standing types and representatives of Jesus Christ," is a mystery which I leave others to penetrate. In speaking of the American church, however, let it be distinctly understood that I mean the *great mass* of the religious organizations of our land. There are exceptions, and I thank God that there are. Noble men may be found, scattered all over these Northern States, of whom Henry Ward Beecher, of Brooklyn; Samuel J. May, of Syracuse; and my esteemed friend (Rev. R. R. Raymond) on the platform, are shining examples; and let me say further, that, upon these men lies the duty to inspire our ranks with high religious faith and zeal, and to cheer us on in the great mission of the slave's redemption from his chains.

One is struck with the difference between the attitude of the American church towards the anti-slavery movement, and that occupied by the churches in England towards a similar movement in that country. There, the church, true to its mission of ameliorating, elevating and improving the condition of mankind, came forward promptly, bound up the wounds of the West Indian slave, and restored him to his liberty. There, the question of emancipation was a high religious question. It was demanded in the name of humanity, and according to the law of the living God. The Sharps, the Clarksons, the Wilberforces, the Buxtons, the Burchells, and the Knibbs were alike famous for their piety and for their philanthropy. The anti-slavery movement *there* was not an anti-church movement, for the reason that the church took its full share in prosecuting that movement: and the anti-slavery movement in this country will cease to be an anti-church movement, when the church of this country shall assume a favorable instead of a hostile position towards that movement.

Americans! your republican politics, not less than your republican religion, are flagrantly inconsistent. You boast of your love of liberty, your superior civilization, and your pure Christianity, while the whole political power of the nation (as embodied in the two great political parties) is solemnly pledged to support and perpetuate the enslavement of three millions of your countrymen. You hurl your anathemas at the crowned headed tyrants of Russia and Austria and pride yourselves on your Democratic institutions, while you yourselves consent to be the mere *tools* and *body-guards* of the tyrants of Virginia and Carolina. You invite to your shores fugitives of oppression from abroad, honor them with banquets, greet them with ovations, cheer them, toast them, salute them, protect them, and pour out your money to them like water; but the fugitives from your own land you advertise, hunt, arrest, shoot, and kill. You glory in your refinement and your universal education; yet you maintain a system as barbarous and dreadful as ever stained the character of a nation—a system begun in avarice, supported in pride, and perpetuated in cruelty. You shed tears over fallen Hungary, and make the sad story of her wrongs the theme of your poets, statesmen, and orators, till your gallant sons are ready to fly to arms to vindicate her cause against the oppressor; but, in regard to the ten thousand wrongs of the American slave, you would enforce the strictest silence, and would hail him as an enemy of the nation who dares to make those wrongs the subject of public discourse! You are all on fire at the mention of liberty for France or for Ireland; but are as cold as an iceberg at the thought of liberty for the enslaved of America. You discourse eloquently on the dignity of labor; yet, you sustain a system which, in its very essence, casts a stigma upon labor. You can bare your bosom to the storm of British artillery to throw off a three-penny tax on tea; and yet wring the last hard earned farthing from the grasp of the black laborers of your country. You profess to believe "that, of one blood, God made all nations of men to dwell on the face of all the earth," and hath commanded all men, everywhere, to love one another; yet you notoriously hate (and glory in your hatred) all men whose skins are not colored like your own. You declare before the world, and are understood by the world to declare that you *"hold these truths to be self-evident, that all men are created equal; and are endowed by their Creator with certain inalienable rights; and that among these are, life, liberty, and the pursuit of happiness;* and yet, you hold securely, in a bondage which, according to your own Thomas Jefferson, *"is worse than ages of that which your fathers rose in rebellion to oppose," a seventh part* of the inhabitants of your country.

Fellow-citizens, I will not enlarge further on your national inconsistencies. The existence of slavery in this country brands your republicanism as a sham, your humanity as a base pretense, and your Christianity as a lie. It destroys your moral power abroad: it corrupts your politicians at home. It saps the foundation of religion; it makes your name a hissing and a bye-word to a mocking earth. It is the antagonistic force in your government, the only thing that seriously disturbs and endangers your *Union.* It fetters your progress; it is the enemy of improvement; the deadly foe of education; it fosters pride; it breeds insolence; it promotes vice; it shelters crime; it is a curse to the earth that supports it; and yet you cling to it as if it were the sheet anchor of all your hopes. Oh! be warned! be warned! a horrible reptile is coiled up in your nation's bosom; the venomous creature is nursing at the tender breast of your youthful republic; *for the love of God, tear away,* and fling from you the hideous monster, and *let the weight of twenty millions crush and destroy it forever!*

But it is answered in reply to all this, that precisely what I have now denounced is, in fact, guaranteed and sanctioned by the Constitution of the United States; that, the right to hold, and to hunt slaves is a part of that Constitution framed by the illustrious Fathers of this Republic.

Then, I dare to affirm, notwithstanding all I have said before, your fathers stooped, basely stooped

> "To palter with us in a double sense:
> And keep the word of promise to the ear,
> But break it to the heart."

And instead of being the honest men I have before declared them to be, they were the veriest impostors that ever practised on mankind. This is the inevitable conclusion, and from it there is no escape; but I differ from those who charge this baseness on the framers of the Constitution of the United States. It is a slander upon their memory, at least, so I believe. There is not time now to argue the constitutional question at length; nor have I the ability to discuss it as it ought to be discussed. The subject has been handled with masterly power by Lysander Spooner, Esq., by William Goodell, by Samuel E. Sewall, Esq., and last, though not least, by Gerritt Smith, Esq. These gentlemen have, as I think, fully and clearly vindicated the Constitution from any design to support slavery for an hour.

Fellow-citizens! there is no matter in respect to which the people of the North have allowed themselves to be so ruinously imposed upon as that of the pro-slavery character of the Constitution. In that instrument I hold there is neither warrant, license, nor sanction of the hateful thing; but interpreted, as it ought to be interpreted, the Constitution is a GLORIOUS LIBERTY DOCUMENT. Read its preamble, consider its purposes. Is slavery among them? Is is at the gateway? or is it in the temple? it is neither. While I do not intend to argue this question on the present occasion, let me ask, if it be not somewhat singular that, if the Constitution were intended to be, by its framers and adopters, a slaveholding instrument, why neither slavery, slaveholding, nor slave can anywhere be found in it. What would be thought of an instrument, drawn up, legally drawn up, for the purpose of entitling the city of Rochester to a tract of land, in which no mention of land was made? Now, there are certain rules of interpretation for the proper understanding of all legal instruments. These rules are well established. They are plain, common-sense rules, such as you and I, and all of us, can understand and apply, without having passed years in the study of law. I scout the idea that the question of the constitutionality, or unconstitutionality of slavery, is not a question for the people. I hold that every American citizen has a right to form an opinion of the constitution, and to propagate that opinion, and to use all honorable means to make his opinion the prevailing one. Without this right, the liberty of an American citizen would be as insecure as that of a Frenchman. Ex-Vice-President Dallas tells us that the constitution is an object to which no American mind can be too attentive, and no American heart too devoted. He further says, the Constitution, in its words, is plain and intelligible, and is meant for the home-bred, unsophisticated understandings of our fellow-citizens. Senator Berrien tells us that the Constitution is the fundamental law, that which controls all others. The charter of our liberties, which every citizen has a personal interest in understanding thoroughly. The testimony of Senator Breese, Lewis Cass, and many others that might be named, who are everywhere esteemed as sound lawyers, so regard the constitution. I take it, therefore, that it is not presumption in a private citizen to form an opinion of that instrument.

Now, take the Constitution according to its plain reading, and I defy the presentation of a single pro-slavery clause in it. On the other hand, it will be found to contain principles and purposes, entirely hostile to the existence of slavery.

I have detained my audience entirely too long already. At some future period I will gladly avail myself of an opportunity to give this subject a full and fair discussion.

Allow me to say, in conclusion, notwithstanding the dark picture I have this day presented, of the state of the nation, I do not despair of this country. There are forces in operation which must inevitably work the downfall of slavery. "The arm of the Lord is not shortened," and the doom of slavery is certain. I, therefore, leave off where I began, with hope. While drawing encouragement from "the Declaration of Independence," the great principles it contains, and the genius of American Institutions, my spirit is also cheered by the obvious tendencies of the age. Nations do not now stand in the same relation to each other that they did ages ago. No nation can now shut itself up from the surrounding world and trot round in the same old path of its fathers without interference. The time was when such could be done. Long established customs of hurtful character could formerly fence themselves in, and do their evil work with social impunity. Knowledge was then confined and enjoyed by the privileged few, and the multitude walked on in mental darkness. But a change has now come over the affairs of mankind. Walled cities and empires have become unfashionable. The arm of commerce has borne away the gates of the strong city. Intelligence is penetrating the darkest corners of the globe. It makes its pathway over and under the sea, as well as on the earth. Wind, steam, and lightning are its chartered agents. Oceans no longer divide, but link nations together. From Boston to London is now a holiday excursion. Space is comparatively annihilated.—Thoughts expressed on one side of the Atlantic are distinctly heard on the other.

The far off and almost fabulous Pacific rolls in grandeur at our feet. The Celestial Empire, the mystery of ages, is being solved. The fiat of the Almighty, "Let there be Light," has not yet spent its force. No abuse, no outrage whether in taste, sport or avarice, can now hide itself from the all-pervading light. The iron shoe, and crippled foot of China must be seen in contrast with nature. Africa must rise and put on her yet unwoven garment. "Ethiopia shall stretch out her hand unto God." In the fervent aspirations of William Lloyd Garrison, I say, and let every heart join in saying it:

"God speed the year of jubilee
  The wide world o'er!
When from their galling chains set free,
Th' oppress'd shall vilely bend the knee,
And wear the yoke of tyranny
  Like brutes no more.
That year will come, and freedom's reign,
To man his plundered rights again
  Restore.

"God speed the day when human blood
  Shall cease to flow!
In every clime be understood,
The claims of human brotherhood,
And each return for evil, good,
  Not blow for blow;
That day will come all feuds to end,
And change into a faithful friend
  Each foe.

"God speed the hour, the glorious hour,
  When none on earth
Shall exercise a lordly power,
Nor in a tyrant's presence cower;
But to all manhood's stature tower,
  By equal birth!
That hour will come, to each, to all,
And from his prison-house, to thrall
  Go forth.

"Until that year, day, hour, arrive,
With head, and heart, and hand I'll strive,
To break the rod, and rend the gyve,
The spoiler of his prey deprive—
So witness Heaven!
And never from my chosen post,
Whate'er the peril or the cost,
Be driven."

In the following extract from the speech delivered before the American Antislavery Society in New York in May, 1853, Frederick Douglass showed a statesmanlike knowledge of the political situation in this country as presented by the conflicting forces of slavery and freedom. Here we see how he understood the national economic problems of tariff and free trade in their bearing on the effort for the liberation of the slave. He undoubtedly had a more intelligent grasp of things than the so-called statesmen of the time, who had spent years in advancing compromising measures which merely postponed the ultimate solution of a serious problem.

THE SLAVERY PARTY

By Frederick Douglass

Sir, it is evident that there is in this country a purely slavery party—a party which exists for no other earthly purpose but to promote the interests of slavery. The presence of this party is felt everywhere in the republic. It is known by no particular name, and has assumed no definite shape; but its branches reach far and wide in the church and in the state. This shapeless and nameless party is not intangible in other and more important respects. That party, sir, has determined upon a fixed, definite, and comprehensive policy toward the whole colored population of the United States. What that policy is, it becomes us as abolitionists, and especially does it become the colored people themselves, to consider and to understand fully. We ought to know who our

[1] Frederick Douglas, *My Bondage and Freedom*, 441-450.

enemies are, where they are, and what are their objects and measures. Well, sir, here is my version of it—not original with me—but mine because I hold it to be true.

I understand this policy to comprehend five cardinal objects. They are these: 1st, The complete suppression of all anti-slavery discussion. 2d, The expatriation of the entire free people of color from the United States. 3d, The unending perpetuation of slavery in this republic. 4th, The nationalization of slavery to the extent of making slavery respected in every state of the Union. 5th, The extension of slavery over Mexico and the entire South American states.

Sir, these objects are forcibly presented to us in the stern logic of passing events; in the facts which are and have been passing around us during the last three years. The country has been and is now dividing on these grand issues. In their magnitude, these issues cast all others into the shade, depriving them of all life and vitality. Old party ties are broken. Like is finding its like on either side of these great issues, and the great battle is at hand. For the present, the best representative of the slavery party in politics is the democratic party. Its great head for the present is President Pierce, whose boast it was, before his election, that his whole life had been consistent with the interests of slavery, that he is above reproach on that score. In his inaugural address he reassures the south on this point. Well, the head of the slave power being in power, it is natural that the pro-slavery elements should cluster around the administration, and this is rapidly being done. A fraternization is going on. The stringent protectionists and the free-traders strike hands. The supporters of Fillmore are becoming the supporters of Pierce. The silver-gray whig shakes hands with the hunker democrat; the former only differing from the latter in name. They are of one heart, one mind, and the union is natural and perhaps inevitable. Both hate negroes; both hate progress; both hate the "higher law"; both hate William H. Seward; both hate the free democratic party; and upon this hateful basis they are forming a union of hatred. "Pilate and Herod are thus made friends." Even the central organ of the whig party is extending its beggar hand for a morsel from the table of slavery democracy, and when spurned from the feast by the more deserving, it pockets the insult; when kicked on one side it turns the other, and perseveres in its importunities. The fact is, that paper comprehends the demands of the times; it understands the age and its issues; it wisely sees that slavery and freedom are the great antagonistic forces in the country, and it goes to its own side. Silver grays and hunkers all understand this. They are, therefore, rapidly sinking all other questions to nothing, compared with the increasing demands of slavery. They are collecting, arranging, and consolidating their forces for the accomplishment of their appointed work.

The keystone to the arch of this grand union of the slavery party of the United States is the compromise of 1850. In that compromise we have all the objects of our slaveholding policy specified. It is, sir, favorable to this view of the designs of the slave power, that both the whig and the democratic party bent lower, sunk deeper, and strained harder, in their conventions, preparatory to the late presidential election, to meet the demands of the slavery party than at any previous time in their history. Never did parties come before the northern people with propositions of such undisguised contempt for the moral sentiment and the religious ideas of that people. They virtually asked them to unite in a war upon free speech, and upon conscience, and to drive the Almighty presence from the councils of the nation. Resting their platforms upon the fugitive slave bill, they boldly asked the people for political power to execute the horrible and hell-black provisions of that bill. The history of that election reveals, with great clearness, the extent to which slavery has shot its leprous distillment through the life-blood of the nation. The party most thoroughly opposed to the cause of justice and humanity, triumphed; while the party suspected of a leaning toward liberty was overwhelmingly defeated, some say annihilated.

But here is a still more important fact, illustrating the designs of the slave power. It is a fact full of meaning, that no sooner did the democratic slavery party come into power, than a system of legislation was presented to the legislatures of the northern states, designed to put the states in harmony with the fugitive slave law, and the malignant bearing of the national government toward the colored inhabitants of the country. This whole movement on the part of the states bears the evidence of having one origin, emanating from one head, and urged forward by one power. It was simultaneous, uniform, and general, and looked to one end. It was intended to put thorns under feet already bleeding; to crush a people already bowed down; to enslave a people already but half free; in a word, it was intended to discourage, dishearten, and drive the free colored people out of the country. In looking at the recent black law of Illinois, one is struck dumb with its enormity. It would seem that the men who enacted that law had not only banished from their minds all sense of justice, but all sense of shame. It coolly proposes to sell the bodies and souls of the black to increase the intelligence and refinement of the whites; to rob every black stranger who ventures among them, to increase their literary fund.

While this is going on in the states, a pro-slavery, political board of health is established at Washington. Senators Hale, Chase, and Sumner are robbed of a part of their senatorial dignity and consequence as representing sovereign states, because they have refused to be inoculated with the slavery virus. Among the services which a senator is expected by his state to perform, are many that can only be done efficiently on committees; and, in saying to these honorable senators, you shall not serve on the committees of this body, the slavery party took the responsibility of robbing and insulting the states that sent them. It is an attempt at Washington to decide for the states who shall be sent to the senate. Sir, it strikes me that this aggression on the part of the slave power did not meet at the hands of the proscribed senators the rebuke which we had a right to expect would be administered. It seems to me that an opportunity was lost, that the great principle of senatorial equality was left undefended, at a time when its vindication was sternly demanded. But it is not to the purpose of my present statement to criticise the conduct of our friends. I am persuaded that much ought to be left to the discretion of anti-slavery men in congress, and charges of recreancy should never be made but on the most sufficient grounds. For, of all the places in the world where an anti-slavery man needs the confidence and encouragement of friends, I take Washington to be that place.

Let me now call attention to the social influences which are operating and coöperating with the slavery party of the country, designed to contribute to one or all of the grand objects aimed at by that party. We see here the black man attacked in his vital interests; prejudice and hate are excited against him; enmity is stirred up between him and other laborers. The Irish people, warm-hearted, generous, and sympathizing with the oppressed everywhere, when they stand upon their own green island, are instantly taught, on arriving in this Christian country, to hate and despise the colored people. They are taught to believe that we eat the bread which of right belongs to them. The cruel lie is told the Irish, that our adversity is essential to their prosperity. Sir, the Irish-American will find out his mistake one day. He will find that in assuming our avocation he also has assumed our degradation. But for the present we are sufferers. The old employments by which we have heretofore gained our livelihood are gradually, and it may be inevitably, passing into other hands. Every hour sees us elbowed out of some employment to make room perhaps for some newly-arrived emigrants, whose hunger and color are thought to give them a title to especial favor. White men are becoming house-servants, cooks and stewards, common laborers, and flunkeys to our gentry, and, for aught I see, they adjust themselves to their stations with all becoming obsequiousness. This fact proves that if we cannot rise to the whites, the whites can fall to us. Now, sir, look once more. While the colored people are thus elbowed out of employment; while the enmity of emigrants is being excited against us; while state after state enacts laws against us; while we are hunted down, like wild game, and oppressed with a general feeling of insecurity,—the American colonization society—that old offender against the best interests and slanderer of the colored people—awakens to new life, and vigorously presses its scheme upon the consideration of the people and the government. New papers are started—some for the north and some for the south—and each in its tone adapting itself to its latitude. Government, state and national, is called upon for appropriations to enable the society to send us out of the country by steam! They want steamers to carry letters and negroes to Africa. Evidently this society looks upon our "extremity as its opportunity," and we may expect that it will use the occasion well. They do not deplore, but glory, in our misfortune.

But, sir, I must hasten. I have thus briefly given my view of one aspect of the present condition and future prospects of the colored people of the United States. And what I have said is far from encouraging to my afflicted people. I have seen the cloud gather upon the sable brows of some who hear me. I confess the case looks black enough. Sir, I am not a hopeful man. I think I am apt even to undercalculate the benefits of the future. Yet, sir, in this seemingly desperate case, I do not despair for my people. There is a bright side to almost every picture of this kind; and ours is no exception to the general rule. If the influences against us are strong, those for us are also strong. To the inquiry, will our enemies prevail in the execution of their designs, in my God and in my soul, I believe they will not. Let us look at the first object sought for by the slavery party of the country, viz: the suppression of anti-slavery discussion. They desire to suppress discussion on this subject, with a view to the peace of the slaveholder and the security of slavery. Now, sir, neither the principle nor the subordinate objects here declared can be at all gained by the slave power, and for this reason: It involves the proposition to padlock the lips of the whites, in order to secure the fetters on the limbs of the blacks. The right of speech, precious and priceless, cannot, will not, be surrendered to slavery. Its suppression is asked for, as I have said, to give peace and security to slaveholders. Sir, that thing cannot be done. God has interposed an insuperable obstacle to any such result. "There can be no peace, saith my God, to the wicked." Suppose it were possible to put down this discussion, what would it avail the guilty slaveholder, pillowed as he is upon the heaving bosoms of ruined souls? He could not have a peaceful spirit. If every anti-slavery tongue in the nation were silent—every anti-slavery organization dissolved—every anti-slavery press demolished—every anti-slavery periodical, paper, book, pamphlet, or what not, were searched out, gathered together, deliberately burned to ashes, and their ashes given to the four winds of heaven, still, still the slaveholder could have "no peace." In every pulsation of his heart, in every throb of his life, in every glance of his eye, in the breeze that soothes, and in the thunder that startles, would be waked up an accuser, whose cause is, "Thou art, verily, guilty concerning thy brother."[1]

When it seemed that the effort in the North to nullify the Fugitive Slave Law had failed and that without molestation the bondmen escaping from their masters could be

[1] Douglass, *My Bondage and My Freedom*, pp. 451-456.

apprehended and returned to their owners, the problem of the Negro seemed to have no other solution than a most radical one. A larger number of the antislavery leaders of both races, therefore, began to espouse the principle of "No union with slaveholders," advanced by William Lloyd Garrison years before when he was mobbed in Boston for advocating the breakup of the republic.

In the folllowing speeches of Charles Lenox Remond this high ground is fearlessly taken. He was speaking in the New England Antislavery Convention upon the resolution in favor of the dissolution of the Union. Unlike Frederick Douglass, Remond permitted himself to be influenced too much by the effort to secure the recognition of the social and civic rights of the free Negro in the North. If the Fugitive Slave Law could thus nationalize the institution and impress all free men into the service of reclaiming bondmen escaping from their masters, the free Negro in the North might be much better off should the connection between the slaveholding and non-slaveholding States be severed. Here Remond either manifested a lack of judgment, or a lack of interest in the slave. While the condition of the free Negro in the North might thereby have been improved, the wretched slave in the South certainly would have had less chance for freedom without the Union than when attached to one section endeavoring to make the whole nation free. Frederick Douglass always had sufficient foresight to see the results of such a policy and he was never won to the advocacy of such extreme measures. Remond's speech, however, is significant in showing the gravity of that crisis.

SPEECH BEFORE THE NEW ENGLAND ANTI-SLAVERY CONVENTION

BY CHARLES LENOX REMOND

Fellow-Countryman: I cannot begin by saying "Fellow-citizens," for that would be an unwarrantable assumption, under the circumstances of the case. I do not, Mr. Chairman, intend to speak at length; but I feel this evening, as I have felt on former occasions, that the testimony of colored persons was wanted on this platform, and especially at this time.

I do not presume, either, Mr. Chairman, on rising to speak, that I can hope to entertain the audience long upon the resolution now under consideration, in favor of a dissolution of the Union. I need not remind those who are present, that this subject is by no means a new one to a New England Anti-Slavery Convention. But while, sir, it may be old, and even trite, still, it may be worthy of our consideration at the present time; and I may say, as our esteemed friend Samuel J. May said this afternoon, that in the few remarks I have to make I shall not address myself to abolitionists, but to those who stand in the distance, or sit in the distance, and have yet, like Mr. Furness, of Philadelphia, to "take sides" in this enterprise; and if I shall succeed in interesting but one new mind upon this subject, that shall be honor enough in the humble effort I am to make.

It seems to me, Mr. Chairman, that we have enough of intellect, enough of respectability, in a word, sufficient of social influence, to carry this glorious cause in our own State, if we cannot carry it further. If it is true, that there was a time when Napoleon Bonaparte feared the pen and the voice of a single woman more than all the power of Russia, certainly we may feel the force of the remark I have made. [Cheers.] [Miss Stone had just left the platform.]

Now, sir, I am not among the number of those who despond for the success of this movement for the dissolution of this Union; I am among the number hopeful of that glorious event; and that, too, while I feel that the remark may sound strange, coming from one of my complexion. I regret that it is necessary for a colored man, for a black man or a red man, ever to refer to his complexion on the anti-slavery platform; but it does unfortunately happen that everything hinges upon that circumstance. It is the gist of this matter; and if I could feel fully satisfied that every man and every woman within the hearing of my voice was free from that feeling, I should feel that there was a moral certainty of the liberation of Anthony Burns in the city of Boston. [Cheers.]

We have been told here this evening, Mr. Chairman, that the

great trouble with Massachusetts men is to be found in their pockets or their purses. This is true to a certain extent; but is it not also true, that, outside of their pockets and their purses, there is a want of interest in the real, bona fide victims of American slavery? In other words, do we not need to have the complexion of the slave population of our country changed, at least in imagination, in order that the work may be done? I know, Sir, that men do not argue upon this question as they would then argue; I know that they do not write as they would then write; I know that they do not believe as they would then believe; I know that they do not preach as they would then preach; I know that they do not pray as they would pray, with this change of complexion.

Now, since my friend Prince, of Essex, called attention this afternoon to the character of the colored people, allow me to ask you to look in that direction for a moment; for while men live in Boston, go upon 'Change, walk up and down the public streets, all the while coming in contact with colored people, they do not understand their character; they do not know that, notwithstanding the constant pressure, from the commencement of our nation's history, which has been exerted upon their manhood, their morality, upon all that is noble, magnanimous and generous in their characters, they have exhibited as many instances of noble manhood, in proportion to their number, as have been displayed by their more favored brethren of a white complexion. It was said here by Mr. Prince that the colored race is at once morally and physically brave. Do not consider me, Mr. Chairman, in alluding to this subject, as feeling vain in regard to it; I only ask that the whole truth respecting my people may be known, and there I will leave the success of their cause. But I ask the people not to act blindly with regard to it; not to make up their opinions with this great weight of prejudice on their minds. I ask them to look upon this question impartially, generously, magnanimously, patriotically, and I believe they will be converted to our movement.

Sir, I have taken note, for the last eighteen years, of the course pursued by colored people in anti-slavery meetings, for there was a time when the number of colored people present was greater than at the present time; and yesterday, I had evidence that there was some courage left with them yet. I refer to this incident only as an illustration of the character of this people generally in our country. There was a meeting of anti-slavery friends in the basement of Tremont Temple, and a call was made for persons to come forward and give in their names, that they might be called upon, at any moment, to discharge not only a responsible, but dangerous duty; and my heart has not been so much encouraged for many a long day as when I witnessed a large number of the colored men present walk up to that stand, with an unfaltering step, and enroll their names. [Applause.]

Why is it that the anti-slavery cause should recommend itself to every well-wisher of his country? Because there are men, white men, who have never been deprived of their citizenship, nor subjected to persecution, outrage and insult, who are honored for the patriotism they have exhibited; and if the demonstration of that feeling, or principle, or sentiment, or whatever you may please to call it, is worthy of honor in the white man, then it is also worthy of honor in the colored man; and the last evening that I had the privilege of speaking in this house, I endeavored, briefly, to make it clear that, on every occasion where manhood and courage have been required in this country, the number of colored people volunteering their services has been equal to that of white people, in proportion to their number, from the earliest moment of our nation's existence. [Cheers.]

Why is it that men stand aloof from this subject? Why do they look coldly upon the discussion of the question of the dissolution of the Union? I think I may safely say, Sir, that the courage and patriotism of the colored man is of a higher character than that of the white man. There is not a man of fair complexion before me who has not something in this country to protect which the colored man does not possess; and, Sir, when I see them, in the moment of danger, willing to discharge their duty to the country, I have a proof that they are the friends, and not the enemies of the country. Then, why are they treated in this manner? Why are the people not ready to go for a dissolution of the Union? If they were white, the people would say, without hesitation, "Let this Union be dissolved!"

But there is another consideration. I ask white men of what value the American Union is to them, north of Mason and Dixon's line, and I find some of them have considerable trouble in making answer. I know there is a more potent influence than money, and that is the social influence south of Mason and Dixon's line. But what have the citizens of Boston to gain from it to-night? I am glad that one of our popular city papers has to-day asked, although indirectly, of what value is the American Union to the citizens of Boston and of the Commonwealth of Massachusetts, if they must perform such work as is being performed in and around the Court House at the present time? Look at it, gentlemen, carefully, and tell me, if you please, citizens of Boston,—white as you are, educated, as you are, wealthy, as you may be, influential, as you may be,—tell me what reward you are receiving for this almost idolatrous advocacy and defense of the American Union. Has the South honored you? When and where? Has she given you office? When? All I can gather from this whole matter is, that it is the work of education. If the editors of newspapers in Boston would right-about-face to-morrow, and recommend a different course of policy from that which has been hitherto pursued, you would soon discover a change. If the popular lyceum lecturers, instead of ridiculing the black man and traducing the black man's friends, would come up and speak in their behalf, you would find public sentiment changing in this matter. It is immaterial whether we have one organization or a hundred in this part of our country. I am satisfied that all we require to secure the success of the anti-slavery enterprise is right deeds and right words upon this subject. We want the sympathies of men on the side of the slave; we want men understanding their own rights, and daring to defend them.

I went into State street to-day, and I heard a man say—"The black niggers would do well enough in this community; the great difficulty is with the d—d white niggers." What sort of negro hatred could prompt a man to say more? I heard a poor ignorant Irishman say, within the last forty-eight hours—"Hustle the niggers out of Court Square." I heard others say, "Kick the niggers!" "Drive them out of the country," etc. And these Irishmen are in the city of Boston, and in the United States, only on sufferance. I cannot but settle down in the conviction, that were it not for this spirit of Negro hate, we should not hear them say these things. I therefore call upon this audience, in the name of their country, their principles and their professions, to forget the arguments of Stephen S. Foster, to forget the appeals of my beloved friends, Wendell Phillips and William Lloyd Garrison, to shut their eyes to the character of the gentlemen who sit before and around me, and to go back to revolutionary times, and study the character of old John Adams, and Samuel Adams, and John Hancock, and tell me what there is in the character of these men to warrant the position which you, as citizens of Massachusetts, occupy to slavery and to this slaveholding Union at the present time. Can any man deny that, if John Adams, and Samuel Adams, and John Hancock, were alive to-day, they would, in view of the transactions in the city of Boston, demand the immediate dissolution of the Union? [Applause.] I believe in my soul they would. And why? Because they would hold in too high estimation their own liberties to submit to such outrages. I have said before, and I repeat it again, even in view of the humble position I occupy as a black man in the State of Massachusetts, I would rather be ten thousand times blacker than I am than to be the proudest pale face that walks State Street to-day, doing the bidding of the slaveholder. [Loud cheers.]

Am I asked, Mr. Chairman, why I made this rough remark? If I am, I will answer. It has become not only a part of our education, but almost part and parcel of our nature, to look upon the colored man in this country as born to the vile inheritance of slavery, from his cradle to his grave; to have the word slave written on his brow; to do the bidding of the pale face; to go and come at his call. He must not presume to imitate the white man; if he shall, away with him to Africa on the one hand, or banish him from the State on the other. But the white man, he can go to Bunker Hill, and look upon that stone which commemorates the noble deeds of his fathers; he can go to Lexington, and bow before the memory of men who fought and bled for liberty; and from that place, he can go to Cambridge, and there be educated under the most favorable auspices; and then he can come to Boston, and live on Beacon Street or Park Street, and he can go up and down the streets, and be everywhere treated with respect and honor; and when he goes upon a steamboat, the officers do not tell him he cannot have a berth to sleep in; when he goes to a hotel he is not told that that is no place for "niggers"; when he goes before a Court, he does not find that none of his own color can sit in the jury box; but every white man is presumed to be a sovereign in this country, and qualified to meet any man in the world. But where is their manhood to-day? Men are found ready to be, here, what the most contemptible man disdains to be in South Carolina or Virginia—a negro catcher. The Southerner will not perform such devilish work; but men born in Boston, and educated at Cambridge, volunteer to do it! Why? Simply because it is the custom of the times.

I ask men to throw themselves back upon their manhood; women to throw themselves back upon their womanhood, and go into the Court House,—if it must be that Anthony Burns is to be delivered up,—I do not believe that it will be necessary for any man to shoulder a musket, or carry a dagger in his bosom. Let them go there to-morrow; and then, if the victim is brought out, let some one cry out, "Rescue that man!" and I believe, as if by magic, he will be rescued. [Loud cheers.] All that is wanted is the right voice, at the right time, and in the right place, and the work will be done. In God's name, cannot that spirit be infused into the people?

Friends! God has made us men. If you will recognize us as such, we will conduct ourselves in a manner worthy your regard and protection. All we want is a fair chance; and just in proportion as this is granted will this recognition be made. I ask no man for his sympathy. I am simply asking of the majority, because we are in a minority, an opportunity to develop the faculties which the Creator has given us. I tell you, my friends, if we were equal in numbers to-morrow, we should not ask your aid; into our own hands we would take the vindication of our rights.

The friend who preceded me (Miss Wright) wanted to know what was to be done, in case the Union was dissolved,—she could not see what was to be gained by it. Sir, if the Union should be dissolved, leave this whole question with the slave population, and they will take care of it. [Applause.] It is the North that practically keeps them in slavery; and hence I say, that the work is with Boston men, with Massachusetts men, with New England men. When New England shall be right, then the work will be accomplished.

If you could only be black, friends, for eight and forty hours, how would you reason on this question? [Cheers.] Talk about the eloquence of the colored man! We should not have a chance to get up, with our poor speech, so many would be eager to occupy the platform. We should have a whole host of eloquent speakers. I met Mr. Choate in the street to-day, and having a stranger friend with me, I pointed him out to him; and I could not but think, as I passed him, that if Mr. Choate would come to this New England Convention, and speak as he is qualified to speak on this subject, and admit that he had been mistaken—mistaken long ago—it would do more to immortalize his name than all the victories he ever gained upon the public forum. [Cheers.]

I would say, in conclusion, Mr. Chairman, to our friends present, do not go away from this meeting feeling prejudiced against it, but go from here and resolve what you will do when that poor fugitive is taken away. One statement I wish to make. The reports are various respecting the proceedings in the court-room. The audience are undoubtedly every one of them aware that there has been some testimony presented to-day going to show a discrepancy in the time when the slaveholders and their counsel say Burns left Virginia and the time when he was actually seen in Boston; and I have since heard, from persons interested in that direction, that considerable confidence is felt that he will be discharged. I have heard that the man claiming to be Burns's master now offers to sell him for four hundred dollars. I hope that he will not have the privilege of taking four hundred cents. I hope that if there is a Commissioner in Boston mean enough to be willing to give up Burns, he will not be purchased: for a lesson will be read from that circumstance, which will do more to aid the cause of the three and a half millions in bonds than any purchase could do. I remember reading, when I was a boy, an account of a British general, who, many years ago, was wounded three times in a battle, yet he would not consent to be taken from his horse; but, receiving a fresh wound, he fell from his horse, and just before he expired, he heard the shout—"They fly!—they fly!" "Who fly?" he asked. "Our enemies," was the reply. "Then," said he, "I die happy." I hope that in this case we may hear the cry—"They fly!" And when we ask, "Who fly?" that we may hear the answer, "The slaveholders!" That shall be glory enough, and a shout shall go up that Massachusetts is redeemed. [Loud cheers.]

I am reminded of another report, which comes from a good source, that in the event of Commissioner Loring giving Burns his freedom, or whether he shall or not, the slaveholder and his friends have determined to carry him off in the face of the purchase money, and the remonstrances and wishes of the people. I hope, therefore, that the friends will be prepared to meet any exigency that may arise, and to vindicate the laws of eternal justice and right.

I know, Mr. Chairman, that I am not, as a general thing, a peacemaker. I am irritable, excitable, quarrelsome—I confess it, Sir, and my prayer to God is, that I may never cease to be irritable, that I may never cease to be excitable, that I may never cease to be quarrelsome, until the last slave shall be made free in our country, and the colored man's manhood acknowledged. [Loud applause.] [1]

As the situation grew still more critical before any signs of improvement were evident, orators like Remond became much more embittered against the nation and its functionaries. Not only had the holding of slaves been finally acquiesced into in the North, but the proslavery movement had opened the sores of bleeding Kansas and the Dred Scott decision had finally aligned the judiciary along with the executive and legislative departments in nationalizing slavery and depriving the Negro of all rights and considerations except the tender mercies of the wicked. In this speech of Charles Lenox Remond before the Massachusetts Antislavery Society on the 10th of July, 1857, therefore, he insisted that the only way out of the difficulty was the dissolution of the Union with slaveholders.

AN ANTI-SLAVERY DISCOURSE

By Charles Lenox Remond

Mr. President, and Ladies and Gentlemen: I hardly need inform those who are gathered together here to-day, that I take some satisfaction in responding to the kind invitation of the Committee of the Massachusetts A. S. Society, for more reasons, perhaps, than would at first appear to many who are present. We have been informed, by the gentleman who preceded our respected President (Mr. Jackson), that this is a repetition of eighty years'

[1] *Liberator*, June 23, 1854.

standing of the demonstration of the American people on the side of liberty and independence. The reason why I, above all others, take pleasure in coming to this platform, is not to exhibit, if I may so express myself, the commonplace idea of a colored man's speaking in public, nor is it the grateful associations that may appear to other minds, on another account, or for other reasons, but it is that I may have the satisfaction of saying, in a word, that I hold all demonstrations on this day, outside of the gatherings similar to the one of which we form a part, as so many mockeries and insults to a large number of our fellow-countrymen. To-day there are, on the Southern plantations, between three and four millions, to whom the popular Fourth of July in the United States of America is a most palpable insult; and to every white American who has any sympathy whatever with the oppressed, the day is also a mockery. Why, sir, I have been informed, since I came into this grove, that on this platform sit one or two men recently from Virginia, known and owned there as slaves. I ask you, Mr. Chairman, and I ask this audience, what must be the emotions of these men, who are now on their way from Virginia, through the free State of Massachusetts, to Canada, where alone they can be free, happy, or out of danger? I ask you if I say too much when I say, that to the slave, the popular Fourth of July in the United States is an insult? And hence I was glad to hear our esteemed friend, Francis Jackson, inquire if we are willing to take our places here to-day upon the glorious motto of "No Union with Slaveholders"; if we are willing to subscribe to the declaration that shall affirm our purpose to be to dissolve this slaveholding Union. [Applause.] I do not know how others may feel; I do not expect to get a hearty response to that expression; but the time is coming when a larger number than is gathered here to-day will subscribe to the idea of a dissolution of the Union as the only means of their own safety, as well as of the emancipation of the slave.

Sir, I do not care, so far as I am concerned, to view even the deeds committed by the greatest men of the Revolution, nor the purposes which they achieved. I do not care whether the statue recently erected to commemorate the deeds of Joseph Warren be deserved or not; I do not care whether the great majority of the reminiscences that cluster around the history of this day be veritable or not; I do know, in my heart, that every slave, on every plantation, has the right from his God and Creator to be free, and that is enough to warrant me in saying, that we cannot come here for a better or a nobler purpose than to help forward the effort to dissolve the American Union, because, if the Union shall be dissolved, if for no other purpose than for the emancipation of the slave, it will be glory enough for me to engage in it. [Applause.] Hence, sir, I do not feel, as many may feel today, to make an appeal over the prostrate form of some slave mother; nor do I care to repeat the sayings of some noble slave father; nor do I ask the men on my right what they have to say. I have only to speak for myself; to speak for freedom for myself; to determine for freedom for myself; and in doing so, I speak and determine for the freedom of every slave on every plantation, and for the fugitives on my right hand; and in so speaking, I speak for those before me as emphatically as I can for the blackest man that lives or suffers in our country. I subscribe, Mr. Chairman, to the remark made by our esteemed friend, Mr. Foss, in the cars, while coming here to-day; that I have not a word to say about the evils of American slavery, as they are detailed on the one hand, and retailed on the other. The time has come for us to make the ground upon which we stand to-day sacred to the cause of liberty; and when we make the ground of Framingham thus sacred, we do away with the necessity for the disgraceful underground railroad of our country, that transports such men as these fugitives to the dominions of the British Queen, in order that they may secure their inalienable rights; we do away with the dishonor that now gathers around and over the State of Massachusetts, which makes it necessary for any man or any woman to pass beyond our border before he or she can be free. Talk to me of Bunker Hill, and tell me that a fugitive passed through Boston to-day! Talk about Lexington, and tell me a slave mother must be kept secreted in Boston! Talk to me of commemorating the memory of Joseph Warren, while thirty thousand fugitive slaves are in Canada! I will scout the memory of the Revolution, the memory of Washington, and Adams, and Hancock, until the soil of Massachusetts shall be as free to every fugitive, and as free to me, as it is to the descendants of any of them. [Loud applause.] And until we shall do this, we talk in vain, and celebrate in vain.

O, sir, I long to see the day when Massachusetts, and every New England State, shall be the only Canada needful to the American slave. I see CHARLES SUMNER, on the one hand, in Europe, trying to recover from illness and physical prostration, the result of American slavery; on the other hand, I see Kansas prostrate and bleeding, the result of American slavery. Before me, I see HORACE GREELEY, kicked and cuffed in the city of Washington, as the result of slavery. I look at Massachusetts, and I see our State, as an entire State, silently acquiescing in the recent disgraceful decision given by Judge Taney in the United States Supreme Court, whereby it is declared that the black man in the United States has no rights which the white man is bound to respect! Shame on Judge Taney! Shame on the United States Supreme Court! Shame on Massachusetts, that she does not vindicate herself from the insult cast upon her through my own body, and through the body of every colored man in the State! [Loud cheers.] My God and Creator has given me rights which you are as much bound to respect as those of the whitest man among you, if I make the exhibitions of a man. And black men did make the exhibition of manhood at Bunker Hill, and Lexington, and Concord, as I can well testify. But in view of the ingratitude of the American people, in view of the baseness of such men as Judge Taney, in view of the dough-face character that degrades our State, I regret exceedingly that there is one single drop of blood in my own veins that mingle with the blood of the men who engaged in the strife on Bunker Hill and at Lexington. Better that any such man had folded his hands and crossed his knees, during the American Revolution, if this is the reward we are to derive from such hypocrites, such cowards, such panders to American slavery, as Judge Taney and his co-operators.

Mr. Chairman, I will not dwell upon this theme. I am not the man to speak to a white audience on the Fourth of July. I am reminded by everything over me, beneath me, and all around me, of my shame and degradation; and I shall take my seat on this occasion by stating to every white man present, who does not feel that the time has come when the rights of the colored man should be restored to him, that I am among the number who would embrace this day, this moment, to strike the last fetter from the limbs of the last slave, if it were in my power to do so, and leave the consequences to those at whose instigation it has been fastened upon them.

I look around the country, and behold one other demonstration, and with the mention of that, I shall take my seat. During the last year, not a few exhibitions have been made, in various parts of our country, of the purposes of American slavery the year to come; but there was no stronger demonstration than that made during the late Presidential canvass by the American people; and whatever may have been said prior to that time of the general sentiment of our country, the election of James Buchanan to the Presidency has placed that question beyond doubt and cavil, and has determined that the American people, by an overwhelming majority, are on the side of slavery, with all its infernalism. Now, sir, it belongs to the true friends who are present to go forward, determined that this state of things shall be altered, and it can only be altered by the largest application and the freest promulgation of the doctrine set forth by the American and Massachusetts Anti-Slavery Societies. I am glad, therefore, to utter my testimony from a platform where they are represented; and let me say, friends, whether you believe it or not, that if the cause of universal liberty shall ever be established in our country, within our day and generation, it can only be by the promulgation to the country of the most radical type of Anti-Slavery, known as the "Garrison doctrine." [Applause.] [1]

To justify the wisdom of revolution, not a few Negro orators boldly lauded Toussaint Louverture, whose efforts in stirring up the slaves in Haiti to kill off their masters and establish the independence of that country had, for years, caused the American slaveholders to live in eternal dread of servile insurrection. In the following oration by James Theodore Holly, delivered in 1857, one observes, not only the expected eulogies, but a vindication of the capacity of the Negro for self-government and civilized progress as demonstrated by historical events of the Haitian revolution and the subsequent acts of the people after their national independence.

[1] *Liberator,* July 10, 1857.

THE AUSPICIOUS DAWN OF NEGRO RULE

By Theodore Holly

Toussaint, by his acute genius and daring prowess, made himself the most efficient instrument in accomplishing these important results, contemplated by the three French Commissioners, who brought the last decrees of the National Assembly of France, proclaiming liberty throughout the island to all the inhabitants thereof; and thus, like another Washington, proved himself the regenerator and savior of his country.

On this account, therefore, he was solemnly invested with the executive authority of the colony; and their labors having been thus brought to such a satisfactory and auspicious result, two of the Commissioners returned home to France.

No man was more competent to sway the civil destinies of these enfranchised bondmen than he who had preserved such an unbounded control over them as their military chieftain, and led them on to glorious deeds amid the fortunes of warfare recently waged in that island. And no one else could hold that responsible position of an official mediator between them and the government of France, with so great a surety and pledge of their continued freedom, as Toussaint L'Ouverture. And there was no other man, in fine, that these rightfully jealous freemen would have permitted to carry out such stringent measures in the island, so nearly verging to serfdom, which were so necessary at that time in order to restore industry, but one of their own caste whose unreserved devotion to the cause of their freedom placed him beyond the suspicion of any treacherous design to re-enslave them.

Hence, by these eminent characteristics possessed by Toussaint in a super-excellent degree, he was the very man for the hour; and the only one fitted for the governorship of the colony calculated to preserve the interests of all concerned.

The leading Commissioners of France, then in the island, duly recognized this fact, and did not dispute with him the claim to this responsible position. Thus had the genius of Toussaint developed itself to meet an emergency that no other man in the world was so peculiarly prepared to fulfil; and thereby he has added another inextinguishable proof of the capacity of the Negro for self-government.

But if the combination of causes, which thus pointed him out as the only man that could safely undertake the fulfillment of the gubernatorial duties, are such manifest proofs of Negro capacity; then the manner in which we shall see that he afterwards discharged the duties of that official station, goes still further to magnify the self-evident fact of Negro capability.

The means that he adapted to heal the internecine dissensions that threatened civil turmoil; and the manner that he successfully counteracted the machinations of the ambitious General Hedouville, a French Commissioner that remained in the colony, who desired to overthrow Toussaint, showed that the Negro chieftain was no novice in the secret of government.

He also established commercial relations between that island and foreign nations; and he is said to be the first statesman of modern times who promulgated the doctrine of free trade and reduced it to practice. He also desired to secure a constitutional government to St. Domingo, and for this purpose he assembled around him a select council of the most eminent men in the colony, who drew up a form of constitution under his supervision and approval, and which he transmitted, with a commendatory letter to Napoleon Bonaparte, then First Consul of France, in order to obtain the sanction of the imperial government.

But that great bad man did not even acknowledge its receipt to Toussaint; but in his mad ambition he silently meditated when he should safely dislodge the Negro chief from his responsible position, as the necessary prelude to the re-enslavement of his sable brethren, whose freedom was secure against his nefarious designs, so long as Toussaint stood at the helm of affairs in the colony.

But decidedly the crowning act of Toussaint Louverture's statesmanship was the enactment of the Rural Code, by the operation of which he was successful in restoring industrial prosperity to the island, which had been sadly ruined by the late events of sanguinary warfare. He effectually solved the problem of immediate emancipation and unimpaired industry, by having the emancipated slaves produce thereafter as much of the usual staple productions of the country as was produced under the horrible regime of slavery; nevertheless, the lash was entirely abolished, and a system of wages adopted, instead of the uncompensated toil of the lacerated and delving bondman. In fact, the island reached the highest degree of prosperity that it ever attained under the Negro governorship of Toussaint.

The rural code, by which so much was accomplished, instead of being the horrible nightmare of despotism—worse than slavery, that some of the pro-slavery calumniators of Negro freedom and rule would have us believe; was, in fact, nothing more than a prudent government regulation of labor—a regulation which made labor the first necessity of a people in a state of freedom,—a regulation which struck a death blow at idleness, the parent of poverty and all the vices—a regulation, in fine, which might be adopted with advantage in every civilized country in the world, and thereby extinguish two-thirds of the pauperism, vagrancy and crime, that curse these nations of the earth—and thus lessen the need for poorhouses, police officers, and prisons, that are now sustained at such an enormous expense, for the relief of the poor and the correction of felons.

This Haytian Code compelled every vagabond or loafer about the towns and cities, who had no visible means of an honest livelihood, to find an employer and work to do in the rural districts. And if no private employer could be found, then the government employed such on its rural estates, until they had found a private employer. The hours and days of labor were prescribed by this code, and the terms of agreement and compensation between employer and employed were also determined by its provisions. Thus, there could be no private imposition on the laborers; and, as a further security against such a spirit, the government maintained rural magistrates and a rural police, whose duty it was to see to the faithful execution of the law on both sides.

By the arrangement of this excellent and celebrated code everybody in the commonwealth was sure of work and compensation for the same, either from private employers or from the government. Nobody needed to fear being starved for want of work to support himself, as is often the case among the laborers of Europe, and is fast coming to pass in the densely populated communities of this country, where labor is left to take care of itself under the private exploitation of mercenary capitalists. Under this code nobody needed to fear being exploited on by such unprincipled and usurious men, who willingly take advantage of the poor to pay them starvation prices for their labor; because, against such, the law of Toussaint secured to each laborer a living compensation.

By the operation of this code, towns and cities were cleared of all those idle persons who calculate to live by their wits, and who commit nine-tenths of all the crimes that afflict civilized society. All such were compelled to be engaged at active industrial labors, and thus rendered a help to themselves and a blessing to the community at large.

By this industrial regulation, everything flourished in the island in an unprecedented degree; and the Negro genius of Toussaint, by a bold and straight-forward provision for the regulation and protection of his emancipated brethren, effected that high degree of prosperity in Hayti, which all the wisdom of the British nation has not been able to accomplish in her emancipated West India colonies, in consequence of her miserable shuffling in establishing Coolie and Chinese apprenticeship—that semi-system of slavery—in order to gratify the prejudices of her pro-slavery colonial planters; and because of the baneful influence of absentee landlordism, which seems to be an inseparable incident of the British system of property.

Thus did the Negro government of St. Domingo show more paternal solicitude for the well being of her free citizens than they ever could have enjoyed under the capricious despotism of individual masters who might pretend to care for them; and thus did it more truly subserve the purposes of a government than any or all of the similar organizations of civilization, whose only care and object seem to be the protection of the feudal rights of property in the hands of the wealthy few; leaving the honest labor of the many unprotected, and the poor laborer left to starve, or to become a criminal, to be punished either by incarceration in the jails, prisons and dungeons provided for common felons; or executed on the gallows as the greatest of malefactors.

The genius of Toussaint by towering so far above the common ideas of this age in relation to the true purposes of government; and by carrying out his bold problem with such eminent success, has thereby emblazoned on the historic page of the world's statesmanship a fame more enduring than Pitt, who laid the foundation of a perpetual fund to liquidate the national debt of England.

I say Toussaint has carved for himself a more enduring fame, because his scheme was more useful to mankind. The Negro, statesman devised a plan that comprehended in its scope the well being of the masses of humanity. But Pitt only laid a scheme whereby the few hereditary paupers pensioned on a whole nation, with the absurd right to govern it, might still continue to plunge their country deeper and deeper into debt, to subserve their own extravagant purposes; and then provide for the payment of the same out of the blood and sweat, and bones of the delving operatives and colliers of Great Britain. Thus, Toussaint by the evident superiority of his statesmanship has left on the pages of the world's statute book an enduring and irrefutable testimony of the capacity of the Negro for self-government and the loftiest achievements in national statesmanship.

And Toussaint showed that he had not mistaken his position by proving himself equal to that trying emergency when that demigod of the historian Abbott, Napoleon Bonaparte, First Consul of France, conceived the infernal design of re-enslaving the heroic blacks of St. Domingo; and who for the execution of this nefarious purpose sent the flower of the French Army, and a naval fleet of fifty-six vessels, under command of General Leclerc, the husband of Pauline, the voluptuous and abandoned sister of Napoleon.

When this formidable expedition arrived on the coast of St. Domingo, the Commander found Toussaint and his heroic compeers ready to defend their God-given liberty against even the terrors of the godless First Consul of France. Wheresoever these minions of slavery and despotism made their sacrilegious advances. devastation and death reigned under the exasperated genius of Toussaint.

He made that bold resolution and unalterable determination which, in ancient times, would have entitled him to be deified among the gods; that resolution was to reduce the fair Eden-like Isle of Hispaniola to a desolate waste like Sahara; and suffer every black to be immolated in a manly defense of his liberty, rather than the infernal and accursed system of Negro slavery should again be established on that soil. He considered it far better that his sable countrymen should be DEAD FREEMEN THAN LIVING SLAVES.[1]

Emerging from this chaos of conflicting opinions in counteracting the efforts of the rebellion, the friends of freedom

[1] Holley, *The Auspicious Dawn of Negro Rule.*

found themselves inevitably directed to Frederick Douglass for advice as to the part his race should play in this upheaval. Douglass early advocated the enlistment of Negroes and slaves in the ranks as soldiers rather than as servants for the officers in the army. Driven to the position of employing all means of rehabilitating the Union armies decimated by the militant Confederacy, the Federal Government finally decided to adopt this policy. The following speeches show the mind of the great man and how he functioned at this critical time in the history of the nation.

A UNION SPEECH

By Frederick Douglass

Mr. President and Fellow-Citizens: I shall not attempt to follow Judge Kelley and Miss Dickinson in their eloquent and thrilling appeals to colored men to enlist in the service of the United States. They have left nothing to be desired on that point. I propose to look at the subject in a plain and practical common-sense light. There are obviously two views to be taken of such enlistments—a broad view and a narrow view. I am willing to take both, and consider both. The narrow view of this subject is that which respects the matter of dollars and cents. There are those among us who say they are in favor of taking a hand in the tremendous war, but they add they wish to do so on terms of equality with white men. They say if they enter the service, endure all hardships, perils and suffering—if they make bare their breasts, and with strong arms and courageous hearts confront rebel cannons, and wring victory from the jaws of death, they should have the same pay, the same rations, the same bounty, and the same favorable conditions every way afforded to other men.

I shall not oppose this view. There is something deep down in the soul of every man present which assents to the justice of the claim thus made, and honors the manhood and self-respect which insists upon it. [Applause.] I say at once, in peace and in war, I am content with nothing for the black man short of equal and exact justice. The only question I have, and the point at which I differ from those who refuse to enlist, is whether the colored man is more likely to obtain justice and equality while refusing to assist in putting down this tremendous rebellion than he would be if he should promptly, generously and earnestly give his hand and heart to the salvation of the country in this its day of calamity and peril. Nothing can be more plain, nothing more certain than that the speediest and best possible way open to us to manhood, equal rights and elevation, is that we enter this service. For my own part, I hold that if the Government of the United States offered nothing more, as an inducement to colored men to enlist, than bare subsistence and arms, considering the moral effect of compliance upon ourselves, it would be the wisest and best thing for us to enlist. [Applause.] There is something ennobling in the possession of arms, and we of all other people in the world stand in need of their ennobling influence.

The case presented in the present war, and the light in which every colored man is bound to view it, may be stated thus. There are two governments struggling now for the possession of and endeavoring to bear rule over the United States—one has its capital in Richmond, and is represented by Mr. Jefferson Davis, and the other has its capital at Washington, and is represented by "Honest Old Abe." [Cheers and long-continued applause.] These two governments are to-day face to face, confronting each other with vast armies, and grappling each other upon many a bloody field, North and South, on the banks of the Mississippi, and under the shadows of the Alleghenies. Now, the question for every colored man is, or ought to be, what attitude is assumed by these respective governments and armies towards the rights and liberties of the colored race in this country; which is for us, and which against us! [Cries of, "That's the question."]

Now, I think there can be no doubt as to the attitude of the Richmond or Confederate Government. Wherever else there has been concealment, here all is frank, open, and diabolically straightforward. Jefferson Davis and his government make no secret as to the cause of this war, and they do not conceal the purpose of the war. That purpose is nothing more or less than to make the slavery of the African race universal and perpetual on this continent. It is not only evident from the history and logic of events, but the declared purpose of the atrocious war now being waged against the country. Some, indeed, have denied that slavery has anything to do with the war, but the very same men who do this affirm it in the same breath in which they deny it, for they tell you that the abolitionists are the cause of the war. Now, if the abolitionists are the cause of the war, they are the cause of it only because they have sought the abolition of slavery. View it in any way you please, therefore, the rebels are fighting for the existence of slavery—they are fighting for the privilege, and horrid privilege, of sundering the dearest ties of human nature—of trafficking in slaves and the souls of men—for the ghastly privilege of scourging women and selling innocent children. [Cries of, "That's true."]

I say this is not the concealed object of the war, but the openly confessed and shamelessly proclaimed object of the war. Vice-President Stephens has stated, with the utmost clearness and precision, the difference between the fundamental ideas of the Confederate Government and those of the Federal Government. One is based upon the idea that colored men are an inferior race, who may be enslaved and plundered forever and to the heart's content of any men of a different complexion, while the Federal Government recognizes the natural and fundamental equality of all men. [Applause.]

I say, again, we all know that this Jefferson Davis government holds out to us nothing but fetters, chains, auction-blocks, bludgeons, branding-irons, and eternal slavery and degradation. If it triumphs in this contest, woe, woe, ten thousand woes, to the black man! Such of us as are free, in all the likelihoods of the case, would be given over to the most excruciating tortures, while the last hope of the long-crushed bondman would be extinguished forever. [Sensation.]

Now, what is the attitude of the Washington government towards the colored race? What reasons have we to desire its triumph in the present contest? Mind, I do not ask what was its attitude towards us before this bloody rebellion broke out. I do not ask what was its disposition when it was controlled by the very men who are now fighting to destroy it when they could no longer control it. I do not even ask what it was two years ago, when McClellan shamelessly gave out that in a war between loyal slaves and disloyal masters, he would take the side of the masters against the slaves—when he openly proclaimed his purpose to put down slave insurrections with an iron hand—when glorious Ben. Butler [Cheers and applause], now stunned into a conversion to anti-slavery principles (which I have every reason to believe sincere), proffered his services to the Governor of Maryland, to suppress a slave insurrection, while treason ran riot in that State, and the warm, red blood of Massachusetts soldiers still stained the pavements of Baltimore.

I do not ask what was the attitude of this government when many of the officers and men who had undertaken to defend it openly threatened to throw down their arms and leave the service if men of color should step forward to defend it, and be invested with the dignity of soldiers. Moreover, I do not ask what was the position of this government when our loyal camps were made slave-hunting grounds, and United States officers performed the disgusting duty of slave dogs to hunt down slaves for rebel masters. These were all the dark and terrible days for the republic. I do not ask you about the dead past. I bring you to the living present. Events more mighty than men, eternal Providence, all-wise and all-controlling, have placed us in new relations to the government and the government to us. What that government is to us to-day, and what it will be to-morrow, is made evident by a very few facts. Look at them, colored men. Slavery in the District of Columbia is abolished forever; slavery in all the territories of the United States is abolished forever; the foreign slave trade, with its ten thousand revolting abominations, is rendered impossible; slavery in ten States of the Union is abolished forever; slavery in the five remaining States is as certain to follow the same fate as the night is to follow the day. The independence of Hayti is recognized; her Minister sits beside our Prime Minister, Mr. Seward, and dines at his table in Washington, while colored men are excluded from the cars in Philadelphia; showing that a black man's complexion in Washington, in the presence of the Federal Government, is less offensive than in the city of brotherly love. Citizenship is no longer denied us under this government.

Under the interpretation of our rights by Attorney General Bates, we are American citizens. We can import goods, own and sail ships, and travel in foreign countries with American passports in our pockets; and now, so far from there being any opposition, so far from excluding us from the army as soldiers, the President at Washington, the Cabinet and the Congress, the generals commanding and the whole army of the nation unite in giving us one thunderous welcome to share with them in the honor and glory of suppressing treason and upholding the star-spangled banner. The revolution is tremendous, and it becomes us as wise men to recognize the change, and to shape our action accordingly. [Cheers and cries of, "We will."]

I hold that the Federal Government was never, in its essence, anything but an antislavery government. Abolish slavery tomorrow, and not a sentence or syllable of the Constitution need be altered. It was purposely so framed so to give no claim, no sanction to the claim of property in man. If in its origin slavery had any relation to the government, it was only as the scaffolding to the magnificent structure, to be removed as soon as the building was completed. There is in the Constitution no East, no West, no North, no South, no black, no white, no slave, no slaveholder, but all are citizens who are of American birth.

Such is the government, fellow-citizens, you are now called upon to uphold with your arms. Such is the government that you are called upon to co-operate with in burying rebellion and slavery in a common grave. [Applause.] Never since the world began was a better chance offered to a long enslaved and oppressed people. The opportunity is given us to be men. With one courageous resolution we may blot out the hand-writing of ages against us. Once let the black man get upon his person the brass letters U. S.; let him get an eagle on his button, and a musket on his shoulder, and bullets in his pocket, and there is no power on the earth or under the earth which can deny that he has earned the right of citizenship in the United States. [Laughter and applause.] I say again, this is our chance, and woe betide us if we fail to embrace it. The immortal bard hath told us:

> "There is a tide in the affairs of men,
> Which, taken at the flood, leads on to fortune.
> Omitted, all the voyage of their life
> Is bound in shallows and in miseries.
> We must take the current when it serves,
> Or lose our ventures."

Do not flatter yourselves, my friends, that you are more important to the government than the government is to you. You stand but as the plank to the ship. This rebellion can be put down without your help. Slavery can be abolished by white men; but liberty so won for the black man, while it may leave him an object of pity, can never make him an object of respect.

Depend upon it, this is no time for hesitation. Do you say you want the same pay that white men get? I believe that the justice and magnanimity of your country will speedily grant it. But will you be overnice about this matter? Do you get as good wages now as white men get by staying out of the service? Don't you work for less every day than white men get? You know you do. Do I hear you say you want black officers? Very well, and I have not the slightest doubt that in the progress of this war we shall see black officers, black colonels, and generals even. But is it not ridiculous in us in all at once refusing to be commanded by white men in time of war, when we are everywhere commanded by white men in time of peace? Do I hear you say still that you are a son, and want your mother provided for in your absence?—a husband, and want your wife cared for?—a brother, and want your sister secured against want? I honor you for your solicitude. Your mothers, your wives, and your sisters ought to be cared for, and an association of gentlemen, composed of responsible white and colored men, is now being organized in this city for this very purpose.

Do I hear you say you offered your services to Pennsylvania and were refused? I know it. But what of that? The State is not more than the nation. The greater includes the lesser. Because the State refuses, you should all the more readily turn to the United States. [Applause.] When the children fall out, they should refer their quarrel to the parent. "You came unto your own, and your own received you not." But the broad gates of the United States stand open night and day. Citizenship in the United States will, in the end, secure your citizenship in the State.

Young men of Philadelphia, you are without excuse. The hour has arrived, and your place is in the Union army. Remember that the musket—the United States musket with its bayonet of steel—is better than all mere parchment guarantees of liberty. In your hands that musket means liberty; and should your constitutional right at the close of this war be denied, which, in the nature of things, it cannot be, your brethren are safe while you have a Constitution which proclaims your right to keep and bear arms. [Immense cheering.]

"MEN OF COLOR, TO ARMS!"

BY FREDERICK DOUGLASS

When first the rebel cannon shattered the walls of Sumter and drove away its starving garrison, I predicted that the war then and there inaugurated would not be fought out entirely by white men. Every month's experience during these dreary years has confirmed that opinion. A war undertaken and brazenly carried on for the perpetual enslavement of colored men, calls logically and loudly for colored men to help suppress it. Only a moderate share of sagacity was needed to see that the arm of the slave was the best defense against the arm of the slaveholder. Hence with every reverse to the national arms, with every exulting shout of victory raised by the slaveholding rebels, I have implored the imperiled nation to unchain against her foes, her powerful black hand. Slowly and reluctantly that appeal is beginning to be heeded. Stop not now to complain that it was not heeded sooner. It may or it may not have been best that it should not. This is not the time to discuss that question. Leave it to the future. When the war is over, the country is saved, peace is established, and the black man's rights are secured, as they will be, history with an impartial hand will dispose of that and sundry other questions. Action! Action! not criticism, is the plain duty of this hour. Words are now useful only as they stimulate to blows. The office of speech now is only to point out when, where, and how to strike to the best advantage. There is no time to delay. The tide is at its flood that leads on to fortune. From East to West, from North to South, the sky is written all over, "Now or never." Liberty won by white men would lose half its luster. "Who would be free themselves must strike the blow." "Better even die free, than to live slaves." This is the sentiment of every brave colored man amongst us. There are weak and cowardly men in all nations. We have them amongst us. They tell you this is the "white man's war"; that you will be no "better off after than before the war;"

that the getting of you into the army is to "sacrifice you on the first opportunity." Believe them not; cowards themselves, they do not wish to have their cowardice shamed by your brave example. Leave them to their timidity, or to whatever motive may hold them back. I have not thought lightly of the words I am now addressing you. The counsel I give comes of close observation of the great struggle now in progress, and of the deep conviction that this is your hour and mine. In good earnest then, and after the best deliberation, I now for the first time during this war feel at liberty to call and counsel you to arms. By every consideration which binds you to your enslaved fellow-countrymen, and the peace and welfare of your country; by every aspiration which you cherish for the freedom and equality of yourselves and your children; by all the ties of blood and identity which make us one with the brave black men now fighting our battles in Louisiana and in South Carolina, I urge you to fly to arms, and smite with death the power that would bury the government and your liberty in the same hopeless grave. I wish I could tell you that the State of New York calls you to this high honor. For the moment her constituted authorities are silent on the subject. They will speak by and by, and doubtless on the right side; but we are not compelled to wait for her. We can get at the throat of treason and slavery through the State of Massachusetts. She was first in the War of Independence; first to break the chains of her slaves; first to make the black man equal before the law; first to admit colored children to her common schools, and she was first to answer with her blood the alarm cry of the nation, when its capital was menaced by rebels. You know her patriotic governor, and you know Charles Sumner. I need not add more.

Massachusetts now welcomes you to arms as soldiers. She has but a small colored population from which to recruit. She has full leave of the general government to send one regiment to the war, and she has undertaken to do it. Go quickly and help fill up the first colored regiment from the North. I am authorized to assure you that you will receive the same wages, the same rations, the same equipments, the same protection, the same treatment, and the same bounty, secured to the white soldiers. You will be led by able and skillful officers, men who will take especial pride in your efficiency and success. They will be quick to accord to you all the honor you shall merit by your valor, and see that your rights and feelings are respected by other soldiers. I have assured myself on these points, and can speak with authority. More than twenty years of unswerving devotion to our common cause may give me some humble claim to be trusted at this momentous crisis. I will not argue. To do so implies hesitation and doubt, and you do not hesitate. You do not doubt. The day dawns; the morning star is bright upon the horizon! The iron gate of our prison stands half open. One gallant rush from the North will fling it wide open, while four millions of our brothers and sisters shall march out into liberty. The chance is now given you to end in a day the bondage of centuries, and to rise in one bound from social degradation to the plane of common equality with all other varieties of men. Remember Denmark Vesey of Charleston; remember Nathaniel Turner of Southampton; remember Shields Green and Copeland, who followed noble John Brown, and fell as glorious martyrs for the cause of the slave. Remember that in a contest with oppression, the Almighty has no attribute which can take sides with oppressors. The case is before you. This is our golden opportunity. Let us accept it, and forever wipe out the dark reproaches unsparingly hurled against us by our enemies. Let us win for ourselves the gratitude of our country, and the best blessings of our posterity through all time. The nucleus of this first regiment is now in camp at Readville, a short distance from Boston. I will undertake to forward to Boston all persons adjudged fit to be mustered into the regiment, who shall apply to me at any time within the next two weeks.[1]

In the midst of the fighting of the Civil War and immediately thereafter the freedmen faced the problem of economic adjustment and education. How they dealt with this situation is eloquently presented by Dr. J. Sella Martin,[2]

[1] Rochester, March 2, 1863, *Life and Times of Frederick Douglass*, pp. 344-346.

[2] John Sella Martin was born in Charlotte, North Carolina. He was a slave of a master who sold him when he was just a child. He spent a part of his life in Georgia, from which he escaped in 1856. He then resided some time in Chicago, studied for the ministry at Detroit, and took charge of a church at Buffalo. He first attracted attention when he came to Boston and was introduced to the public at Tremont Temple by Rev. M. Kalloch, for whom he preached several weeks during the latter's vacation. After supplying the pulpit for some time at Lawrence, he took charge of the Joy Street Baptist Church in Boston. He preached thereafter in churches in New York, Washington, and then engaged in politics. He was for a time the editor of the *National Era*, a position in which he

addressing the Antislavery Conference held in Paris on August 26 and 27, 1867.

A SPEECH BEFORE THE PARIS ANTISLAVERY CONFERENCE, AUGUST 27, 1867

By J. Sella Martin

Mr. President, Ladies and Gentlemen: Mr. Garrison justly rejoices that the statute-books of his country have been cleansed from the thousand clauses that sanctioned its greatest crime and curse; and even I, as a Negro, can rejoice with him that it is not now as it formerly was, when every white man who escaped persecution did so by carrying a lie in his right hand. Looking at the results of emancipation from the standpoint of a white man, there are many things to make the flush of triumph deepen into a blush of shame.

The Negroes are free as to their chains, but everywhere their prospects are darkened by prejudice and proscription, which Fred Douglass forcibly calls the shadow of Slavery. And this fact shows how deeply corrupted the Americans were by that system which they deliberately made their own, in defiance of every claim of justice for those who helped them to win the battle of national independence, and who, in their generous confidence, came again to the rescue when these same breakers of faith were sinking in the waters of strife upon which they had so confidently entered at the beginning of the late war. There is, nevertheless, a hopeful sign about the present state of things, and that is, that even those who used to vilify the Negro are now beginning to apologize for his present state. Yet I undertake to say that the Negro needs no apology. What is the Negro? Why, the popular notion is that he is a coward. Yet he has proved that he will fight, though for one I have no high eulogy to pass upon him for doing that which is the last resort of a cur that cannot run away. I know the whites have another measurement for brute force. While the Negro behaved like a Christian—like the old English slaves who waited

evinced considerable literary ability. In person, he was of mixed blood, gentlemanly in his appearance and refined in his manner. He was one of the most eloquent men of his time. He visited England three times. He also traveled in other countries; and he was in Paris when he delivered the address given in this work.

for the advance of civilization to gradually melt rather than to break their chains—the whites called him a brute, too degraded to wish for freedom or try to win it. But as soon as he began to act like a brute and to revel in the dreadful orgies of war, then they called him a man. Wendell Phillips truly says that the Negro race is the only one in history which, unaided, broke its chains of bondage. I do not know what gradual emancipation would have brought with it. It is claimed that it would have brought a great deal; preparation for freedom to both master and slave; that it would have prevented the dreadful spectacles which the destitution and starvation, during this transition period of the freedmen, have called for the pity and aid of the world. But I know this: we did not get gradual emancipation, and that the slaveholders refused to have it; and I know, also, that such emancipation as the Negro has got was won partly by his wisdom in waiting till those who had united in oppressing him got too far apart even to join their weapons in putting down a Negro insurrection, and partly by a bravery equal to his brethren of St. Domingo. When events justified the Negro in joining the contest, his ready submission to discipline, his fidelity in helping those who, through necessity only, had become his friends, and his willing assault upon strongholds in which he had to walk over hidden torpedoes, which was considered rather hard walking for white men, made him a place in history that needs no apology. Whatever, therefore, may be the value of physical courage, he is entitled to it.

The Negro, too, is a man that will work. Wise men would have excused him if the first days of his freedom had been spent in visiting the cities which slavery never allowed him to see. Had he feasted his eyes upon the fine things—for which, it is said, he has a taste—displayed in the shop windows, he would have followed very elegant examples. There would have been no wonder in his desire and effort to leave a form of labour which suggested even the most painful reminiscences of murdered kindred, ruined wives and daughters, and degrading submission. And yet whenever they could get work the majority have remained to do it. When they could get paid for their work they have worked to profit; and when they have made money, they have learned to save it. Nobody with any sense denies that there may be a large number of lazy Negroes who will not work; the carrion from which the vultures of the pro-Slavery press get their food; and it would be a sad thing for commerce if there were no lazy Negroes, for the race would have to be removed from the American Continent and the cultivation of cotton, for fear of being corrupted into laziness and vagabondage by the too numerous examples of the white race. But this I do contend for: that for a people ignorant of the laws of contract, and beneath the general stimulus to industry which long habit of enterprise, and long enjoyment of the fruits of labour bring for them, to rise from the conditions of bondage, and without any system of constraint, under great uncertainty of getting paid, cheated by those whom they often take at first for their best friends—for such a people to give the world from their industry, in four years after the unparalleled devastation of the late war, within two-thirds the amount of cotton it got before the war began, is to prove beyond question their capacity and willingness to work. Why, Sir, on the Sea Islands, one year's labour by a few thousand freedmen gave the United States Government, which employed them, 1,000,120 francs' profit, and three years of labour made the Negroes the largest purchasers of the abandoned lands which were sold for unpaid taxes on these very islands, where, only two years before, they were held as slaves.

The Negro will learn. He has been denied the capacity for it; and in cases where the falsehood could not be dodged, as it could not in the case of Toussaint and Christophe, the pure Negro rulers of Hayti, it has been contended that they were exceptions. As though anybody took Lord Brougham, or the Emperor Napoleon, or Longfellow, Bryant and Beecher, as the rule among the white race as to capacity. Cannot they learn? Why, sir, one of the meanest men I ever saw was a black man; he was a Negro slaveholder, and he kept only the company of white men. The simple fact is this; prejudice and proscription in free society during the time of slavery kept the white people away from the Negroes, so that they knew, and still know, but little of colored people; and the slaveholder, though knowing better, found it to his interest to keep his knowledge to himself; or else it would have been known, that in New York and Boston, in New Orleans and Mobile, there are to be found some of the most accomplished colored men and women to be found anywhere, some of them of such unmixed African blood that they cannot be robbed of their virtues and attainments by that Anglo-Saxon pride of race which believes in no blood it has not corrupted by the vices of amalgamation.

But a new phase—many new phases of Negro capacity are being developed by the opportunities of this transition state of the freedmen, and by the efforts of the various Freedmen's Societies.

Take my own society, for instance—the American Missionary Association—for which I am one of the delegation at this conference along with the Rev. J. A. Thome. This Association, organized more than thirty years ago to fight against the foul and anti-Christian dogmas and practices of slavery, and supported by the self-sacrificing efforts of such men as Lewis and Arthur Tappan, was the first to begin the work of education among the freedmen. Its first year's work, after the breaking out of the war, did not bring more than fifty or sixty teachers into the field, because the freedmen could not be got at. But as the South could be reached, so eager was the rush of slaves to learn, that the resources of the Government were inadequate to furnish houses and tents to teach them in. And those who mistook this real thirst after knowledge for mere curiosity in the slave to find out what his master feared in a book, have been undeceived by the increasing number of scholars from week to week, and from year to year, as well as by the regularity and punctuality of their attendance, and the progress they make in their studies. The American Missionary Association has in the field nearly 500 teachers, who teach not less than 150,000 scholars. And from every one of them we have the strongest testimony of the most uniform character, that the Negroes, old and young, are eager and apt scholars, and that a great many of them are endowed with most extraordinary natural powers. Whatever the philanthropy of a country may do, governments are made up of elements too neutralizing to each other for them to be carried away by mere sentiment. Hood got off the satire that the abolitionists had tried to wash the Negroes white, and, failing that, they were going to gild them. But governments have no such temptation, and it must be taken as the best of all proofs of Negro capacity, that the Freedmen's Bureau of Washington has gone on from year to year, spending its 25,000,000 of francs per annum in aid of the Freedmen, much of which goes towards education.

The Negro can be elevated. He has a moral nature that shrinks from bloodshed, and his imitative power is the chief feature of difference between him and the race which has perished from its own native soil, because the instinct of revenge could never be subdued in it; no excuse for the white race, whose every act of intercourse with the poor red men has been as treacherous and as bloody as the policy and code of these poor savages. The Negro is a lover of family and home and some of the most touching records of this transition state are to be found in the efforts of husbands to find the wives, and wives their husbands, that slavery tore from them, and for parents to find their children, and children their parents. There is to be added to this unselfishness to high moral and social characteristics his love of religion. It may be true that he is, in this respect, peculiarly endowed, or it may be simply, that in being denied access to the family hearth, and in being driven away from the seat of justice and the altar of the Lord, he has contracted a deep religious trust, by having to make an appeal from these unfaithful exponents of Christianity to the author of Christianity Himself. Whatever may be the cause, the effect is, that wherever there are to be found a dozen Negroes together you will get a prayer-meeting. Now the Association that I represent recognises this fact, and believing not only that the fact ought to be turned to account in getting the confidence of these people, but, believing also, that those evangelical principles which have made the English-speaking race what it is, wherever on the globe it may be, are destined to go on subduing the world to the author of those principles, though empires fall and races decay, till the whole world shall be filled with the knowledge of the Lord, they have been true to their convictions, while adopting the wisest policy in sending the Bible along with the spelling book. Mr. Garrison says his Society is the largest non-ecclesiastical Freedmen's Aid Society in America. The term ecclesiastical we do not accept, because we are supported by, and employ in, our work, members of every evangelical sect. But the term "religious but non-sectarian" we can and do accept. We are not unmindful of the advantages to the world that are to grow out of the civilization and Christianization of the Freedmen in commercial, social and political points of view. Europe and the north will get better cotton and more of it from free men than they did from slaves, and the corresponding increase of their export trade to clothe and satisfy these people, whose daughters must dress, and whose wives will demand luxuries, will not be the least of their gains. We know that a people who can defy the semi-tropical climate of the Southern States, and who possess the secret of the culture of that staple in which the whole world takes such an interest, if they are once educated will put the supply of cotton on a basis of permanency that no white laborers can put it upon for many generations; and we know, too, if the Negro is educated and made prosperous that he must be the main link of binding the South to the North. His gratitude for his freedom and his love of home and country, along with his love of peace, guarantees permanency in our political relations to the South, more surely than would a colony of New Englanders. But, Sir, above all these considerations with us, there arises this one, that a civilized and converted population of Africans in America means the civilization, in no very distant day, of Africa itself. England and France spend every year their millions to maintain squadrons on the coast of Africa, but the slave-trade still goes on. The whole civilized world has sent missionaries to Christianize the Africans, and but little headway has been made in the work, because of the deadly nature of the climate to the white. But if our labors are aided, as they ought to be, by the good people of every country, we shall send educated Christian coloured men from America proof against the deadly diseases of the climate, possessing a claim to the confidence of the natives in sameness of complexion, and carrying the principles of truth against those of error to an ardent-natured people, with natures of their own as ardent to dry up the fountain-head of the slave-trade, and so stop the stream for ever, and to attack superstition with the strongest weapon next to truth itself—the ability to live where it prevails, and to command the confidence and sympathy of the natives.[1]

[1] *Special Report of the Anti-Slavery Conference held in Paris on the 26th and 27th of August 1867*, pp. 49-52.

CHAPTER VII

DELIBERATIVE ORATORY—SPEECHES OF NEGRO CONGRESSMEN

Negro spokesmen considered in connection with the status of the race, as it has been said above, have not generally figured in deliberative oratory. As this style of oratory, however, is not restricted altogether to that of the assembly, a large number of the speeches of Negroes may be thus classified. Some authorities in this field thus designate any speech before a number of people who listen as judges, when the object of the speaker is to induce his hearers to accept or reject a given policy for the future. In their struggles against the evils of caste, the Negro spokesmen have been compelled to devote most of their time to this very sort of effort.

During the reconstruction, however, a few Negroes had the opportunity to indulge in the oratory of the assembly in their capacity as members of State conventions and legislatures, and of both branches of Congress. The oratory in this case did not differ widely from that of ante-bellum days. Many of the disabilities from which the Negro suffered prior to emancipation were carried over into freedom, inasmuch as it was impossible to change immediately the nature of the whites. As a majority, they did not welcome the Negroes in politics, except so far as they could be used for party purposes, and did not accord them social privileges. The Negro statesmen, then, both in assemblies and before other groups, concerned themselves primarily with the defense of the rights which had recently been guaranteed to them by State and national legislation.

Yet it must not be said that the Negro orators selfishly devoted their energies to the protection of their people.

While this was the mainspring of their action, they nevertheless delivered logical discourse on the most important questions of the day. Some of the most effective speeches made in behalf of removing the political disabilities from which the southern whites suffered as a result of their participation in the rebellion, were delivered by Negroes feeling sympathy for their former masters and desiring the coöperation of all for the common good. The Negro statesmen, moreover, took part in the discussions upon education, internal improvements, economic development, and foreign affairs. Some of these discourses would do credit to persons who were much further removed from the influences of slavery.

The first of such speeches were efforts to establish the claims of Negro members to seats in Congress. Most of such elections were contested; and when decided in their favor unreconstructed members of Congress sought to eliminate Negro Congressmen by invoking the principle of the Dred Scott decision to the effect that the Negro was not a citizen of the United States and could not exercise such functions. The following speeches of Menard, Bruce, and Langston illustrate this point.

THE NEGRO'S FIRST SPEECH IN CONGRESS, MADE BY JOHN WILLIS MENARD IN DEFENSE OF HIS ELECTION TO CONGRESS WHEN HIS SEAT WAS CONTESTED AND WON BY HIS POLITICAL OPPONENT [1]

Mr. Speaker: I appear here more to acknowledge this high privilege than to make an argument before this House. It was

[1] John Willis Menard, the first Negro to be heard as a Representative in the Nation's Council, was born in Kaskaskia, Illinois, April 3, 1838. The first eighteen years of his life were spent on a farm. It was then decided that he should be given broader educational opportunities. So he was sent to Sparta, Illinois, to school. Upon completing the course of study there, he took the college course at Iberia College, where he fitted himself for the honorable part he subsequently bore in the reconstruction history of the Negro.

In the spring of 1862, he was appointed to a clerkship in the Department of the Interior—being the first colored man to hold such a position in Washington. The feeling against this innovation was so bitter that he found his position anything but a bed of roses.

Shortly after this, the question which has ever agitated the American public, certainly not my intention at first to take any part in this case at all; but as I have been sent here by the votes of nearly nine thousand electors, I would feel myself recreant to the duty imposed upon me if I did not defend their rights on this floor. I wish it to be well understood, before I go further, that in the disposition of this case I do not expect, nor do I ask, that there shall be any favor shown me on account of my race, or the former condition of that race. I wish the case to be decided on its own merits, and nothing else. As I said before the Committee of Election, Mr. Hunt, who contests my seat, is not properly a contestant before this House, for the reason that he has not complied with the law of Congress in serving notice upon me of his intention to contest my seat. The returns of the Board of Canvassers of the State of Louisiana were published officially on the twenty-fifth of November, and the gentleman had sufficient time to comply with the law of Congress if he had chosen to do so. When Congress convened on the seventh of December, he presented to the Speaker of this House a protest against my taking my seat. I did not know the nature of that protest until about the middle of January, when the case was called up before the committee.

Upon this point of notice I desire to call the attention of the House to this fact: that General Sheldon, who ran on the same ticket that I did as a candidate for the Forty-first Congress, was declared to be elected upon the same grounds that I was, and he wrote to the Chairman of the Committee of Elections to find out his opinion with regard to this question of notice. Mr. Hunt, it seems, failed to give him notice also; and I understood when I

"What shall we do with the Negro?" assumed considerable importance. Colonization seemed to many to offer the only practical solution. An Englishman named Dodge proffered to the government a large tract of land in Balize, Central America, for this purpose. In casting about for some one to investigate the feasibility of the proposed plan, the Commissioner of Immigration selected Mr. Menard to make the investigation. He was commissioned, proceeded to Balize, was officially received by the Governor, made his investigation, and subsequently published a report; but nothing further was heard of this colonization movement.

In 1865 Mr. Menard moved to New Orleans, where he at once took a prominent part in the work of reconstruction. Freely participating in local politics, he was soon appointed Inspector of Customs, and afterward a Commissioner of Streets. During this time he published an ably edited newspaper, *The Radical Standard.* In 1868 he received the nomination for the unexpired term of the Fortieth Congress, running on the same ticket with General Sheldon, who ran for the full term of the Forty-first Congress. Each received the same vote and was given a certificate of election by the Governor. General Sheldon was seated, but the political atmosphere was as yet too full of the taint which slavery had left—and Mr. Menard was rejected, but allowed full pay.

was last in New Orleans that it is the opinion of the Chairman of the Committee of Elections that the case of Mr. Sheldon is a very clear one. I am very sorry that the Chairman of the Committee of Elections did not give me the benefit of that opinion.

I am of opinion that when Congress enacted that law it certainly intended that every contestant should comply with its requirements, and I can see no reason why the law should be set aside in this case any more than in any other; and I think that if Mr. Hunt did not know the law of Congress, he was a very poor subject to be sent to Congress.

Now, sir, the Committee of Elections, in their report, have cited the New Hampshire case of Perkins *vs.* Morrison; but they take as a precedent the action of the minority of the committee in that case—which is very strange, indeed—and they give us no benefit from the report of the majority of that committee. I ask the Clerk to read from that majority report the passage which I have marked. . . .

Mr. Speaker, in the matter of redistricting the State of Louisiana, the Governor had no authority of law whatever to send his precept for an election to fill this vacancy to any other district than the new one made by the Legislature on the twenty-second of August, eighteen hundred and sixty-eight. He could not have ordered an election to fill this vacancy under a law which had not been repealed.

There is another point to which I wish to call the attention of this House. The State was redistricted before Colonel Mann died. Therefore, at the time when he died his district was intact, and no change was made in it after his death. And the voters in that portion of the new district, who were formerly within the districts that elected Mr. Newsham and Mr. Vidal to this House were no longer constituents of those gentlemen, but had become the constituents of Mr. Mann. So far as the law is concerned, Mr. Mann represented the new district as it now stands. And when he died, and there was a vacancy in that new district, the Governor of the State had no power whatever to order an election in the old district to fill the vacancy, but the election had to be held by law within the territorial limits of the new district. The Legislature of Louisiana, according to the Constitution of the United States, had the power to change the districts. Therefore the Governor was, by the new redistricting act, to order an election to fill the vacancy within the new district.

Now, I would call attention to another point. If it be admitted that the election was legal, and that the Legislature had full power to create new districts, I ask a moment's attention while I compare the vote on the third of November with the vote cast in the preceding April election on the ratification of the constitution. In the first, second, third, tenth and eleventh wards of the city of New Orleans, which are included in the new Second Congressional District, the vote for the constitution in April was 7,373. In the same ward on the third of November there were only 125 votes; showing a falling off of 7,248 votes in the space of six months. In the parish of Jefferson, on the seventeenth and eighteenth days of April, eighteen hundred and sixty-eight, the votes for the constitution were 3,133. On the third of November following, the Republican votes in that parish were only 662; showing a falling off in six months of 2,470 votes. This is sufficient to show to any reasonable person that the loyal voters in this portion of the district were deprived of the right to go to the polls and cast their ballots. Now, this falling off was caused by the intimidations and threats made and the frauds practiced in those parishes. And I now ask Congress, on behalf of the loyal people of my district, to set aside the returns of votes from those parishes, so as to give the rebels there no more encouragement for their systematic plan of fraud and intimidation. And if the votes of those two parishes are thrown out, I will then have, in the remainder of the district, a majority over Mr. Hunt, my contestant, of 3,341 votes. And as I hold the certificate of election from the Governor, I hold that I should be recognized and admitted to this body as the legal Representative of the district in which a vacancy was created by the death of my predecessor, Mr. Mann. There is no evidence whatever that there was any fraud in the election in the remaining five parishes of the district. Our vote in November compares favorably with the vote cast in April for the constitution. And I think Congress should rcognize the right of the voters of those parishes to be represented here. Had the same Republican vote been cast in November that was cast in April in the parishes of Orleans and Jefferson, I would still have a majority over Mr. Hunt of several hundred votes.

It will be noticed that under the new registration for the election of November, there were 20,314 voters registered in the five wards of the city of New Orleans comprised in the Second Congressional District of Louisiana. The total vote in those wards cast at the election, admitting all of them to have been legal, were 11,660, showing that over 8,500 legal voters were deprived of the right to vote in consequence of the condition of things then existing in Louisiana, and I have every reason to believe, judging from the election in April previous, that those 8,500 were Republican voters. I ask this House to give these men—most of whom were colored—some consideration, and not allow the rebel votes to be counted against them. If this is done, it is possible that at the next election loyal men will have a chance to express their will through the ballot-box. And according to the registration for the parish of Jefferson, there were then 5,969 voters, while the total number of votes cast on the third of November was 2,886; showing that in that parish alone there were 3,083 loyal voters who were deprived of their right to vote in consequence of the intimidation and lawlessness there.[1]

AN ADDRESS DELIVERED TO THE UNITED STATES SENATE IN BEHALF OF ADMITTING P. B. S. PINCHBACK AS SENATOR FROM THE STATE OF LOUISIANA

By B. K. Bruce[2]

When I entered upon my duties here as Senator from Mississippi, the question ceased to be novel, and had already been elaborately and exhaustively discussed. So far as opportunity has permitted me to do so, I have dispassionately examined the question in the light of the discussion, and I venture my views now with the diffidence inspired by my limited experience in the consideration of such questions and by a just appreciation of the learning and ability of the gentlemen who have already attempted to elucidate and determine this case.

[1] *Congressional Globe*, 40th Cong., 3rd Sess., Appendix, 1684, 1685.

[2] Blanche K. Bruce of Floreyville, Mississippi, was born in Prince Edward County, Virginia, March 1, 1841. A man of limited education, he became, in 1869, a planter in Mississippi. Later he became a member of the Mississippi levee board, served in several local offices, and finally was elected, in 1875, to the United States Senate, where he served till 1881. Mr. Bruce died at Washington, D. C., March 17, 1898.—*Biographical Congressional Directory*, p. 420.

I believe, Mr. President, whatever seeming informalities may attach to the manner in which the will of the people was ascertained, Mr. Pinchback is the representative of a majority of the legal voters of Louisiana, and is entitled to a seat in the Senate. In the election of 1872, the white population of the state exceeded, by the census of 1872, the colored population by about two thousand, including in the white estimate 6,300 foreigners, only half of whom were naturalized. This estimate, at the same ratio in each race, would give a large majority of colored voters. The census and registration up to 1872 substantially agree, and both sustain this conclusion. The census of 1875, taken in pursuance of an article of the State constitution, gives, after including the foreign population (naturalized and unnaturalized) in the white aggregate, a majority of 45,695 colored population.

This view of the question is submitted not as determining the contest, but as an offset to the allegation that Mr. Pinchback does not fairly represent the popular will of the State, and as a presumption in favor of the legal title of the assembly that elected him.

The State government elected in 1872, and permanently inaugurated in January, 1873, in the face of contest and opposition, obtained for its authority recognition of the inferior and supreme courts of the State. When organized violence threatened its existence and the United States Government was appealed to for troops to sustain it, the national Executive, in pursuance of his constitutional authority and duty, responded to the demand made for help, prefacing said action by an authoritative declaration, made through the Attorney General, addressed to Lieutenant-Governor Pinchback, then Acting Governor, of date of December 17, 1872, that said Pinchback was "recognized as the lawful executive of Louisiana, and the body assembled at Mechanics' Institute as the lawful Legislature of the State"; and similar recognition of his successor was subsequently given. When in September, 1874, an attempt was made to overthrow the government, the President again interposed with the Army and Navy for its protection and the maintenance of its authority.

This government has proceeded to enact and enforce laws for three years, which not only affect life, liberty, and property, but which have received the general obedience of the citizens of the State. The present government also has frequently been brought in official contact with the United States Congress—through its legislatures of 1873 and 1875, by memorials and joint resolutions addressed to the respective Houses; and through its executive, by credentials, borne by Congressmen and by Senators—and in no instance has the sufficiency of the executive's credentials been questioned, in either House, except in the matter of the senatorial claimant.

Now, Sir, shall we admit by our action on this case that for three years the State of Louisiana has not had a lawful Legislature; that its laws have been made by an unauthorized mob; that the President of the United States actively, and Congress, by non-action at least, have sustained and perpetuated this abnormal, illegal, wrongful condition of things, thereby justifying and provoking the indignant and violent protests of one portion of the people of that State, and inviting them to renewed and continued agitation and violence? Such action by us would be unjust to the claimant, a great wrong to the people who sent him here, and cruel even to that class who have awaited an opportunity to bring to their support the overwhelming moral power of the nation in the pursuit of their illusion—which has so nearly ruined the future of that fair State—a government based upon the prejudices of caste.

I respectfully ask attention of Senators to another view of this subject, which is not without weight in determining the obligations of this body to the State of Louisiana and in ascertaining the title of the claimant. If the assumption that the present government inaugurated in 1873 is without legal authority and usurpation is true, the remedy for the state of things was to be found in the exercise of Congress through the joint action of the two Houses of the powers conferred under the guaranteeing clause of the Constitution relative to republican forms of government in the several States.

Failing to exercise her power and perform her duty in this direction, and thus practically perpetuating the present government, I submit that, in my judgment, we cannot now ignore our obligation to give the State her full representation on the score of the alleged irregularity of the government through which she has expressed her will; and there does seem to me, in this connection, something incongruous in the proposition that we may impose upon the people a government without legal sanction and demand their obedience to and support thereof, said government meanwhile determining the character of its successions and thus perpetuating its talent, and yet are powerless to admit a Senator elected thereby.

In my judgment, this question shall at this juncture be considered and decided not on abstract but practical grounds. Whatever wrongs have been done and mistakes made in Louisiana by either party, the present order of things is accepted by the people of the State and by the nation, and will be maintained as final settlement of the political issues that have divided the people there; and no changes in the administration of public affairs can or will be made except by the people, through the ballot, under the existing government and laws of the Commonwealth.

Under these circumstances, holding the question in abeyance is, in my judgment, an unconstitutional deprivation of a State, and a provocation of popular disquietude; and in the interest of good-will and good government, the most judicious and consistent course is to admit the claimant to his seat.

I desire, Mr. President, to make a personal reference to the claimant. I would not attempt one or deem one proper were it not that his personal character has been assailed.

As a father, I know him to be affectionate; as a husband, the idol of a pleasant home and cheerful fireside; as a citizen, loyal, brave, and true. And in his character and success we behold an admirable illustration of the excellence of our republican institutions.[1]

A SPEECH DELIVERED IN MARCH, 1876, WHEN IT BECAME NECESSARY FOR THE SENATE TO INTRODUCE A RESOLUTION APPOINTING A COMMITTEE TO INVESTIGATE ELECTION PRACTICES IN MISSISSIPPI

By B. K. Bruce

The conduct of the late election in Mississippi affected not merely the fortunes of the partisans—as the same were necessarily involved in the defeat or success of the respective parties to the contest—but put in question and jeopardy the sacred rights of the

[1] *Congressional Record*, First Session, pp. 1444-1445.

citizens; and the investigation contemplated in the pending resolution has for its object not the determination of the question whether the offices shall be held and the public affairs of the State be administered by democrats or republicans, but the higher and more important end, the protection in all their purity and significance of the political rights of the people and the free institutions of the country.

The evidence in hand and accessible will show beyond peradventure that in many parts of the State corrupt and violent influences were brought to bear upon the registrars of voters, thus materially affecting the character of the voting or poll lists; upon the inspectors of election, prejudicially and unfairly, thereby changing the number of votes cast; and finally threats and violence were practiced directly upon the masses of voters in such measures and strength as to produce grave apprehensions for personal safety and as to deter them from the exercise of their political franchises.

It will not accord with the laws of nature or history to brand colored people a race of cowards. On more than one historic field, beginning in 1776 and coming down to the centennial year of the Republic, they have attested in blood their courage as well as a love of liberty. I ask Senators to believe that no consideration of fear or personal danger has kept us quiet and forbearing under the provocations and wrongs that have so sorely tried our souls. But feeling kindly towards our white fellow-citizens, appreciating the good purposes and offices of the better classes, and, above all, abhorring war of races, we determined to wait until such time as an appeal to the good sense and justice of the American people could be made.

The sober American judgment must obtain in the South as elsewhere in the Republic, that the only distinctions upon which parties can be safely organized and in harmony with our institutions are differences of opinion relative to principles and policies of government, and that differences of religion, nationality, or race can neither with safety nor propriety be permitted for a moment to enter into the party contests of the day. The unanimity with which the colored voters act with a party is not referable to any race prejudice on their part. On the contrary, they invite the political co-operation of their white brethren, and vote as a unit because proscribed as such. They deprecate the establishment of the color line by the opposition, not only because the act is unwise, but because it isolates them from the white men of the South and forces them, in sheer self-protection, and against their inclination, to act seemingly upon the basis of a race prejudice that they neither respect nor entertain. They not only recognize the equality of citizenship and the right of every man to hold without proscription any position of honor and trust to which the confidence of the people may elevate him; but owing nothing to race, birth, or surroundings, they above all other classes, in the community, are interested to see prejudices drop out of both politics and the businesses of the country, and success in life proceed upon the integrity and merit of the man who seeks it. . . . But withal, as they progress in intelligence and appreciation of the dignity of their prerogatives as citizens, they as an evidence of growth begin to realize the significance of the proverb, "When thou doest well for thyself, men shall praise thee"; and are disposed to exact the same protection and concessions of rights that are conferred upon other citizens by the Constitution, and that too without humiliation involved in the enforced abandonment of their political convictions.

I have confidence, not only in my country and her institutions, but in the endurance, capacity and destiny of my people. We will, as opportunity offers and ability serves, seek our places, sometimes in the field of literary arts, science and the professions. More frequently mechanical pursuits will attract and elicit our efforts; more still of my people will find employment and livelihood as the cultivators of the soil. The bulk of this people—by surroundings, habits, adaptation, and choice will continue to find their homes in the South and constitute the masses of its yeomanry. We will there, probably of our own volition and more abundantly than in the past, produce the great staples that will contribute to the basis of foreign exchange, and in giving the nation a balance of trade, and minister to the wants and comforts and build up the prosperity of the whole land. Whatever our ultimate position in the composite civilization of the Republic and whatever varying fortunes attend our career, we will not forget our instincts for freedom nor our love for country.[1]

[1] *Congressional Record*, 44th Congress, First Session, pp. 2100-2105.

SPEECH IN THE CASE OF HIS CONTESTED ELECTION

By John R. Lynch[1]

The House having under consideration the contested election case of Lynch *vs.* Chalmers from the sixth Congressional district of Mississippi——

Mr. Lynch (the contestant), said:

Mr. Speaker: In presenting this case to the House and to the country I will not discuss the legal questions that are involved; nor will I review the testimony that has been taken. These points have been and will be forcibly presented by members of the committee who have familiarized themselves with the case. I will content myself with calling public attention to the disreputable system of elections of which the pending case is a natural and necessary outgrowth.

Out of 21,143 votes polled the contestee actually received about 5,000. In the counties of Adams, Claiborne, Jefferson, Washington and Wilkinson something over 5,000 votes were counted and returned for him that were polled against him. Giving him the benefit of these frauds, he was still defeated by a majority of 663. His pretended claim to the seat is based upon the action of election commissioners or county returning boards in several counties in throwing out over 5,000 Republican tickets that had been received, counted, and returned by the precinct inspectors. Over 3,000 of these tickets were thrown out for the alleged reason that the election officers failed to comply with some technical requirement of the law; such for instance as a failure on the part of the election clerks to send up with the returns a list of the names of those who voted.

WARREN COUNTY

In Warren County all the Republican tickets except those polled in the first ward of the city of Vicksburg were thrown out, for the

[1] John R. Lynch, of Natchez, Mississippi, was born in Concordia Parish, Louisiana, September 10, 1847. He attended evening school at Natchez for a few months, and by private study acquired a good English education. He engaged in the business of photography at Natchez until 1869, when Governor Ames appointed him a justice of the peace. Mr. Lynch served in the 43rd, 44th, and 47th Congresses, and was elected to the 45th Congress, but was counted out. Later he served as Fourth Auditor of Treasury Department under President Harrison, and as a paymaster in the Volunteer Army during the Spanish-American War.—*Biographical Congressional Directory*, p. 662.

alleged reason that they had on their face the usual and ordinary printer's dashes, which the contestee claimed to be a distinguishing mark. The rejection of these tickets was the most disgraceful act in the whole questionable business. Warren County, which includes the city of Vicksburg, is the county and city in which General Chalmers now claims to live and where he is presumed to be well, if not favorably known. Although the election machinery in Warren, as in all the other counties in the district, was in the hands of his partisan friends and supporters, but where, I am pleased to be able to say, the election was fair and the count honest, up to the time the returns were made to the county commissioners, the county gave a majority of 1,052 against him. No one supposed for a moment that the commissioners could be induced or even seduced into committing this great outrage, especially as the precinct inspectors had positively refused to reject these tickets in spite of the appeals that were made to them to do so.

But General Chalmers, who seems to be equal to any emergency when his personal interests are at stake, appeared before this board in the person of his law partner and, without notice to his opponent, without allowing the other side an opportunity to take exceptions to the jurisdiction of the board or to present the other side of the question on the merits of the case, insisted upon the commission, without delay, of this great wrong, although they had ten days under the law in which to make their returns to the Secretary of State. The opinion is prevalent in Warren County to-day that this board of election commissioners, which consisted of three men of only ordinary intelligence, would not have committed this outrage upon popular suffrage, as one of them frankly admitted to me, had both sides of the question been presented at the time. But the contestee, through his law partner, made them believe that it was their sworn duty to act exactly in accordance with his advice and agreeably to his instructions. In fact it can be truly said that he virtually decided the case himself; and as his modesty is not equal to his ambition, it is not strange that he decided the case in his own favor.

But there is another fact in support of the assertion that the commissioners acted agreeably to instructions furnished from General Chalmers' law office. The result of the election in the first ward of the city of Vicksburg was as follows: Chalmers, 168;

Lynch, 57. The 57 Republican tickets polled in that ward were exactly like those that were declared by the commissioners to be unlawful and yet these 57 tickets were declared to be lawful and were, therefore, counted and returned as such. If all of the other tickets voted by the Republicans in the county were unlawful on account of the printer's dashes, then these were unlawful also, for they were all exactly alike. When the commissioners were asked why they did not throw these out also, their answer was because they were not protested against. The reason they were not protested against is no doubt due to the fact that the contestee had a large majority in that ward. The charge, therefore, made by the Vicksburg *Herald*, the ablest Democratic paper published in the State, that the Republican tickets in that county were not thrown out because they had a few printer's dashes on them, but because they did not have the name of Chalmers on them, is unquestionably true. The assertion that the illiterate Republican voters were enabled to distinguish the tickets of the two parties by these dashes is untrue, because every ward in the city and every precinct in the county was supplied with counterfeit Republican tickets, the only difference between the genuine and counterfeit Republican tickets was that the latter had the name of Chalmers instead of Lynch on them for Congress. The printer's dashes, therefore, could not possibly operate to the disadvantage of Mr. Chalmers.

RACE PREJUDICE

In reading one of Gath's letters to the Cincinnati *Enquirer* shortly after the election of 1880, I saw the following:

> "The *Tribune* interviewed General Chalmers, of Mississippi, yesterday, who coolly said: 'I think about 5,000 votes for Lynch were thrown out in the district, out of 15,000 in all. As self-preservation is the first law of nature, I am in favor of using every means short of violence to preserve the intelligent white people of Mississippi in supreme control of political affairs. They are justified in using every means that wit or money, short of open bribery, can procure. If this is Chalmerism,' he concluded, 'I am proud of it.' "

The words "short of violence," and "short of open bribery" were no doubt used for purposes of embellishment and smooth reading. The facts would have been more accurately stated, as expressive of the purposes and methods of the element of which that gentleman is a recognized opponent, had these qualifying words been omitted. But the language the gentleman is reported to have used, as quoted above, is hardly less than a libel upon the most intelligent and respectable white people of Mississippi. That General Chalmers is authorized to speak for the Bourbons of Mississippi, I unhesitatingly admit. That he is authorized to speak for the conservative white people of Mississippi, I most emphatically deny. That he does not and has not expressed their feelings, sentiments, and wishes, either in his utterances or methods, I most positively assert. No one, I presume, will deny that whenever there is a conflict between wealth and intelligence upon the one side and poverty and ignorance upon the other, the former can always wield a controlling influence, or at least hold the latter within legitimate bounds, and that too without resorting to any lawless or questionable means for that purpose. Whenever fraud and violence are resorted to, upon the plea that they are necessary to prevent the ascendancy of ignorance over intelligence, the impression that is naturally created upon the public mind is that the order of intelligence is either very inferior or else there is no antagonism or conflict between these elements.

I deny that race prejudice has anything to do with fraud and violence at elections in the Southern States. There is not half as much race feeling at the South as many of the Bourbon leaders in that section would have the country believe. The antagonisms that exist there to-day are not based on antipathies of race, but they are based on antipathies of parties. The race feeling was strong shortly after the war, but it has now very nearly died out. Colored men are not now persecuted in the section from which I come on account of their color, but Republicans, white and colored, are persecuted in many localities on account of their politics. More colored than white men are thus persecuted, simply because they constitute in larger numbers the opposition to the Democratic party. The opposition to me as the candidate of the Republican party for Congress was no more intense than it would have been had the Republicans nominated an aristocrat of the *ante-bellum* period who fought on the side of the Confederacy during the late war.

The barrier to my success was not due to my color; it was due to my politics.

Bruce, Douglass, Langston, or any other reputable colored man, as the candidate of the Republican party for the Presidency in 1880, would have come just as near carrying Mississippi as did General Garfield. The Southern Bourbons are simply determined not to tolerate honest differences of opinion upon political questions. They make no distinction between those who have the courage, the manliness, and the independence to array themselves in opposition to Bourbon methods and measures. It matters not what name the opposition may assume nor of what elements it may be composed. They may call themselves Republicans, or Greenbackers as in some localities, or Independents as in others, or Readjusters as in Virginia. The fact that they oppose the ascendancy of Bourbon Democracy makes them, from a Bourbon standpoint, enemies to the South, to its interests, and to its people. All that is needed at the South to-day is the inculcation of a just and liberal public sentiment which will destroy political proscription and intolerance. That being done, a full vote, a free ballot, and a fair count will necessarily follow, for it is an indisputable fact that fraud and violence have, as the basis of their existence, proscription and intolerance. [Applause.]

THE SOLID SOUTH

That the South is solidly Democratic at the expense of the purity of elections is no longer a disputed question. Every intelligent man knows it and every candid man admits it. Many of those who defend the methods of Southern Bourbons, do so upon the plea that wealth and intelligence ought not to be governed by poverty and ignorance, and, as the wealth and intelligence of the South are identified with the Democratic party, and the poverty and ignorance with the Republican party, it necessarily follows that Democratic success is essential to the ascendancy of the intelligent and property-owning classes. According to their reasoning, therefore, the country ought to countenance and justify fraud and violence on their part. Let us inquire into this a little. The claim that the Democratic party at the South embraces within its membership all of the wealth and the intelligence of that section has not the slightest foundation in fact. I know whereof I speak when I assert that the opposition to the Democratic organization in the State of Mississippi, for instance, embraces within its membership a large per cent. of the wealth, the intelligence, and the moral worth of that commonwealth. It is equally true that the Democratic party embraces within its membership some of the most ignorant and depraved of our population.

True, the Republican party at the South has a larger percentage of the illiterate voters than has the Democratic party, but it is also true that both parties contain a sufficient number of each of these classes to prevent either from being accepted as the exclusive representative of either class. Under the existing order of things it is impossible to make wealth and intelligence the basis of party organization in any one of the Southern States. If it be true that the Democratic organization at the South is the exclusive representative of the wealth and the intelligence of that section, why is it they do not establish by law an educational or a property qualification for electors? I think I can inform the country why it is they have attempted nothing of the kind. It is because they know that they cannot disfranchise the illiterate Republican voter without disfranchising at the same time and in the same way the illiterate Democratic voter. It is because they cannot disfranchise the poverty-stricken Republican voter without disfranchising at the same time and in the same way the poverty-stricken Democratic voter. This is the "self-preservation" which they consider to be the "first law of nature."

I admit that a much larger number of Republican than Democratic voters would be thus disfranchised, but a sufficient number of Democrats would be disfranchised to create a public sentiment which would destroy the Democratic organization and drive the party from power. As to that party being the exclusive representative of political morality, the facts presented in this case go far to disprove that claim. I assert with feelings of deep mortification and profound regret that in the official person of the contestee in this case the country is presented with a living monument of rifled ballot-boxes, stifled public justice, and a prostituted suffrage. Although the gentleman has occupied a seat upon this floor during the last five years, yet no one knows better than he does himself that he has never—with possibly one exception, 1878, when the Republicans made no organized opposition—received as many as one-third of the votes polled at any election at which he was a candidate. With all of their boasted intelligence and independence it is an unfortunate fact that Southern Democrats are particularly noted for their subserviency to party leadership. They rely chiefly upon their party leaders and local newspapers for political instruction and direction and they generally do or allow to be done whatever their leaders and party papers advise, whether it be right or wrong, fair or unfair. Under these circumstances it can be truly alleged that the contestee in this case is more responsible for the frauds and outrages that were committed in his behalf and for his benefit than any one else.

I am satisfied that had he gone before the people of the sixth district and told them that while he was ambitious to represent them in Congress, yet as an honorable man he could not afford to countenance or encourage any fraudulent or questionable methods to bring about that result, the election would have been fair and the count honest throughout the district. But it is an unfortunate fact that no such words as these were ever known to fall from his lips. On the contrary, the fraudulent acts that were committed by a portion of his friends and supporters, and which resulted in his being returned to a seat upon this floor, were received by him with either silent acquiescence or public approval. His chief aim, his sole object, seems to have been to occupy a seat upon this floor, regardless of the means by which that result might be brought about. I can assure the House and the country of the fact that it gives me no pleasure to feel compelled, in vindicating the cause of truth and justice, to use such strong language in referring to my distinguished opponent, because, aside from his questionable election methods, he is a gentleman whose ability, eloquence, and genial disposition are calculated to commend him to the appreciation and respect of those with whom he may be officially or socially connected. Gladly would I acquit him of ever having countenanced or encouraged the commission of election frauds if the facts would only warrant me in so doing.

But, Mr. Speaker, must it be assumed that the commission of these crimes and these outrages are encouraged by the wealth and the intelligence of the sixth district of Mississippi? In the name of those who in *ante-bellum* days gave tone and character to Southern society, under the supervision and direction of some of whom

I received my early training, and by whom I was taught to seek through a laudable and commendable ambition the realization and accomplishment of those things which can be honorably achieved only by those who are imbued with and actuated by the highest, noblest, and most exalted aspirations, I must enter my earnest and emphatic protest against such an unjust, unfair, and unreasonable assumption. While I admit that the late war, which was disastrous in its results so far as many of the Southern white people were concerned, produced a marked and lamentable decadence in the public morals of that section, yet I know, of my own personal knowledge, that there are, even in the sixth district of Mississippi, white men and Democrats who are admitted by all who know them to be men of honor, character, and integrity. When, therefore, the contestee attempts to make it appear that these men endorse and defend the methods by which he was returned to a seat upon this floor, he thereby becomes a maligner of his section and a traducer of the most intelligent and respectable portion of his own people.

I can assert whereof I know to be a fact that there are thousands of Democrats in the sixth district of Mississippi, many of whom voted for the contestee, but who know and admit that he was fairly and honestly defeated and that he reflects no credit upon himself, his party, and his State in claiming a seat upon such a flimsy and ridiculous plea as the one set up by him in this case. The worst that can be said about these law-abiding Democrats is, that through a mistaken zeal for the success of their party they remain, as a rule, reticent and inactive, while the ignorant and immoral are allowed to debauch the suffrage in the interest of the Democratic party, and thus bring odium and disgrace upon their State and party.

Both of the great political parties of the day are no doubt anxious to bring about a cessation of the agitation of sectionalism. They differ only as to the basis upon which this agitation shall cease. The Democrats who are in favor of upholding and defending the Bourbon system of fraudulent elections, as illustrated in this case, for instance, are anxious to bring about a cessation of sectional agitation upon the basis of a violent and fraudulent suppression of the popular will. The Republicans, on the other hand, and I am pleased to be able to say, thousands of honest Democrats as well, are anxious that this agitation shall cease, upon such conditions as will secure to all citizens the equal protection of the laws, and a willing acquiescence in the lawfully expressed will of the majority. As an humble member of the great Republican party, I have no hesitation in declaring it to be the unchangeable determination of that party to continue to wage a persistent war upon Bourbon methods at the South until the right of every citizen to cast his ballot for the man or the party of his choice and have that ballot fairly and honestly counted shall have been acquiesced in from one end of the country to the other. [Applause on the Republican side.]

Mr. Speaker, so far as this case is concerned it is not a question of party. It is one that appeals to the patriotism and justice of the American people. You are called upon to determine in this case whether or not 10,000 voters of one party in a district shall be allowed through systematic frauds and ballot-box manipulation to be equal to 20,000 voters of the other party in a district where the election is fairly and honestly conducted. You are called upon to determine whether or not in a district containing about 40,000 voters, 30,000 of them shall be allowed through the commission and perpetration of flagitious crimes to be practically disfranchised and the 10,000 alone to have voice and representation upon this floor. You are called upon to determine whether or not these grave offenses against law, justice, and public morals shall receive the condemnation or approbation of the national House of Representatives. To the Democratic members of the House who are the chosen representatives of a willing constituency and whose titles are not saturated with the crime of fraud, I have this to say: that you will accept the fraudulent methods and practices that were resorted to in behalf of the contestee in this case as your standard of political morality is what I have been too charitable to believe and too generous to assert. That any considerable number of Representatives of any party can give these offenses the sanction of their approval is what I cannot and will not believe until that fact has been unmistakably demonstrated.

I am aware of the fact that Southern Republicans are sometimes reproached because they do not make forcible resistance to the perpetration of these frauds; but it must be remembered that the frauds are always committed under some sort of color of law. The five thousand and more Republican tickets that were thrown out in the sixth district of Mississippi were thrown out by men whose sworn duty it was to make true and correct returns of all the votes polled in their respective counties. In counties where not less than 5,000 votes were counted and returned for the contestee that were polled against him, the frauds were either committed by the sworn officers themselves or by accomplices who had been selected for that purpose. The frauds are always committed either by the sworn officers of the law or by others with their knowledge and approval. What lawful redress have Republicans, then, except to do just what I am now doing?

You certainly cannot expect them to resort to mob-law and brute force, or to use what may be milder language, inaugurate a revolution. My opinion is that revolution is not the remedy to be applied in such cases. Our system of government is supposed to be one of law and order, resting upon the consent of the governed, as expressed through the peaceful medium of the ballot. In all localities where the local public sentiment is so dishonest, so corrupt, and so demoralized as to tolerate the commission of election frauds, and shield the perpetrators from justice, such people must be made to understand that there is patriotism enough in this country and sufficient love of justice and fair play in the hearts of the American people to prevent any party from gaining the ascendancy in the Government that relies upon a fraudulent ballot and a false return as the chief source of its support.

BRAVERY AND FIDELITY OF THE COLORED PEOPLE

The impartial historian will record the fact that the colored people of the South have contended for their rights with a bravery and a gallantry that is worthy of the highest commendation. Being, unfortunately, in dependent circumstances, with the preponderance of the wealth and intelligence against them in some localities, yet they have bravely refused to surrender their honest convictions, even upon the altar of their personal necessities. They have said to those upon whom they depended: You may deprive me for the time being of the opportunity of making an honest living; you may take the bread out of the mouths of my hungry and dependent family; you may close the school-house door in the face of my children; yea, more, you may take that which no man can give, my life, my manhood, my principles you cannot have! [Applause.] Even when the flag of your country was trailing in the dust of treason and rebellion; when the Constitution was ignored, and the lawfully chosen and legally-constituted authorities of the Government were disregarded and disobeyed; although the bondman's yoke of oppression was then upon their necks, yet they were then true and loyal to their Government, and faithful to the flag of their country. [Applause.]

They were faithful and true to you then; they are no less so today. And yet they ask no special favors as a class; they ask no special protection as a race. They feel that they purchased their inheritance when upon the battlefields of their country they watered the tree of liberty with the precious blood that flowed from their loyal veins. [Loud applause.] They ask no favors; they demand what they deserve and must have, an equal chance in the race of life. They feel that they are a part and parcel of you, bone of your bone, flesh of your flesh. Your institutions are their institutions, and your Government is their Government. You cannot consent to the elimination of the colored man from the body-politic, especially through questionable and fraudulent methods, without consenting to your own downfall and to your own destruction. That the colored people of the United States have made and are making material progress in the acquisition of knowledge, the accumulation of wealth, and in the development of a high order of civilization are facts known, recognized, and admitted by all except those who are too blind to see them or too prejudiced to admit them.

The condition of the colored people of this country today is a living contradiction of the prophecies of those who have predicted that the two races could not live upon the same continent together upon terms of political equality. In spite of these predictions we are here today, clothed with the same rights, the same privileges, and the same immunities, with complete political assimilation; loyal to the same Government, true to the same flag; yielding obedience to the same laws, revering the same institutions; actuated by the same patriotic impulses, imbued with the same noble ambition; entertaining the same hopes, seeking the gratification and satisfaction of the same aspirations; identified with the same interests, speaking the same language; professing the same religion, worshiping the same God. The colored man asks you in this particular instance to give effect to his ballot, not for his sake alone, but for yours as well. He asks you to recognize the fact that he has the right to assist you in defending, protecting, and upholding our Government and perpetuating our institutions. You must, then, as I am sure you will, condemn the crimes against our institutions, against law, against justice, and against public morals that were committed in this case.

CONCLUSION

In conclusion, Mr. Speaker, I regret to be compelled to say that it seems to be the settled determination of the Bourbon party at the South that we must either have a centralized Government or no Government at all. They seem to be determined that if they cannot destroy the Government in one way they will in another; for it is an incontrovertible and indisputable fact that the sanctity and the purity of the ballot is the chief pillar in our governmental structure. Destroy that pillar, and the structure must necessarily fall. I speak today not in behalf of my party, but in behalf of my country. I hope that I speak not as a partisan, but as a patriot. If the party to which I belong and to which I feel that I owe allegiance cannot commend itself to the approbation and support of a majority of the American people upon its merits, then it does not deserve success. Political parties under our system of Government are supposed to be organized for the purpose of advocating certain political principles and to carry into effect certain public policies. Upon all such questions we may honestly differ and make such differences the basis of party organization. But upon questions affecting the stability of the Government and the perpetuity of our institutions, we are at least presumed to be a united, harmonious and indissoluble people.

Mr. Speaker, this disgraceful system of election frauds in several of the Southern States, through and by which that section was made solid in its support of one of the great political parties of the day ought, must, and will be destroyed. [Applause.] The people of this great country are too intelligent and patriotic to tolerate a continuance of such outrages upon our elective system. Such methods and such practices are contrary to the spirit of the age in which we live and to the civilization of the nineteenth century. That there may exist in all parts of our country—North, South, East, and West—and among all races and classes of our people peace, happiness, concord, and fraternal feeling upon such conditions as will secure to all exact justice and the equal protection of the laws is the aim, the object, the hope, and the aspiration of every patriotic American citizen. For the accomplishment of these grand and noble purposes and the attainment of these commendable and patriotic ends, I invoke, in the language of the immortal Lincoln, the considerate judgment of mankind and the gracious favor of almighty God. [Great applause.] [1]

[During the delivery of the above speech, the hour having expired, the time was, by unanimous consent, extended to its conclusion.]

After establishing their right to serve in Congress one of the first concerns of the Negro members was to induce this body to enact the necessary laws to protect the freedmen in the enjoyment of their rights so easily jeopardized at that time by the agents of disorder throughout the South. The following speeches of Hiram Revels [2] in the Senate and of Jefferson F. Long [3] in the House are typical of these eloquent pleas for peace and order.

[1] *Congressional Record.*

[2] Hiram R. Revels was born at Fayetteville, North Carolina, September 1, 1822. Being unable to obtain an education in his own State, he moved to Indiana and there began study for the ministry. At the outbreak of the Civil War, Mr. Revels assisted in the organization of the first two Negro regiments in Maryland. Having made a record for service among his people in the central States, he went to Mississippi and there became interested in managing the freedmen's affairs. He was elected to several local offices and in 1870 was elected to fill an unexpired term in the United States Senate. After his retirement from Congress, Mr. Revels served as president of Alcorn University at Rodney, Mississippi, and later as pastor of the African Methodist Episcopal Church at Richmond, Indiana. He died January 16, 1901, at Aberdeen, Mississippi.—*Biographical Congressional Directory*, p. 763.

[3] Jefferson F. Long was born in Crawford County, Georgia, March 3, 1836. Some time thereafter he moved to Macon, Bibb County, where, under the direction of his owner, he learned the tailor's trade. Prior to his election to the third session of the 41st Congress, Mr. Long conducted, in Macon, a thriving business as a merchant tailor. His patronage, which consisted largely of that of whites, was much decreased after his term in Congress, due no doubt to their resentment of his activities in politics. Mr. Long was a good speaker, a Christian gentleman, and a man of many fine qualities. Upon his death in Macon, February 4, 1900, his loss was mourned alike by whites and Negroes.—Chaplain T. G. Steward, *Fifty Years in the Gospel Ministry*, p. 129. Letter from Mrs. A. L. Rucker, Atlanta, Ga., daughter of Mr. Long, October, 1921.

SPEECH ON THE GEORGIA BILL

By Hiram R. Revels

Mr. President, I rise at this particular juncture in the discussion of the Georgia bill with feelings which perhaps never before entered into the experience of any member of this body. I rise, too, with misgivings as to the propriety of lifting my voice at this early period after my admission into the Senate. Perhaps it were wiser for me, so inexperienced in the details of senatorial duties, to have remained a passive listener in the progress of this debate; but when I remember that my term is short, and that the issues with which this bill is fraught are momentous in their present and future influence upon the well-being of my race, I would seem indifferent to the importance of the hour and recreant to the high trust imposed upon me if I hesitated to lend my voice on behalf of the loyal people of the South. I therefore waive all thoughts as to the propriety of taking a part in this discussion. When questions arise which bear upon the safety and protection of the loyal white and colored population of those States lately in rebellion I cannot allow any thought as to mere propriety to enter into my consideration of duty. The responsibilities of being the exponent of such a constituency as I have the honor to represent are fully appreciated by me. I bear about me daily the keenest sense of their weight, and that feeling prompts me now to lift my voice for the first time in this Council Chamber of the nation; and, sir, I stand today on this floor to appeal for protection from the strong arm of the Government for her loyal children, irrespective of color and race, who are citizens of the Southern States, and particularly the State of Georgia.

I am well aware, sir, that the idea is abroad that an antagonism exists between the whites and blacks, that that race which the nation raised from the degradation of slavery, and endowed with the full and unqualified rights and privileges of citizenship, are intent upon power, at whatever price it can be gained. It has been the well-considered purpose and aim of a class not confined to the South to spread this charge over the land, and their efforts are as vigorous today to educate the people of this nation into that belief as they were at the close of the war. It was not uncommon to find this same class, even during the rebellion, prognosticating a servile war.

It may have been that the "wish was father to the thought." And, sir, as the recognized representative of my downtrodden people, I deny the charge, and hurl it back into the teeth of those who make it, and who, I believe, have not a true and conscientious desire to further the interests of the whole South. Certainly no one possessing any personal knowledge of the colored population of my own or other States need be reminded of the noble conduct of that people under the most trying circumstances in the history of the late war, when they were beyond the protection of the Federal forces. While the confederate army pressed into its ranks every white male capable of bearing arms, the mothers, wives, daughters, and sisters of the Southern soldiers were left defenseless and in the power of the blacks, upon whom the chains of slavery were still riveted; and to bind those chains the closer was the real issue for which so much life and property was sacrificed.

And now, sir, I ask, how did that race act? Did they in those days of confederate weakness and impotence evince the malignity of which we hear so much? Granting, for the sake of argument, that they were ignorant and besotted, which I do not believe, yet with all their supposed ignorance and credulity they in their way understood as fully as you or I the awful import of the contest. They knew if the gallant corps of national soldiers were beaten back and their flag trailed in the dust that it was the presage of still heavier bondage. They longed, too, as their fathers did before them, for the advent of that epoch over which was shed the hallowed light of inspiration itself. They desired, too, with their fathers, to welcome the feet of the stranger shod with the peaceful preparation of good news. Weary years of bondage had told their tale of sorrow to the court of Heaven. In the councils of the great Father of all they knew the adjudication of their case, albeit delayed for years, in which patient suffering had nearly exhausted itself, would in the end bring to them the boon for which they sighed—God's most blessed gift to His creatures—the inestimable boon of liberty. They waited, and they waited patiently. In the absence of their masters they protected the virtue and chastity of defenseless women. Think, sir, for a moment, what the condition of this land would be today if the slave population had risen in servile insurrection against those who month by month were fighting to perpetuate that institution which brought to them all the evils of which they complained. Where would have been the security for property, female chastity, and childhood's innocence? The bloody counterpart of such a story of cruelty and wrong would have been paralleled only in those chapters of Jewish history as recorded by Josephus, or in the still later atrocities of that reign of terror which sent the unfortunate Louis XVI and Marie Antoinette to the scaffold. Nay, the deeds in that drama of cold-blooded butchery would have out-Heroded the most diabolical acts of Herod himself.

Mr. President, I maintain that the past record of my race is a true index of the feelings which today animate them. They bear toward their former masters no revengeful thoughts, no hatred, no animosities. They aim not to elevate themselves by sacrificing one single interest of their white fellow-citizens. They ask but the rights which are theirs by God's universal law, and which are the natural outgrowth, the logical sequence of the condition in which the legislative enactments of this nation have placed them. They appeal to you and to me to see that they receive that protection which alone will enable them to pursue their daily avocations with success and enjoy the liberties of citizenship on the same footing with their white neighbors and friends. I do not desire simply to defend my own race from unjust and unmerited charges, but I also desire to place upon record an expression of my full and entire confidence in the integrity of purpose with which I believe the President, Congress, and the Republican party will meet these questions so prolific of weal or woe, not only to my own people, but to the whole South. They have been, so far as I can read the history of the times, influenced by no spirit of petty tyranny. The poet has well said that:

> "It is excellent
> To have a giant's strength; but it is tryannous
> To use it like a giant."

And how have they used that power lodged in them by the people? In acts of cruelty and oppression toward those who sought to rend in twain this goodly fabric of our fathers, the priceless heritage of so much hardship and endurance in revolutionary times? Let the reconstruction enactments answer the interrogation. No poor words of mine are needed to defend the wise and beneficent legislation which has been extended alike to white and colored citizens. The Republican party is not inflamed, as some would fain have the country believe, against the white population of the South. Its borders are wide enough for all truly loyal men to find within them peace and repose from the din and discord of angry faction. And be that loyal man white or black, that great party of our Republic will, if consistent with the record it has already made for posterity, throw around him the same impartial security in his pursuit of liberty and happiness. If a certain class at the South had accepted in good faith the benevolent overtures which were offered to them with no niggard hand today would not find our land still harassed with feuds and contentions.

I remarked, Mr. President, that I rose to plead for protection for the defenseless race who now send their delegation to the seat of Government to sue for that which this Congress alone can secure to them. And here let me say further, that the people of the North owe to the colored race a deep obligation which it is no easy matter to fulfill. When the Federal armies were thinned by death and disaster, and somber clouds overhung the length and breadth of the Republic, and the very air was pregnant with the rumors of foreign interferences—in those dark days of defeat, whose memories even yet haunt us as an ugly dream, from what source did our nation in its seeming death throes gain additional and new-found power? It was the sable sons of the South that valiantly rushed to the rescue, and but for their intrepidity and ardent daring many a northern fireside would miss today paternal counsels or a brother's love.

Sir, I repeat the fact that the colored race saved to the noble women of New England and the Middle States men on whom they lean today for security and safety. Many of my race, the representatives of these men on the field of battle, sleep in the countless graves of the South. If those quiet resting-places of our honored dead could speak today what a mighty voice, like to the rushing of a mighty wind, would come up from those sepulchral homes! Could we resist the eloquent pleadings of their appeal? Ah, sir, I think that this question of immediate and ample protection for the loyal people of Georgia would lose its legal technicalities, and we would cease to hesitate in our provision for their instant relief. Again, I regret this delay on other grounds. The taunt is frequently flung at us that a Nemesis more terrible than the Greek personation of the anger of the gods awaits her hour of direful retribution. We are told that at no distant day a great uprising of the American people will demand that the reconstruction acts of Congress be undone and blotted forever from the annals of legislative enactment. I inquire, sir, if this delay in affording protection to the loyalists of the State of Georgia does not lend an uncomfortable significance to this boasting sneer with which we so often meet? Delay is perilous at best; for it is as true in legislation as in physic, that the longer we procrastinate to apply the proper remedies the more chronic becomes the malady that we seek to heal.

> "The land wants such
> As dare with rigor execute the laws.
> Her festered members must be lanced and tended.
> He's a bad surgeon that for pity spares
> The part corrupted till the gangrene spread
> And all the body perish. He that's merciful
> Unto the bad is cruel to the good."

Mr. President, I favor the motion to strike out so much of the bill under debate as tends to abridge the term of the existing Legislature of Georgia. Let me, then, as briefly as possible, review the history of the case which so urgently claims our prompt action. In the month of November, 1867, an election was held by the authority of the reconstruction policy of this Congress in the State of Georgia. Its object was to settle by the ballot of her whole people, white and colored, whether it was expedient to summon a convention which should frame a constitution for civil government in that State. A certain class of the population declined to take any part in the election. The vote cast at election represented thirty thousand white and eighty thousand colored citizens of the State. It was a majority, too, of the registered vote, and in consequence a convention was called. A number of the delegates who formed that convention were colored. By its authority a constitution was framed just and equitable in all its provisions. Race, color, or former condition of servitude found no barrier in any of its ample enactments, and it extended to those lately in armed rebellion all the privileges of its impartial requirements. This constitution was submitted to the people of the State for ratification. Every effort which human ingenuity could call into requisition to defeat its adoption was resorted to. The loyal population of the State was victorious; and notwithstanding the determination of some to defeat the constitution that same class sought under its provisions to procure the nomination for all the offices within the gift of the people. A number were declared elected as county officers and members of the General Assembly.

Under the authority given by the act of Congress of June 25, 1868, the Legislature thus elected convened on the 4th of July of the same year in Atlanta. The act of Congress to which I refer reaffirmed certain qualifications which were demanded from all persons who were to hold office in the reconstructed States. After some delay a resolution was adopted by the Legislature of Georgia declaring that that body was duly qualified, and thus began the civil government in the State. Peace and harmony seemed at last to have met together, truth and justice to have kissed each other. But their reign was of short duration. By and by the reconstruction acts of Congress began to be questioned, and it was alleged that they were unconstitutional; and the Legislature which was elected under the constitution framed and supported by colored men declared that a man having more than an eighth of African blood in his veins was ineligible to office or a seat in the Legislature of the State of Georgia. These very men, to whom the Republican party extended all the rights and privileges of citizenship, whom they were empowered, if deemed expedient, to cut off forever from such beneficent grants, were the men to deny political equality to a large majority of their fellow-citizens. In the month of September, 1868, twenty-eight members of the Legislature were expelled from that body, and upon the assumption of the strange and startling hypothesis just mentioned they continued to legislate in open violation of the constitution. That constitution required by its provisions the establishment of a system of free schools. Such provisions were wholly abortive, indeed a dead letter, for none were established. The courts of law, at least so far as colored men were regarded, were a shameless mockery of justice. And here an illustration, perhaps, will the better give point to my last remark. A case in which was involved the question whether or not a colored man was eligible to one of the county offices was taken before the superior court, and the judge upon the bench rendered as his judicial opinion that a man of color was not entitled to hold office. I am told, sir, that the colored man in question is a graduate of Oberlin, Ohio, and served with honor as a commissioned officer in the Union Army during the late war. Is any comment needed in this body upon such a condition of affairs in the State of Georgia? Sir, I trust not.

Then, again, these facts were presented for the calm consideration of Congress in the following December, and the results of their deliberation may be seen in the report of the Committee on the Judiciary toward the close of January of last year. Congress took no action to remedy this state of affairs and aid the people of Georgia in obtaining the rights clearly guaranteed to them by the provisions of their State constitution.

In December last, at the earnest recommendation of the President, the act of the 22d of that month was adopted. It provided for the reassembling of the parties declared to have been elected by the general commanding that district, the restoration of the expelled persons of the Legislature, and the rejection of disqualified persons by that body. The present Legislature of Georgia has adopted the fourteenth and fifteenth amendments to the Constitution of the United States and the fundamental conditions required by the act of June 25, 1868. The reconstructed State of Georgia now offers herself, through the constitutionally elected Senators, as meet and fit for the recognition and admission by this Congress.

I have thus rapidly gone over the history of the events which have transpired in the State of Georgia till I have come to the legislation of the present time. The Committee on Reconstruction in the other House prepared and presented a bill providing for the admission of the State on similar grounds to those on which my own State and Virginia were allowed to take their places in the Union. An amendment, however, was proposed in the House and adopted, the aim and purport of which is to legalize the organization of 1868, and declare that the terms of the members of the Legislature, who have so recently qualified for a fair and just recognition by Congress, shall expire before they have completed their full term of two years under the constitution. Again, this amendment seeks to retain in office, whether approved by the Legislature of the State or not, the judges who have declared, in opposition to the constitution and the law, that in the State of Georgia at least there exists a distinction as to race and color, so far as civil and political rights are concerned. If there be any meaning in the words of the constitution of that State no such class distinction as this exists; and, sir, I am at a loss to determine upon what grounds we are called upon to hedge in by congressional enactment any public servant who may still give utterance to such doctrines, which are part and parcel of the effete civilization of our Republic. If the Legislature of Georgia thinks it right and proper to place in positions of trust and responsibility men of this school of political thought, certainly I shall not offer one objection. But let that Legislature assume the risk, as it is its true province, and let it also bear the consequences.

I do not believe that it can be proved that the State of Georgia has ever been beyond the control of Congress, nor that she has ever become fully admitted into the Union or entitled to representation since her impotent efforts to promote rebellion; and that therefore, when the act now under consideration and properly amended shall have been adopted, the government of that State and the Legislature of that State will enter upon the terms of office, will assume the powers for good and right and justice which are prescribed in the constitution of that State, and that under the circumstances the Senate will not deny to the loyal men of Georgia the recognition of their recent victory.

And now, sir, I protest in the name of truth and human rights against any and every attempt to fetter the hands of one hundred thousand white and colored citizens of the State of Georgia. Sir, I now leave this question to the consideration of this body, and I wish my last words upon the great issues involved in the bill before us to be my solemn and earnest demand for full and prompt protection for the helpless loyal people of Georgia.

I appeal to the legislative enactments of this Congress, and ask if now, in the hour when a reconstructed State most needs support, this Senate, which hitherto has done so nobly, will not give it such legislation as it needs.[1]

[1] *Congressional Globe*, 41st Congress, Second Session, pp. 1986-1988.

SPEECH ON DISORDERS IN THE SOUTH

By Jefferson F. Long

Mr. Speaker the object of the bill before the House is to modify the test-oath. As a citizen of the South, living in Georgia, born and raised in that State, having been there during the war and up to the present time, I know the condition of affairs in that State. Now, sir, we propose here today to modify the test-oath, and to give to those men in the rebel States who are disloyal today to the government this favor. We propose, sir, to remove political disabilities from the very men who were the leaders of the Ku Klux and who have committed midnight outrages in that State.

What do those men say? Before their disabilities are removed they say, "We will remain quiet until all of our disabilities are removed, and then we shall again take the lead." Why, Mr. Speaker, in my State since emancipation there have been over five hundred loyal men shot down by the disloyal men there, and not one of those who took part in committing those outrages has ever been brought to justice. Do we, then, really propose here today, when the country is not ready for it, when those disloyal people still hate this Government, when loyal men dare not carry the "stars and stripes" through our streets, for if they do they will be turned out of employment, to relieve from political disability the very men who have committed these Ku Klux outrages? I think that I am doing my duty to my constituents and my duty to my country when I vote against any such proposition.

Yes, sir; I do mean that murders and outrages are being committed there. I received no longer ago than this morning a letter from a man in my State, a loyal man who was appointed postmaster by the President, stating that he was beaten in the streets a few days ago. I have also received information from the lower part of Georgia that disloyal men went in the midnight disguised and took a loyal man out and shot him; and not one of them has been brought to justice. Loyal men are constantly being cruelly beaten. When we take the men who commit these outrages before judges and juries we find that they are in the hands of the very Ku Klux themselves who protect them.

Mr. Speaker, I propose, as a man raised as a slave, my mother a slave before me, and my ancestry slaves as far back as I can trace them, yet holding no animosity to the law-abiding people of my State, and those who are willing to stand by the Government, while I am willing to remove the disabilities of all such who will support the Government, still I propose for one, knowing the condition of things there in Georgia, not to vote for any modification of the test-oath in favor of disloyal men.

Gentlemen on the other side of the House have complimented men on this side. I hope the blood of the Ku Klux has not got upon this side; I hope not. If this House removes the disabilities of disloyal men by modifying the test-oath, I venture to prophesy you will again have trouble from the very same men who gave you trouble before.[1]

SPEECH ON THE ENFORCEMENT OF THE FOURTEENTH AMENDMENT

By R. C. DeLarge[2]

Mr. Speaker: I had supposed that in the consideration of this matter of legislation for the South party lines would not have been so distinctly drawn, but that we would have at least first endeavored to ascertain whether or not there was any necessity for the legislation, and then decide what kind of legislation would be best. I say I did not expect that party lines would be drawn so distinctly while considering a matter of such grave import.

I believe that if there was a single gentleman upon the floor of this House who, before the commencement of this debate, doubted that lawlessness, confusion, and anarchy existed in some portions of the South, he is at least cured of that doubt by this time. Gentlemen upon both sides of the House have in their speeches acknowledged, and, by the evidence produced, proven to my satisfaction, and, I believe, to the satisfaction of a majority of the members of this House, that such a state of affairs does exist in some portions of the southern states.

I am free to say that none can bring the charge to my door of ever having acted in a manner that would be termed illiberal. I

[1] *Congressional Globe*, 41st Congress, Third Session, p. 881.

[2] Robert C. DeLarge was born at Aiken, South Carolina, March 15, 1842. He received only a limited education and chose to pursue the occupation of farming. He entered politics in 1868, held several local and State offices, was elected to the 42nd Congress, and on February 15, 1874, became a trial justice at Charleston.—*Biographical Congressional Directory*, p. 497.

am also free to say that I, like other gentlemen upon the floor of this House, have the honor of representing a district in which no case of outlawry has ever occurred. Since the time of reconstruction no outrage has been committed in my district; and I say frankly to you today that until within the last few months no one upon the face of God's earth could have convinced me that any secret organization existed in my State for the purpose of committing murder, arson, or other outrages upon the lives, liberty, and property of the people; and, sir, I sincerely deplore and lament the abundance of that evidence which so plainly proves the existence of such an organization today. Would to God, sir, that the fair fame of the State of my birth, and which I have the honor in part to represent, had not been marred by the wicked deeds of these outlaws, who shrink from no cruelty, who spare no sex nor station to carry out their devilish purposes.

But, sir, I cannot shut my eyes to facts; I cannot refuse to yield my faith to tales of horror so fully proven; and I am thoroughly convinced that it is necessary to do something to cure these awful wrongs. I am free to admit that neither the Republicans of my State nor the Democrats of that State can shake their garments and say that they have had no hand in bringing about this condition of affairs. Both parties are responsible for it. As a member of the Republican party I may state, while demanding legislation on behalf of all the citizens there, that both parties to a considerable extent are responsible for this condition of things. Sir, it is necessary that we should legislate upon this subject. The Governor of my State has called upon the Executive of this country for assistance and protection. He has stated distinctly in that call that he is unable to preserve the public peace in some districts of that State. That is something which we must all admit. That is not denied by the Democrats of South Carolina. Some of them doubtless rejoice in this, because they can throw the blame, as they think, upon the administration of the State, which is in the hands of their political foes. It is not now the question, what is the cause which has brought about this condition of affairs. It is useless, except for the purpose of gaining partisan credit or fixing partisan odium, now to charge the blame here or there. But, sir, the naked facts stare us in the face, that this condition of affairs does exist, and that it is necessary for the strong arm of the law to interpose and protect the people in their lives, liberty, and property.

Just here allow me to make a suggestion. If the gentlemen on this side of the House propose to legislate for the benefit of the people of the South, I tell them, and say it fully conscious of the responsibility that rests upon me in saying it, that while legislation is necessary, yet unless they are ready to concede along with this legislation for the protection of the loyal people of the South some accompanying measure to go hand in hand with this and remove as far as in our power rests some of the evils that have brought about the existing condition of things, neither this legislation nor any other that you may pass from now until the hour of doom will be of any benefit. I speak knowing what I say.

Mr. Speaker, when the Governor of my State the other day called in council the leading men of that State, to consider the condition of affairs there and to advise what measure would be best for the protection of the people, whom did he call together? The major portion of the men whom he convened were men resting under political disabilities imposed by the fourteenth amendment. In good faith I ask gentlemen on this side of the House, and gentlemen on the other side, whether it is reasonable to expect that these men should be interested, in any shape or form, in using their influence and best endeavors for the preservation of the public peace, when they have nothing to look for politically in the future? You say they should have the moral and material interest of their State at heart, though even always to be denied a participation in its honors. You may insist that the true patriot seeks no personal ends in the acts of patriotism. All this is true; but, Mr. Speaker, men are but men everywhere, and you ought not to expect of those whom you daily call by opprobrious epithets, whom you daily remind of their political sins, whom you persistently exclude from places of the smallest trust in the Government you have created, to be very earnest to coöperate with you in the work of establishing and fortifying governments set up in hostility to the whole tone of their prejudices, their convictions, and their sympathies. What ought to be is one thing, what in the weakness and fallibility of human nature will be is quite another thing. The statesman regards the actual and acts upon it; the desirable, the possible, and even the probable furnishes but poor basis for political action.

If I had time I would enumerate some of the causes which have brought about the existing state of affairs. I am not here to apologize for murderers; I am not here to defend any one who has committed any act of impropriety or wrong. But, sir, it is a fact, I do not give it as any or even the slightest excuse for the Democrats of my State, who, by their influence secretly or by joining in armed organization, have brought about this condition of affairs—it is a fact, unfortunately for us, that our party has done some things which give color to the charge that it is responsible to some degree for the evils which afflict us.

When I heard the gentleman from New York (Mr. Cox) on Tuesday last hurl his shafts against the members of my race, charging that through their ignorance they had brought about these excesses, I thought he should have remembered that for the ignorance of that portion of the people he and his party associates are responsible, not those people themselves. While there may have been extravagance and corruption resulting from the placing of improper men in official positions—and this is part of the cause of the existing state of things—these evils have been brought about by men identified with the race to which the gentleman from New York belongs, and not by our race.

Many men like himself, in order to get a better position in society or officially, came down among us, and, not knowing them, we placed them in position. If we, through ignorance, have placed them in position, have placed them in power, and they have deceived us, it is no fault of ours. In this connection I desire to have read a part of the remarks of the gentleman from New York on Tuesday last.

The Clerk read as follows:

"South Carolina has been infested by the worst local government ever vouchsafed to a people. Ignorance, bribery, and corruption are common in her Legislature. Bonds by the million are issued, the public debt increased, and nothing to show for it. The debt in 1860 was but $3,691,574. It was last year $11,429,711; and this year no one knows whether it is twenty or thirty millions, nor how much is counterfeit or genuine! Her rulers contrived new burdens in order to blunder more. On a full valuation of real and personal property of $183,913,367 the people pay this year sixteen mills on the dollar as a State tax and four mills county tax.

"This is for 1870 and 1871, and amounts in all to $4,095,047, to which $300,000 is to be added for poll tax. In other words, the value of the property is reduced from $489,000,000 before the war to $188,000,000, and the tax raised from $400,000 to $4,250,000, or ten times as much. It is two and a half per cent, on a full valuation, and only chronic insecurity and disorder as the consideration! This is done by those who pay no taxes, who squander what is paid, who use the means to arm negro militia and create a situation of terror, from which men rush into secret societies for defense of homes, mothers, sisters, wives, and children.

"Add to these grievances the intolerable exactions of the Federal Government, not only in taxes, but in laws, and it should give us pause before we place that people at the mercy of an inferior race, a vindictive party, a court-martial, and a hostile President. The people in their agony in that State actually clamored for United States troops to save them from the rapacity and murder of the negro bands and their white allies. Can we not understand why men, born free, should rise, or, if not rise with safety, that they are compelled to hide in Ku Klux or other secret clans, and strike against this ruin and desolation, peculation and violence, and that, too, when it is done by those who are not of their race and but lately in their midst?

Mr. de Large. I desire to correct the statement made by the gentleman from New York, that the State tax of South Carolina for 1870 is only nine mills on the dollar, for 1871, seven mills, not as he states, sixteen mills. I have already alluded to the ignorance referred to in the gentleman's remarks. Before closing I desire to say that I hope the House will adopt the substitute of the gentleman from Ohio. I am prepared to vote for that substitute, while I am free to admit that I did not intend to vote for the bill as originally reported.[1]

[1] *Congressional Globe*, 42nd Congress, First Session, pp. 230-231.

THE SOUTHERN SITUATION[1]

By Joseph H. Rainey

Mr. Speaker, in approaching the subject now under consideration I do so with a deep sense of its magnitude and importance, and in full recognition of the fact that a remedy is needed to meet the evil now existing in most of the Southern States, but especially in that one, which I have the honor to represent in part, the State of South Carolina. The enormity of the crimes constantly perpetrated there finds no parallel in the history of this Republic in her very darkest days. There was a time when the early settlers of New England were compelled to enter the fields, their homes, even the very sanctuary itself, armed to the full extent of their means. While the people were offering their worship to God within those humble walls their voices kept time with the tread of the sentry outside. But, sir, it must be borne in mind that at the time referred to civilization had but just begun its work upon this continent. The surroundings were unpropitious, and as yet the grand capabilities of this fair land lay dormant under the fierce tread of the red man. But as civilization advanced with its steady and resistless sway it drove back those wild cohorts and compelled them to give way to the march of improvement. In course of time superior intelligence made its impress and established its dominion upon this continent. That intelligence, with an influence like that of the sun rising in the east and spreading its broad rays like a garment of light, gave life and gladness to the dark and barbaric land of America.

Surely, sir, it were but reasonable to hope that this sacred influence should never have been overshadowed, and that in the history of other nations, no less than in our own past, we might find beacon lights for our guidance. In part this has been realized, and might have reached the height of our expectations if it had not been for the blasting effects of slavery, whose deadly pall has so long spread its folds over this nation, to the destruction of

[1] Joseph H. Rainey was born of slave parents at Georgetown, S. C., June 21, 1832. He received a limited education. After following the trade of a barber, he was compelled, in 1862, to work on Confederate fortifications. From this work he escaped, going to the West Indies, where he remained till the end of the war. Upon his return to the United States, he entered politics. He served in the 42nd, 43rd, 44th, and 45th Congresses, and died at Georgetown, S. C., August 1, 1887.—*Biographical Congressional Directory*, p. 757.

peace, union, and concord. Most particularly has its baneful influence been felt in the South, causing the people to be at once restless and discontented. Even now, sir, after the great conflict between slavery and freedom, after the triumph achieved at such a cost, we can yet see the traces of the disastrous strife and the remains of disease in the body-politic of the South. In proof of this witness the frequent outrages perpetrated upon our loyal men. The prevailing spirit of the Southerner is either to rule or to ruin. Voters must perforce succumb to their wishes or else risk life itself in the attempt to maintain a simple right of common manhood.

The suggestions of the shrewdest Democratic papers have proved unavailing in controlling the votes of the loyal whites and blacks of the South. Their innuendoes have been evaded. The people emphatically decline to dispose of their rights for a mess of pottage. In this particular the Democracy of the North found themselves foiled and their money needless. But with a spirit more demon-like than that of a Nero or a Caligula, there has been concocted another plan, destructive, ay, diabolical in its character, worthy only of hearts without regard for God or man, fit for such deeds as those deserving the name of men would shudder to perform. Is it asked, what are those deeds? Let those who liberally contributed to the supply of arms and ammunition in the late rebellious States answer the question. Soon after the close of the war there had grown up in the South a very widely-spread willingness to comply with the requirements of the law. But as the clemency and magnanimity of the General Government became manifest once again did the monster rebellion lift its hydra head in renewed defiance, cruel and cowardly, fearing the light of day, hiding itself under the shadow of the night as more befitting its bloody and accursed work.

I need not, Mr. Speaker, recite here the murderous deeds committed both in North and South Carolina. I could touch the feelings of this House by the story of widows and orphans now wandering amid the ravines of the rural counties of my native State seeking protection and maintenance from others who are yet unable, on account of their own poverty, to grant them aid. I could dwell upon the sorrows of poor women, with their helpless infants, cast upon the world, homeless and destitute, deprived of their natural protectors by the red hand of the midnight assassin. I could appeal to you, members upon this floor, as husbands and fathers, to picture to yourselves the desolation of your own happy firesides should you be suddenly snatched away from your loved ones. Think of gray-haired men, whose fourscore years are almost numbered, the venerated heads of peaceful households, without warning, murdered for political opinion's sake. In proof I send to the desk the following article and ask the Clerk to read. It is taken from the Spartanburg (South Carolina) Republican, March 29, 1871.

The Clerk read as follows:

"Horrible Attempt at Murder by Disguised Men.—One of the most cowardly and inhuman attempts at murder known in the annals of crime was made last Wednesday night, the 22d instant, by a band of disguised men upon the person of Dr. J. Winsmith at his home about twelve miles from town. The doctor, a man nearly seventy years of age, had been to town during the day and was seen and talked with by many of our citizens. Returning home late, he soon afterward retired, worn out and exhausted by the labors of the day. A little after midnight he was aroused by some one knocking violently at his front door. The knocking was soon afterward repeated at his chamber door, which opens immediately upon the front yard. The doctor arose, opened the door, and saw two men in disguise standing before him. As soon as he appeared one of the men cried out, 'Come on, boys! Here's the damned old rascal.' The doctor immediately stepped back into the room, picked up two single-barreled pistols lying upon the bureau, and returned to the open door. At his reappearance the men retreated behind some cedar trees standing in the yard. The doctor, in his night clothes, boldly stepped out into the yard and followed them. On reaching the trees he fired, but with what effect he does not know. He continued to advance, when twenty or thirty shots were fired at him by men crouched behind an orange hedge. He fired his remaining pistol and then attempted to return to the house. Before reaching it, however, he sank upon the ground exhausted by the loss of blood, and pain, occasioned by seven wounds which he had received in various parts of his body. As soon as he fell the assassins mounted their horses and rode away.

"The doctor was carried into the house upon a quilt, borne by his wife and some colored female servants. The colored men on the premises fled on the approach of the murderers, and the colored women being afraid to venture out, Mrs. Winsmith herself was obliged to walk three quarters of a mile to the house of her nephew, Dr. William Smith, for assistance. The physician has been with Dr. Winsmith day and night since the difficulty occurred, and thinks, we learn, that there is a possible chance of the doctor's recovery.

"The occasion of this terrible outrage can be only the fact that Dr. Winsmith is a Republican. One of the largest land-holders and tax-payers in the county, courteous in manner, kind in disposition, and upright and just in all his dealings with his fellow men, he has ever been regarded as one of the leading citizens of the county. For many years prior to the war he represented the people in the Legislature, and immediately after the war he was sent to the Senate. Because he has dared become a Republican, believing that in the doctrines of true republicanism only can the State and country find lasting peace and prosperity, he has become the doomed victim of the murderous Ku Klux Klan.

"The tragedy has cast a gloom over the entire community, and while we are glad to say that it has generally been condemned, yet we regret to state that no step has yet been taken to trace out and punish the perpetrators of the act. The judge of this circuit is sitting on his bench; the machinery of justice is in working order; but there can be found no hand bold enough to set it in motion. The courts of justice seem paralyzed when they have to meet such issues as this. Daily reports come to us of men throughout the country being whipped; of schoolhouses for colored children being closed, and of parties being driven from their houses and their families. Even here in town there are some who fear to sleep at their own homes and in their own beds. The law affords no protection for life and property in this county, and the sooner the country knows it and finds a remedy for it, the better it will be. Better a thousand times the rule of the bayonet than the humiliating lash of the Ku Klux and the murderous bullet of the midnight assassin."

Mr. Rainey. The gentleman to whom reference is made in the

article read, is certainly one of the most inoffensive individuals I have ever known. He is a gentleman of refinement, culture, and sterling worth, a Carolinian of the old school, an associate of the late Hon. John C. Calhoun, being neither a pauper nor a pensioner, but living in comparative affluence and ease upon his own possessions, respected by all fair-minded and unprejudiced citizens who know him. Accepting the situation, he joined the Republican party in the fall of 1870; and for this alliance, and this alone, he has been vehemently assailed and murderously assaulted. By all the warm and kindly sympathies of our common humanity, I implore you to do something for this suffering people, and stand not upon the order of your doing. Could I exhume the murdered men and women of the South, Mr. Speaker, and array their ghastly forms before your eyes, I should not need remove the mantle from them, because their very presence would appeal, in tones of plaintive eloquence, which would be louder than a million tongues. They could indeed—

> "A tale unfold whose lightest word
> Would harrow up thy soul."

It has been asserted that protection for the colored people only has been demanded; and in this there is a certain degree of truth, because they are noted for their steadfastness to the Union and the cause of liberty as guaranteed by the Constitution. But, on the other hand, this protection is equally desired for those loyal whites, some to the manner born, others who, in the exercise of their natural rights as American citizens, have seen fit to remove thither from other sections of the States, and who are now undergoing persecution simply on account of their activity in carrying out Union principles and loyal sentiments in the South. Their efforts have contributed largely to further reconstruction and the restoration of the southern states to the old fellowship of the Federal compact. It is indeed hard that their reward for their well-meant earnestness should be that of being violently treated, and even forced to flee from the homes of their choice. It will be a foul stain upon the escutcheon of our land if such atrocities be tamely suffered longer to continue.

In the dawn of our freedom our young Republic was widely recognized and proudly proclaimed to the world the refuge, the safe asylum of the oppressed of all lands. Shall it be said that at this day, through mere indifference and culpable neglect, this grand boast of ours is become a mere form of words, an utter fraud? I earnestly hope not! And yet, if we stand with folded arms and idle hands, while the cries of our oppressed brethren sound in our ears, what will it be but a proof to all men that we are utterly unfit for our glorious mission, unworthy our noble privileges, as the greatest of republics, the champions of freedom for all men? I would that every individual man in this whole nation could be aroused to a sense of his own part and duty in this great question. When we call to mind the fact that this persecution is waged against men for the simple reason that they dare to vote with the party which has saved the Union intact by the lavish expenditure of blood and treasure, and has borne the nation safely through the fearful crisis of these last few years, our hearts swell with an overwhelming indignation.

The question is sometimes asked, Why do not the courts of law afford redress? Why the necessity of appealing to Congress? We answer that the courts are in many instances under the control of those who are wholly inimical to the impartial administration of law and equity. What benefit would result from appeal to tribunals whose officers are secretly in sympathy with the very evil against which we are striving?

But to return to the point in question. If the Negroes, numbering one-eighth of the population of these United States, would only cast their votes in the interest of the Democratic party, all open measures against them would be immediately suspended, and their rights, as American citizens, recognized. But as to the real results of such a state of affairs, and speaking in behalf of those with whom I am conversant, I can only say that we love freedom more, vastly more, than slavery; consequently we hope to keep clear of the Democrats!

In most of the arguments to which I have listened the positions taken are predicated upon the ground of the unconstitutionality of the bill introduced by the gentleman from Ohio (Mr. Shallabarger). For my part, I am not prepared, Mr. Speaker, to argue this question from a constitutional standpoint alone. I take the ground that, in my opinion, lies far above the interpretation put upon the provisions of the Constitution. I stand upon the broad plane of right; I look to the urgent, the importunate demands of the present emergency; and while I am far from advocating any step not in harmony with that sacred law of our land, while I would not violate the lightest word of that chart which has so well guided us in the past, yet I desire that so broad and liberal a construction be placed upon its provisions as will insure protection to the humblest citizen, without regard to rank, creed or color. Tell me nothing of a constitution which fails to shelter beneath its rightful power the people of a country!

I believe when the fathers of our country framed the Constitution they made the provisions so broad that the humblest, as well as the loftiest citizen, could be protected in his inalienable rights. It was designed to be, and is, the bulwark of freedom, and the strong tower of defense, against foreign invasion and domestic violence. I desire to direct your attention to what is imbodied in the preamble, and would observe that it was adopted after a liberal and protracted discussion on every article composing the great American Magna Charta. And like a keystone to an arch it made the work complete. Here is what it declares:

"We, the people of the United States, in order to form a more perfect Union, establish justice, insure domestic tranquillity, provide for the common defense, promote the general welfare, and secure the blessings of liberty to ourselves and our posterity, do ordain and establish this Constitution for the United States of America."

If the Constitution which we uphold and support as the fundamental law of the United States is inadequate to afford security to life, liberty, and property—if, I say, this inadequacy is proven, then its work is done, then it should no longer be recognized as the Magna Charta of a great and free people; the sooner it is set aside the better for the liberties of the nation. It has been asserted on this floor that the Republican party is answerable for the existing state of affairs in the South. I am here to deny this, and to illustrate, I will say that in the State of South Carolina there is no disturbance of an alarming character in any one of the counties in which the Republicans have a majority. The troubles are usually in those sections in which the Democrats have predominance in power, and, not content with this, desire to be supreme.

I say to the gentlemen of the Opposition, and to the entire membership of the Democratic party, that upon your hands rests the blood of the loyal men of the South. Disclaim it as you will the stain is there to prove your criminality before God and the world in the day of retribution which will surely come. I pity the man or party of men who would seek to ride into power over the dead body of a legitimate opponent.

It has been further stated that peace reigned in the rebellious States from 1865 until the enactment of the reconstruction laws. The reason of this is obvious. Previous to that time they felt themselves regarded as condemned traitors, subject to the penalties of the law. They stood awaiting the sentence of the nation to be expressed by Congress. Subsequently the enactments of that body, framed with a spirit of magnanimity worthy a great and noble nation, proved that, far from a vindictive course, they desired to deal with them with clemency and kindness. This merciful plan of action proved to be a mistake, for cowardice, emboldened by the line of policy of the President, began to feel that judgment long delayed meant forgiveness without repentance. Their tactics were changed, and again a warlike attitude was assumed, not indeed directly against the General Government, but against those who upon southern soil were yet the staunch supporters of its powers. Thus is it evident that if only the props which support such a fabric could be removed the structure must necessarily fall, to be built again by other hands. This is the animus of the Ku Klux Klan, which is now spreading devastation through the once fair and tranquil South.

If the country there is impoverished it has certainly not been caused by the fault of those who love the Union, but it is simply the result of a disastrous war madly waged against the best Government known to the world. The murder of unarmed men and the maltreating of helpless women can never make restitution for the losses which are the simply inevitable consequence of the rebellion. The faithfulness of my race during the entire war, in supporting and protecting the families of their masters, speaks volumes in their behalf as to the real kindliness of their feelings toward the white people of the South.

In conclusion, sir, I would say that it is in no spirit of bitterness against the southern people that I have spoken to-day. There are many among them for whom I entertain a profound regard, having known them in former and brighter days of their history. I have always felt a pride in the prestige of my native State, noted as she has been for her noble sons, with their lofty intellect or tried statesmanship. But it is not possible for me to speak in quiet and studied words of those unworthy her ancient and honorable name, who at this very day are doing all they can do to deface her fair records of the past and bring the old State into disrepute.

I can say for my people that we ardently desire peace for ourselves and for the whole nation. Come what will, we are fully determined to stand by the Republican party and the Government. As to our fate, "we are not wood, we are not stone," but men, with feelings and sensibilities like other men whose skin is of a lighter hue.

When myself and colleagues shall leave these Halls and turn our footsteps toward our southern homes we know not but that the assassin may await our coming, as marked for his vengeance. Should this befall, we would bid Congress and our country to remember that 'twas—

"Bloody treason flourished over us."

Be it as it may, we have resolved to be loyal and firm, "and if we perish, we perish!" I earnestly hope the bill will pass.[1]

The fight for the recognition of the Negro as a citizen and a man assumed the form of an effort led by Charles Sumner to protect the Negro by laws guaranteeing the civil rights of all regardless of race or color or previous condition of servitude. The measures embodying these principles commonly referred to as the Civil Rights Bill caused alarm among the spokesmen of the unreconstructed South. In their attack on the principle of liberty, they evoked from several Negro congressmen forceful speeches which deserve honorable mention. The first one below delivered by Robert Brown Elliott was considered one of the most eloquent addresses ever delivered before that body.

[1] *Congressional Globe,* Part 1, First Session, 42nd Congress, pp. 393-395.

THE CIVIL RIGHTS BILL[1]

BY R. B. ELLIOTT

WHILE I am sincerely grateful for this high mark of courtesy that has been accorded to me by this House, it is a matter of regret to me that it is necessary at this day that I should rise in the presence of an American Congress to advocate a bill which simply asserts equal rights and equal public privileges for all classes of American citizens. I regret, sir, that the dark hue of my skin may lend a color to the imputation that I am controlled by motives personal to myself in my advocacy of this great measure of national justice. Sir, the motive that impels me is restricted by no such narrow boundary, but is as broad as your Constitution. I advocate it, sir, because it is right. The bill, however, not only appeals to your justice, but it demands a response from your gratitude.

In the events that led to the achievement of American Independence the Negro was not an inactive or unconcerned spectator. He bore his part bravely upon many battle-fields, although uncheered by that certain hope of political elevation which victory would secure to the white man. The tall granite shaft, which a grateful State has reared above its sons who fell in defending Fort Griswold against the attack of Benedict Arnold, bears the name of Jordan, Freeman, and other brave men of the African race who there cemented with their blood the corner-stone of the Republic. In the State which I have the honor in part to represent the rifle of the black man rang out against the troops of the British crown in the darkest days of the American Revolution. Said General Greene, who has been justly termed the Washington of the North, in a letter written by him to Alexander Hamilton, on the 10th day of January, 1781, from the vicinity of Camden, South Carolina:

"There is no such thing as national character or national sentiment. The inhabitants are numerous, but they would be formidable abroad rather than at home. There is a great spirit of enterprise among the black people, and those that come out as volunteers are not a little formidable to the enemy."

[1] Robert Brown Elliott was born in Boston, Massachusetts, August 11, 1842. He was educated in England, and upon his return to the United States entered local politics in the State of South Carolina. Mr. Elliott was elected to the 42nd Congress and resigned before the term had expired; he was reëlected to the 43rd Congress and again resigned, this time to accept the office of sheriff.—*Biographical Congressional Directory*, p. 517.

At the battle of New Orleans, under the immortal Jackson, a colored regiment held the extreme right of the American line unflinchingly, and drove back the British column that pressed upon them, at the point of the bayonet. So marked was their valor on that occasion that it evoked from their great commander the warmest encomiums, as will be seen from his dispatch announcing the brilliant victory.

As the gentleman from Kentucky, (Mr. Beck), who seems to be the leading exponent on this floor of the party that is arrayed against the principle of this bill, has been pleased, in season and out of season, to cast odium upon the negro and to vaunt the chivalry of his State, I may be pardoned for calling attention to another portion of the same dispatch. Referring to the various regiments under his command, and their conduct on that field which terminated the second war of American Independence, General Jackson says:

"At the very moment when the entire discomfiture of the enemy was looked for with a confidence amounting to certainty, the Kentucky reënforcements, in whom so much reliance had been placed, ingloriously fled."

In quoting this indisputable piece of history, I do so only by way of admonition and not to question the well-attested gallantry of the true Kentuckian, and to suggest to the gentleman that it would be well that he should not flaunt his heraldry so proudly while he bears this bar-sinister on the military escutcheon of his State—a State which answered the call of the Republic in 1861, when treason thundered at the very gates of the capital, by coldly declaring her neutrality in the impending struggle. The Negro, true to that patriotism and love of country that have ever characterized and marked his history on this continent, came to the aid of the Government in its efforts to maintain the Constitution. To that Government he now appeals; that Constitution he now invokes for protection against outrage and unjust prejudices founded upon caste.

But, sir, we are told by the distinguished gentleman from Georgia (Mr. Stephens) that Congress has no power under the Constitution to pass such a law, and that the passage of such an act is in direct contravention of the rights of the States. I cannot assent to any such proposition. The constitution of a free government ought always to be construed in favor of human rights. Indeed, the thirteenth, fourteenth, and fifteenth amendments, in positive words, invest Congress with the power to protect the citizen in his civil and political rights. Now, sir, what are civil rights? Rights natural, modified by civil society. Mr. Lieber says:

"By civil liberty is meant, not only the absence of individual restraint, but liberty within the social system and political organism—a combination of principles and laws which acknowledge, protect, and favor the dignity of man.* * * Civil liberty is the result of man's two-fold character as an individual and social being, so soon as both are equally respected."—Leiber on *Civil Liberty*, Page 25.

Alexander Hamilton, the right-hand man of Washington in the perilous days of the then infant Republic, the great interpreter and expounder of the Constitution, says:

"Natural liberty is a gift of the beneficent Creator to the whole human race; civil liberty is founded on it; civil liberty is only natural liberty modified and secured by civil society."—Hamilton's *History of the American Republic*, vol. 1, page 70.

In the French constitution of June, 1793, we find this grand and noble declaration:

"Government is instituted to insure to man the free use of his natural and inalienable rights. These rights are equality, liberty, security, property. All men are equal by nature and before the law. * * * Law is the same for all, be it protective or penal. Freedom is the power by which man can do what does not interfere with the rights of another; its basis is nature, its standard is justice, its protection is law, its moral boundary is the maxim: 'Do not unto others what you do not wish they should do unto you.' "

Are we then, sir, with the amendments to our Constitution staring us in the face; with these grand truths of history before our eyes; with innumerable wrongs daily inflicted upon five million citizens demanding redress, to commit this question to the diversity of State legislation? In the words of Hamilton—

"Is it the interest of the Government to sacrifice individual rights to the preservation of the rights of an artificial being, called States? There can be no truer principle than this, that every individual of the community at large has an equal right to the protection of Government. Can this be a free Government if partial distinctions are tolerated or maintained?"

The rights contended for in this bill are among "the sacred rights of mankind, which are not to be rummaged for among old parchments or musty records; they are written as with a sunbeam, in the whole volume of human nature, by the hand of the Divinity itself, and can never be erased or obscured by mortal power."

But the Slaughter-house cases!—the Slaughter-house cases!

The honorable gentleman from Kentucky, always swift to sustain the failing and dishonored cause of proscription, rushes forward and flaunts in our faces the decision of the Supreme Court of the United States in the Slaughter-house cases, and in that act he has been willingly aided by the gentleman from Georgia. Hitherto, in the contests which have marked the progress of the cause of equal civil rights, our opponents have appealed sometimes to custom, sometimes to prejudice, more often to pride of race, but they have never sought to shield themselves behind the Supreme Court. But now, for the first time, we are told that we are barred by a decision of that court, from which there is no appeal. If this be true we must stay our hands. The cause of equal civil rights must pause at the command of a power whose edicts must be obeyed till the fundamental law of our country is changed.

Has the honorable gentleman from Kentucky considered well the claim he now advances? If it were not disrespectful I would ask, has he ever read the decision which he now tells us is an insuperable barrier to the adoption of this great measure of justice?

In the consideration of this subject, has not the judgment of the gentleman from Georgia been warped by the ghost of the dead doctrines of State-rights? Has he been altogether free from prejudices engendered by long training in that school of politics that well-nigh destroyed this Government?

Mr. Speaker, I venture to say here in the presence of the gentleman from Kentucky, and the gentleman from Georgia, and in the presence of the whole country, that there is not a line or word, not a thought or dictum even, in the decision of the Supreme Court in the great Slaughter-house cases which casts a shadow of doubt on the right of Congress to pass the pending bill, or to adopt such other legislation as it may judge proper and necessary to secure perfect equality before the law to every citizen of the Republic. Sir, I protest against the dishonor now cast upon our Supreme Court by both the gentleman from Kentucky and the gentleman from Georgia. In other days, when the whole country was bowing beneath the yoke of slavery, when press, pulpit, platform, Congress, and courts felt the fatal power of the slave oligarchy, I remember a decision of that court which no American now reads without shame and humiliation. But those days are past. The Supreme Court of today is a tribunal as true to freedom as any department of this Government, and I am honored with the opportunity of repelling a deep disgrace which the gentleman from Kentucky, backed and sustained as he is by the gentleman from Georgia, seeks to put upon it.

What were these Slaughter-house cases? The gentleman should be aware that a decision of any court should be examined in the light of the exact question which is brought before it for decision. That is all that gives authority to any decision.

The State of Louisiana, by act of her Legislature, had conferred on certain persons the exclusive right to maintain stock-landings and slaughter-houses within the city of New Orleans, or the parishes of Orleans, Jefferson, and Saint Bernard, in that State. The corporation which was thereby chartered were invested with the sole and exclusive privilege of conducting and carrying on the live-stock, landing, and slaughter-house business within the limits designated.

The supreme court of Louisiana sustained the validity of the act conferring these exclusive privileges, and the plaintiffs in error brought the case before the Supreme Court of the United States for review. The plaintiffs in error contended that the act in question was void, because, first, it established a monopoly which was in derogation of common right and in contravention of the common law; and, second, that the grant of such exclusive privileges was in violation of the thirteenth and fourteenth amendments of the Constitution of the United States.

It thus appears from a simple statement of the case that the question which was before the court was not whether a State law which denied to a particular portion of her citizens the rights conferred on her citizens generally, on account of race, color, or previous condition of servitude, was unconstitutional because in conflict with the recent amendments, but whether an act which conferred on certain citizens exclusive privileges for police purposes was in conflict therewith, because imposing an involuntary servitude forbidden by the thirteenth amendment, or abridging the rights and immunities of citizens of the United States, or denying the equal protection of the laws, prohibited by the fourteenth amendment.

On the part of the defendants in error it was maintained that the act was the exercise of the ordinary and unquestionable power of the State to make regulation for the health and comfort of society—the exercise of the police power of the State, defined by Chancellor Kent to be "the right to interdict unwholesome trades, slaughter-houses, operations offensive to the senses, the deposit of powder, the application of steam-power to propel cars, the building with combustible materials, and the burial of the dead in the midst of dense masses of population, on the general and rational principle that every person ought so to use his own property as not to injure his neighbors, and that private interests must be made subservient to the general interests of the community."

The decision of the Supreme Court is to be found in the 16th volume of Wallace's Reports, and was delivered by Associate Justice Miller. The court holds, first, that the act in question is a legitimate and warrantable exercise of the police power of the State in regulating the business of stock-handling and slaughtering in the city of New Orleans and the territory immediately contiguous. Having held this, the court proceeds to discuss the question whether the conferring of exclusive privileges, such as those conferred by the act in question, is the imposing of an involuntary servitude, the abridging of the rights and immunities of citizens of the United States, or the denial to any person within the jurisdiction of the State of the equal protection of the laws.

That the act is not the imposition of an involuntary servitude the court holds to be clear, and they next proceed to examine the remaining questions arising under the fourteenth amendment. Upon this question the court holds that the leading and comprehensive purpose of the thirteenth, fourteenth, and fifteenth amendments was to secure the complete freedom of the race, which, by the events of the war, had been wrested from the unwilling grasp of their owners. I know no finer or more just picture, albeit painted in the neutral tints of true judicial impartiality, of the motives and events which led to these amendments. Has the gentleman from Kentucky read these passages which I now quote? Or has the gentleman from Georgia considered well the force of the language therein used? Says the court on page 70:

"The process of restoring to their proper relations with the Federal Government and with the other States those which had sided with the rebellion, undertaken under the proclamation of President Johnson in 1865, and before the assembling of Congress, developed the fact that, notwithstanding the formal recognition by those States of the abolition of slavery, the condition of the slave race would, without further protection of the Federal Government, be almost as bad as it was before. Among the first acts of legislation adopted by several of the States in the legislative bodies which claimed to be in their normal relations with the Federal Government, were laws which imposed upon the colored race onerous disabilities and burdens, and curtailed their rights in the pursuit of life, liberty and property to such an extent that their freedom was of little value, while they had lost the protection which they had received from their former owners from motives both of interest and humanity.

"They were in some States forbidden to appear in the towns in any other character than menial servants. They were required to reside on and cultivate the soil, without the right to purchase or own it. They were excluded from any occupations of gain, and were not permitted to give testimony in the courts in any case where a white man was a party. It was said that their lives were at the mercy of bad men, either because the laws for their protection were insufficient or were not enforced.

"These circumstances, whatever of falsehood or misconception may have been mingled with their presentation, forced upon the statesmen who had conducted the Federal Government in safety through the crisis of rebellion, and who supposed that by the thirteenth article of amendment they had secured the result of their labors, the conviction that something more was necessary in the way of constitutional protection to the unfortunate race who had suffered so much. They accordingly passed through Congress the proposition for the fourteenth amendment, and they declined to treat as restored to their full participation in the Government of the Union the States which had been in insurrection until they ratified that article by a formal vote of their legislative bodies.

"Before we proceed to examine more critically the provisions of this amendment, on which the plaintiffs in error rely, let us complete and dismiss the history of the recent amendments, as that history relates to the general purpose which pervades them all. A few years' experience satisfied the thoughtful men who had been the authors of the other two amendments that, notwithstanding the restraints of those articles on the States and the laws passed under the additional powers granted to Congress, these were inadequate for the protection of life, liberty, and property, without which freedom to the slave was no boon. They were in all those States denied the right of suffrage. The laws were administered by the white man alone. It was urged that a race of men distinctively marked as was the Negro, living in the midst of another and dominant race, could never be fully secured in their person and their property without the right of suffrage.

"Hence the fifteenth amendment, which declares that 'the right of a citizen of the United States to vote shall not be denied or abridged by any State on account of race, color, or previous condition of servitude.' The Negro having, by the fourteenth amendment, been declared to be a citizen of the United States, is thus made a voter in every State of the Union.

"We repeat, then, in the light of this recapitulation of events almost too recent to be called history, but which are familiar to us all, and on the most casual examination of the language of these amendments, no one can fail to be impressed with the one pervading purpose found in them all, lying at the foundation of each, and without which none of them would have been even suggested: we mean the freedom of the slave race, the security and firm establishment of that freedom, and the protection of the newly-made freeman and citizen from the oppressions of those who had formerly exercised unlimited dominion over him. It is true that only the fifteenth amendment in terms mentions the Negro by speaking of his color and his slavery. But it is just as true that each of the other articles was addressed to the grievances of that race, and designed to remedy them, as the fifteenth.''

These amendments, one and all, are thus declared to have as their all-pervading design and end the security to the recently enslaved race, not only their nominal freedom, but their complete protection from those who had formerly exercised unlimited dominion over them. It is in this broad light that all these amendments must be read, the purpose to secure the perfect equality before the law of all citizens of the United States. What you give to one class you must give to all; what you deny to one class you shall deny to all, unless in the exercise of the common and universal police power of the State you find it needful to confer exclusive privileges on certain citizens, to be held and exercised still for the common good of all.

Such are the doctrines of the Slaughter-house Cases—doctrines worthy of the Republic, worthy of the age, worthy of the great tribunal which thus loftily and impressively enunciates them. Do they—I put it to any man, be he lawyer or not; I put it to the gentleman from Georgia—do they give color even to the claim that this Congress may not now legislate against a plain discrimination made by State laws or State customs against that very race for whose complete freedom and protection these great amendments were elaborated and adopted? Is it pretended, I ask the honorable gentleman from Kentucky or the honorable gentleman from Georgia—is it pretended anywhere that the evils of which we complain, our exclusion from the public inn, from the saloon and table of the steamboat, from the sleeping-coach on the railway, from the right of sepulture in the public burial-ground, are an exercise of the police power of the State? Is such oppression and injustice nothing but the exercise by the State of the right to make regulations for the health, comfort, and security of all her citizens? Is it merely enacting that one man shall so use his own as not to injure another's? Are the colored people to be assimilated to an unwholesome trade or to combustible materials, to be interdicted, to be shut up within prescribed limits? Let the gentleman from Kentucky or the gentleman from Georgia answer. Let the country know to what extent even the audacious prejudice of the gentleman from Kentucky will drive him, and how far even the gentleman from Georgia will permit himself to be led captive by the unrighteous teachings of a false political faith.

If we are to be likened in legal view to "unwholesome trades," to "large and offensive collections of animals," to "noxious slaughter-houses," to "the offal and stench which attend on certain manufactures," let it be avowed. If that is still the doctrine of the political party to which the gentlemen belong, let it be put upon record. If State laws which deny us the common rights and privileges of other citizens, upon no possible or conceivable ground save one of prejudice, or of "taste," as the gentleman from Texas termed it, and as I suppose the gentlemen will prefer to call it, are to be placed under the protection of a decision which affirms the right of a State to regulate the police of her great cities, then the decision is in conflict with the bill before us. No man will dare maintain such a doctrine. It is as shocking to the legal mind as it is offensive to the heart and conscience of all who love justice or respect manhood. I am astonished that the gentleman from Kentucky or the gentleman from Georgia should have been so grossly misled as to rise here and assert that the decision of the Supreme Court in these cases was a denial to Congress of the power to legislate against discriminations on account of race, color, or previous condition of servitude, because that court has decided that exclusive privileges conferred for the common protection of the lives and health of the whole community are not in violation of the recent amendments. The only ground upon which the grant of exclusive privileges to a portion of the community is ever defended is that the substantial good of all is promoted; that in truth it is for the welfare of the whole community that certain persons should alone pursue certain occupations. It is not the special benefit conferred on the few that moves the legislature, but the ultimate and real benefit of all, even of those who are denied the right to pursue those specified occupations. Does the gentleman from Kentucky say that my good is promoted when I am excluded from the public inn? Is the health or safety of the community promoted? Doubtless his prejudice is gratified. Doubtless his democratic instincts are pleased; but will he or his able coadjutor say that such exclusion is a lawful exercise of the police power of the State, or that it is not a denial to me of the equal protection of the laws? They will not so say.

But each of these gentlemen quote at some length from the decision of the court to show that the court recognizes a difference between citizenship of the United States and citizenship of the States. That is true, and no man here who supports this bill questions or overlooks the difference. There are privileges and immunities which belong to me as a citizen of the United States, and there are other privileges and immunities which belong to me as a citizen of my State. The former are under the protection of the Constitution and laws of the United States, and the latter are under the protection of the constitution and laws of my State. But what of that? Are the rights which I now claim—the right to enjoy the common public conveniences of travel on public highways, of rest and refreshment at public inns, of education in public schools, of burial in public cemeteries—rights which I hold as a citizen of the United States or of my State? Or, to state the question more exactly, is not the denial of such privileges to me a denial to me of the equal protection of the laws? For it is under this clause of the fourteenth amendment that we place the present bill, no State shall "deny to any person within its jurisdiction the equal protection of the laws." No matter, therefore, whether his rights are held under the United States or under his particular State, he is equally protected by this amendment. He is always and everywhere entitled to the equal protection of the laws. All discrimination is forbidden; and while the rights of citizens of a State as such are not defined or conferred by the Constitution of the United States, yet all discrimination, all denial of equality before the law, all denial of the equal protection of the laws, whether State or national laws, is forbidden.

The distinction between the two kinds of citizenship is clear, and the Supreme Court have clearly pointed out this distinction, but they have nowhere written a word or line which denies to Congress the power to prevent a denial of equality of rights, whether those rights exist by virtue of citizenship of the United States or of a State. Let honorable members mark well this distinction. There are rights which are conferred on us by the United States. There are other rights conferred on us by the States of which we are individually the citizens. The fourteenth amendment does not forbid a State to deny to all its citizens any of those rights which the State itself has conferred, with certain exceptions, which are pointed out in the decision which we are examining. What it does forbid is inequality, is discrimination, or, to use the words of the amendment itself, is the denial "to any person within its jurisdiction the equal protection of the laws." If a State denies to me rights which are common to all her other citizens, she violates this amendment, unless she can show, as was shown in the Slaughter-house Cases, that she does it in the legitimate exercise of her police power. If she abridges the rights of all her citizens equally, unless those rights are specially guarded by the Constitution of the United States, she does not violate this amendment. This is not to put the rights which I hold by virtue of my citizenship of South Carolina under the protection of the national Government; it is not to blot out or overlook in the slightest particular the distinction between rights held under the United States and the rights held under the States; but it seeks to secure equality, to prevent discrimination, to confer as complete and ample protection on the humblest as on the highest.

The gentleman from Kentucky, in the course of the speech to which I am now replying, made a reference to the State of Massachusetts which betrays again the confusion which exists in his mind on this precise point. He tells us that Massachusetts excludes from the ballot-box all who cannot read and write, and points to that fact as the exercise of a right which this bill would abridge or impair. The honorable gentleman from Massachusetts (Mr. Dawes) answered him truly and well, but I submit that he did not make the best reply. Why did he not ask the gentleman from Kentucky if Massachusetts had ever discriminated against any of her citizens on account of color, or race, or previous condition of servitude? When did Massachusetts sully her proud record by placing on her statute-book any law which admitted to the ballot the white man and shut out the black man? She has never done it; she will not do it; she cannot do it so long as we have a Supreme Court which reads the Constitution of our country with the eyes of justice; nor can Massachusetts or Kentucky deny to any man, on account of his race, color, or previous condition of servitude, that perfect equality of protection under the laws so long as Congress shall exercise the power to enforce, by appropriate legislation, the great and unquestionable securities embodied in the fourteenth amendment to the Constitution.

But, sir, a few words more as to the suffrage regulation of Massachusetts. It is true that Massachusetts in 1857, finding that her illiterate population was being constantly augmented by the continual influx of ignorant emigrants, placed in her constitution the least possible limitation consistent with manhood suffrage to stay this tide of foreign ignorance. Its benefit has been fully demonstrated in the intelligent character of the voters of that honored Commonwealth, reflected so conspicuously in the able Representatives she has today upon this floor. But neither is the inference of the gentleman from Kentucky legitimate, nor do the statistics of the census of 1870, drawn from his own State, sustain his astounding assumption. According to the statistics we find the whole white population of that State is 1,098,692; the whole colored population 222,210. Of the whole white population who cannot write we find 201,077; of the whole colored population who cannot write, 126,048; giving us, as will be seen, 96,162 colored persons who can write to 897,615 white persons who can write. Now, the ratio of the colored population to the white is as 1 to 5, and the ratio of the illiterate colored population to the whole colored population is as 1 to 2; the ratio of the illiterate white population is to the whole white population as 1 is to 5. Reducing this, we have only a preponderance of three-tenths in favor of the whites as to literacy, notwithstanding the advantages which they have always enjoyed and do now enjoy of free-school privileges, and this, too, taking solely into account the single item of being unable to write; for with regard to the inability to read, there is no discrimination in the statistics between the white and colored population. There is, moreover, a peculiar felicity in these statistics with regard to the State of Kentucky, quoted so opportunely for me by the honorable gentleman; for I find that the population of that State, both with regard to its white and colored populations, bears the same relative rank in regard to the white and colored population of the United States; and, therefore, while one Negro would be disfranchised were the limitation of Massachusetts put in force, nearly three white men would at the same time be deprived of the right of suffrage—a consummation which I think would be far more acceptable to the colored people of that State than to the whites.

Now, sir, having spoken as to the intention of the prohibition imposed by Massachusetts, I may be pardoned for a slight inquiry as to the effect of this prohibition. First, it did not in any way abridge or curtail the exercise of the suffrage by any person who at that time enjoyed such right. Nor did it discriminate between the illiterate native and the illiterate foreigner. Being enacted for the good of the entire Commonwealth, like all just laws, its obligations fell equally and impartially upon all its citizens. And as a justification for such a measure, it is a fact too well known almost for mention here that Massachusetts had, from the beginning of her history, recognized the inestimable value of an educated ballot, by not only maintaining a system of free schools, but also enforcing an attendance thereupon, as one of the safeguards for the preservation of a real republican form of government. Recurring then, sir, to the possible contingency alluded to by the gentleman from Kentucky, should the State of Kentucky, having first established a system of common schools whose doors shall swing open freely to all, as contemplated by the provisions of this bill, adopt a provision similar to that of Massachusetts, no one would have cause justly to complain. And if in the coming years the result of such legislation should produce a constituency rivaling that of the old Bay State, no one would be more highly gratified than I.

Mr. Speaker, I have neither the time nor the inclination to notice the many illogical and forced conclusions, the numerous transfers of terms, or the vulgar insinuations which further incumber the argument of the gentleman from Kentucky. Reason and argument are worse than wasted upon those who meet every demand for political and civil liberty by such ribaldry as this—extracted from the speech of the gentleman from Kentucky:

"I suppose there are gentlemen on this floor who would arrest, imprison, and fine a young woman in any State of the South if she were to refuse to marry a Negro man on account of color, race, or previous condition of servitude, in the event of his making her a proposal of marriage, and her refusing on that ground. That would be depriving him of a right he had under the amendment, and Congress would be asked to take it up and say, "This insolent white woman must be taught to know that it is a misdemeanor to deny a man marriage because of race, color, or previous condition of servitude''; and Congress will be urged to say after a while that that sort of thing must be put a stop to, and your conventions of colored men will come here asking you to enforce that right.''

Now, sir, recurring to the venerable and distinguished gentleman from Georgia (Mr. Stephens), who has added his remonstrance against the passage of this bill, permit me to say that I share in the feeling of high personal regard for that gentleman which pervades this House. His years, his ability, and his long experience in public affairs entitle him to the measure of consideration which has been accorded to him on this floor. But in this discussion I cannot and I will not forget that the welfare and rights of my whole race in this country are involved. When, therefore, the honorable gentleman from Georgia lends his voice and influence to defeat this measure, I do not shrink from saying that it is not from him that the American House of Representatives should take lessons in matters touching human rights or the joint relations of the State and national governments. While the honorable gentleman contented himself with harmless speculations in his study, or in the columns of a newspaper, we might well smile at the impotence of his efforts to turn back the advancing tide of opinion and progress; but, when he comes again upon this national arena, and throws himself with all his power and influence across the path which leads to the full enfranchisement of my race, I meet him only as an adversary; nor shall age or any other consideration restrain me from saying that he now offers his Government, which he has done his utmost to destroy, a very poor return for its magnanimous treatment, to come here and seek to continue, by the assertion of doctrines obnoxious to the true principles of our Government, the burdens and oppressions which rest upon five millions of his countrymen who never failed to lift their earnest prayers for the success of this Government when the gentleman was seeking to break up the Union of these States and to blot the American Republic from the galaxy of nations. [Loud applause.]

Sir, it is scarcely twelve years since that gentleman shocked the civilized world by announcing the birth of a government which rested on human slavery as its corner-stone. The progress of events has swept away that pseudo-government which rested on greed, pride, and tyranny; and the race whom he then ruthlessly spurned and trampled on are here to meet him in debate, and to demand that the rights which are enjoyed by their former oppressors—who vainly sought to overthrow a Government which they could not prostitute to the base uses of slavery—shall be accorded to those who even in the darkness of slavery kept their allegiance true to freedom and the Union. Sir, the gentleman from Georgia has learned much since 1861; but he is still a laggard. Let him put away entirely the false and fatal theories which have so greatly marred an otherwise enviable record. Let him accept, in its fullness and beneficence, the great doctrine that American citizenship carries with it every civil and political right which manhood can confer. Let him lend his influence, with all his masterly ability, to complete the proud structure of legislation which makes this nation worthy of the great declaration which heralded its birth, and he will have done that which will most nearly redeem his reputation in the eyes of the world, and best vindicate the wisdom of that policy which has permitted him to regain his seat upon this floor.

To the diatribe of the gentleman from Virginia (Mr. Harris), who spoke on yesterday, and who so far transcended the limits of decency and propriety as to announce upon this floor that his remarks were addressed to white men alone, I shall have no word of reply. Let him feel that a Negro was not only too magnanimous to smite him in his weakness, but was even charitable enough to grant him the mercy of his silence. [Laughter and applause on the floor and in the galleries.] I shall, sir, leave to others less charitable the unenviable and fatiguing task of sifting out of that mass of chaff the few grains of sense that may, perchance, deserve notice. Assuring the gentleman that the Negro in this country aims at a higher degree of intellect than that exhibited by him in this debate, I cheerfully commend him to the commiseration of all intelligent men the world over—black men as well as white men.

Sir, equality before the law is now the broad, universal, glorious rule and mandate of the Republic. No State can violate that. Kentucky and Georgia may crowd their statute-books with retrograde and barbarous legislation; they may rejoice in the odious eminence of their consistent hostility to all the great steps of human progress which have marked our national history since slavery tore down the stars and stripes on Fort Sumter; but, if Congress shall do its duty, if Congress shall enforce the great guarantees which the Supreme Court has declared to be the one pervading purpose of all the recent amendments, then their unwise and unenlightened conduct will fall with the same weight upon the gentlemen from those States who now lend their influence to defeat this bill, as upon the poorest slave who once had no rights which the honorable gentlemen were bound to respect.

But, sir, not only does the decision in the Slaughter-house Cases contain nothing which suggests a doubt of the power of Congress to pass the pending bill, but it contains an express recognition and affirmance of such power. I quote now from page 81 of the volume:

" 'Nor shall any State deny to any person within its jurisdiction the equal protection of the laws.'

In the light of the history of these amendments, and the pervading purpose of them, which we have already discussed, it is not difficult to give a meaning to this clause. The existence of laws in the States where the newly emancipated Negroes resided, which discriminated with gross injustice and hardship against them as a class, was the evil to be remedied by this clause, and by it such laws are forbidden.

If, however, the States did not conform their laws to its requirements, then, by the fifth section of the article of amendment, Congress was authorized to enforce it by suitable legislation. We doubt very much whether any action of a State not directed by way of discrimination against the Negroes as a class, or on account of their race, will ever be held to come within the purview of this provision. It is so clearly a provision for that race and that emergency, that a strong case would be necessary for its application to any other. But as it is a State that is to be dealt with, and not alone the validity of its laws, we may safely leave that matter until Congress shall have exercised its power, or some case of State oppression, by denial of equal justice in its courts shall have claimed a decision at our hands."

No language could convey a more complete assertion of the power of Congress over the subject embraced in the present bill than is here expressed. If the States do not conform to the requirements of this clause, if they continue to deny to any person within their jurisdiction the equal protection of the laws, or as the Supreme Court had said, "deny equal justice in its courts," then Congress is here said to have power to enforce the constitutional guarantee by appropriate legislation. That is the power which this bill now seeks to put in exercise. It proposes to enforce the constitutional guarantee against inequality and discrimination by appropriate legislation. It does not seek to confer new rights, nor to place rights conferred by State citizenship under the protection of the United States, but simply to prevent and forbid inequality and discrimination on account of race, color, or previous condition of servitude. Never was there a bill more completely within the constitutional power of Congress. Never was there a bill which appealed for support more strongly to that sense of justice and fair-play which has been said, and in the main with justice, to be a characteristic of the Anglo-Saxon race. The Constitution warrants it; the Supreme Court sanctions it; justice demands it.

Sir, I have replied to the extent of my ability to the arguments which have been presented by the opponents of this measure. I have replied also to some of the legal propositions advanced by gentlemen on the other side; and now that I am about to conclude, I am deeply sensible of the imperfect manner in which I have performed the task. Technically, this bill is to decide upon the civil status of the colored American citizen; a point disputed at the very formation of our present Government, when by a short-sighted policy, a policy repugnant to true republican government, one Negro counted as three-fifths of a man. The logical result of this mistake of the framers of the Constitution strengthened the cancer of slavery, which finally spread its poisonous tentacles over the southern portion of the body-politic. To arrest its growth and save the nation we have passed through the harrowing operation of internecine war, dreaded at all times, resorted to at the last extremity, like the surgeon's knife, but absolutely necessary to extirpate the disease which threatened with the life of the nation the overthrow of civil and political liberty on this continent. In that dire extremity the members of the race which I have the honor in part to represent—the race which pleads for justice at your hands today, forgetful of their inhuman and brutalizing servitude at the South, their degradation and ostracism at the North—flew willingly and gallantly to the support of the national Government. Their sufferings, assistance, privations, and trials in the swamps and in the rice-fields, their valor on the land and on the sea, is a part of the ever-glorious record which makes up the history of a nation preserved, and might, should I urge the claim, incline you to respect and guarantee their rights and privileges as citizens of our common Republic. But I remember that valor, devotion, and loyalty are not always rewarded according to their just deserts, and that after the battle some who have borne the brunt of the fray may, through neglect or contempt, be assigned to a subordinate place, while the enemies in war may be preferred to the sufferers.

The results of the war, as seen in reconstruction, have settled forever the political status of my race. The passage of this bill will determine the civil status, not only of the Negro, but of any other class of citizens who may feel themselves discriminated against. It will form the cap-stone of that temple of liberty, begun on this continent under discouraging circumstances, carried on in spite of the sneers of monarchists and the cavils of pretended friends of freedom, until at last it stands in all its beautiful symmetry and proportions, a building the grandest which the world has ever seen, realizing the most sanguine expectations and the highest hopes of those who, in the name of equal, impartial, and universal liberty, laid the foundation stones.

The Holy Scriptures tell us of an humble hand-maiden who long, faithfully and patiently gleaned in the rich fields of her wealthy kinsman; and we are told further that at last, in spite of her humble antecedents, she found complete favor in his sight. For over two centuries our race has "reaped down your fields." The cries and woes which we have uttered have "entered into the ears of the Lord of Sabaoth," and we are at last politically free. The last vestiture only is needed—civil rights. Having gained this, we may, with hearts overflowing with gratitude, and thankful that our prayer has been granted, repeat the prayer of Ruth: "Entreat me not to leave thee, or to return from following after thee; for whither thou goest, I will go; and where thou lodgest, I will lodge; thy people shall be my people, and thy God my God; where thou diest, will I die, and there will I be buried; the Lord do so to me, and more also, if aught but death part thee and me."[1] [Great applause.]

CIVIL RIGHTS BILL[2]

BY RICHARD H. CAIN

Mr. Speaker, I feel called upon more particularly by the remarks of the gentleman from North Carolina (Mr. Vance) on civil rights to express my views. For a number of days this question has been discussed, and various have been the opinions expressed as to whether or not the pending bill should be passed in its present form or whether it should be modified to meet the objections entertained by a number of gentlemen whose duty it will be to give their votes for or against its passage. It has been assumed that to pass this bill in its present form Congress would manifest a tendency to override the Constitution of the country and violate the rights of the States.

Whether it be true or false is yet to be seen. I take it, so far as the constitutional question is concerned, if the colored people under the law, under the amendments to the Constitution, have become invested with all the rights of citizenship, then they carry with them all rights and immunities accruing to and belonging to a citizen of the United States. If four, or nearly five, million people have been lifted from the thralldom of slavery and made free; if the Government by its amendments to the Constitution has guaranteed to them all rights and immunities, as to other citizens, they must necessarily therefore carry along with them all the privileges enjoyed by all other citizens of the Republic.

Sir, the gentleman from North Carolina (Mr. Vance) who spoke on the questions stated some objections, to which I desire to address a few words of reply. He said it would enforce social rights, and therefore would be detrimental to the interests of both the whites and the blacks of the country. My conception of the effect of this

[1] *Congressional Record*, Vol. II, Part 1, 43rd Congress, First Session, pp. 407-410.

[2] Richard H. Cain was born in Greenbrier County, Virginia, April 12, 1825. In 1831, he moved with his father to Gallipolis, Ohio. Of limited education prior to his marriage, and having entered the ministry at an early age, he found it to his advantage, at the age of 35 years, to undertake formal study at a recognized school of learning. This was Wilberforce University. Following a career as clergyman, missionary, and politician, he easily became popular. He was elected to the 43rd Congress and reëlected to the 45th from South Carolina. After his retirement from Congress, Mr. Cain was elected the fourteenth bishop of the African Methodist Episcopal Church. He died in Washington, January 18, 1887.—*Biographical Congressional Directory*, p. 434.

bill, if it be passed into a law, will be simply to place the colored men of this country upon the same footing with every other citizen under the law, and will not at all enforce social relationship with any other class of persons in the country whatsoever. It is merely a matter of law. What we desire is that our civil rights shall be guaranteed by law as they are guaranteed to every other class of persons; and when that is done all other things will come in as a necessary sequence, the enforcement of the rights following the enactment of the law.

Sir, social equality is a right which every man, every woman, and every class of persons have within their own control. They have a right to form their own acquaintances, to establish their own social relationships. Its establishment and regulation is not within the province of legislation. No laws enacted by legislators can compel social equality. Now, what is it we desire? What we desire is this: inasmuch as we have been raised to the dignity, to the honor, to the position of our manhood, we ask that the laws of this country should guarantee all the rights and immunities belonging to that proud position, to be enforced all over this broad land.

Sir, the gentleman states that in the State of North Carolina the colored people enjoy all their rights as far as the highways are concerned; that in the hotels, and in the railroad cars, and in the various public places of resort, they have all the rights and all the immunities accorded to any other class of citizens of the United States. Now, it may not have come under his observation, but it has under mine, that such really is not the case; and the reason why I know and feel it more than he does is because my face is painted black and his is painted white. We who have the color—I may say the objectionable color—know and feel all this. A few days ago, in passing from South Carolina to this city, I entered a place of public resort where hungry men are fed, but I did not dare—I could not without trouble—sit down to the table. I could not sit down at Wilmington or at Weldon without entering into a contest, which I did not desire to do. My colleague, the gentleman who so eloquently spoke on this subject the other day (Mr. Elliott), a few months ago entered a restaurant at Wilmington and sat down to be served, and while there a gentleman stepped up to him and said, "You can not eat here." All the other gentlemen upon the railroad as passengers were eating there; he had only twenty minutes, and was compelled to leave the restaurant or have a fight for it. He showed fight, however, and got his dinner; but he has never been back there since. Coming here last week I felt we did not desire to draw revolvers and present the bold front of warriors, and therefore we ordered our dinners to be brought into the cars, but even there we found the existence of this feeling; for, although we had paid a dollar apiece for our meals, to be brought by the servants into the cars, still there was objection on the part of the railroad people to our eating our meals in the cars, because they said we were putting on airs. They refused us in the restaurant, and then did not desire that we should eat our meals in the cars, although we paid for them. Yet this was in the noble State of North Carolina.

Mr. Speaker, the colored men of the South do not want the adoption of any force measure. No; they do not want anything by force. All they ask is that you will give them, by statutory enactment under the fundamental law, the right to enjoy precisely the same privileges accorded to every other class of citizens.

The gentleman, moreover, has told us that if we pass this civil-rights bill we will thereby rob the colored men of the South of the friendship of the whites. Now, I am at a loss to see how the friendship of our white friends can be lost to us by simply saying we should be permitted to enjoy the rights enjoyed by other citizens. I have a higher opinion of the friendship of the southern men than to suppose any such thing. I know them too well. I know their friendship will not be lost by the passage of this bill. For eight years I have been in South Carolina, and I have found this to be the fact, that the higher class, comprising gentlemen of learning and refinement, are less opposed to this measure than are those who do not occupy so high a position in the social scale.

Sir, I think that there will be no difficulty. But I do think this, that there will be more trouble if we do not have those rights. I regard it important, therefore, that we should make the law so strong that no man can infringe those rights.

But, says the gentleman from North Carolina, some ambitious colored man will, when this law is passed, enter a hotel or railroad car, and thus create disturbance. If it be his right, then there is no vaulting ambition in his enjoying that right. And if he can pay for his seat in a first-class car or his room in a hotel, I see no objection to his enjoying it. But the gentleman says more. He cited, on the school question, the evidence of South Carolina, and says the South Carolina University has been destroyed by virtue of bringing into contact the white students with the colored. I think not. It is true that a small number of students left the institution, but the institution still remains. The buildings are there as erect as ever; the faculty are there as attentive to their duties as ever they were; the students are coming in as they did before. It is true, sir, that there is a mixture of students now; that there are colored and white students of law and medicine sitting side by side; it is true, sir, that the prejudice of some of the professors was so strong that it drove them out of the institution; but the philanthropy and good sense of others were such that they remained; and thus we have still the institution going on, and because some students have left, it cannot be reasonably argued that the usefulness of the institution has been destroyed. The University of South Carolina has not been destroyed.

But the gentleman says more. The colored man cannot stand, he says, where this antagonism exists, and he deprecates the idea of antagonizing the races. The gentleman says there is no antagonism on his part. I think there is not antagonism so far as the country is concerned. So far as my observation extends, it goes to prove this: that there is a general acceptance upon the part of the larger and better class of the whites of the South of the situation, and that they regard the education and the development of the colored people as essential to their welfare, and the peace, happiness, and prosperity of the whole country. Many of them, including the best minds of the South, are earnestly engaged in seeking to make this great system of education permanent in all the States. I do not believe, therefore, that it is possible there can be such an antagonism. Why, sir, in Massachusetts there is no such antagonism. There the colored and the white children go to school side by side. In Rhode Island there is not that antagonism. There they are educated side by side in the high schools. In New York, in the highest schools, are to be found of late colored men and colored women. Even old democratic New York does not refuse to give the colored people their rights, and there is no antagonism. A few days ago, when in New York, I made it my business to find out what was the position of matters there in this respect. I ascertained that there are, I think, seven colored ladies in the highest school in New York, and I believe they stand No. 1 in their class, side by side with members of the best and most refined families of the citizens of New York, and without any objection to their presence.

I cannot understand how it is that our southern friends, or a certain class of them, always bring back this old ghost of prejudice and of antagonism. There was a time, not very far distant in the past, when this antagonism was not recognized, when a feeling of fraternization between the white and the colored races existed, that made them kindred to each other. But since our emancipation, since liberty has come, and only since—only since we have stood up clothed in our manhood, only since we have proceeded to take hold and help advance the civilization of this nation—it is only since then that this bugbear is brought up against us again. Sir, the progress of the age demands that the colored man of this country shall be lifted by law into the enjoyment of every right, and that every appliance which is accorded to the German, to the Irishman, to the Englishman, and every foreigner, shall be given to him; and I shall give some reasons why I demand this in the name of justice.

For two hundred years the colored men of this nation have assisted in building up its commercial interests. There are in this country nearly five millions of us, and for a space of two hundred and forty-seven years we have been hewers of wood and drawers of water; but we have been with you in promoting all the interests of the country. My distinguished colleague, who defended the civil rights of our race the other day on this floor, set this forth so clearly that I need not dwell upon it at this time.

I propose to state just this: that we have been identified with the interests of this country from its very foundation. The cotton crop of this country has been raised and its rice-fields have been tilled by the hands of our race. All along as the march of progress, as the march of commerce, as the development of your resources has been widening and expanding and spreading, as your vessels have gone on every sea, with the stars and stripes waving over them, and carried your commerce everywhere, there the black man's labor has gone to enrich your country and to augment the grandeur of your nationality. This was done in the time of slavery. And if, for the space of time I have noted, we have been hewers of wood and drawers of water; if we have made your cotton-fields blossom as the rose; if we have made your rice-fields wave with luxuriant harvests; if we have made your corn-fields rejoice; if we have sweated and toiled to build up the prosperity of the whole country by the productions of our labor, I submit, now that the war has made a change, now that we are free—I submit to the nation whether it is not fair and right that we should come in and enjoy to the fullest extent our freedom and liberty.

A word now as to the question of education. Sir, I know that, indeed, some of our Republican friends are even a little weak on the school clause of this bill; but, sir, the education of the race, the education of the nation, is paramount to all other considerations. I regard it important, therefore, that the colored people should take place in the educational march of this nation, and I would suggest that there should be no discrimination. It is against discrimination in this particular that we complain.

Sir, if you look over the reports of superintendents of schools in the several States, you will find, I think, evidences sufficient to warrant Congress in passing the civil-rights bill as it now stands. The report of the commissioner of education of California shows that, under the operation of law and of prejudice, the colored children of that State are practically excluded from schooling. Here is a case where a large class of children are growing up in our midst in a state of ignorance and semi-barbarism. Take the report of the superintendent of education of Indiana, and you will find that while efforts have been made in some places to educate the colored children, yet the prejudice is so great that it debars the colored children from enjoying all the rights which they ought to enjoy under the law. In Illinois, too, the superintendent of education makes this statement: that, while the law guarantees education to every child, yet such are the operations among the school trustees that they almost ignore, in some places, the education of colored children.

All we ask is that you, the legislators of the nation, shall pass a law so strong and so powerful that no one shall be able to elude it and destroy our rights under the Constitution and laws of our country. That is all we ask.

But, Mr. Speaker, the gentleman from North Carolina (Mr.

Vance) asks that the colored man shall place himself in an attitude to receive his rights. I ask, what attitude can we assume? We have tilled your soil, and during the rude shock of war, until our hour came, we were docile during that long, dark night, waiting patiently the coming day. In the Southern States during that war our men and women stood behind their masters; they tilled the soil, and there were no insurrections in all the broad lands of the South; the wives and daughters of the slaveholders were as sacred then as they were before; and. the history of the war does not record a single event, a single instance, in which the colored people were unfaithful, even in slavery; nor does the history of the war record the fact that on the other side, on the side of the Union, there were any colored men who were not willing at all times to give their lives for their country. Sir, upon both sides we waited patiently. I was a student at Wilberforce University, in Ohio, when the tocsin of war was sounded, when Fort Sumter was fired upon, and I never shall forget the thrill that ran through my soul when I thought of the coming consequences of that shot. There were one hundred and fifteen of us, students at that university, who, anxious to vindicate the stars and stripes, made up a company, and offered our services to the governor of Ohio; and, sir, we were told that this was a white man's war and that the negro had nothing to do with it. Sir, we returned—docile, patient, waiting, casting our eyes to the heavens whence help always comes. We knew that there would come a period in the history of this nation when our strong black arms would be needed. We waited patiently; we waited until Massachusetts, through her noble governor, sounded the alarm, and we hastened then to hear the summons and obey it.

Sir, as I before remarked, we were peaceful on both sides. When the call was made on the side of the Union, we were ready; when the call was made for us to obey orders on the other side, in the confederacy, we humbly performed our tasks, and waited patiently. But, sir, the time came when we were called for; and, I ask, who can say that when that call was made, the colored men did not respond as readily and as rapidly as did any other class of your citizens? Sir, I need not speak of the history of this bloody war. It will carry down to coming generations the valor of our soldiers on the battle-field. Fort Wagner will stand forever as a monument of that valor, and until Vicksburg shall be wiped from the galaxy of battles in the great contest for human liberty that valor will be recognized.

And for what, Mr. Speaker, and gentlemen, was the great war made? The gentleman from North Carolina (Mr. Vance) announced before he sat down, in answer to an interrogatory by a gentleman on this side of the House, that they went into the war conscientiously before God. So be it. Then we simply come and plead conscientiously before God that these are our rights, and we want them. We plead conscientiously before God, believing that these are our rights by inheritance, and by the inexorable decree of Almighty God.

We believe in the Declaration of Independence, that all men are born free and equal, and are endowed by their Creator with certain inalienable rights, among which are life, liberty, and the pursuit of happiness. And we further believe that to secure those rights governments are instituted. And we further believe that when governments cease to subserve those ends the people should change them.

I have been astonished at the course which gentlemen on the other side have taken in discussing this bill. They plant themselves right behind the Constitution, and declare that the rights of the State ought not to be invaded. Now, if you will take the history of the war of the rebellion, as published by the Clerk of this House, you will see that in 1860 the whole country, each side, was earnest in seeking to make such amendments to the Constitution as would forever secure slavery and keep the Union together under the circumstances. The resolutions passed, and the sentiments expressed in speeches at that time, if examined by gentlemen, will be found to bear out all that I have indicated. It was felt in 1860 that anything that would keep the "wayward sisters" from going astray was desirable. They were then ready and willing to make any amendments.

And now, when the civil rights of our race are hanging upon the issue, they on the other side are not willing to concede to us such amendments as will guarantee them; indeed, they seek to impair the force of existing amendments to the Constitution of the United States, which would carry out the purpose.

I think it is proper and just that the civil-rights bill should be passed. Some think it would be better to modify it, to strike out the school clause, or to so modify it that some of the State constitutions should not be infringed. I regard it essential to us and the people of this country that we should be secured in this if in nothing else. I cannot regard that our rights will be secured until the jury-box and the school-room, those great palladiums of our liberty, shall have been opened to us. Then we will be willing to take our chances with other men.

We do not want any discriminations to be made. If discriminations are made in regard to schools, then there will be accomplished just what we are fighting against. If you say that the schools in the State of Georgia, for instance, shall be allowed to discriminate against colored people, then you will have discriminations made against us. We do not want any discriminations. I do not ask any legislation for the colored people of this country that is not applied to the white people. All that we ask is equal laws, equal legislation, and equal rights throughout the length and breadth of this land.

The gentleman from North Carolina (Mr. Vance) also says that the colored men should not come here begging at the doors of Congress for their rights. I agree with him. I want to say that we do not come here begging for our rights. We come here clothed in the garb of American citizenship. We come demanding our rights in the name of justice. We come, with no arrogance on our part, asking that this great nation, which laid the foundations of civilization and progress more deeply and more securely than any other nation on the face of the earth, guarantee us protection from outrage. We come here, five millions of people—more than composed this whole nation when it had its great tea-party in Boston Harbor, and demanded its rights at the point of the bayonet—asking that unjust discriminations against us be forbidden. We come here in the name of justice, equity, and law, in the name of our children, in the name of our country, petitioning for our rights.

Our rights will yet be accorded to us, I believe, from the feeling that has been exhibited on this floor of the growing sentiment of the country. Rapid as the weaver's shuttle, swift as the lightning's flash, such progress is being made that our rights will be accorded to us ere long. I believe the nation is perfectly willing to accord this measure of justice, if only those who represent the people here would say the word. Let it be proclaimed that henceforth all the children of this land shall be free; that the stars and stripes, waving over all, shall secure to every one equal rights, and the nation will say "amen."

Let the civil-rights bill be passed this day, and five million black men, women, and children, all over the land, will begin a new song of rejoicing, and the thirty-five millions of noble-hearted Anglo-Saxons will join in the shout of joy. Thus will the great mission be fulfilled of giving to all the people equal rights.

Inasmuch as we have toiled with you in building up this nation; inasmuch as we have suffered side by side with you in the war; inasmuch as we have together passed through affliction and pestilence, let there be now a fulfillment of the sublime thought of our fathers—let all men enjoy equal liberty and equal rights.

In this hour, when you are about to put the cap-stone on the mighty structure of government, I ask you to grant us this measure, because it is right. Grant this, and we shall go home with our hearts filled with gladness. I want to "shake hands over the bloody chasm." The gentleman from North Carolina has said he desires to have forever buried the memory of the recent war. I agree with him. Representing a South Carolina constituency, I desire to bury forever the tomahawk. I have voted in this House with a free heart to declare Universal amnesty. Inasmuch as general amnesty has been proclaimed, I would hardly have expected there would be any objection on this floor to the civil-rights bill, giving to all men the equal rights of citizens. There should be no more contest. Amnesty and civil rights should go together. Gentlemen on the other side will admit that we have been faithful; and now, when we propose to bury the hatchet, let us shake hands upon this measure of justice; and if heretofore we have been enemies, let us be friends now and forever.

Our wives and our children have high hopes and aspirations; their longings for manhood and womanhood are equal to those of any other race. The same sentiment of patriotism and of gratitude, the same spirit of national pride that animates the hearts of other citizens animates theirs. In the name of the dead soldiers of our race, whose bodies lie at Petersburgh and on other battle-fields of the South; in the name of the widows and orphans they have left behind; in the name of the widows of the confederate soldiers who fell upon the same fields, I conjure you let this righteous act be done. I appeal to you in the name of God and humanity to give us our rights, for we ask nothing more. [Loud applause.] [1]

CIVIL RIGHTS BILL

By James T. Rapier [2]

Mr. Speaker, I had hoped there would be no protracted discussion on the civil-rights bill. It has been debated all over the country for the last seven years; twice it has done duty in our national political campaigns; and in every minor election during that time it has been pressed into service for the purpose of intimidating the weak white men who are inclined to support the republican ticket. I was certain until now that most persons were acquainted with its provisions, that they understood its meaning; therefore it was no longer to them the monster it had been depicted, that was to break down all social barriers, and compel one man to recognize another socially, whether agreeable to him or not.

I must confess it is somewhat embarrassing for a colored man to urge the passage of this bill, because if he exhibit an earnestness in the matter and express a desire for its immediate passage, straightway he is charged with a desire for social equality, as explained by the demagogue and understood by the ignorant white man. But then it is just as embarrassing for him not to do so, for, if he remains silent while the struggle is being carried on around, and for him, he is liable to be charged with a want of interest in a matter that concerns him more than any one else, which is enough to make his friends desert his cause. So in steering away from Scylla I may run upon Charybdis. But the anomalous, and I may add the supremely ridiculous, position of the negro at this time, in this country, compel me to say something. Here his condition

[1] *Congressional Record*, Vol. II, Pt. 1, 43rd Congress, 1st Session, pp. 565-567.

[2] James T. Rapier was born at Florence, Alabama, in 1840. He was sent to Canada to be educated, and while there was given the opportunity to recite before the late King Edward VII, then Prince of Wales, who was at that time visiting the United States and Canada. Prior to his election to Congress, Mr. Rapier held several local offices in Alabama and also aspired to become Secretary-of-State. In this contest he was defeated by one Nicholas Davis, a white man. Mr. Rapier was a partisan in the split in the Republican Party in his State, aligning himself with one Spencer, a Republican leader of that date. Losing in this contest, he lost also his ability to win votes and so was defeated in his attempt to seek reëlection to the 44th Congress. Soon thereafter, Mr. Rapier gave his attention to farming and was highly successful as a cotton planter.—*Biographical Congressional Directory*, p. 760, and a statement of Thomas Walker, a local officer in Alabama during the reconstructive period.

is without a comparison, parallel alone to itself. Just think that the law recognizes my right upon this floor as a law-maker, but that there is no law to secure to me any accommodations whatever while traveling here to discharge my duties as a Representative of a large and wealthy constituency. Here I am the peer of the proudest, but on a steamboat or car I am not equal to the most degraded. Is not this most anomalous and ridiculous?

What little I shall say will be more in the way of stating the case than otherwise, for I am certain I can add nothing to the arguments already made in behalf of the bill. If in the course of my remarks I should use language that may be considered inelegant, I have only to say that it shall be as elegant as that used by the opposition in discussing this measure; if undignified, it shall not be more so than my subject; if ridiculous, I enter the plea that the example has been set by the democratic side of the House, which claims the right to set examples. I wish to say in justice to myself that no one regrets more than I do the necessity that compels one to the manner born to come in these Halls with hat in hand (so to speak) to ask at the hands of his political peers the same public rights they enjoy. And I shall feel ashamed for my country if there be any foreigners present, who have been lured to our shores by the popular but untruthful declaration that this land is the asylum of the oppressed, to hear a member of the highest legislative body in the world declare from his place, upon his responsibility as a Representative, that notwithstanding his political position he has no civil rights that another class is bound to respect. Here a foreigner can learn what he cannot learn in any other country, that it is possible for a man to be half free and half slave, or, in other words, he will see that it is possible for a man to enjoy political rights while he is denied civil ones; here he will see a man legislating for a free people, while his own chains of civil slavery hang about him, and are far more galling than any the foreigner left behind him; here he will see what is not to be seen elsewhere, that position is no mantle of protection in our "land of the free and home of the brave"; for I am subjected to far more outrages and indignities in coming to and going from this capital in discharge of my public duties than any criminal in the country providing he be white. Instead of my position shielding me from insult, it too often invites it.

Let me cite a case. Not many months ago Mr. Cardoza, treasurer of the State of South Carolina, was on his way home from the West. His route lay through Atlanta. There he made request for a sleeping-berth. Not only was he refused this, but was denied a seat in a first-class carriage, and the parties went so far as to threaten to take his life because he insisted upon his rights as a traveler. He was compelled, a most elegant and accomplished gentleman, to take a seat in the dirty smoking-car, along with the traveling rabble, or else be left, to the detriment of his public duties.

I affirm, without the fear of contradiction, that any white ex-convict (I care not what may have been his crime, nor whether the hair on the shaven side of his head has had time to grow out or not) may start with me to-day to Montgomery, that all the way down he will be treated as a gentleman, while I will be treated as the convict. He will be allowed a berth in a sleeping-car with all its comforts, while I will be forced into a dirty, rough box with the drunkards, apple-sellers, railroad hands, and next to any dead that may be in transit, regardless of how far decomposition may have progressed. Sentinels are placed at the doors of the better coaches, with positive instructions to keep persons of color out; and I must do them the justice to say that they guard these sacred portals with a vigilance that would have done credit to the flaming swords at the gates of Eden. Tender, pure, intelligent young ladies are forced to travel in this way if they are guilty of the crime of color, the only unpardonable sin known in our Christian and Bible lands, where sinning against the Holy Ghost (whatever that may be) sinks into insignificance when compared with the sin of color. If from any cause we are compelled to lay over, the best bed in the hotel is his if he can pay for it, while I am invariably turned away, hungry and cold, to stand around the railroad station until the departure of the next train, it matters not how long, thereby endangering my health, while my life and property are at the mercy of any highwayman who may wish to murder and rob me.

And I state without the fear of being gainsaid, the statement of the gentleman from Tennessee to the contrary notwithstanding, that there is not an inn between Washington and Montgomery, a distance of more than a thousand miles, that will accommodate me to a bed or meal. Now, then, is there a man upon this floor who is so heartless, whose breast is so void of the better feelings, as to say that this brutal custom needs no regulation? I hold that it does and that Congress is the body to regulate it. Authority for its action is found not only in the fourteenth amendment to the Constitution, but by virtue of that amendment (which makes all persons born here citizens) authority is found in article 4, section 2, of the Federal Constitution, which declares in positive language "that the citizens of each State shall have the same rights as the citizens of the several States." Let me read Mr. Brightly's comment upon this clause; he is considered good authority, I believe. In describing the several rights he says they may be all comprehended under the following general heads: "Protection by the Government; the enjoyment of life and liberty, with the right to acquire and possess property of every kind, and to pursue and obtain happiness and safety; the right of a citizen of one State to pass through or to reside in any other State for purposes of trade, agriculture, professional pursuits, or otherwise."

It is very clear that the right of locomotion without hindrance and everything pertaining thereto is embraced in this clause; and every lawyer knows if any white man in ante bellum times had been refused first-class passage in a steamboat or car, who was free from any contagious disease, and was compelled to go on deck of a boat or into a baggage car, and any accident had happened to him while he occupied that place, a lawsuit would have followed and damages would have been given by any jury to the plaintiff; and whether any accident had happened or not in the case I have referred to, a suit would have been brought for a denial of rights, and no one doubts what would have been the verdict. White men had rights then that common carriers were compelled to respect, and I demand the same for the colored men now.

Mr. Speaker, whether this deduction from the clause of the Constitution just read was applicable to the Negro prior to the adoption of the several late amendments to our organic law is not now a question, but that it does apply to him in his new relations no intelligent man will dispute. Therefore I come to the national, instead of going to the local Legislatures for relief, as has been suggested, because the grievance is national and not local; because Congress is the law-making power of the General Government, whose duty it is to see that there be no unjust and odious discriminations made between its citizens. I look to the Government in the place of the several States, because it claims my first allegiance, exacts at my hands strict obedience to its laws, and because it promises in the implied contract between every citizen and the Government to protect my life and property. I have fulfilled my part of the contract to the extent I have been called upon, and I demand that the Government, through Congress, do likewise. Every day my life and property are exposed, are left to the mercy of others, and will be so as long as every hotel-keeper, railroad conductor, and steamboat captain can refuse me with impunity the accommodations common to other travelers. I hold further, if the Government cannot secure to a citizen his guaranteed rights it ought not to call upon him to perform the same duties that are performed by another class of citizens who are in the free and full enjoyment of every civil and political right.

Sir, I submit that I am degraded as long as I am denied the public privileges common to other men, and that the members of this House are correspondingly degraded by recognizing my political equality while I occupy such a humiliating position. What a singular attitude for law-makers of this great nation to assume, rather come down to me than allow me to go up to them. Sir, did you ever reflect that this is the only Christian country where poor, finite man is held responsible for the crimes of the infinite God whom you profess to worship? But it is; I am held to answer for the crime of color, when I was not consulted in the matter. Had I been consulted, and my future fully described, I think I should have objected to being born in this gospel land. The excuse offered for all this inhuman treatment is that they consider the Negro inferior to the white man, intellectually and morally. This reason might have been offered and probably accepted as truth some years ago, but no one now believes him incapable of a high order of culture, except some one who is himself below the average of mankind in natural endowments. This is not the reason, as I shall show before I have done.

Sir, there is a cowardly propensity in the human heart that delights in oppressing somebody else, and in the gratification of this base desire we always select a victim that can be outraged with safety. As a general thing, the Jew has been the subject in most parts of the world; but here the Negro is the most available for this purpose; for this reason in part he was seized upon, and not because he is naturally inferior to any one else. Instead of his enemies believing him to be incapable of a high order of mental culture, they have shown that they believe the reverse to be true, by taking the most elaborate pains to prevent his development. And the smaller the caliber of the white man the more frantically has he fought to prevent the intellectual and moral progress of the Negro, for the simple but good reason that he has most to fear from such a result. He does not wish to see the Negro approach the high moral standard of a man and gentleman.

Let me call your attention to a case in point. Some time since a well-dressed colored man was traveling from Augusta to Montgomery. The train on which he was stopped at a dinner-house. The crowd around the depot, seeing him well dressed, fine-looking, and polite, concluded he must be a gentleman (which was more than their righteous souls could stand), and straightway they commenced to abuse him. And, sir, he had to go into the baggage-car, open his trunks, show his cards. faro-bank, dice, &c., before they would give him any peace; or, in other words, he was forced to give satisfactory evidence that he was not a man who was working to elevate the moral and intellectual standards of the negro before they would respect him. I have always found more prejudice existing in the breasts of men who have feeble minds and are conscious of it, than in the breasts of those who have towering intellects and are aware of it. Henry Ward Beecher reflected the feelings of the latter class when on a certain occasion he said: "Turn the Negro loose; I am not afraid to run the race of life with him." He could afford to say this, all white men cannot; but what does the other class say? "Build a Chinese wall between the Negro and the schoolhouse, discourage in him pride of character and honest ambition, cut him off from every avenue that leads to the higher grounds of intelligence and usefulness, and then challenge him to a contest upon the highway of life to decide the question of superiority of race." By their acts, not by their words, the civilized world can and will judge how honest my opponents are in their declarations that I am naturally inferior to them. No one is surprised that this class opposes the passage of the civil-rights bill, for if the Negro were allowed the same opportunities, the same rights of locomotion, the same rights to comfort in travel, how could they prove themselves better than the Negro?

Mr. Speaker, it was said, I believe, by the gentleman from Kentucky (Mr. Beck), that the people of the South, particularly his State, were willing to accord to the colored man all the rights they believe him guaranteed by the Constitution. No one doubts this assertion. But the difficulty is they do not acknowledge that I am entitled to any rights under the organic law. I am forced to this conclusion by reading the platforms of the democratic party in the several States. Which one declares that that party believes in the constitutionality of the Reconstruction Acts or the several amendments? But upon the other hand, they question the constitutionality of every measure that is advanced to ameliorate the condition of the colored man; and so skeptical have the democracy become respecting the Constitution, brought about by their unsuccessful efforts to find constitutional objections to every step that is taken to elevate the Negro, that now they begin to doubt the constitutionality of the Constitution itself. The most they have agreed to do is to obey present laws bearing on manhood suffrage until they are repealed by Congress or decided to be unconstitutional by the Supreme Court.

Let me read what the platform of the democratic party in Alabama has to say on this point:

The democratic and conservative party of the State of Alabama, in entering upon the contest for the redemption of the State government from the radical usurpers who now control it, adopt and declare as their platform—

1. That we stand ready to obey the Constitution of the United States and the laws passed in pursuance thereof, and the constitution and laws of the State of Alabama, so long as they remain in force and unrepealed.

I will, however, take the gentleman at his word; but must be allowed to ask if so, why was it, even after the several amendments had been officially announced to be part of the Federal Constitution, that his State and others refused to allow the Negro to testify in their courts against a white man? If they believed he should be educated (and surely this is a right), why was it that his schoolhouses were burned down, and the teachers who had gone down on errands of mercy to carry light into dark places driven off, and in some places killed? If they believe the Negro should vote (another right, as I understand the Constitution), why was it that Ku Klux Klans were organized to prevent him from exercising the right of an American citizen, namely, casting the ballot—the very thing they said he had a right to do?

The professed belief and practice are sadly at variance, and must be intelligently harmonized before I can be made to believe that they are willing to acknowledge that I have any rights under the Constitution or elsewhere. He boasts of the magnanimity of Kentucky in allowing the Negro to vote without qualification, while to enjoy the same privilege in Massachusetts he is required to read the constitution of that State. He was very unhappy in this comparison. Why, sir, his State does not allow the Negro to vote at all. When was the constitution of Kentucky amended so as to grant him the elective franchise? They vote there by virtue of the fifteenth amendment alone, independent of the laws and constitution of that Commonwealth; and they would today disfranchise him if it could be done without affecting her white population. The Old Bay State waited for no "act of Congress" to force her to do justice to all of her citizens, but in ante bellum days provided in her constitution that all male persons who could read and write should be entitled to suffrage. That was a case of equality before the law, and who had a right to complain? There is nothing now in the amended Federal Constitution to prevent Kentucky from adopting the same kind of clause in her constitution, when the convention meets to revise the organic law of that State, I venture the assertion that you will never hear a word about it; but it will not be out of any regard for her colored citizens, but the respect for that army of fifty thousand ignorant white men she has within her borders, many of whom I see every time I pass through that State, standing around the several depots continually harping on the stereotyped phrase, "The damned Negro won't work."

I would not be surprised though if she should do better in the future. I remember when a foreigner was just as unpopular in Kentucky as the Negro is now; when the majority of the people of that State were opposed to according the foreigner the same rights they claimed for themselves; when that class of people were mobbed in the streets of her principal cities on account of their political faith, just as they have done the Negro for the last seven years. But what do you see today? One of that then proscribed class is Kentucky's chief Representative upon this floor. Is not this an evidence of a returning sense of justice? If so, would it not be reasonable to predict that she will in the near future send one of her now proscribed class to aid him in representing her interests upon this floor?

Mr. Speaker, there is another member of this body who has opposed the passage of this bill very earnestly, whose position in the country and peculiar relations to the Government compel me to refer to him before I conclude. I allude to the gentleman from Georgia (Mr. Stephens). He returns to this House after an absence of many years with the same old ideas respecting State-rights that he carried away with him. He has not advanced a step; but unfortunately for him the American people have, and no longer consider him a fit expounder of our organic law. Following to its legitimate conclusion the doctrine of State-rights (which of itself is secession), he deserted the flag of his country, followed his State out of the Union, and a long and bloody war followed. With its results most men are acquainted and recognizant; but he, Bourbon-like, comes back saying the very same things he used to say, and swearing by the same gods he swore by in other days. He seems not to know that the ideas which he so ably advanced for so many years were by the war swept away, along with that system of slavery which he intended should be the chief corner-stone, precious and elect, of the transitory kingdom over which he was second ruler.

Sir, the most of us have seen the play of Rip Van Winkle, who was said to have slept twenty years in the Catskill Mountains. On his return he found that the small trees had grown up to be large ones; the village of Falling Waters had improved beyond his recollection; the little children that used to play around his knees and ride into the village upon his back had grown up to be men and women and assumed the responsibilities of life; most of his friends, including Nick Vedder, had gone to that bourn whence no traveler returns; but, saddest of all, his child, "Mene," could not remember him. No one can see him in his efforts to recall the scenes of other days without being moved almost to tears. This, however, is fiction. The life and actions of the gentleman from Georgia most happily illustrate this character. This is a case where truth is stranger than fiction; and when he comes into these Halls advocating the same old ideas after an absence of so many years, during which time we have had a conflict of arms such as the world never saw, that revolutionized the entire body-politic, he stamps himself a living "Rip Van Winkle."

I reiterate, that the principles of "State-rights," for the recognition of which, he now contends, are the ones that were in controversy during our late civil strife. The arguments pro and con were heard in the roar of battle, amid the shrieks of the wounded, and the groans of the dying; and the decision was rendered amid shouts of victory by the Union soldiers. With it all appear to be familiar except him, and for his information I will state that upon this question an appeal was taken from the forum to the sword, the highest tribunal known to man, that it was then and there decided that National rights are paramount to State-rights, and that liberty and equality before the law should be coextensive with the jurisdiction of the Stars and Stripes. And I will further inform him that the bill now pending is simply to give practical effect to that decision.

I sympathize with him in his inability to understand this great change. When he left here the Negro was a chattel, exposed for sale in the market places within a stone's throw of the Capitol; so near that the shadow of the Goddess of Liberty reflected by the rising sun would fall within the slave-pen as a forcible reminder that there was no hopeful day, nothing bright in the future, for the poor slave. Then no Negro was allowed to enter these Halls and hear discussions on subjects that most interested him. The words of lofty cheer that fell from the lips of Wade, Giddings, Julian, and others were not allowed to fall upon his ear. Then, not more than three Negroes were allowed to assemble at any place in the capital of the nation without special permission from the city authorities. But on his return he finds that the slave-pens have been torn down, and upon their ruins temples of learning have been erected; he finds that the Goddess of Liberty is no longer compelled to cover her radiant face while she weeps for our national shame, but looks with pride and satisfaction upon a free and regenerated land; he finds that the laws and regulations respecting the assembling of Negroes are no longer in force, but on the contrary he can see on any public holiday the Butler Zouaves, a fine-looking company of colored men, on parade.

Imagine, if you can, what would have been the effect of such a sight in this city twelve years ago. Then one Negro soldier would have caused utter consternation. Congress would have adjourned; the Cabinet would have sought protection elsewhere; the President would have declared martial law; troops and marines would have been ordered out; and I cannot tell all that would have happened; but now such a sight does not excite a ripple on the current of affairs; but over all, and worse to him than all, he finds the Negro here, not only a listener but a participant in debate. While I sympathize with him in his inability to comprehend this marvelous change, I must say in all earnestness that one who cannot understand and adjust himself to the new order of things is poorly qualified to teach this nation the meaning of our amended Constitution. The tenacity with which he sticks to his purpose through all the vicissitudes of life is commendable, though his views be objectionable.

While the chief of the late confederacy is away in Europe fleeing the wrath to come in the shape of Joe Johnson's history of the war, his lieutenant, with a boldness that must challenge the admiration of the most impudent, comes into these Halls and seeks to commit the nation, through Congress, to the doctrine of State-rights, and thus save it from the general wreck that followed the collapse of the rebellion. He had no other business here. Read his speech on the pending bill; his argument was cunning, far more ingenious than ingenuous. He does not deny the need or justness of the measure, but claims that the several States have exclusive jurisdiction of the same. I am not so willing as some others to believe in the sincerity of his assertions concerning the rights of the colored man. If he were honest in this matter, why is it he never recommended such a measure to the Georgia Legislature? If the several States had secured to all classes within their borders the rights contemplated in this bill, we would have had no need to come here; but they having failed to do their duty, after having had ample opportunity, the General Government is called upon to exercise its rights in the matter.

Mr. Speaker, time will not allow me to review the history of the American Negro, but I must pause here long enough to say that he has not been properly treated by this nation; he has purchased and paid for all, and for more, than he has yet received. Whatever liberty he enjoys has been paid for over and over again by more than two hundred years of forced toil; and for such citizenship as is allowed him he paid the full measure of his blood, the dearest price required at the hands of any citizen. In every contest, from the beginning of the revolutionary struggle down to the war between the States, has he been prominent. But we all remember in our late war when the Government was so hard pressed for troops to sustain the cause of the Union, when it was so difficult to fill up the ranks that had been so fearfully decimated by disease and the bullet; when every train that carried to the front a number of fresh soldiers brought back a corresponding number of wounded and sick ones; when grave doubts as to the success of the Union arms had seized upon the minds of some of the most sanguine friends of the Government; when strong men took counsel of their fears; when those who had all their lives received the fostering care of the nation were hesitating as to their duty in that trying hour, and others questioning if it were not better to allow the star of this Republic to go down and thus be blotted out from the great map of nations than to continue the bloodshed; when gloom and despair were widespread; when the last ray of hope had nearly sunk below our political horizon, how the Negro then came forward and offered himself as a sacrifice in the place of the nation, made bare his breast to the steel, and in it received the thrusts of the bayonet that were aimed at the life of the nation by the soldiers of that government in which the gentleman from Georgia figured as second officer.

Sir, the valor of the colored soldier was tested on many a battlefield, and today his bones lie bleaching beside every hill and in every valley from the Potomac to the Gulf; whose mute eloquence in behalf of equal rights for all before the law, is and ought to be far more persuasive than any poor language I can command.

Mr. Speaker, nothing short of a complete acknowledgement of my manhood will satisfy me. I have no compromises to make, and shall unwillingly accept any. If I were to say that I would be content with less than any other member upon this floor I would forfeit whatever respect any one here might entertain for me, and would thereby furnish the best possible evidence that I do not and cannot appreciate the rights of a freeman. Just what I am charged with by my political enemies. I cannot willingly accept anything less than my full measure of rights as a man, because I am unwilling to present myself as a candidate for the brand of inferiority, which will be as plain and lasting as the mark of Cain. If I am to be thus branded, the country must do it against my solemn protest.

Sir, in order that I might know something of the feelings of a freeman, a privilege denied me in the land of my birth, I left home last year and traveled six months in foreign lands, and the moment I put my foot upon the deck of a ship that unfurled a foreign flag from its mast-head, distinctions on account of my color ceased. I am not aware that my presence on board the steamer put her off her course. I believe we made the trip in the usual time. It was in other countries than my own that I was not a stranger, that I could approach a hotel without the fear that the door would be slammed in my face. Sir, I feel this humiliation very keenly; it dwarfs my manhood, and certainly it impairs my usefulness as a citizen.

The other day when the centennial bill was under discussion I would have been glad to say a word in its favor, but how could I? How would I appear at the centennial celebration of our national freedom, with my own galling chains of slavery hanging about me? I could no more rejoice on that occasion in my present condition than the Jews could sing in their wonted style as they sat as captives beside the Babylonish streams; but I look forward to the day when I shall be in the full enjoyment of the rights of a freeman, with the same hope they indulged, that they would again return to their native land. I can no more forget my manhood, than they could forget Jerusalem.

After all, this question resolves itself to this: either I am a man or I am not a man. If one, I am entitled to all the rights, privileges, and immunities common to any other class in this country; if not a man, I have no right to vote, no right to a seat here; if no right to vote, then 20 per cent. of the members on this floor have no right here, but, on the contrary, hold their seats in violation of law. If the Negro has no right to vote, then one-eighth of your Senate consists of members who have no shadow of a claim to the places they occupy; and if no right to a vote, a half-dozen governors in the South figure as usurpers.

This is the legitimate conclusion of the argument, that the Negro is not a man and is not entitled to all the public rights common to other men, and you cannot escape it. But when I press my claims I am asked, "Is it good policy?" My answer is, "Policy is out of the question; it has nothing to do with it; that you can have no policy in dealing with your citizens; that there must be one law for all; that in this case justice is the only standard to be used, and you can no more divide justice than you can divide Deity." On the other hand, I am told that I must respect the prejudices of others. Now, sir, no one respects reasonable and intelligent prejudice more than I. I respect religious prejudices, for example; these I can comprehend. But how can I have respect for the prejudices that prompt a man to turn up his nose at the males of a certain race, while at the same time he has a fondness for the females of the same race to the extent of cohabitation? Out of four poor unfortunate colored women, who from poverty were forced to go to the lying-in branch of the Freedman's Hospital here in the District last year, three gave birth to children whose fathers were white men, and I venture to say that if they were members of this body, would vote against the civil rights Bill. Do you, can you wonder at my want of respect for this kind of prejudice? To make me feel uncomfortable appears to be the highest ambition of many white men. It is to them a positive luxury, which they seek to indulge at every opportunity.

I have never sought to compel any one, white or black, to associate with me, and never shall; nor do I wish to be compelled to associate with any one. If a man does not wish to ride with me in the street-car, I shall not object to his hiring a private conveyance; if he does not wish to ride with me from here to Baltimore, who shall complain if he charter a special train? For a man to carry out his prejudices in this way would be manly, and would leave no cause for complaint, but to crowd me out of the usual conveyance into an uncomfortable place with persons for whose manners I have a dislike, whose language is not fit for ears polite, is decidedly unmanly and cannot be submitted to tamely by any one who has a particle of self-respect.

Sir, this whole thing grows out of a desire to establish a system of "caste," an anti-republican principle, in our free country. In Europe they have princes, dukes, lords, etc., in contradistinction to the middle classes and peasants. Further East they have the brahmans or priests, who rank above the sudras or laborers. In those countries distinctions are based upon blood and position. Every one there understands the custom and no one complains. They, poor innocent creatures, pity our condition, look down upon us with a kind of royal compassion, because they think we have no tangible lines of distinction, and therefore speak of our society as being vulgar. But let not our friends beyond the seas lay the flattering unction to their souls that we are without distinctive lines; that we have no nobility; for we are blessed with both. Our distinction is color (which would necessarily exclude the brahmans), and our lines are much broader than anything they know of. Here a drunken white man is not only equal to a drunken negro (as would be the case anywhere else), but superior to the most sober and orderly one; here an ignorant white man is not only the equal of an unlettered Negro, but is superior to the most cultivated; here our nobility cohabit with our female peasants, and then throw up their hands in holy horror when a male of the same class enters a restaurant to get a meal, and if he insist upon being accommodated our scion of royalty will leave and go to the arms of his colored mistress and there pour out his soul's complaint, tell her of the impudence of the "damned nigger" in coming to a table where a white man was sitting.

What poor, simple-minded creatures these foreigners are. They labor under the delusion that they monopolize the knowledge of the courtesies due from one gentleman to another. How I rejoice to know that it is a delusion. Sir, I wish some of them could have been present to hear the representative of the F. F. V.'s upon this floor (and I am told that that is the highest degree that society has yet reached in this country) address one of his peers, who dared asked him a question, in this style: "I am talking to white men." Suppose Mr. Gladstone—who knows no man but by merit —who in violation of our custom entertained the colored jubilee singers at his home last summer, or the Duke de Broglie, had been present and heard this eloquent remark drop from the lips of this classical and knightly member, would they not have hung their heads in shame at their ignorance of politeness, and would they not have returned home, repaired to their libraries, and betaken themselves to the study of Chesterfield on manners? With all these absurdities staring them in the face, who can wonder that foreigners laugh at our ideas of distinction?

Mr. Speaker, though there is not a line in this bill the democracy approve of, yet they made the most noise about the school clause. Dispatches are freely sent over the wires as to what will be done with the common-school system in the several Southern States in the event this bill becomes a law. I am not surprised at this, but, on the other hand, I looked for it. Now what is the force of that school clause? It simply provides that all the children in every State where there is a school system supported in whole or in part by general taxation shall have equal advantages of school privileges. So that if perfect and ample accommodations are not made convenient for all the children, then any child has the right to go to any school where they do exist. And that is all there is in this school clause. I want some one to tell me of any measure that was intended to benefit the Negro that they have approved of. Of which one did they fail to predict evil? They declared if the Negroes were emancipated that the country would be laid waste, and that in the end he would starve, because he could not take care of himself. But this was a mistake. When the reconstruction acts were passed and the colored men in my State were called upon to express through the ballot whether Alabama should return to the Union or not, white men threw up their hands in holy horror and declared if the Negro voted that never again would they deposit another ballot. But how does the matter stand now? Some of those very men are in the republican ranks, and I have known them to grow hoarse in shouting for our platforms and candidates. They hurrah for our principles with all the enthusiasm of a new-born soul, and, sir, so zealous have they become that in looking at them I am amazed, and am often led to doubt my own faith and feel ashamed for my lukewarmness. And those who have not joined our party are doing their utmost to have the Negro vote with them. I have met them in the cabins night and day where they were imploring him, for the sake of old times, to come up and vote with them.

I submit, Mr. Speaker, that political prejudices prompt the democracy to oppose this bill as much as anything else. In the campaign of 1868 Joe Williams, an uncouth and rather notorious colored man, was employed as a general democratic canvasser in the South. He was invited to Montgomery to enlighten us, and while there he stopped at one of the best hotels in the city, one that would not dare entertain me. He was introduced at the meeting by the chairman of the democratic executive committee as a learned and elegant, as well as eloquent, gentleman. In North Alabama he was invited to speak at the Seymour and Blair barbecue, and did address one of the largest audiences, composed largely of ladies, that ever assembled in that part of the State. This I can prove by my simon-pure democratic colleague, Mr. Sloss, for he was chairman of the committee of arrangements on that occasion, and I never saw him so radiant with good humor in all my life as when he had the honor of introducing "his friend," Mr. Williams. In that case they were extending their courtesies to a coarse, vulgar stranger, because he was a democrat, while at the same time they were hunting me down as the partridge on the mount, night and day, with their Ku Klux Klan, simply because I was a republican and refused to bow at the foot of their Baal. I might enumerate many instances of this kind, but I forbear. But to come down to a later period, the Greeley campaign. The colored men who were employed to canvass North Carolina in the interest of the democratic party were received at all the hotels as other men and treated, I am informed, with marked distinction. And in the State of Louisiana a very prominent colored gentleman saw proper to espouse the Greeley cause, and when the fight was over and the McEnery government saw fit to send on a committee to Washington to present their case to the President, this colored gentleman was selected as one of that committee. On arriving in the city of New Orleans prior to his departure he was taken to the Saint Charles, the most aristocratic hotel in the South. When they started he occupied a berth in the sleeping-car; at every eating-house he was treated like the rest of them, no distinction whatever. And when they arrived at Montgomery, I was at the depot, just starting for New York. Not only did the conductor refuse to allow me a berth in the sleeping-car, but I was also denied a seat in the first-class carriage. Now, what was the difference between us? Nothing but our political faith. To prove this I have only to say that just a few months before this happened, he, along with Frederick Douglass and others, was denied the same privileges he enjoyed in coming here. And now that he has returned to the right party again I can tell him that never more will he ride in another sleeping-car in the South unless this bill becomes law. There never was a truer saying than that circumstances alter cases.

Mr. Speaker, to call this land the asylum of the oppressed is a misnomer, for upon all sides I am treated as a pariah. I hold that the solution of this whole matter is to enact such laws and prescribe such penalties for their violation as will prevent any person from discriminating against another in public places on account of color. No one asks, no one seeks the passage of a law that will interfere with any one's private affairs. But I do ask the enactment of a law to secure me in the enjoyment of public privileges. But when I ask this I am told that I must wait for public opinion; that it is a matter that cannot be forced by law. While I admit that public opinion is a power, and in many cases is a law of itself, yet I cannot lose sight of the fact that both statute law, and the law of necessity manufacture public opinion. I remember, it was unpopular to enlist Negro soldiers in our late war, and after they enlisted it was equally unpopular to have them fight in the same battles; but when it became a necessity in both cases, public opinion soon came around to that point. No white father objected to the Negro's becoming food for powder if thereby his son could be saved. No white woman objected to the Negro marching in the same ranks and fighting in the same battles if by that her husband could escape burial in our savannas and return to her and her little ones.

Suppose there had been no reconstruction acts nor amendments to the Constitution, when would public opinion in the South have suggested the propriety of giving me the ballot? Unaided by law when would public opinion have prompted the Administration to appoint members of my race to represent this Government at foreign courts? It is said by some well-meaning men that the colored man has now every right under the common law; in reply I wish to say that that kind of law commands very little respect when applied to the rights of colored men in my portion of the country; the only law that we have any regard for is uncommon law of the most positive character. And I repeat, if you will place upon your statute-books laws that will protect me in my rights, that public opinion will speedily follow.

Mr. Speaker, I trust this bill will become law, because it is a necessity, and because it will put an end to all legislation on this subject. It does not and cannot contemplate any such ideas as social equality; nor is there any man upon this floor so silly as to believe that there can be any law enacted or enforced that would compel one man to recognize another as his equal socially; if there be, he ought not to be here, and I have only to say that they have sent him to the wrong public building. I would oppose such a bill as earnestly as the gentleman from North Carolina, whose associations and cultivations have been of such a nature as to lead him to select the crow as his standard of grandeur and excellence in the place of the eagle, the hero of all birds and our national emblem of pride and power. I will tell him that I have seen many of his race to whose level I should object to being dragged.

Sir, it matters not how much men may differ upon the question of State and national rights; there is one class of rights, however, that we all agree upon, namely, individual rights, which includes the right of every man to select associates for himself and family, and to say who shall and who shall not visit at his house. This right is God-given and custom-sanctioned, and there is, and there can be no power overruling your decision in this matter. Let this bill become law and not only will it do much toward giving rest to this weary country on this subject, completing the manhood of my race and perfecting his citizenship, but it will take him from the political arena as a topic of discussion where he has done duty for the last fifty years, and thus freed from anxiety respecting his political standing, hundreds of us will abandon the political fields who are there from necessity, and not from choice, and enter other and more pleasant ones; and thus relieved, it will be the aim of the colored man as well as his duty and interest, to become a good citizen, and to do all in his power to advance the interests of a common country.

SPEECH ON THE CIVIL-RIGHTS BILL [1]

By John R. Lynch

Mr. Speaker, I was not particularly anxious to take part in this debate, and would not have done so but for the fact that this bill

[1] *Congressional Record*, Vol. II, Part V, 43rd Congress, 1st Session, pp. 4782-4786.

has created a great deal of discussion both in and outside of the halls of Congress. In order to answer successfully the arguments that have been made against the bill, I deem it necessary, if my time will allow me to do so, to discuss the question from three stand-points—legal, social, and political. I confess, Mr. Speaker, that it is with hesitancy that I shall attempt to make a few remarks upon the legal question involved; not that I entertain any doubts as to the constitutionality of the pending bill, but because that branch of the subject has been so ably, successfully, and satisfactorily discussed by other gentlemen who have spoken in the affirmative of the question. The importance of the subject, however, is my apology to the House for submitting a few remarks upon this point in addition to what has already been said.

Constitutionality of the Bill

It is a fact well known by those who are at all familiar with the history of our Government that the great question of State rights—absolute State sovereignty as understood by the Calhoun school of politicians—has been a continuous source of political agitation for a great many years. In fact, for a number of years anterior to the rebellion this was the chief topic of political discussion. It continued to agitate the public mind from year to year and from time to time until the question was finally settled upon the field of battle. The war, however, did not result in the recognition of what may be called a centralized government, nor did it result in the destruction of the independent functions of the several States, except in certain particulars. But it did result in the recognition, and I hope the acceptance, of what may be called a medium between these two extremes; and this medium position or liberal policy has been incorporated in the Federal Constitution through the recent amendments to that instrument. But many of our constitutional lawyers of to-day are men who received their legal and political training during the discussion of the great question of State rights and under the tutorship of those who were identified with the Calhoun school of impracticable State rights theorists; they having been taught to believe that the Constitution as it was justified the construction they placed upon it, and this impression having been so indelibly and unalterably fixed upon their minds that recent changes, alterations, and amendments have failed to bring about a corresponding change in their construction of the Constitution. In fact, they seem to forget that the Constitution as it is is not in every respect the Constitution as it was.

We have a practical illustration of the correctness of this assertion in the person of the distinguished gentleman from Georgia (Mr. Stephens), and I believe my colleague, who sits near me (Mr. Lamar), and others who agree with them in their construction of the Constitution. But believing as I do that the Constitution as a whole should be so construed as to carry out the intention of the framers of the recent amendments, it will not be surprising to the House and to the country when I assert that it is impossible for me to agree with those who so construe the Constitution as to arrive at the erroneous conclusion that the pending bill is in violation of that instrument. It is not my purpose, however, to give the House simply the benefit of my own opinion upon the question, but to endeavor to show to your satisfaction, if possible, that the construction which I place upon the Constitution is precisely in accordance with that placed upon it by the highest judicial tribunal in the land, the Supreme Court of the United States. And this brings us to the celebrated Slaughter-house cases. But before referring to the decision of the court in detail, I will take this occasion to remark that, for the purposes of this debate at least, I accept as correct the theory that Congress cannot constitutionally pass any law unless it has expressed constitutional grant of power to do so; that the constitutional right of Congress to pass a law must not be implied, but expressed; and that in the absence of such expressed constitutional grant of power the right does not exist. In other words:

"The powers not delegated to the United States by the Constitution, nor prohibited by it to the States, are reserved to the States respectively, or to the people."

I repeat, that for the purposes of this debate at least, I accept as correct this theory. After having read over the decision of the court in these Slaughter-house cases several times very carefully, I have been brought very forcibly to this conclusion: that so far as this decision refers to the question of civil rights—the kind of civil rights referred to in this bill—it means this and nothing more:

that whatever right or power a State may have had prior to the ratification of the fourteenth amendment it still has, except in certain particulars. In other words, the fourteenth amendment was not intended, in the opinion of the court, to confer upon the Federal Government additional powers in general terms, but only in certain particulars. What are those particulars wherein the fourteenth amendment confers upon the Federal Government powers which it did not have before? The right to prevent distinctions and discriminations between the citizens of the United States and of the several States whenever such distinctions and discriminations are made on account of race, color, or previous condition of servitude; and that distinctions and discriminations made upon any other ground than these are not prohibited by the fourteenth amendment. As the discrimination referred to in the Slaughter-house cases was not made upon either of these grounds, it did not come within the constitutional prohibition. As the pending bill refers only to such discriminations as are made on account of race, color, or previous condition of servitude, it necessarily follows that the bill is in harmony with the Constitution as construed by the Supreme Court.

I will now ask the Clerk to read the following extract from the decision upon which the legal gentlemen on the other side of the House have chiefly relied to sustain them in the assertion that the court has virtually decided the pending bill to be unconstitutional.

The Clerk read as follows:

"Of the privileges and immunities of the citizens of the United States, and of the privileges and immunities of the citizens of the State, and what they respectively are, we will presently consider; but we wish to state here that it is only the former which are placed by this clause under the protection of the Federal Constitution, and that the latter, whatever they may be, are not intended to have any additional protection by this paragraph of the amendment.

If, then, there is a difference between the privileges and immunities belonging to a citizen of the United States as such, and those belonging to the citizen of the State as such, the latter must rest for their security and protection where they have heretofore rested, for they are not embraced by this paragraph of the amendment."

Mr. Lynch. If the court had said nothing more on the question of civil rights, then there would probably be some force in the argument. But after explaining at length why the case before it did not come within the constitutional prohibition, the court says:

"Having shown that the privileges and immunities relied on in the argument are those which belong to citizens of the States as such, and that they are left to the State government for security and protection, and not by this article placed under the special care of the Federal Government, we may hold ourselves excused from defining the privileges and immunities of citizens of the United States which no State can abridge until some case involving those privileges may make it necessary to do so."

But there are some democrats, and if I am not mistaken the gentleman from Georgia (Mr. Stephens) is one among the number, who are willing to admit that the recent amendments to the Constitution guarantee to the colored citizens all of the rights, privileges, and immunities that are enjoyed by white citizens. But they say that it is the province of the several States, and not that of the Federal Government, to enforce these constitutional guarantees. This is the most important point in the whole argument. Upon its decision this bill must stand or fall. We will now suppose that the constitutional guarantee of equal rights is conceded, which is an important concession for those calling themselves Jeffersonian democrats to make. The question that now presents itself is, has the Federal Government the constitutional right to enforce by suitable and appropriate legislation the guarantees herein referred to? Gentlemen on the other side of the House answer the question in the negative; but the Supreme Court answers the question in the following unmistakable language:

"Nor shall any State deny to any person within its jurisdiction the equal protection of the laws. In the light of the history of these amendments and the pervading purpose of them, which we have already discussed, it is not difficult to give a meaning to this clause. The existence of laws in the States where the newly emancipated Negroes resided, which discriminated with gross injustice and hardship against them as a class, was the evil to be remedied by this clause, and by it such laws are forbidden.

If, however, the States did not conform their laws to its requirements, then by the fifth section of the article of amendment Congress was authorized to enforce it by suitable legislation. We doubt very much whether any action of a State not directed by way of discrimination against the Negroes as a class, or on account of their race, will ever be held to come within the purview of this provision."

It will be seen from the above that the constitutional right of Congress to pass this bill is fully conceded by the Supreme Court. But before leaving this subject, I desire to call attention to a short legal argument that was made by a distinguished lawyer in the other end of the Capitol (if it is parliamentary to do so) when the bill was under consideration before that body:

"Mr. Carpenter. Mr. President, as I shall vote against this bill in its present form, I wish to state very briefly why I shall do so. Without discussing other provisions of the bill, one makes it impossible for me to vote for it, and that is the provision in regard to State juries. I know of no more power in the Government of the United States to determine the component elements of a State jury than of a State bench or of a State Legislature. I can see no argument which shows the powers of this Government to organize State juries that does not apply to State Legislatures; a power which, in my judgment, is clearly not conferred upon this Government. I cannot vote for a bill as an entirety which contains even one provision which I deem unconstitutional. For that reason I shall vote against this bill."

The Clerk will now read the fourth section of the bill; the section referred to by the distinguished Wisconsin Senator.

The Clerk read as follows:

"Sec. 4. That no citizen possessing all other qualifications which are or may be prescribed by law shall be disqualified for service as juror in any court, national or State, by reason of race, color, or previous condition of servitude; and any officers or other persons charged with any duty in the selection or summoning of jurors who shall exclude or fail to summon any citizen for the reason above named shall, on conviction thereof, be deemed guilty of a misdemeanor and be fined not less than $1,000 nor more than $5,000."

MR. LYNCH. The position assumed by the eminent lawyer is so unreasonable, untenable, and illogical that it would have surprised me had it been taken by an ordinary village lawyer of inferior acquirements. There is nothing in this section that will justify the assertion that it contemplates regulating State juries. It simply contemplates carrying into effect the constitutional prohibition against distinctions on account of race or color.

There is also a constitution prohibition against religious proscription. Let us suppose that another section conferred the power on Congress to enforce the provisions of that article by appropriate legislation; then suppose a State should pass a law disqualifying from voting, holding office, or serving on juries all persons who may be identified with a certain religious denomination; would the distinguished Wisconsin Senator then contend that Congress would have no right to pass a law prohibiting this discrimination, in the face of the constitutional prohibition and the right conferred upon Congress to enforce it by appropriate legislation? I contend that any provision in the constitution or laws of any State that is in conflict with the Constitution of the United States is absolutely null and void; for the Constitution itself declared that:

"This Constitution and the laws of the United States which shall be made in pursuance thereof * * * * shall be the supreme law of the land; and the judges in every state shall be bound thereby, anything in the constitution or laws of any State to the contrary notwithstanding."

The Constitution further declares that:

"No State shall make or enforce any law which shall abridge the privileges or immunities of citizens of the United States, * * * * nor deny to any person within its jurisdiction the equal protection of the laws."

And that:

"The Congress shall have power to enforce this article by appropriate legislation."

As the Supreme Court has decided that the above constitutional provision was intended to confer upon Congress the power to prevent distinctions and discriminations when made on account of race or color, I contend that the power of Congress in this respect is applicable to every office under the constitution and laws of any State. Some may think that this is extraordinary power; but such is not the case. For any State can, without violating the fourteenth or fifteenth amendments and the provisions of this bill, prohibit any one from voting, holding office, or serving on juries in their respective States, who cannot read and write, or who does not own a certain amount of property, or who shall not have resided in the State for a certain number of months, days, or years. The only thing these amendments prevent them from doing in this respect is making the color of a person or the race with which any person may be identified a ground of disqualification from the enjoyment of any of these privileges. The question seems to me to be so clear that further argument is unnecessary.

Civil Rights and Social Equality

I will now endeavor to answer the arguments of those who have been contending that the passage of this bill is an effort to bring about social equality between the races. That the passage of this bill can in any manner affect the social status of any one seems to me to be absurd and ridiculous. I have never believed for a moment that social equality could be brought about even between persons of the same race. I have always believed that social distinctions existed among white persons the same as among colored people. But those who contend that the passage of this bill will have a tendency to bring about social equality between the races virtually and substantially admit that there are no social distinctions among white people whatever, but that all white persons, regardless of their moral character, are the social equals of each other; for if by conferring upon colored people the same rights and privileges that are now exercised and enjoyed by whites indiscriminately will result in bringing about social equality between the races, then the same process of reasoning must necessarily bring us to the conclusion that there are no social distinctions among whites, because all white persons, regardless of their social standing, are permitted to enjoy these rights. See then how unreasonable, unjust, and false is the assertion that social equality is involved in this legislation. I cannot believe that gentlemen on the other side of the House mean what they say when they admit, as they do, that the immoral, the ignorant and the degraded of their own race are the social equals of themselves, and their families. If they do, then I can only assure them that they do not put as high an estimate upon their own social standing as respectable and intelligent colored people place upon theirs; for there are hundreds and thousands of white people of both sexes whom I know to be the social inferiors of respectable and intelligent colored people. I can then assure that portion of my democratic friends on the other side of the House whom I regard as my social inferiors that if at any time I should meet any one of you at a hotel and occupy a seat at the same table with you, or the same seat in a car with you, do not think that I have thereby accepted you as my social equal. Not at all. But if any one should attempt to discriminate against you for no other reason than because you are identified with a particular race or religious sect, I would regard it as an outrage; as a violation of the principles of republicanism; and I would be in favor of protecting you in the exercise and enjoyment of your rights by suitable and appropriate legislation.

No, Mr. Speaker, it is not social rights that we desire. We have enough of that already. What we ask is protection in the enjoyment of public rights. Rights which are or should be accorded to every citizen alike. Under our present system of race distinctions a white woman of a questionable social standing, yea, I may say, of an admitted immoral character, can go to any public place or upon any public conveyance and be the recipient of the same treatment, and the same courtesy, and the same respect that is usually accorded to the most refined and virtuous; but let an intelligent, modest, refined colored lady present herself and ask that the same privileges be accorded to her that have just been accorded to her social inferior of the white race, and in nine cases out of ten, except in certain portions of the country, she will not only be refused, but insulted for making the request.

Mr. Speaker, I ask the members of this House in all candor, is this right? I appeal to your sensitive feelings as husbands, fathers, and brothers, is this just? You who have affectionate companions, attractive daughters, and loving sisters, is this just? If you have any of the ingredients of manhood in your composition you will answer the question most emphatically, No! What a sad commentary upon our system of government, our religion, and our civilization! Think of it for a moment; here am I, a member of your honorable body, representing one of the largest and wealthiest districts in the State of Mississippi, and possibly in the South; a district composed of persons of different races, religions, and nationalities; and yet, when I leave my home to come to the capital of the nation, to take part in the deliberations of the House and to participate with you in making laws for the government of this great Republic, in coming through the God-forsaken States of Kentucky and Tennessee, if I come by the way of Louisville or Chattanooga, I am treated, not as an American citizen, but as a brute. Forced to occupy a filthy smoking-car both night and day, with drunkards, gamblers, and criminals; and for what? Not that I am unable or unwilling to pay my way; not that I am obnoxious in my personal appearance or disrespectful in my conduct; but simply because I happen to be of a darker complexion. If this treatment was confined to persons of our own sex we could possibly afford to endure it. But such is not the case. Our wives and our daughters, our sisters and our mothers are subjected to the same insults and to the same uncivilized treatment. You may ask why we do not institute civil suits in the State courts. What a farce! Talk about instituting a civil-rights suit in the State courts of Kentucky, for instance, where the decision of the judge is virtually rendered before he enters the court-house, and the verdict of the jury substantially rendered before it is impaneled. The only moments of my life when I am necessarily compelled to question my loyalty to my Government or my devotion to the flag of my country is when I read of outrages having been committed upon innocent colored people and the perpetrators go unwhipped of justice, and when I leave my home to go traveling.

Mr. Speaker, if this unjust discrimination is to be longer tolerated by the American people, which I do not, cannot, and will not believe until I am forced to do so, then I can only say with sorrow and regret that our boasted civilization is a fraud; our republican institutions a failure; our social system a disgrace; and our religion a complete hypocrisy. But I have an abiding confidence—(though I must confess that that confidence was seriously shaken a little over two months ago)—but still I have an abiding confidence in the patriotism of this people, in their devotion to the cause of human rights, and in the stability of our republican institutions. I hope that I will not be deceived. I love the land that gave me birth; I love the Stars and Stripes. This country is where I intend to live, where I expect to die. To preserve the honor of the national flag and to maintain perpetually the Union of the States hundreds, and I may say thousands, of noble, brave, and true-hearted colored men have fought, bled, and died. And now, Mr. Speaker, I ask, can it be possible that that flag under which they fought is to be a shield and a protection to all races and classes of persons except the colored race? God forbid!

The School Clause

The enemies of this bill have been trying very hard to create the impression that it is the object of its advocates to bring about a compulsory system of mixed schools. It is not my intention at this time to enter into a discussion of the question as to the propriety or impropriety of mixed schools; as to whether or not such a system is essential to destroy race distinctions and break down race prejudices. I will leave these questions to be discussed by those who have given the subject a more thorough consideration. The question that now presents itself to our minds is, what will be the effect of this legislation on the public-school system of the country, and more especially in the South? It is to this question that I now propose to speak. I regard this school clause as the most harmless provision in the bill. If it were true that the passage of this bill with the school clause in it would tolerate the existence of none but a system of mixed free schools, then I would question very seriously the propriety of retaining such a clause; but such is not the case. If I understand the bill correctly (and I think I do), it simply confers upon all citizens, or rather recognizes the right which has already been conferred upon all citizens, to send their children to any public free school that is supported in whole or in part by taxation, the exercise of the right to remain a matter of option as it now is—nothing compulsory about it. That the passage of this bill can result in breaking up the public-school system in any State is absurd. The men who make these reckless assertions are very well aware of the fact, or else they are guilty of unpardonable ignorance, that every right and privilege that is enumerated in this bill has already been conferred upon all citizens alike in at least one-half of the States of this Union by State legislation. In every Southern State where the republican party is in power a civil-rights bill is in force that is more severe in its penalties than are the penalties in this bill. We find mixed-school clauses in some of their State constitutions. If, then, the passage of this bill, which does not confer upon the colored people of such States any rights that they do not possess already, will result in breaking up the public-school system in their respective States, why is it that State legislation has not broken them up? This proves very conclusively, I think, that there is nothing in the argument whatever, and that the school clause is the most harmless provision in the bill. My opinion is that the passage of this bill just as it passed the Senate will bring about mixed schools practically only in localities where one or the other of the two races is small in numbers, and that in localities where both races are large in numbers separate schools and separate institutions of learning will continue to exist, for a number of years at least.

I now ask the Clerk to read the following editorial, which appeared in a democratic paper in my own State when the bill was under discussion in the Senate. This is from the Jackson *Clarion*, the leading conservative paper in the State, the editor of which is known to be a moderate, reasonable, and sensible man.

The Clerk read as follows:

THE CIVIL-RIGHTS BILL AND OUR PUBLIC-SCHOOL SYSTEM

"The question has been asked what effect will the civil-rights bill have on the public-school system of our State if it should become a law? Our opinion is that it will have none at all. The provisions of the bill do not necessarily break up the separate-school system, unless the people interested choose that they shall do so; and there is no reason to believe that the colored people of this State are dissatisfied with the system as it is, or that they are not content to let well enough alone. As a people, they have not shown a disposition to thrust themselves where they are not wanted, or rather had no right to go. While they have been naturally tenacious of their newly acquired privileges, their general conduct will bear them witness that they have shown consideration for the feelings of the whites.

The race line in politics never would have been drawn if opposition had not been made to their enjoyment of equal privileges in the Government and under the laws after they were emancipated.

As to our public-school system, so far as it bears upon the races, we have heard no complaint whatever. It is not asserted that it is operated more advantageously to the whites than to the blacks. Its benefits are shared alike by all; and we do not believe the colored people, if left to the guidance of their own judgment, will consent to jeopardize these benefits in a vain attempt to acquire something better.''

Mr. Lynch. The question may be asked, however, if the colored people in a majority of the States are entitled by State legislation to all of the rights and privileges enumerated in this bill, and if they will not insist upon mixing the children in the public schools in all localities, what is the necessity of retaining this clause? The reasons are numerous, but I will only mention a few of them. In the first place, it is contrary to our system of government to discriminate by law between persons on account of their race, their color, their religion, or the place of their birth. It is just as wrong and just as contrary to republicanism to provide by law for the education of children who may be identified with a certain race in separate schools to themselves, as to provide by law for the education of children who may be identified with a certain religious denomination in separate schools to themselves. The duty of the law-maker is to know no race, no color, no religion, no nationality, except to prevent distinctions on any of these grounds, so far as the law is concerned.

The colored people in asking the passage of this bill just as it passed the Senate do not thereby admit that their children can be better educated in white than in colored schools; nor that white teachers because they are white are better qualified to teach than colored ones. But they recognize the fact that the distinction when made and tolerated by law is an unjust and odious proscription; that you make their color a ground of objection, and consequently a crime. This is what we most earnestly protest against. Let us confer upon all citizens, then, the rights to which they are entitled under the Constitution; and then if they choose to have their children educated in separate schools, as they do in my own State, then both races will be satisfied, because they will know that the separation is their own voluntary act and not legislative compulsion.

Another reason why the school clause ought to be retained is because the Negro question ought to be removed from the politics of the country. It has been a disturbing element in the country ever since the Declaration of Independence, and it will continue to be so long as the colored man is denied any right or privilege that is enjoyed by the white man. Pass this bill as it passed the Senate, and there will be nothing more for the colored people to ask or expect in the way of civil rights. Equal rights having been made an accomplished fact, opposition to the exercise thereof will gradually pass away, and the everlasting Negro question will then be removed from the politics of the country for the first time since the existence of the Government. Let us, then, be just as well as generous. Let us confer upon the colored citizens equal rights, and, my word for it, they will exercise their rights with moderation and with wise discretion.

Civil Rights from a Political Standpoint

I now come to the most important part of my subject—civil rights from a political standpoint. In discussing this branch of the subject, I do not deem it necessary to make any appeal to the republican members whatever in behalf of this bill. It is presumed, and correctly, too, I hope, that every republican member of the House will vote for this bill. The country expects it, the colored people ask it, the republican party promised it, and justice demands it. It is not necessary therefore for me to appeal to republicans in behalf of a measure that they are known to be in favor of.

But it has been suggested that it is not necessary for me to make an appeal to the democratic, conservative, or liberal republican members in behalf of this measure; that they will go against it to a man. This may be true, but I prefer to judge them by their acts. I will not condemn them in advance. But I desire to call the attention of the democratic members of the House to one or two things in connection with the history of their organization.

Your party went before the country in 1872 with a pledge that it would protect the colored people in all of their rights and privileges under the Constitution, and to convince them of your sincerity you nominated as your standard-bearer one who had proved himself to be their life-long friend and advocate. But the colored people did not believe that you were sincere, and consequently did not trust you. As the promise was made unconditionally, however, their refusal to trust you does not relieve you from the performance of the promise. Think for a moment what the effect of your votes upon this bill will be. If you vote in favor of this measure, which will be nothing more than redeeming the promises made by you in 1872, it will convince the colored people that they were mistaken when they supposed that you made the promise for no other purpose than to deceive them. But if you should vote against this bill, which I am afraid you intend to do, you will thereby convince them that they were not mistaken when they supposed that you made the promise for no other purpose than to deceive them. It can have no other effect than to increase their suspicion, strengthen their doubts, and intensify their devotion to the republican party. It will demonstrate to the country and to the world that you attempted in 1872 to obtain power under false pretenses. I once heard a very eminent lawyer make the remark that the crime of obtaining money or goods under false pretenses is in his opinion the next crime to murder. I ask the democratic and conservative members of the House will you, by voting against this bill, convict yourselves of attempting in 1872 to obtain power under false pretenses?

I will take this occasion to say to my democratic friends, that I do not wish to be understood as endeavoring to convey the idea that all of the prominent men who were identified with the so-called liberal movement in 1872 were actuated by improper motives, that they made promises which they never intended to redeem. Far from it. I confess, Mr. Speaker, that some of the best and most steadfast friends the colored people in this country have ever had were identified with that movement. Even the man whom you selected, from necessity and not from choice, as your standard-bearer on that occasion is one whose memory will ever live in the hearts of the colored people of this country as one of their best, their strongest, and most consistent friends.

They will ever cherish his memory, in consequence of his life-long devotion to the cause of liberty, humanity, and justice—for his earnest, continuous, persistent, and consistent advocacy of what he was pleased to term manhood suffrage. In voting against him so unanimously as the colored voters did, it was not because they questioned his honesty, or his devotion to the cause of equal rights, but they recognized the fact that he made the same mistake that many of our great men have made—he allowed his ambition to control his better judgment. While the colored voters would have cheerfully supported him for the Presidency under different circumstances, they could not give their votes to elevate him to that position through such a questionable channel as that selected by him in 1872. But since he has passed away, they are willing to remember only his virtues and to forget his faults. I might refer to several other illustrious names that were identified with that movement and whose fidelity to the cause of civil rights can never be questioned, but time will not allow me to do so.

I will now refer to some of the unfortunate remarks that were made by some gentlemen on the other side of the House during the last session—especially those made by the gentleman from North Carolina (Mr. Robbins) and those made by the gentleman from Virginia (Mr. Harris). These two gentlemen are evidently strong believers in the exploded theory of white superiority and negro inferiority. But in order to show what a difference of opinion exists among men, with regard to man's superiority over man, it gives me pleasure to assure those two gentlemen that if at any time either of them should become so generous as to admit that I, for instance, am his equal, I would certainly regard it as anything else but complimentary to myself. This may be regarded as a little selfish, but as all of us are selfish to some extent, I must confess that I am no exception to the general rule. The gentleman from North Carolina admits, ironically, that the colored people, even when in bondage and ignorance, could equal, if not excel, the whites in some things—dancing, singing, and eloquence, for instance. We will admit, for the sake of the argument, that in this the gentleman is correct, and will ask the question, Why is it that the colored people could equal the whites in these respects, while in bondage and ignorance, but not in others? The answer is an easy one: You could not prevent them from dancing unless you kept them continually tied; you could not prevent them from singing unless you kept them continually gagged; could not prevent them from being eloquent unless you deprived them of the power of speech; but you could and did prevent them from becoming educated for fear that they would equal you in every other respect; for no educated people can be held in bondage. If the argument proves anything, therefore, it is only this: That if the colored people while in bondage and ignorance could equal the whites in these respects, give them their freedom and allow them to become educated and they will equal the whites in every other respect. At any rate I cannot see how any reasonable man can object to giving them an opportunity to do so if they can. It does not become southern white men, in my opinion, to boast about the ignorance of the colored people, when you know that their ignorance is the result of the enforcement of your unjust laws. Any one would suppose, from the style and the manner of the gentleman from North Carolina, that the white man's government of the State from which he comes is one of the best States in the Union for white men to live in at least. But I will ask the Clerk to read, for the information of that gentleman, the following article from a democratic paper in my own State.

The Clerk read as follows:

"The following from the Charlotte *Democrat* is a hard hit: 'The Legislature of Mississippi has just elected a Negro to represent that State in the United States Senate. The white men who recently moved from Cabarrus County, North Carolina, to Mississippi, to better their condition, will please report the situation and say which they like best, white rule in North Carolina or black rule in Mississippi.'

We do not see the point of the joke. The 'white men who moved from Cabarrus will doubtless report' that they have not realized, and do not expect to, any serious inconvenience from the election of Bruce. It is better to be endured than the inconvenience of eking out a starveling existence in a worn-out State like North Carolina. Besides, when we look to the executive offices of the two States we will find that the governor of North Carolina claims to be as stanch a republican as his excellency of Mississippi. And then contrast the financial condition of the two States. There is poor old North Carolina burdened with a debt of $30,000,000, with interest accumulating so rapidly that she is unable to pay it, much less the principal. The debt of Mississippi, on the other hand, is but three millions, and with her wonderful recuperative powers it can be wiped out in a few years by the economical management solemnly promised by those in charge of her State government.

The men 'who moved from Cabarrus' will 'look upon this picture, and on this,' and conclude that they have bettered their condition, notwithstanding affairs are not entirely as they would have them. A warm welcome to them."

MR. LYNCH. So far as the gentleman from Virginia is concerned, the gentleman who so far forgot himself as to be disrespectful to one of his fellow-members, I have only this remark to make: Having served in the Legislature of my own State several years, where I had the privilege of meeting some of the best, the ablest, and I may add, the bitterest democrats in the State, it gives me pleasure to be able to say, that with all of their bitterness upon political questions, they never failed to preserve and maintain that degree of dignity, self-respect, and parliamentary decorum which always characterized intelligent legislators and well-bred gentlemen. Take, for instance, my eloquent and distinguished colleague (Mr. Lamar) on the other side of the House, and I venture to assert that he will never declare upon this floor, or elsewhere that he is only addressing white men. No, sir; Mississippians do not send such men to Congress, nor even to their State Legislature. For if they did, it would not only be a sad and serious reflection upon their intelligence, but it would be a humiliating disgrace to the State.

Such sentiments as those uttered by the gentleman from North Carolina and the gentleman from Virginia are certainly calculated to do the southern white people a great deal more harm than it is possible for them to do the colored people. In consequence of which I can say to those two gentlemen, that I know of no stronger rebuke than the language of the Saviour of the world when praying for His persecutors: "Father, forgive them; for they know not what they do."

The South Not Opposed to Civil Rights

The opposition to civil rights in the South is not so general or intense as a great many would have the country believe. It is a mistaken idea that all of the white people in the South outside of the republican party are bitterly opposed to this bill. In my own State, and especially in my own district, the democrats as a rule are indifferent as to its fate. It is true they would not vote for it, but they reason from this standpoint: The civil-rights bill does not confer upon the colored people of Mississippi any rights that they are not entitled to already under the constitution and laws of the State. We certainly have no objection, then, to allowing the colored people in other States to enjoy the same rights that they are entitled to in our own State. To illustrate this point more forcibly, I ask the Clerk to read the following article from the ablest conservative paper in the State, a paper, however, that is opposed to the White League. This article was published when the civil-rights bill was under discussion in the Senate last winter.

The Clerk read as follows:

"A civil-rights bill is before the Senate. As we have civil-rights here in Mississippi and elsewhere in the South, we do not understand why southern representatives should concern themselves about applying the measure to other portions of the country; or what practical interest we have in the question. On the 29th, Senator Norwood, of Georgia, one of the mediocrities to whom expediency has assigned a place for which he is unfitted, delivered himself of a weak and driveling speech on the subject in which he did what he was able to keep alive sectional strife and the prejudices of race. We will venture to say that his colleague, General Gordon, who was a true soldier when the war was raging, will not be drawn into the mischievous controversy which demagogues from both sections, and especially latter-day fire-eaters who have become intensely enraged since the surrender, take delight in carrying on."

Mr. Lynch. What is true of Mississippi in this respect is true of nearly every State where a civil-rights bill is in force. In proof of this, I ask the Clerk to read the following remarks made by the present democratic governor of Arkansas during his candidacy for that office.

The Clerk read as follows:

"But I hear it whispered round and about that the Southern States, and Arkansas among them, are to be overhauled by Congress this winter, and in some way reconstructed, because the colored man has no law giving him civil rights in those States. Upon this pretext we are to be upset and worked over. My fellow-citizens, one and all, upon this proposition Arkansas is at home and quite comfortable. In the acts of the Legislature of 1873, pages 15-19 (No. 12), we have a 'civil-rights bill,' which is now in force—almost a copy, if I mistake not, of the bill Mr. Sumner shortened his life in vainly trying to get Congress to pass. If Congress next winter can get up one more definite, more minute, and more specific in giving rights to the colored man, I would be pleased to look upon and observe it. That act is now in force, as I said, and I know of no one who wants to repeal it, and certainly I do not want it repealed; and will not favor its repeal; and I do hope, if our opponents do start in this direction before Congress, they will call attention to it directly. If there is any complaint with and among our colored friends as to the terms of this act, or as to its not being enforced, I have not heard of them, and I am persuaded there have been none."

Mr. Lynch. It will be seen from the above that if Mr. Garland means what he says, which remains to be seen, the democratic or conservative party in Arkansas is in favor of civil rights for the colored people. Why? Simply because, the republican Legislature having passed the bill, democrats now see that it is not such a bad thing after all. But if the Legislature had failed to pass it, as in Alabama for instance, White League demagogues would have appealed to the passions and prejudices of the whites, and made them believe that this legislation is intended to bring about a revolution in society. The opposition to civil rights in the South, therefore, is confined almost exclusively to States under democratic control, or States where the Legislature has failed or refused to pass a civil-rights bill. I ask the republican members of the House, then, will you refuse or fail to do justice to the colored man in obedience to the behests of three or four democratic States in the South? If so, then the republican party is not made of that material which I have always supposed it was.

Public Opinion

Some well-meaning men have made the remark that the discussion of the civil-rights question has produced a great deal of bad feeling in certain portions of the South, in consequence of which they regret the discussion of the question and the possibility of the passage of the pending bill. That the discussion of the question has produced some bad feeling I am willing to admit; but allow me to assure you, Mr. Speaker, that the opposition to the pending bill is not half so intense in the South today as was the opposition to the reconstruction acts of Congress. As long as congressional action is delayed in the passage of this bill, the more intense this feeling will be. But let the bill once pass and become a law, and you will find that in a few months reasonable men, liberal men, moderate men, sensible men, who now question the propriety of passing this bill, will arrive at the conclusion that it is not such a bad thing as they supposed it was. They will find that democratic predictions have not and will not be realized. They will find that there is no more social equality than before. That whites and blacks do not intermarry any more than they did before the passage of the bill. In short, they will find that there is nothing in the bill but the recognition by law of the equal rights of all citizens before the law. My honest opinion is that the passage of this bill will have a tendency to harmonize the apparently conflicting interests between the two races. It will have a tendency to bring them more closely together in all matters pertaining to their public and political duties. It will cause them to know, appreciate, and respect the rights and privileges of each other more than ever before. In the language of my distinguished colleague on the other side of the house, "They will know one another, and love one another."

Conclusion

In conclusion, Mr. Speaker, I say to the republican members of the House that the passage of this bill is expected by you. If any of our democratic friends will vote for it, we will be agreeably surprised. But if republicans should vote against it, we will be sorely disappointed; it will be to us a source of deep mortification as well as profound regret. We will feel as though we are deserted in the house of our friends. But I have no fears whatever in this respect. You have stood by the colored people of this country when it was more unpopular to do so than it is to pass this bill. You have fulfilled every promise thus far, and I have no reason to believe that you will not fulfill this one. Then give us this bill. The white man's government Negro-hating democracy will, in my judgment, soon pass out of existence. The progressive spirit of the American people will not much longer tolerate the existence of an organization that lives upon the passions and prejudices of the hour. But when that party shall have passed away, the republican party of today will not be left in undisputed control of the Government; but a young, powerful, and more vigorous organization will rise up to take the place of the democracy of today. This organization may not have opposition to the Negro the principal plank in its platform; it may take him by the right hand and concede him every right in good faith that is enjoyed by the whites; it may confer upon him honor and position. But if you, as leaders of the republican party, will remain true to the principles upon which the party came into power, as I am satisfied you will, then no other party, however just, liberal, or fair it may be, will ever be able to detach any considerable number of colored voters from the national organization. Of course, in matters pertaining to their local State affairs, they will divide up to some extent, as they sometimes should, whenever they can be assured that their rights and privileges are not involved in the contest. But in all national contests, I feel safe in predicting that they will remain true to the great party of freedom and equal rights.

I appeal to all the members of the House—republicans and democrats conservatives and liberals—to join with us in the passage of this bill, which has for its object the protection of human rights. And when every man, woman, and child can feel and know that his, her, and their rights are fully protected by the strong arm of a generous and grateful Republic, then we can all truthfully say that this beautiful land of ours, over which the Star Spangled Banner so triumphantly waves, is, in truth and in fact, the "land of the free and the home of the brave."[1]

[1] *Congressional Record,* Vol. 3, Part II, 43rd Cong., 2nd Session, pp. 943-947.

Some important speeches of the Negro dealt with various topics. J. H. Rainey's speech on education shows an interest in social uplift in general as well as in the welfare of his own particular group. The speeches of J. M. Langston and George H. White, following this, deal with the defense of the race in general.

A SPEECH MADE IN REPLY TO AN ATTACK UPON THE COLORED STATE LEGISLATORS OF SOUTH CAROLINA BY REPRESENTATIVE COX OF NEW YORK

By Joseph H. Rainey

The remarks made by the gentleman from New York in relation to the colored people of South Carolina escaped my hearing, as I was in the rear of the Hall when they were made, and I did not know that any utterance of that kind had emanated from him. I have always entertained a high regard for the gentleman from New York, because I believed him to be a useful member of the House. He is a gentleman of talent and of fine education, and I have thought heretofore that he would certainly be charitable toward a race of people who have never enjoyed the same advantages that he has. If the colored people of South Carolina had been accorded the same advantages—if they had had the same wealth and surroundings which the gentleman from New York has had, they would have shown to this nation that their color was no obstacle to their holding positions of trust, political or otherwise. Not having had these advantages, we cannot at the present time compete with the favored race of this country; but perhaps if our lives are spared, and if the gentleman from New York and other gentlemen on that side of the House will only accord to us right and justice, we shall show to them that we can be useful, intelligent citizens of this country. But if they will continue to proscribe us, if they will continue to cultivate prejudice against us, if they will continue to decry the Negro and crush him under foot, then you cannot expect the Negro to rise while the Democrats are trampling upon him and his rights. We ask you, sir, to do by the Negro as you ought to do by him in justice.

If the Democrats are such staunch friends of the Negro, why is it that when propositions are offered here and elsewhere looking to the elevation of the colored race, and the extension of right and justice to them, do the Democrats array themselves in unbroken phalanx, and vote against every such measure? You, gentlemen of that side of the House, have voted against all the recent amendments of the Constitution, and the laws enforcing the same. Why did you do it? I answer, because those measures had a tendency to give to the poor Negro his just rights, and because they proposed to knock off his shackles and give him freedom of speech, freedom of action, and the opportunity of education, that he might elevate himself to the dignity of manhood.

Now you come to us and say that you are our best friends. We would that we could look upon you as such. We would that your votes as recorded in the *Globe* from day to day could only demonstrate it. But your votes, your actions, and the constant cultivation of your cherished prejudices prove to the Negroes of the entire country that the Democrats are in opposition to them, and if they (the Democrats) could have sway our race would have no foothold here.

Now, sir, I have not time to vindicate fully the course of action of the colored people of South Carolina. We are certainly in the majority there; I admit that we are as two to one. Sir, I ask this House, I ask the country, I ask white men, I ask Democrats, I ask Republicans whether the Negroes have presumed to take improper advantage of the majority they hold in that State by disregarding the interest of the minority? They have not. Our convention which met in 1868, and in which the Negroes were in a large majority, did not pass any proscriptive or disfranchising acts, but adopted a liberal constitution, securing alike equal rights to all citizens, white and black, male and female, as far as possible. Mark you, we did not discriminate, although we had a majority. Our constitution towers up in its majesty with provisions for the equal protection of all classes of citizens. Notwithstanding our majority there, we have never attempted to deprive any man in that State of the rights and immunities to which he is entitled under the Constitution of this Government. You cannot point me to a single act passed by our Legislature, at any time, which had a tendency to reflect upon or oppress any white citizen of South Carolina. You cannot show me one enactment by which the majority in our State have undertaken to crush the white men because the latter are in a minority.

I say to you, gentlemen of the Democratic party, that I want you to deal justly with the people composing my race. I am here representing a Republican constituency made up of white and colored men. I say to you deal with us justly; be charitable toward us. An opportunity will soon present itself when we can test whether you on that side of the House are the best friends of the oppressed and ill-treated Negro race. When the civil rights bill comes before you, when that bill comes up upon its merits asking you to give civil rights of the Negro, I will then see who are our best friends on that side of the House.

I will say to the gentleman from New York that I am sorry I am constrained to make these remarks. I wish to say to him that I do not mind what he may have said against the Negroes of South Carolina. Neither his friendship nor his enmity will change the sentiment of the loyal men of that State. We are determined to stand by this Government. We are determined to use judiciously and wisely the prerogative conferred upon us by the Republican party. The democratic party may woo us, they may court us and try to get us to worship at their shrine, but I will tell the gentleman that we are republicans by instinct, and we will be Republicans so long as God will allow our proper senses to hold sway over us.[1]

SPEECH ON EDUCATION

By J. H. Rainey

Mr. Speaker: I have been an attentive listener to the discussions on House bill No. 1043. This bill, as you are aware, has for its object the education of the people, and proposes to that end that the proceeds accruing from the sale of all public lands should be set apart as a sacred fund for that object. Viewing it in this light, one may well be surprised at the manner in which the entire subject has been treated by the Opposition. It is truly marvelous to observe the manifest antipathy exhibited toward measures that are brought before this House having for their purpose the amelioration and improvement of the masses.

[1] *Congressional Globe*, 42nd Congress, 2nd Session, 1442, 1443.

It ought not to be forgotten that we are the custodians of the interests of the whole people, sent here direct from their hands to represent their claims and interests before Congress, and, I may add, the whole country. Why, sir, those illiterate and somewhat neglected people are the actual bone and sinew of the country, and at this time may be safely numbered among the stanchest supporters of its institutions. Their efficiency, bravery, and power were known to the country in its darkest days and dire necessities, the testimony of which is stamped in bloody stains upon many a battlefield. These gallant and true men, many of whom have passed away, have left their fatherless children as a heritage and trust to this Government. Yea, the whole people are deeply interested in this subject of education; therefore, we should endeavor to reflect as best we can their opinions, wishes, and desires in this regard.

I feel confident in saying that the populace is eager for education, and are looking with an ardent desire to the General Government to aid them in this particular. Educational facilities are needed alike by all classes, both white and black. There is an appalling array of the illiterate made in the admirable report of the Commissioner of Education, a forcible tabular statement of which has been brought to the notice of this House by the distinguished gentleman from Massachusetts (Mr. Hoar). Surely this ought to be sufficient to disarm all hostility to this laudable and much-needed measure; but instead of that, it meets with every conceivable objection and opposition from those who profess to be the friends and advocates of universal education. By some the bill under consideration is said to be unconstitutional; by others, centralizing power in the hands of the General Government which by right belongs to individual States.

The gentleman from Georgia (Mr. McIntyre) expressed his apprehensions that this was a plan to mix the schools throughout the country. What of that? Suppose it should be so, what harm would result therefrom? Why this fear of the Negro since he has been a freedman, when in the past he was almost a household god, gamboling and playing with the children of his old master? And occasionally it was plain to be seen that there was a strong family resemblance between them.

Now, since he is no longer a slave, one would suppose him a

leper, to hear the objections expressed against his equality before the law. Sir, this is the remnant of the old pro-slavery spirit, which must eventually give place to more humane and elevating ideas. Schools have been mixed in Massachusetts, Rhode Island, and other States, and no detriment has occurred. Why this fear of competition with a Negro? All they ask for is an equal chance in life, with equal advantages, and they will prove themselves to be worthy American citizens. In the southern States it was a pride in the past to exult in the extraordinary ability of a few representative men, while the poorer classes were kept illiterate and in gross ignorance; consequently completely under the control of their leaders, all of whom were Democrats.

The Republican party propose by this measure now pending to educate the masses so that they will be enabled to judge for themselves in all matters appertaining to their interests, and by an intelligent expression of their manhood annihilate the remnant of that oligarchical spirit of exclusiveness which was so prominent in the past. Sir, it appears to me as though gentlemen on this floor have lost sight of the fact that the besom of war has swept over this country, and that there is a change in the condition of affairs; that the people are the rightful rulers, and those in power are but their servants.

During the last Congress we had under consideration a bill for the establishing of a system of national education, but adverse arguments were urged against the proposition, which resulted in its defeat. It was said then, as now, that it was unwise and inexpedient for such a bill to pass Congress, because it looked forward to centralization of Government, and an eventual invasion and trespass upon State rights. In my opinion, if the doctrine of State rights was not destroyed in the heated conflict of the late war, there are little or no apprehensions of such a contingency in the passage of this bill.

The decision of the sword is conceded to be the most arbitrary of all decisions which we have on record, and it might be added that they are written in blood and will assuredly withstand, all corrosive arguments to the contrary notwithstanding. The results of the rebellion have decided some things, and, in my judgment, defined the boundaries of State rights. Sir, speaking of centralization, all powerful Governments have a tendency in that direction, and those who have not are showing this day their sad want of power to control their internal affairs, and at the same time exercise a salutary influence on the actions and affairs of other nations.

In the old Roman empire, proud though it was, boasting of its many conquests and its almost unlimitable extent of territory, feeling themselves secured by a supposed high order of civilization, they grew indifferent to their best interests in this regard, and as a natural sequence their power waned, and they are only known to us as a nation through the pages of history. The nations of modern Europe most respected are those which have succeeded partly in centralizing their power, and I can see no difference in this respect with republics and monarchical governments. I am confident—yea, it is inevitable—that if this Government expects to control this vast extent of territory now in its possession, with an almost annual augmentation thereto, it must, of necessity, become somewhat centralized or it cannot stand.

Mr. Speaker, I have no argument to advance for or against the constitutionality of this bill; that I cheerfully submit to abler hands. It was said, however, by the gentleman from Pennsylvania (Mr. Storm) and others, that it is grossly unconstitutional; therefore more objectionable than the Ku Klux bill was. Such strictures are frequently heard from the Democracy. Nothing, in fact, appears to be constitutional to them that emanates or originates with the Republicans; consequently, the force of the argument is not felt to any extent. But admitting the assertion with all of the force and potency with which it is constantly uttered, I ask if it is a perversion of the spirit of the Constitution to invoke the sanction of that sacred instrument upon such a laudable measure as this, having for its aim the advancement of the whole people intellectually; thereby raising them to a higher plane, from which they may observe the beneficent workings of this, the greatest and most magnanimous of Governments.

The natural result of this mental improvement will be to impart a better understanding of our institutions, and thus cultivate a loyal disposition and lofty appreciation for them. The military prowess and demonstrative superiority of the Prussians, when compared to the French, especially in the late war, is attributable to the fact that the masses of the former were better educated and trained than those of the latter. The leavening spirit of the German philosophers has, apparently, pervaded all classes of the population of that entire empire. It is not necessary to detail the result that has passed into history, the lesson of which should not be lost on this continent. With these truths confronting us what is best to be done? Why, educate the people to a higher standard of citizenship. If this is done by the aid of the General Government its fruits will be seen in every department, and its power felt in every emergency.

Now, I am in favor of Government aid in this respect, for it will materially assist and eventually succeed in obliterating sectional feeling and differences of opinion, and thus foster a unit of sentiment that is so desirable by all true patriots, who are ever ready to acknowledge its essentiality to harmony, concord, and perpetual peace; thereby aiding the industries of our country and developing our vast national resources. If this had been done years ago there would have been a better understanding and more fraternal feeling between the North and the South, which would have annihilated that obstinate, hostile spirit which engendered the late "unpleasantness." The recent trials of the Ku Klux at Columbia, South Carolina, furnish a striking proof, which is beyond controversion, for the criminals themselves confessed an utter destitution of general information that did not fail to excite the commiseration of the presiding judges.

This lamentable condition of things demands a remedy at the hand of our powerful and generous Government. The evidence is conclusive; therefore it is not necessary that arguments should be multiplied on this point. The report of the Commissioner of Education presents an astonishing anomaly in its tabular statements setting forth the illiterate of all classes in the United States. We find that out of a population of over thirty-eight millions, over two and one-half millions in the southern States over twenty-one years old are unable to read and write, and over one million in the northern States.

I find in the report of the superintendent of education of the State which I have the honor in part to represent, the following interesting statement: there are 206,610 school children between the ages of six and sixteen, with a total attendance of only 66,056, the greater portion of the remainder being unable to attend for the want of educational facilities, although there has been one hundred and four school-houses erected during the year 1871, at a cost of $13,254, and fifty-two rented in addition thereto. There are employed in that State 1,898 teachers, at a cost of over two hundred and sixty-one thousand dollars per annum.

Sir, I now ask is not this statement of sufficient force to baffle opposition, and awaken a lively interest on the part of this House favorable to this great popular necessity? Think of it, only 66,056 children attending school out of a school population of 206,610 in one State in the Union. What must be the exhibit of all the States? But for all this the people are not to blame for their insufficiency of information. They are eager for knowledge, and the cry is still for more. I have seen, much to my admiration, old gray-headed men, formerly slaves, learning the alphabet, and straining their blunted senses in quest of knowledge, and this, too, after the hard toils of the day. The delight with which they behold their little children striving to read while seated around their humble firesides is pleasurable to behold, as a hopeful sign of what the once oppressed will be when they shall have drunk deep from the perennial stream of knowledge. What we want is schools, and more of them. We want them strung along the highways and byways of this country.

Mr. Speaker, I would have it known that this ignorance is wide-spread; it is not confined to any one State. This mental midnight, we might justly say, is a national calamity, and not necessarily sectional. We should therefore avail ourselves of every laudable means in our power to avert its direful effects. The great remedy, in my judgment, is free schools, established and aided by the Government throughout the land. The following statistics will demonstrate what I have said:

In Illinois, in the year 1870, the number of white pupils was 826,829; number of colored pupils, 6,210; number of school-houses, 10,381; number of school districts with no schools, 390; number of scholars attending school, 706,780. By this you will perceive that there are over 126,000 children not attending school in this State.

In Indiana, in the years 1867 and 1868, the number of school children was 591,661; number attending school, 436,736; average daily attendance, 283,340; amount expended for tuition, $1,474,-832.49.

The population of Maine, in 1870, was 630,423; number of school children, 228,167; number enrolled, 126,946; number not enrolled, 90,335; average attendance, 100,815. Average duration of schools only four months and twenty days.

The population of Louisiana in 1870 was 716,394; school population, 254,533; number enrolled, 50,000; average attendance, 40,000; number not registered, 204,533; making a total absence from school in that State of 214,533.

The school population of Arkansas in 1870 was 180,000; number enrolled, 100,000; average attendance, 60,000; number not enrolled, 80,000; average absence of those enrolled, 40,000; total average absence, 120,000.

Can we look at these facts unmoved? Do they not call for our deliberate and earnest action? Surely they do.

There is another fact which should not be lost sight of: our country is comparatively new; the want of skilled labor is felt in all the branches of its progressive industries. If the Government can utilize any portion of its immense domain for the furtherance of these ends, it will thus be dispensing its benefits and wealth to another class besides railroad corporations, who already have too much of what in right and equity belongs to the people. Millions of fertile acres have been disposed of in a prodigal manner to these opulent, dictatorial corporations. At present they have too much power and influence at their command, and in certain States in this Union they shape and control legislation to a great extent. My fears are that if Congress continues to assist them by further grants of the public domain, they will eventually become the dictators of national legislation.

The plan embraced in this bill thwarts their designs, and will in a measure protect the Government from such a misfortune, and the people from such a catastrophe. In fact, the people have long since rendered a verdict on this subject— "No more public lands to corporations." If this verdict holds good, the public possessions, henceforth, will be held in fee-simple for the sole benefit of the people.

I shall remind the House of one thing more, then I shall have done. The youth now springing up to manhood will be the future lawmakers and rulers of our country. That they should be intelligent and thoroughly educated is a prime necessity and of great importance, which is admitted by all and denied by none. All that may be done with this end in view will be returned with an increased interest.

I truly hope that those who oppose this bill will reconsider their opposition, and give it their vote when the question shall again be before the House. For one, I shall give it my hearty support, believing it to be just and beneficial in its provisions.[1]

A SPEECH LAUDATORY OF THE NEGRO

By J. M. Langston[2]

If there is anything that I would gladly see, it is "Our country first on land, and first on sea," and it is natural for me, coming into this body, as I do, from the Old Dominion that gave life to Washington and birth to Jefferson to come with the sentiment I have just expressed. I have seen American masters of ships wronged in foreign countries, and finally successfully defended by the Government through the vigorous and manly efforts of our representatives abroad. I recollect among the very last things that occurred when I had the honor of representing this Government abroad was this fact, first, that an old shipmaster said to me in our legation, "When you go home, if you ever have the opportunity to say a word for us, say it, say it freely and say it positively, and so emancipate us, that on the great sea, as well as at home, we may feel the consciousness that we are Americans."

I promised that shipmaster that if ever I had the opportunity of speaking for our shipping I would do it, and do it fearlessly and thoroughly. One of these days, in this august body, I trust that I shall have the opportunity of saying a word. But how can we make our land and our Government great in the estimation of others, except as finally we plant ourselves as a nation on those fundamental, far-reaching, eternal principles underlying all democracies and perpetuating all republics?

I would speak today to you, not in any other wise than as I

[1] *Congressional Globe*, 2nd Session, 42nd Congress, Appendix, pp. 15-17.

[2] John Mercer Langston was born in Louisa County, Virginia, December 14, 1829. He distinguished himself as an educator and won many honors in his field. Mr. Langston served also in many civic and political offices prior to his election to the 51st Congress. Due to the contest he was forced to make for his seat, Mr. Langston served actually a very short time in Congress. He died in Washington, D. C., November 15, 1897.—*Biographical Congressional Directory*, p. 643.

would defend the Constitution of my country, planting myself on those doctrines of the Declaration so clearly and forcibly enunciated in these words:

"We hold these truths to be self-evident; that all men are created equal; that they are endowed by their Creator with certain unalienable rights; that among these are life, liberty and the pursuit of happiness. That to secure these rights governments are instituted among men, deriving their just powers from the consent of the governed."

Ah, Mr. Chairman, the day has come to us now when we are to recur in our thoughts and reach in our purposes those olden times of this Republic when our fathers built, as Christ did, "on the rock," that His church might stand, and now that our Government may stand.

Why, the feeling in the country seems to be today that silver is the thing; and a man said to me the other day, when the silver bill had been laid aside for the time being, "Ah, sir, your cause has been sold for thirty pieces of silver."

MR. JOSEPH D. TAYLOR. The "elections bill," you mean, was laid aside.

MR. LANGSTON. Yes; I mean when the election bill was laid aside. But I said: "Not so, sir, for we live in the United States of America, in the midst of schoolhouses, in the midst of schools, in the midst of churches, in the midst of Christians, and we have built our nation on other material than that which shall find any class of our population, politicians or statesmen, finally willing to sell the cause of liberty, the rights of the humblest citizen of our Government, for anything like a compromise, even in silver." [Applause on the Republican side.]

Why, on what are we built and where do we go? Our nation is built first on those fundamental laws given in the midst of the flame and smoke of Sinai, and across the gateway of the old Mosaic system it was written, "He that stealeth a man and selleth him, or if he be found in his hands, he shall surely die"; and in the light of this law slavery has gone. We find that there was in the same law, enunciated so clearly and so beautifully by Him, "who spake as never man spake," the maxim that "Whatever you would that men should do unto you, do ye even so unto them." And we built on that afterwards. But here is the declaration which we have built on, and that is this Constitution, which we have amended, not because it needed amendment, but that there might be no mistake as to the question of whether a black man might be free or slave; whether he should continue ignorant and a discredit to you by having been born in this country. In his nativity, he finds the fact that he is an American, and the law must protect him in that character. [Loud applause on the Republican side.]

But my friend on the other side of the House the other day referred to what was done in 1815. He alluded to the fact that great men moved in that day, and I watched for him to come down to the position of General Jackson on the Negro question, because I wanted to hear him on that; but he tarried at the Hartford convention and did not come on down to the victory that was won at New Orleans, when the great general of that day called his troops about him and gave utterance to sentiments that the Negro loves and some men hate even up to this hour. [Applause on the Republican side.] Ah, General Jackson was not a bad man, although he was a Democrat in some senses of the word. [Laughter.]

I would that the Democrats of the United States would accept the doctrines of that great and venerable man who, firm and true to the last, was able to see, beyond the curl of a man's hair and beyond the color of his face, the fact that he was a man and the fact that he could be a patriotic American. [Applause on the Republican side.] Now, if you will permit me I will read a few words from the utterance of that distinguished man on this subject, to show that he could call us citizens of the United States, American citizens, and, in addressing us, could use language which became the lips of a brave and valiant American general:

"Soldiers—"

He says, in addressing his black troops after the war:

"—soldiers, when on the banks of the Mobile I called you to take up arms, inviting you to partake in the perils and glory of your white fellow-citizens—"

Ah, my white fellow-citizens on the other side of the House [laughter], and my white fellow-citizens on every side of the

House, and my white fellow-citizens in every section of the country, black as we are no man shall go ahead of us in devotion to this country, in devotion to its free institutions, for we hold our lives, our property, and our sacred honor in pledge to the welfare of our country and of all our fellow-citizens. [Applause on the Republican side.] Do you want men to fight; call us and we will come. Do you want men to tarry at home and take care of your wives, take care of your children, take care of your homes and protect your interests; call on us. And when the time is past, if you can find a Negro who has betrayed you in a single case put your finger on him and we will aid you in lynching him. [Applause.] But he cannot be found.

Oh, no. What a wonderful chapter that is, that the men who lived near where General Jackson uttered these words, in the State of Louisiana, and in the States of the South, all along the line of battle, could go away leaving everything in the hands of the Negro and come back and find that it had been guarded, thoroughly protected. For that alone, if for no other reason, the Negro might well be accorded the freedom and justice that are his right, and he would be if those men had only been fair and true to him. Now, you see, General Jackson calls us your "fellow-citizens" by referring to the white man as our "white fellow-citizens." [Laughter.] That certainly is legal and logical. He says further:

"I expected much from you, for I was not ignorant that you possessed qualities most formidable to an invading enemy. I knew with what fortitude you could endure hunger and thirst and the fatigues of the campaign. I knew well how you loved your native country—"

"Your native country." Oh, yes; this is our native country. We do not have to go abroad to find our native country, for Jackson has told us we need not go. Some men want us to go to Africa and to the isles of the sea, but, blessed be the name of this grand old Democrat, he has taught us another lesson; he has taught us that this is our home; and in the name of Jackson, whose shade is about me now, I declare in this sacred place that we are here to stay and never will go away. [Laughter.] Why, we can not go. How can I get out of this country?

I undertook to leave Virginia, and the first thing I knew I was back there. I moved away and located in Ohio, but I could not stay. I came to the District of Columbia, but I could not stay here. I went abroad, but I could not stay there. When I returned and undertook to go away again, by a curious adjustment of Providence, I found myself in Virginia; and today, by a curious adjustment of Providence, I find myself standing in this august and wonderful presence. We cannot control ourselves in these things.

Do you think that the Negro would have come to this country to find slavery when the white man came here to find liberty? Yet, when the white men were landing on the eastern shores of the continent and beginning to build our nationality, the Negro came in chains to the southward; and, as the white men became great in numbers, the Negroes multiplied, until finally, in the great struggle for liberty, when, in its far-reaching and broad sweep slavery had stricken down the liberties of the people, and the fight had to come, the Negro, in the midst of the thunder of the great contest, is called from his slumbers, comes forth from his rags a free man, and enters upon real life the equal of his white fellow-citizen. [Applause on the Republican side.] Here we are and here we are to stay. And I give my Democratic friends a warning that they may oppress us as much as they will, but still we shall remain. Abuse us as you will, gentlemen, we will increase and multiply until, instead of finding every day five hundred black babies turning up their bright eyes to greet the rays of the sun, the number shall be five thousand and shall still go on increasing. [Laughter and applause.]

There is no way to get rid of us. [Laughter.] It is our native country.

"And that you as well as ourselves had to defend what man holds most dear, parents, wife, children, and property. You have done more than I have expected. In addition to the previous qualities I before knew you to possess, I found among you a noble enthusiasm which leads to the performance of great things."

And we will not disappoint you in that.

"Soldiers! the President of the United States shall hear how praiseworthy was your conduct in the hour of danger, and the representatives of the American people will give you the praise your exploits entitle you to. Your general anticipates them in applauding your noble ardor."

We are simply fellow-citizens. We have always been fellow-citizens. We are nothing but fellow-citizens today, and fellow-citizens in permanent residence in this our native country.

But this is not the only testimony. I can offer on this subject Southern testimony which goes further than this. Gentlemen are very timid about us; not only timid, but anxious. But where do you find the very first judicial opinion, broad and comprehensive, recognizing the Negro of this country not only as a citizen, but as an elector? Suppose I should state here, Mr. Chairman, that in this matter we must follow the lead of the South? Suppose I should say that as a matter of fact the enunciation in that behalf, clear and distinct, was made not by a Northern judge, but by a Southern judge, and that this judge was the first lawyer of the State of North Carolina? I will say so; and I will astonish you by reading (if you have not read it) from the learned opinion of Chief Justice Gaston, as given in the case of the State vs. Manuel. A Negro boy, having assaulted a white boy, was brought to trial and found guilty; the punishment adjudged was thirty-nine lashes at the whipping post.

A young white lawyer said to gentlemen of Fayetteville, N. C.: "Raise a little purse and I will take this case before the supreme court of the State; I will ask Judge Gaston to pass on the case, and I believe he will decide that no colored man, even though born a slave, if subsequently emancipated, as Manuel has been, can be punished at the whipping post, because by reason of his nativity he is an American citizen." The money was raised and the case carried to the supreme court. Judge Gaston sat in that case and delivered the opinion. Now, what do my Democratic friends think he said? Mark you, I read from the opinion of a North Carolina judge. Listen:

"According to the laws of this State (North Carolina) all the human beings within it who are not slaves fall within one of two classes. Whatever distinctions may have existed in the Roman laws between citizens and free inhabitants, they are unknown to our institutions. Before our Revolution all free persons born within the dominions of the King of Great Britain, whatever their color or complexion, were native-born British subjects; those born out of his allegiance were aliens. Slavery did not exist in England, but it did in the British colonies. Slaves were not, in legal parlance, persons, but property. The moment the incapacity, the disqualification of slavery was removed, they became persons, and were then either British subjects or not British subjects, according as they were or were not born within the allegiance of the British King.

Upon the Revolution no other change took place in the laws of North Carolina than was consequent on the transition from a colony dependent on a European king to a free and sovereign State; slaves remained slaves; British subjects in North Carolina become North Carolina freemen; foreigners, until made members of the State, remained aliens; slaves manumitted here became freemen; and therefore, if born within North Carolina, are citizens of North Carolina, and all free persons born within the State are born citizens of the State. The Constitution extended the elective franchise to every freeman who had arrived at the age of twenty-one and paid a public tax, and it is a matter of universal notoriety that under it free persons, without regard to color, claimed and exercised the franchise until it was taken from freemen of color a few years since by our amended constitution."

North Carolina started this doctrine and we accept it.

And on this question of citizenship, allow me to read the opinion of Hon. Edward Bates, given by him as Attorney-General of the United States, in 1862, in response to the question propounded by the then Secretary of the Treasury, Salmon P. Chase, "Are colored men citizens of the United States, and therefore competent to command American vessels?"

"1. In every civilized country the individual is born to duties and rights, the duty of allegiance and the right to protection; and these are correlative obligations, the one the price of the other, and they constitute the all-sufficient bond of union between the individual and his country, and the country he is born in is prima facie his country.

2. And our Constitution in speaking of natural-born citizens uses no affirmative language to make them such, but only recognizes and reaffirms the universal principle, common to all nations and as old as political society, that the people born in the country do constitute the nation, and, as individuals, are natural members of the body politic.

3. In the United States it is too late to deny the political rights and obligations conferred and imposed by nativity, for our laws do not pretend to create or enact them, but do assume and recognize them as things known to all men, because pre-existent and natural, and therefore things of which the laws must take cognizance.

4. It is strenuously insisted by some that 'persons of color,' though born in the country, are not capable of being citizens of the United States. As far as the Constitution is concerned, this is a naked assumption, for the Constitution contains not one word upon the subject.

5. There are some who, abandoning the untenable objection of color, still contend that no person descended from Negroes of the African race can be a citizen of the United States. Here the objection is not color, but race only. * * * The Constitution certainly does not forbid it, but is silent about race as it is about color.

6. But it is said that African Negroes are a degraded race, and that all who are tainted with that degradation are forever disqualified for the functions of citizenship. I can hardly comprehend the thought of the absolute incompatibility of degradation and citizenship; I thought that they often went together.

7. Our nationality was created and our political Government exists by written law, and inasmuch as that law does not exclude persons of that descent, and as its terms are manifestly broad enough to include them, it follows inevitably that such persons born in the country must be citizens unless the fact of African descent be so incompatible with the fact of citizenship that the two can not exist together.''

Being citizens, being electors, we are confronted today as distinctly as in 1861-'65 with the question of slavery or freedom, with the question whether every American citizen may wield the ballot in this country freely and according to his own judgment in the interest of the welfare of our common country. It does not matter how black we are; it does not matter how ignorant we are; it does not matter what our race may be; it does not matter whether we were degraded or not; the question presented today under our amended Constitution, as under the Constitution without amendment, is, shall every freeman, shall every American citizen, shall every American elector in the North and in the South, everywhere in the country, be permitted to wield a free ballot in the interests of our common country and our free institutions? [Applause.]

Here lies the difference: The old Democratic party used to maintain that this right should be accorded to every American citizen; the new Democratic party is fighting it. But, thank God, the genuine Americans—mainly found in the Republican party—some few in the Democratic party, but through mistake [laughter]—are standing up bravely and truly today to meet this question intelligently and patriotically.

"Oh," but the Democrats say, "you got beaten at the last election." In one sense we did and in one sense we did not. "Whom the Lord loveth he chasteneth." [Laughter.] We have only been chastened a little to make us more firm, and more solid, and the more certain in the high march that is before us to the "promised land" in the midst of our own homes to which God would lead us in the establishment of an all-comprehensive freedom and equality of right.

How dark it was in 1861! How dark it was in 1850! Ah! compromises were made; the great orators spoke; the great parties resolved; and the friends of freedom came well-nigh to despair. But the voice of the faithful and the true was still heard; and finally in the thunder of great guns, in the midst of terrible smoke as of the Mountain of Sinai, and in the flashes of light that made every slave in the land glad, emancipation was declared and the country was saved. [Applause.]

But, Mr. Chairman, it is sneeringly said that the Republican party laid aside the elections bill in the Senate. But it was only for a little while; it was only to take it up again; that was all. And they have taken it up now in earnest. And if the elections shall come around shortly you will see the change when the people have been forgotten who failed to do their duty in connection with the matter. Yes, they have taken up the elections bill again, and those people who yielded it for awhile, who laid it aside to address themselves to other matters, have gone back to the solid, patriotic conviction that at last liberty is the whitest and brightest jewel in the firmament, and that the greatest heritage of American citizenship is to be free. [Applause.]

Why, sir, the Democrats talk of carrying the election in 1892. How could they carry it? They could not do it by any fair means. But our Democratic friends do not talk of fair means any more. They avoid all that. [Laughter.] A gentleman who spoke the other day, and talked of free ballots and all that sort of thing, was asked against whom he made the charges. He said "The Democratic party." Why should we not so charge it under the circumstances? I would like to see somebody put his finger on something that the Democratic party has done from the beginning that looks like favoring freedom or favoring the colored men in this country, at whose friends on this floor strange words have been hurled. How peculiarly our friends are characterized! You can hardly believe the language that is used towards them. I have some of it here before me, studied, selected, written, and rewritten it must have been, but yet very peculiar language. I have read it a good many times, but I never saw anything like it before. Here is a specimen:

"Mr. Speaker, I am heartily tired and sick of this eternal cant and hypocrisy. I think the time has come to tear off the thin veil which covers it, and to express our opinions about this business and the fellows who are engaged in it.

What is this bill, anyhow? It is urged on the pretense that it is necessary to secure fair elections. But every honest man of intelligence knows that that is a mere subterfuge. It originates in a section of the Union which has grown enormously rich at the expense of the West and South. It observes the development and rapid growth in political power of the West and South with ever-increasing alarm. Conscious that unity of interest will, as a matter of self-defense, ultimate inevitably in bringing about some unity of action between the West and South, this bill is thrown as a firebrand into our politics, with the hope of passing it under the spur of partisan prejudice and pressure, thereby delaying that political adhesion already approaching in other sections, and using it to perpetuate as long as possible a local advantage.

Fair elections! Sir, it will be a sad day for this Republic when the people can be no longer trusted with the ballot box. Virtue is the very essence of popular liberty; but equally so is liberty the essence of public virtue. These gentlemen say they can no longer trust the States and the people with their own ballot box. They hold it has become necessary to have an army of officials, without direct responsibility to the voters, to watch, to supervise, and, if need be, to punish them. If, indeed, it be true that patriotism and public sentiment and public morals have come to this low ebb, then are we approaching that starless night into whose eternal shadows has disappeared nearly every effort at popular government which mankind, striving for higher and nobler ideas of liberty, have ever made in the history of the world. I do not believe it.

I can still trust with perfect confidence the people of all or any of the States of the American Union. I had rather confide the ballot box to the plain people of the land, risk its purity to their patriotism and its safety to their hands, than trust it to any band of partisan mercenaries, with badges on their lapels and batons or bayonets in their hands, appointed by any Federal administration that ever was or shall be.

Against whom, specially and professedly, is this haughty insolence directed? Against whom are these charges of fraud and crime, these burning and intolerable insults, leveled? The democratic party. Forget not, gentlemen, that that party represents a large majority of all the people of the whole country, and a full round million majority of the white voters of the United States, the sons of the warriors and matrons who won the battles of the Revolution and laid broad and deep the foundations of the Republic. They can not be intimidated by a threat nor overawed by a menace."

There is no need to continue this. It is found on every page of the RECORD.

In this connection I wish to quote in contrast what is said so ably by the President in his last annual message:

"But it is said that this legislation will revive race animosities, and some have even suggested that when the peaceful methods of fraud are made impossible they may be supplanted by intimidation and violence. If the proposed law gives to any qualified elector, by a hair's weight, more than his equal influence, or detracts by so much from any other qualified elector, it is fatally impeached. But if the law is equal and the animosities it is to evoke grow out of the fact that some electors have been accustomed to exercise the franchise for others as well as for themselves, then these animosities ought not to be confessed without shame and can not be given any weight in the discussion without dishonor. No choice is left to me but to enforce with vigor all laws intended to secure to the citizen his constitutional rights, and to recommend that the inadequacies of such laws be promptly remedied. If to promote with zeal and ready interests every project for the development of its material interests, its rivers, harbors, mines, and factories, and the intelligence, peace, and security under the law of its communities and its homes, is not accepted as sufficient evidence of friendliness to any State or section, I can not add connivance at election practices that not only disturb local results, but rob the electors of other States and sections of their most priceless political rights."

Eight millions of people who stand behind me today, a few in the West and all over the South, command me to say to you that so long as there is a name akin to that of HOAR in New England we will honor and revere it because that man has been true to us in the Senate. [Applause on the Republican side.] But it would not have made any difference. We do not forget our friends.

You recollect that there was a Hoar who went South once, and he went to Charleston, S. C., going there as the agent of the great State of Massachusetts. He appeared in the name of the sovereignty of that great State as a lawyer, not to "steal Negroes," but to inquire in the courts of that State as to whether it was legal for a colored citizen of the State of Massachusetts, sailing into the harbor of Charleston on a Northern vessel, to be arrested and imprisoned and adjudged a free Negro and sold into interminable slavery. He was accompanied by his sweet, elegant, charming daughter, a young lady of Boston. He appeared, and very soon a committee of gentlemen of property waited on him. "What is your business here, sir?" He said, "I have come," as I have described, "in the name of the Commonwealth in which I live, to look after matters of interest to the great body of the people of our State."

"We give you, sir, one hour's notice to take your trunk and leave this city, and if you are not gone within that time we will tar and we will feather you." And at the end of that time the committee waited on him again. He was a little behind time. And, Mr. Chairman, it is recorded in history that the presence of his daughter alone saved him from their clutches.

MR. MORSE. That is as true as Gospel.

MR. LANGSTON. And coming around to Philadelphia, a Whig national convention was in session, and this noble man of Massachusetts, this grand man, was called on for a speech. How do you think he opened his address?

"Fellow-citizens, having escaped the bloody clutches of the slaveholders of the South, I take a great deal of pleasure in addressing you."

Ah, Mr. Chairman, this spirit does not know white man or black man. All stand equal before it, as they should stand equal before the law. When I stand here today speaking for the cause of the people of my State, my native State, the State of Virginia, I am pleading for her people, both white and black. I am speaking for white men as well as for Negroes; for white men in my State are proscribed, and they are denied a free ballot, though their "locks be flaxen and their eyes blue." I might cite you the case of a man, a friend of mine, residing in Chase City, the postmaster at that place, appointed through my efforts: He writes me:

"I can not go to the polls on election day to vote for you because I was proscribed already for my support of you. My family were proscribed, my children at the school, and we are all hated because I vote the republican ticket."

And that is no uncommon or isolated case. But go into another county, if you will. Go with me to my beautiful city of Petersburgh. They sometimes say I do not live there, but if you will go with me down there I will show you that I do live there and live at home. [Laughter.] One man said, "I do not believe you live in Petersburgh, because you have a house in Washington." Well, unfortunately, I have got a house in Washington, because it sometimes happens that a colored man can have two houses, one in which he lives and one where he does not live. [Laughter.] White men, of course, may have three or four without question.

MR. ATKINSON, of West Virginia. Some do not have any.

MR. LANGSTON. That is true. But most Negroes now have their own homes.

Come down there with me. Let me introduce you to a fine-looking man with splendid hair, noble face, fine bearing, the picture of intelligence. He leaves his table on election day and gets to the door of his office, where he is met and asked:

"Where are you going?"

"Going to vote."

"Are you going to vote for that fellow?"

"What do you mean?" he asks.

"Why, are you going to vote for Langston?"

"Yes, I am. Langston is a Republican. There is only one Republican running, and I always vote the Republican ticket. Here is my ticket. I am on the way to vote for him."

He went and voted. What was the result? The next morning at 5 o'clock, when he stepped out of his door, he found it all draped with crape. What was going to be done? Why, he voted for a Republican yesterday, and this crape was significant. What was the result? He was proscribed, his children were proscribed. They point their fingers at his children as they are on the way to school, and when they get to the school they call his children names. And I plead the cause here today, Mr. Chairman, not only of 7,000,000 Negroes of the South, but of the white men in all the South who have accepted the principles of the fathers and dedicated their faith to Republican doctrine. [Applause on the Republican side.] And I do not apologize for it.

I appeal to any and every democrat on this floor, if it is not true, that I state hastily here, too hastily to make myself well understood, the doctrine, first, that the white men of the South have maintained that Negroes are citizens upon their nativity; secondly, the decision of Judge Gaston, who ruled that we are entitled to the elective franchise upon a property qualification in North Carolina; and then, thirdly and lastly, if it is not true today in the South that white men may not vote the Republican ticket with greater facility or larger freedom from proscription than negroes themselves? Oh, you ought to come down there and see it. You ought to see an intelligent, fine-looking white girl, well dressed, well behaved, bearing herself like a lady, passing along the street with a rabble of white men saying, "Your father voted for a damned Negro and we will show you," and frightening that sweet American girl.

Do you like that spirit? I do not. I will never be the coward to say that I do. And I would pass bills and pile up penalties and put behind every bill soldiers until they rose to the top of the mountains and kissed the stars, to put these women and these men in the sure consciousness of their protection by law. [Applause on the republican side.]

Now, oppress Negroes if you must, but for God's sake stop oppressing white voters. [Applause on the Republican side.] Deny to the Negro the ballot if you will, but for God's sake do not take the ballot from your own brothers with flaxen hair and blue eyes! And yet that is done.

Now, another speaker says, "Why don't you make Bruce President? Why don't you make Langston President?" I want to plead guilty to some things here. I think we have honored Mr. Bruce a good deal. He is a splendid gentleman. He is one of the class of good-looking colored men on this continent, and you will excuse me if I tell you we have got some of the finest looking Negroes on this continent that you ever saw. And then we have got so many. You think you have got millions in the United States, but go with me where I used to live when I was your representative, and let me show you hundreds of thousands there, so black on one side of the island and so light on the other, and let me introduce you to that living monument of fine appearance and culture and magnificent appointments in every respect, the man who used to be president of the Republic of Hayti.

When Rear Admiral Cooper visited me on his ship, the Tennessee, I said, "Admiral, do not you want to see a splendid man; do not you want to see the best-looking black man in the world; do not you want to see a great man, the impersonation of learning and culture, a man who many a day escorted Mrs. Dix to dinner in Paris, who towered up there in all his beauty as a gentleman admired by every representative of every foreign country?" The old admiral said, "I would like to see him." And I made arrangements whereby on the next morning, at 10 o'clock, we went to the national palace, the White House of that country, where we were received in fine style, the national band playing what they thought was our national air:

> "John Brown's body lies moldering in the grave,
> But his soul is marching on."

[Applause and laughter on the Republican side.]

That will be your national air one of these days, in the good time coming. Our bands shall play it, our choristers shall sing it, and we as a Christian nation shall march on under the banner of the Republican party to national and local victory under the impulse and purpose which that song will awaken in our souls.

We entered the palace, and very soon we were in the presence of this magnificent man of more than 300 pounds' weight. His hair was as white as the snow, his face as black as the night, his face the face of Webster, his manner polite, genteel, and elegant, like the manner of Wendell Phillips. He was the impersonation of culture. And when I said to him in French: "Mr. President, I have the honor to present to you a rear admiral of the American Navy," the bow he made, out of his high regard for our free institutions and our noble country and our magnificent nation, was charming in the extreme.

And shortly we took the usual elegant drink of magnificent champagne without ice, as is the custom in this country. [Laughter.] When the rear admiral was about ready to go he said, "Now, minister, make my speech to the President. Tell the President that my goodly ship, the Tennessee, has carried me into the waters of every civilized nation; that I have looked into the faces of kings and queens, emperors and empresses, and the executives of all sorts of men and governments; and say to him that I seem now, in the presence of this President, to stand in the presence of the man whom we call the Father of our Country, 'First in war, first in peace, and first in the hearts of his countrymen.' I feel that I stand in the presence of Washington himself." I threw it into French, as I could then, and then these great men advanced with tears in their eyes and gave each other the warm palm; and I said to them, "Ah! gentlemen, this is the Great Republic of the North extending her warm palm in sympathy to this Negro republic."

It is prophetic of what? That American influences shall prevail with reference to the Negro race of this country on the continent and in the isles of the sea. We are here on the continent; we are here living on the continent as a part of a great nation. God is with us; the people are with us, and we are with you, and we are in the South to remain; coming gently towards the North, increasing day by day, to wield the ballot, the free ballot, given to us by the Government that we defended in its possession, and we will wield it to make our country great on the land and great on the sea, matchless in the ship, and matchless in industry, with mankind to applaud our magnificent pride of country, emulating the white man in our endeavors to realize the glory and distinction which the fathers knew this country would attain in the future; and to that end may God help us. [Loud applause on the Republican side.] [1]

A SPEECH IN DEFENSE OF THE NEGRO RACE

By George H. White [2]

I want to enter a plea for the colored man, the colored woman, the colored boy, and the colored girl of this country. I would not thus digress from the question at issue and detain the House in a discussion of the interests of this particular people at this time but for the constant and the persistent efforts of certain gentlemen upon this floor to mold and rivet public sentiment against us as a people and to lose no opportunity to hold up the unfortunate few who commit crimes and depredations and lead lives of infamy and shame, as other races do, as fair specimens of representatives of the entire colored race. And at no time, perhaps, during the Fifty-sixth Congress were these charges and countercharges, containing, as they do, slanderous statements, more persistently magnified and pressed upon the attention of the nation than during the considera-

[1] *Congressional Record,* 51st Congress, 2nd Session, pp. 1479-1483.

[2] The Honorable George H. White's speech, *Defense of the Negro Race—Charges Answered,* was delivered in the House of Representatives, January 29, 1901.

George Henry White of Tarboro, North Carolina, was born at Rosindale, North Carolina, December 18, 1852. He acquired a good education, practiced law, and entered politics. After serving in several local and State offices, Mr. White was elected to the 55th and reëlected to the 56th Congress.—*Biographical Congressional Directory,* p. 877.

tion of the recent reapportionment bill, which is now a law. As stated some days ago on this floor by me, I then sought diligently to obtain an opportunity to answer some of the statements made by gentlemen from different States, but the privilege was denied me; and I therefore must embrace this opportunity to say, out of season, perhaps, that which I was not permitted to say in season.

In the catalogue of members of Congress in this House perhaps none has been more persistent in his determination to bring the black man into disrepute and, with a labored effort, to show that he was unworthy of the right of citizenship than my colleague from North Carolina, Mr. Kitchin. During the first session of this Congress, while the Constitutional amendment was pending in North Carolina, he labored long and hard to show that the white race was at all times and under all circumstances superior to the Negro by inheritance if not otherwise, and the excuse for his party supporting that amendment, which has since been adopted, was that an illiterate Negro was unfit to participate in making the laws of a sovereign State and the administration and execution of them; but an illiterate white man living by his side, with no more or perhaps not so much property, with no more exalted character, no higher thoughts of civilization, no more knowledge of the handicraft of government, had by birth, because he was white, inherited some peculiar qualification, clear, I presume, only in the mind of the gentleman who endeavored to impress it upon others, that entitled him to vote, though he knew nothing whatever of letters. It is true, in my opinion, that men brood over things at times which they would have exist until they fool themselves and actually, sometimes honestly, believe that such things do exist.

I would like to call the gentleman's attention to the fact that the Constitution of the United States forbids the granting of any title of nobility to any citizen thereof, and while it does not in letters forbid the inheritance of this superior caste, I believe in the fertile imagination of the gentleman promulgating it, his position is at least in conflict with the spirit of that organic law of the land. He insists and, I believe, has introduced a resolution in this House for the repeal of the fifteenth amendment to the Constitution. As an excuse for his peculiar notions about the exercise of the right of franchise by citizens of the United States of different nationality, perhaps it would not be amiss to call the attention of this House to a few facts and figures surrounding his birth and rearing. To begin with, he was born in one of the counties in my district, Halifax, a rather significant name.

I might state as a further general fact that the Democrats of North Carolina got possession of the State and local government since my last election in 1898, and that I bid adieu to these historic walls on the fourth day of next March, and that the brother of Mr. Kitchin will succeed me. Comment is unnecessary. In the town where this young gentleman was born, at the general election last August for the adoption of the constitutional amendment, and the general election for state and county officers, Scotland Neck had a registered white vote of 395, most of whom of course were Democrats, and a registered colored vote of 534, virtually if not all of whom were Republicans, and so voted. When the count was announced, however, there were 831 Democrats to 75 Republicans; but in the town of Halifax, the same county, the result was much more pronounced.

In that town the registered Republican vote was 345, and the total registered vote of the township was 539, but when the count was announced it stood 990 Democrats to 41 Republicans, or 492 more Democratic votes counted than were registered votes in the township. Comment here is unnecessary, nor do I think it necessary for anyone to wonder at the peculiar notion my colleague has with reference to the manner of voting and the method of counting these votes, nor is it to be a wonder that he is a member of this Congress, having been brought up and educated in such wonderful notions of dealing out fair-handed justice to his fellow-man.

It would be unfair, however, for me to leave the inference upon the minds of those who hear me that all of the white people of the State of North Carolina hold views with Mr. Kitchin and think as he does. Thank God, there are many noble exceptions to the example he sets, that, too, in the Democratic party; men who have never been afraid that one uneducated, poor, depressed Negro could put to flight and chase into degradation two educated, wealthy, thrifty white men. There never has been, nor ever will be, any Negro domination in that State, and no one knows it any better than the Democratic party. It is a convenient howl, however, often resorted to in order to consummate a diabolical purpose by scaring the weak and gullible whites into support of measures and men suitable to the demagogue and the ambitious office seeker, whose crave for office overshadows and puts to flight all other considerations, fair or unfair.

As I stated on a former occasion, this young statesman has ample time to learn better and more useful knowledge than he has exhibited in many of his speeches upon this floor, and I again plead for him the statute of youth for the wild and spasmodic notions which he has endeavored to rivet upon his colleagues and this country. But I regret that Mr. Kitchin is not alone upon this floor in these peculiar notions advanced.

It is an undisputed fact that the Negro vote in the State of Alabama, as well as most of the other Southern States, has been effectively suppressed, either one way or the other—in some instances by constitutional amendment and State legislation, in others by cold-blooded fraud and intimidation, but whatever the method pursued, it is not denied, but frankly admitted in the speeches in this House, that the black vote has been eliminated to a large extent. Then, when some of us insist that the plain letter of the Constitution of the United States, which all of us have sworn to support, should be carried out, as expressed in the second section of the fourteenth amendment thereof, to wit:

Representatives shall be apportioned among the several States according to their respective numbers, counting the whole number of persons in each State, excluding Indians not taxed. But when the right to vote at any election for the choice of electors for President and Vice-President of the United States, Representatives in Congress, the executive and judicial officers of a State, or the members of a legislature thereof, is denied to any of the male inhabitants of such State, being twenty-one years of age, and citizens of the United States, or in any way abridged, except for participation in rebellion, or other crime, the basis of representation therein shall be reduced in proportion which the number of such male citizens shall bear to the whole number of male citizens twenty-one years of age in such State.

That section makes the duty of every member of Congress plain, and yet the gentleman from Alabama (Mr. Underwood) says that the attempt to enforce this section of the organic law is the throwing down of firebrands, and notifies the world that this attempt to execute the highest law of the land will be retaliated by the South, and the inference is that the Negro will be even more severely punished than the horrors through which he has already come.

Let me make it plain: The divine law, as well as most of the State laws, says in substance: "He that sheddeth man's blood, by man shall his blood be shed." A highwayman commits murder, and when the officers of the law undertake to arrest, try, and punish him commensurate with the enormity of his crime, he straightens himself up to his full height and defiantly says to them: "Let me alone; I will not be arrested, I will not be tried, I'll have none of the execution of your laws, and in the event you attempt to execute your laws upon me, I will see to it that many more men, women, or children are murdered."

Here's the plain letter of the Constitution, the plain, simple, sworn duty of every member of Congress; yet these gentlemen from the South say, "Yes, we have violated your Constitution of the nation; we regard it as a local necessity; and now, if you undertake to punish us as the Constitution prescribes, we will see to it that our former deeds of disloyalty to that instrument, our former acts of disfranchisement and opposition to the highest law of the land will be repeated many fold."

Not content with all that has been done to the black man, not because of any deeds that he has done, Mr. Underwood advances the startling information that these people have been thrust upon the whites of the South, forgetting, perhaps, the horrors of the slave trade, the unspeakable horrors of the transit from the shores of Africa by means of the middle passage to the American clime; the enforced bondage of the blacks and their descendants for two and a half centuries in the United States, now, for the first time perhaps in the history of our lives, the information comes that these poor, helpless, and in the main inoffensive people were thrust upon our Southern brethren.

Individually, and so far as my race is concerned, I care but little about the reduction of Southern representation, except in so far as it becomes my duty to aid in the proper execution of all the laws of the land in whatever sphere in which I may be placed. Such reduction in representation, it is true, would make more secure the installment of the great Republican party in power for many years to come in all its branches, and at the same time enable the great party to be able to dispense with the further support of the loyal Negro vote; and I might here parenthetically state that there are some members of the Republican party today—"lily whites," if you please—who, after receiving the unalloyed support of the Negro vote for over thirty years, now feel that they have grown a little too good for association with him politically, and are disposed to dump him overboard. I am glad to observe, however, that this class constitutes a very small percentage of those to whom we have always looked for friendship and protection.

I wish to quote from another Southern gentleman, not so young as my other friends, and who always commands attention in this House by his wit and humor, even though his speeches may not be edifying and instructive. I refer to Mr. Otey, of Virginia, and quote from him in a recent speech on this floor, as follows:

"Justice is merely relative. It can exist between equals. It can exist among homogeneous people—among equals. Among heterogeneous people it never has and, in the very nature of things, it never will obtain. It can exist among lions, but between lions and lambs, never. If justice were absolute, lions must of necessity perish. Open his ponderous jaws and find the strong teeth which God has made expressly to chew lamb's flesh! When the Society for the Prevention of Cruelty to Animals shall overcome this difficulty, men may hope to settle the race question along sentimental lines, not sooner.

These thoughts on the Negro are from the pen, in the main, of one who has studied the Negro question, and it was after I heard the gentleman from North Carolina, and after the introduction of the Crumpacker bill, that they occurred to me peculiarly appropriate."

I am wholly at sea as to just what Mr. Otey had in view in advancing the thoughts contained in the above quotation, unless he wished to extend the simile and apply the lion as a white man and the Negro as a lamb. In that case we will gladly accept the comparison, for of all animals known in God's creation the lamb is the most inoffensive, and has been in all ages held up as a badge of innocence. But what will my good friend of Virginia do with the Bible, for God says that He created all men of one flesh and blood? Again, we insist on having one race—the lion clothed with great strength, vicious, and with destructive propensities, while the other is weak, good natured, inoffensive, and useful—what will he do with all the heterogeneous intermediate animals, ranging all the way from the pure lion to the pure lamb, found on the plantations of every Southern State in the Union?

I regard his borrowed thoughts, as he admits they are, as very inaptly applied. However, it has perhaps served the purpose of which he intended it—the attempt to show the inferiority of the one and the superiority of the other. I fear I am giving too much time in the consideration of these personal comments of members of Congress, but I trust I will be pardoned for making a passing reference to one more gentleman—Mr. Wilson of South Carolina—who, in the early part of this month, made a speech, some parts of which did great credit to him, showing, as it did, capacity for collating, arranging, and advancing thoughts of others and of making a pretty strong argument out of a very poor case.

If he had stopped there, while not agreeing with him, many of us would have been forced to admit that he had done well. But his purpose was incomplete until he dragged in the reconstruction days and held up to scorn and ridicule the few ignorant, gullible, and perhaps purchasable Negroes who served in the State legislature of South Carolina over thirty years ago. Not a word did he say about the unscrupulous white men, in the main bummers who followed in the wake of the Federal Army and settled themselves in the Southern States, and preyed upon the ignorant and unskilled minds of the colored people, looted the States of their wealth, brought into lowest disrepute the ignorant colored people, then hied away to their Northern homes for ease and comfort the balance of their lives, or joined the Democratic party to obtain social recognition, and have greatly aided in depressing and further degrading those whom they had used as tools to accomplish a diabolical purpose.

These few ignorant men who chanced at that time to hold office are given as a reason why the black man should not be permitted to participate in the affairs of the Government which he is forced to pay taxes to support. He insists that they, the Southern whites, are the black man's best friend, and that they are taking him by the hand and trying to lift him up; that they are educating him. For all that he and all Southern people have done in this regard,

I wish in behalf of the colored people of the South to extend our thanks. We are not ungrateful to friends, but feel that our toil has made our friends able to contribute the stinty pittance which we have received at their hands.

I read in a Democratic paper a few days ago, the Washington *Times*, an extract taken from a South Carolina paper, which was intended to exhibit the eagerness with which the Negro is grasping every opportunity for educating himself. The clipping showed that the money for each white child in the State ranged from three to five times as much per capita as was given to each colored child. This is helping us some, but not to the extent that one would infer from the gentleman's speech. . . . With all these odds against us, we are forging our way ahead, slowly, perhaps, but surely. You may tie us and then taunt us for a lack of bravery, but one day we will break the bonds. You may use our labor for two and a half centuries and then taunt us for our poverty, but let me remind you we will not always remain poor. You may withhold even the knowledge of how to read God's word and learn the way from earth to glory and then taunt us for our ignorance, but we will remind you that there is plenty of room at the top, and we are climbing.

After enforced debauchery, with the many kindred horrors incident to slavery, it comes with ill grace from the perpetrators of these deeds to hold up the shortcomings of some of our race to ridicule and scorn.

"The new man, the slave who has grown out of the ashes of thirty-five years ago, is inducted into the political and social system, cast into the arena of manhood, where he constitutes a new element and becomes a competitor for all its emoluments. He is put upon trial to test his ability to be counted worthy of freedom, worthy of the elective franchise; and after thirty-five years of struggling against almost insurmountable odds, under conditions but little removed from slavery itself, he asks fair and just judgment, not of those whose prejudice has endeavored to forestall, to frustrate his every forward movement, rather those who have lent a helping hand, that he might demonstrate the truth of the fatherhood of God and the brotherhood of man."[1]

[1] *Congressional Record*, 56th Cong., 2nd Session, 1634-1638.

CHAPTER VIII

SPEECHES OF NEGRO CONGRESSMEN OUTSIDE OF CONGRESS

Some few speeches of these Negro Congressmen delivered during the epoch outside of Congress but bearing on the Negro problem, are also worth noting in estimating the eloquence of the men then representing the Negro in politics. The following speech of A. J. Ransier and the two of J. M. Langston belong to this class.

SPEECH DELIVERED AT CHARLESTON, S. C., MARCH 9, 1871

By A. J. Ransier[1]

Gentlemen: It affords me pleasure always to meet my friends, and when under existing circumstances the compliment of this serenade has been paid me, it is an additional evidence of the confidence reposed in me, not only as a public man, but as your immediate representative. This, gentlemen, is not the only occasion upon which you have indicated an approval of my humble efforts in the field of politics. I remember, in the dark days of 1864, you indicated your confidence when you placed upon me the responsibility of pioneering certain movements looking to results that have been in great part attained. When, in 1865, the first Republican Convention was held in South Carolina, where colored men met and expressed, and without molestation, their opinions as to their condition, you invited me through the delegation to represent at Washington their grievances. In 1868, when, under the reconstruction Acts of Congress, South Carolina was called upon

[1] Alonzo J. Ransier was born at Charleston, South Carolina, January 3, 1836. He received a limited education, entered politics, and held various offices. In 1868, he was a presidential elector, casting a vote for Grant and Colfax, while four years later he was a delegate to the Republican National Convention. He served as a member of the 42nd Congress and died at Charleston, S. C., August 17, 1882.—*Biographical Congressional Directory*, p. 759.

to frame her Constitution and Government agreeably to those Acts, you tendered me a unanimous nomination as a member of that Convention; and subsequently, in 1870, through your representatives, you gave me a unanimous nomination as a candidate for the office of Lieutenant-Governor of the State of South Carolina: and at a still later period you again tendered me a unanimous nomination for the position of Congressman for this District, and those are compliments of which any public man may well be proud and for which I am thankful. Gentlemen, I have tried to do my duty, and if at any time I have failed, it was not because I did not care to succeed, or that I was indifferent to your interests. Gentlemen, though the Republican party, as an organization, has achieved glorious victories in the past, though the majority of us as a race have, through trying ordeals, made marked progress, we are called upon today to pass upon questions in which the entire past and the future are intimately wrapped up and interwoven. Holding the position which I do, gentlemen, and coming amongst you after an absence of nearly four months, at a time, too, when the gravest questions in which is wrapped up the good name of the Republican party, and the interests of all as a people are being discussed, it would seem proper that I should say a word in addition to the acknowledgment of the compliment you kindly tendered me.

All over the country the belief obtains that the situation of affairs in our State is most deplorable. No longer can it be said that these reports are traceable to Democratic sources alone. Representations of this kind have been made by good, bad and indifferent Republicans as well as Democrats: by those who look at everything through a sort of mental magnifying glass, and by others who are actuated by a variety of motives by which the country has been to some extent deceived. Representations are made against our party in a spirit of recklessness which to me is perfectly astounding. That things are not in a satisfactory condition in this State is too true; there are many things of which just complaint might be made. That it is possible, and has been so ever since the Republican party has held the ascendancy in the State to get along with lower rates of taxation by a more judicious expenditure of the public funds, and that we might have selected better men to fill our most important offices, cannot be denied; but neither do exaggerated representations made by our opponents, nor reckless and injudicious public speeches made by Republicans against their own party and public men, help the situation. I am no apologist for thieves; for if I were, I do not think I would have occupied for so long a time a place in your confidence. On the contrary, I am in favor of a most thorough investigation of the official conduct of any and every public officer in connection with the discharge of whose duties there is anything like well-grounded suspicion; and to this effect have I spoken time and again. Nor am I lukewarm on the subject of better government in South Carolina than that which seems to be bearing heavily on all classes and conditions of society today. Still, recognizing that which I believe to be true that such is the determined opposition to the Republican party and its doctrines by our opponents that no administration of our affairs, however honest, just and economical, would satisfy any considerable portion of the Democratic masses in the State of South Carolina, and satisfied that the principles and policy of the great Republican party to which I belong is best adapted for the promotion of good government to all classes of men, our party leaders should be judicious in dealing with the situation. A leading public journal thus forcibly says: "A political leader should not be disingenuous with his own party friends; indeed, he should not 'run amuck' against the administration he is impliedly supposed to support. If there are causes of weakness or occasions for correction and amendment, these should be administered in the frankness and confidence of private counsel, and not in the wide forum of public debate. This is not the place to expose one's own weakness or unroll the calendar of defects which may be better corrected in the confidence of the caucus." In the spirit of this suggestion, I would ask for an advised action on the part of the Republicans throughout the State. I would ask you to calmly consider the state of affairs as they are presented to us today, and if you cannot reach those who have brought this ruin upon us through the medium of the Courts instituted by us as a party, and by the officials whose duty it is to prosecute those who violate the law, then let them be forever discarded from the party. And, again, when you are called upon in your primary meetings in your county and State nominating conventions, let each man act as if, by his individual vote, he could wipe out the odium resting upon our party, and help to remove the evils that afflict us at present. Let him feel, black or white, that the country holds him responsible for the shortcomings of his party, and that it demands of him the elevation to public positions of men who are above suspicion. Let each man feel that upon him individually rests the work of reform; let each man feel that he is responsible for every dollar of the public money fraudulently used; for every school-house closed against his children; for every dollar of taxation in excess of the reasonable and legitimate expenses of the State; in short, let every man feel that society at large will hold him and the party accountable for every misdeed in the administration of government, and will credit him with every honest effort in the interest of the people, and in the interest of good government, whereby the community as a whole is best protected and the equal rights of all guaranteed and made safe. [Applause.] This, gentlemen, is the line of argument which I had hoped to present to you. It is not for us to deny those charges which may be proven to be true, while it is for us to deal in the confidence of a caucus, and by other judicious means, without giving the Democrats weapons with which to beat out our brains [cheers—a voice cried "Good enough"]. For I say tonight, with the full knowledge of the fact that what I may say here tonight will go out to the country, and in view of my responsibilities to my immediate constituents and to society at large, and in view of my responsibilities as a member of Congress, I say that Republicanism is best calculated for the welfare of the Democrats as well as Republicans. It is the government of the people made by the people and for the people, and you dare not, as a Republican, trample on any right of a Democrat, or trifle with the important interest of the people, while at the same time it is your duty to prevent them from trampling upon any of yours. [Applause.] And the best way to effect this is to keep the power within the party. [Applause. A voice—"That's so."] We must not think that because the colored people are in the majority now that we are privileged to be indifferent to the interests of others. As a country we have prospered, we have multiplied our vast resources from Maine to California, while we have increased our industries, and added vastly to our capital, and peopled our cities and towns with tenfold their number; we have rescued within the last ten years an entire race from bondage; we have not only emancipated, but we have enfranchised and clothed this race with the habilaments of citizenship.

But we find ourselves today, as a race, passing through a crisis. The colored people in the United States, with all the grand achievements of the past ten years, are today passing through the crisis of their political history in this country. We present to the world a noble spectacle, a record unparalleled in the annals of any people similarly situated. No race has been subjected to such a scathing fire of criticism; no people have had such tremendous disadvantages to labor under. And I feel free to say, no race in a similar position could have acquitted themselves more creditably; but now, in this trying epoch of our history, we seem to forget much that we should remember, we must not trifle with our responsibilities and let slip our best opportunities to prove our fitness for government. We are charged as giving evidence in some localities of unfitness in this direction; it is for us in this crisis to deny as best we may those allegations against the colored men as a race as to their ability to manage the affairs of government. The country accepts in a great part the representations made by our opponents as to the situation of affairs in this State. It rests with you to remove every just cause of complaint, remembering that by every unworthy man you elevate to office, by every scoundrel you keep in office, you justify the public opinion in the country adverse to the well-being of the Republican party in this State, and to the fitness of the colored man for franchise. The Tax-Payers' Convention was composed of gentlemen, most of whom, I believe, I am acquainted with. As to politics, it seems we must ever differ. Their representations are founded, however false, to a considerable extent, upon the bad management of the Republican party, and I believe that many Republicans in the State of South Carolina are giving their movements strength and aid, in the hope of accomplishing certain results. They will be deceived, of course. If any Republican thinks that in any possible contingency they as a class are going to support him for office, he will be most wofully deceived. They are not going to do it. I read the reply to the memorial of the "Tax-Payers' Convention," and when the committee of distinguished gentlemen reach the national capital and present their memorial, they will find that President Grant has already received Mr. Cardozo's paper, and already understands the situation, and will be able to make up a just judgment. I do not want any one to misunderstand me. That I believe there is a necessity for a correction of abuses in the State I have already stated. I have already said we could have done better; that I believe we have elected some men to position who are corrupt, and who hold offices now to the disgrace of the party and to the injury of the State. We cannot and must not repeat this thing. Everybody, perhaps, knows that I am colored, and I am very naturally proud when we do well; and when we do not, I could wish that I was not one of it. My hopes and aspirations are wrapped up with the race to which I belong. I want to see it live and prosper as I believe God intended that it should. And while the country may hold the colored people in South Carolina responsible for bad government, I want to say, in the name of that Republicanism to which I belong and which I represent, that the country would be justified in so doing by virtue of the fact that the colored people in South Carolina are in the majority—the white vote being 50,000 and the colored vote 80,000; therefore, the colored people would justly be held responsible for the affairs of the Government; and, to that extent, they ought to feel the necessity of wiping out every stain and of removing every wrong from self-interest, if not from a sense of decency, from the love of good government.

But to return to the subject. There are those who have devoted their lives to the doctrine of civil and political equality, and have given their time and labor to the promotion of the colored men, who are anxiously watching us, and bid us do our duty; who would feel mortification and regret should we trifle with our vast responsibility as citizens. I believe that there is sufficient virtue and common sense, and pride of race, and love of country, in the breasts of the rank and the file of the colored people to secure to us an improved condition of affairs. Let each man in our primary meetings, and in our conventions, feel that his country's welfare, and his own political salvation depends upon his actions and vote; and as I have previously exhorted you, act as if by your individual vote you could effect the reform so much needed, so much desired. And now, gentlemen, in conclusion, let me thank you most heartily for this compliment. As long as I am in possession of my senses, I shall try to deserve your confidence and support, and to the extent of my ability to work for your interests and your welfare. And when, in the next campaign you are called upon, as you will be, to select men for our important offices, see to it that they are men whom you can trust, men who will not deceive nor disgrace you. As to myself, I shall go against any man, be he black or white, whose past conduct in or out of office does not give us the assurance of better government, cost me what it may. Again, gentlemen, I thank you for your more than kind and cordial welcome.[1]

THE OTHER PHASE OF RECONSTRUCTION

By J. M. Langston [2]

The thoughtful and patriotic American, animated by other than partisan and sectional considerations and feelings, turns with delight from the contemplation of the belligerent to the pacific phase of reconstruction.

Four years of bloody contest, characterized by all the evils attendant in the most aggravated form upon a civil strife of gigantic proportions; and twelve years of effort at reconciliation and readjustment, marked by displays of cruel, unrestrained fury, controlled only by military power, brings us, in all earnestness of soul, to inquire: "Is there no method by which the problem of reconstruction may be satisfactorily solved in some peaceful manner?"

Rising above party considerations, seeming sectional interests, as well as individual aggrandizement, we should study well every lesson of history, every lesson suggested by the precepts of Christianity, every lesson taught in sound political philosophy, having reference to this problem, which of all others commands consideration and intelligent solution.

In this discussion, we have to do with one of the important sections of our country; one divided into great States, populated by millions of people, peculiar not less in their present than in their former condition and relations.

[1] *The Daily Union Herald* (Columbia, S. C.), March 20, 1874.

[2] Hon. John M. Langston addressed the people of Jersey City, N. J., on the evening of April 17, 1877, upon "The Other Phase of Reconstruction." The audience was large and enthusiastic, and listened earnestly to the words of the eloquent and able defender of the policy which proposes to protect the rights of his people by peaceful rather than by belligerent means.

Three Classes in the South

Sixteen years ago there were three distinct classes composing the population of the South; the first, the slaveholding class, the lords of the land and the lash; the next, the class known as the "poor whites," the under grade of Southern society; and, thirdly, the negroes, slaves, chattels personal. The first class were not only the owners of the wealth, but they possessed the education and the intelligence, the social and political influence, of their various communities. From this class came, as well the old political leaders, as the military chieftains, who led the rank and file of the Southern army in the late rebellion. From this class, too, came the purpose and the energy which at once originated and sustained the revolt against the Government, and the attempt to organize the Southern Confederacy. If any single class may be called the "master class" of the South, occupying commanding place, and wielding controlling influence in the politics of that section, that class is the one of which I now speak. Deprived by the war largely of its property, its numbers considerably reduced by the same cause, its compact and easily moved organization, not a little impaired, disappearing from politics for several years during the earlier period of reconstruction, within the past two or three years it has rallied, reorganized, assumed again political control, and once more promises to dominate the entire section. Louisiana and South Carolina seem just now passing from Republican control to that of this particular class. The latest Republican Governors, more learned, more efficient, more distinguished for exalted elements of personal character and statesmanship, surrender to the more commanding political and moral power of this class. Chamberlain gives place to Hampton! and Packard, it is thought, must surrender to Nicholls!

The Poor Whites, in the days of slavery, cherished no love for the class of which I have spoken, and the latter had even greater affection for the slave than for the poor white. But things have changed. The poor white, called to the army as a common soldier, was taught that the white men of the South, rich and poor, had a common cause for which they were called to struggle, to suffer, and to die, if need were, against the encroachments of a usurping and tyrannical Federal Government. He was taught to admire, and to love even, that class which furnished the daring and dashing leader, who commanded those forces which went out to do battle gallantly in defense of this common cause. No poor white man of the South fails today to entertain and express high admiration for Lee, "Stonewall" Jackson, Johnston, and Hood. United then in admiration of their leaders, political and military, and devoted to a common cause, which they hold, if one may judge by their words and deeds, as dear as life, there is a bond of sympathy and union existing between them which is as firm and abiding as the cause which they love and would conserve. Thus far, neither the offers of peaceful reconstruction, nor the menace of armed efforts at readjustment, have, as yet, reached and subdued these classes, united in such common sympathy and purpose.

Of the Negroes, formerly slaves, loyal to the Government at all times and under the most trying circumstances, Republican, not only by instinct, but from considerations of self-preservation as well as patriotism, the loftiest words of commendation may be spoken without fear of overstatement in their behalf. Emancipated, made citizens, given civil rights and political powers, and the opportunity to rise officially to the highest place in the gift of any Republican majority, they have, in the main, shown themselves moderate and manly in their behavior. It was natural for them not to follow the leadership of the white classes referred to; while it was, on the other hand, natural for them to follow the leadership of that other class, the new-comer from the North, added to the Southern population by the war, contemptuously called "The Carpet-Bagger"; for this class came as the representative of that sentiment and power, which made them free and promised their enfranchisement and protection; bringing them schools and books; to their more needy, food and clothing; and everywhere showing himself the friend of that power, so ill defined to the Negro intellect, which had brought the goodly things of freedom and equal rights to him who was formerly a slave.

Following the leadership of this class the Negro as naturally allied himself to the Republican party as the old master class did to the Democratic: and here commenced that gulf of difference which has continued to widen, as Reconstruction has been fixed by constitutional enactment, and endorsed by the public sentiment of the country.

Of course the Republican immigrant, American by birth and education, reared in the midst of free institutions, and taught to value manhood, freedom and equal rights, obedient to law, and yet tenacious of every right, privilege, and immunity belonging to him, conceding nothing but what he demanded, and demanding nothing but what he conceded,—I say it was impossible for such class to locate in the South, surrounded by the newly-emancipated and enfranchised Negro, without becoming political leaders and representative characters in the work of Reconstruction. Their influence, of course, while it tended to enlighten the Negro and establish him in his freedom, tended to draw him away from the control of the classes in whose midst he had lived, been enslaved, and served, to those who came the representatives of freedom and conservators of the Republican party.

It did not improve the feeling of the defeated classes of the South to contemplate, at first, the amendments of the Constitution of the United States, which not only established the freedom of the slave, but established his citizenship beyond question, and putting into his hands the ballot, making him the political equal of his former owner. Objecting not only to the law, but to that practice under it, which to him made it intolerable, the former master class became greatly exasperated, and resolving, if possible, to overcome this condition of things, organized bands of "White-liners," "Ku-Klux," and "Bull-dozers," and entered upon that systematic warfare upon Republicans, white and colored, which, resulting in violence, intimidation and murder, has necessitated the use of the army to maintain the peace, and protect the loyal people of the South against that domestic violence, which at times seemed to threaten utter destruction, interfering even with legislatures, and disturbing the operations of the Government.

This condition of things has continued from 1865, growing rapidly worse, up to and through the last Presidential Canvass, and seemingly, culminating in the massacres of South Carolina and Louisiana during the summer and fall of last year.

Were I to tarry here in my description of classes composing the population of the South, I should do great injustice to two other classes, of whom I make mention with special pleasure. I refer first, to the very respectable class of white men found in the South, known as original Union men, latterly sneeringly called "Scallawags"; and, secondly, to a considerable class of white men who going into the rebel army and being defeated in honorable warfare, have accepted the situation in good faith, and yield a cordial obedience to the law. These, too, have also been sneeringly designated by the same appellation.

If I might be permitted to particularize still further, I would mention, for the purpose of bringing to your attention, with due emphasis, all the peculiar classes with which we have to deal in settling the Southern problem—a class of white men peculiarly and intimately related to the colored class by ties of blood and kinship. I refer to a class of white men who have not hesitated to establish the relations named, by recognizing, in many instances, the offspring of their slave women as their own children, not infrequently providing for their education, and otherwise manifesting a fatherly interest and affection for such children. How far such offspring, the children of white men by colored women, in many cases educated, as intimated, by their fathers, are to aid in bridging the social and political differences between the classes of the South, white and colored, Providence only knows and will determine. The prediction that this class will play, in the future, an important part in this work may not prove wholly unwise.

The classes now described are diverse in origin, unlike in instinct, and have by no means enjoyed equal educational advantages; in fact, the Negro and the poor white were wholly without educational opportunities during the days of slavery. One great class were formerly the slave-masters; another, their slaves; a third, the poor whites, during the existence of slavery, were almost as destitute of civil and political rights and privileges as the slaves themselves; and, in fact, his social and moral condition was even lower than that of the Negro. And these classes differ widely in political purpose and affiliation, as well as in political understanding and aspiration. Is it possible to bring these classes to such agreement with regard to their common welfare, the material and moral good of their section, and thus remove the differences, political and other, to which reference has been made, and also to establish peace, good order, and consequent prosperity and happiness, under the Constitution, as the results of Pacific Reconstruction?

Difficulties of Peaceful Reconstruction

The proposition of peaceful Reconstruction is surrounded with serious difficulties awaiting solution. The first of these is found in the fact that the dominant classes of the South, united in purpose, and animated by common feelings, forming a compact social and political organization, easily and effectively wielded, as necessity required, has hitherto formed a firm alliance with the Democratic party, which promises through its influence, direct and indirect, success to their sectional plans and measures. This party, always false in the presence of high moral and patriotic requirement, stands ready to promise all things in return for any support which brings it success and power. Its leaders act as if it had been organized, and were still maintained, rather to achieve mere party success, and party ends, than the enduring good of all sections of the country, the lasting welfare of all the people. This party taught, first of all, the false doctrine of State Sovereignty as opposed to the supremacy of the National Government; and it today must be held responsible for the blighting consequences which have followed therefrom. It is responsible, too, in no insignificant sense, for the late Rebellion, in connection with which there is no feature of its conduct, as a party, as far as the South is concerned, or the Government, which reflects upon it special credit. Having promised to aid the South in its attempts to make practical the lessons of political philosophy, which it had taught, in the hour of trial it proved itself cowardly, and ever after as unworthy of confidence. If, as a party, it affected to give the Government support, its acts proved insincere and pretentious.

Estimated in the light of its past record, weighing its purpose and integrity in the light of its recent behavior, one must conclude that the sagacious and earnest leaders of the South, always requiring, in those with whom they deal, decision, courage and truth, cannot longer confide in such party, nor trust the destiny of their section to its control. The character and behavior of the Democratic Party, so inconsistent and unreliable, furnish ground of hope for good to the South. As the Southern leaders lose confidence in this party, its teachings and its policy, its disposition and ability to discharge its promises, the alliance mentioned will be weakened, sooner or later annulled, and other and more advantageous affiliations sought and formed. The conduct of prominent leaders, members of the House of Representatives, from the South in the last session of Congress, in connection with certain decisions of the Electoral Commission, bears, with peculiar force, upon this particular point. It is admitted on all sides that it was the vote of Southern men—men who were expected to vote with filibustering Democrats from the North—which thwarted the purpose of such Democratic members, and sustained the action of the Commission. This must be regarded as a step in the direction of just and peaceful Reconstruction. With this beginning, we may reasonably hope for an ending as beneficent as it is wise.

A second difficulty is found in the indisposition, heretofore existing on the part of the dominant class of the South, to brook opposition of opinion and judgment in matters of politics. Taught from their cradles by the influences of their peculiar institution, as it formerly existed, to believe themselves the owners and masters of men, and learning early, and witnessing constantly, the utter dependence of the non-slaveholding whites, living in their midst, upon their power and whim, it was altogether natural, inevitable, that they acquired the habit of command, exacting ready and unquestioning acquiescence. Politically, the course of treatment pursued by the Government toward the South on all subjects relating to that section, affecting its interests, directly or remotely, really or imaginarily, compromising too often, even at the expense of Freedom and National Honor, has tended greatly, and not unnaturally, to create and foster the feeling to which reference has been made.

The experience of the past sixteen years, the lessons of law and ethics, freedom and equal rights, free thought and free speech, the right of every individual, without denial and unchallenged, to form and express his own judgment, being amenable, according to law only, for the abuse of this privilege, have done much to correct this state of mind, and to beget and sustain largely, a spirit of honest difference of sentiment, even on political subjects. The progress made in this direction, though far from being all we could wish, is of great value and promises well.

Free thought, free discussion, earnest and honest agitation are the indispensable conditions of reformation and progress in the

South, as well as everywhere else, among all people. Is this condition possible by means of peaceful Reconstruction?

A third difficulty following close upon the one just named, although distinct from it, is found in the inaccessibility of the masses, as well as leaders, now, as heretofore, dominant in the South. Will they hear? Can they be reached? The first question is partially answered in what has already been said. It may be added that: "The old wall of partition has been broken down," and the teacher and the agitator are now in their midst. If allowed to remain their influence must tell for good. The little leaven may leaven the whole lump.

Following the revolution, which has just been wrought in the South, breaking up institutions, changing the system of labor, necessitating the remodeling of law and legislation, the establishment of other and better educational organizations, the submission of the political and the religious opinion of the people to a new crucial test, the deposing of many old, and the advancement of other leaders, the condition of the public mind, now upon inquiry, the best, the most gifted and learned, seeking knowledge, makes this the time preëminently to speak and be heard. The public address, the considerate editorial, the pamphlet or book, in which are discussed, with wisdom and moderation, the problems of Reconcilement and Pacification, the material and moral welfare of the South, its just local self-government, will be read, and their sentiments considered and diffused to the good of all the people. This is the hour for its performance, and this is the work which should be done for the South. The truth and the light should be given the people of this section.

A fourth difficulty connected with Peaceful Reconstruction is discoverable in the fear of many that efforts in that behalf tend to jeopardize the rights of the colored people, through the probable success of the Democratic party.

If what has already been said be true, there can be no well-founded fear that peaceful Reconstruction in the South would result in the success of the Democratic party, and in jeopardizing the liberty and rights of the emancipated class. Many good men, earnest and tried friends of the colored people, find it difficult to give their consent to the new policy of Pacification for the reasons here indicated. The Democratic party, they justly fear, and they would keep it out of power at all hazards. The liberty and rights of the colored American they would sustain, even by the use of the Army and Navy. Such purpose I endorse and shall sustain, whenever needful as far as possible, without violating the rights of others, and doing violence and damage to the interests of all concerned, the black as well as the white man.

In the first place, mere party success is not, in my judgment, indispensable to the greater good we should seek to accomplish, nor, in any sense, comparable with it. Party, I hold as a means. The end to be gained is the incomparable and enduring good of the people. The success of the Democratic party does not follow necessarily the adoption of the policy of pacific Reconstruction. On the other hand, I fear the continuance of the use of the Army in the South will hasten such result in the defeat of the Republican Party. Let us not, in our anxiety as to Democratic success, fail to secure the continued success of the Party of Freedom.

But will Pacific Reconstruction prove injurious to the colored citizen? I believe not. I believe it will prove to him, as to all other residents of the South, an inestimable blessing. Of all others thus located, he is most ill prepared for a continuance of political strife, so costly of time, industry, the fruits of toil, personal safety, life, liberty, and pursuit of happiness. Reconciliation—the peace, the rest, the opportunity and blessings which come of this, he needs. And if he is to gain positive footing as a citizen of character, means, and influence where he lives, this he must have. With harmony and good neighborhood existing between him and the white classes, his life, under the 13th, 14th, and 15th Amendments of the Constitution of the United States and the laws passed in pursuance thereof, with his liberty and rights duly protected, as emergency may require, by the State or Federal Government, will prove, it may be, at times rugged and hard, but on the whole, successful and profitable. Relieved from too pressing and absorbing political excitement, he will cultivate industry more thoroughly and advantageously, locate his family, educate his children, accumulate wealth, and improve himself in all those things which pertain to dignified life.

He will become, in this way, a valuable and influential member of society, respected and honored, it may be, by his neighbors and fellow-citizens. He will become, indeed, interested in all matters which concern the State in which he lives, and like his fellow-citizens, by voice and vote, advance and conserve the welfare of the community. He will become self-reliant and self-supporting; no longer a pariah, but a man and citizen in fact. Having passed thus his life in honest industry and noble endeavor, winning honors, official and other, no distinctions made against him on account of his color—distinctions offensive and harassing—he spends his declining years in the midst of a happy family, his children respected, as they show themselves honest, honorable and worthy. Is this condition possible? May we justly contemplate this as the promise of Peaceful Reconstruction to the former slave? God grant that it may be so!

I will not pass, I will not treat as a thing of small account, the hatred, intense and seemingly implacable, exhibited since the war by the dominant class of the South against the enfranchised colored citizen. The intensity and the implacability of this feeling cannot be denied, and this fact we must not fail to appreciate. In an amicable readjustment, however, and under the milder sway of truth and justice, law and liberty, it is to be hoped that the condition of things indicated will be established, and an intelligent and permanent friendship secured between these classes.

Several important circumstances, now existing facts, must contribute directly and largely to the accomplishment of this result. The improved condition of the colored people, their advancement in education, property, and social character, in their knowledge of their rights as well as their courage to assert earnestly their claim thereto; the presence and residence of many Northern white men in the South, with their broad and liberal education, their knowledge and appreciation of the beautiful and ennobling lessons of Christian civilization, their value of manhood and the best methods of developing and fostering its noblest qualities, their energy, their industry, their thrift, their progress, their love of liberty, equal rights, and free institutions; the influence of the native-Union white man of the South, his brave assertion of loyal sentiments, and his fearless maintenance of the doctrines of our amended Constitution and the equal rights of all, as therein enunciated, must all aid in producing and sustaining such state of society.

The last and crowning difficulty which I shall mention is the wrong political education of the white classes of the South. The tendency of political thought in the South has always been towards aristocracy and feudal institutions—the right of the few to govern, that right being founded upon wealth, landed estates, and consequent social position and influence. It may be stated with truth that the central and controlling idea of the American Government, tersely and graphically described by Abraham Lincon as—"The government of the people, by the people, and for the people," has never been incorporated in the political judgment or policy of the South. How else could it be, with the overshadowing institution of slavery existing there for quite two hundred and forty-five years; while under this institution 365,000 slaveholders constituted the body of property-holders, and the ruling class, to all intents and purposes! In addition to this political heresy, through the teachings of certain eminent and distinguished Southern statesmen, the doctrine of State-Rights and Secession prevailed, and was tenaciously held generally.

Besides, the South had not accepted as the basis of political action, prior to the war, those great and fundamental principles which distinguished the American Revolution. The principles of the Declaration, the doctrines of the Constitution, the sentiments of the wisest and best statesmanship of the country, were generally treated as "glittering generalities," void of practical significance. But now they profess to accept all these; and no one is found to advocate the re-enslavement of the Negro, or to oppose Universal Suffrage. Freedom and popular government are accepted and established facts. Everybody admits the utter absurdity and impracticability of secession, and yields a cordial and supreme allegiance to the General Government. Indeed, professedly, all the results of the war are accepted, including the amendments of the Constitution and the Reconstruction acts, so-called. Taught, in a baptism of blood, the utter absurdity and futility of their former political training, its unreasonableness and want of foundation in truth, it is to be hoped that, like wise men, the Southern statesmen will build anew upon sounder principles of philosophy and law, as illustrated in the history of the best and most exalted civilization of mankind.

More than this. Revolutions always prove moral sources of education to the people. The Revolution of the South will form no exception to this rule. And among the valuable fruits which it will bring to the people finally, as I believe, is a system of Common Schools, founded and supported by the State, aided, it may be, by the National Government, which will become nurseries no less of liberty and labor, learning and piety, than sentiments of humane consideration and kindly regard of the one class for the other. The humanizing influences of letters, the liberalizing tendencies of knowledge, the purity of purposes and elevation of character produced by culture, the new feelings and consequent change of habits and conduct, products of enlightenment, must be treated as positive moral agencies, having to do with the problem which we are now considering.

In a carefully prepared address, delivered by the Hon. Roscoe Conkling, at Utica, New York, during the late Presidential Campaign, occurs the following truthful statement: "Two hundred years ago two hostile systems of civilization started on this continent. They came from other lands. One was the idea of free thought and action, of equal rights for all; of dignity of labor—the idea that every man was his own master and peer of any other man before the law, however poor and humble his calling, however hard his lot. This idea, and the system it founded, were planted at the North.

"The other was the idea of aristocracy and caste, of lawful superiority of man over man, of the right of one class to dominate another and appropriate its labor, and to enjoy class immunity and privilege. This idea, with the system it founded, was planted in the South."

Our late war was, indeed, nothing other than the last bloody contest of these two ideas and systems in mighty and desperate appeal to arms for the mastery. The result of the contest has been chronicled; and the mastery—the eternal mastery of the Northern idea and system, matchless in the glory of its triumph, promising, in peace, prosperity, and happiness, such priceless blessings to the entire country, must, shall be maintained! If the professions of the dominant classes at the South are sincere, if they have put away indeed the old things and really accept the new, the task of Reconcilement and Pacification is easy, and, accomplished, our nation moves forward henceforth, cultivating the one idea and the one system, thereby achieving the largest possible results under a common, harmonious, Christian civilization.

THE REPUBLICAN PLAN OF PACIFIC RECONSTRUCTION

The Republican party, at its late National Convention, expressed, with clearness and force, its judgment and purpose as to the permanent pacification of the South, and the complete protection of all its citizens in the free enjoyment of all their rights. Its expression on the subject is significant, and is alluded to here as wise and true. The third section of the platform reads:

"The permanent pacification of the Southern section of the Union, the complete protection of all its citizens in the free enjoyment of all their rights, are duties to which the Republican Party is sacredly pledged. The power to provide for the enforcement of the principles embodied in the recent Constitutional amendments is vested by those amendments in the Congress of the United States, and we declare it to be the solemn obligation of the Legislative and Executive Departments of the Government to put into immediate and vigorous exercise all their constitutional powers for removing any just cause of discontent on the part of any class, and securing to every American citizen complete liberty and exact equality in the exercise of all civil, political and public rights. To this end we imperatively demand a Congress and Chief Executive whose courage and fidelity to these duties shall not falter until these results are placed beyond dispute or recall."

Commenting upon this portion of the platform, President Hayes, in his letter of acceptance, says:

"The resolution of the convention on the subject of the permanent pacification of the country, and the complete protection of all its citizens in the free enjoyment of all their constitutional rights, is timely and of great importance. The condition of the Southern States attracts the attention and commands the sympathy of the people of the whole Union in their progressive recovery from the effects of the war. Their first necessity is an intelligent and honest administration of government, which will protect all classes of citizens in all their political and private rights. What the South most needs is peace, and peace depends upon the supremacy of law.

"There can be no enduring peace if the constitutional rights of any portion of the people are habitually disregarded. A division of political parties, resting merely upon distinctions of race or upon sectional lines, is always unfortunate, and may be disastrous. The welfare of the South, alike with that of every other part of the country, depends upon the attractions it can offer to labor and immigration, and to capital. But laborers will not go, and capital will not be ventured, where the Constitution and laws are set at defiance, and distraction, apprehension and alarm take the place of peace-loving and law-abiding social life. All parts of the Constitution are sacred, and must be sacredly observed—the parts that are new, no less than the parts that are old. The moral and material prosperity of the Southern States can be most effectively advanced by a hearty and generous recognition of the rights of all by all, a recognition without reserve or exception. With such a recognition fully accorded, it will be practicable to promote, by the influence of all legitimate agencies of the general Government, the effort of the people of these States to obtain for themselves the blessings of honest and capable local government. If elected, I shall consider it not only my duty, but it will be my ardent desire to labor for the attainment of this end. Let me assure my countrymen of the Southern States that, if I shall be charged with the duty of organizing an Administration, it will be one which will regard and cherish their truest interests, the interests of the white and the colored people, both and equally, and which will put forth its best efforts in behalf of a civil policy which will wipe out forever the distinction between the North and the South in our common country."

True to this declaration, faithful to the promise it contains, President Hayes, in his Inaugural Address, elaborates and enforces the same sentiments in the following words:

"The permanent pacification of the country upon such principles and by such measures as will secure the complete protection of all its citizens in the free enjoyment of all their constitutional rights is now the one subject in all our public affairs which all thoughtful and patriotic citizens regard as of supreme importance.

"Many of the calamitous effects of the tremendous revolution which has passed over the Southern States still remain. The immeasurable benefits which will surely follow, sooner or later, the hearty and generous acceptance of the legitimate results of that revolution have not yet been realized. Difficult and embarrassing questions meet us at the threshold of this subject. The people of those States are still impoverished, and the inestimable blessing of wise, honest, and peaceful local self-government is not fully enjoyed. Whatever difference of opinion may exist as to the cause of this condition of things, the fact is clear that, in the progress of events, the time has come when such government is the imperative necessity required by all the varied interests, public and private, of those States. But it must not be forgotten that only a local government which recognizes and maintains inviolate the rights of all is a true self-government.

"With respect to the two distinct races whose peculiar relations to each other have brought upon us the deplorable complications and perplexities which exist in those States, it must be a government which guards the interests of both races carefully and equally. It must be a government which submits loyally and heartily to the Constitution and the laws—the laws of the nation and the laws of the States themselves—accepting and obeying faithfully the whole Constitution as it is.

"Resting upon this sure and substantial foundation, the superstructure of beneficent local governments can be built up and not otherwise. In furtherance of such obedience to the letter and the spirit of the Constitution, and in behalf of all that its attainment implies, all so-called party interests lose their apparent importance, and party lines may well be permitted to fade into insignificance. The question we have to consider for the immediate welfare of those States of the Union is the question of government or no government, of social order and all the peaceful industries and the happiness that belong to it, or a return to barbarism.

"It is a question in which every citizen of the nation is deeply interested, and with respect to which we ought not to be, in a partisan sense, either Republicans or Democrats, but fellow-citizens and fellowmen, to whom the interests of a common country and a common humanity are dear."

These utterances—the one, that of the great National Party, which is responsible for the conduct of our Federal and State affairs beyond question for the past sixteen years; the other the utterances of a sagacious and judicious statesman occupying conspicuous place among the leaders of the party—teach the threefold lesson: first, that Pacific Reconstruction, if possible, ought to be accomplished; second, that, if accomplished, it is to be done only in the adoption of "such principles and measures as will secure the complete protection of all citizens in the free enjoyment of all their constitutional rights''; and, third, that such attempts at Pacification are not only not inconsistent, but are in perfect accord with the principles and doctrines of genuine Republicanism. The lessons of history, not less than the precepts of our religion and the fundamental principles of wise statesmanship, justify and sustain such treatment of the Southern section of our country. But how shall this peaceful theory of Reconstruction, so beautiful in ideal, whose results are so delightful to contemplate, be reduced to practice without injustice to any, and with the largest good to all?

I have designated the various classes composing the population of the South. I have indicated certain difficulties, and in that connection dwelt upon changes of institutions, and feelings of the people, which, as I suppose, have taken place; and I have presented in the language of the platform lately adopted, and in the language of his letter of acceptance and his Inaugural Address, the sentiments of the Republican party and the President of the United States, with regard to this subject. And now, with the field before us, the difficulties of its cultivation presented, the practical, all-important question of how we shall proceed confronts us.

Peaceful Reconstruction Possible

The importance, the magnitude, and difficulty, as well as the necessity, of Reconstruction by peaceful means will be conceded. And however we may regret it, it will be conceded that the method heretofore pursued proves by no means satisfactory in its results. Whether this failure is owing to the unhandsome and obnoxious conduct of political adventurers; the unnecessary and too constant political excitement and agitation of the people, the injudicious and oppressive acts of Republican legislatures and officials, the former composed, frequently, largely of ignorant, unqualified, and impecunious persons, white and black, and the latter frequently not only incompetent, but offensive and exasperating in their conduct; the too frequent interference by the National Government in State affairs with the Army, seemingly for party purposes; the general bad temper and purpose of the native dominant white class—whatever the cause, as to the failure of the former method, there is but one opinion. The failure is a fact, and some new and, if possible, better method must be tried. This, the welfare of those immediately concerned, as well as the general good of the country in all its material and moral interests, requires.

We must remember, however, in dealing with this subject, that there is to be no compromise, no surrender of principle, no betrayal of plighted faith. And there need not be; for with us it is not a question of new principles and measures; it is simply a matter of administration, or policy involving the mode of applying the principles and measures, already accepted and fixed in the Constitution and the laws.

The present Administration, in its efforts at pacification in dealing with States, classes, races and individuals, proposes, as one must believe, to stand on the law, as now written and determined, insisting upon the cordial recognition of the equal rights of all citizens, the practical guarantee of their protection in such rights, the establishment and maintenance of such condition of good order and peace as to encourage immigration, the introduction of capital, and the advancement of labor, as well as the inauguration of such local self-governments as in all their departments and acts shall be harmonious with the altered status of the former slave, the new provisions of the Constitution, and the enactment of the State and General Government passed in accordance therewith. Occupying such position, and insisting upon such conditions as precedent and indispensable, the good omens of its initial efforts promise a happy success. The acceptance of these conditions as precedent and indispensable, constitutes the only correct and sure test of the willingness and the fitness of the dominant white classes of the South, for properly considering and appreciating efforts for the permanent pacification of that section. Did such condition of public feeling exist, discoverable in the acts and utterances of the leading and influential men of the South, in their treatment of the classes and persons differing with them in political sentiments and party relations, in the solution and determination of those questions, material, educational and political, which more especially affect the newly enfranchised people, we might wisely give ourselves no further anxiety with regard to this subject, resting assured that the general management of it by the Government would improve and sustain it.

Our anxieties, our fears come of the fact, that too little such public feeling is now discernible; and that it is to be created and fostered largely by agencies and influences brought to bear mainly from without, and through the instrumentality of the Government, upon those who are to be reconciled and made obedient, law-abiding subjects of the State. The thing to be done, then, is to manifest in bold and decisive manner, such impartial and patriotic disposition and purpose, with reference to the management of the Southern problem, as to convince all concerned of the sincerity and wisdom of the pacific yet positive intentions of the Government and country with regard to their case. In this way, win their confidence, if possible, and secure an earnest and hearty response to such beneficent purposes. We do not calculate wisely regarding human impulses, nor the power of kindness over the hearts of men, if the result does not prove satisfactory.

The acts, expressive of such disposition and purpose—whether by the appointment of a distinguished former Rebel to the Cabinet, and prominent Southern men of the same class to conspicuous official positions, are matters of detail, which may be very properly, under the law and the admonitions of public opinion, entrusted to the President. It must be insisted, however, as both wise and just, that, in the distribution of official patronage, Republicans, especially native Whites and Blacks of the South, shall not be neglected, and that the recognition accorded them shall be of equal dignity and responsibility with that accorded the other class. For in this way the aristocratic feeling already mentioned, the hatred of the Negro, and the political repellency existing between the classes, will be the more speedily corrected and removed. It must also be insisted, where no such domestic violence as that described in the Constitution exists in a State, although there exist therein dispute as to the fact and legality of one of two governments, that the Federal army shall not be used to interfere therewith; but decision as to the dispute shall be made under the law in accordance with the mode and methods provided thereby. Thus an exciting, irritating, and exasperating cause is removed, and Government and people remitted to the established methods of the law. The experience, the habits of thought and feeling of Americans, ill prepare them for tolerating the use of the army in the settlement of political differences; and in the presence of any such real or supposed condition of things, permanent peace is impossible in any section of our country.

The Contemplation of Reconcilement and Peace Established

The pleasing contemplation of the people of the South, engaging in the wise and profitable cultivation of all the industries, agricultural and other, peculiar to and remunerative in that section; human life and human rights, without regard to class or color, properly valued and protected; just local self-government established; the vexed and trying question of reconstruction settled; the union of our States and the Government no longer endangered by any exciting sectional dispute, but adjusted upon enduring principles of justice, law, and liberty, excites in our minds the deepest feelings of hope, the profoundest purpose to do all that is practicable to secure such consummation, so devoutly to be wished.

This condition of reconcilement and peace secured, in the prosperity and happiness of our country, heretofore "rent by fratricidal strife," we shall realize the picture so strikingly drawn by the Bard of Avon when dwelling upon the restoration of Peace at the close of civil war:

> "No more the thirsty Erinnys of this soil
> Shall daub her lips with her own children's blood;
> No more shall trenching war channel her fields,
> Nor bruise her flow'rets with the armed hoofs
> Of hostile paces: those opposed eyes,
> Which—like the meteors of a troubled heaven,
> All of one nature, of one substance bred—
> Did lately meet in the intestine shock
> And furious close of civil butchery,
> Shall now, in mutual, well-beseeming ranks,
> March all one way, and be no more oppos'd
> Against acquaintance, kindred, and allies:
> The edge of war, like an ill-sheathed knife,
> No more shall cut his master."[1]

[1] Langston, *Lectures, etc.*, 209-231.

EQUALITY BEFORE THE LAW

By John Mercer Langston [1]

Mr. President and Friends: I thank you for the invitation which brings me before you at this time, to address you upon this most interesting occasion. I am not unmindful of the fact that I stand in the presence of instructors, eminently distinguished for the work which they have done in the cause of truth and humanity. Oberlin was a pioneer in the labor of abolition. It is foremost in the work of bringing about equality of the Negro before the law. Thirty years ago, on the first day of last March, it was my good fortune, a boy seeking an education, to see Oberlin for the first time. Here I discovered at once that I breathed a new atmosphere. Though poor, and a colored boy, I found no distinction made against me in your hotel, in your institution of learning, in your family circle. I come here today with a heart full of gratitude, to say to you in this public way, that I not only thank you for what you did for me individually, but for what you did for the cause whose success makes this day the colored American a citizen sustained in all the rights, privileges, and immunities of American citizenship by law.

As our country advances in civilization, prosperity and happiness, cultivating things which appertain to literature, science, and law, may your Oberlin, as in the past, so in all the future, go forward, cultivating a noble, patriotic, Christian leadership. In the name of the Negro, so largely blest and benefited by your institution, I bid you a hearty God-speed.

Mr. President, within less than a quarter of a century, within the last fifteen years, the colored American has been raised from the condition of four-footed beasts and creeping things to the level of enfranchised manhood. Within this period the slave oligarchy of the land has been overthrown, and the nation itself emancipated from its barbarous rule. The compromise measures of 1850, including the Fugitive Slave law, together with the whole body of law enacted in the interest of slavery, then accepted as finalities, and the power of leading political parties pledged to their maintenance, have, with those parties, been utterly nullified and destroyed. In their stead we have a purified constitution and legis-

[1] Delivered at Oberlin on the anniversary of the adoption of the Fifteenth Amendment, May 17, 1874.

lation no longer construed and enforced to sanction and support inhumanity and crime, but to sustain and perpetuate the freedom and the rights of us all.

Indeed, two nations have been born in a day. For in the death of slavery, and through the change indicated, the colored American has been spoken into the new life of liberty and law; while new, other and better purposes, aspirations and feelings, have possessed and moved the soul of his fellow-countrymen. The moral atmosphere of the land is no longer that of slavery and hate; as far as the late slave, even, is concerned, it is largely that of freedom and fraternal appreciation.

Not forgetting the struggle and sacrifice of the people, the matchless courage and endurance of our soldiery, necessary to the salvation of the Government and Union, our freedom and that reconstruction of sentiment and law essential to their support, it is eminently proper that we all leave our ordinary callings this day, to join in cordial commemoration of our emancipation, the triumph of a movement whose comprehensive results profit and bless without discrimination as to color or race.

Hon. Benjamin F. Butler, on the 4th day of July last, in addressing his fellow-citizens of Massachusetts, at Framingham, used the following language, as I conceive, with propriety and truth:

"But another and, it may not be too much to say, greater event has arisen within this generation. The rebellion sought to undo all that '76 had done, and to dissolve the nation then born, and to set aside the Declaration that all men are created equal, with certain inalienable rights, among which are life, liberty and the pursuit of happiness. The war that ensued in suppressing this treasonable design demanded so much greater effort, so much more terrible sacrifice, and has imprinted itself upon the people with so much more sharpness and freshness, that we of the present, and still more they of the coming generation, almost forgetting '76, will remember '61 and '65, and the wrongs inflicted upon our fathers by King George and his ministers will be obliterated by the remembrance of the Proclamation of Emancipation, the assassination of the President, the restoration of the Union, and the reconstruction of the country in one united, and as we fondly trust, never to be dissevered nation."

The laws of a nation are no more the indices of its public sentiment and its civilization than of its promise of progress toward the permanent establishment of freedom and equal rights. The histories of the empires of the past, no less than the nations of the present, bear testimony to the truthfulness of this statement. Because this is so, her laws, no less than her literature and science, constitute the glory of a nation, and render her influence lasting. This is particularly illustrated in the case of Rome, immortalized, certainly, not less by her laws than her letters or her arms. Hence the sages, the jurists, and the statesmen of all ages, since Justinian, have dwelt with delight and admiration upon the excellences and beauties of Roman jurisprudence. Of the civil law Chancellor Kent eloquently says: "It was created and matured on the banks of the Tiber, by the successive wisdom of Roman statesmen, magistrates and sages; and after governing the greatest people in the ancient world for the space of thirteen or fourteen centuries, and undergoing extraordinary vicissitudes after the fall of the Western Empire, it was revived, admired and studied in northern Europe, on account of the variety and excellence of its general principles. It is now taught and obeyed not only in France, Spain, Germany, Holland, and Scotland, but in the islands of the Indian Ocean and on the banks of the Mississippi and the St. Lawrence. So true, it seems, are the words of d'Augesseau, that "the grand destinies of Rome are not yet accomplished; she reigns throughout the world by her reason, after having ceased to reign by her authority." And the reason through which she here reigns is the reason of the law.

It is no more interesting to the patriot than to the philanthropist to trace the changes which have been made during the last decade in our legislation and law. Nor is there anything in these changes to cause regret or fear to the wise and sagacious lawyer or statesman. This is particularly true since, in the changes made, we essay no novel experiments in legislation and law, but such as are justified by principles drawn from the fountains of our jurisprudence, the Roman civil and the common law. It has been truthfully stated that the common law has made no distinction on account of race or color. None is now made in England or in any other Christian country of Europe. Nor is there any such distinction made, to my knowledge, in the whole body of the Roman civil law.

Among the changes that have been wrought in the law of our country, in the order of importance and dignity, I would mention, first, that slavery abolished, not by State but national enactment, can never again in the history of our country be justified or defended on the ground that it is a municipal institution, the creature of State law. Henceforth, as our emancipation has been decreed by national declaration, our freedom is shielded and protected by the strong arm of national law. Go where we may, now, like the atmosphere about us, law protects us in our locomotion, our utterance, and our pursuit of happiness. And to this leading and fundamental fact of the law the people and the various States of the Union are adjusting themselves with grace and wisdom. It would be difficult to find a sane man in our country who would seriously advocate the abrogation of the 13th amendment to the Constitution.

In our emancipation it is fixed by law that the place where we are born is *ipso facto* our country; and this gives us a domicile, a home. As in slavery we had no self-ownership, nor interest in anything external to ourselves, so we were without country and legal settlement. While slavery existed, even the free colored American was in no better condition; and hence exhortations, prompted in many instances by considerations of philanthropy and good-will, were not infrequently made to him to leave his native land, to seek residence and home elsewhere, in distant and inhospitable regions. These exhortations did not always pass unheeded; for eventually a national organization was formed, having for its sole purpose the transportation to Africa of such colored men as might desire to leave the land of their birth to find settlement in that country. And through the influence of the African Colonization Society not a few, even, of our most energetic, enterprising, industrious and able colored men, not to mention thousands of the humbler class, have been carried abroad.

It may be that, in the providence of God, these persons, self-expatriated, may have been instrumental in building up a respectable and promising government in Liberia, and that those who have supported the Colonization Society have been philanthropically disposed, both as regards the class transported and the native African. It is still true, however, that the emancipated American has hitherto been driven or compelled to consent to expatriation because denied legal home and settlement in the land of his nativity. Expatriation is no longer thus compelled; for it is now settled in the law, with respect to the colored, as well as all other native-born Americans, that the country of his birth, even this beautiful and goodly land, is his country. Nothing, therefore, appertaining to it, its rich and inexhaustible resources, its industry and commerce, its education and religion, its law and Government, the glory and perpetuity of its free institutions and Union, can be without lively and permanent interest to him, as to all others who, either by birth or adoption, legitimately claim it as their country.

With emancipation, then, comes also that which is dearer to the true patriot than life itself: country and home. And this doctrine of the law, in the broad and comprehensive application explained, is now accepted without serious objection by leading jurists and statesmen.

The law has also forever determined, and to our advantage, that nativity, without any regard to nationality or complexion, settles, absolutely, the question of citizenship. One can hardly understand how citizenship, predicated upon birth, could have ever found place among the vexed questions of the law; certainly American law. We have only to read, however, the official opinions given by leading and representative American lawyers, in slaveholding times, to gain full knowledge to the existence of this fact. According to these opinions our color, race and degradation, all or either, rendered the colored American incapable of being or becoming a citizen of the United States. As early as November 7th, 1821, during the official term of President Monroe, the Hon. William Wirt, of Virginia, then acting as Attorney-General of the United States, in answer to the question propounded by the Secretary of the Treasury, "whether free persons of color are, in Virginia, citizens of the United States within the intent and meaning of the acts regulating foreign and coasting trade, so as to be qualified to command vessels," replied, saying, among other things: "Free Negroes and mulattoes can satisfy the requisitions of age and residence as well as the white man; and if nativity, residence and allegiance combined (without the rights and privileges of a white man) are sufficient to make him a citizen of the United States, in the sense of the Constitution, then free Negroes and mulattoes are eligible to those high offices" (of President, Senator or Representative), "and may command the purse and sword of the nation." After able and elaborate argument to show that nativity in the case of the colored American does not give citizenship, according to the meaning of the Constitution of the United States, Mr. Wirt concludes his opinion in these words: "Upon the whole, I am of the opinion that free persons of color, in Virginia, are not citizens of the United States, within the intent and meaning of the acts regulating foreign and coasting trade, so as to be qualified to command vessels."

This subject was further discussed in 1843, when the Hon. John C. Spencer, then Secretary of the Treasury, submitted to Hon. H. S. Legare, Attorney-General of the United States, in behalf of the Commissioner of the General Land Office, with request that his opinion be given thereon, "whether a free man of color, in the case presented, can be admitted to the privileges of a pre-emptioner under the act of September 4, 1841." In answering this question, Mr. Legare held: "It is not necessary, in my view of the matter, to discuss the question how far a free man of color may be a citizen in the highest sense of that word that is, one who enjoys in the fullest manner all the *jura civitatis* under the Constitution of the United States. It is the plain meaning of the act to give the right of pre-emption to all denizens; any foreigner who had filed his declaration of intention to become a citizen is rendered at once capable of holding land." Continuing, he says: "Now, free people of color are not aliens; they enjoy universally (while there has been no express statutory provision to the contrary) the rights of denizens."

This opinion of the learned Attorney-General, while it admits the free man of color to the privileges of a pre-emptioner under the act mentioned, places him legally in a nondescript condition, erroneously assuming, as we clearly undertake to say, that there are degrees and grades of American citizenship. These opinions accord well with the dicta of the Dred Scott decision, of which we have lively remembrance.

But a change was wrought in the feeling and conviction of our country, as indicated in the election of Abraham Lincoln President of the United States. On the 22d day of September, 1862, he issued his preliminary Emancipation Proclamation. On the 29th day of the following November Salmon P. Chase, then Secretary of the Treasury, propounded to Edward Bates, then Attorney-General, the same question in substance which had been put in 1821 to William Wirt, viz.: "Are colored men citizens of the United States, and therefore competent to command American vessels?" The reasoning and the conclusion reached by Edward Bates were entirely different from that of his predecessor, William Wirt. Nor does Edward Bates leave the colored American in the anomalous condition of a "denizen." In his masterly and exhaustive opinion, creditable alike to his ability and learning, his patriotism and philanthropy, he maintains that "free men of color, if born in the United States, are citizens of the United States; and, if otherwise qualified, are competent, according to the acts of Congress, to be masters of vessels engaged in the coasting trade. In the course of his argument he says:

1. "In every civilized country the individual is born to duties and rights, the duty of allegiance and the right to protection, and these are correlative obligations, the one the price of the other, and they constitute the all-sufficient bond of union between the individual and his country, and the country he is born in is *prima facie* his country.

2. "And our Constitution, in speaking of natural-born citizens, uses no affirmative language to make them such, but only recognizes and reaffirms the universal principle, common to all nations and as old as political society, that the people born in the country do constitute the nation, and, as individuals, are natural members of the body politic.

3. "In the United States it is too late to deny the political rights and obligations conferred and imposed by nativity; for our laws do not pretend to create or enact them, but do assume and recognize them as things known to all men, because pre-existent and natural, and, therefore, things of which the laws must take cognizance.

4. "It is strenuously insisted by some that 'persons of color,' though born in the country, are not capable of being citizens of the United States. As far as the Constitution is concerned, this is a naked assumption, for the Constitution contains not one word upon the subject.

5. "There are some who, abandoning the untenable objection of color, still contend that no person descended from Negroes of the African race can be a citizen of the United States. Here the objection is not color but race only. * * * * The Constitution certainly does not forbid it, but is silent about race as it is about color.

6. "But it is said that African Negroes are a degraded race, and that all who are tainted with that degradation are forever disquali-

fied for the functions of citizenship. I can hardly comprehend the thought of the absolute incompatibility of degradation and citizenship; I thought that they often went together.

7. "Our nationality was created and our political government exists by written law, and inasmuch as that law does not exclude persons of that descent, and as its terms are manifestly broad enough to include them, it follows, inevitably, that such persons born in the country must be citizens unless the fact of African descent be so incompatible with the fact of citizenship that the two cannot exist together."

When it is recollected that these broad propositions with regard to citizenship predicated upon nativity, and in the case of free colored men, were enunciated prior to the first day of January, 1863, before emancipation, before even the 13th amendment of the Constitution was adopted; when the law stood precisely as it was, when Wirt and Legare gave their opinions it must be conceded that Bates was not only thoroughly read in the law, but bold and sagacious. For these propositions have all passed, through the 14th amendment, into the Constitution of the United States, and are sustained by a wise and well-defined public judgment.

With freedom decreed by law, citizenship sanctioned and sustained thereby, the duty of allegiance on the one part, and the right of protection on the other recognized and enforced, even if considerations of political necessity had not intervened, the gift of the ballot to the colored American could not have long been delayed. The 15th amendment is the logical and legal consequences of the 13th and 14th amendments of the Constitution. Considerations of political necessity, as indicated, no doubt hastened the adoption of this amendment. But in the progress of legal development in our country, consequent upon the triumph of the abolition movement, its coming was inevitable. And, therefore, as its legal necessity, as well as political, is recognized and admitted, opposition to it has well-nigh disappeared. Indeed, so far from there being anything like general and organized opposition to the exercise of political powers by the enfranchised American, the people accept it as a fit and natural fact.

Great as the change has been with regard to the legal status of the colored American, in his freedom, his enfranchisement, and the exercise of political powers, he is not yet given the full exercise and enjoyment of all the rights which appertain by law to American citizenship. Such as are still denied him are withheld on the plea that their recognition would result in social equality, and his demand for them is met by considerations derived from individual and domestic opposition. Such reasoning is no more destitute of logic than law. While I hold that opinion sound which does not accept mere prejudice and caprice instead of the promptings of nature, guided by cultivated taste and wise judgment as the true basis of social recognition; and believing, too, that in a Christian community, social recognition may justly be pronounced a duty, I would not deal in this discussion with matters of society. I would justify the claim of the colored American to complete equality of rights and privileges upon well considered and accepted principles of law.

As showing the condition and treatment of the colored citizens of this country, anterior to the introduction of the Civil Rights Bill, so called, into the United States Senate, by the late Hon. Charles Sumner, I ask your attention to the following words from a letter written by him:

"I wish a bill carefully drawn, supplementary to the existing Civil Rights Law, by which all citizens shall be protected in equal rights:

"1. On railroads, steamboats and public conveyances, being public carriers.

"2. At all houses in the nature of 'inns.'

"3. All licensed houses of public amusement.

"4. At all common schools.

"Can you do this? I would follow as much as possible the language of the existing Civil Rights Law, and make the new bill supplementary."

It will be seen from this very clear and definite statement of the Senator, that in his judgment, in spite of and contrary to common law rules applied in the case, certainly of all others, and recognized as fully settled, the colored citizen was denied those accommodations, facilities, advantages and privileges, furnished ordinarily by common carriers, inn-keepers, at public places of amusement and common schools; and which are so indispensable to rational and useful enjoyment of life, that without them citizenship itself loses much of its value, and liberty seems little more than a crime.

The judicial axiom, *omnes homines æquales sunt,* is said to have been given the world by the jurisconsults of the Antonine era. From the Roman, the French people inherited this legal sentiment; and, through the learning, the wisdom and patriotism of Thomas Jefferson and his Revolutionary compatriots, it was made the chief corner-stone of jurisprudence and politics. In considering the injustice done the colored American denying him common school advantages on general and equal terms with all others, impartial treatment in the conveyances of common carriers, by sea and land, and the enjoyment of the usual accommodations afforded travelers at public inns, and in vindicating his claim to the same, it is well to bear in mind this fundamental and immutable principle upon which the fathers built, and in the light of which our law ought to be construed and enforced. This observation has especial significance as regards the obligations and liabilities of common carriers and inn-keepers; for from the civil law we have borrowed those principles largely which have controlling force in respect to these subjects. It is manifest, in view of this statement, that the law with regard to these topics is neither novel nor unsettled; and when the colored American asks its due enforcement in his behalf, he makes no unnatural and strange demand.

Denied, generally, equal school advantages, the colored citizen demands them in the name of that equality of rights and privileges which is the vital element of American law. Equal in freedom, sustained by law; equal in citizenship, defined and supported by the law; equal in the exercise of political powers, regulated and sanctioned by law; by what refinement of reasoning, or tenet of law. can the denial of common school and other educational advantages be justified? To answer, that so readeth the statute, is only to drive us back of the letter to the reasonableness, the soul of the law, in the name of which we would, as we do, demand the repeal of that enactment which is not only not law, but contrary to its simplest requirements. It may be true that that which ought to be law is not always so written; but, in this matter, that only ought to remain upon the statute book, to be enforced as to citizens and voters, which is law in the truest and best sense.

Without dwelling upon the advantages of a thorough common school education, I will content myself by offering several considerations against the proscriptive, and in favor of the common school. A common school should be one to which all citizens may send their children, not by favor, but by right. It is established and supported by the Government; its criterion is a public foundation; and one citizen has as rightful claim upon its privileges and advantages as any other. The money set apart to its organization and support, whatever the sources whence it is drawn, whether from taxation or appropriation, having been dedicated to the public use, belongs as much to one as to another citizen; and no principle of law can be adduced to justify any arbitrary classification which excludes the child of any citizen or class of citizens from equal enjoyment of the advantages purchased by such fund, it being the common property of every citizen equally, by reason of its public dedication.

Schools which tend to separate the children of the country in their feelings, aspirations and purposes, which foster and perpetuate sentiments of caste, hatred, and ill-will, which breed a sense of degradation on the one part and of superiority on the other, which beget clannish notions rather than teach and impress an omnipresent and living principle and faith that we are all Americans, in no wise realize our ideal of common schools, while they are contrary to the spirit of our laws and institutions.

Two separate school systems, tolerating discriminations in favor of one class against another, inflating on the one part, degrading on the other; two separate school systems, I say, tolerating such state of feeling and sentiment on the part of the classes instructed respectively in accordance therewith, cannot educate these classes to live harmoniously together, meeting the responsibilities and discharging the duties imposed by a common government in the interest of a common country.

The object of the common school is two-fold. In the first place it should bring to every child, especially the poor child, a reasonable degree of elementary education. In the second place it should furnish a common education, one similar and equal to all pupils attending it. Thus furnished, our sons enter upon business or professional walks with an equal start in life. Such education the Government owes to all classes of the people.

The obligations and liabilities of the common carrier of passengers can, in no sense, be made dependent upon the nationality or color of those with whom he deals. He may not, according to law, answer his engagements to one class and justify non-performance or neglect as to another by considerations drawn from race. His contract is originally and fundamentally with the entire community, and with all its members he is held to equal and impartial obligation. On this subject the rules of law are definite, clear, and satisfactory. These rules may be stated concisely as follows: It is the duty of the common carrier of passengers to receive all persons applying and who do not refuse to obey any reasonable regulations imposed, who are not guilty of gross and vulgar habits of conduct, whose characters are not doubtful, dissolute or suspicious or unequivocally bad, and whose object in seeking conveyance is not to interfere with the interests or patronage of the carrier so as to make his business less lucrative.

And, in the second place, common carriers may not impose upon passengers oppressive and grossly unreasonable orders and regulations. Were there doubt in regard to the obligation of common carriers as indicated, the authorities are abundant and might be quoted at large. Here, however, I need not make quotations. The only question which can arise as between myself and any intelligent lawyer, is as to whether the regulation made by common carriers of passengers generally in this country, by which white passengers and colored ones are separated on steamboats, railroad cars, and stage coaches, greatly to the disadvantage, inconvenience, and dissatisfaction of the latter class, is reasonable. As to this question, I leave such lawyer to the books and his own conscience. We have advanced so far on this subject, in thought, feeling, and purpose, that the day cannot be distant when there will be found among us no one to justify such regulations by common carriers, and when they will be made to adjust themselves, in their orders and regulations with regard thereto, to the rules of the common law. The grievance of the citizen in this particular is neither imaginary nor sentimental. His experience of sadness and pain attests its reality, and the awakening sense of the people generally, as discovered in their expressions, the decisions of several of our courts, and the recent legislation of a few States, shows that this particular discrimination, inequitable as it is illegal, cannot long be tolerated in any section of our country.

The law with regard to inn-keepers is not less explicit and rigid. They are not allowed to accommodate or refuse to accommodate wayfaring persons according to their own foolish prejudices or the senseless and cruel hatred of their guests.

Their duties are defined in the following language, the very words of the law:

"Inns were allowed for the benefit of travelers, who have certain privileges whilst they are in their journeys, and are in a more peculiar manner protected by law.

"If one who keeps a common inn refuses to receive a traveler as a guest into his house, or to find him victuals or lodging upon his tendering a reasonable price for the same, the inn-keeper is liable to render damages in an action at the suit of the party grieved, and may also be indicted and fined at the suit of the King.

"An inn-keeper is not, if he has suitable room, at liberty to refuse to receive a guest who is ready and able to pay him a suitable compensation. On the contrary, he is bound to receive him, and if, upon false pretences, he refuses, he is liable to an action."

These are doctrines as old as the common law itself; indeed, older, for they come down to us from Gaius and Papinian. All discriminations made, therefore, by the keepers of public houses in the nature of inns, to the disadvantage of the colored citizen, and contrary to the usual treatment accorded travelers, is not only wrong morally, but utterly illegal. To this judgment the public mind must soon come.

Had I the time, and were it not too great a trespass upon your patience, I should be glad to speak of the injustice and illegality, as well as inhumanity, of our exclusion, in some localities, from jury, public places of learning and amusement, the church and the cemetery. I will only say, however (and in this statement I claim the instincts, not less than the well-formed judgment of mankind, in our behalf), that such exclusion at least seems remarkable, and is difficult of defense upon any considerations of humanity, law, or Christianity. Such exclusion is the more remarkable and indefensible since we are fellow-citizens, wielding like political powers, eligible to the same high official positions, responsible to the same degree and in the same manner for the discharge of the duties they impose; interested in the progress and civilization of a common country, and anxious, like all others, that its destiny be glorious and matchless. It is strange, indeed, that the colored American may find place in the Senate, but is denied access and welcome to the public place of learning, the theater, the church and the graveyard, upon terms accorded to all others.

But, Mr. President and friends, it ill becomes us to complain; we may not tarry to find fault. The change in public sentiment, the reform in our national legislation and jurisprudence, which we this day commemorate, transcendent and admirable, augurs and guarantees to all American citizens complete equality before the law, in the protection and enjoyment of all those rights and privileges which pertain to manhood, enfranchised and dignified. To us the 13th amendment of our Constitution, abolishing slavery and perpetuating freedom; the 14th amendment establishing citizenship and prohibiting the enactment of any law which shall abridge the privileges or immunities of citizens of the United States, or which shall deny the equal protection of the laws to all American citizens; and the 15th amendment, which declares that the RIGHT of citizens of the United States to vote shall not be denied or abridged by the United States or by any State, on account of race, color, or previous condition of servitude, are national utterances which not only recognize, but sustain and perpetuate our freedom and rights.

To the colored American, more than to all others, the language of these amendments is not vain. To use the language of the late Hon. Charles Sumner, "within the sphere of their influence no person can be created, no person can be born, with civil or political privileges not enjoyed equally by all his fellow-citizens; nor can any institution be established recognizing distinction of birth. Here is the great charter of every human being, drawing vital breath upon this soil, whatever may be his condition and whoever may be his parents. He may be poor, weak, humble or black; he may be of Caucasian, Jewish, Indian or Ethiopian race; he may be of French, German, English or Irish extraction; but before the Constitution all these distinctions disappear. He is not poor, weak, humble or black; nor is he Caucasian, Jew, Indian or Ethiopian; nor is he French, German, English or Irish—he is a man, the equal of all his fellow-men. He is one of the children of the State, which like an impartial parent, regards all its offspring with an equal care. To some it may justly allot higher duties according to higher capacities; but it welcomes all to its equal hospitable board. The State, imitating the Divine Justice, is no respecter of persons."

With freedom established in our own country, and equality before the law promised in early Federal, if not State legislation, we may well consider our duty with regard to the abolition of slavery, the establishment of freedom and free institutions upon the American continent, especially in the island of the seas, where slavery is maintained by despotic Spanish rule, and where the people declaring slavery abolished, and appealing to the civilized world for sympathy and justification of their course, have staked all upon "the dread arbitrament of war." There can be no peace on our continent, there can be no harmony among its people till slavery is everywhere abolished and freedom established and protected by law; the people themselves, making for themselves, and supporting their own government. Every nation, whether its home be an island or upon a continent, if oppressed, ought to have, like our own, a "new birth of freedom," and its "government of the people, by the people, and for the people," shall prove at once its strength and support.

Our sympathies especially go towards the struggling patriots of Cuba. We would see the "Queen of the Antilles" free from Spanish rule; her slaves all freemen, and herself advancing in her freedom, across the way of national greatness and renown. Or if her million and a half inhabitants, with their thousands of rich and fertile fields, are unable to support national independence and unity, let her not look for protection from, or annexation to, a country and government despotic and oppressive in its policy. By its proximity to our shores, by the ties of blood which connect its population and ours; by the examples presented in our Revolutionary conflict, when France furnished succor and aid to our struggling but heroic fathers; by the lessons and examples of international law and history; by all the pledges made by our nation in favor of freedom and equal rights, the oppressed and suffering people of Cuba may justly expect, demand our sympathies and support in their struggle for freedom and independence. Especially let the colored American realize that where battle is made against despotism and oppression, wherever humanity struggles for national existence and recognition, there his sympathies should be felt, his word and succor inspiriting, encouraging and supporting. Today let us send our word of sympathy to the struggling thousands of Cuba, among whom, as well as among the people of Porto Rico, we hope soon to see slavery, indeed, abolished, free institutions firmly established, and good order, prosperity and happiness secured. This accomplished, our continent is dedicated to freedom and free institutions; and the nations which compose its population will enjoy sure promise of national greatness and glory. Freedom and free institutions should be as broad as our continent. Among no nation here should there be found any enslaved or oppressed. "Compromises between right and wrong, under pretence of expediency," should disappear forever; our house should be no longer divided against itself; a new corner-stone should be built into the edifice of our national, continental liberty, and those who "guard and support the structure," should accept, in all its comprehensiveness, the sentiment that all men are created equal, and that governments are established among men to defend and protect their inalienable rights to life, liberty, and the pursuit of happiness.[1]

[1] *Lectures and Addresses of John M. Langston*, pp. 141-161.

CHAPTER IX

ORATORY IN THE SOLUTION OF THE RACE PROBLEM

Outside of Congress there were Negroes of consequence voicing the sentiment of the rank and file of the race on important questions. In fact, with the exception of the speeches of R. B. Elliott, the great orations of that day were not delivered in Congress. While most of the Negroes who served in that body were as a rule abler than the average white member, they were not always equal to the many outstanding Negroes so circumstanced as not to have a constituency thus to honor them. On questions vitally concerning the race, the Negro usually found comfort in the oratory of Frederick Douglass. This situation obtained for a generation after the collapse of reconstruction.

The first great upheaval deeply affecting the Negro throughout the country after the Civil War was the exodus of 1879. It was a turning point in the readjustment of the Negro after freedom. The reconstruction had been undone, and the Negro, during the later seventies, had to readjust himself so as to accept the situation in the South, or to go to a more hospitable place. The majority of them, in the nature of their circumstances, had to remain where they were, but a few, better circumstanced than others, were moved to migrate to the West. Whether or not this was a wise policy was debated throughout the North and South. Seeing the serious economic loss to that section, the planters endeavored first to persuade the Negroes to remain, but when they failed to do this they brought to bear such force as they could indirectly by handicapping the migrants in securing transportation.

The Negroes were divided on the question for the reason

that many of those interested in politics still hoped that they might regain control in certain parts of the South. Others were disposed to abandon the South altogether with hopes of building on a surer foundation in the Northern or Western States. The speeches of Frederick Douglass and Richard T. Greener, which follow, present these points of view.

THE NEGRO EXODUS FROM THE GULF STATES[1]

By Frederick Douglass

The Negro, long deemed to be too indolent and stupid to discover and adopt any rational measure to secure and defend his rights as a man, may now be congratulated upon the telling contradiction which he has recently and strikingly given to this withering disparagement and reproach. He has discovered and adopted a measure which may assist very materially in the solution of some of the vital problems involved in his sudden elevation from slavery to freedom, and from chattelhood to manhood and citizenship. He has shown that Mississippi can originate more than one plan, and that there is a possible plan for the oppressed, as well as for the oppressor. He has not chosen to copy the example of his would-be enslavers. It is to his credit that he has steadily refused to resort to those extreme measures of repression and retaliation to which the cruel wrongs he has suffered might have tempted a less docile and forgiving race. He has not imitated the plan of the oppressed tenant, who sneaks in ambush and shoots his landlord, as in Ireland; nor the example of the Indian, who meets the invader of his hunting-ground with scalping-knife and tomahawk; he has not learned his lesson from the freed serfs of Russia, and organized assassination against tyrant princes and nobles; nor has he copied the example of his own race in Santo Domingo, who taught their French oppressors by fire and sword the danger of goading too far the "energy that slumbers in the black man's arm."

On the contrary, he has adopted a simple, lawful and peaceable measure. It is emigration—the quiet withdrawal of his valuable bones and muscles from a condition of things which he considers

[1] Read at Saratoga Springs before the American Social Science Association, Sept. 12, 1879—*Journal of Social Science*, May, 1880. Vol. 11.

no longer tolerable. Innocent as this remedy is for the manifold ills, which he has thus far borne with marvellous patience, fortitude, and forbearance, it is none the less significant and effective. Nothing has occurred since the abolition of slavery, which has excited a deeper interest among thoughtful men in all sections of the country, than has this Exodus. In the simple fact that a few thousand freedmen have deliberately laid down the shovel and the hoe, quitted the sugar and cotton fields of Mississippi and Louisiana, and sought homes in Kansas, and that thousands more are seriously meditating upon following their example, the sober thinking minds of the South have discovered a new and startling peril to the welfare and civilization of that section of our country. Already apprehension and alarm have led to noisy and frantic efforts on the part of the South to arrest and put an end to what it considers a ruinous evil.

It cannot be denied that there is much reason for this apprehension. This Exodus has revealed to southern men the humiliating fact that the prosperity and civilization of the South are at the mercy of the despised and hated Negro. That it is for him, more than for any other, to say what shall be the future of the late Confederate States; that within their ample borders, he alone can stand between the contending powers of savage and civilized life; that the giving or withholding of his labor will bless or blast their beautiful country. Important as manual labor is everywhere, it is nowhere more important than in the more southern of the United States. Machinery may continue to do, as it has done, much of the work of the North, but the work of the South requires bone, sinew and muscle of the strongest and most enduring kind for its performance. Labor in that section must know no pause. Her soil is prolific with life and energy. All the forces of nature within her borders are wonderfully vigorous, persistent and active. Aided by an almost perpetual summer, abundantly supplied with heat and moisture, her soil readily and rapidly covers itself with noxious weeds, dense forests and impenetrable jungles, natural hiding places for devouring wolves and loathsome reptiles. Only a few years of non-tillage would be required to give the sunny and fruitful South to the bats and owls of a desolate wilderness. From this condition, shocking for a southern man to contemplate, it is now seen that nothing less powerful than the naked iron arm of the

Negro can save her. For him, as a southern laborer, there is no competitor or substitute. The thought of filling his place by any other variety of the human family will be found utterly impracticable. Neither Chinaman, German, Norwegian nor Swede can drive him from the sugar and cotton fields of Louisiana and Mississippi. They would certainly perish in the black bottoms of those states if they could be induced, which they cannot, to try the experiment. Nature itself in those states comes to the rescue of the Negro; fights his battles and enables him to exact conditions from those who would unfairly treat and oppress him. Besides being dependent upon the roughest and flintiest kind of labor, the climate of the South makes such labor uninviting and harshly repulsive to the white man. He dreads it, shrinks from it and refuses it. He shuns the burning sun of the fields, and seeks the shade of the verandas. On the contrary, the Negro walks, labors, or sleeps in the sunlight unharmed. The standing apology for slavery was based upon a knowledge of this fact. It was said that the world must have cotton and sugar, and that only the Negro could supply this want, and that he could be induced to do it only under the "beneficent whip" of some bloodthirsty Legree. The last part of this argument has been happily disproved by the large crops of these productions since emancipation; but the first part of it stands firm, unassailed and unassailable. It served him well years ago, when in the bitterest extremity of his destitution. But for it he would have perished when he dropped out of slavery. It saved him then and will save him again.

Emancipation came to him surrounded by exceedingly unfriendly circumstances. It was not the choice or consent of the people among whom he lived, but against a death struggle on their part to prevent it. His chains were broken in the tempest and whirlwind of civil war. Without food, without shelter, without land, without money or friends, he, with his children, his sick, his aged and helpless, was turned loose and naked to the open sky. The announcement of his freedom was instantly followed by an order from his old master to quit his old quarters and to seek bread thereafter from the hands of those who had given him his freedom. A desperate extremity was this forced upon him at the outset of his freedom, and the world watched with humane anxiety to see what would become of him. His peril was imminent; starvation stared him in the face.

Even if climate, and other natural causes, did not protect the Negro from all competition in the labor market of the South, inevitable social causes would probably effect the same result. The slave system of that section left behind it, as in the nature of the case it must, manners, customs and conditions, to which free white laboring men will not be in haste to submit themselves and their families. They do not emigrate from the free North, where labor is respected, to a lately enslaved South, where labor has been whipped, chained and degraded for centuries. Naturally enough such emigration follows the lines of latitude in which they who compose it were born. Not from South to North, but from East to West "the course of empire takes its way." Hence, it is seen that the dependence of the planters, landowners and old master-class of the South upon the Negro, however galling and humiliating to Southern pride and power, is nearly complete and perfect. There is only one mode of escape for them, and that mode they will certainly not adopt. It is to take off their own coats, cease to whittle sticks and talk politics at the cross-roads, and go themselves to work in their broad and sunny fields of cotton and sugar. An invitation to do this is about as harsh and distasteful to all their inclinations as would be an invitation to step down into their graves. With the Negro, all this is different. Neither natural, artificial nor traditional causes stand in the way of the freedman to such labor in the South. Neither heat, nor the fever demon that lurks in her tangled and oozy swamps, affrights him, and he stands today the admitted author of whatever prosperity, beauty, and civilization are now possessed by the South. He is the arbiter of her destiny.

This, then, is the high vantage ground of the Negro; he has labor, the South wants it, and must have it or perish. Since he is free he can now give it, or withhold it; use it where he is, or take it elsewhere, as he pleases. His labor made him a slave, and his labor can, if he will, make him free, comfortable and independent. It is more to him than either fire, sword, ballot-boxes, or bayonet. It touches the heart of the South through its pocket.

It will not be soon forgotten that, at the close of a five hours' speech by the late Senator Sumner, in which he advocated, with unequalled learning and eloquence, the enfranchisement of the freedmen, he was met in the senate with the argument that legislation at that point would be utterly superfluous; that the Negro was rapidly dying out and must inevitably and speedily disappear. Inhuman and shocking as was this consignment of millions of human beings to extinction, the extremity of the Negro, at that date, did not contradict but favored the prophecy. The policy of the old master-class, dictated by passion, pride and revenge, was then to make the freedom of the Negro a greater calamity to him, if possible, than had been his slavery. But happily, both for the old master-class, and the recently emancipated, there came, as there will come now, the sober, second thought. The old master-class then found that it had made a great mistake. It had driven away the means of its own support. It had destroyed the hands and left the mouths. It had starved the Negro and starved itself. Not even to gratify its own anger and resentment could it afford to allow its fields to go uncultivated, and its tables to go unsupplied with food. Hence the freedman, less from humanity than cupidity, less from choice than necessity, was speedily called back to labor and life. But now, after fourteen years of service, and fourteen years of separation from visible presence of slavery, during which he has shown both disposition and ability to supply the labor market of the South, and that he could do so far better as a freeman than he ever did as a slave; that more cotton and sugar can be raised by the same hands under the inspiration of liberty and hope than can be raised under the influence of bondage and the whip,—he is again, alas! in the deepest trouble,—without a home; again out under the open sky, with his wife and his little ones. He lines the sunny banks of the Mississippi, fluttering in rags and wretchedness; he stands mournfully imploring hard-hearted steamboat captains to take him on board; while the friends of the emigration movement are diligently soliciting funds all over the North to help him away from his old home to the modern Canaan of Kansas.

The Cause of It

Several causes have been assigned for this truly desperate and pitiable spectacle. Many of these are, upon their face, superficial, insufficient and ridiculous. Adepts in political trickery and duplicity, who will never go straight to a point, when they can go crooked, explain the Exodus as a cunning scheme to force a certain nomination upon the Republican party in 1880. It does not appear how such an effect is to follow such a cause. For, if the Negroes are to leave the South, as the advocates of the Exodus tell us, and settle in the North, where all their rights are protected, the country need not trouble itself about securing a President whose chief recommendation is supposed to be his will and power to protect the Negro in the South; and the nomination is thus rendered unnecessary by the success of the measure which made it necessary. Again, we are told that greedy speculators in Kansas have adopted this plan to sell and increase the value of their land. This cannot be,—men of this class are usually shrewd. They do not seek to sell land to those who have no money,—and they are too sharp to believe that they can increase the value of their property by inviting to its neighborhood a class of people against whom there is an intense and bitter popular prejudice. Malignant emissaries from the North, it is said, have been circulating among the freedmen, talking to them and deluding them with promises of the great things which will be done for them if they will only go to Kansas. Plainly enough this theory fails for the want of even the show of probable motive. The North can have no motive to cripple industry at the South, or elsewhere, in this country. If she were malignant enough, which she is not, she is not blind enough to her own interest to do any such thing. She sees and feels that an injury to any part of this country is an injury to the whole of it.

Again, it is said, that this Exodus is all the work of the defeated and disappointed demagogues, white and black, who have been hurled from place and power by the men of property and intelligence in the South. There may be some truth in this theory. Human nature is capable of resentment. It would not be strange if people who have been degraded and driven from place and power by brute force and by fraud, were to resent the outrage in any way they safely could. But it is still further said that the Exodus is peculiarly the work of Senator Windom. His resolution and speech in the Senate, last winter, are said to have set this black ball in motion, and much wrath has been poured out upon that humane Senator for his part in the movement. It need not be denied that there is truth in this allegation. Senator Windom's speech and resolution certainly did serve as a powerful stimulus to this emigration. Until he spoke there was no general stampede from the cotton and sugar plantations of Mississippi and Louisiana. There can be no doubt, either, that the freedmen received erroneous notions from some quarter what the Government was likely to do for them in the new country to which they are now going. They may have been told of "forty acres and a mule," and some of them may have believed and acted upon it. But it is manifest that the real cause of this extraordinary Exodus lies deeper down than any point touched by any of the causes thus far alleged. Political tricksters, land speculators, defeated office seekers, Northern malignants, speeches and resolutions in the Senate, unaided by other causes, could not, of themselves, have set such a multitudinous Exodus in motion. The colored race is a remarkably home-loving race. It has done little in the way of voluntary colonization. It shrinks from the untried and unknown. It thinks its own locality the best in the world. Of all the galling conditions to which the Negro was subjected in the days of his bondage, the worst was the liability of separation from home and friends. His love of home and his dread of change made him even partially content in slavery. He could endure the smart of the lash, worked to the utmost of his power, and be content till the thought of being sent away from the scenes of his childhood and youth was thrust upon his heart.

But argument is less needed upon this point than testimony. We have the story of the emigrants themselves, and if any can reveal the true cause of this Exodus they can. They have spoken, and their story is before the country. It is a sad story, disgraceful and scandalous to our age and country. Much of their testimony has been given under the solemnity of an oath. They tell us with great unanimity that they are very badly treated at the South. The land owners, planters, and the old master-class generally, deal unfairly with them, having had their labor for nothing when they were slaves. These men, now they are free, endeavor by various devices to get it for next to nothing; work as hard, faithfully and constantly as they may, live as plainly and as sparingly as they may, they are no better off at the end of the year than at the beginning. They say that they are the dupes and victims of cunning and fraud in signing contracts which they cannot read and cannot fully understand; that they are compelled to trade at stores owned in whole or in part by their employers, and that they are paid with orders and not with money. They say that they have to pay double the value of nearly everything they buy; that they are compelled to pay a rental of ten dollars a year for an acre of ground that will not bring thirty dollars under the hammer; that land owners are in league to prevent land-owning by Negroes; that when they work the land on shares they barely make a living; that outside the towns and cities no provision is made for education, and, ground down as they are, they cannot themselves employ teachers to instruct their children; that they are not only the victims of fraud and cunning, but of violence and intimidation; that from their very poverty the temples of justice are not open to them; that the jury box is virtually closed; that the murder of a black man by a white man is followed by no conviction or punishment. They say further, that a crime for which a white man goes free a black man is severely punished; that impunity and encouragement are given by the wealthy and respectable classes to men of the baser sort who delight in midnight raids upon the defenceless; that their ignorance of letters has put them at the mercy of men bent upon making their freedom a greater evil to them than was their slavery; that the law is the refuge of crime rather than of innocence; that even the old slave driver's whip has reappeared, and the inhuman and disgusting spectacle of the chain-gang is beginning to be seen; that the government of every Southern State is now in the hands of the old slave oligarchy, and that both departments of the National Government soon will be in the same hands. They believe that when the Government, State and National, shall be in the control of the old masters of the South, they will find means for reducing the freedmen to a condition analogous to slavery. They despair of any change for the better, declaring that everything is waxing worse for the Negro, and that his only means of safety is to leave the South.

It must be admitted, if this brief statement of complaints be only half true, the explanation of the Exodus and the justification of the persons composing it, are full and ample. The complaints they make against Southern society are such as every man of common honesty and humanity must wish ill founded; unhappily, however, there is nothing in the nature of these complaints to make them doubtful or surprising. The unjust conduct charged against the late slaveholders is eminently probable. It is an inheritance from the long exercise of irresponsible power by man over man. It is not a question of the natural inferiority of the Negro, or the color of his skin. Tyranny is the same proud and selfish thing everywhere, and with all races and colors. What the Negro is now suffering at the hands of his former master, the white emancipated serfs of Russia are now suffering from the lords and nobles by whom they were formerly held as slaves. In form and appearance the emancipation of the latter was upon better terms than in the case of the Negro. The Empire, unlike the Republic, gave the free serfs three acres of land,—a start in the world. But the selection and bestowment of this land was unhappily confided to the care of the lords and nobles, their former masters. Thus the lamb was committed to the care of the wolf; hence the organized assassination now going on in that country, and it will be well for our Southern States if they escape a like fate. The world is slow to learn that no man can wrong his brother without doing a greater wrong to himself; something may, however, be learned from the lessons of alarm and consternation which are now written all over Russia.

But in contemplating this Exodus, it should be kept in mind that the way of an oppressed people from bondage to freedom is never smooth. There is ever in such transition much to overcome on both sides. Neither the master nor the emancipated slave can at once shake off the habits and manners of a long-established past condition. The form may be abolished, but the spirit survives and lingers about the scenes of its former life. The slave brings into the new relation much of the dependence and servility of slavery, and the master brings much of his pride, selfishness and love of power. The influence of feudalism has not yet disappeared from Europe. Norman pride is still visible in England, though centuries have passed since the Saxon was the slave of the Norman; and long years must elapse before all traces of slavery shall disappear from our country. Suffering and hardships made the Saxon strong, —and suffering and hardships will make the Anglo-African strong.

The Exodus as a Policy

Very evidently there are to be asked and answered many important questions, before the friends of humanity can be properly called upon to give their support to this emigration movement. A natural and primary inquiry is: What does it mean? How much ground is it meant to cover? Is the total removal of the whole five millions of colored people from the South contemplated? Or is it proposed to remove only a part? And if only a part, why a part and not the whole? A vindication of the rights of the many can not be less important than the same to the few. If the few are to be removed because of the intolerable oppression which prevails in the South, why not the many also? If exodus is good for any, must it not be equally good for all? Then, if the whole five millions are to leave the South, as a doomed country,—left as Lot left Sodom, or driven out as the Moors were driven out of Spain,—there is next a question of ways and means to be considered. Has any definite estimate of the cost of this removal been made? How shall the one or two hundred millions of dollars which such removal would require be obtained? Shall it be appropriated by Congress, or voluntarily be contributed by the public? Manifestly, with such a debt upon the nation as the war for the Union has created, Congress is not likely to be in a hurry to make any such appropriation. It would much more willingly and readily enact the necessary legislation to protect the freedmen where they are than appropriate $200,000,000 to help them away to Kansas, or elsewhere in the North. But suppose, as already suggested, the matter shall not be left at all to Congress, but remitted to the voluntary contributions from the people. Then a swarm of Conways and Tandys must be employed to circulate over the country, hat in hand, soliciting and collecting these contributions; representing to the people, everywhere, that the cause of the Negro is lost in the South; that his only hope and deliverance from a condition of things worse than slavery is,—removal to Kansas, or to some country outside the Southern States. Then, would such an arrangement, such an apostleship of despair, be beneficial or prejudicial to the cause of the freedman?

Precisely and plainly, this is a feature of the emigration movement which is open to serious objection. Voluntary, spontaneous, self-sustained emigration on the part of the freedmen may or may not be commendable. It is a matter with which they alone have to do. The public is not called upon to say or do anything for or against it; but when the public is called upon to take sides, declare its views, organize emigration societies, appoint and send out agents to make speeches and collect money,—to help the freedmen from the South,—it may very properly object. The public may not wish to be responsible for the measure, or for the disheartening doctrines by which the measure is supported. Objection may properly be made upon many grounds. It may well enough be said that the Negro question is not so desperate as the advocates of this Exodus would have the public believe; that there is still hope that the Negro will ultimately have his rights as a man, and be fully protected in the South; that in several of the old slave States his citizenship and his right to vote are already respected and protected; that the same, in time, will be secured for the Negro in the other States; that the world was not the work of a day; that even in free New England, all the evils generated by slavery did not disappear in a century after the abolition of the system, if, indeed, they have yet entirely disappeared.

Within the last forty years, a dark and shocking picture might be given of the persecution of the Negro and his friends, even in the now preeminently free State of Massachusetts. It is not more than twenty years ago that Boston supplied a pistol club, if not a rifle club, to break up an abolition meeting; and that one of her most eminent citizens had to be guarded to and from his house (Wendell Phillips) to escape the hand of mobocratic assassins, armed in the interest of slavery. The Negro on the Sound boats between New York and Boston, though a respectable, educated gentleman, was driven forward of the wheels, and must sleep, if he slept at all, upon the naked deck in the open air. Upon no condition except that of a servant or slave could he be permitted to go into a cabin. All the handicrafts of New England were closed to him. The appearance of a black man in any workshop or ship yard, as a mechanic, would have scattered the whole gang of white hands at once. The poor Negro was not admitted into the factories to work, or as an apprentice to any trade. He was barber, waiter, white-washer and wood-sawer. All of what were called respectable employments, by a power superior to legal enactments, were denied him. But none of these things have moved the Negro from New England, and it is well for him that he has remained there. Bad as is the condition of the Negro today at the South, there was a time when it was flagrantly and incomparably worse. A few years ago he had nothing; he did not have himself, his labor and his rights to dispose of as should best suit his own happiness. But he has now even more. He has a standing in the supreme law of the land, in the Constitution of the United States, not to be changed or affected by any conjunction of circumstances likely to occur in the immediate or remote future. The Fourteenth Amendment makes him a citizen, and the Fifteenth makes him a voter. With power behind him at work for him, and which cannot be taken from him, the Negro of the South may wisely bide his time.

The situation at this moment is exceptional and transient. The permanent powers of the Government are all on his side. What though for the moment the hand of violence strikes down the Negro's rights in the South? Those rights will revive, survive and flourish again. They are not the only people who have been in a moment of popular passion maltreated and driven from the polls. The Irish and Dutch have frequently been so treated; Boston, Baltimore and New York have been the scenes of this lawless violence; but those scenes have now disappeared. A Hebrew may even now be rudely repulsed from the door of a hotel; but he will not on that account get up another Exodus, as he did three thousand years ago, but will quietly "put money in his purse" and bide his time, knowing that the rising tide of civilization will eventually float him, as it floats all other varieties of the human family, to whom floating in any condition is possible. Of one thing we may be certain (and it is a thing which is destined to be made very prominent not long hence), the Negro will either be counted at the polls, or not counted in the basis of representation. The South must let the Negro vote, or surrender its representation in Congress. The chosen horn of this dilemma will finally be to let the Negro vote, and vote unmolested. Let us have all the indignant and fiery declamation which the warm hearts of our youthful orators can pour out against Southern meanness, "White Leagues," "Bulldozers," and other "Dark Lantern" organizations, but let us have a little calm, clear reason as well. The latter is a safer guide than the former. On this great occasion we want light rather than heat; thought, rather than feeling; a comprehensive view and appreciation of what the Negro has already on his side, as well as the disadvantages against which he has thus far been compelled to struggle, and still has to struggle.

THE EXODUS ILL-TIMED

Without abating one jot of our horror and indignation at the outrages committed in some parts of the Southern States against the Negro, we cannot but regard the present agitation of an African Exodus from the South as ill-timed, and in some respects hurtful. We stand today at the beginning of a grand and beneficent reaction. There is a growing recognition of the duty and obligation of the American people to guard, protect and defend the personal and political rights of all the people of the States; to uphold the principles upon which rebellion was suppressed, slavery abolished, and the country saved from dismemberment and ruin. We see and feel today, as we have not seen and felt before, that the time for conciliation, and trusting to the honor of the late rebels and slaveholders, has past. The President of the United States, himself, while, still liberal, just and generous towards the South, has yet sounded a halt in that direction, and has bravely, firmly and ably asserted the constitutional authority, to maintain the public peace in every State in the Union, and upon every day in the year; and has maintained this ground against all the powers of House and Senate. We stand at the gateway of a marked and decided change in the statesmanship of our rulers. Every day brings fresh and increasing evidence that we are, and of right ought to be, a nation; that Confederate notions of the nature and powers of our Government ought to have perished in the rebellion which they supported; that they are anachronisms and superstitions, and no longer fit to be above ground. National ideas are springing up all around us; the oppressor of the Negro is seen to be the enemy of the peace, prosperity and honor of the country. The attempt to nullify the national election laws; to starve the officer where they could not destroy the office; to attack the national credit when they could not prevent successful resumption; to paralyze the Constitution where they could neither prevent nor set it aside, has all worked against the old slaveholding element, and in the interest of the Negro. They have made it evident that the sceptre of political power must soon pass from the party of reaction, revolution, rebellion and slavery, to the party of constitution, liberty and progress.

At a time like this, so full of hope and courage, it is unfortunate that a cry of despair should be raised in behalf of the colored people of the South; unfortunate that men are going over the country begging in the name of the poor colored man of the South, and telling the people that the Government has no power to enforce the Constitution and Laws in that section, and that there is no hope for the poor Negro, but to plant him in the new soil of Kansas and Nebraska. These men do the colored people of the South a real damage. They give their enemies an advantage in the argument for their manhood and freedom. They assume the inability of the colored people of the South to take care of themselves. The country will be told of the hundreds who go to Kansas, but not of the thousands who stay in Mississippi and Louisiana. They will be told of the destitute who require material aid, but not of the multitude who are bravely sustaining themselves where they are. In Georgia the Negroes are paying taxes upon six millions of dollars; in Louisiana upon forty or fifty millions, and upon unascertained sums elsewhere in the Southern States. Why should a people who have made such progress in the course of a few years now be humiliated and scandalized by Exodus agents, begging money to remove them from their home; especially at a time when every indication favors the position that the wrongs and hardships which they suffer are soon to be redressed?

It Surrenders a Great Principle

Besides the objections thus stated, it is manifest that the public and noisy advocacy of a general stampede of the colored people from the South to the North, is necessarily an abandonment of the great and paramount principle of protection to person and property in every State of the Union. It is an evasion of a solemn obligation and duty. The business of this nation is to protect its citizens where they are, not to transport them where they will not need protection. The best that can be said of this exodus in this respect is that it is an attempt to climb up some other than the right way; it is an expedient, a half-way measure, and tends to weaken in the public mind a sense of the absolute right, power and duty of the Government, inasmuch as it concedes, by implication at least, that on the soil of the South, the law of the land cannot command obedience; the ballot box cannot be kept pure; peaceable elections cannot be held; the Constitution cannot be enforced; and the lives and liberties of loyal and peaceable citizens cannot be protected. It is a surrender, a premature, disheartening surrender, since it would make freedom and free institutions depend upon migration rather than protection; by flight, rather than by right; by going into a strange land, rather than by staying in one's own. It leaves the whole question of equal rights on the soil of the South open and still to be settled, with the moral influence of Exodus against us; since it is a confession of the utter impracticability of equal rights and equal protection in any State, where those rights may be struck down by violence.

It does not appear that the friends of freedom should spend either time or talent in furtherance of this Exodus as a desirable measure either for the North or the South; for the blacks of the South or the whites of the North. If the people of this country cannot be protected in every State of this Union, the Government of the United States is shorn of its rightful dignity and power; the late rebellion has triumphed; the sovereignty of the nation is an empty name, and the power and authority in individual States is greater than the power and authority of the United States.

Better to Stay Than to Go

While necessity often compels men to migrate; to leave their old homes and seek new ones; to sever old ties and create new ones; to do this the necessity should be obvious and imperative. It should be a last resort and only adopted after carefully considering what is against the measure as well as what is in favor of it. There are prodigal sons everywhere, who are ready to demand the portion of goods that would fall to them and betake themselves to a strange country. Something is ever lost in the process of migration, and much is sacrificed at home for what is gained abroad. A world of wisdom is in the saying of Mr. Emerson, "that those who made Rome worth going to stayed there." Three moves from house to house are said to be worse than a fire. That a rolling stone gathers no moss has passed into the world's wisdom. The colored people of the South, just beginning to accumulate a little property, and to lay the foundation of families, should not be in haste to sell that little and be off to the banks of the Mississippi. The habit of roaming from place to place in pursuit of better conditions of existence is by no means a good one. A man should never leave his home for a new one till he has earnestly endeavored to make his immediate surroundings accord with his wishes. The time and energy expended in wandering about from place to place, if employed in making him comfortable where he is, will, in nine cases out of ten, prove the best investment. No people ever did much for themselves or for the world, without the sense and inspiration of native land; of a fixed home; of familiar neighborhood, and common associations. The fact of being to the manor born has an elevating power upon the mind and heart of a man. It is a more cheerful thing to be able to say, "I was born here and know all the people," than to say, "I am a stranger here and know none of the people." It cannot be doubted, that in so far as this Exodus tends to promote restlessness in the colored people of the South, to unsettle their feeling of home and to sacrifice positive advantages where they are, for fancied ones in Kansas or elsewhere, it is an evil. Some have sold their little homes at a sacrifice, their chickens, mules and pigs, to follow the Exodus. Let it be understood that you are going, and you advertise the fact that your mule has lost half his value—for your staying with him makes half his value. Let the colored people of Georgia offer their six millions worth of property for sale, with the purpose to leave Georgia, and they will not realize half its value. Land is not worth much where there are no people to occupy it, and a mule is not worth much where there is no one to use it.

A Mistake and a Failure

It may safely be asserted that, whether advocated and commended to favor on the ground that it will increase the political power of the Republican party, and thus help to make a solid North against a solid South; or upon the ground that it will increase the power and influence of the colored people as a political element, and enable them the better to protect their rights, and ensure their moral and social elevation, the Exodus will prove a disappointment, a mistake and a failure; because, as to strengthening the Republican party, the emigrants will go only to those States where the Republican party is strong and solid enough already without their votes; and in respect to the other part of the argument, it will fail, because it takes colored voters from a section of the country where they are sufficiently numerous to elect some of their number to places of honor and profit, and places them in a country where their proportion to other classes will be so small as not to be recognized as a political element, or entitled to be represented by one of themselves; and further, because, go where they will, they must, for a time, inevitably carry with them poverty, ignorance and other repulsive incidents inherited from their former conditions as slaves; a circumstance which is about as likely to make votes for Democrats as for Republicans, and to raise up bitter prejudices against them, as to raise up friends for them. No people can be much respected in this country, where all are eligible to office, that cannot point to any one of their class in an honorable, responsible position. In sending a few men to Congress, the Negroes of the South have done much to dispel prejudice and raise themselves in the estimation of the country and the world. By staying where they are, they may be able to send abler, better and more effective representatives of their race to Congress, than it was possible for them to send at first, because of their want of education, and their recent liberation from bondage. In the South the Negro has at least the possibility of power; in the North he has no such possibility, and it is for him to say how well he can afford to part with this possible power.

But another argument in favor of this emigration is, that having a numerical superiority in Mississippi, Louisiana and South Carolina, and thereby possessing the ability to choose some of their own number to represent them in the state and nation, they are necessarily brought into antagonism with the white race, and invite the very political persecution of which they complain. So they are told that the best remedy for this persecution is to surrender the right and advantage given them by the Constitution and the Government, of electing men of color to office. They are not to overcome prejudice and persecution where it is, but to go where it is not; not to stand where they are, and demand the full constitutional protection which the Government is solemnly bound to give, but to go where the protection of the Government is not needed. Plainly enough this is an evasion of a solemn obligation and duty, an attempt to climb up some other way; a half-way measure, a makeshift, a miserable substitution of expediency for right. For an egg, it gives the Negro a stone. The dissemination of this doctrine by the agents of emigration cannot but do the cause of equal rights much harm. It lets the public mind down from the high ground of a great national duty to a miserable compromise, in which wrong surrenders nothing, and right everything. The South is not to repent its crimes, and submit to the Constitution in common with all other parts of the country, but such repentance and submission is to be conveniently made unnecessary by removing the temptation to commit violations of the Law and the Constitution. Men may be pardoned for refusing their assent to a measure supported upon a principle so unsound, subversive and pernicious. The nation should be held steadily to the high and paramount principle, that allegiance and protection are inseparable; that this Government is solemnly bound to protect and defend the lives and liberties of all its citizens, of whatever race or color, or of whatever political or religious opinion, and to do this in every State and territory within the American Union. Then, again, is there to be no stopping-place for the Negro? Suppose that by-and-by some "Sand Lot Orator" shall arise in Kansas, as in California, and take it into his head to stir up the mob against the Negro, as he stirred up the mob against the Chinese? What then? Must the Negro have another Exodus? Does not one Exodus invite another, and in advocating one do we not sustain the demand for another?

Plainly enough, the Exodus is less harmful in itself than are the arguments by which it is supported. The one is the result of a feeling of outrage and despair; but the other comes of cool, selfish calculation. One is the result of honest despair, and appeals powerfully to the sympathies of men; the other is an appeal to our selfishness, which shrinks from doing right because the way is difficult.

The South the Best Market for the Black Man's Labor

Not only is the South the best locality for the Negro on the ground of his political powers and possibilities, but it is best for him as a field of labor. He is there, as he is nowhere else, an absolute necessity. He has a monopoly of the labor market. His labor is the only labor which can successfully offer itself for sale in that market. This, with a little wisdom and firmness, will enable him to sell his labor there on terms more favorable to himself than he can elsewhere. As there are no competitors or substitutes, he can demand living prices with the certainty that the demand will be complied with. Exodus would deprive him of this advantage.

It would take him from a country where the land owners and planters must have his labor, or allow their fields to go untilled and their purses unsupplied with cash; to a country where the land owners are able and proud to do their own work, and do not need to hire hands except for limited periods at certain seasons of the year. The effect of this will be to send the Negro to the towns and cities to compete with white labor. With what result, let the past tell. They will be crowded into lanes and alleys, cellars and garrets, poorly provided with the necessaries of life, and will gradually die out. The Negro, as already intimated, its preeminently a Southern man. He is so both in constitution and habits, in body as well as mind. He will not only take with him to the North, Southern modes of labor, but Southern modes of life. The careless and improvident habits of the South cannot be set aside in a generation. If they are adhered to in the North, in the fierce winds and snows of Kansas and Nebraska, the emigration must be large to keep up their numbers. It would appear, therefore, that neither the laws of politics, labor nor climate favor this Exodus. It does not conform to the laws of healthy emigration which proceeds not from South to North, not from heat to cold, but from East to West, and in climates to which the emigrants are more or less adapted and accustomed.

The North Gate of the South Must Be Kept Open

As an assertion of power by a people hitherto held in bitter contempt; as an emphatic and stinging protest against high-handed, greedy and shameless injustice to the weak and defenceless; as a means of opening the blind eyes of oppressors to their folly and peril, the Exodus has done valuable service. Whether it has accomplished all of which it is capable in this particular direction for the present, is a question which may well be considered. With a moderate degree of intelligent leadership among the laboring class at the South, properly handling the justice of their cause, and wisely using the Exodus example, they can easily exact better terms for their labor than ever before. Exodus is medicine, not food; it is for disease, not health; it is not to be taken from choice, but necessity. In anything like a normal condition of things the South is the best place for the Negro. Nowhere else is there for him a promise of a happier future. Let him stay there if he can, and save both the South and himself to civilization. While, however, it may be the highest wisdom under the circumstances for the freedmen to stay where they are, no encouragement should be given to any measures of coercion to keep them there. The American people are bound, if they are or can be bound to anything, to keep the North gate of the South open to black and white, and to all the people. The time to assert a right, Webster says, is when it is called in quetsion. If it is attempted by force or fraud to compel the colored people to stay, then they should by all means go; go quickly, and die, if need be, in the attempt. Thus far and to this extent any man may be an emigrationist. In no case must the Negro be "bottled up" or "caged up." He must be left free, like every other American citizen, to choose his own local habitation, and to go where he shall like. Though it may not be for his interest to leave the South, his right and power to leave it may be his best means of making it possible for him to stay there in peace. Woe to the oppressed and destitute of all countries and races if the rich and powerful are to decide when and where they shall go or stay. The deserving hired man gets his wages increased when he can tell his employer that he can get better wages elsewhere. And when all hope is gone from the hearts of the laboring classes of the old world, they can come across the sea to the new. If they could not do that their crushed hearts would break under increasing burdens. The right to emigrate is one of the most useful and precious of all rights. But not only to the oppressed, to the oppressor also, is the free use of this right necessary. To attempt to keep these freedmen in the South, who are spirited enough to undertake the risks and hardships of emigration, would involve great possible danger to all concerned. Ignorant and cowardly as the Negro may be, he has been known to fight bravely for his liberty. He went down to Harper's Ferry with John Brown, and fought as bravely and died as nobly as any. There have been Nathaniel Turners and Denmark Veseys among them in the United States, Joseph Cinques, Madison Washingtons and Tillmans on the sea, and Toussaint L'Ouvertures on land. Even his enemies, during the late war, had to confess that the Negro is a good fighter, when once in a fight. If he runs, it is only as all men will run, when they are whipped.

This is no time to trifle with the rights of men. All Europe today is studded with the material for a wild conflagration. Every day brings us news of plots and conspiracies against oppressive power. An able writer in the *North American Review* for July, himself a Nihilist, in a powerful article defends the extremest measures of his party, and shows that the treatment of the emancipated peasants by the government and landed aristocracy of Russia is very similar to that now practiced towards the freedmen by the landed aristocracy of the South. Like causes will produce like effects, the world over. It will not be wise for the Southern slaveholders and their successors to shape their policy upon the presumption that the Negro's cowardice or forbearance has no limit. The fever of freedom is already in the Negro's blood. He is not just what he was fourteen years ago. To forcibly dam up the stream of emigration would be a measure of extreme madness as well as oppression. It would be exposing the heart of the oppressor to the pistol and dagger, and his home to fire and pillage. The cry of "Land and Liberty," the watchword of the Nihilistic party in Russia, has a music in it sweet to the ear of all oppressed peoples, and well it shall be for the landholders of the South if they shall learn wisdom in time and adopt such a course of just treatment towards the landless laborers of the South in the future as shall make this popular watchword uncontagious and unknown among their laborers, and further stampede to the North wholly unknown, indescribable and impossible.

THE EMIGRATION OF COLORED CITIZENS FROM THE SOUTHERN STATES [1]

By R. T. Greener [2]

The land question is no new one; at the present time there are difficulties in England, Ireland, Scotland, and India with regard to this tenure of land; and when we come to study them, we find

[1] Read at Saratoga Springs, before the American Social Science Association, September 12, 1874.

[2] Richard T. Greener was born in Philadelphia, Pennsylvania, but went to Boston to live at five years of age. He there attended the grammar school at Cambridge, and then spent two years preparing for college at Oberlin, Ohio. He finished his preparation for college at Phillips Academy, Andover, Massachusetts. He then entered Harvard where he was graduated with the degree of Bachelor Arts in 1870 at the age of twenty-six, being the first Negro to be thus honored by that Institution. He was immediately made principal of the male department of the Institute for Colored Youth, Philadelphia. Mr. Greener next served as principal of the Sumner High School in Washington, in the District of Columbia. That same year, he accepted a position in

many cases analogous to those in America. There are remarkable coincidences and wonderful similarities of conditions, complaints and demands, which show conclusively that injustice and wrong, and disregard of rights and abuses of privilege are not confined to any one country, race or class. As a rule, capital takes advantage of the needs of labor. Landlords in every country oppress tenants, and sometimes disregard the welfare of the humbler agricultural laborer. The race in power lords it over the humbler; and if any change takes place from such normal condition, it only comes after a fierce outbreak of pent-up passion, or smouldering fires of wrong; or because some bold champion of the people rises to denounce oppression and demand redress. It has been fourteen years since the Confederacy collapsed, and eleven years since reconstruction. The South has now had for three years home rule, "Autonomy"; and yet, instead of the renewed prosperity, harmony of races, and absence of political violence and lawlessness, which we were promised, we find demoralized credit, shameless repudiation, and organized lawlessness—rendering the condition of the Negro tenant class worse than at any period since slavery. So deplorable and abject indeed is it that expatriation and escape to Liberia, or the West, seems the only hope, as it is the continued dream of the Negroes, old and young, in the six Southern States. We are accustomed to blame the Southern whites for the ultimate and approximate causes of this sad state of affairs. They are deeply responsible. I do not hesitate to place upon their shoulders all they deserve; but the North is not wholly innocent. We legislate for the interests of four million blacks just freed from bondage, demoralized by four years of war, and for two million

the office of the United States Attorney for the District of Columbia. Two months later, he was elected Professor of Metaphysics and Logic in the University of Columbia, South Carolina. This chair he accepted and filled with great credit until 1877 when the University was closed by the Hampton Legislature. When in South Carolina, he took part in revising the course of study for the school system of that State. He also completed his law studies which he began in Philadelphia, and was admitted to practice before the Supreme Court of that State.

Leaving South Carolina in 1877, he became Instructor in the Law Department in Howard University, and on the death of John H. Cook, in 1879, he was elected Dean. He then accepted a position under the First Controller of the United States Treasury which he held until 1882 when he began the active practice of law. Being active in politics, Mr. Greener figured conspicuously in the organization of his party, and at times delivered addresses and lectured throughout the country. He served as Consul at Bombay, and later at Vladivostok.

rebellious whites, landless, hopeless, thankful at that time, even if their lives were spared, and we ignore all the precedents of history—the West Indies, Ireland, Russia and Germany. We threw the Negro without anything, the carpet-bagger with his musket, the ex-Confederate disarmed, pell-mell together, and told them to work out the problem.

After the war it was difficult to purchase land because the old master was not disposed to sell. With the downfall of reconstruction a new lease of life was given to Southern barbarity and lawlessness. As usual, the Negro was the principal sufferer. Negro representation went first; next the educational system, which the carpet-bagger had brought to the South, was crippled by insufficient appropriations. Majorities were overcome by shot-gun intimidation, or secretly by the tissue ballot. Radical office-holders were forced to resign, robbed of their property by "due process of law," and driven North. The jury-box and representation the Negro was forced to give up; but after enduring all this, he found himself charged exorbitantly for the most necessary articles of food. His land was rented to him at fabulous prices. His cabin was likely to be raided at any time, whenever capricious lust, or a dreadful thirst for blood was roused. He saw his crop dwindling day by day; he saw himself growing poorer and getting into debt; his labor squandered between exacting landlords and rapacious store-keepers. It was then the Negro resolved to give up the fruitless contest so long and hopelessly waged, and try his fortune in the great West, of which he had heard and read so much during the past ten years.

Immediate Causes of the Exodus

To quote from the St. Louis Memorial: "The story is about the same, in each instance; great privation and want from excessive rent exacted for land; connected with the murder of colored neighbors and friends, and threats of personal violence to themselves; the tenor of which statement is that of suffering and terror. Election days and Christmas, by the concurrent testimony, seem to have been preferred for killing the 'smart man,' while robbery and personal violence, in one form and another, seem to have run the year around. Here they are in multitudes, not often alone, but women and children, old and middle-aged and young, and with common consent, leaving their old home for an unnatural climate, and facing storms and unknown dangers to go to northern Kansas. Why? Among them little is said of hope in the future; it is all of fear in the past. They are not drawn by the attractions of Kansas, they are driven by the terrors of Mississippi and Louisiana.'' The thriftless habits of work, engendered by southern life; the utter lack of foresight found in white and black alike, are powerful agents in bringing about the Exodus. The universal credit system is fostered by the planters, and kept up by the wily store-keeper; the insecurity of the holdings (long leases being unknown), is such that, if the Negro succeeds in raising a good crop, he has no guaranty that he can keep his patch the next year. The prices charged for the necessaries of life may be noticed. These are copied from the original documents brought by the refugees: $1.50 per lb. for tobacco; molasses, $1.50 per gallon; filling out a contract, $2.50; meal, per bushel, $2.00, not worth more than $1; pork, per barrel, $30.

''Again, the political difference of opinion which exists in the South is another important cause. There, political convictions rank with religious opinions in intensity. The over-production of cotton is another cause, by the low price of that staple. Then the fact that the Negro owns neither land, nor presses, cotton-gin, and implements, but buys mules, rents land, and purchases his provisions at an advance, often thirty and forty per cent., is sufficient cause for the Exodus. If we add that the landlord has a first claim on the crop, a law which is identical with the Scotch law of hypotheca, we shall see reasons enough for a failure, and for the disposition to seek a happier home elsewhere. It can not be denied that there are instances where the Negroes find themselves hopelessly involved; and seeing no prospect of any compensation, have at once repudiated their contracts and their country. This, of course, does not apply to those who have mules, carts, implements, and other utensils, which keep them attached closer to the soil. The law protects the landlord, and his claim always has the precedence. It is a punishable offence to remove any portion of the crop from the plantation before the landlord's claim is met. Next comes the store-keeper with his bill of six months. If anything were left for the poor Negro when all these demands are satisfied, it would partake of the nature of a genuine miracle.''

Advantages of the Exodus to the Negro

This emigration will benefit the Negro, who is now too much inclined to stay where he is put. At the South he never knows his own possibilities. Then again, the South is a wretched place for any people to develop in, and this is especially true of the Negro; because, like all subject races, he imitates the life about him. The Negro at the South is in a demoralized condition, and no jury will convict for political offences committed against him. Chief Justice Waite, at Charleston, in the case of the Ellerton rioters, could not charge the jury in favor of liberty and protection. District attorneys are appointed at the recommendation of known rebels and sympathizers and assassins. Of course, they will not do their duty; hence, the Negro dares not look for justice in the courts—once proudly called the palladium of English liberty. The use of the military power to enforce any right is repudiated at the North. But I remember it was employed quite efficaciously to return Anthony Burns and Simms, fugitive slaves, some years ago. I need not enumerate the demoralizing features of Southern life, the reckless disregard for human life, the lack of thrift, drinking customs, gaming, horse-racing, etc. The Negro needs contact with all that is healthful and developing in modern civilization, and by emigration the Negro will learn to love thrift, and unlearn many bad habits and improvident notions acquired from preceding generations.

The exclusive devotion of the Negro to the culture of cotton and rice is demoralizing to him. They drag women and children into the field, with no commissioner of labor to look out for outraged childhood and impaired maternity. I do not expect this argument to find favor with those who think the Negro has no other future before him than to cultivate sugar, cotton and rice. On the politico-economic side a partial Exodus will benefit those who remain, by raising the wage fund, increasing the demand, and insuring better treatment to those who are left; the fact of the Exodus being a preventive check, if I may borrow a phrase from Mr. Malthus. It will remove the Negro from the incessant whirl of politics, in which, like all dark races, he is governed more by feeling than selfish interest.

At present the Negro stands in the way of his own advancement, by reason of political fidelity, and the very excess of population, not diminished since the war, and yet not so systematically diffused and employed. Even Senator Butler, of South Carolina, says: "We have too much cheap Negro labor in the South." As to wages, the average Negro can earn higher wages and live more comfortably at the North, even if confined to humble employments, than he can at the South. When we add such trifles as protection, school privileges, free suffrage and Christian influences, we transcend the limits of legitimate comparison. That the departure of the few will benefit the many might be abundantly illustrated by the condition of Ireland after the famine of 1848, or England after the Lancashire distress, when Canon Girdlestone, Mr. Froude and Goldwin Smith counseled emigration.

I assume that the predominance of the Negro in politics at the South is gone for a generation at least. The South will not have it and the North has exhibited no very marked disposition to enforce it. If it be ever desirable again, let it come when the children of the present black colonists go back to the mother land, improved in all that makes good citizens by a sojourn in the West.

Objections to the Exodus

There are few opponents of the Exodus. Most of them are only negative objectors. The only class positively objecting is the planting class. At Vicksburg, and in Washington County (Miss.), they objected vehemently and loudly. Foreign labor, they say, would cost money. Not one planter in ten is able to make further outlay. During the change of laborers, even, they would go to rack and ruin. The Negro is the only one who can do their work. To go now will ruin the cotton crop, and, hence, affect the North as well as the South.

No one disputes the right of the Negro to go West, now that he is free. We accord to all men the right to improve their condition by change of residence or employment. Nearly all of the objectors, white and black, have grave doubts as to our ability to stand this severe Northern climate. They fear we may not find work adapted to our limited peculiar powers; may not meet with kind friends and genial sympathy. We must endure privations and meet with ostracism at the North. Mechanics will not work with Negroes. The Negro remembers Slavery, Black Codes, Ku-Klux, Sister Sallie's plan, tissue ballots, the murder of Dr. Dostie and Randolph in South Carolina, Caldwell and Dixon in Mississippi, and says: "My relatives and friends who have gone North since the war tell a different story. They have held no offices, but they are free. They sleep in peace at night; what they earn is paid them, if not, they can appeal to the courts. They vote without fear of the shot-gun, and their children go to school. It is true the Northern people do not love us so well as you did, and hence the intermixture of races is not so promiscuous there as here. This we shall try to endure, if we go North, with patience and Christian resignation. We have never heard of the people at the North paying in ten, twenty-five and fifty cent scrip, payable four years hence, nor charging $2.00 a plug for tobacco, and $2.50 for witnessing a contract. While we may not have so much social equality as with you, we shall have more political equality and man to man justice. You charge $15.00 and $25.00 per acre for worn-out land; we can buy better in Kansas and Nebraska at $2.50 an acre. We had rather die free at the North than live as paupers and pariahs here, only nominally free. You thought Kansas not too cold for us in 1854-5; we are not afraid to try it now."

The most important opponent of the Exodus is Marshal Frederick Douglass, my distinguished antagonist in this discussion, who, I sincerely regret, is not here to lend to his able and ingenious argument the magic of his presence and the influence of his eloquent voice. The greatest Negro whom America has produced, having suffered all that our race could endure, and having been elevated higher than any other Negro, he cannot lack sympathy with any movement which concerns his race, and hence, any objection coming from him challenges attention, and demands to be answered. Age, long service, and a naturally keen and analytic mind would presume a soundness of view on almost any topic of national importance or race interest. It is, therefore, with the highest regard for the honesty of Mr. Douglass's views that I venture to reply to some of his objections. Mr. Douglass has not been an inactive opponent. He has written elaborate resolutions, made at least six speeches, spoken at the Methodist Conference, and been interviewed on the Exodus. While time has modified his extreme views, and more recent events have blunted the edge of his sarcasm, and while most of his objections are of the negative rather than the positive order, against the methods and men who seek to help the movement, rather than against the Exodus itself, still the morale of his influence is in opposition. Mr. Douglass's arguments, as I have been able to find them in speeches, resolutions, and the paper just read, are briefly these:

1. Emigration is not the proper nor permanent remedy.

2. The Government ought to protect colored citizens at the South; to encourage emigration gives the Government a chance to shirk its duty; while the advocates of the measure leave Equal Rights, Protection and Allegiance open questions.

3. The colored race should be warned against a nomadic life and habits of wandering.

4. African emigration and migration to the West are analogous; the failure of the one is prophetic of the other.

5. The Negro now is potentially able to elect some members of his race at the South to Congress; this is impossible at the North.

6. At the South he has a monopoly of the supply of labor; at the West he would not have it. At the South, land owners must have laborers or starve; Western land owners are independent.

7. The Exodus does not conform to "the laws of civilizing emigration," as the carrying of a language, literature, etc., of a superior race to an inferior; nor does it conform to "the law of geography." These, according to Mr. Douglass, "require for healthy emigration that it proceed from East to West, not from South to North, and not far away from latitudes and climates in which the emigrants were born."

To these objections first, it may be said, no favorer of migration claims it as the sole, proper or only permanent remedy for the aggravated relation of landlord and tenant at the South. It is approved of as one remedy, thus far the most salutary, in stopping lawlessness and exactions. The reciprocity of allegiance and protection is granted; but it is asked, "How can the United States Government protect its black citizens while the fallacy of State rights and undefinable 'home rule' or 'autonomy,' prevent interference?" The Duke of Argyle believes that "there is no abstract limit to the right of the State to do anything." "In the interest of economy," says he, "it may pass sumptuary laws, or regulate the wages of farm laborers." This is under a monarchy. With us, neither Government nor courts may interfere with contracts, either to enforce the terms or insure justice, when the local sentiment is opposed. The Government does not protect the Negro because it finds itself powerless to do so. As a general rule, the Negro may well be warned against a wandering life; but in the present instance such advice is gratuitous.

The failure of the analogy drawn between African colonization and migration to the West may be stated in this way; the one was worked up by slave-owners in the interest of slavery; this one springs spontaneously, according to Mr. Douglass's view, from the class considering itself aggrieved; one led out of the country to a comparative wilderness; the other directs to better land and larger opportunities here at home. The one took the Negro to contend with barbarism. This places him under more civilizing influences than he has ever enjoyed, involving no change of allegiance nor serious differences of climate. If the colored people are "potentially" able to elect one of their own race to Congress, they cannot now make that potentiality possible. Emigration surely cannot lessen the potentiality, since the emigrants will remain citizens. I am inclined to think it will not diminish the probability. If I remember correctly, Massachusetts first elected colored men to her General Court; Ohio has nominated one, and Illinois has a colored representative.

Mr. Douglass is rather misleading and fails again in his analogy, when he infers that the Negro must go West as a civilizer or not go at all. He goes out from the house of bondage up from the land of Egypt, directed, I am inclined to think, by the same mighty hand which pointed out the way to Israel:

"By day, along the astonished land,
The cloudy pillar glided slow;
By night, Arabia's crimsoned sand,
Returned the fiery column's glow."

If by the laws of geography, to which, unfortunately, this new Exodus does not conform, Mr. Douglass means that colonization, migration or civilization proceed best within the isothermal lines, we may concede the law, but all history shows exceptions remarkable and instructive.

The Phœnicians sailed West and North; the Greek colonies were at all known points; the Dutch and English have not been hindered by isothermal lines, penetrating far away from the latitudes in which they were born. Magna Græcia, in distinction from Hellas, and Mr. Dilke's "Greater Britain," are pertinent illustrations of the unsoundness of this seeming historical statement. If it were even philosophically correct, there is no analogy in the examples; the Southern Negro, if he emigrates to Washington Territory or Arizona, would not be as far from home as the Aryan race now is by its excessive waves of migration from the Black and Caspian Seas. When Mr. Douglass grants in his paper that if the half is true of what the Negro suffers, the Exodus is justified,—he grants all that any advocate of it asks. It is from causes, which he condemns, denounces, deplores and considers disgraceful, that we say, "emigrate, and if you can, better your condition."

The Exodus is complained of as a "policy." We might answer, it is a result, not a policy in the ordinary sense, although, as a safe check to certain ulterior causes, we might well commend it to oppressed people anywhere as a measure of policy.

We are told, aphoristically, that the Negro's labor made him free, and therefore, it can make him "free, comfortable, and independent." The assumed fact is not exactly clear, and the conclusion is scarcely warranted by the Negro's statements of his condition, according to Mr. Douglass.

We are called upon to say whether we would remove a part, or all of the colored people from the South. "A part," we answer, "if that will insure protection and just treatment for the rest; the whole, if they can be protected in no other way." "But where will you get money to remove them?" is the new horn to the dilemma. "Congress cannot give it, because of the public debt," and yet Congress (what Congress?) would rather spend $200,000,000 to protect them where they are." In short, Mr. Douglass grants the Negro's misery, but tells him to wait, his present state is "exceptional and transient," his rights "will revive, survive and flourish"; but the poor frightened, half-starved Negroes, crouching along the Mississippi, fear this will not happen until they have literally passed over. Mr. Douglass is not willing to have Congress nor capitalists help these houseless wanderers, to whom we gave nothing when we freed them. We did better than that by fugitives forty years ago, and I see no good reason why Northern philanthropy should close its hand and ears now to a cry which is as despairing as that which rang from Ireland in 1848, or from the yellow fever sufferers, a twelvemonth ago. We see capital employed to build better houses for the poor, to transport young children to the West; why shall we not try to help those who are trying as best they may to help themselves? The statement that Massachusetts was once Mississippi, is a favorite one of Mr. Douglass, and has been reiterated so often as to lead the unwary to believe that the Marshal of the District of Columbia thinks it true. I am more inclined to ascribe it to the orator's love of antithesis; so incorrect, so unjust, and for Frederick Douglass, so unkind would such a remark be.

To say to the emigrants, "Better stay than go," is analogous to saying "Be ye warmed and filled, notwithstanding ye give not those things which are needful for the body." Nor do proverbs add protection to the one argument any more than food and raiment to the other.

The Exodus may be a failure and a mistake, but whether it is or not, it has no connection with the power of the Republican party, or the retention of political power by the Negro. Both may be benefited, and it may fail; both may be injured by it, and it may nevertheless succeed. This is a specimen *non sequitur,* very familiar in arguments against the present migration.

We are assured that there will be misery and want resulting from this "ill-timed" movement. Doubtless there will be; every movement having in it the elements of good, has brought some hardship:

> "Never morning wore
> To evening, but some heart did break."

The crucial test, however, is whether there will be more misery and want by migrating than by remaining; we think not.

Another distinguished gentleman, a financier, a banker, a political economist, Ex-Secretary McCulloh, in his seventh Harvard lecture, thinks the Exodus unfortunate. He also has faith that all will be well. With a refinement of unconscious sarcasm, he quotes Charles Sumner, and says to the Negroes, "stick, fight it out where you are, if it takes not merely the present, but many other summers." But the Ex-Secretary, less cautious than Mr.

Douglass, says, if they (the colored people) were forced to go, they should be returned, even with the aid of the Government. Here is much sympathy enclosed in a dubious sentence. We do not know whether financial aid, or bayonet aid is to return these refugees, and nothing is said of their possible condition after they are returned. With such matters of detail the optimist and the doctrinaire have no concern. I shall call on Henry Jackson to answer Mr. Douglass and Mr. McCulloh: "I left the South because I could not make a living. Year before last I made ten bales of cotton, and never got a cent for it. I sued for it but could not get anything; they wanted me to pawn my horse and begin over again; but I told them I was going to sell my horse and go away. I would not go back to the South again because I could not live; cannot live there and give $2 for meal, and $30 for a barrel of pork, $10 an acre for land, $5 for ginning cotton, and then being cheated out of everything after I made it. My wife is along with me. I reckon I have money enough to get to Kansas."

Best Time to Emigrate

The western lands are waiting for settlers, and are being rapidly filled up by Swedes, Norwegians, Mennonites, Icelanders and Poles, why should not the Negro participate? Six hundred thousand acres of public land have been taken up since June 30, 1878; 50,000 families have gone westward under the homestead law, exclusive of those who have small sums to invest. Why shall we debar the Negro? Irish Catholics have raised a fund of $100,000 to assist their poor from the large cities. The Hebrews have also an excellent association for the same purpose. These aid societies hold meetings and solicit funds. No one denounces them or impugns the motives of their advocates. What will benefit Irish, Hebrew, Swede, and Norwegian, cannot be decidedly injurious to the colored race alone.

How Will They Be Treated in the West?

Governor St. John, of Kansas, is authority on this point. "Up to the present writing, about 3,000 destitute refugees have arrived, the most of whom have been cared for by our committee. We have been very successful in securing for them employment, and thus placed them in a position that they soon became self-sustaining, and no longer required aid. These people seem to be honest, and of good habits; are certainly industrious and anxious to work, and, so far as they have been tried, have proved to be faithful and excellent laborers.'' Sir George Campbell[1] says, ''In Kansas City, and still more in the suburbs of Kansas proper, the Negroes are much more numerous than I have yet seen. On the Kansas side, they form quite a large proportion of the population. They are certainly subject to no indignity or ill-usage; * * * Here the Negroes seem to have quite taken to work at trades; I saw them doing building work, both alone and assisting white men, and also painting and other tradesmen's work. On the Kansas side, I found a Negro blacksmith, with an establishment of his own; he was an old man and very 'Negro.' He grumbled just like a white. * * * He came from Tennessee, after emancipation; had not been back there, and did not want to go. * * * I also saw black women keeping apple stalls and engaged in other such occupations. In these States, which I may call intermediate between black and white countries (States), the blacks evidently have no difficulty.''

What is true of Kansas is true of the Indian Territory. A recent traveller there, writes: ''The cozy homes and promising fields were the property of freedmen; every ploughboy you see has been a slave. All the farms along our route today belong to freedmen, to whom the Creeks accord every right and privilege they enjoy themselves,—annuity lands, offices and honors. * * * Every home gives proof of thrift. New fences, addition to the cabins, new barns and out-houses, catch the eye on every hand, except the school-house and church; these appear to be going to decay, but it is only in the rude buildings that this is true. Both church and school are prosperous.''

At the South the Negro, under adverse conditions, is not a great land owner, but yet he is not wholly landless. In South Carolina he owns 20,000 acres; in Georgia pays taxes on $6,000,000, mostly in land; and in Mississippi and Louisiana it is estimated he pays taxes on between $10,000,000 and $20,000,000, the greater portion in land.

Emigration is no new thing, beginning with Senator Windom's speech. It began in 1840 and has kept up ever since. You may remember some of the old pictures of the emigrant with bundle

[1] "Black and White in the United States."

on his shoulder. He went alone formerly, and was often taken back at the Government's expense; now he takes his family, and cannot be taken back against his will. In Kansas there are now five or six colonies, some of them established since 1870; Baxter Springs, Nicodemus, Morton City, and Singleton. The reports from all are favorable. The people are said to be thrifty, intelligent and willing to work. All are paying for their land by instalments, at prices from $1.25 to $6.00 per acre. If, dissatisfied with Kansas, they wish to "move on," no one interferes with them. Mississippi, in spite of her Constitution, which says, "No citizen shall be prevented from emigrating on any pretence whatever," attempts to keep them back by libelling the steamboats for carrying excessive numbers. The Negroes are also detained by writs gotten up on spurious charges. In short, the Southern landlord now demands more than the lord paramount in the middle ages; the tenant must be a permanent fixture to the land. Georgia and South Carolina have already revived the law of Edward VI. (Act I, c. 3, 1381), and sell idle vagrants, or farm them out to service in gangs, as their prejudice dictates.

The Political Side of the Exodus

We are told it is a political scheme. To insure success as a political movement, 60,000 colored voters should be distributed in certain States before November, 1879, the end of the period allowed for legal residence. If the Exodus were promoted by politicians, we should find 20,000 Negroes going to Pennsylvania, 20,000 to New Jersey, 10,000 at least to New York, the same number for Indiana, and a spare 5,000 for Connecticut. This could not be done under $2,000,000, even had it begun six months ago. Thus far at the North, not $20,000 has been raised to help the refugees, notwithstanding $100,000,000 would not be idly spent to help the Negro and end this vexed question. It is estimated that 15,000 have gone West within eight months; 150 leave New Orleans each week. All are not going to Kansas. Many are wisely pushing farther North. As a class, they differ from the West India Negroes after their emancipation. The Southern Negro did not relapse into barbarism; he manifests a disposition and an adaptability to work. That he is industrious is shown by the immense cotton crop, just reported as contributing to the exportable products of the nation, $189,000,000 per annum.

No view of the movement would be complete which did not notice the relation of the colored people of the country to this flight from oppression. The first stage is passed, the appeal to white philanthropists. My notion is the second is here, the appeal to ourselves. We must organize societies, contribute our dimes, and form a network of communication between the South and every principal point North and West. We should raise $200,000 to form a company; we should have a National Executive Committee, and have agents to buy land, procure cheap transportation, disseminate accurate information, and see to it that they are neither deluded nor defrauded. Such an organization, working through our churches and benevolent societies, would do more to develop our race than all the philanthropic measures designed to aid us since the war.

The Exodus Will Go On

The little rill has started on its course toward the great sea of humanity. It moves slowly on by virtue of the eternal law of gravitation, which leads peoples and individuals toward peace, protection and happiness. Today it is a slender thread and makes way with difficulty amid the rocks and tangled growth; but it has already burst through serious impediments, showing itself possessed of a mighty current. It started in Mississippi, but it is even now being rapidly fed by other rills and streams from the territory through which it flows. Believing that it comes from God, and feeling convinced that it bears only blessings in its course for that race so long tossed, so ill-treated, so sadly misunderstood, I greet its tiny line, and almost see in the near future its magnificent broad bosom, bearing proudly onward, until at last, like the travel-worn and battle-scarred Greeks of old, there bursts upon its sight the sea, the broad sea of universal freedom and protection.

This address below is one delivered at various times by the famous orator, Joseph C. Price, who, although he passed away in the prime of life, made the impression, both in this country and abroad, as one of the most eloquent men of any race and of any time. His views as to the plight of the Negro and the remedies for the uplift of the race are set forth in this address.

THE RACE PROBLEM STATED

By Joseph C. Price[1]

Ladies and Gentlemen: I gratefully acknowledge the honor in being permitted to speak in this intelligent and representative presence, upon some phase of the Race Problem. Such a discussion in this metropolitan city is both a measurement of its interest in the satisfactory solution of the race question, and an indication that it is not simply a "race" or "southern," but a "national" problem, in its origin, nature and results.

The American atmosphere is full of the Race Problem. The leading daily papers crowd their columns with it. The more elaborate monthly magazines invite the freest and fullest discussion of it. In the North and in the South alike, men and women are industriously seeking its solution. The ripest scholarship and most profound learning represented by our brightest intellects, are making generous contributions to this end. Caucasian and Negro are rivaling each other in the endeavor to discover the element that will enter as a peaceful means in the harmonious adjustment of the as yet unadjusted racial relations in the South.

Where so much is being said, pro and con, I cannot even hope for a moment to say anything new on this all-absorbing American topic: but as I am sometimes taken for a Negro, on account of my slight identity with that race, I will not be considered at all pre-

[1] Joseph C. Price was born in Elizabeth City, North Carolina, February 10, 1854. Notwithstanding his father was a slave, his mother was a free woman, and, according to the regulation of slavery, the child followed the condition of the mother. At the age of nine years he went with his mother to New Bern, North Carolina, where he spent the largest part of his life. He began his serious study at the Lowell Normal School of New Bern. After mastering the fundamentals, he commenced teaching in the public school of Wilson, North Carolina. He then entered Shaw University, but abandoned that institution for Lincoln University. At Lincoln, he distinguished himself as an orator, winning most of the contests which he entered. He was graduated as the valedictorian of his class in 1879. He remained at the institution, however, to study theology, completing the course in two rather than in three years.

Early in his career he had embraced the faith of the African Methodist Episcopal Zion Church. In recognition of his ability he was selected to speak at the Ecumenical Conference in London where he distinguished himself by perhaps the shortest speech he ever made. In England, he collected a considerable sum of money with which he began the establishment of Livingstone College in Salisbury, North Carolina. Gifted as an orator, desired here and there, he popularized his school and secured for it contributions sufficient to lay the foundation for its present progress. He was cut down in the prime of life before he had time to do a good many things expected of him because of the most promising beginning which he had made.

sumptuous in attempting to humbly represent him by an expression of opinion on the problem of the hour.

I may further add, that I am prompted to this endeavor from the fact that the Negro is so frequently, and almost unpardonably, misrepresented as to his candid and unbiassed position in the race problem discussions. In fact, one of the signs of encouragement in all of the debates as to the relation of the dual races in the South arises from the presence of Negroes in the arena, who are eminently competent to speak for themselves,—and in no uncertain sound.

It is necessary, before the bar of public opinion, as well as in the Civil Courts, to have evidence from both sides. The Negro is gradually waking up to the realization of the responsibility resting on him, and to the necessity of his helping, as best he can, to make plain the situation as it is.

In keeping with this idea, it shall be my purpose, for a short time tonight, to address myself to this subject,—THE RACE PROBLEM STATED.

The widespread concern, and I may add, the growing alarm, over the rapid increase of the Negroes in this country, gives some of us the impression that we are coming to another serious stage in the development of the race question; hence, to many of us, this is not the time for the covert use of language, their delusive charms of glittering generalities, nor the dazzling display of pyrotechnic oratory. There are vital issues at stake. These issues involve certain eternal and incontrovertible principles. Upon these principles will be determined the inalienable rights, the liberty, and the pursuit of happiness of a whole race of men; the prosperity of one of the most fertile sections of our land,—a section whose immeasurable resources have scarcely been touched with the quickening spirit of the age; and the safety and perpetuity of a country whose beckoning hand is stretched out to every nation under the sun, and within whose broad and illimitable domain all races of the globe are destined to feel the impulse of a magnetic Americanism.

With such issues at stake, I cannot be insensible to the gravity and responsibility of the occasion. I have been kindly requested to come here and give you my candid opinion on the race problem.

I would be unworthy of your invitation, lacking in the instincts of true manliness, an enemy to my race, to the South and to the country,—did I not speak to you out of my experience, observation and convictions, the truth as I feel and as I know it.

A Race Problem Not Unnatural

The race problem is not of Negro origin. The Negro washes his hands of this responsibility. The Negro Question finds it beginning in 1620. The present race problem is the last unsettled phase of the slave question. Slavery, it is true, is settled forever, because it was settled right. The principle of freedom so permeates the American consciousness, that all of the standing army and floating navy cannot fasten that wrong, that iniquity, that hydra-headed monster, on this country again. The South, even, would now vote "No" on the impossible question of reenslavement.

But this attitude on the part of the South is a development,—for it is a matter of history that it once fought to make a new republic out of the wreck of the old, whose corner-stone should be human slavery. In that struggle, freedom triumphed. But the South was more conquered than convinced; it was overpowered rather than fully persuaded. The Confederacy surrendered its sword at Appomattox, but did not there surrender its convictions. It has taken twenty-five years of freedom, with its unparalleled progress and marvelous impulse to southern activities, to convince the South that freedom is more profitable than slavery.

It took a quarter of a century to produce a Henry W. Grady,—so able, so eloquent in expressions of loyalty to the Stars and Stripes; so impassioned in utterances of devotion to the union of states, and so full of fervid admiration of the history, struggles and triumphs of the influences of Plymouth Rock. Just after the war, such a man with such environments and entertaining such sentiments, would have been considered a southern monstrosity, and an enemy to his section and its people; but his declarations in the new light of today made him an idol in the South, and an object of admiring wonder in the North.

Some say,—How changed. I answer, "Yes." But let us not forget that this change has come only on one phase of the race problem, and that this phase was settled by the bloody arbitrament of arms.

But on all the resultants of slavery and the war, there is nothing like a unanimity of sentiment in the South. It was not so hard to give up the principle of slavery as it was to surrender the property in the slave. And, just here, it is not difficult to discover one of the discordant elements in the race problem of today. The ruling classes in the South had their fortunes scattered and their commercial activities paralyzed by the war. In the Negro centered all the wealth of the South. He was the soul of its industrial machinery. His freedom, therefore, was galling to the body politic in the South, not only because he was free but because, through his freedom, they became poor. This feeling, for a long time, was the source of antipathy against the Negro,—for as he moved among the master-class as a freeman, he was constantly reminding them of their losses.

But I believe that in proportion as the South recovers its lost fortunes, through industrial development, and the Negro becomes more and more an indispensable factor in this development, the intensity of feeling on this account will be mitigated. And it is my observation that such a feeling is not as prevalent now as it was just after the war.

A New Phase of the Race Problem Now Confronts the South

The South has yet to realize that, not only is freedom better than slavery and that free-labor is better than slave-labor (which it now admits); it must also face the logical conclusion of its own assertion, that a freeman is better than a slave and has greater powers, and therefore should have wider scope as a man, and as an industrial factor. And such a conclusion will be a long step in the solution of the race problem, and a great advance toward southern prosperity; for the great need of the South today is industrial power, and the development of this power is imperative, not only for the speedy recovery of lost fortunes and the rapid strengthening of paralyzed energies, but as an unfailing agency in unifying the interests and making common the destiny of both races in the South, and in the nation as well.

Other Elements in the Problem

The emancipation of the slave, and the loss of property in that act, are not the only elements that have made possible the race problem in this country.

When the property in human form was recognized as a man and brother, by the amendments to the Constitution, it was considered an insult added to the injuries already sustained through him. Our friends in the South did not recognize that this step was a necessity, and not an insult; for freedom implies manhood. In fact, there is no true freedom (anything else is a mere mockery of the name) that does not give full recognition and assent to that cardinal principle of humanity,—the fatherhood of God and the brotherhood of man.

We remember that under the peculiar institution the slave was a thing, chattel (that is, cattle). The system as such, and the laws of the country protecting it, did not operate on the principle that the Negro was a member of the human family even. The auction-block, painful separations of parents and children, husbands and wives, the ruthless sundering of the tenderest ties of which the human heart is capable, were evidences of this sad truth.

Under the training of such a system for centuries, it is not an anomaly that the South, just after the unpleasantness, was not prepared to welcome the Negro as a bona-fide member of the human brotherhood, or that we now have a race problem.

Some went so far as to argue that the Negro did not have a soul. One man put his assertions in book form on this subject. I do not hesitate to say that there are men living now who have not yet satisfied themselves of the common origin of the Negro. They believe him, not circumstantially, but inherently inferior, and different from the ordinary family of mankind; hence the hesitancy, the downright refusal to accord him his place in the one family of which God is the common father.

On this question of the humanity of the Negro, it is encouraging to know that the South does not stand where it stood twenty-five or fifty years ago. The man who tried to prove that the Negro was soulless, if he were living today, could not be persuaded to attempt such a stupendous piece of nonsense; for now we have men in the South who have grown famous among southerners because of their advocacy of the brotherhood of men. *Our brother in black, his freedom and his future,*—by Dr. A. B. Haygood of Georgia, is an illustration of this fact.

It will be observed that in the discussion thus far of the race problem, I am something of an optimist;—not absolutely so, however.

If emancipation, loss of property in the freedmen, and the humanity of the Negro, were the only elements of inharmony between the races, it would not take us very long to solve the race problem. In all these phases of the question, it is my observation that great progress has been made; and while the South may not be unanimous in its sentiment even on these phases, still it is evident that its advance has been beyond the expectation of some of the most sanguine of us.

Negro Citizenship the Knotty Element in the Problem

The great discordant element between the races, that which makes the so-called race problem, is Negro Citizenship and its consequent eligibility to office. If there is a race problem, here are its centripetal and centrifugal forces. It is, indeed, the great stone of offence, and many think the rock of a great southern and national disaster.

Neither the South nor the country was prepared for the sudden emancipation of the Negro. Yesterday a slave,—today a freeman,—the next day a citizen, and the next an office-holder and ruler,—was a little too much, in the opinion of some. As the dominant sentiment in the South persistently opposed all of the endeavors leading to this crowning point, it is not strange that they should now say, "This final consummation shall not be realized"; for to the sensitive nerve of a southerner this is the most irreconcilable resultant of the war, and the "unkindest cut of all," the rebounds of their own action. The concession of equal manhood rights to what they call "an alien race" is to them not a necessity, nor a legitimate outcome of freedom, but an added insult to a people already stung with defeat. Some of the southern leaders declare that this part of the law of the land shall not be carried out. "The ballot of the Negro must be suppressed," they say, "especially in states where he is in the majority." Some have gone so far as to threaten a call to arms before it shall be done.

This defiance, in many parts of the South, to the Constitution and the rights of men is no secret. The Ku-Klux Klan, Winchester Rifles, tissue ballots, the Eight Box System, Red Shirters,—are but varying phases of the same great opposition to Negro citizenship.

The cruel discrimination on lines of public travel, railroad and steamboat, and the lack of eating accommodations on the railroads for respectable colored people, are also reminders of the race issue in the South.

It is an undisguised truth that colored men pay first-class fare on railroads in most of the states of the South without receiving the accommodations for which they pay. This condition of things is not only unjust, but it is ungrateful; for the Negroes not only construct the railroads of the South, but through their labor they contribute largely to their support. It is not a pleasant thing for the Negro to dwell upon when he calls to mind the fact that after he has contributed his indispensable labor to the construction of a road, and after he has been taxed to build new roads, not a member of his race can be accorded a decent car, or a decent seat in a waiting room. Growing intelligence will not be content with such a condition of affairs.

From Washington to Jacksonville there is not, so far as my experience goes, a place for a colored lady or gentleman, however refined or intelligent, however well dressed and behaved, to take a meal, except it be in the kitchen of the railroad eating houses, or at a window, in a bag, at some dining room. I speak out of a bitter experience on this matter. If there is an exception to this statement, it simply proves the rule.

Is it unreasonable, is it unbusinesslike, is it impudence to ask that decent accommodation be accorded colored passengers who are compelled to travel upon our southern roads? No. Humanity, not to speak of justice, demands it.

From what Dr. Haygood said recently through the *Atlanta Constitution* on this matter, these discriminations are not to be attributed to irresponsible conductors and brakemen on the railroads, but to the bond-holders in Wall Street. This may be true, but it is rather strange, however, that there are no such discriminations between Washington and New York, or between New York and Boston; and the owners of which can also be traced to Wall Street and to State Street.

Thus far we have been trying to show some of the elements that enter into the race problem. But why is the idea of a problem suggested by the situation in the South?

The Problem Stated

The southern question is simply this,—How long can we deny to men their inalienable and constitutional rights, the denial of which they most keenly feel, even when no complaint is made, without a serious conflict involving not only the section and races immediately concerned, but the nation as well?

It is seriously asked,—"Can such a condition continue with impunity?" The question is not, whether the races can live side by side in peace, but whether the two races can live together in harmony, with the one denying the natural and constitutional rights of the other. Can the one persist in not recognizing the political and civil privileges,—privileges conceded by the highest tribunal of the land,—of the other, with no ultimate harm to both?

Can this problem be solved? Or, in other words,—Will the South ever concede to the Negro his unrestricted privileges as a citizen, and thereby solve this problem?

I believe it will; and so far as the Negro is concerned, he is ready to do his part, to take his step in this direction, even at the sacrifice of the non-essentials involved in its solution.

The South is, providentially, the home of the Negro as a mass in this country, and he is willing and ready to live in peace with his white brethren under any conditions save those which violate the very instinct of his being and imply the surrender of his manhood and God-given rights. For the sake of the progress and prosperity of the South he is ready and willing to make any terms that are reasonable, just and fair; but a compromise that reverses the Declaration of Independence, nullifies the national constitution, and is contrary to the genius of this republic, ought not be asked of any race living under the stars and stripes; and if asked, ought never to be granted.

In the face of the Negro's increasing intelligence and marvelous fecundity, we are asked,—Can a race conflict be avoided? This depends on one or two things: first, the avoidance of the conflict depends upon the changed attitude of the South toward the legal status of the Negro. Secondly, the conflict may be avoided by the utter disappearance of the Negro, through amalgamation or deportation.

As we have already intimated, present indications are against the latter. The Negroes are not disappearing, or dying out; they are not being lost through amalgamation. From four millions they have grown to eight millions in less than a quarter of a century. And it is worthy of consideration to note that the Negro is not only growing larger in numbers, but more solid in blackness as well.

It is a mere waste of time to speak of expatriation or deportation as a way of escape from giving the Negro his due under the Constitution. He has been in the South too long; his feet are too deeply imbedded in its soil to be decoyed away as a mass by adroit national appropriations, or wily schemes of "Appeals to Pharaoh."

More is true. The Negro is so interwoven into the industrial life of the South that if he desired to go and the nation made its appropriation, the whites of the South would oppose it.

But you ask, "Are the Negroes to remain in the South then, and be forever subjected to political persecution, mob violence and a denial of their rights as men and as citizens?"

I answer, "No." We must remember that the Negroes are in a formative period, and that we are but twenty-five years removed from a most degrading slavery. There must be time for the growth of new ideas, and for the dissemination of a humane and patriotic sentiment.

I have faith in the better element in the South which is every day increasing, notwithstanding it is still in the minority. Race prejudices and antipathies, whether between Patricians and Plebeians, Normans and Saxons, or Negroes and southern whites, are not to be removed in a day,—especially when these prejudices are the stubborn growth of centuries. As these prejudices have deepened into convictions because of a certain adverse condition of the Negro, they will not be fully removed until the conditions are changed that helped to produce them. The white man of the South has evolved into his present attitude by the environments which logically drove him to it; and he can only be effectually and permanently changed by a correspondent change, not of the position, but of the character of the environment.

Will Additional Law, or Statutory Enactments, Solve the Problem?

Wherever there is lawlessness, or disorder, or mob violence of any kind, law is always in order to restrain and punish the law-breakers. The law-abiding element in the South is not afraid of law; for law is only a terror to the evil-doer; but legislation without a sentiment to sustain it cannot solve the problem. We have tried it for twenty-five years, and it has been a dead letter.

The Negro does not ask for any new laws for him as a black man; he seeks no special legislation. He only asks for the enforcement of the law as it is, and not for him as a black man, but only as it should be exercised for any other American citizen.

Time and patience will be large elements in the solution of the problem: vituperation will avail us nothing. We cannot legislate men out of their prejudices or remove their antipathies by abuse. There must be a gradual growth from within that must remove the convictions from without.

I may be too much of an optimist, but I confess to more confidence in the South of the future than even Mr. Grady. He was of the opinion that the South would never concede to the Negro the untrammelled exercise of his franchise or tolerate his influence as a political factor in the South. I try to look at this whole matter in the light of a progressive civilization and the advance of an enlightened Christianity.

In the city of New York less than a quarter of a century ago, there were separate street cars for colored people, and they had to wait until the "Jim-Crow Car" came along before they could ride. Such a thing, so far as street cars are concerned, is unknown anywhere in the South today.

In the memory of men now living, colored people were only allowed to ride on the outside of stages running between Boston and Cambridge. Prudence Crandall, whose house was burned to the ground because she dared, in Connecticut, to teach Negro boys and girls to read and write, died only a few months ago.

Even now, in metropolitan cities like New York, Brooklyn and Washington, colored men are denied a dozen times a day (or as often as they may apply) a decent meal at restaurants and a comfortable bed at hotels, simply because they belong to another race.

The Assumptions of the South

The South refused to concede to the Negro his constitutional rights, on assumptions; and these assumptions are based on false alarms, filled with fear. First, it is assumed that in denying the Negro free speech and a free ballot is the only way to save that section from misrule and bankruptcy; "for," they say, "the Negro is seeking the control of the government, and, through this control, the domination of the whites." This is not true. To give the Negro his rights, or to guarantee to him a free ballot does not necessarily argue that the ignorant, poor and vicious will control the intelligent, wealthy and virtuous. If this were so, the poor, ignorant whites, who are in the majority among the whites, would be in control throughout the South. These poor whites have all their constitutional rights, yet they do not hold the offices, nor manage the finances of that section. The Negroes believe in an intelligent administration of government as much as anybody else; they seriously object to putting the incompetent in places of power and responsibility: they do not desire to be officered by ignorant men.

The Negroes enter their protest, however, to the presumption that all the intelligence or capability is in one party, or one race. There are colored men in the South who compare favorably in intelligence and character with white men in that section, and the only objection urged against them is their race identity.

Mr. Grady said, in his Dallas speech, that "Ignorance may struggle up to intelligence, and out of the corruptible may come the incorruptible; but the white men must rule this country"—implying in that statement that the citizenship of the Negro must not enter as an element in the control of the affairs of the South, even if he is intelligent and possesses unblemished character.

But the Negro is not seeking supremacy through the ballot, he is not after power, but protection,—not control, but rights. He has no desire to rule the whites, but he does insist that the whites shall rule him only on the principle of humanity and justice. The Negro is after friends, more than supremacy. If he does not find them in one set of men, he seeks them in another; if not in one section of the country, he looks to another. But it does not argue that to give the Negro a free ballot where he is in the majority, means mismanagement and financial ruin to the county or district in which he resides; for there are counties in the South, in Virginia and North Carolina, where the Negro is in the majority and where he has a free ballot,—but the illiterate and vicious do not hold the offices, and the general condition of these counties compares very favorably with those counties in which the whites have the majority and control.

Secondly: The South assumes that the reconstruction period is coequal with eternity; for this period, especially from a South Carolina point of view, is constantly brought forward to illustrate what would be the state of things in the South if the Negroes were not suppressed. In this matter it is forgotten that the schemes for plunder were not the work of black men wholly; they are more attributable to bad, vicious and unscrupulous intelligent white men than to ignorant Negroes. If good white men had taken hold of the Negro and made him an ally, many of the southern states would have been saved much of the disgrace of the reconstruction period.

But the assumption that, because the Negro, intoxicated with freedom and blinded by ignorance, was not prepared for the exercise of his franchise just after the war, is therefore not prepared for it twenty-five years afterwards (and, as some assert, will not be equal to it in a hundred years, if ever), is, to say the least, unreasonable, especially in the light of the rapid progress of the race since that time. It is my opinion that the average colored voter among the masses of the blacks is not far behind the average voter among the masses of the whites in the South; and as to plunder, a few white state officials have relieved a few southern states of more "boodle" since the war than all the Negroes appropriated during the whole reconstruction period.

That the reconstruction period operated to the detriment of the Negro and the South I will not deny; and yet that period was not without some evidence of intelligent management; for it is true, as stated by Mr. W. H. Anderson of the Detroit *Plaindealer*, in writing on this period, "That he (the Negro) established state constitutions that were models of a republican form of government; he abolished the property qualification, which opened up the ballot-box to the poor whites; he established a system of public schools, which was hitherto unknown in that section; he abolished the barbarous penal systems, established equality and uniformity of taxation; introduced the township system of self-government; and, with generous motives, removed the political disabilities of men who had fought to render slavery more secure, and who now rail at his capacity."

Thirdly: It is further assumed that the Negro is seeking social equality in demanding his constitutional rights, and that a cession of civil privileges means this.

There never was a greater mistake. The South was never more at sea on an issue. The Negro does not desire and does not seek social equality with the whites. Such an equality does not obtain among the Negroes themselves. A glance at the remarkable variety of shades of complexion among the colored people is evidence beyond doubt that the social equality tendency is not pressed by Negroes. In fact, the Negroes seek to avoid it, but it is forced upon them in a manner that corrupts both blacks and whites. The Negro in his own race has the rare privilege of choosing any color, from the snowy white to the ebony black.

The colored man or woman does not seek a seat in a car free from tobacco smoke and juice, or profanity and obscenity, or ask for a meal in a decent dining room because he desires to be in the society of whites, but because he desires comfort, protection and nourishment.

There are a great many whites whom the Negroes refuse to accept on social equality as quickly and even more quickly than these whites would hesitate to accept them.

There are states in the South where the Negro has a free ballot, and there are railroads in the South where Negroes have first-class accommodations on the cars, when they pay for it; and yet there is no more social equality in these states than in others where this right is denied.

Let me ask, in conclusion, WHAT OF THE FUTURE?

I repeat, that I have confidence not only in the better element, progressive, humane and patriotic, of the South; but I have also an unswerving faith in the appearance of a better, brighter day in that section,—a day filled with the gladdening light of freedom, prosperity and peace; for, as the South has seen some of the errors of the past, I believe it will come to discover the aggravating and retarding delusions of the present.

Not to believe in such an era is to doubt the ultimate triumph of truth over error, of right over wrong, and to question the victories of the onward sweep and universal conquest of the subduing, humanizing and eternal principles of the enlightened Christian civilization of the nineteenth century. To this end, there is nothing more essential than widespread intelligence, as well as an all-conquering, consistent Christianity.

WHAT CAN THE NORTH DO toward hastening this happy consummation? The North can help by holding tenaciously to its principles of humanity and justice, even under the spell of winsome oratory. Let the North continue to send its capital and its skill into the South to rebuild her waste places and utilize her great natural resources;—for I believe that a dollar carries with it a remarkable civilizing and humanizing influence. Let our friends in the North persist in pushing, with increased industry and unflagging ardor, the work of education among the ignorant blacks and whites in that section. Let the North insist that there be national appropriations for the education of the people.

When the North followed in the wake of the army with the spelling-book and the Bible, they then handled the key to the solution of this great problem; and we are satisfied that the work of the last twenty-five years has brought them encouragement and hope for the future. That section from which went the ideas that undermined the foundation and first threatened the fall of slavery,—that section from which marched the armies that saved the union and perpetuated human freedom; that section from which has gone millions of money to make the freeman an intelligent citizen, and the nation more secure through this intelligence,—cannot now afford to turn its back on those ideas, nor to say, or even to intimate, to the living or dead heroes of that struggle that they suffered or died in vain. For the work which those ideas started will never be completed, and the whole duty of the North never fully done until the last vestige of the peculiar institution is destroyed, and the smoking and dying embers of that fire which its hands have kindled shall have been forever extinguished.[1]

[1] J. C. Price, *The Race Problem Stated,* passim.

CHAPTER X

THE PANEGYRIC

ANOTHER form of oratory, the panegyric, has been frequently indulged in by spokesmen of all races and especially such groups as the freedmen. Gratitude is natural in man. From the Negro, then, there have been evoked such expressions of appreciation of the services of their benefactors. Many of these speeches not only reflect the thought of a race, but meet the requirements of the most elaborate orations. The distinguished dead who received such praise from the Negro orators were largely William Lloyd Garrison, the ardent abolitionist; Abraham Lincoln, the great emancipator; and Charles Sumner, the champion of human rights. These speeches as they appear here require no comment.

EULOGY OF CHARLES SUMNER[1]

BY R. B. ELLIOTT

Mr. President, Ladies and Gentlemen: The boon of a noble human life cannot be appropriated by any single nation or race. It is a part of the common wealth of the world; a treasure, a guide and an inspiration to all men in all lands and through all ages. The earthly activities of this life are circumscribed by time and space; but the divine and essential genius which informs and inspires that life is boundless in the sweep of its influence, and immortal in the energy of its activity. In the great All Hail Hereafter, in that mysterious and glorious Future, which the heart of man, touched, as I firmly believe, by a divine intimation, is ever painting with more or less of conscious fondness, those mighty spirits moving in new majesty and power on their great missions of Truth and Love, will have laid aside the limitations which fet-

[1] Delivered in Boston in Faneuil Hall in 1874.

tered them here and become the apparent and acknowledged leaders and voices of humanity itself.

Charles Sumner, in his mortal limitations, was an American; more narrowly, he was a Massachusetts man; more narrowly still, he was a white man: but today what nation shall claim him, what State shall appropriate him, what race shall boast him? He was the fair consummate flower of humanity. He was the fruit of the ages. He was the child of the Past and the promise of the Future. The whole world, could it but know its relations, would mourn his departure, and mankind everywhere would join in his honors.

But, fellow-citizens, if any fraction of humanity may claim a peculiar right to do honor to the memory of this great common benefactor of the world, surely it is the colored race in these United States. To other men his services may seem only a vast accession of strength to a cause already moving with steady and assured advance; to us, to the colored race, he is and ever will be the great leader in political life, whose ponderous and incessant blows battered down the walls of our prison house, and whose strong hand led us forth into the sunlight of Freedom. I do not seek to appropriate him to my race: but I do feel today that my race might almost bid the race to which by blood he belonged to stand aside while we to whose welfare his life was so completely given advance to do grateful honor to him who was our great Benefactor and Friend. "To the illustrious the whole world is a sepulchre." To Charles Sumner the whole civilized world has paid its honors, and now we meet to give some formal testimony of our profound reverence for the personal gifts and powers, for the measure of unselfish devotion, which he gave to *us*.

If I could on this occasion frame into articulate words the feelings of our hearts, if I could but half express the depth and sincerity of that gratitude which dwells in all our hearts, I might hope to rise to the height of the feelings of this hour. But that may not be.

This is Faneuil Hall. Here, within this venerable shelter, so fitly styled "The Cradle of Liberty," a little more than twenty-eight years ago the voice of Charles Sumner was first heard in that great warfare to which his after life was so completely devoted. His tones were trumpet-like. Listen to them: "Let Massachusetts, then, be aroused. Let all her children be summoned to this holy cause. There are questions of ordinary politics in which men may remain neutral; but neurality now is treason to liberty, to humanity, and to the fundamental principles of free institutions. * * * Massachusetts *must* continue foremost in the cause of Freedom."

Brave, glorious words! But how few then to echo them! Twenty-eight years only have passed, and here in that same Faneuil Hall that prostrate race against whose further enslavement Charles Sumner then thundered his protest and warning, have met beneath the protection of the laws not only of Massachusetts, but of the American Republic, to do honor to that splendid career then and there begun, which witnessed the final overthrow of Slavery and the citizenship of its victims throughout the Republic.

From that hour, in this Hall, in November, 1845, Charles Sumner may be said to have entered on his life-work. With what splendid equipments of mind, of heart, of body, did he advance to the conflict! No knightlier figure ever moved forth to ancient jousts. No braver heart ever enlisted in Freedom's cause. No scholarship more complete and affluent, since Milton, has placed its gifts and graces at the shrine of Justice and public Honor.

He little dreamed, I have ventured to think, of the severity of the sacrifices or the glory of the achievements which lay in the pathway on which he then entered. The mad and remorseless spirit of Slavery which then aroused his courage and drew him to the conflict, moved steadily forward to its purposes. Texas was annexed; the whole North, the entire national domain, was converted into the hunting ground of slavery; but Charles Sumner was lifted by Massachusetts into the Senate of the United States. The voice which had awakened the echoes of this historic hall in November, 1845, was transferred to that central point to rouse the sleeping conscience of the whole nation. With these vows, uttered likewise in this Hall, he entered upon his august duties in the Senate, "To vindicate Freedom and oppose Slavery, so far as I may constitutionally—with earnestness, and yet, I trust, without personal unkindness on my part—is the object near my heart. Would that my voice, leaving this crowded hall tonight, could traverse the hills and valleys of New England, that it could run along the rivers and lakes of my country, lighting in every heart a beacon-flame to arouse the slumberers throughout the land! Others may become indifferent to these principles, bartering them for political success, vain and short-lived, or forgetting the visions of youth in the dreams of age. Whenever I forget them, whenever I become indifferent to them, whenever I cease to be constant in maintaining them, through good report and evil report, in any future combinations of party, then may 'my tongue cleave to the roof of my mouth, may my right hand forget its cunning.' "

From the hour he entered the Senate the combat narrowed and deepened. The dreadful Fugitive-Slave law hung its pall over the whole land. The spirit of Slavery was omnipresent, ruling Courts, Congress, Churches. In all this fierce conflict, above the loudest din, ever sounded his courageous, clarion voice. What cause was ever honored by nobler efforts of research, of argument, of historical illustration, of classical adornments, of strong-hearted, resounding and lofty eloquence? But above all other utterances was the constant and conspicuous enunciation of the highest moral principles as applicable to all political action and duty. Hear him: "Sir, I have never been a politician. The slave of principles, I call no party master. By sentiment, education and conviction a friend of Human Rights in their utmost expansion, I have ever most sincerely embraced the Democratic Idea,—not, indeed, as represented or professed by any party, but according to its real significance, as transfigured in the Declaration of Independence and in the injunctions of Christianity. Amidst the vicissitudes of public affairs, I shall hold fast always to this idea, and to any political party that truly embraces it."

With such sentiments planted and cultivated into full growth and vigor into the very soil of his moral nature, he presented himself to the country and the world in his first Senatorial speech in August, 1852, upon the repeal of the Fugitive-Slave law. Reading that massive and noble argument again in the light of twenty years of subsequent events, how difficult to realize the prodigious moral energy which it at once demanded and displayed! The argument is ample and conclusive: the historical proofs are abundant; the eloquence is noble and affecting; but high above all rises the grandeur of the moral convictions which underlie and inspire all its wealth of argumentation and oratory. With proud and undaunted spirit he thus denounces that wicked enactment: "Sir, the Slave Act violates the Constitution and shocks the Public Conscience. With modesty, and yet with firmness, let me add, sir, it offends against the Divine Law.

"No such enactment is entitled to support. As the throne of God is above every earthly throne, so are his laws and statutes above all the laws and statutes of men. The mandates of an earthly power are to be discussed; those of Heaven must at once be performed; nor can we suffer ourselves to be drawn into any compacts in opposition to God." Words worthy, are they not, fellow-citizens, of the noblest of the martyrs and confessors of any age? One year before, his faithful friend, Theodore Parker, a name ever sacred in the hearts of those who love Freedom and Truth, had written him, "I hope you will build on the Rock of Ages and look to Eternity for your justification." How truly did he build on the Rock of Ages! Yet, while he looked to eternity, time has brought him his abundant justification!

Upon the lofty arena of the Senate he now struggled incessantly with the intellectual gladiators whom slavery ever had as her champions. The heat and din of the conflict grew greater at every step. Yet there he stood, proud, defiant, uncomplaining, aggressive. How heavy the strain on his great but sensitive nature, so finely cultured, his words of acknowledgment of the cordial support which Massachusetts ever gave him, will attest. Hear him at Worcester: "After months of constant, anxious service in another place, away from Massachusetts, I am permitted to stand among you again, my fellow-citizens, and to draw satisfaction and strength from your generous presence. Life is full of change and contrast. From slave soil I have come to free soil. From the tainted breath of slavery I have passed into the bracing air of Freedom. And the heated antagonism of debate, shooting forth its fiery cinders, is changed into this brimming, overflowing welcome, while I seem to lean on the great heart of our beloved Commonwealth, as it palpitates audibly in this crowded assembly."

A little later, Slavery, in its rapid march, assailed the time-honored barrier which the compromise of a former generation had set up against its advance over our vast Northwestern territories. Mr. Sumner was now at the height of his powers. His age was forty-three; his senatorial experience was such as to confirm his confidence in his own powers, and to concentrate upon him the confidence and admiration of the friends of Freedom. History has been to me the delight and study of my life, but I know of no figure in history which commands more of my admiration than that of Charles Sumner in the Senate of the United States, from the hour when Douglas presented his ill-omened measure for the repeal of the Missouri Compromise until the blow of the assassin laid him low. Here was the perfection of moral constancy and daring. Here was sleepless vigilance, unwearying labor, hopefulness born only of deepest faith, buoyant resolution caring nothing for human odds, but serenely abiding in the perfect peace which the unselfish service of Truth alone can bring. The issues then before the country awakened his profoundest alarm. The balance seemed to him to be about to pass from Freedom to Slavery. The American Republic, so solemnly dedicated by the Fathers to Freedom, seemed about to cut loose from all her ancient moorings. The imminence and greatness of the danger oppressed him. Listen to these words, opening that speech which seems to me perhaps the most perfect of his life, in which he first opposed the removal of the Landmark of Freedom: "Mr. President, I approach this discussion with awe. The mighty question, with untold issues, oppresses me. Like a portentous cloud, surcharged with irresistible storm and ruin, it seems to fill the whole heavens, making me painfully conscious how unequal to the occasion I am, —how unequal, also, is all that I can say to all that I feel." But listen, also, to these words of lofty cheer which fitly close the same speech, in which, rising on the wings of Faith, he looks beyond the storm raging around him, and contemplates that purer and final "UNION contemplated at the beginning, against which the storms of faction and the assaults of foreign power shall beat in vain, as upon the Rock of Ages,—and LIBERTY, seeking a firm foothold, WILL HAVE AT LAST WHEREON TO STAND AND MOVE THE WORLD."

To such a man, to a faith so clear-sighted, to a spirit so faithful to God and His Truth, no disaster or defeat, my fellow-citizens, can ever come. Victory sits forever on his trumphant crest.

And in his last final protest against that measureless wrong, see how, from the oppression of temporary defeat, he rises to joyous heights of serene moral confidence: "Sir, more clearly than ever before I now penetrate that great Future when Slavery must disappear. Proudly I discern the flag of my country, as it ripples in every breeze, at last in reality, as in name, the Flag of Freedom, —undoubted, pure, and irresistible. Sorrowfully I bend before the wrong you commit. Joyfully I welcome the promises of the Future."

But the sacred Landmark of Freedom for which he pleaded was ruthlessly swept away, and two years later the country was convulsed by the outrages of the Slave Power on the plains of Kansas. The conflict raged equally in the halls of Congress, where Slavery sought to gather the fruits of this great wrong by the organization of the territory of Kansas as a slave state.

Against this measure Charles Sumner uttered the magnificent Philippic entitled so aptly "The Crime against Kansas," thus expressing in a single phrase the moral aspects and character of that whole passage of history.

In that speech he developed new powers of denunciation and invective. From the impressive exordium beginning, "Mr. President, you are now called to redress a great wrong"—on through the ample statement, the exhaustive narrative, the irresistible argument, the fiery invective, the pathetic appeal, to those last words of the memorable peroration,—"In the name of the Heavenly Father, whose service is perfect Freedom, I make this last appeal," —he spoke with absolute fidelity to the convictions of his own heart and of the aroused conscience of the free North. It was the full discharge, aye, the explosion, of the slumbering volcano of moral indignation which slavery had aroused in thirty years of continuous and intolerable aggressions. It was the voice of the Declaration of Independence calling back the recreant sons to the faith and practice of the fathers. It was, as Whittier said, "a grand and terrible Philippic, worthy of the great occasion; the severe and awful truth which the sharp agony of the national crisis demanded." It was more than a speech, it was an event. It was more than a half battle, it was a *battle* crowned with glorious victory. It was a scene and a speech to be compared only with the great triumphs of oratory,—Demosthenes pleading for Athenian liberty, Cicero thundering against the oppressor of Sicily, Burke arraigning the Scourge of India.

But why do I thus characterize that great utterance? Two days after its delivery it received a demonstration of its quality and power more impressive and startling than any which attended the former masterpieces of human speech. Slavery, in the person of a representative in Congress from South Carolina, struck him to the floor and covered him with murderous blows. It was, as another has eloquently said, "our champion beaten to the ground for the noblest word Massachusetts ever spoke in the Senate."

The effect of this assault upon the fortunes of the two struggling powers—freedom and slavery—was significant. Each rushed to the support of its champion. Brooks was hailed throughout the South as the chivalrous exponent of slavery, while Charles Sumner ceased to be the assailant merely of slavery, and became the champion and martyr of free speech and the sacred right of parliamentary debate.

Alas—do we not still say alas—that "that noble head," as Emerson then said, "so comely and so wise, must be the target for a pair of bullies to beat with clubs!" Yet that blood was precious testimony for truth and freedom. In an instant the civilized world stood by the side of Sumner. What neither moral force, nor finished scholarship, nor commanding eloquence could do, this final brutality achieved; and from that day the hot and furious wrath of every freedom-loving heart fell upon that institution whose agent and representative had thus outraged humanity itself. America and Europe rang with a shout of horror. This historic Hall echoed with fitting words of indignant eloquence. "It is," said one still living, "it is a blow not merely at Massachusetts, a blow not merely at the name and fame of our common country; it is a blow at constitutional liberty all the world over; it is a stab at the cause of universal freedom. It is aimed at all men, everywhere, who are struggling for what we now regard as our great birthright, and which we intend to transmit unimpaired to our latest posterity. * * * Forever, forever and aye, that stain will plead in silence for liberty, wherever man is enslaved, for humanity all over the world, for truth and for justice, now and forever."

Months and years of bodily suffering followed this outrage, borne, as all his life's experiences were borne, with unsurpassed fortitude, but with longings inexpressible for a return to the activities and dangers of the conflict in which he was now the central figure. While recalling this devotion of her great Senator, let me not forget to pay a tribute to that generous and true commonwealth which he so truly represented. If Charles Sumner was faithful, so was Massachusetts. The proud State felt, and felt truly, that his vacant chair was her truest representative until he to whom it belonged should reoccupy it. While still prostrated and unable to resume his duties, Massachusetts by a vote approaching unanimity, reëlected him as her Senator,—State and Senator, true to each other, worthy of each other.

But while resting among the Alleghanies of our own country, or seeking health on foreign shores, his heart was never absent from the Great Cause. What tributes do his brief utterances bear to the unwavering fidelity of his soul! Speaking to a sympathizing friend, he says, "Oh, no. My suffering is little, in comparison with daily occurrences. The poorest slave is in danger of worse outrages every moment of his life." Again, he writes to the young men of Fitchburg, "We have been told that the 'duties of life are more than life'; and I assure you that the hardest part of my present lot is the enforced absence from public duties, and especially from that seat, where, as a Senator from Massachusetts, it is my right, and also my strong desire at this moment, to be heard."

Again he writes, "With sorrow inexpressible I am constrained to all the care and reserve of an invalid. More than four months have passed since you clasped my hand as I lay bleeding in the Senate Chamber. This is hard, very hard, for me to bear, for I long to do something, at this critical moment, for the Cause. What is life worth without action?"

Again, while lingering at Savoy, subjected to daily treatment by fire, he writes, "It is with a pang unspeakable that I find myself thus arrested in the labors of life and in the duties of my position. This is harder to bear than the fire."

No testimonies of this noble life will be more precious than these longings of this great heart for the duties of his position.

At last, on the 4th of June, 1860, he was permitted to reënter upon those scenes of Senatorial debate from which, four years before, he had been so cruelly withdrawn. Butler and Brooks were both dead. The memories of his outrage and sufferings must have filled his mind, yet see how he puts by all personal considerations and remembers only the Cause for which he is to speak: "Mr. President, I have no personal griefs to utter,—only a vulgar egotism could intrude such into this Chamber; I have no personal wrongs to avenge,—only a brutish nature could attempt to wield that vengeance which belongs to the Lord. The years that have intervened and the tombs that have opened since I spoke, have their voices, which I cannot fail to hear. Besides, what am I, what is any man among the living or among the dead, compared with the question before us?"

With these simple and yet pathetic allusions he commenced that most exhaustive delineation of the spirit, methods, and effects of slavery, which, under its singularly felicitous title, "The Barbarism of Slavery," will remain a monument of research, of invective, and of impassioned eloquence.

From this time the great drama moved rapidly to its catastrophe. The slave power writhed beneath the effect of this awful arraignment at the bar of the world's judgment. It saw in secession from the Union and the establishment of a separate slave-holding Confederacy, its only hope and safety. Abraham Lincoln became President, and in April, 1861, the bombardment of Fort Sumter in Charleston harbor sounded the tocsin of civil war throughout the land. Into that struggle Charles Sumner entered without hesitation and without alarm. His only anxiety had been to keep the North clear of the deadly spirit of compromise. Let justice be done him here. His moral equilibrium and courage were never more conspicuous. Many had joined him in his fierce assaults on slavery who now shrunk back from the gulf of war and disunion which seemed to open before them. Compromises were suggested on all sides,—compromises, too, which would have robbed freedom of all her advantage and left the slave to his hopeless bondage. Let no Negro forget,—nay, let no American forget,—that Charles Sumner never sullied his lips with degrading compromise.

Duty was his master; justice ruled him; and to every suggestion of compromise with slavery he responded, "Get thee behind me, Satan!"

His inflexible spirit may be seen in these words to Governor Andrew: "TIMEO DANAOS ET DONA FERENTES. Don't let these words be ever out of your mind, when you think of any proposition from the slave masters. *They are all essentially false, with treason in their hearts if not on their tongues.* How can it be otherwise? Slavery is a falsehood, and its supporters are all perverted and changed. Punic in faith, Punic in character, you are to meet all that they do or say with denial or distrust. I know these men and see through their plot. The time has not yet come to touch the chords which I wish to awaken. *But I see my way clear.* O, God! Let Massachusetts keep true. It is all I ask."

Again, to the same friend he writes, "More than the loss of forty forts, arsenals, or the national capital, *I fear the loss of our principles.* * * * Keep firm, and do not listen to any proposition."

Fellow-citizens, I am a Negro,—one of the victim race. My heart bows in gratitude to every man who struck a blow for the liberty of my race. But how can I fail to remember that alone, *alone,* of all the great leaders of our cause at Washington, Charles Sumner kept his faith to Freedom, stern and true. What measure of honor shall we not pay to him whose only prayer, amidst the abounding dangers of that hour, was, "Oh, God! let Massachusetts keep true"? Lincoln, Seward, Adams,—eulogy even cannot claim such absolute fidelity for either of them. History, I venture to predict, will point to this passage in the life of Charles Sumner as the highest proof of the superior and faultless tone of his moral nature. What a majestic moral figure! Let us bear it in our hearts as the crowning gift and glory of his life.

But humanity swept onward; timid compromisers were overwhelmed by the logic of events; and at last God held this great nation face to face with its duty. The death-grapple rocked and agonized the land. Released from the Delilah bands of compromise, the Samson of the North resumed and reasserted his resistless strength. In the van of every effort and policy which sought the overthrow of slavery or the triumph of freedom, was Charles Sumner: "EMANCIPATION, our best WEAPON," is the inspiriting title of a speech bearing so early a date as October 1, 1861. "Welcome to Fugitive Slaves" was a Senatorial utterance of December 4, 1861. With tireless industry, working in all directions: in legislation for the support of our armies; for maintaining our public credit; in inspiring the President to his full duty; in guarding our relations with other nations; above all, in saving the nation from the fatal mistake of Mr. Lincoln's Louisiana scheme of reconstruction, he sustained, encouraged, vindicated, and ennobled the national cause.

The triumph of the national arms in the spring of 1865 threw upon the National Government the unparalleled task of reëstablishing civil government in the rebellious States. The work of destruction was ended, and the work of rebuilding must be begun. The ill-advised and ill-starred attempts of Andrew Johnson complicated the problem already bristling with difficulties, constitutional and legal, and beset with dangers, political and moral. The moral intrepidity and prescience of Mr. Sumner was earliest to detect the false political theories which then so widely prevailed. With wonted boldness he denounced the Presidential scheme of reconstruction, and summoned Congress and the country to its duty. In a series of Senatorial efforts he proclaimed and emphasized in the ear of the nation the paramount duty of guarding the results of the war by "irreversible constitutional guarantees." Especially did he denounce the injustice and wickedness of any settlement which left the colored race of the South under the hands of their former masters. This was an axiom in his arguments, the postulate of his reasonings. From this starting point he readily reached that conclusion, finally accepted by the country and enacted into our national laws and Constitution, that the colored race must be made citizens of the United States and voters in their respective States. The Declaration of Independence, with its lofty and immortal truth—"All men are created FREE and EQUAL,"—was to him a clear and constant guide. In this grand, germinal truth he saw the only true and final rule of government, and he pressed towards its practical realization with eager and unfaltering steps. He had heard this sacred tenet of the Fathers flouted in the Senate as a "self-evident lie," but he only bore it the more proudly and conspicuously on his shield until he could gratefully say, "The Declaration of Independence, so lately a dishonored tradition, is now the rubric and faith of the Republic." God be praised! He found at last that *"Union, where Liberty, seeking a firm foothold, might have whereon to stand and move the world."*

Once only in all this splendid and faithful career did Charles Sumner part company with the great mass of the friends of Freedom, and on this he needs no silence. Differing, as I could not but differ, from his judgment in the last national campaign, I point to it today as one of the highest proofs of his utter devotion to the call of duty. Still was he true, utterly true, to his convictions, to the commanding voice of Conscience. He had been faithful in defeat; could he be faithful in success? Draw no veil of silence over this passage; but write it high on his monument,—that in old age, when the weary frame longed for repose, he could again brace himself for the conflict in which nearly all of the friends of a lifetime stood arrayed against him.

> "Nothing is here for tears; nothing to wail
> Or knock the breast; no weakness, no contempt,
> Dispraise or blame; nothing but well and fair."

As his life was wholly consecrated to duty, so his death was wanting in no element of moral grandeur. He fell with armor on, with face still inflexibly turned towards present duties, fronting eternity with the simple trust which God gives to his faithful servant. With no vague dread or anxiety concerning the future, he bore his earthly cares and duties to the threshold of eternity, and laid down the burdens of life only at the feet of his Divine Master. "Don't let my Civil-Rights Bill fail," was his fitting adieu to earth and greetings to Heaven.

Fellow-citizens, the life of Charles Sumner needs no interpreter. It is an open, illuminated page. The ends he aimed at were always high; the means he used were always direct. Neither deception nor indirection, neither concealment nor disguise of any kind or degree, had place in his nature or methods. By open means he sought open ends. He walked in the sunlight, and wrote his heart's inmost purpose on his forehead.

His activity and capacity of intellectual labor was almost unequaled. Confined somewhat by the overshadowing nature of the antislavery cause in the range of his topics, he multiplied his blows and redoubled the energy of his assaults upon that great enemy of his country's peace. Here his vigor knew no bounds. He laid all ages and lands under contribution. Scholarship in all its walks—history, art, literature, science—all these he made his aids and servitors.

But who does not see that these are not his glory? He was a scholar among scholars; an orator of consummate power; a statesman familiar with the structure of governments and the social forces of the world. But he was greater and better than one or all of these: he was a man of *absolute rectitude of purpose and of life.* His personal purity was perfect and unquestioned everywhere. He carried morals into politics. And this is the *greatness* of Charles Sumner,—that by the power of his moral enthusiasm he rescued the nation from its shameful subservience to the demands of material and commercial interests, and guided it up to the high plane of justice and right. Above his other great qualities towers that moral greatness to which scholarship, oratory, and statesmanship are but secondary and insignificant. He was just because he *loved* justice; he was right because he *loved* right. Let this be his record and epitaph.

To have lived such a life was glory enough. Success was not needed to perfect its star-bright, immortal beauty. But success came. What amazing contrasts did his life witness! He heard the hundred guns which Boston fired for the passage of the Fugitive-Slave act; and he saw Boston sending forth, with honors and blessings, a regiment of fugitive slaves to save that Union which the crime of her Webster had imperiled. He saw Franklin Pierce employing the power of the nation to force back one helpless fugitive to the hell of slavery; and he saw Abraham Lincoln write the edict of Emancipation. He heard Taney declare that "the black man had no rights which the white man was bound to respect"; and he welcomed Revels to his seat as a Senator of the United States.

But as defeat could not damp his ardor, so success could not abate his zeal. He fell while bearing aloft the same banner of human rights which, twenty-eight years before, he had unfurled and lifted in this hall.

The blessings of the poor are his laurels. One sacred thought, duty,—presided over his life, inspiring him in youth, guiding him in manhood, strengthening him in age. Be it ours to walk by the light of this pure example. Be it ours to copy this stainless integrity, his supreme devotion to humanity, his profound faith in truth, and his unconquerable moral enthusiasm.

Adieu! great Servant and Apostle of Liberty! If others forget thee, thy fame shall be guarded by the millions of that emancipated race whose gratitude shall be more enduring than monumental marble or brass.

AN ORATION IN MEMORY OF ABRAHAM LINCOLN[1]

By Frederick Douglass

Friends and Fellow-citizens:

I warmly congratulate you upon the highly interesting object which has caused you to assemble in such numbers and spirit as you have today. This occasion is in some respects remarkable. Wise and thoughtful men of our race, who shall come after us, and study the lesson of our history in the United States; who shall survey the long and dreary spaces over which we have traveled; who shall count the links in the great chain of events by which we have reached our present position, will make a note of this occasion; they will think of it and speak of it with a sense of manly pride and complacency.

I congratulate you, also, upon the very favorable circumstances in which we meet today. They are high, inspiring, and uncommon. They lend grace, glory, and significance to the object for which we have met. Nowhere else in this great country, with its uncounted towns and cities, unlimited wealth, and immeasurable territory extending from sea to sea, could conditions be found more favorable to the success of this occasion than here.

We stand today at the national center to perform something like a national act—an act which is to go into history; and we are here where every pulsation of the national heart can be heard, felt, and reciprocated. A thousand wires, fed with thought and winged with lightning, put us in instantaneous communication with the loyal and true men all over this country.

Few facts could better illustrate the vast and wonderful change which has taken place in our condition as a people than the fact of our assembling here for the purpose we have today. Harmless, beautiful, proper, and praiseworthy as this demonstration is, I cannot forget that no such demonstration would have been tolerated here twenty years ago. The spirit of slavery and barbarism,

[1] This oration was delivered by Frederick Douglass on the occasion of the unveiling of the Freedmen's Monument in memory of Abraham Lincoln, in Lincoln Park, Washington, D. C., April 14, 1876.

which still lingers to blight and destroy in some dark and distant parts of our country, would have made our assembling here the signal and excuse for opening upon us all the flood-gates of wrath and violence. That we are here in peace today is a compliment and a credit to American civilization, and a prophecy of still greater national enlightenment and progress in the future. I refer to the past not in malice, for this is no day for malice; but simply to place more distinctly in front the gratifying and glorious change which has come both to our white fellow-citizens and ourselves, and to congratulate all upon the contrast between now and then; the new dispensation of freedom with its thousand blessings to both races, and the old dispensation of slavery with its ten thousand evils to both races—white and black. In view, then, of the past, the present, and the future, with the long and dark history of our bondage behind us, and with liberty, progress, and enlightenment before us, I again congratulate you upon this auspicious day and hour.

Friends and fellow-citizens, the story of our presence here is soon and easily told. We are here in the District of Columbia, here in the city of Washington, the most luminous point of American territory; a city recently transformed and made beautiful in its body and in its spirit; we are here in the place where the ablest and best men of the country are sent to devise the policy, enact the laws, and shape the destiny of the Republic; we are here, with the stately pillars and majestic dome of the Capitol of the nation looking down upon us; we are here, with the broad earth freshly adorned with the foliage and flowers of spring for our church, and all races, colors, and conditions of men for our congregation—in a word, we are here to express, as best we may, by appropriate forms and ceremonies, our grateful sense of the vast, high, and preëminent services rendered to ourselves, to our race, to our country, and to the whole world by Abraham Lincoln.

The sentiment that brings us here to-day is one of the noblest that can stir and thrill the human heart. It has crowned and made glorious the high places of all civilized nations with the grandest and most enduring works of art, designed to illustrate the characters and perpetuate the memories of great public men. It is the sentiment which from year to year adorns with fragrant and beautiful flowers the graves of our loyal, brave, and patriotic soldiers who fell in defence of the Union and liberty. It is the sentiment of gratitude and appreciation, which often, in the presence of many who hear me, has filled yonder heights of Arlington with the eloquence of eulogy and the sublime enthusiasm of poetry and song; a sentiment which can never die while the Republic lives.

For the first time in the history of our people, and in the history of the whole American people, we join in this high worship, and march conspicuously in the line of this time-honored custom. First things are always interesting, and this is one of our first things. It is the first time that, in this form and manner, we have sought to do honor to an American great man, however deserving and illustrious. I commend the fact to notice; let it be told in every part of the Republic; let men of all parties and opinions hear it; let those who despise us, not less than those who respect us, know that now and here, in the spirit of liberty, loyalty, and gratitude, let it be known everywhere, and by everybody who takes an interest in human progress and in the amelioration of the condition of mankind, that, in the presence and with the approval of the members of the American House of Representatives, reflecting the general sentiment of the country; that in the presence of that august body, the American Senate, representing the highest intelligence and the calmest judgment of the country; in the presence of the Supreme Court and Chief-Justice of the United States, to whose decisions we all patriotically bow; in the presence and under the steady eye of the honored and trusted President of the United States, with the members of his wise and patriotic Cabinet, we, the colored people, newly emancipated and rejoicing in our blood-bought freedom, near the close of the first century in the life of this Republic, have now and here unveiled, set apart, and dedicated a monument of enduring granite and bronze, in every line, feature, and figure of which the men of this generation may read, and those of after-coming generations may read, something of the exalted character and great works of Abraham Lincoln, the first martyr President of the United States.

Fellow-citizens, in what we have said and done today, and in what we may say and do hereafter, we disclaim everything like arrogance and assumption. We claim for ourselves no superior devotion to the character, history, and memory of the illustrious name whose monument we have here dedicated today. We fully comprehend the relation of Abraham Lincoln both to ourselves and to the white people of the United States. Truth is proper and beautiful at all times and in all places, and it is never more proper and beautiful in any case than when speaking of a great public man whose example is likely to be commended for honor and imitation long after his departure to the solemn shades, the silent continents of eternity. It must be admitted, truth compels me to admit, even here in the presence of the monument we have erected to his memory, Abraham Lincoln was not, in the fullest sense of the word, either our man or our model. In his interests, in his associations, in his habits of thought, and in his prejudices, he was a white man.

He was preëminently the white man's President, entirely devoted to the welfare of white men. He was ready and willing at any time during the first years of his administration to deny, postpone, and sacrifice the rights of humanity in the colored people to promote the welfare of the white people of this country. In all his education and feeling he was an American of the Americans. He came into the Presidential chair upon one principle alone, namely, opposition to the extension of slavery. His arguments in furtherance of this policy had their motive and mainspring in his patriotic devotion to the interests of his own race. To protect, defend, and perpetuate slavery in the states where it existed Abraham Lincoln was not less ready than any other President to draw the sword of the nation. He was ready to execute all the supposed guarantees of the United States Constitution in favor of the slave system anywhere inside the slave states. He was willing to pursue, recapture, and send back the fugitive slave to his master, and to suppress a slave rising for liberty, though his guilty master were already in arms against the Government. The race to which we belong were not the special objects of his consideration. Knowing this, I concede to you, my white fellow-citizens, a preëminence in this worship at once full and supreme. First, midst, and last, you and yours were the objects of his deepest affection and his most earnest solicitude. You are the children of Abraham Lincoln. We are at best only his step-children; children by adoption, children by forces of circumstances and necessity. To you it especially belongs to sound his praises, to preserve and perpetuate his memory, to multiply his statues, to hang his pictures high upon your walls, and commend his example, for to you he was a great and glorious friend and benefactor. Instead of supplanting you at his altar, we would exhort you to build high his monuments; let them be of the most costly material, of the most cunning workmanship; let their forms be symmetrical, beautiful, and perfect; let their bases be upon solid rocks, and their summits lean against the unchanging blue, overhanging sky, and let them endure forever! But while in the abundance of your wealth, and in the fullness of your just and patriotic devotion, you do all this, we entreat you to despise not the humble offering we this day unveil to view; for while Abraham Lincoln saved for you a country, he delivered us from a bondage, according to Jefferson, one hour of which was worse than ages of the oppression your fathers rose in rebellion to oppose.

Fellow-citizens, ours is no new-born zeal and devotion—merely a thing of this moment. The name of Abraham Lincon was near and dear to our hearts in the darkest and most perilous hours of the Republic. We were no more ashamed of him when shrouded in clouds of darkness, of doubt, and defeat than when we saw him crowned with victory, honor, and glory. Our faith in him was often taxed and strained to the uttermost, but it never failed. When he tarried long in the mountain; when he strangely told us that we were the cause of the war; when he still more strangely told us that we were to leave the land in which we were born; when he refused to employ our arms in defence of the Union; when, after accepting our services as colored soldiers, he refused to retaliate our murder and torture as colored prisoners; when he told us he would save the Union if he could with slavery; when he revoked the Proclamation of Emancipation of General Fremont; when he refused to remove the popular commander of the Army of the Potomac, in the days of its inaction and defeat, who was more zealous in his efforts to protect slavery than to suppress rebellion; when we saw all this, and more, we were at times grieved, stunned, and greatly bewildered; but our hearts believed while they ached and bled. Nor was this, even at that time, a blind and unreasoning superstition. Despite the mist and haze that surrounded him; despite the tumult, the hurry, and confusion of the hour, we were able to take a comprehensive view of Abraham Lincoln, and to make reasonable allowance for the circumstances of his position. We saw him, measured him, and estimated him; not by stray utterances to injudicious and tedious delegations, who often tried his patience; not by isolated facts torn from their connection; not by any partial and imperfect glimpses, caught at inopportune moments; but by a broad survey, in the light of the stern logic of great events, and in view of that divinity which shapes our ends, rough hew them how we will, we came to the conclusion that the hour and the man of our redemption had somehow met in the person of Abraham Lincoln. It mattered little to us what language he might employ on special occasions; it mattered little to us, when we fully knew him, whether he was swift or slow in his movements; it was enough for us that Abraham Lincoln was at the head of a great movement, and was in living and earnest sympathy with that movement, which, in the nature of things, must go on until slavery should be utterly and forever abolished in the United States.

When, therefore, it shall be asked what we have to do with the memory of Abraham Lincoln, or what Abraham Lincoln had to do with us, the answer is ready, full, and complete. Though he loved Cæsar less than Rome, though the Union was more to him than our freedom or our future, under his wise and beneficent rule we saw ourselves gradually lifted from the depths of slavery to the heights of liberty and manhood; under his wise and beneficent rule, and by measures approved and vigorously pressed by him, we saw that the handwriting of ages, in the form of prejudice and proscription, was rapidly fading away from the face of our whole country; under his rule, and in due time, about as soon after all as the country could tolerate the strange spectacle, we saw our brave sons and brothers laying off the rags of bondage, and being clothed all over in the blue uniforms of the soldiers of the United States; under his rule we saw two hundred thousand of our dark and dusky people responding to the call of Abraham Lincoln, and with muskets on their shoulders, and eagles on their buttons, timing their high footsteps to liberty and union under the national flag; under his rule we saw the independence of the black republic of Hayti, the special object of slaveholding aversion and horror, fully recognized, and her minister, a colored gentleman, duly received here in the city of Washington; under his rule we saw the internal slave-trade, which so long disgraced the nation, abolished, and slavery abolished in the District of Columbia; under his rule we saw for the first time the law enforced against the foreign slave-trade, and the first slave-trader hanged like any other pirate or murderer; under his rule, assisted by the greatest captain of our age, and his inspiration, we saw the Confederate States, based upon the idea that our race must be slaves, and slaves forever, battered to pieces and scattered to the four winds; under his rule, and in the fullness of time, we saw Abraham Lincoln, after giving the slaveholders three months' grace in which to save their hateful slave system, penning the immortal paper, which, though special in its language, was general in its principles and effect, making slavery forever impossible in the United States. Though we waited long, we saw all this and more.

Can any colored man, or any white man friendly to the freedom of all men, ever forget the night which followed the first day of January, 1863, when the world was to see if Abraham Lincoln would prove to be as good as his word? I shall never forget that memorable night, when in a distant city I waited and watched at a public meeting, with three thousand others not less anxious than myself, for the word of deliverance which we have heard read today. Nor shall I ever forget the outburst of joy and thanksgiving that rent the air when the lightning brought to us the emancipation proclamation. In that happy hour we forgot all delay, and forgot all tardiness, forgot that the President had bribed the rebels to lay down their arms by a promise to withhold the bolt which would smite the slave-system with destruction; and we were thenceforward willing to allow the President all the latitude of time, phraseology, and every honorable device that statesmanship might require for the achievement of a great and beneficent measure of liberty and progress.

Fellow-citizens, there is little necessity on this occasion to speak at length and critically of this great and good man, and of his high mission in the world. That ground has been fully occupied and completely covered both here and elsewhere. The whole field of fact and fancy has been gleaned and garnered. Any man can say things that are true of Abraham Lincoln, but no man can say anything that is new of Abraham Lincoln. His personal traits and public acts are better known to the American people than are those of any other man of his age. He was a mystery to no man who saw him and heard him. Though high in position, the humblest could approach him and feel at home in his presence. Though deep, he was transparent; though strong, he was gentle; though decided and pronounced in his convictions, he was tolerant towards those who differed from him, and patient under reproaches. Even those who only knew him through his public utterances obtained a tolerably clear idea of his character and personality. The image of the man went out with his words, and those who read them knew him.

I have said that President Lincoln was a white man, and shared the prejudices common to his countrymen towards the colored race. Looking back to his times and to the condition of his country, we are compelled to admit that this unfriendly feeling on his part may be safely set down as one element of his wonderful success in organizing the loyal American people for the tremendous conflict before them, and bringing them safely through that conflict. His great mission was to accomplish two things: first, to save his country from dismemberment and ruin; and, second, to free his country from the great crime of slavery. To do one or the other, or both, he must have the earnest sympathy and the powerful coöperation of his loyal fellow-countrymen. Without this primary and essential condition to success his efforts must have been vain and utterly fruitless. Had he put the abolition of slavery before the salvation of the Union, he would have inevitably driven from him a powerful class of the American people and rendered resistance to rebellion impossible. Viewed from the genuine abolition ground, Mr. Lincoln seemed tardy, cold, dull, and indifferent; but measuring him by the sentiment of his country, a sentiment he was bound as a statesman to consult, he was swift, zealous, radical, and determined.

Though Mr. Lincoln shared the prejudices of his white fellow-countrymen against the Negro, it is hardly necessary to say that in his heart of hearts he loathed and hated slavery. . . .[1] The man who could say, "Fondly do we hope, fervently do we pray, that this mighty scourge of war shall soon pass away, yet if God wills it continue till all the wealth piled by two hundred years of bondage shall have been wasted, and each drop of blood drawn by the lash shall have been paid for by one drawn by the sword, the

[1] "I am naturally anti-slavery. If slavery is not wrong, nothing is wrong. I cannot remember when I did not so think and feel."—*Letter of Mr. Lincoln to Mr. Hodges, of Kentucky, April 4, 1864.*

judgments of the Lord are true and righteous altogether,'' gives all needed proof of his feeling on the subject of slavery. He was willing, while the South was loyal, that it should have its pound of flesh, because he thought that it was so nominated in the bond; but farther than this no earthly power could make him go.

Fellow-citizens, whatever else in this world may be partial, unjust, and uncertain, time, time! is impartial, just, and certain in its action. In the realm of mind, as well as in the realm of matter, it is a great worker, and often works wonders. The honest and comprehensive statesman, clearly discerning the needs of his country, and earnestly endeavoring to do his whole duty, though covered and blistered with reproaches, may safely leave his course to the silent judgment of time. Few great public men have ever been the victims of fiercer denunciation than Abraham Lincoln was during his administration. He was often wounded in the house of his friends. Reproaches came thick and fast upon him from within and from without, and from opposite quarters. He was assailed by Abolitionists; he was assailed by slaveholders; he was assailed by the men who were for peace at any price; he was assailed by those who were for a more vigorous prosecution of the war; he was assailed for not making the war an abolition war; and he was bitterly assailed for making the war an abolition war.

But now behold the change: the judgment of the present hour is, that taking him for all in all, measuring the tremendous magnitude of the work before him, considering the necessary means to ends, and surveying the end from the beginning, infinite wisdom has seldom sent any man into the world better fitted for his mission than Abraham Lincoln. His birth, his training, and his natural endowments, both mental and physical, were strongly in his favor. Born and reared among the lowly, a stranger to wealth and luxury, compelled to grapple single-handed with the flintiest hardships of life, from tender youth to sturdy manhood, he grew strong in the manly and heroic qualities demanded by the great mission to which he was called by the votes of his countrymen. The hard condition of his early life, which would have depressed and broken down weaker men, only gave greater life, vigor, and buoyancy to the heroic spirit of Abraham Lincoln. He was ready for any kind and any quality of work. What other young men dreaded in the shape of toil, he took hold of with the utmost cheerfulness.

"A spade, a rake, a hoe,
A pick-axe, or a bill;
A hook to reap, a scythe to mow,
A flail, or what you will."

All day long he could split heavy rails in the woods, and half the night long he could study his English Grammar by the uncertain flare and glare of the light made by a pine-knot. He was at home on the land with his axe, with his maul, with gluts, and his wedges; and he was equally at home on water, with his oars, with his poles, with his planks, and with his boat-hooks. And whether in his flat-boat on the Mississippi River, or at the fireside of his frontier cabin, he was a man of work. A son of toil himself, he was linked in brotherly sympathy with the sons of toil in every loyal part of the Republic. This very fact gave him tremendous power with the American people, and materially contributed not only to selecting him to the Presidency, but in sustaining his administration of the Government.

Upon his inauguration as President of the United States, an office, even when assumed under the most favorable conditions, fitted to tax and strain the largest abilities, Abraham Lincoln was met by a tremendous crisis. He was called upon not merely to administer the Government, but to decide, in the face of terrible odds, the fate of the Republic.

A formidable rebellion rose in his path before him; the Union was already practically dissolved; his country was torn and rent asunder at the center. Hostile armies were already organized against the Republic, armed with the munitions of war which the Republic had provided for its own defence. The tremendous question for him to decide was whether his country should survive the crisis and flourish, or be dismembered and perish. His predecessor in office had already decided the question in favor of national dismemberment, by denying to it the right of self-defence and self-preservation—a right which belongs to the meanest insect.

Happily for the country, happily for you and for me, the judgment of James Buchanan, the patrician, was not the judgment of Abraham Lincoln, the plebeian. He brought his strong common sense, sharpened in the school of adversity, to bear upon the question. He did not hesitate, he did not doubt, he did not falter; but at once resolved that at whatever peril, at whatever cost, the union of the States should be preserved. A patriot himself, his faith was strong and unwavering in the patriotism of his countrymen. Timid men said before Mr. Lincoln's inauguration, that we had seen the last President of the United States. A voice in influential quarters said, "Let the Union slide." Some said that a Union maintained by the sword was worthless. Others said a rebellion of 8,000,000 cannot be suppressed; but in the midst of all this tumult and timidity, and against all this, Abraham Lincoln was clear in his duty, and had an oath in heaven. He calmly and bravely heard the voice of doubt and fear all around him; but he had an oath in heaven, and there was not power enough on earth to make this honest boatman, back-woodsman, and broad-handed splitter of rails evade or violate that sacred oath. He had not been schooled in the ethics of slavery; his plain life had favored his love of truth. He had not been taught that treason and perjury were the proof of honor and honesty. His moral training was against his saying one thing when he meant another. The trust that Abraham Lincoln had in himself and in the people was surprising and grand, but it was also enlightened and well founded. He knew the American people better than they knew themselves, and his truth was based upon this knowledge.

Fellow-citizens, the fourteenth day of April, 1865, of which this is the eleventh anniversary, is now and will ever remain a memorable day in the annals of this Republic. It was on the evening of this day, while a fierce and sanguinary rebellion was in the last stages of its desolating power; while its armies were broken and scattered before the invincible armies of Grant and Sherman; while a great nation, torn and rent by war, was already beginning to raise to the skies loud anthems of joy at the dawn of peace, it was startled, amazed, and overwhelmed by the crowning crime of slavery—the assassination of Abraham Lincoln. It was a new crime, a pure act of malice. No purpose of the rebellion was to be served by it. It was the simple gratification of a hell-black spirit of revenge. But it has done good after all. It has filled the country with a deeper abhorrence of slavery and a deeper love for the great liberator.

Had Abraham Lincoln died from any of the numerous ills to

which flesh is heir; had he reached that good old age of which his vigorous constitution and his temperate habits gave promise; had he been permitted to see the end of his great work; had the solemn curtain of death come down but gradually—we should still have been smitten with a heavy grief, and treasured his name lovingly. But dying as he did die, by the red hand of violence, killed, assassinated, taken off without warning, not because of personal hate—for no man who knew Abraham Lincoln could hate him—but because of his fidelity to union and liberty, he is doubly dear to us, and his memory will be precious forever.

Fellow-citizens, I end, as I began, with congratulations. We have done a good work for our race today. In doing honor to the memory of our friend and liberator, we have been doing highest honors to ourselves and those who come after us; we have been fastening ourselves to a name and fame imperishable and immortal; we have also been defending ourselves from a blighting scandal. When now it shall be said that the colored man is soulless, that he has no appreciation of benefits or benefactors; when the foul reproach of ingratitude is hurled at us, and it is attempted to scourge us beyond the range of human brotherhood, we may calmly point to the monument we have this day erected to the memory of Abraham Lincoln.

ADDRESS DELIVERED AT THE DEDICATION OF THE ROBERT GOULD SHAW MONUMENT IN BOSTON, MAY 31, 1897

By Booker T. Washington

Mr. Chairman and Fellow Citizens: In this presence, and on this sacred and memorable day, in the deeds and death of our hero, we recall the old, old story, ever old, yet ever new, that when it was the will of the Father to lift humanity out of wretchedness and bondage, the precious task was delegated to him who among ten thousand was altogether lovely, and was willing to make himself of no reputation that he might save and lift up others.

If that heart could throb and those lips could speak, what would be the sentiment and words that Robert Gould Shaw would have us feel and speak at this hour? He would not have us to dwell long on the mistakes, the injustice, the criticisms of the days—

"Of storm and cloud, of doubt and fears,
Which across the eternal sky must lower,
Before the glorious noon appears."

He would have us bind up with his own undying fame and memory and retain by the side of his monument, the name of John A. Andrew, who, with prophetic vision and strong arm, helped to make the existence of the 54th regiment possible; and that of George L. Stearns, who, with hidden generosity and a great, sweet heart, helped to turn the darkest hour into day, and in doing so freely gave service, fortune and life itself to the cause which this day commemorates. Nor would he have us forget those brother officers, living and dead, who, by their baptism in blood and fire, in defense of Union and freedom, gave us an example of the highest and purest patriotism.

To you who fought so valiantly in the ranks, the scarred and scattered remnant of the 54th regiment, who with empty sleeve and wanting leg, have honored this occasion with your presence, to you your commander is not dead. Though Boston erected no monument and history recorded no story, in you and the loyal race you represent, Robert Gould Shaw would have a monument which time could not wear away.

But an occasion like this is too great, too sacred for mere individual eulogy. The individual is the instrument, national virtue the end. That which was 300 years being woven into the warp and woof of our democratic institutions could not be effaced by a single battle, as magnificent as was that battle; that which for three centuries had bound master and slave, yea, North and South, to a body of death, could not be blotted out by four years of war, could not be atoned for by shot and sword, nor by blood and tears.

Not many days ago, in the heart of the South, in a large gathering of the people of my race, there were heard from many lips praises and thanksgiving to God for his goodness in setting them free from physical slavery. In the midst of that assembly a Southern white man arose, with gray hair and trembling hands, the former owner of many slaves, and from his quivering lips there came the words: "My friends, you forget in your rejoicing that in setting you free, God was also good to me and my race in setting us free." But there is a higher and deeper sense in which both races must be free than that represented by the bill of sale. The black man who cannot let love and sympathy go out to the white man is but half free. The white man who would close the shop or factory against a black man seeking an honest living is but half free. The white man who retards his own development by opposing a black man is but half free. The full measure of the fruit of Fort Wagner and all this monument stands for will not be realized until every man covered with a black skin shall by patient and natural effort, grow to that height in industry, property, intelligence and moral responsibility, where no man in all our land will be tempted to degrade himself by withholding from his black brother any opportunity which he himself would possess.

Until that time comes this monument will stand for effort, not victory complete. What these heroic souls of the 54th regiment began we must complete. It must be completed not in malice, not in narrowness; nor artificial progress, nor in efforts at mere temporary political gain, nor in abuse of another section or race. Standing as I do today in the home of Garrison and Phillips and Sumner, my heart goes out to those who wore the gray as well as to those clothed in the blue; to those who returned defeated, to destitute homes, to face blasted hopes and a shattered political and industrial system. To them there can be no prouder reward for defeat than by a supreme effort to place the Negro on that footing where he will add material, intellectual and civil strength to every department of the State.

This work must be completed in the public school, industrial school and college. The most of it must be completed in the effort of the Negro himself, in his effort to withstand temptation, to economize, to exercise thrift, to disregard the superficial for the real, the shadow for the substance, to be great and yet small, in his effort to be patient in the laying of a firm foundation, to grow so strong in skill and knowledge that he shall place his service in demand by reason of his intrinsic and superior worth. All this makes the key that unlocks every door of opportunity, and all others fail. In this battle of peace the rich and poor, the black and white may have a part.

What lessons has this occasion for the future? What of hope, what of encouragement, what of caution? "Watchman, tell us of the night; what the signs of promise are." If through me, an humble representative, nearly ten millions of my people might be permitted to send a message to Massachusetts, to the survivors of the 54th regiment, to the committee whose untiring energy has made this memorial possible, to the family who gave their only boy that we might have life more abundantly, that message would be, "Tell them that the sacrifice was not in vain, that up from the depth of ignorance and poverty we are coming, and if we come through oppression out of the struggle, we are gaining strength. By the way of the school, the well-cultivated field, the skilled hand, the Christian home, we are coming up; that we propose to invite all who will to step up and occupy this position with us. Tell them that we are learning that standing ground for a race, as for an individual, must be laid in intelligence, industry, thrift and property, not as an end, but as a means to the highest privileges; that we are learning that neither the conqueror's bullet nor the fiat of law could make an ignorant voter an intelligent voter, could make a dependent man an independent man, could give one citizen respect for another, a bank account, nor a foot of land, nor an enlightened fireside. Tell them that as grateful as we are to artist and patriotism for placing the figures of Shaw and his comrades in physical form of beauty and magnificence, that, after all, the real monument, the greater monument, is being slowly but safely builded among the lowly in the South, in the struggles and sacrifices of a race to justify all that has been done and suffered for it.

One of the wishes that lay nearest Colonel Shaw's heart was, that his black troops might be permitted to fight by the side of the white soldiers. Have we not lived to see that wish realized, and will it not be more so in the future? Not at Wagner, not with rifle and bayonet, but on the field of peace, in the battle of industry, in the struggle for good government, in the lifting up of the lowest to the fullest opportunities. In this we shall fight by the side of the white man, North and South. And if this be true, as under God's guidance it will, that old flag, that emblem of progress and security, which brave Sergeant Carney never permitted to fall to the ground, will still be borne aloft by Southern soldier and Northern soldier, and, in a more potent and higher sense, we shall all realize that—

> "The slave's chain and the master's alike broken;
> The one curse of the race held both in tether;
> They are rising, all are rising—
> The black and the white together."

WILLIAM LLOYD GARRISON: A CENTENNIAL ORATION[1]

By Reverdy C. Ransom[2]

Friends, Citizens: We have assembled here tonight to celebrate the one hundredth birth of William Lloyd Garrison. Not far from this city he was born. Within the gates of this city, made famous by some of America's most famous men, he spent more than two-thirds of his long and eventful career, enriching its history and adding to the glory of its renown. This place, of all places, is in keeping with the hour. It is most appropriate that we should meet in Faneuil Hall, the cradle of American liberty, a spot hallowed and made sacred by the statesmen, soldiers, orators, scholars, and reformers who have given expression to burning truths and found a hearing within these walls. Of all people it is most fitting that the Negro Americans of Boston should be the ones to take the lead in demonstrating to their fellow-citizens, and to the world, that his high character is cherished with affection, and the priceless value of his unselfish labors in their behalf shall forever be guarded as a sacred trust.

Only succeeding generations and centuries can tell the carrying power of a man's life. Some men, whose contemporaries thought their title to enduring fame secure, have not been judged worthy

[1] Delivered in Faneuil Hall, Boston, December 10, 1905.

[2] Bishop Reverdy C. Ransom early connected himself with the African Methodist Episcopal Church to which he owes most of the honors which he has enjoyed. He was educated at Wilberforce University. After serving in several large cities as pastor of popular churches, he became the editor of the *African Methodist Episcopal Review* which he ably edited until 1924 when he was chosen and consecrated Bishop of his denomination.

As an orator, Bishop Ransom has few equals. His addresses are not mere outbursts of eloquence, but show the conviction of the man as to the claims of the Negro to recognition in this country and the procedure to be followed in reaching this end. He has, therefore, taken the advanced position of espousing forward-looking movements securing to the Negro the rights which have been denied him by the reactionaries now in control of the State and Federal governments.

in a later time to have their names recorded among the makers of history. Some men are noted, some are distinguished, some are famous,—only a few are great.

The men whose deeds are born to live in history do not appear more than once or twice in a century. Of the millions of men who toil and strive, the number is not large whose perceptible influence reaches beyond the generation in which they lived. It does not take long to call the roll of honor of any generation, and when this roll is put to the test of the unprejudiced scrutiny of a century, only a very small and select company have sufficient carrying power to reach into a second century. When the roll of the centuries is called, we may mention almost in a single breath the names which belong to the ages. Abraham and Moses stand out clearly against the horizon of thirty centuries. St. Paul, from his Roman prison, in the days of the Cæsars, is still an articulate and authoritative voice; Savonarola, rising from the ashes of his funeral-pyre in the streets of Florence, still pleads for civic righteousness; the sound of Martin Luther's hammer nailing his thesis to the door of his Wittenburg church continues to echo around the world; the battle-cry of Cromwell's Ironsides shouting, "The Lord of Hosts!" still causes the tyrant and the despot to tremble upon their thrones; out of the fire and blood of the French Revolution, "Liberty and Equality" survive; Abraham Lincoln comes from the backwoods of Kentucky, and the prairies of Illinois, to receive the approval of all succeeding generations of mankind for his Proclamation of Emancipation; John Brown was hung at Harper's Ferry that his soul might go marching on in the tread of every Northern regiment that fought for the "Union forever"; William Lloyd Garrison, mobbed in the streets of Boston for pleading the cause of the slave, lived to see freedom triumph, and tonight, a century after his birth, his name is cherished, not only in America, but around the world, wherever men aspire to individual liberty and personal freedom.

William Lloyd Garrison was in earnest. He neither temporized nor compromised with the enemies of human freedom. He gave up all those comforts, honors, and rewards which his unusual talents would easily have won for him in behalf of the cause of freedom which he espoused. He stood for righteousness with all the rugged strength of a prophet. Like some Elijah of the Gilead forests, he pleaded with this nation to turn away from the false gods it had enshrined upon the altars of human liberty. Like some John the Baptist crying in the wilderness, he called upon this nation to repent of its sin of human slavery, and to bring forth the fruits of its repentance in immediate emancipation.

William Lloyd Garrison was born in Newburyport, Mass., Dec. 10, 1805. He came of very poor and obscure parentage. His father, who was a seafaring man, early abandoned the family for causes supposed to relate to his intemperance. The whole career of Garrison was a struggle against poverty. His educational advantages were limited. He became a printer's apprentice when quite a lad, and learned the printing trade. When he launched his paper, *The Liberator,* which was to deal such destructive blows to slavery, the type was set by his own hands. The motto of *The Liberator* was "Our country is the world, our countrymen mankind."

Garrison did not worship the golden calf. His course could not be changed, nor his opinion influenced by threats of violence or the bribe of gold. Money could not persuade him to open his mouth against the truth, or buy his silence from uncompromising denunciation of the wrong. He put manhood above money, humanity above race, the justice of God above the justices of the Supreme Court, and conscience above the Constitution. Because he took his stand upon New Testament righteousness as taught by Christ, he was regarded as a fanatic in a Christian land. When he declared that "he determined at every hazard to lift up a standard of emancipation in the eyes of the nation, within sight of Bunker Hill and in the birthplace of liberty," he was regarded as a public enemy, in a nation conceived in liberty and dedicated to freedom!

Garrison drew his arguments from the Bible and the Declaration of Independence, only to be jeered as a wild enthusiast. He would not retreat a single inch from the straight path of liberty and justice. He refused to purchase peace at the price of freedom. He would not drift with the current of the public opinion of his day. His course was upstream; his battle against the tide. He undertook to create a right public sentiment on the question of freedom ,a task as great as it was difficult. Garrison thundered warnings to arouse the public conscience before the lightnings of his righteous wrath and the shafts of his invincible logic wounded the defenders of slavery in all the vulnerable joints of their armor. He declared: "Let Southern oppressors tremble—let their secret abettors tremble; let their Northern apologists tremble; let all the enemies of the persecuted blacks tremble." For such utterances as these his name throughout the nation became one of obloquy and reproach.

He was not bound to the slave by the ties of race, but by the bond of common humanity which he considered a stronger tie. In his struggle for freedom there was no hope of personal gain; he deliberately chose the pathway of financial loss and poverty. There were set before his eyes no prospect of honor, no pathways leading to promotion, no voice of popular approval, save that of his conscience and his God. His friends and neighbors looked upon him as one who brought a stigma upon the fair name of the city in which he lived. The business interests regarded him as an influence which disturbed and injured the relations of commerce and of trade; the Church opposed him; the press denounced him; the State regarded him as an enemy of the established order; the North repudiated him; the South burned him in effigy. Yet, almost single-handed and alone, Garrison continued to fight on, declaring that "his reliance for the deliverance of the oppressed universally is upon the nature of man, the inherent wrongfulness of oppression, the power of truth, and the omnipotence of God." After the greatest civil war that ever immersed a nation in a baptism of blood and tears, Garrison, unlike most reformers, lived to see the triumph of the cause for which he fought and every slave not only acknowledged as a free man, but clothed with the dignity and powers of American citizenship. William Lloyd Garrison has passed from us, but the monumental character of his work and the influence of his life shall never perish. While there are wrongs to be righted, despots to be attacked, oppressors to be overthrown, peace to find and advocate, and freedom a voice, the name of William Lloyd Garrison will live.

Those who would honor Garrison and perpetuate his memory and his fame must meet the problems that confront them with the same courage and in the same uncompromising spirit that Garrison met the burning questions of the day. Those who would honor Garrison in one breath, while compromising our manhood and advocating the surrender of our political rights in another, not only dishonor his memory, not only trample the flag of our country with violent and unholy feet, but they spit upon the grave which holds the sacred dust of this chiefest of the apostles of freedom.

The status of the Negro in this country was not settled by emancipation; the 15th Amendment to the Constitution, which it was confidently believed would clothe him forever with political influence and power, is more bitterly opposed today than it was a quarter of a century ago. The place which the Negro is to occupy is still a vital and burning question. The newspaper press and magazines are full of it; literature veils its discussion of the theme under the guise of romance; political campaigns are waged with this question as a paramount issue; it is written into the national platform of great political parties; it tinges legislation; it has invaded the domain of dramatic art, until today, it is enacted upon the stage; philanthropy, scholarship, and religion are, each from their point of view, more industriously engaged in its solution than they have been in any previous generation. If the life and labors of Garrison, and the illustrious men and women who stood with him, have a message for the present, we should seek to interpret its meaning and lay the lesson to heart.

The scenes have shifted, but the stage is the same; the leading characters have not changed. We still have with us powerful influences trying to keep the Negro down by unjust and humiliating legislation and degrading treatment; while, on the other hand, the Negro and his friends are still contending for the same privileges and opportunities that are freely accorded to other citizens whose skins do not happen to be black. We, of this nation, are slow to learn the lessons taught by history; the passions which feed on prejudice and tyranny can neither be mollified nor checked by subjection, surrender, or compromise. Self-appointed representatives of the Negro, his enemies and his would-be friends, are pointing to many diverse paths, each claiming that the one they have marked for his feet is the proper one in which he should walk. There is but one direction in which the Negro should steadfastly look and but one path in which he should firmly plant his feet—that is, toward the realization of complete manhood and equality, and the full justice that belongs to an American citizen clothed with all of his constitutional power.

This is a crucial hour for the Negro American; men are seeking today to fix his industrial, political, and social status under freedom as completely as they did under slavery. As this nation continued unstable, so long as it rested upon the foundation-stones of slavery so will it remain insecure as long as one-eighth of its citizens can be openly shorn of political power, while confessedly they are denied "life, liberty, and the pursuit of happiness." We have no animosity against the South or against Southern people. We would see the wounds left by the War of the Rebellion healed; but we would have them healed so effectually that they could not be trodden upon and made to bleed afresh by inhuman barbarities and unjust legislation; we would have the wounds of this nation bound up by the hands of those who are friendly to the patient, so that they might not remain a political running sore. We would have the bitter memories of the war effaced, but they cannot fade while the spirit of slavery walks before the nation in a new guise. We, too, would have a reunited country; but we would have the reunion to include not only white men North and South, but a union so endearing, because so just, as to embrace all of our fellow-countrymen, regardless of section or of race.

* * * * * *

It is not a man's right, it is his duty to support and defend his family and his home; he should therefore resist any influence exerted to prevent him from maintaining his dependents in comfort; while he should oppose with his life the invader or despoiler of his home. God has created man with a mind capable of infinite development and growth; it is not, therefore, a man's right, it is his duty to improve his mind and to educate his children; he should not, therefore, submit to conditions which would compel them to grow up in ignorance. Man belongs to society; it is his duty to make his personal contribution of the best that is within him to the common good; he can do this only as he is given opportunity freely to associate with his fellow-man. He should, therefore, seek to overthrow the artificial social barriers which would intervene to separate him from realizing the highest and best there are within him by freedom of association. It is man's duty to be loyal to his country and his flag, but when his country becomes a land of oppression and his flag an emblem of injustice and wrong, it becomes as much his duty to attack the enemies within the nation as to resist the foreign invader. Tyrants and tyranny everywhere should be attacked and overthrown.

This is a period of transition in the relations of the Negro to this nation. The question which America is trying to answer, and which it must soon definitely settle, is this: What kind of Negroes do the American people want? That they must have the Negro in some relation is no longer a question of serious debate. The Negro is here 10,000,000 strong, and, for weal or woe, he is here to stay—he is here to remain forever. In the government he is a political factor; in education and in wealth he is leaping forward with giant strides; he counts his taxable property by the millions, his educated men and women by the scores of thousands; in the South he is the backbone of industry; in every phase of American life his presence may be noted; he is also as thoroughly imbued with American principles and ideals as any class of people beneath our flag. When Garrison started his fight for freedom, it was the prevailing sentiment that the Negro could have no place in this country save that of a slave, but he has proven himself to be more valuable as a free man than as a slave. What kind of Negroes do the American people want? Do they want a voteless Negro in a Republic founded upon universal suffrage? Do they want a Negro who shall not be permitted to participate in the government which he must support with his treasure and defend with his blood? Do they want a Negro who shall consent to be set apart as forming a distinct industrial class, permitted to rise no higher than the level of serfs or peasants? Do they want a Negro who shall accept an inferior social position, not as a degradation, but as the just operation of the laws of caste based upon color? Do they want a Negro who will avoid friction between the races by consenting to occupy the place to which white men may choose to assign him? What kind of a Negro do the American people want? Do they want a Negro who will accept the doctrine, that however high he may rise in the scale of character, wealth, and education, he may never hope to associate as an equal with white men? Do white men believe that 10,000,000 blacks, after having imbibed the spirit of American institutions, and having exercised the rights of free men for more than a generation, will ever accept a place of permanent inferiority in the Republic? Taught by the Declaration of Independence, sustained by the Constitution of the United States, enlightened by the education of our schools, this nation can no more resist the advancing tread of the hosts of the oncoming blacks than it can bind the stars or halt the resistless motion of the tide.

The answer which the American people may give to the question proposed cannot be final. There is another question of greater importance which must be answered by the Negro, and by the Negro alone: What kind of an American does the Negro intend to be? The answer to this question he must seek and find in every field of human activity and endeavor. First, he must answer it by negation. He does not intend to be an alien in the land of his birth, nor an outcast in the home of his fathers. He will not consent to his elimination as a political factor; he will refuse to camp forever on the borders of the industrial world; as an American he will consider that his destiny is united by indissoluble bonds with the destiny of America forever; he will strive less to be a great Negro in this Republic and more to be an influential and useful American. As intelligence is one of the chief safeguards of the Republic, he will educate his children. Knowing that a people whose morals are above reproach cannot perish, he will ally himself on the side of the forces of righteousness; having been the object of injustice and wrong, he will be the foe of anarchy and the advocate of the supremacy of law. As an American citizen, he will allow no man to protest his title, either at home or abroad. He will insist more and more, not only upon voting, but upon being voted for, to occupy any position within the gift of the nation. As an American whose title to citizenship is without blemish or flaw, he will resist without compromise every law upon the statute-books which is aimed at his degradation as a human being and humiliation as a citizen. He will be no less ambitious and aspiring than his fellow-countrymen; he will assert himself, not as a Negro, but as a man; he will beat no retreat in the face of his enemies and opposers; his gifted sons and daughters, children of genius who may be born to him, will make their contribution to the progress of humanity on these shores, accepting nothing but the honors and rewards that belong to merit. What kind of an American does the Negro intend to be? He intends to be an American who will never mar the image of God, reproach the dignity of his manhood, or tarnish the fair title of his citizenship, by apologizing to men or angels for associating as an equal, with some other American who does not happen to be black. He will place the love of country above the love of race; he will consider no task too difficult, no sacrifice too great, in his effort to emancipate his country from the un-Christlike feelings of race hatred and the American bondage of prejudice. There is nothing that injustice so much respects, that Americans so much admire, and the world so much applauds, as a man who stands erect like a man, has the courage to speak in the tones of a man, and to act fearlessly a man's part.

There are two views of the Negro question now at last clearly defined. One is that the Negro should stoop to conquer; that he should accept in silence the denial of his political rights; that he should not brave the displeasure of white men by protesting when he is segregated in humiliating ways upon the public carriers and in places of public entertainment; that he may educate his children, buy land, and save money, but he must not insist upon his children taking their place in the body politic to which their character and intelligence entitle them; he must not insist on ruling the land which he owns or farms; he must have no voice as to how the money he has accumulated is to be expended through taxation and various forms of public improvement. There are others who believe that the Negro owes this nation no apology for his presence in the United States; that, being black, he is still no less a man; that he should not yield one syllable of his title to American citizenship; that he should refuse to be assigned to an inferior plane by his fellow-countrymen; though foes conspire against him and powerful friends desert him, he should refuse to abdicate his sovereignty as a citizen, and to lay down his honor as a man.

If Americans become surfeited with wealth, haughty with the boasting pride of race superiority, morally corrupt in the high places of honor and of trust, enervated through the pursuit of pleasure, or the political bondmen of some strong man plotting to seize the reins of power, the Negro American will continue his steadfast devotion to the flag, and the unyielding assertion of his constitutional rights, that "this government of the people, for the people, and by the people, may not perish from the earth."

It is so marvelous as to be like a miracle of God, to behold the transformation that has taken place in the position of the Negro in this land since William Lloyd Garrison first saw the light of a century ago. When the Negro had no voice, Garrison pleaded his cause; tonight the descendants of the slave stand in Faneuil Hall, while from ocean to ocean every foot of American soil is dedicated to freedom. The Negro American has found his voice; he is able to speak for himself; he stands upon this famous platform here and thinks it no presumption to declare that he seeks nothing more, and will be satisfied with nothing less than the full measure of American citizenship!

I feel inspired tonight. The spirits of the champions of freedom hover near. High above the stars, Lincoln and Garrison, Sumner and Phillips, Douglass and Lovejoy, look down to behold their prayers answered, their labors rewarded, and their prophecies fulfilled. They were patriots; the true saviors of a nation that esteemed them not. They have left us a priceless heritage. Is there to be found among us now one who would so dishonor the memory of these sainted dead; one so lost to love of country and loyalty to his race, as to offer to sell our birthright for a mess of pottage? When we were slaves, Garrison labored to make us free; when our manhood was denied, he proclaimed it. Shall we in the day of freedom be less loyal to our country and true to ourselves than were the friends who stood for us in our night of woe? Many victories have been won for us; there are still greater victories we must win for ourselves. The proclamation of freedom and the bestowal of citizenship were not the ultimate goal we started out to reach, they were but the beginnings of progress. We, of this generation, must so act our part that, a century hence, our children and our children's children may honor our memory and be inspired to press on as they receive from us untarnished the banner of freedom, of manhood, and of equality among men.

The Negro went aboard the ship of state when she was first launched upon the uncertain waters of our national existence. He booked as through passenger until she should reach "the utmost sea-mark of her farthest sail." When those in command treated him with injustice and brutality, he did not mutiny or rebel; when placed before the mast as a lookout, he did not fall asleep at his post. He has helped to keep her from being wrecked upon the rocks of treachery; he has imperiled his life by standing manfully to his task while she out-rode the fury of a threatening sea; when the pirate-craft of rebellion bore down upon her and sought to place the black flag of disunion at her masthead, he was one of the first to respond when the captain called all hands up on deck. If the enemies of liberty should ever again attempt to wreck our ship of state, the Negro American will stand by the guns; he will not desert her when she is sinking, but with the principles of the Declaration of Independence nailed to the masthead, with the flag afloat, he would prefer rather to perish with her than to be numbered among those who deserted her when assailed by an overwhelming foe. If she weathers the storms that beat upon her, outsails the enemies that pursue her, avoids the rocks that threaten her, and anchors at last in the port of her desired haven, black Americans and white Americans, locked together in brotherly embrace, will pledge each other to remain aboard forever on terms of equality, because they shall have learned by experience that neither one of them can be saved, except they thus abide in the ship.

For the present our strivings are not in vain. The injustice that leans upon the arm of oppression for support must fall; truth perverted or suppressed gains in momentum while it waits; generations may perish, but humanity will survive; out of the present conflict of opinion and the differences of race and color that divide, once the tides of immigration have ceased to flow to our shores, this nation will evolve a people who shall be one in purpose, one in spirit, one in destiny—a composite American by the commingling of blood.

LINCOLN, THE MAN OF THE HOUR[1]

By M. C. B. Mason[2]

Genius is unanswerable and inexplicable. Who can tell how Shakespeare, the profligate horse tender, in ten years became the world's greatest poet; how Napoleon, the unknown Corsican, be-

[1] Delivered on various occasions by the orator.

[2] M. C. B. Mason was born in Houma, Louisiana, in 1859. He entered school at the age of twelve, and became a minister in 1877. He then completed the college course at New Orleans University, and later did some post-graduate work there leading to the degree of Master of Arts. In 1891 he was appointed Field Secretary of the Freedmen's Aid Society. In 1893 he was elected Assistant Corresponding Secretary of this same society, and in 1896 was chosen Corresponding Secretary of the General Conference, a position which no Negro, up to that time, had held. Retiring from this position in 1912, he served as the National Organizer of the National Association for the Advancement of Colored People. In all of these efforts, he made the impression of an able scholar, an unusual orator, and a logical lecturer. He died in 1912.

came the world's greatest military leader; how Moses, the slave boy of Egypt, became the world's greatest lawgiver and philanthropist; how Abraham Lincoln, the rail-splitter, became the world's greatest statesman and emancipator?

Surely, my friends, genius is always unanswerable and inexplicable, for somehow Lincoln seemed to have combined in himself all the elements of greatness in the men of genius who had preceded him, for he had the wisdom of a Socrates, the statesmanship of a Washington, the diplomacy of a Pericles, the unselfish devotion of a Moses, the lofty vision of a St. Paul, and, in his relation toward his fellow-men, who can doubt but that he had much of the spirit of the Man of Galilee?

Such a man was Abraham Lincoln, the man of the hour, concerning whom it might have been said as it was said of John, "He was a man sent from God." And it is inspiring to see this man—this Divinely called man, if you please—standing yonder at Washington during those terrible days of the '60s, holding firmly and steadily and patiently the reins of government. Always conceding, but never receding; constantly giving up nonessentials in order that the one great purpose of his life, namely, the safety of the Union and emancipation of the slave, might be conserved; called incompetent by his cabinet, a weakling by his party, a traitor by the abolitionists, a tyrant by the South, yet he held on firmly, steadily, patiently, "with malice toward none, with charity for all"—he held on till the hour of God's providence came, when, with one stroke of his pen, he saved a nation and emancipated the slave.

Lincoln did not spring into greatness by one bound. His growth was steady and constant. Born in a log cabin, he struggled against poverty and hardships, against difficulties and discouragements, and arose in spite of them all, out of ignorance and obscurity into knowledge and power and influence. Taught his A, B, C's by his stepmother, he at once began the work of self-culture by the faithful use of a few standard books. These were the Bible, Bunyan's Pilgrim's Progress, Æsop's Fables, and a short history of the life of Washington. These classics he read and reread until he had fully mastered them, and, as it were, with hooks of steel he fastened the essentials into his very being. Stretched out at full length on the dirt floor of his cabin home, with the light of a pine knot for his lamp, book in hand, he kept up the work of preparation. He learned his first lessons in arithmetic on a wooden shovel, wiping it off and scraping it to make more room for new figures when a new lesson was given him. In this manner, with only three or four months in school, amid poverty and distress, he kept at the work of getting ready, until he had trained and disciplined his mental and moral power beyond that attained by many a college or university graduate.

Here is an evidence of his innate strength and power. He was willing to pay the price, to fight against the most stupendous odds, if only he could prepare himself for a life of highest usefulness. In all these stirring events of his early life, when he was subjecting himself to such systematic and rigid preparation, nothing is clearer than that his aim was not to further personal ambition for office or power, but to make of himself an efficient servant for his country.

It is important here to note that in this formative period of Lincoln's life the ethical and moral side of his education was not neglected. He learned to distinguish clearly between the right and the wrong, the good and the evil, and the clearness of his moral perception was the basis for the declaration of those principles which made him in the truest sense the greatest statesman of his age.

It is the clearness of perception which marks the difference between right and wrong which makes Lincoln an inspiration to every struggling youth of every race to high and lofty service, to be and to do his best. For it was by manly and heroic effort, by constant and rigid self-denial, by strict adherence to the truth, by absolute obedience to conscience and duty, that he lifted himself up out of morbid mediocrity, out of ignorance and self-conceit, into a broad and refined manhood that immediately won for him the respect and admiration of the civilized world.

Lincoln's successful fight over environment and inherited ignorance gives us a study in heredity. His mother could not read, and his father was not only ignorant, but was stupid and slothful, and the Kentucky neighborhood in which he was born, and where he spent his early days, was not only without educational advantages, but was absolutely devoid of the educational spirit. Against these great odds, Lincoln began his fight. His native soil was not indigenous to the growth of men. A whole generation had not made a single man who could really be called great. Slavery had choked the avenues, poisoned the atmosphere, and greatness seemed impossible. This man, however, was equal to the emergency. He was a green spot in the desert, a root out of dry ground. He made the soil rich by his sweat and tears; he made the cabin a college by his industry and pluck; and climbed so high an altitude that he found pure air and grew in spite of his environments. Studied side by side with Lincoln, Hugo's great creation becomes a living reality, and reveals the fact that men, if they would but fight, can overcome heredity and grow out of ignorance and poverty and malice and envy, into intelligence and power and tenderness and love.

Lincoln's first attempt for political preferment was doomed to failure. In 1832, his father having moved to Illinois, he was appointed by the governor of that state captain of a company in the Black Hawk War. Unlike some of our more fortunate public men, his company did not engage in a single combat, and he came back home with no blazing war record to give him political prestige. His manly qualities, however, had won for him the respect and esteem, not only of his company, but of all who came within his limited acquaintance. Accordingly, he was nominated for the state legislature, but was defeated. The singular incident about the contest which marked Lincoln as the coming man was, that although defeated, he received every vote in his own county, the vote of the other counties in the district, where he was not well known electing his opponent. Defeat, however, neither discouraged nor dismayed him. The two years following he kept up his work of studying men and books, supporting himself in the meantime by keeping a country store, and with no better success as a surveyor, until his horse and few rude instruments were sold for debt. These failures, both in political and business life, coming so close together, would have completely soured and discouraged the average man. Not so with Lincoln. His greatness was here manifest, and he went on in the even tenor of his way, with that cheerfulness and good humor that made him the center of admiration by friend and foe alike.

At the next election, when he was twenty-five years old, he triumphed signally, and was elected to the Illinois legislature by a large majority, and was continued in this position for eight consecutive years. Still anxious to acquire knowledge, he borrowed such books as he could and in this way qualified himself for the bar. As a lawyer he attracted attention far and wide, and his clearness of statement, his rugged honesty, his dogged fearlessness, and his uncompromising fair play made for him a great reputation as a lawyer and political debater, and soon he became the most effective speaker in the entire West.

Lincoln had early begun to hate the institution of slavery. When, as a flat-boatman in New Orleans, he saw the accursed auction block separating husband and wife, mother and child, his righteous soul was stirred to its very depths, and out of his indignation at this terrible spectacle, he declared, "If I ever get a chance at that thing, I will hit it and hit it hard, by the eternal God."

Here as a member of the Illinois legislature he began the fight against slavery, which was ultimately to end in its entire overthrow and utter annihilation. At the very moment when Garrison was dragged through the streets of Boston for his abolition sentiments, and Lovejoy was slain by a mob for printing a paper against slavery, Lincoln showed the courage of his convictions, with only one man to stand by him, by entering his protest in the Illinois legislature, that the institution of slavery was founded both on injustice and bad policy.

In 1846, Lincoln was elected to Congress, and thus came for the first time in the arena of national politics. He continued his fight against slavery and brought in a bill for gradual emancipation in the District of Columbia, with compensation to the slave owners for their slaves thus emancipated. This concession on Lincoln's part to pay the slave owners for their slaves who should be set free was characteristic of the honesty and fair play of the man, and made his future position on the slave question absolutely impregnable, and rallied the nation to his support when he subsequently signed the Emancipation Proclamation.

The slavery question was now one of absorbing interest and rapidly forging to the front as a burning issue in national politics. In order to get the real situation before us, a casual review of the history of slavery in America may be necessary if not interesting. In 1619, one year before the Mayflower landed in Massachusetts, a Dutch ship landed at Jamestown with a carload of slaves. Their importation continued until 1808, when the constitutional prohibition against it took effect. During all these years, from 1619 until 1808, covering 188 years, the number of slaves by importation and birth had vastly increased in the South, and although the traffic had slightly increased in several states of the North, the number of slaves there was not large enough at any time to threaten the peace of the community, or to become of any political significance. Evidently the leading members of the convention at the time of the adoption of the Constitution of the United States did not believe in slavery, and supposed that after 1808, when the further importation would cease, slavery would gradually die out and become entirely extinct. Washington, in his will, freed his slaves and expressed the hope that some plan might be adopted by which slavery could be abolished in this country, and Thomas Jefferson, the writer of the Declaration of Independence, speaking of the institution of slavery, at one time said: "I tremble for my country when I think that God is just and that his justice cannot sleep forever." Other leading men, like Franklin, Adams and Patrick Henry, were all opposed to it.

The invention of the cotton gin in 1792 had made slavery very profitable in the South, and she was determined that the system should be perpetuated. Accordingly, a compromise was secured, by which, first, the time of the prohibition of the importation of slaves should be extended twenty years; second, a provision for the return of runaway slaves; third, the existence of slavery in the states recognized as a basis of representation in Congress. This compromise was a great victory for the slaveholding states, for it gave a new impetus to the slave trade, made the institution of slavery constitutional, and put the South in the saddle by virtue of the increased representation which she thereby secured. From that very moment, slavery became a political power, and the South, not content with its victory, used every possible means to maintain it where it then existed, and to extend it in other sections of the country.

The conscience of the North was slowly rising against this iniquity, and parties began to organize for its overthrow. The slave oligarchy, crazed by its power, threatened even at that early date to leave the Union if their demands were not complied with. To satisfy them and to save the Union, compromise after compromise was made, but all of them were broken by the South and her friends. The Missouri Compromise, however, proved to be the measure which finally broke the backbone of slavery. This compromise, as you remember, was made in 1820 on the admission of Missouri as a slave state, with a distinct provision that slavery should never thereafter be admitted in the Northwest Territory. This compromise was ruthlessly overthrown and broken in 1854, and at once the slumbering passion of the North arose with a mighty protest; slavery was declared to be a public nuisance, and the Republican party was organized with the declaration of principles that slavery be confined where it then existed, and should not be permitted under any circumstances to be extended in the Northwest Territory or in any other section of the Union.

The crisis had now come. The North, for so many years quiescent, was now aggressive. Lincoln again came to the front as one of the leaders and most effective speakers of the new party. Its first campaign was made in 1856, with John C. Fremont as the nominee, and, though defeated, it received a surprisingly large vote and carried several states.

The one event which brought Lincoln into national prominence was his debate with Judge Douglas in 1858. Douglas spoke in favor of the extension of slavery, or "squatter sovereignty," as it was then called. Lincoln spoke for the restriction of slavery and against its extension in Kansas, which state was then applying for admission into the Union. The debates drew great crowds and became at once of national significance. Judge Douglas was a man of the schools, highly cultured, eloquent, and of commanding appearance; Lincoln was without the preparation of the schools, thoroughly lacking in refinement and the conventionalities of society, but his statements were clear and forcible, his logic irresistible and his powerful arguments carried conviction everywhere. What now was the essential difference between Lincoln and Douglas? Douglas plead for the Constitution; Lincoln plead for justice and fair play. Douglas was on the side of that which was expedient; Lincoln was on the side of that which was just and righteous. Lincoln believed fully in that principle of the Declaration of Independence, "that all men are created equal and endowed with certain inalienable rights, among which are life, liberty and the pursuit of happiness." On this doctrine of equal rights and fair play he staked his case and ultimately won.

In the very beginning of the debate Lincoln struck the keynote of the whole question when he said—I quote him verbatim: "The real issue in this country is the eternal struggle between these two principles, right and wrong, throughout the world. They are the two principles that have stood face to face from the beginning of time and will ever continue to struggle. One is the common right of humanity and the other the divine right of kings. It is the same principle in whatever shape it develops itself. It is the same spirit that says: 'You work and toil and earn bread and I will eat it.' "

Upon this basis of right against wrong, of freedom against slavery, Lincoln made his fight. He foresaw with the eye of a prophet and a statesman, that union and liberty, freedom and slavery, could not exist together, that one or the other must finally fall. It was upon the enunciation of this great truth that Lincoln gave expression to that immortal sentence that completely overwhelmed Douglas and made Lincoln preëminently the man of the hour. "Under the operation of the policy of the compromise, the slavery agitation has not only not ceased but has constantly augmented. In my opinion it will not cease until a crisis has been reached and passed. A house divided against itself cannot stand. I believe this government cannot endure permanently half slave and half free. I do not expect the Union to be dissolved; I do not expect the house to fall, but I do expect it will cease to be divided. It will become all one thing or all the other. Either the opponents of slavery will prevent the further spread of it and place it where the public mind shall rest in the belief that it is in the course of ultimate extinction, or its advocates will push it forward until it shall become alike lawful in all the states, old as well as new, North as well as South."

This argument struck the deathblow to "squatter sovereignty" and the extension of slavery. Lincoln, as it has been facetiously said, lost the senatorship but gained the presidency. The nation was now stirred to its very depths. At this critical time several events occurred which added fuel to the flames. It seems as if Almighty God with long-suffering patience was at last permitting the slave power to dash itself to pieces and grind itself into powder. The Fugitive Slave Act, by which slaves were dragged through the streets of Boston, shook that ancestral stronghold of freedom to its very foundation; the Dred Scott Decision of the Supreme Court, which declared that a Negro had no rights which a white man should respect, showing that the slave power had at last gotten hold of the Supreme Court, the very foundation of justice; the attempted murder of Senator Sumner by a Southern slave holder; the attempt to force slavery into Kansas; the execution of John Brown, and the publication of "Uncle Tom's Cabin," all these events stirred up the sleeping conscience of the North and sounded the death knell of slavery.

At the Chicago convention of 1860, Lincoln was nominated for the presidency. It was a great victory for the man from a log cabin over Chase, and Stanton, and especially Seward, whom everyone supposed would receive the nomination. The Democratic party was hopelessly divided, and, strange to say, the division was made by the masterful work of Lincoln in his debates with Douglas two years before. Accordingly, four parties were in the field, the regular Democratic party, headed by Breckinridge of Kentucky; the Popular Sovereignty party, a split from the Democratic party, headed by Douglas of Illinois, Lincoln's recent antagonist; the Constitutional Union party, headed by John Bell of Tennessee, and the Republican party, headed by Abraham Lincoln of Illinois. After one of the most stirring and bitter campaigns in the history of the country, Lincoln was triumphantly elected, receiving 180 out of 303 electoral votes. The crisis was now on. Lincoln, fearing assassination, journeyed secretly to Washington for the inauguration and easily eluded the friends of secession, who threatened to take his life. The scenes at the inauguration were strange and pathetic. Douglas, his famous rival, held his hat; Chief Justice Taney, of Dred Scott fame, gave the oath of office; Seward, Chase and Stanton, chosen members of his cabinet and former candidates for the presidency, were about him, and with these surroundings he plead for peace before the seceding states should return, and pledged himself to see that the laws were faithfully executed.

No ruler in all the world's history ever faced such perilous conditions as confronted Lincoln when he assumed the reins of government. The situation was not only grave, it was, indeed, alarming. South Carolina, the home of nullification, became the mother of secession and opened fire on the nation's flag at Fort Sumter. South Carolina, it would seem, has a peculiar history, for, from Calhoun to Tillman, she has been an eyesore and a nuisance in our national life. State after state seceded until all the slave-holding states, with a few exceptions, had gone out of the Union. Jefferson Davis, then United States Senator from Mississippi, resigned his position to accept the presidency of the rebellious states, and it is a strange coincidence of history that a Negro, in the person of Hiram R. Revels, was elected to take his place and became the first Negro United States Senator in the history of the republic.

In this hour of severest trial Lincoln's cabinet was either openly against him or apparently indifferent. Four of them, Chase, Stanton, Seward, and Cameron, had been recent candidates for the presidency. When Lincoln faced his cabinet for the first time, not a man who sat before him was a personal friend or had any real sympathy for him as an individual. Every man of them thought himself superior to him and did not hesitate to let him know it at every possible opportunity. To add to the gravity of the position trouble arose with England over the forcible seizure of Mason and Slidell. Under these perilous conditions, with his own country torn, disordered, belligerent, with his cabinet suspicious and fault-finding, and facing hostilities with a powerful foreign foe, Lincoln assumed the presidency and undertook the stupendous task of saving the nation, and emancipating the slaves. He was, however, equal to the emergency. Calm, patient, diplomatic, with boundless compassion and heroic self-denial, he worked by day and by night for the closing of hostilities and for the preservation of the nation.

No one will doubt that for this special work God had been for many years preparing him. Day by day he mastered the problems as they came before him. His endurance, his fertility of resources, his courage, his even temper, his tender-heartedness, his comprehensive grasp of the difficult questions of diplomacy—these essential evidences of a great ruler surprised his friends, dumbfounded his enemies, and made him complete master of the situation.

Lincoln's desire to save the Union at all cost and all hazard lost him almost the entire support of the abolition element—indeed, many of them became his bitterest enemies. Unable to see the width and breadth of his statesmanship, they called him a traitor to the cause of the freedom of the slaves and an enemy to his country. To Horace Greeley, who was constantly chiding him for not issuing the Emancipation Proclamation, he wrote:

"If I could save the Union without freeing any slave, I would do it; and if I could save it by freeing all the slaves, I would do it; and if I could do it by freeing some and by leaving others, I would also do that."

Here was statesmanship of an unusual order. Lincoln knew that the one great central idea around which all the patriotism of the North might in the end declare allegiance, was the preservation of the Union. This secured, slavery in the very nature of the case would be ultimately abolished.

During these critical days when the mighty heart of great Lincoln was bearing such a load, there were two distinguished citizens, among other patriots, who came forward to aid and cheer him. I refer to Henry Ward Beecher and Frederick Douglass. Beecher's services at this time in England were invaluable. England wanted Southern cotton for her mills and was afraid if slavery was abolished her interests would suffer. Accordingly, she was about to recognize the Southern Confederacy with Jefferson Davis as president, which in itself would have been a death blow to the Union cause. In a series of addresses in the great cities of the Empire, London, Liverpool, Manchester, Glasgow, at first the audiences hissed and insulted him, but Beecher stood his ground for fair play and noninterference. He secured a complete triumph. England saw the error of her ways and made a complete somersault, the result of which was to weaken and discomfit the Confederacy gradually. Frederick Douglass at home performed a task equally as important. He fired the North with his eloquent pleas for the emancipation of his brethren and the preservation of the Union, and did yeoman service in the organization and equipment of colored soldiers, who fought so bravely for the Union and the overthrow of slavery.

In the hour of Lincoln's greatest need, the churches of the North came to his rescue. In the homes of the people, on the streets, and even on the railway trains, they prayed audibly and openly for the president and for the success of Union arms. An incident is told of the meeting on a railway train of a Quaker woman of the North, who was praying for the Union, and a Confederate woman of the South, who was praying for the success of Jefferson Davis and his cause. The Southern woman remonstrated with the Northern woman, saying that she was praying to God for the success of the Confederate army, and how did she expect God to answer her who was praying for the success of the Union army, to which the Quaker woman immediately replied: "The good Lord does not pay any attention to thee, for he thinks thee is joking."

The General Conference of the Methodist Episcopal Church, in session at Philadelphia in 1864, sent a delegation to Mr. Lincoln, pledging him their prayers and hearty support. To this delegation, Mr. Lincoln replied:

"In response to your address, allow me to attest the accuracy of its historical statements; endorse the sentiment it expresses; and thank you, in the nation's name, for the sure promise it gives.

"Nobly sustained as the government has been by all the churches, I would utter nothing which might, in the least, appear invidious against any. Yet, without this, it may fairly be said that the Methodist Episcopal Church, not less devoted than the rest, is, by its greater numbers, the most important of all. It is no fault in others that the Methodist Church sends more soldiers to the field, more nurses to the hospitals, and more prayers to Heaven than any. God bless the Methodist Church—bless all the churches—and blessed be God, Who, in this our great trial, giveth us the churches."

As commander in chief of the army, Lincoln's resources were taxed to the very utmost, but even here in this trying ordeal he was preëminently the man of the hour. Forced to make important changes from time to time, he was, nevertheless, always true to his generals. When he found that Grant was a man that would fight and would ultimately bring the war to a triumphant close, he gave him the right of way and stood by him without reserve. Once when Grant's critics urged Lincoln to remove him as commander of the army, charging him with drinking too freely, Lincoln himself replied: "What does Grant drink?" "Whiskey," said the man. "Well," said Lincoln, "just find out what particular brand he uses and I will send a barrel to my other generals."

The adroit, diplomatic manner by which he handled the question of emancipation showed the breadth and depth of his splendid statesmanship. An error at that time would have been fatal to the preservation of the Union as well as the freedom of the slave. He waited patiently while both friends and foes slandered and abused him; waited till the Union was ready; waited till the psychological moment; waited till the hour of God's providence came, when he resolutely fulfilled the promise he had made many years before when a humble flat-boatsman in New Orleans. And when the hour had fully come he struck the fatal blow which emancipated the slave and blotted out forever from the face of this Union that iniquity of all iniquities, human slavery.

This act was the great statesman's master stroke. By it he discomfited the Confederacy, rallied the patriotism of the North as nothing else could have done, saved the Union and made effective the proclamation which he had issued. It came not a moment too soon, for from that moment defeat was turned into victory, and Grant and Sherman kept the rebels on the run till Lee surrendered at Appomattox.

Lincoln's second inaugural address, like his Gettysburg speech, is a classic. Besides, it reveals the innate strength and courage of the man when face to face with duty. In that remarkable sentence in which he declares he will push the war to a successful close, Lincoln said: "Fondly do we hope, fervently do we pray, that this mighty scourge of war may speedily pass away, but if God will that it continue till all the wealth piled up by the bondsman's 250 years of unrequited toil shall be sunk, and till every drop of blood drawn with a lash shall be paid with another drawn with a sword, as was said three thousand years ago, so still must it be said, 'The judgments of the Lord are true and righteous altogether.' "

At length the hour came. Lincoln himself knew that it was near. Speaking to Harriet Beecher Stowe, the author of "Uncle Tom's Cabin," he said: "Whichever way it goes, I will not last long." On the night of April 14, 1865, only forty days after he had been inaugurated, while in Ford's theater, the assassin's bullet felled the great man to the earth, and he passed to the Great Beyond the next morning at seven o'clock. His work was done, his course was finished, he had kept the faith, and he went to his eternal reward. For God had let him live long enough to see the close of the war and the adoption of the thirteenth amendment to the Constitution.

Standing here tonight, my fellow citizens, on this one hundredth anniversary of his birth, what is the lesson he leaves us? To be honest, industrious and true, to be useful and intelligent citizens, to make ourselves absolutely necessary to the life of every community in which we live, to acquire property and lands, to keep out of the saloon, out of the police courts, to be sober, industrious, to be patient, to be bold, to endure and to be in our virtuous lives a standing argument for the wisdom of his action by which our liberty was secured.

Lincoln, thou art not dead. The assassin's bullet did not strike thee; it touched only the hem of thy garment and bruised and shattered the house in which thou didst live. Thou art living still, living in the lives of thy countrymen, yea, in the life of the world, and inspiring now, as thou didst then, to sublime courage and heroic self-denial. Verily, as some one has facetiously said: "Thou art the tallest white angel of a thousand years."

ABRAHAM LINCOLN AND FIFTY YEARS OF FREEDOM[1]

By Alexander Walters[2]

The distinguished person whom we pause to honor was not born great, if to be born great means to be born in a mansion, surrounded at the start of life with opulence, "dangled on the knee of indulgence and charmed to sleep by the voice of liveried servants"; if this is the measure of greatness, then Abraham Lincoln was not born great,—but if to be born great is to be ushered into the world with embryonic qualities of heart, elements calculated to unfold into the making of the stature of a complete man, a manly man, a brave, a God-fearing man—a statesman equal to the greatest emergency of a nation, then the little fellow of destiny who

[1] Delivered on various occasions by Bishop Walters.

[2] Bishop Alexander Walters was one of the prominent figures of the African Methodist Episcopal Church. He was doubtless the outstanding bishop of his connection during his time. He rendered his church valuable service as an educator and minister in Kentucky, California and Tennessee. In these efforts he made such a favorable impression that he easily attained the highest position in his connection.

Differing widely from the conservative element in the race, Bishop Walters advocated the division of the Negro vote, thinking that as long as the race is slavishly attached to one party, it can never hope to figure as a factor in politics. Consequently, he advocated the election of Woodrow Wilson in 1912, and was instrumental in diverting from their former allegiance a considerable number of Negro voters in support of the War President. For this, Bishop Walters was at times severely criticized, but his example was salutary in pointing the way for a new day for the Negro as a full citizen.

made his initial bow to the goddess of light in Hardin County, Kentucky, February 12, 1809, was born great.

If to achieve greatness is to win the hearts of one's youthful companions, one's associates in professional life, and to merit the confidence and genuine love of a nation to the extent of securing its greatest honors and to perform the mightiest work of a century, then Abraham Lincoln achieved greatness.

. . . .

The assertion has been made that President Lincoln was not in favor of universal freedom. I beg to take issue with this view.

A careful study of this sincere, just, and sympathetic man will serve to show that from his earliest years he was against slavery. He declared again and again: "If slavery is not wrong, nothing is wrong; I cannot remember when I did not so think and feel."

Back in the thirties this young man clad in homespun was standing in the slave-mart of New Orleans, watching husbands and wives being separated forever, and children being doomed never again to look into the faces of their parents. As the hammer of the auctioneer fell, this young flat-boatman, with quivering lips, turned to his companion and said: "If ever I get a chance to hit that thing (slavery), I will hit it hard, by the Eternal God I will."

In March, 1839, he had placed upon the House Journal of Illinois a formal protest against pro-slavery resolutions which he could get but one other member beside himself to sign. Long before he was made President, in a speech at Charleston, Illinois, he said: "Yes, we will speak for freedom, and against slavery, as long as the Constitution of our country guarantees free speech, until everywhere on this wide land the sun shall shine, and the rain shall fall, and the winds shall blow upon no man who goes forth to unrequited toil."

While in Congress in 1848 he offered a bill to abolish slavery in the District of Columbia. It was his opinion that Congress had control over the institution of slavery in the District of Columbia and the territories, and he evidenced his desire for the freedom of the slaves by offering a bill to abolish it in the District, and he afterwards strenuously advocated the elimination of slavery from the territories.

In 1864, about the time of the repeal of the Fugitive Slave Law, President Lincoln said to some gentlemen from the West: "There have been men base enough to propose to me to return to slavery our black warriors of Port Hudson and Olustee, and thus win the respect of the masters they fought. Should I do so, I should deserve to be damned in time and eternity.''

Through all the mighty struggle of the Civil War when bowed in sorrow, and when it was truly said of him ''That he was a man of sorrows and acquainted with grief,'' he was ever heard to say, ''It is my desire that all men be free.''

If President Lincoln were not in favor of the freedom of the slaves, why did he write the Emancipation Proclamation without the knowledge of his Cabinet and, when reading it to them, inform them that he did not do so to have them make any changes, but simply to apprise them of its contents? I answer, because he saw the time had come, the opportune time for which he had longed, when he, as President of these United States, could free the slaves. The South was so certain that it was Mr. Lincoln's intention to liberate the slaves, that, upon his election as President, they seceded from the Union. They felt that the institution which they had struggled so long to maintain was doomed.

His famous letter to Horace Greeley, so diplomatically written, shows him to be in favor of the emancipation of slaves. Said he: ''My paramount object is to save the Union, and not either to save or destroy slavery. If I could save the Union without freeing any slaves I would do it; if I could save it by freeing all the slaves I would do it; and if I could do it by freeing some and leaving others alone, I would also do that. I shall try to correct errors when shown to be errors, and I shall adopt new views as fast as they shall appear to be true views. I have here stated my purpose according to my views of official duty, and I intend no modification of my oft-expressed personal wish that all men everywhere could be free.''

Had President Lincoln not desired the freedom of the slaves would he have written this last sentence?

Professor Pickens, of Talladega College, says: ''He was a patriot statesman; although he abhorred slavery in his own inclination, he was wise enough to see that the question of slavery was subordinate to the immediate object of saving the Union. If slavery is not wrong, nothing is wrong; he declared as his private opinion; but it was his public duty and his oath to save the Union, regardless of slavery. His logic and clear seizure of the main point stood him in good stead against the over-zealous Abolitionists on the one hand, while on the other hand, as soon as the interests of Negro freedom and the interests of the Union coincided, the same unchanged and consistent logic answered those who assailed him on constitutional grounds."

Mr. Lincoln believed that the Constitution protected slavery in the States wherein it existed, and his aim was to let it alone where it had a constitutional right to exist. Not because he thought slavery right, but because of his respect for the law.

His original position was that, since slavery was protected by the law, the friends of freedom would have to abide their time and continue to create sentiment sufficient to change the law and thus overthrow the iniquitous institution. This is the only interpretation that can be put upon his doctrine. "The house divided against itself."

Is it reasonable to think that a man so thoughtful and sincere as was Mr. Lincoln could give a life to the advocacy of the freedom of the slaves, and in his heart not be in favor of their liberation? Mr. Lincoln often expressed ideas on the emancipation calculated to jeopardize his political future, which he would not have done but for the fact that in his heart of hearts he was committed to the cause of freedom.

The slaves hailed him as their savior, which he proved to be by emancipating 4,000,000 of them, and he will be held in loving remembrance by Afro-Americans as long as the world shall stand.

It is fitting that we assemble ourselves together on the anniversary of his birth to honor his memory, and tell of his noble deeds to the rising generation.

President Lincoln was truly a great man; a giant in intellect, a peerless diplomat, a fearless advocate of the rights of humanity and a wise ruler. In council he stood head and shoulders above the members of his Cabinet and other advisers, notwithstanding he was surrounded by some of the greatest scholars and statesmen of his time.

Allow me to apply to Lincoln the words of Wendell Phillips in his address "Touissant L'Ouverture":

"Lincoln was greater than Cæsar; Cæsar fought to further his ambition and to extend a great empire. Lincoln was an advocate of principle, justice, and fair play. He was greater than Alexander; Alexander fought for glory—to conquer all the world, all at the sacrifice of happy homes and the desolation and ruin of countries. Lincoln sacrificed comfort and ease to save a nation and liberate an enslaved people. He was greater than Napoleon; Napoleon made wives to be widows, and children to be fatherless and homeless, and drenched Europe and Egypt in blood for fame and the desire to found a greater empire than the Roman dynasty; but Lincoln perished because he dared to defend an oppressed people."

When the last scarred veteran shall gather around the last campfire and shall rehearse stories of valor, he will close his tale of sorrow with the name of Lincoln.

When the last poet shall compose his last poem on America's great struggle,—yea, of the victories of Vicksburg, Fort Donelson, Lookout Mountain, Gettysburg, Appomattox, Petersburg, and the fall of Richmond, he will close it by paying a tribute to the memory of the sainted Lincoln.

When the last statesman of the world shall pronounce a farewell anathema upon the world's oppression, when he shall write the names of those foremost in the work of emancipation, after he shall have written the name of Moses,—long ere he reaches the name of Wilberforce or Clarkson, he shall have written high on the scroll of fame the name of Lincoln.

When the last flag bearing the "Stars and Stripes" shall wave over this great commonwealth, telling of its glory and tremendous influence, on the wings of the eagle upon the staff of that flag will be written for her to bear away on the eternal breezes the name of the immortal Lincoln,—the savior of his country, the Emancipator of its people.

. . . .

The dying legacy bequeathed to the American nation by the martyred Lincoln was a united country and a free people. It gave us a nation which today stands first in the galaxy of the nations of the world—in character, thought, wealth, and all the qualities which make for the highest civilizations—a glorious country, whose natural resources stand unsurpassed.

All honor to Mr. Lincoln, the nation's Chieftain, the giant of the conflict, the statesman of the age, the immortal Emancipator;

and all honor to the men who wore the blue, both white and black; and all honor to the men and women who gave their sons to the cause and furnished the sinews of war; and all praise be to the God of Heaven who was behind the conflict controlling all.

If we would properly honor this great and good man we must finish the work which he so nobly began,—the lifting up of the Negro race to the highest point of civilization. This can be accomplished: first, by being good and loyal citizens ourselves, and by teaching our children to be the same.

The ground work of our material advancement is industry. As a race we are generally industrious, but we need to become more skillfully so. Unskilled labor cannot compete with skilled labor, neither North nor South. In the past you gave us certain positions as the result of sympathy, not because we could perform the work as skillfully as others.

The sentiment which actuated you to help us was a noble one, but that kind of sentiment is a thing of the past; now we are required to stand or fall according to our merits. When goods are to be manufactured, machines constructed, houses and bridges built, clothing fashioned, or any sort of work performed, none but skilled workmen are considered; there are a great number of employers that care but little about the color of the workmen; with them the question is, can he do the work?

We must continue the struggle for our civil and political rights. I have no sympathy with that class of leaders who are advising the Negro to eschew politics in deference to color prejudice.

Does it make for permanent peace to deny to millions of citizens their political rights when they are equal to the average electorate in intelligence and character? Fitness, and not color or previous condition of servitude, should be the standard of recognition in political matters. Indeed the Negro should not be denied any civil or political right on account of his color, and to the extent this is done there is bound to be disquietude in the nation.

We have already seen that temporizing with slavery at the formation of the Union resulted in a hundred years of strife and bitterness, and finally brought on devastation and death. And may we not profit by this bitter experience? The enlightened American conscience will not tolerate injustice forever. The same spirit of liberty and fair play which enveloped the nation in the days of

Mr. Lincoln and that was recognized by his astute mind, clear to his mental vision and so profoundly appreciated by his keen sense of justice and which he had the courage to foster against all opposition, is abroad in our land today, will ultimately triumph.

Mr. Lincoln was the first to suggest to his party the enfranchisement of the Negro. He wrote Governor Hahn, of Louisiana, advising that the ballot should be given to the colored man; said he, "Let in, as for instance, the very intelligent and especially those who have fought gallantly in our ranks. They would probably help in some trying time in the future to keep the jewel of liberty in the family of freedom."

It seems to me right and proper on this memorable day, when the nation has stopped to consider the work of the man above all others who started the Negro on his upward way, that we should appeal to the enlightened conscience of the nation, to unloose further the fetters which bind the black man, especially the industrial bands placed upon him in the North. I appeal to the white people of the South, the sentiment-makers of that section, to create sentiment in favor of law and order, and that they demand a cessation of lynchings. I appeal to the legislature of the South to allow the civil and political door of hope to remain open to my people, and in all things which make for quietness and permanent peace, let us be brethren.

The Negro should no longer be considered a serf, but a citizen of this glorious Republic which both white and black alike have done so much to develop.

Mr. Edwin D. Mead, in the New York *Independent* of January 21, 1909, says, "Has the country been faithful to Lincoln's memory and task? Has the evolution of emancipation been pushed with proper persistence and earnestness? Are we ceasing our discrimination against men because they are black? It is not a question put by North to South. It is a question put to Springfield, Illinois, the old home of Lincoln himself, as directly as to men in Maryland busy with their pitiful disfranchising chicanery." To the still lingering cry of "black men down" this salutary Commemoration rings back, the "all men up," whose echoes after forty years were growing faint in too many American hearts.

Had they not grown faint in many, the recent words of Justice Harlan, so like Lincoln's own, upon the Berea College decision confirming the Kentucky law that, however they themselves desired it, and even in private institutions, a black boy and white boy may not study together the rule of three or the law of gravitation, the Golden Rule, or the Emancipation Proclamation,—would have aroused a vastly profounder and louder response.

"If the views of the highest court of Kentucky be sound, that commonwealth may, without infringing on the Constitution of the United States, forbid the association in the same private school of pupils of the Anglo-Saxon and Latin races respectively, or pupils of Christian and Jewish faith respectively. Have we become so inoculated with prejudice of race that any American government professedly based on the principles of freedom and charged with the protection of all citizens alike can make distinctions between such citizens in the manner of their voluntary meeting for innocent purposes, simply because of their respective races? If the court be right, then the State may make it a crime for white and colored persons to frequent the same market-places at the same time or to appear in an assemblage of citizens convened to consider questions of a public or political nature, in which all citizens without regard to race are equally interested; and other illustrations would show the mischievous, not to say cruel, character of the statute in question, and how inconsistent such legislation is with the principle of the equality of citizens before the law."

Mr. Mead further says that Abraham Lincoln was called upon to make his memorable and mighty protest with reference to a single race. In our time the problem becomes vastly more complex and pressing.

But, however complex, there is but one way of solving it—the simple, Christian, fraternal way. It is well for us that the Lincoln centennial comes to say this to us persuasively and commandingly.[1]

[1] Walters, *Abraham Lincoln and Fifty Years of Freedom.*

ADDRESS OF WILLIAM H. LEWIS, ASSISTANT ATTORNEY-GENERAL OF THE UNITED STATES, BEFORE THE MASSACHUSETTS HOUSE OF REPRESENTATIVES, FEB. 12, 1913 [1]

Mr. Speaker and Members of the House of Representatives:

The power of the House to summon forthwith any citizen of the Commonwealth has never been resisted; and so by designation of the Honorable Speaker, in accordance with the order of the House, I am here in answer to your summons. You have invited me as a member of the liberated race, to address you upon this Lincoln's Birthday in commemoration of the 50th Anniversary of the Emancipation Proclamation. Words would be futile to express my deep appreciation of this high honor, however unworthily bestowed. Twice before have I met this honorable House. I came first as an humble petitioner seeking redress against discrimination on account of color. You then granted my prayer. Some years later, I came as a member of this House, the last representative of my race to sit in this body. You treated me then as a man and an equal. And now the honors of an invited guest I shall cherish as long as memory lasts.

Today is the anniversary of the birth of Abraham Lincoln, the preserver of the Union, the liberator of a race. "The mystic chords of memory," stretching from heart to heart of millions of Americans at this hour, "swell the chorus of thanksgiving" to the Almighty for the life, character and service of the great President.

Four brief crucial years he represented the soul of the Union

[1] William H. Lewis was born in Berkeley, Virginia, in 1868. He attended school at an early age, and by peddling matches and doing odd jobs, he managed to make his way through the Virginia Normal and Collegiate Institute. He then attended Amherst College where he was graduated in 1892. At Amherst he distinguished himself as captain of the college football team, as an orator, and as a debater. He won the prizes in two of the most important contests, and was finally chosen by his class at graduation to deliver the class day oration.

He next studied law at Harvard University where he continued as a football player with a national reputation. After completing the course in law, Mr. Lewis settled in Cambridge and practiced in Boston. Entering politics about the same time, he was elected City Councilman of Cambridge in 1899, 1900 and 1901. In 1902 he was elected to the State Legislature. In 1903 he was appointed by President Roosevelt to the position of Third Assistant United States District Attorney with headquarters in Boston. He was promoted to Second Assistant United States District Attorney in 1904. and was made head of the Naturalization Bureau from 1903 to 1909. In 1911 he was appointed by President Taft to the position of Assistant Attorney General of the United States.

struggling for immortality—for perpetuity; in him was the spirit of liberty struggling for a new birth among the children of men.

"Slavery must die," he said, "that the Union may live."

We have a Union today because we have Emancipation; we have Emancipation because we have a united country. Though nearly 50 years have elapsed since his martyr death and we see his images everywhere, yet Lincoln is no mere legendary figure of an heroic age done in colors, cast in bronze, or sculptured in marble; he is a living, vital force in American politics and statecraft. The people repeat his wise sayings; politicians invoke his principles; men of many political stripes profess to be following in his footsteps. We of this generation can almost see him in the flesh and blood and hear falling from his lips the sublime words of Gettysburg, the divine music of the Second Inaugural and the immortal Proclamation of Emancipation. We see this man of mighty thews and sinews, his feet firmly planted in mother earth, his head towering in the heavens. He lived among men but he walked with God. He was himself intensely human, but his sense of right, of justice, seemed to surpass the wisdom of men. A true child of nature, he beheld the races of men in the raw without the artificial trappings of civilization and the adventitious circumstances of birth or wealth or place, and could see no difference in their natural rights.

"The Negro is a man," said he, "my ancient faith tells me that all men are created equal."

As a man he was brave yet gentle, strong yet tender and sympathetic, with the intellect of a philosopher, yet with the heart of a little child. As a statesman he was prudent, wise, sagacious, far seeing and true. As President he was firm, magnanimous, merciful and just. As a liberator and benefactor of mankind, he has no peer in all human history.

As Lowell said in his famous commemoration ode, it still must be said:

"Great captains, with their guns and drums,
Disturb our judgment for the hour,
But at last silence comes;
These are all gone, and, standing like a tower,
Our children shall behold his fame,
The kindly-earnest, brave, foreseeing man,

Sagacious, patient, dreading praise, not blame,
New birth of our new soil, the first American."

There are only three great charters of freedom among Anglo-Saxon peoples, the Magna Charta which the barons wrung from King John at Runnymede, the Declaration of Independence which a few colonials threw at the head of an obstinate king, the Emancipation Proclamation which Lincoln cast into the balance for the Union. The Magna Charta gave freedom to the nobility; the Declaration of Independence brought freedom down to the plain people; the Proclamation of Abraham Lincoln set free the under man and proclaimed liberty to the slave and the serf throughout the world.

Massachusetts had no small part in the second great charter of liberty. This is attested not only by the signatures of Hancock, the Adamses, Paine and Gerry, to that great document, but here is Boston, Concord, Lexington and Bunker Hill, and a thousand memorials of the revolution besides. Great indeed as was the part that Massachusetts played in achieving independence, greater still was her share in the Emancipation of the slave. Lincoln himself said that Boston had done more to bring on the war than any other city; and when Emancipation had been achieved he generously credited the result "to the logic and moral power of Garrison and the anti-slavery people."

This day, therefore, belongs to Massachusetts. It is a part of her glorious history. Emancipation was but the triumph of Puritan principle—the right of each individual to eat his bread out of the sweat of his own brow or not at all. The history of the abolition of slavery in America could not be written with Massachusetts left out; the history of Massachusetts herself, since the revolution, would be but a dreary, barren waste without the chapter of her part in the Emancipation.

The House does well to pause in its deliberations to commemorate this anniversary. In 1837 your predecessors threw open the old Hall of Representatives to the first meeting of the New England Anti-Slavery Society. A year later, the legislature adopted resolutions against the slave trade, for the abolition of slavery in the District of Columbia, and the prohibition of slavery in the territories.

The fathers early enacted that there should be neither bond slaves nor villenage amongst us except captives taken in just wars and those condemned judicially to serve. When it was attempted to land the first cargo of slaves upon her soil, the people seized them and sent them back to their own country and clime. In spite of the prayers and resolutions and acts of the early fathers, a form of slavery grew up here, but it was milder than the English villenage: it resembled apprenticeship except in the duration. The slave had many of the rights of free men; the right to marry and the right to testify in court. Either with the decision of Somerset's case in England or the adoption of the first Constitution of the Commonwealth, during the revolution, that institution passed away forever. The voices of freedom were first raised here. Whittier, Lowell and Longfellow sang the songs of Emancipation. Garrison, Phillips and Parker were the prophets and disciples of Lincoln. In the darkest days of slavery, John Quincy Adams held aloft the torch of liberty and fed its flame with his own intrepid spirit. Sumner was the scourge of God, the conscience of the state incarnate.

The people of Massachusetts were not only idealists, dreamers, and moulders of public opinion, but when 30 years of agitation had reached its culmination in the Civil War, Massachusetts sent 150,000 of her sons to sustain upon the battlefields of the republic the ideals which she had advocated in the Halls of Congress, in the forum and the market place. The people of Massachusetts, true to their history and traditions, have abolished here, so far as laws can do so, every discrimination between race and color, and every inequality between man and man.

I have recalled these things for no vainglorious purpose. We should remind ourselves constantly that we have a history behind us, that we have a character to sustain. Are we of this generation worthy descendants of tea spillers and abolitionists? Are we living up to the traditions of the Commonwealth, to the principles of the fathers in relation to the treatment of citizens of color? I have observed with aching heart and agonizing spirit during the last 20 years not only the growing coldness and indifference on the part of our people to the fate of the Negro elsewhere; but here in our own city the breaking up of the old ties of friendship that once existed between people of color and all classes of citizens, just after Emancipation, the gradual falling away of that sympathy and support upon which we could always confidently rely in every crisis. I have watched the spirit of race prejudice raise its sinister shape in the labor market, in the business house, the real estate exchange, in public places, and even in our schools, colleges and churches.

I say all this with pain and sorrow. I would be the last to "soil my own nest" or to utter one word that would reflect in the slightest degree upon Massachusetts or her people. I love inexpressibly every foot of Massachusetts soil, from the Berkshires to Essex, from the Cape to the islands off our southern coast. I have studied her history; I know her people, and when I have played out the little game with destiny, I want to rest upon some Massachusetts hillside.

I can never forget the emotions that filled my breast when first I set foot in Boston just a quarter of a century ago, a Negro lad in search of education, freedom, and opportunity. As I walked these sacred streets I lived over the revolution, I saw them peopled with the mighty men of the past. I hastened to make my obeisance first to the spot where Attucks fell, the first martyr of the revolution. I next looked out upon Bunker Hill where Peter Salem stood guard over the fallen Warren. I said to myself, "Here at last no black man need be ashamed of his race, here he has made history." And then to scenes of still another period I turned my gaze. I looked upon the narrow streets where Garrison was mobbed for my sake. I viewed the place where a few brave men gave Shadrach to freedom and to fame. The pictured walls of the old "cradle of liberty" seemed to still echo to the silvery tones of Phillips. The moulded face of Governor Andrew spoke a benediction: "I know not what record of sins awaits me in that other life, but this I do know, I never despised any man because he was ignorant, because he was poor or because he was black."

I felt that here at last was liberty, and here I would make my home.

You say to me, "certainly you can find no fault." I gratefully acknowledge the debt which I owe the people of Massachusetts, but I cannot forget my brethren here. I cannot forget my children, too, who were born here and by the blessings of God and your help I will leave to them and their children a freer and better Massachusetts even than I have found her.

"Eternal vigilance is the price of liberty."

I want upon this day to remind Massachusetts of her old ideals of liberty, justice, equality for all beneath her pure white flag. Laws, customs, institutions are nothing unless behind them stands a vital, living, throbbing public sentiment in favor of their enforcement in the spirit as well as in the letter. My friends, unless we can stay the rising tide of prejudice; unless we can hark back to our old ideals and old faiths, our very statues and memorials will some day mock us and cry shame upon us.

National Emancipation was the culmination of a moral revolution, such as the world has never seen. It was not as Garrison intended, a peaceful revolution, the unanimous verdict of an awakened national conscience. Thirty years of fierce agitation and fiercer politics made an appeal to arms absolutely certain. A conflict of arms brought on by a conflict of opinion was bound to be followed by a conflict of opinion, whichever side won. So for fifty years since Emancipation, there has been more or less conflict over the Negro and his place in the Republic. The results of that conflict have in many instances been oppressive and even disastrous to his freedom. Many things incidental to Emancipation and vital to complete freedom are unfortunately still in the controversial stages. The right of the Negro to cast a ballot on the same qualifications as his other fellow citizens is not yet conceded everywhere. Public sentiment has not yet caught up with the Constitution, nor is it in accord with the principles of true democracy. The right of the Negro to free access to all public places and to exact similar treatment therein is not universal in this country. He is segregated by law in some sections; he is segregated by custom in others. He is subjected to many petty annoyances and injustices and ofttimes deep humiliation solely on account of his color.

The explanation of this reactionary tendency sometimes given is that the Negro is only a generation from slavery. It should not be forgotten that individuals of every other race in history have at some time been held slaves. The bondage of Israel is today only an epic poem. The Greek Slave adorns simply a niche in some palace of art. The Servi of Rome instructed the masters of the world. The Anglo-Saxon has not only worn the Roman and Norman collars, but individuals of that race were sold as slaves in the West Indies as late as the seventeenth century. White men have enslaved white men, black men have enslaved black men. The place of human slavery in the divine economy I do not understand, nor do I defend it; I am glad that the human race has long since passed that stage in its development. No race has a right to lord it over another or seek to degrade it because of a history of servitude; all have passed through this cruel experience; the history of the black race is a little more recent, that is all. The fact of slavery, therefore, should not impose the slightest limitation upon the liberty of the Negro or restriction upon his rights as a man and citizen.

The one great phase of the race question agitating the country today is that of intermarriage and miscegenation. It is a serious question; it is a vital question. No one will deny the right of any man to protect his family stock, or the right of a group to preserve its racial integrity. The facts show, however, that laws, however stringent, will not accomplish it. I submit for the serious consideration of the American people that the only danger of infusion from the Negro side is simply one thing, and that is summed up in one word "injustice." Why is it that thousands of colored men and women go over to the other side, "pass," as we say? It is for no other purpose than to escape the social ostracism and civic disabilities of the Negro. Why is it that we see so many pathetic attempts to be white? It is simply to escape injustice. In a country where every opportunity is open to the white, in business, in society, in government, and the door shut against or reluctantly opened to the black, the natural unconscious effort of the black is to get white. Where black is a badge of an inferior caste position in society, the natural effort of the black is to find some method of escape. I do not advocate intermarriage; I do not defend miscegenation. The same thing is true today as it was true in the time of Lincoln. In his debates with Douglas in 1858, he noted "that among the free states, those which make the colored man the nearest equal to the white have proportionally the fewest mulattoes, the least amalgamation."

I submit therefore, that the only sure way to put an end to this tendency or desire, so far as the Negro is concerned, is to accord him all his public and political rights and to treat each individual upon his merits as a man and citizen, according to him such recognition as his talents, his genius, his services to the community or the state entitles him. Make black, brown, yellow the "open sesame" to the same privileges and the same opportunities as the white, and no one will care to become white.

Upon this day which commemorates the Emancipation of the black and the larger freedom of the white race, the redemption of the state and the birth of a new nation, I would bring to you a message not of blackness and despair but of hope—hope triumphant, hope, that Watts has pictured as blind with one string to her lyre, sees not the star just ahead, but sits supreme at the top of the world.

Emancipation redeemed the precious promises of the Declaration of Independence. It rid the Republic of its one great inconsistency, a government of the people resting upon despotism; it rescued the ship of state from the rocks of slavery and sectionalism, and set her with sails full and chart and compass true once more upon the broad ocean of humanity to lead the world to the haven of true human brotherhood. We have encountered storms and tempests at times; the waves of race antipathy have run high, and the political exigencies of the hour seem to overcast the heavens with clouds of darkness and despair, yet I have never lost faith, because the fathers set her course, and God, the Master Mariner, has ever been at the helm. "In giving freedom to the slave we insured freedom to the free." In a country where all men were free none could be slaves. Emancipation raised labor to its true dignity and gave a new impetus to industry, commerce and civilization. Under free labor men of many climes have come here to help develop the natural resources of the country, and the nation has entered upon a period of progress such as the world has never before witnessed in any time or place.

What of the Negro himself? Has he justified Emancipation? The statistics of his physical, intellectual and material progress are known to all. He has increased his numbers nearly threefold. The Negro population is today nearly three times that of the whole country at the time of the adoption of the Constitution. It is nearly three times that of New England in 1860. He has reduced his illiteracy to 30 per cent. He owns nearly $700,000,000 worth of property including nearly one million homes. He has shown that his tutelage in American civilization has not been vain; that he could live under the most trying and oppressive conditions.

Three milestones in his progress have been reached and passed:

First: The North and South agree that the abolition of slavery was right and just.

Second: The people of the North and South agree that every industrial opportunity shall be given to the Negro.

Third: The right of the Negro to be educated and the duty of the state to see to it that he has every opportunity for education are established. Public opinion has settled forever the right of the Negro to be free to labor and to educate. These three things constitute no slight advance; they are the fundamental rights of civilization.

The prophecy of Lincoln has been fulfilled, that Emancipation would be "An Act which the world will forever applaud and God must forever bless." Moreover, it should not be forgotten, as Bancroft the historian has said, that "it is in part to the aid of the Negro in freedom that the country owes its success, in its movement of regeneration—that the world of mankind owes the continuance of the United States as an example of a republic." The American Negro in freedom has brought new prestige and glory to his country in many ways. Tanner, a Georgia boy, is no longer a Negro artist, but an American artist whose works adorn the galleries of the world. Paul Laurence Dunbar, an American poet, who singing songs of his race, voicing its sorrows and griefs with unrivaled lyric sweetness and purity, has caught the ear of the world. The matchless story of Booker Washington, the American Educator, is told in many tongues and in many lands.

The history of the world has no such chapter as the Negro's fifty years of freedom. *The duty of the hour is to unshackle him and make him wholly free.* When the Negro is free from the vexatious annoyances of color and has only the same problems of life as any other men, his contribution to the general welfare of his country will be greater than ever before.

Whatever be his present disadvantages and inequalities, one thing is absolutely certain, that nowhere else in the world does so large a number of people of African descent enjoy so many rights and privileges as here in America. God has not placed these 10,000,000 here upon the American Continent in the American Republic for naught. There must be some work for them to do. He has given to each race some particular part to play in our great national drama. I predict that within the next 50 years all these discriminations, disfranchisements, and segregation will pass away. Antipathy to color is not natural, and the fear of ten by eighty million of people is only a spook of politics, a ghost summoned to the banquet to frighten the timid and foolish.

I care nothing for the past; I look beyond the present; I see a great country with her territories stretching from the rising to the setting sun, with a climate as varied as a tropical day and an Arctic night, with a soil blessed by the fruits of the earth and nourished by the waters under it; I see a great country tenanted by untold millions of happy, healthy human beings; men of every race that God has made out of one blood to inherit the earth, a great human family, governed by righteousness and justice, not by greed and fear—in which peace and happiness shall reign supreme.

Men more and more are beginning to realize that the common origin and destiny of the human race give to each species the right to occupy the earth in peace, prosperity, and plenty, and that the duty of each race is to promote the happiness of all. The movements for social and industrial justice and the right of the people to rule are world wide.

The American people are fast losing their provincial character. They are today a great world power with interests and possessions upon every part of the globe. Their horizon is the world; they are thinking in terms of the universe, and speaking in the tongues of all men.

With the widening of men's visions they must realize that the basis of true democracy and human brotherhood is the common origin and destiny of the human race; that we are all born alike, live alike, and die alike, that the laws of man's existence make absolutely no distinction.

I wandered recently into Westminster Abbey. I beheld all around me the images and effigies of the illustrious and the great, —kings, rulers, statesmen, poets, patriots, explorers and scientists;

I trampled upon the graves of some; I stood before the tombs of kings, some dead twelve centuries; there the wisest and merriest of monarchs and the most pious and dissolute of kings slept side by side. As illustrating the vanity of triumphs of personal glory, on one side of the Chapel of Henry VII, rests Mary, Queen of Scots and almost directly opposite, all that remains of Elizabeth, her executioner. I stood before the tomb of the great Napoleon; I wandered through his palaces at Versailles and Fontainebleau with all of their magnificence and splendor, and I recalled the period of his power and glory among men, and yet, he too died. Then I passed a potter's field and I looked upon the graves of the unknown, graves of the pauper, and the pleb, and I realized that they were at last equal, those who slept in Valhalla and those who slept in the common burying ground, and that they would each and all hear the first or the second trump of the resurrection "according to the deeds done in the body and the flesh, according to whether they were good or evil." In the democracy of death all are equal. Then men, my brothers, our duty is to make life in human society the same great democracy of equality of rights, of privileges, of opportunities, for all the children of men. There is nothing else worth while.

God grant to the American people this larger view of humanity, this greater conception of human duty. In a movement for democracy, for social and industrial justice, for the complete Emancipation of the Negro from the disabilities of color, Massachusetts must now, as in the past, point the way. If we fail here, with traditions and history such as are ours behind us, can we succeed elsewhere? The Great Emancipator speaks to us at this hour and furnishes the solution for all our race problems. "Let us discard all this quibbling about this man and the other man, this race and the other race, and the other race being inferior and therefore must be placed in an inferior position. Let us discard all these things and unite as one people throughout this land, until we shall once more stand up declaring that 'all men are created equal'."

God grant that the American people, year by year, may grow more like Lincoln in charity, justice, and righteousness to the end that "the government of the people, for the people, by the people, shall not perish from the earth."

THE NEGRO'S DEBT TO LINCOLN[1]

By Robert Russa Moton[2]

When the Pilgrim Fathers set foot upon the shores of America, in 1620, they laid the foundations of our national existence upon the bed-rock of liberty. From that day to this, liberty has been the common bond of our united people. In 1776 the altars of a new nation were set up in the name of liberty, and the flag of freedom unfurled before the nations of the earth. In 1812, in the name of liberty, we bared our youthful might and struck for the freedom of the seas. Again, in '61, when the charter of the nation's birth was assailed, the sons of liberty declared anew the principles of their fathers and liberty became co-extensive with the Union. In '98 the call once more was heard and freedom became co-extensive with the hemisphere. And as we stand in solemn silence here today, there still comes rumbling out of the East the slowly dying echoes of the last great struggle to make freedom co-extensive with the seven seas. Freedom is the life-blood of the nation. Freedom is the heritage bequeathed to all her sons. For all who reflect upon the glory of our Republic, freedom is the underlying philosophy of our national existence.

Conflict of Two Great Forces

But at the same time another influence was working within the nation. While the *Mayflower* was riding at anchor preparing for her voyage from Plymouth, another ship had already arrived at Jamestown. The first was to bear the pioneers of freedom—freedom of thought and freedom of conscience; the latter had already borne the pioneers of bondage, a bondage repressive alike to body, mind, and spirit. Here, then, upon American soil, met, within a year, the two great forces that were to shape the destiny of the

[1] Delivered at the dedication of the Lincoln Monument in Washington, D. C., on May 30, 1922.

[2] Robert Russa Moton was born in Amelia County, Virginia, August 26, 1867. His beginnings were obscure. An opportunity came, however, when he reached Hampton where he was educated under the influence of General Samuel Chapman Armstrong. He later became attached to the staff, and was the Commandant of the Hampton cadets. In this position he served acceptably until the death of Booker T. Washington when he was chosen as his successor. Since then, the services rendered by Dr. Moton have been largely educational, but at the same time, so far-reaching as to touch the life of the Negro in all of its ramifications.

nation. They developed side by side. Freedom was the great compelling force that dominated all, and, like a great and shining light, beckoned the oppressed of every nation to the hospitality of these shores. But slavery, like a brittle thread, was woven year by year into the fabric of the nation's life. They who for themselves sought liberty and paid the price thereof in precious blood and priceless treasure, somehow still found it possible, while defending its eternal principles for themselves, to withhold that same precious boon from others.

And how shall we account for it, except it be that in the providence of God the black race in America was thrust across the path of the onward-marching white race to demonstrate, not only for America, but for the world, whether the principles of freedom are of universal application, and ultimately to extend its blessings to all mankind.

In the process of time, as was inevitable, these great forces—the forces of liberty and the forces of bondage—met in open conflict upon the field of battle. And how strange it is, through the same over-ruling providence, that children of those who bought and sold their fellows into bondage should be among those who cast aside ties of language, of race, of religion, and even of kinship, in order that a people, not of their own race nor of their own creed or color but sharing a common humanity, should have the same measure of liberty and freedom which they themselves enjoyed.

Freedom's Costly Sacrifice

What a costly sacrifice upon the altar of freedom! How costly the world can never know nor justly estimate. The flower of the nation's manhood and the accumulated treasure of two hundred and fifty years of unremitting toil were offered up; and at length, when the bitter strife was over, when the marshaled hosts on both sides had turned again to broken, desolated firesides, a cruel fate, unsatisfied wtih the awful toll of four long years of carnage, struck at the nation's head and brought to the dust the already wearied frame of him whose patient fortitude, whose unembittered charity, whose never-failing trust in the guiding hand of God had brought the nation, weltering through a sea of blood, yet one and indivisible, to quietude and peace. On that day, Abraham Lincoln laid down his life for America, the last and costliest sacrifice upon the altar of freedom.

Today, in this inspiring presence, we raise a symbol of gratitude for all who are blest by that sacrifice. But in all this vast assemblage there are none more grateful, none more reverent, than the twelve million black Americans, who, with their fellow-citizens of every race, pay devout homage to him who was for them, more truly than for any other group, the author of their freedom. There is no question that Abraham Lincoln died to save the Union. It is equally true that to the last extremity he defended the rights of the States. But, when the last veteran has stacked his arms on fame's eternal camping ground; when only the memory of high courage and deep devotion remains to inspire the noble sons of valiant fathers; at such a time, the united voice of grateful posterity will say: The claim of greatness for Abraham Lincoln lies in this, that amid doubt and distrust, against the counsel of chosen advisers, in the hour of the nation's utter peril, he put his trust in God and spoke the word that gave freedom to a race, and vindicated the honor of a nation conceived in liberty and dedicated to the proposition that all men are created equal.

Has the Sacrifice Been Justified?

But some one will ask: Has such a sacrifice been justified? Has such martyrdom produced its worthy fruits? I speak for the Negro race. Upon us, more perhaps than upon any other group of the nation, rests the immediate obligation to justify so dear a price for our emancipation. In answer let me review the Negro's past upon American soil. No group has been more loyal. Whether bond or free, the Negro has served alike his country's need. Let it never be omitted from the nation's annals that the blood of a black man—Crispus Attucks—was the first to be shed for this nation's freedom. So again, when the world was threatened with disaster and the deciding hand of America was lifted to stay the peril, her black soldiers were among the first to cross the treacherous sea and the last to leave the trenches. No one is more sensible than the Negro himself of his incongruous position in the great American Republic. But be it recorded, to his everlasting credit, that no failure to reap the full reward of his sacrifices has ever in the least degree qualified his loyalty or cooled his patriotic fervor.

In like manner has he served his country in the pursuits of peace. From the first blows that won the virgin soil from the wilderness to the sudden marvelous expansion of our industry that went so far to win the late war, the Negro has been the nation's greatest single asset in the development of its resources. Especially is this true in the South where his uncomplaining toil sustained the splendors of that life which gave to the nation a Washington and a Jefferson, a Jackson and a Lee. And afterwards, when devastating war had leveled this fair structure with the ground, the labor of the freedmen restored it to its present proportions, more substantial and more beautiful than before.

While all this was going on, in spite of limitations within and restrictions without, he still found the way, through industry, integrity, and thrift, to acquire 22,000,000 acres of land, 600,000 homes, and 45,000 churches. After less than sixty years of freedom Negroes operate 78 banks, 100 insurance companies, and 50,000 other business enterprises with a combined capital of more than $150,000,000. Besides all this, there are within the race 60,000 professional men, 44,000 school teachers, and 400 newspapers and magazines; while its general illiteracy has been reduced to twenty-six per cent. Still the Negro race is but at the beginning of its development; so that if anything in its history could justify the sacrifice that has been made, it is this: that a race possessing such remarkable capacity for advancement has taken full advantage of its freedom to develop its latent powers for itself and for the nation. A race that has produced a Frederick Douglass in the midst of slavery, and a Booker Washington in the aftermath of reconstruction, has gone far to justify its emancipation. And the nation where such achievement is possible is fully worthy of such heroic sacrifice.

But Lincoln did not die for the Negro alone. He freed a nation as well as a race. Those conflicting forces planted two hundred and fifty years before had slowly divided the nation in spirit, in ideals, and in policy. Passing suddenly beyond the bitterness of controversy, his death served more than war itself to emphasize the enormity of the breach that had developed between the sections. Not until then was there a full realization of the deep significance of his prophetic words: "This nation cannot endure half slave and half free."

That tragic event shocked the conscience of the nation and stirred a great resolve to establish forever the priceless heritage so dearly bought. From that day the noblest minds and hearts, both North and South, were bent on healing the breach and restoring the Union. With a devotion that counted neither personal loss nor gain, Abraham Lincoln held steadfastly to an ideal for the Republic that measured at full value the worth of each race and section, cherishing at the same time the hope that under God all should share alike in the blessings of freedom. Now we rejoice in the far-seeing vision and the unswerving faith that held firmly to its single purpose, even in the midst of reproach, and preserved for all posterity the integrity of the nation.

Lincoln has not died in vain. Slowly through the years that noble spirit has been permeating every section of our land and country. Sixty years ago he stood in lonely grandeur above a torn and bleeding nation, a towering figure of patient righteousness. Today his spirit animates the breasts of millions of his countrymen who unite with us to pay tribute to his lofty character and his immortal deeds.

An Experiment in Human Relationships

And now the whole world turns with anxious hearts and eager eyes toward America. In the providence of God there has been started on these shores the great experiment of the ages—an experiment in human relationships where men and women of every nation, of every race and creed, are thrown together in daily contact. Here we are engaged, consciously or unconsciously, in the great problem of determining how different races can not only live together in peace, but coöperate in working out a higher and better civilization than has yet been achieved. At the extremes the white and black races face each other. Here in America these two races are charged under God with the responsibility of showing the world how individuals, as well as races, may differ most widely in color and inheritance and at the same time make themselves helpful and even indispensable to each other's progress and prosperity. This is especially true in the South where the black man is found in greatest numbers and where the two races are thrown into closest contact. And there today are found black men and white men who are working together in the spirit of Abraham Lincoln to establish in fact what his death established in principle: that a nation conceived in liberty and dedicated to the proposition that all men are created equal, can endure.

As we gather on this consecrated spot his spirit must rejoice that sectional rancours and racial antagonisms are softening more and more into mutual understanding and effective coöperation. And I like to think that here today, while we dedicate this symbol of our gratitude, the nation is dedicated anew by its own determined will to fulfill to the last letter the task imposed upon it by the martyred dead: that here it highly resolves that the humblest citizen, of whatever color or creed, shall enjoy that equal opportunity and unhampered freedom for which the immortal Lincoln gave the last full measure of devotion.

And the progress of events confirms this view. Step by step has the nation been making its way forward in the spirit of the great Emancipator. And nowhere is this more true than in that section which sixty years ago seemed least in accord with his spirit and purpose, yet at this hour, in many things, is vying with the rest of the nation toward the fulfillment of his hopes.

Twelve million black Americans share in the rejoicing of this hour. As yet, no other name so warms the heart or stirs the depths of their gratitude as that of Abraham Lincoln. To him above all others we owe the privilege of sharing as fellow-citizens in the consecration of this spot and the dedication of this shrine. In the name of Lincoln twelve million black Americans pledge to the nation their continued loyalty and their unreserved coöperation in every effort to realize in deeds the lofty principles established by his martyrdom. "With malice toward none, with charity for all, with firmness in the right as God gives us to see the right," may we, one and all, black and white, North and South, strive on to finish the work which he so nobly began: to make America an example for all the world of equal justice and equal opportunity for all.

CHAPTER XI

OPTIMISTIC ORATORY

IMMEDIATELY following the reconstruction, there developed the polemic orator. As the effort to elevate the Negro to citizenship in the South had failed upon the withdrawal of the Federal troops from that section, persons still interested in the race hoped that, by building upon the mere foundation of their physical freedom, they might devise some scheme for their elevation to the status of the whites.

At first, the emphasis was upon religion, with education as a preparation for a larger enjoyment of things spiritual. A generation after the days of reconstruction, however, Booker T. Washington came forward with the idea of emphasizing industrial training for economic efficiency to secure the recognition of the whites. Coming at a time when so much had been done to elevate the Negro by applying the means which had hitherto been instrumental in the uplift of the whites, his policy was militantly attacked by persons who would not accept this program as a finality.

This optimistic doctrine, however, was most eloquently and successfully set forth by this new leader in one of the greatest speeches of modern times at the Atlanta Exposition in 1895. Reading this discourse, which diverges so much from the procedure of others then toiling for the mental development of the Negro, one can readily observe how much confusion in the ranks of such workers would inevitably result.

AN ADDRESS DELIVERED AT THE OPENING OF THE COTTON STATES' EXPOSITION IN ATLANTA, GEORGIA, SEPTEMBER, 1895.

By Booker T. Washington

Mr. President and Gentlemen of the Board of Directors and Citizens: One-third of the population of the South is of the Negro race. No enterprise seeking the material, civil, or moral welfare of this section can disregard this element of our population and reach the highest success. I but convey to you, Mr. President and Directors, the sentiment of the masses of my race when I say that in no way have the value and manhood of the American Negro been more fittingly and generously recognized than by the managers of this magnificent Exposition at every stage of its progress. It is a recognition that will do more to cement the friendship of the two races than any occurrence since the dawn of freedom.

Not only this, but the opportunity here afforded will awaken among us a new era of industrial progress. Ignorant and inexperienced, it is not strange that in the first years of our new life we began at the top instead of at the bottom; that a seat in Congress or the State Legislature was more sought than real estate or industrial skill; that the political convention or stump speaking had more attractions than starting a dairy farm or truck garden.

A ship lost at sea for many days suddenly sighted a friendly vessel. From the mast of the unfortunate vessel was seen a signal: "Water, water; we die of thirst!" The answer from the friendly vessel at once came back: "Cast down your bucket where you are." A second time the signal, "Water, water; send us water!" ran up from the distressed vessel, and was answered: "Cast down your bucket where you are." The captain of the distressed vessel, at last heeding the injunction, cast down his bucket, and it came up full of fresh, sparkling water from the mouth of the Amazon River. To those of my race who depend upon bettering their condition in a foreign land, or who underestimate the importance of cultivating friendly relations with the Southern white man, who is his next door neighbor, I would say: "Cast down your bucket where you are"—cast it down in making friends in every manly way of the people of all races by whom we are surrounded.

Cast it down in agriculture, mechanics, in commerce, in domestic service, and in the professions. And in this connection it is well to bear in mind that whatever other sins the South may be called to bear, when it comes to business, pure and simple, it is in the South that the Negro is given a man's chance in the commercial world, and in nothing is this Exposition more eloquent than in emphasizing this chance. Our greatest danger is, that in the great leap from slavery to freedom we may overlook the fact that the masses of us are to live by the productions of our hands, and fail to keep in mind that we shall prosper in proportion as we learn to dignify and glorify common labor, and put brains and skill into the common occupations of life; shall prosper in proportion as we learn to draw the line between the superficial and the substantial, the ornamental gewgaws of life and the useful. No race can prosper till it learns that there is as much dignity in tilling a field as in writing a poem. It is at the bottom of life we must begin, and not at the top. Nor should we permit our grievances to overshadow our opportunities.

To those of the white race who look to the incoming of those of foreign birth and strange tongue and habits for the prosperity of the South, were I permitted I would repeat what I say to my own race, "Cast down your bucket where you are." Cast it down among the 8,000,000 Negroes whose habits you know, whose fidelity and love you have tested in days when to have proved treacherous meant the ruin of your firesides. Cast down your bucket among these people who have, without strikes and labor wars, tilled your fields, cleared your forests, builded your railroads and cities, and brought forth treasures from the bowels of the earth, and helped make possible this magnificent representation of the progress of the South. Casting down your bucket among my people, helping and encouraging them as you are doing on these grounds, and, with education of head, hand and heart, you will find that they will buy your surplus land, make blossom the waste places in your fields, and run your factories. While doing this, you can be sure in the future, as in the past, that you and your families will be surrounded by the most patient, faithful, law-abiding, and unresentful people that the world has seen. As we have proved our loyalty to you in the past, in nursing your children, watching by the sick bed of your mothers and fathers, and often following them with tear-dimmed eyes to their graves, so in the future, in our humble way, we shall stand by you with a devotion that no foreigner can approach, ready to lay down our lives, if need be, in defense of yours, interlacing our industrial, commercial, civil, and religious life with yours in a way that shall make the interests of both races one. In all things that are purely social we can be as separate as the fingers, yet one as the hand in all things essential to mutual progress.

There is no defense or security for any of us except in the highest intelligence and development of all. If anywhere there are efforts tending to curtail the fullest growth of the Negro, let these efforts be turned into stimulating, encouraging, and making him the most useful and intelligent citizen. Effort or means so invested will pay a thousand per cent interest. These efforts will be twice blessed —blessing him that gives and him that takes.

There is no escape through law of man or God from the inevitable:

"The laws of changeless justice bind
Oppressor with oppressed;
And close as sin and suffering joined
We march to fate abreast."

Nearly sixteen millions of hands will aid you in pulling the load upwards, or they will pull against you the load downwards. We shall constitute one-third and more of the ignorance and crime of the South, or one-third its intelligence and progress; we shall contribute one-third to the business and industrial prosperity of the South, or we shall prove a veritable body of death, stagnating, depressing, retarding every effort to advance the body politic.

Gentlemen of the Exposition, as we present to you our humble effort at an exhibition of our progress, you must not expect overmuch. Starting thirty years ago with ownership here and there in a few quilts and pumpkins and chickens (gathered from miscellaneous sources), remember the path that has led from these to the invention and production of agricultural implements, buggies, steam engines, newspapers, books, statuary, carving, paintings, the management of drug stores and banks has not been trodden without contact with thorns and thistles. While we take pride in what we exhibit as a result of our independent efforts, we do not for a moment forget that our part in this exhibition would fall far short of your expectations but for the constant help that has come to our educational life, not only from the Southern States, but especially from Northern philanthropists, who have made their gifts a constant stream of blessing and encouragement.

The wisest among my race understand that the agitation of questions of social equality is the extremest folly, and that progress in the enjoyment of all the privileges that will come to us must be the result of severe and constant struggle rather than of artificial forcing. No race that has anything to contribute to the markets of the world is long in any degree ostracized. It is important and right that all privileges of the law be ours, but it is vastly more important that we be prepared for the exercise of those privileges. The opportunity to earn a dollar in a factory just now is worth infinitely more than the opportunity to spend a dollar in an opera house.

In conclusion, may I repeat that nothing in thirty years has given us more hope and encouragement, and drawn us so near to you of the white race, as this opportunity offered by the Exposition; and here bending, as it were, over the altar that represents the results of the struggles of your race and mine, both starting practically empty-handed three decades ago, I pledge that, in your effort to work out the great and intricate problem which God has laid at the doors of the South, you shall have at all times the patient, sympathetic help of my race; only let this be constantly in mind that, while from representations in these buildings of the products of field, of forest, of mine, of factory, letters, and art, much good will come, yet far above and beyond material benefits will be the higher good, that let us pray God will come, in a blotting out of sectional differences and racial animosities and suspicions, in a determination to administer absolute justice, in a willing obedience among all classes to the mandates of law. This, coupled with our material prosperity, will bring into our beloved South a new heaven and a new earth.

ADDRESS DELIVERED AT THE HARVARD ALUMNI DINNER IN 1896

By Booker T. Washington[1]

Mr. President and Gentlemen: It would in some measure relieve my embarrassment if I could, even in a slight degree, feel myself worthy of the great honor which you do me today. Why you have called me from the Black Belt of the South, from among my humble people, to share in the honors of this occasion, is not for me to explain; and yet it may not be inappropriate for me to suggest that it seems to me that one of the most vital questions that touch our American life is how to bring the strong, wealthy and learned into helpful touch with the poorest, most ignorant and humblest, and at the same time make the one appreciate the vitalizing, strengthening influence of the other. How shall we make the mansions on yon Beacon Street feel and see the need of the spirits in the lowliest cabin in Alabama cotton fields or Louisiana sugar bottoms? This problem Harvard University is solving, not by bringing itself down, but by bringing the masses up.

If through me, an humble representative, seven millions of my people in the South might be permitted to send a message to Harvard—Harvard that offered up on death's altar young Shaw, and Russell, and Lowell, and scores of others, that we might have a free and united country—that message would be, "Tell them that the sacrifice was not in vain. Tell them that by habits of thrift and economy, by way of the industrial school and college, we are coming. We are crawling up, working up, yea, bursting up. Often through oppression, unjust discrimination and prejudice, but through them all we are coming up, and with proper habits, intelligence and property, there is no power on earth that can permanently stay our progress."

If my life in the past has meant anything in the lifting up of my people and the bringing about of better relations between your race and mine, I assure you from this day it will mean doubly more. In the economy of God there is but one standard by which an individual can succeed—there is but one for a race. This country demands that every race shall measure itself by the Amer-

[1] In 1896 Harvard University honored Mr. Washington by conferring upon him the degree of Master of Arts. This was the first time that a New England college had conferred an honorary degree upon a Negro.

ican standard. By it a race must rise or fall, succeed or fail, and in the last analysis mere sentiment counts for little. During the next half century and more, my race must continue passing through the severe American crucible. We are to be tested in our patience, our forbearance, our perseverance, our power to endure wrong, to withstand temptations, to economize, to acquire and use skill; in our ability to compete, to succeed in commerce, to disregard the superficial for the real, the appearance for the substance, to be great and yet small, learned and yet simple, high and yet the servant of all. This, this is the passport to all that is best in the life of our Republic, and the Negro must possess it, or be debarred.

While we are thus being tested, I beg of you to remember that wherever our life touches yours, we help or hinder. Wherever your life touches ours, you make us stronger or weaker. No member of your race in any part of our country can harm the meanest member of mine without the proudest and bluest blood in Massachusetts being degraded. When Mississippi commits crime, New England commits crime, and in so much, lowers the standard of your civilization. There is no escape—man drags man down, or man lifts man up.

In working out our destiny, while the main center of activity must be with us, we shall need, in a large measure in the years that are to come as we have in the past, the help, the encouragement, the guidance that the strong can give the weak. Thus helped, we of both races in the South soon shall throw off the shackles of racial and sectional prejudice and rise, as Harvard University has risen and as we all should rise, above the clouds of ignorance, narrowness and selfishness, into that atmosphere, that pure sunshine, where it will be our highest ambition to serve man, our brother, regardless of race or previous condition.

FREEDOM THROUGH EDUCATION[1]

By Roscoe Conkling Bruce[2]

We gather to commemorate the resolute and faithful men who fought and fell in the Civil War for nationality and free institu-

[1] An address delivered by Roscoe Conkling Bruce in Sanders Theater, Memorial Hall, Cambridge, Massachusetts, before the Memorial Society of Harvard University on Memorial Day, 1905.

[2] Roscoe Conkling Bruce was born in Washington at the time his father, Senator

tions. Now and then it is urged that the North fought to free the slave; but, looking back over the years, can we say that was all that the men whose names are written upon these walls—Shaw, and Lowell, and Pickering—died for? It was not merely the Sorrow Songs of plantation and swamp, the anguished cry of fugitive slave, the burning eloquence of Frederick Douglass—it was not so much pity as nationality and Anglo-Saxon ideals and institutions that impelled your heroes to strike the fetters from the toiling slave. Your soldiers recognized the fact that fundamental Americanism demands the free play of each individual's best powers in the service of the community. In the interest of social justice, national economy, free institutions, human nature itself, your heroes fought to set my people free.

In camps and fields many a New England soldier with the blue-back spelling book on his knees, had clumsily taught black soldiers and contrabands the first hard lessons in the great mystery of letters. Hard on the heels of the soldiers, when the air was not yet purged of the horrid smell of powder and blood, the schoolma'm ventured. She came to liberate; but, she came with benediction and grace, her power was over the heart and conscience of the people. It was the teacher's service to grant the slave that moral freedom which emancipation of the body made possible; that is the teacher's service at this hour. The free play of each individual's best powers can be secured only through education.

It must be remembered that in slavery Massachusetts and Mississippi, Georgia and Vermont sinned together. Slavery was recognized by statute in 1641 by Massachusetts, in 1650 by Connecticut, in 1661 by Virginia, and later by the other colonies. If emancipation was compassed or in progress throughout the North before 1800, who shall say it was not economic rather than moral reasons that vouchsafed the North this preëminence in public righteousness? Who, then, shall cast the first stone? Slavery was the

Blanch K. Bruce of Mississippi, was serving as United States Senator. He attended the Howard University Academy for a short while, but completed the preparation for college at Phillips Exeter Academy. He then entered Harvard University where he distinguished himself as a debater, as is evidenced by his being chosen class orator. Leaving Harvard, Mr. Bruce became head of the academic department at Tuskegee Institute. From that position, he came to the District of Columbia to serve as Assistant Superintendent in charge of the colored schools. After holding this position fifteen years he resigned to go into business.

nation's sin; freedom through education is the nation's opportunity, the nation's duty to itself.

The fact that in Louisiana, Alabama, Georgia, North and South Carolina, Mississippi, and Virginia over one-half the Negro males of voting age are illiterate, today shows that the nation's duty is not done. Although the total Negro enrollment in the common schools of the South has almost trebled in twenty-six years, it is true that in Georgia, Florida, Alabama, Mississippi, Louisiana, and Arkansas the number of Negro illiterates today exceeds the aggregate Negro population of similar age in 1860; the enlargement of school facilities has lagged far behind the sheer increase in population. Only about one-half the Negro children of school age are enrolled in school and less than one-third of those enrolled attend six months or more. The fundamental principle of the American common school, I mean the impartial disposal of public funds to educate all the children of all the people,—despite substantial improvement in public sentiment, that principle is very far indeed from recognition in Southern practice. Black Americans in the South cast no ballots. And so, not more than one-fifth of the school income, the United States Commissioner of Education very cautiously estimates, goes at present to the support of Negro schools. Says Mr. Carl Holliday, a southern white college professor, in the South Atlantic Quarterly (October, 1904), with unusual candor, "In Alabama where the number of children of school age is almost equally divided between the whites and the blacks, the Negro obtains scarcely more than fifteen per cent of the income for public education. Under such conditions the mental development of the Negro is a matter not of years but of ages."

Of the nine million Negroes in the United States, seven millions live in country districts; the primary problem is that of the peasant. By an automatic process whose current causes are social, the Negro farming population tends to segregate in rather sharply defined areas. For example, in Alabama, there are twelve counties, which form a continuous belt across the state largely coinciding with the cotton soils of the Central Prairie, in each of which the Negroes comprise over seventy per cent of the population. The aggregate population of these counties is nearly half a million, of which eighty-five per cent is Negro; in 1880 the blacks outnumbered the whites by thirty-six to ten, and in 1900 by fifty-five to ten.

Now, the white county Negro seems to occupy a higher level of life and certainly displays a higher industrial efficiency than his black county brother. Comparing twelve white counties in northern Alabama with the twelve black counties, I find that in 1900 fifty-one per cent of the Negroes were illiterate in the white counties as against sixty-seven per cent in the black. In the white counties the Negroes were in charge of less than three thousand agricultural holdings but owned thirty-seven per cent; in the black counties they were in charge of fifty thousand holdings and owned only eight per cent. The white belt produces from one-fourth to one-half bale of cotton to the acre on poor land—the same product that the black belt produces on next to the best land in the South. To no small extent the whites use selected seed, plant an increasing variety of crops, rotate their crops, use fertilizers with intelligence, plow diligently to avert the effects of drouth, readily take to new implements and machinery, stick to their tasks with constancy, and practice many minute economies in production and in consumption. These things are full of instruction and stimulus to the black farmer; but example and stimulus are absent in the black belt. The industrial condition and efficiency and the moral quality of the black farmer in the Alabama black belt have, I believe, improved substantially, but at a snail's pace. The black belt folk are not stolid and stunned; they are good-hearted, hopeful despite the serfmaking proclivities of the crop lien, eager to learn. On the whole, however, the general efficiency of the white county Negro is higher than that of his brother in the black belt and this is largely due to the presence in the one case and the absence in the other of examples of intelligence, thrift, and energy.

You must remember that, in the United States, whereas nineteen per cent of the Negroes engaged in gainful pursuits are grouped as farmers, planters, and overseers, thirty-four per cent are agricultural laborers. Idle a large part of the year, burdened with no particular responsibility, a member of no particular community with position and reputation to make or to sustain, without a home or even a fixed abode, accessible to few of the incentives to probity and thrift and progress that wholesome family life exerts, exposed to the myriad temptations of careless roving—the black farm hand presents a very grave problem.

Is it not abundantly clear that, unless extraordinary effort is put forth, the Negro masses herding in black belts in the way I have suggested, will indefinitely remain below what ought to be our national minimum?—that some of the richest agricultural resources in America will remain undeveloped?—that a vast supply of labor will remain inefficient?—that these slumbering masses of black men and women and children will remain in their helplessness a temptation to unscrupulous shrewdness and a menace to the spirit and practice of Anglo-Saxon institutions? Education is a vast resource; yet the public schools are wretchedly housed, wretchedly furnished, wretchedly taught. Their effort does not vitally connect itself with the actual life and need of these people; if the school arts be ill taught, agriculture and the household arts are hardly taught at all. Now, the moral and industrial regeneration of Negro life in the Black Belt must come from within; the job must be done by teachers, preachers, mechanics, farmers, housewives educated and trained in Negro schools and inspired to help their people. Institutions seeking to contribute to this far-reaching service should educate their students to ideals and train them in habits and arts that they may spread among the masses intelligent methods in farm and garden and household work; patient thrift and sustained industry; clear foresight and prompt initiative; rugged honesty and steady self-control; moral courage, chastity; public spirit and racial confidence and pride. In a school community like Tuskegee all the elements of real life are adequately represented. The students participate to the fullest extent in the whole circle of activities; they gain experience and a reasonable confidence in their own powers and a sense of responsibility. Such school communities, resting upon agriculture as the basic industry, should be established at the center of each of the greater black belts; they should, as President Eliot has recently suggested, receive the nation's aid. Such institutions secure the free play of the best powers of men and women of unusual quality. In a deeper and truer sense than your conquering armies were, a Tuskegee is an instrument of emancipation. I voice today not the prayer of pity, but the august demand of a vast national responsibility.

"The country Negro," says Professor Kelly Miller, "is embalmed . . . in a state of nature, where he will be preserved . . . until his opportunity comes. With the city Negro, on the other hand, it is immediate rescue or destruction." For better schools, better police protection, greater variety of interest, greater personal independence, the Negro flees crop lien, plantation store, and overseer, for the city. Today there are 700,000 Negroes in our large cities. The large number of persons concerned, their steady and rapid increase, their unpreparedness for the new and merciless life, their practical exclusion from the trades, and their congestion in black wards challenge attention. The urban Negro dwells in sullen poverty, his death rate is alarming, he commits excessive crime. "The rich man's wealth is his strong city; the destruction of the poor is their poverty." The starved body, the starved mind, the starved soul predisposed to crime; and poverty starves body, mind, and soul. I cannot forget that behind the marshaled statistics of poverty and crime and death stand suffering, withered hopes, desolate homes, distorted human nature. To me Marlowe's noble art does not more vividly present the eternal tragedy between human aspiration and human power than these dreary statistics portray the awful contrast between the open-hearted buoyancy of the plantation Negro lured to the city's breathless life and the degradation in which he and his children and his children's children find themselves enmeshed. Fundamentally, this situation is due to the fact that the Negro peasant is wholly unprepared for the complications, the composition, the moral stress of city life; and little or no provision is made to train him in the arts and industries by which he might sustain himself. Memphis, Atlanta, Washington, Baltimore, St. Louis, Philadelphia, and New York,—in which the Negro population varies from two per cent of the total in New York to forty-nine per cent in Memphis, and from 36,000 in St. Louis to 87,000 in Washington—contain a total black population of over half a million souls; and in not one of these cities does there exist a Trade School for Negroes even remotely comparable to the Baron de Hirsch School in New York City for immigrant Jews. It is certainly to the interest of the cities to place within reach of their Negro populations not only the usual facilities of good grammar schools and good high schools, but also adequate training directly for economic independence. It is rather more far-seeing to train than to imprison; it costs less in moral liability and in dollars. As to the matter of death rates and some other matters, a modern city is like an ocean liner; yellow fever in the steerage does not stay there. As domestic servant and unskilled laborer, the urban Negro does not offer the city his best powers as an instrument of production. Embittered by an industrial boycott to which he cannot in sufficient numbers oppose high efficiency, at his wit's end for a crust of bread and a couch, his vote is the prompt resource of scamp and scoundrel. For the education and training that shall liberate the black citizen's best powers in the service of the community, it is not pity that pleads—it is social justice and free institutions and the common welfare and the national responsibility.

Dominant opinion North and South is at one in conviction and insistence that the development of the Negro people in America is essential to the progressive well-being of the nation, to the integrity of free institutions in this land; and that this development shall be in a very definite sense separate. Perhaps the most significant fact in recent Negro history is the rapid growth in this rising people, under stress of differential treatment, of self-consciousness and race pride. If this self-consciousness degenerates on occasion into hypersensitiveness and insolence, you must remember that the prejudice often flouts all the equities of democratic life and occasionally revels in excesses which in Jamaica and in Egypt English administration and good sense sternly repress. The rose, I beg you to remember, does not flourish under a millstone; the cactus may.

Discrimination at the soda fountain has been capitalized by the black druggist and is everywhere in the South yielding him "handsome returns"! To the Negro physician race prejudice and differential treatment are in some of their effects a positive asset and bounty. He does not insist in his very salutation upon defining his patient's social inferiority; he is not dreaded as a callous stranger with a terrible knife. The Negro physician's service is largely that of spreading among his people in the multifarious contacts of social life an appreciation of the importance of personal hygiene and good sanitation. It is he who, not only in the sickroom but in all the assemblies of the people, has aroused Negroes to the infectious character of tubercular diseases and the means for checking the advance of the great White Plague. The successful careers of hundreds of Negro physicians and pharmacists in the Lower South is the clearest possible evidence of the opportunities awaiting trained men.

And who can preach the Word of God to black men but a Negro —be he Crummell, with his Oxford education, or the Right Reverend John Jasper, with his "sun-do-move" theology? In country districts, the churches are the centers of organization in Negro life, in potency of influence the preacher overshadows teacher and landholder; but too often the whole weight of the untrained and ignorant preacher's influence is thrown sheer against both material and moral progress. In cities the control of the church over the Negro's life needs strengthening if only for restraint of crime. Everywhere the elaborate ecclesiastical organization should be directed and represented by men of high character and keen intelligence. The divergence in views and sentiments between the older and younger generations of Negroes expresses itself very pointedly in religious matters. The church must remain the House of God, but at the same time the preacher must enrich the formalities of religion not only with the sweet spirit of sociability but also with the serious interests of daily life. The church, as well as the school, must be a social center rich in interest if it is to exercise a reasonable control over the more vigorous elements in the community. The preacher faces a situation in which the utmost tact and intelligence and breadth of appreciation and power of leadership are requisite. Without unduly shocking the ingrained beliefs of the fathers, he must attach the religious sentiment to the moralities of common life. He must preach honesty, chastity, fidelity to contract, home-getting—the religion of character and thrift. How can such service be rendered by an illiterate?—a weakling?

Here and there, particularly in private institutions like Spelman Seminary and Hampton Institute and in Universities like Atlanta and Fisk and Shaw, white teachers—most from the North but some from the South—of the finest culture and the noblest devotion will always, I pray and believe, continue to teach Negro youth in the heart of the South. For this service, the Negro people will always feel as they have always felt—profoundly grateful. But, schools —industrial and normal, elementary and secondary, great and small —even colleges and professional schools,—such separate institutions for Negro students will more and more seek teachers and executive officers in men and women of Negro blood. In point of fact, the teachers of Negroes are today in the vast majority of cases black, and neither South nor North questions for a moment the competency of black men and women for such service or the wholesome effects of such an arrangement upon the spirit and attitude of the students and upon the whole present social situation. The quickening of Negro life must come more and more from within, the uplifting forces in Negro life must be more and more in the hands of Negroes. Now, the fundamental problem of any school is not land and buildings but personnel—the personnel of the teaching body. It is a grievous error to suppose that a good heart and some ability to read and write adequately equip a teacher of the common branches; or that sobriety and some knack with saw and plane and hammer, make a teacher of carpentry. One of the most serious problems that a great institution like Tuskegee, for example, has to face is the dearth of men and women of liberal education, specific training in teaching, and professional spirit and ideals. Negro public schools are everywhere gravely embarrassed by lack of principals and teachers with a sound and thorough education. This issue is now upon us; the demand for well-equipped Negro teachers for all classes of Negro schools is at this moment very far in excess of the supply. The Negro teacher of the best education and the best training is never out of a job; the field of his influence and service is almost limitless.

Where, then, can the teachers, the preachers, the physicians for the Negro people be educated and trained unless the South has colleges and professional schools for selected Negro youth? Now, the truth is that the superior education and training has suffered from popular distrust of the educational value of Greek and Latin in the teaching of Negro youth. A black boy can get education, it has been felt, out of making a horse-shoe or building a wagon; but how out of reading De Senectute? But, the effects of education are really to be sought in the mind and character and growing power of the student; the process is, in any case, essentially intangible, and to estimate the thoroughness of the process and its value for life in terms of the ponderable character of the apparatus is a fundamental error. Anything is practical that is of service to the community. Clear thinking and an insight into human nature certainly have as many practical uses as deftness with hammer and tongs; ordinarily, a teacher influences more people in more important ways than does a blacksmith. In so far as the popular distrust assumes Negro nature to be as unlike human nature as chalk is unlike cheese, I may be permitted to hope the distrust blinks the facts. But, it is unquestionably true that the curriculum of the New England college which New England teachers planted in the South is not adequately adjusted to the life of white youth in New England today, much less to the life of black youth in the lower South. The misfortune is that, while in New England that curriculum has since the sixties been brought into vital relations with present-day conditions, in the South it retains much of the old-time rigor and narrowness and there is much worship of the fetich. The Negro college in the South should admit students who have never studied Latin or Greek, and should enrich its curriculum by the addition of thorough courses in natural science with its applications to trade and industry; in history and social science with special attention to the traditions and progress of Negro peoples in Africa and in America, and to the sociological problems in which Negro life in America is enmeshed today. The Negro college should render its curriculum flexible and more widely serviceable through the introduction of an elective system by the provisions of which the dead languages might give way to the living languages and history and social science, and advanced mathematics to psychology and ethics and the principles and practice of education. And, finally, the Negro university should organize well-equipped schools of education, of engineering, of agriculture alongside of the school of medicine. Some of these reforms have already been compassed or are in progress, I am glad to say, in the best Negro colleges and universities of the South.

It is essential, says President Eliot, "that the teachers, preachers, physicians, lawyers, engineers, and superior mechanics, the leaders of industry throughout the Negro communities of the South, should be trained in superior institutions. If any expect that the Negro teachers of the South can be adequately educated in primary schools or grammar schools or industrial schools pure and simple, I can only say in reply that that is more than we can do in the North with the white race. The only way to have good primary schools and grammar schools in Massachusetts is to have high and normal schools and colleges in which the higher teachers are trained. It must be so throughout the South, the Negro race needs absolutely these higher facilities for education." And yet, for example, after nearly four decades of splendid service, with over a thousand graduates, many of whom are in positions of high trust and responsibility, and with a present enrollment of nearly nine hundred selected Negro youth, the total endowment of Atlanta and Fisk Universities taken together is only $125,000!

When the black soldiers of the sixty-second and sixty-fifth regiments of United States colored infantry were discharged, they contributed a fund of over $6,000 to establish in Missouri a school where their children might enjoy the blessings of a useful education. Those Negro soldiers gave their savings to the same cause for which they had gladly offered their lives—the cause of freedom. The Harvard men who fell in the Civil War gave their lives for social justice, national economy, free institutions, human nature itself. When I stand before the memorial to Robert Gould Shaw, representing in bronze, as your chairman (Professor George Herbert Palmer) has said, "a subject race moving toward freedom, gaining that freedom through its own exertions, yet under the guidance of a people more developed than itself," I am glad to know that a memorial glorified if not by the same art, yet by an equal motive, will be erected to William H. Baldwin, who sought under peace to vouchsafe black Americans opportunity to win a larger freedom. The Baldwin memorial will be erected not on Boston Common but in the heart of the South on soil once tilled by Negro slaves but now consecrated to the education of the children of those slaves under Negro teachers. Baldwin advanced the education and training of selected Negro youth in whose hands may more and more be entrusted the great uplifting forces in Negro life. These two sons of Harvard whose names I would link today, the soldier and the citizen, chiefly served free institutions in America.

Until the fetters fall from the minds and hearts and energies of nine million black Americans, the blood of your heroic soldiers cries aloud from the battle-field and the nation's duty is not done.

BOOKER T. WASHINGTON—A LOVER OF HIS FELLOW-MEN[1]

By William H. Lewis

It is fitting that the Urban League, for the improvement of the conditions of the colored population right at your own doors, should join with Hampton and Tuskegee in this Memorial to Dr. Booker T. Washington, because the objects of the League, of which Dr. Washington was at one time a Director, providing for better sanitary housing, better social conditions, greater industrial opportunities for the thousands of his race in New York, were ever dear to his heart. It is fitting also because the League stands for the principle of coöperation between the races, which begets sympathy and understanding. It recognizes the fact that the colored population will become either a great asset or a dreadful liability to the City, according to whether they are given a fair opportunity to find a place in your social and industrial life, or neglected and treated as strangers within your gates.

It is not of ourselves we have come to speak at this time. We have come to pay our humble tribute of respect to the fallen leader, whose ideas of the economic and social welfare of the race constitute our creed and our program.

That voice, the most eloquent of his day, which once pleaded in this hall for humanity and justice, is hushed forever. The magnetic personality, that so often stood here, the representative of the social, educational, and industrial aspirations of his race, has passed to the silent sepulchre of the dust. No more shall we behold that sturdy, familiar figure. Never more shall we hear that persuasive voice pleading for educational opportunities for the great masses of his people. But the character and influence of Washington still survive. He lives in this magnificent audience gathered here, representing the wealth, the splendor, the intelligence, and public spirit of the great metropolis that he loved so well, upon which he cast a last fond, lingering glance that November afternoon as,

[1] A Memorial Meeting in honor of Dr. Booker T. Washington was held in Carnegie Hall, New York City, on the evening of February 11, 1916. The meeting was held under the auspices of Hampton Institute, Tuskegee Institute, and the National League on Urban Conditions. Hon. Seth Low, Chairman of the Board of Trustees of Tuskegee Institute, presided, and addresses were made by Dr. H. B. Frissell, Hon. W. H. Lewis, Hon. William G. Willcox, Dr. James H. Dillard, and Major R. R. Moton.

sadly but courageously, he began his last journey to Tuskegee and beyond. He lives in millions of homes built by hands of thrift and love, in millions of hopeful, purposeful lives inspired by his teachings. He lives in the thousands of young men and women whom he has sent forth from Tuskegee to teach their fellows how to live healthy, happy, wholesome, human lives. Above all, he lives in that "higher good" which, at Atlanta twenty years ago, he prayed God might come "in blotting out sectional differences and racial animosities and suspicions." If today, in our country, sectionalism happily is on the wane, it is because this slave, with broken chains dangling from his wrists, stretching forth one hand to the North and one to the South to brothers once estranged, said: "You must help each other the other's burden to bear." If today there is a better understanding between the races, a growing feeling of respect for the rights of each other, a spirit of mutual helpfulness and understanding between them, it is because Washington spent his life in cultivating friendships that lay close to his door.

I pledge you here and now, for those of us who knew and loved Dr. Washington, that we will ever pray and strive for that "higher good"; for by this pathway alone can we climb to the summit of complete equality of rights and opportunities in the great American Democracy.

The name and character of Washington will live for years to come, as an example of the heights to which the humblest of any race may attain through service of his fellows. Whether his influence is to be a permanent and abiding force in American life depends upon the future of the institution he founded. In his lifetime he carried Tuskegee upon his heart; in his death Tuskegee rests upon his ashes. That noble institution will either crumble and perish or stand as his enduring monument accordingly as the American people give to it that endowment to which it is entitled because of the inestimable service which it has rendered and is rendering in the solution of the greatest of our problems. His was a practical mind, keen for the essential and fundamental things of life. If he could speak to us at this hour he would ask no memorial of bronze or marble; he would prefer to live in the opportunity given to millions of his race, through Tuskegee, to climb upward slowly but surely through industry and character to complete American citizenship.

The outlines of this marvelous career are known to all because its active period was passed during the lifetime of men not yet old. Born a slave without a name, laid upon a bundle of dirty rags upon the dirt floor of a log cabin, with hardly more thought given to his birth than that of a domestic animal, he had the spark of genius in him; he died a freedman, a citizen of the world. An unlettered slave at the age of seven, he was a Master of Arts at thirty-seven; at forty-two a Doctor of Laws, an American Educator of first rank—the first man of color in the world. So great had been his achievements in uplifting his race in America that Lord Grey invited him to undertake the enormous task of formulating an educational system for the blacks of South Africa.

Surely if ever Abraham Lincoln, upon the eve of whose birthday we stand, needed justification for emancipation it is found in the life, character, and achievements of Booker T. Washington. Washington's life showed that a man could rise from being property himself to inherit the earth; to win, through sacrifice and service to his fellows, immortal fame.

When the shackles fell from his limbs they also fell from his mind, his heart, and soul. No doubt the terrible social and political and industrial conditions in which he found his race after the reconstruction weighed heavily upon him, but he never allowed himself to become discouraged, disheartened, soured, or embittered. He rose superior to race injustice and race prejudice. He so often said that no man could make him hate another; that he would never allow himself to be dragged down by hating any man because of his race or even of his prejudices. He loved the South, its people, and understood them and their sorrow, the terrible experience which had been theirs through the passing of slavery. He sought to assuage her grief, to help bind up her wounds, and to carry the friendly relations which frequently existed between master and slave over into the new life of the freedman. As has been so often said, he became the interpreter of one race to another. He understood both because he was of both. In loving and working for his own race it was easy for him to love and work for all men, so that the man "farthest down," whether in London, Galicia, or Sicily, became the object of his affections and his prayers. In his sympathies for the cause of man he touched the universal. He was a lover of his fellow-men. This is the secret of the greatness of Washington. His was a great soul, in which no bitterness or littleness could even find a lurking place. His was the great heart of Lincoln, "with malice toward none and charity for all." He loved all men, and all men loved him.

When Washington came upon the stage he beheld an emancipated race chained to the soil by the mortgage crop system and other devices; he said to his people: "You must own your own lands, you must own your own farms," and forthwith there was a second emancipation. He beheld the industrial trade and skilled labor passing into other hands; he said: "The hand, as well as the head, must be educated," and forthwith the educational system of America was revolutionized. He saw the black, toiling masses spending all they earned; he said: "Thrift, save; get a bank account. This is the only way." He saw that the political superstructure of our freedom could not last without a solid economic basis laid in thrift, independence, skilled labor, good homes, and good schools, and all the institutions necessary to permanent success. He reared anew the foundations of freedom upon an economic basis. He cemented the friendships of the two races as an essential to permanent progress. He compromised no principle of human rights. In his own way, simple and diplomatic, he advanced the interests and rights of all. He was a statesman, as well as a leader of his race. He was an American orator, educator, and publicist of highest rank and authority.

Washington grew, as Tuskegee grew, in richness, prestige, power, and influence. Tuskegee typifies the man and his achievements. That great institution stands, above all things else, for what Washington intended it should stand, as convincing, ample proof that the colored race has initiative, real constructive ability.

Washington was endowed with great executive and administrative ability, shrewd common sense, and a practical knowledge of men and affairs. His knowledge of human nature was instinctive, intuitive, and sometimes uncanny. He knew the Southern white man better than the Southern white man knew himself, and knew the sure road to his head and heart.

He had a keen sense of humor, characteristic of the race. He could tell a story to enforce or illustrate a point in his argument with telling effect. Strangely enough, this gifted man could make men serious or convulse an audience with laughter, but he was without the gift of pathos, and had few emotions. I have never known him to make an audience weep, unless they were crying with laughter. He had little use for tears because he was an optimist, a strong-hearted, courageous man, whom nothing could discourage. He was a builder, a constructive worker among men. He said an ounce of construction is better than a ton of destruction. His mission was serious. He was in earnest. He was modest in his bearing, with a charming reserve of manner, a simple dignity, perfect poise, and straightforward, sincere, and direct in all his dealings with men.

You, of this generation, who beheld Booker Washington, the idol of his race, the favorite of those in high places—educators, publishers, kings, presidents, philanthropists—must not overlook the humble beginning, privations and sacrifices of his early career. I saw him as a young man, grim, resolute, pursuing the objects of his heart, begging almost from door to door, facing fierce criticism of his own race, including myself, the indifference and unsympathetic ear of others. I saw him again in the full flush of the pride of achievement, the recognized leader of his race, confidant of presidents, everywhere courted and admired. The paths he trod were not all roses; there were thorns and stones, sharp and rough, that beset his way. He wore himself out in the service of his fellows and humanity. He reached the summit, turned a moment, looked back with satisfaction upon the distance he had come, and just before him, all too soon, there fell upon his fading gaze the sunrise of the eternal morning.

And now, my friends, I trust that you will pardon a personal word. For seven years, after leaving college, I belonged to the Boston Radicals, who opposed the policies and program of Booker T. Washington for improving the condition of the masses. It was because I had not risen to the point where I could appreciate or understand the loftiness of his character or the far-reaching influence of his mission. I thought, as a young man, that Latin conquered everything. Washington read it right, labor conquers all. I saw the form. He saw the substance. No power on earth could change his convictions. He was right. I shall never fail to thank the Almighty for the day and the hour when I first saw the truth and became a friend and follower of Booker Washington. For fifteen years I tried to make amends for the injustice I had done.

In all our acquaintanceship he never referred, by word or action, to the many bitter things I had said about him. And now he is gone.

I saw my friend for the last time in August; I think it was the evening of August 22d, when he was turning his step southward. He was worn and tired, his figure emaciated; the light of another day seemed even then upon his countenance, but there was a look of calmness and resignation about him his friends could not fail to note. We realized that the great change was at hand. The clasp of that friendly hand as he said "Good-bye," the hand now cold in death, I shall never forget. I believe that somehow, somewhere, I shall clasp that hand again, meet his full, frank, honest gaze of sympathy and perfect understanding. I am glad to say that he was my friend and I his. To me he is not dead. His sweet and gentle spirit keeps company with me everywhere. His voice comes to me in the silent watches of the night, inspiring and encouraging. I shall never lose faith in man as long as I recall the memory of Booker Washington. Every man, woman, and child of darker skin must feel a greater pride of race, a firmer faith in God, because of the life and character of Booker Washington.

He is dead in his prime, yet he had realized the ambitions and ideals of his youth, something done to advance the Kingdom of God, the cause of his race and his country. As Bernard Shaw said of himself, it might be said of Washington, "he held his life as a flaming torch; he wanted to be thoroughly worn out and burned out when he died." Booker Washington simply burned himself out in the service of his fellows. My humble prayer is that his torch has lighted another among the darker millions of America to lead his race onward and upward.

In the peace of the quiet Sabbath morning, when the harvest season was over, the great soul of Booker Washington passed to his Maker, taking with him his garnered sheaves. The sunrise upon the distant shores greeted a soul as sweet and beautiful as this poor world has ever known, and

"How well he fell asleep!
Like some proud river, widening
Toward the sea;
Calmly and grandly, silently and deep,
Life joined Eternity."

A LIFE OF ACHIEVEMENT[1]

By Robert R. Moton

It is entirely fitting that on the eve of the birthday of the great Emancipator we should gather here to reverently pay our respects to the memory of the one who stands so preëminently as the most unique product of Emancipation. Booker T. Washington's life and work would have alone justified Abraham Lincoln's ideas and actions regarding Emancipation.

The remarks which I shall make this evening are in no sense intended as a eulogy, for that would be absolutely out of harmony with the life and teachings, and, I believe, with the wish of our great leader. My hope is rather to call attention, inadequately, of course, to a few of the great principles which controlled and guided his life, enabling him to perform so great and so beautiful a service for the Negro and for the nation, with the desire that we may therefrom learn lessons and gain inspiration that may help and encourage us for the great work which he left to us all to carry on.

Dr. Washington found a mass of unorganized, unconnected people; untrained in self-direction, with little knowledge of self-support and citizenship; as yet more or less ignorant and poverty stricken, but with a strong desire for education and the possession of property; more or less demoralized and discouraged; as suspicious and distrustful of their own race as of the white race; and, in the main, following no especially constructive leadership; with the relations between the races, to all appearance, growing daily less cordial and friendly, and more cold and businesslike. He found his people, like their more progressive white exemplars, looking with grave suspicion upon any system of education not in accordance with what had previously been in vogue, having the feeling that a farm, or a shop, or a kitchen should have no place in a well-regulated institution, and believing that the pupil should be adjusted to the school, not the school to the pupil.

Few men in the world's history have been able to accomplish in so short a period for so large a mass of people what Dr. Washington was able to accomplish. He organized and enheartened a race, giving them a new idea of education and of life, teaching the

[1] Delivered at a memorial meeting in honor of Booker T. Washington, held in New York City, February 11, 1916.

dignity, grandeur, beauty, and absolute necessity of industry and morality as fundamental things in the development of any people, leading them to a belief in and a respect for their own race, deepening their race pride, their race consciousness, and their race integrity—giving the Negro a definite place in the thought and life of the times. It was a difficult, embarrassing, foreboding race problem which he found; he left a clear, definite, hopeful race program, the letter and spirit of which, if wisely and unselfishly followed, will, without doubt, bring, in the long run, a happy, wholesome, and satisfactory solution, and an adjustment mutually acceptable to all vitally concerned.

He often said: "No man, either white or black, from North or from South, shall drag me down so low as to make me hate him." This, my friends, was his life motto, and yet few men were more sensitive to unfairness or injustice. Misunderstanding and prejudice are apt to affect most people strongly, especially those who are keenly stung, but with Dr. Washington the underlying cause of prejudice and unfairness was of far more interest, and he set himself with all energy and with all patience to dispel ignorance, poverty, inefficiency, and immorality wherever found, not by force and violence of words or of conduct, but by an affectionate, though persistent, courageous, and indomitable common sense, or, rather, uncommon sense.

The press and the platform have emphasized, and justly so, Dr. Washington's great wisdom, his rare tact, his remarkable poise, diplomacy, and self-control. The world has known few men with greater poise and self-control than he possessed. These were very important elements in his character.

But the underlying, fundamental, dominating, controlling principle and characteristic of Dr. Washington's life, that which enabled him to render such a great service to this nation, was his belief in and his love for mankind. All his other qualities, important as they were, were secondary to the great principle which always guided him. He believed in and respected and loved humanity, and this faith was not circumscribed by race, or limited by section, or bounded by color lines. North and South, black and white, were on his heart and in his program. Where ignorance and poverty were greatest, where a human need was most apparent, there his interest was deepest, his words strongest, his great eloquence most convincing, and his energy and force most deeply vitalized and spiritualized. Because he believed in, respected, and loved the Southern white man, he interpreted to his own people with wisdom, with patience, and with kindness the feelings and sentiments of the white South.

Because of Dr. Washington's absolute faith in the possibilities of his own race, because of his pride in his race, because he loved his race, he analyzed and frankly interpreted the Negro to himself, telling him his shortcomings and failings in unvarnished fashion, teaching him what right education means and what it should do for the individual and the race, working out in concrete form in Tuskegee Institute, as well as outside of the institution, his ideas of education. Both in the North and in the South he linked education in a very definite, practical, and necessary way to life, not as life ought to be—the ideal life—but as life really is, in the cabin, on the farm, in the church, in the school, in the alley, in disease, in crime; he taught men that education, whether professional, academic, technical, or industrial, should touch and influence the common, everyday vocations by which men live and move and have their existence.

He interpreted, with kindness and patience and wisdom, the North to the South, the South to the North, the Negro to both, and both to the Negro. He helped tremendously in making peace between races and between sections. He used every opportunity to allay factional strife and bickerings between groups of Negroes. He was truly a peacemaker. He caused the lion and the lamb to lie down together, and a little child—an honest and simple and unselfish Negro—was leading them to real peace on earth and that good-will which the great Nazarene came to bring among men of all races and all nations.

General Armstrong, through Hampton Institute, responded as best he could—and he was a wise, far-seeing man—to the earnest, urgent appeal of this untrained, poverty-stricken, black boy for a chance. He gave him, not money, not even charity as such, but he did give Booker Washington what every American, in the last analysis, believes, deep down in his heart, that every human being should have, an opportunity to make the most of himself—a chance equal to that of any other man. Booker Washington used this chance in developing in every possible way opportunities, chances, for other people, whether in Alabama and the South, the Isles of the Sea, or Africa. He struggled that men might have a chance through the great Tuskegee Normal and Industrial Institute which he founded, for which he labored and sacrificed, and for which he gave his life. He struggled that they might have a chance, not only through Tuskegee Institute, but through other educational institutions of a different character as well. He pleaded for them with rare eloquence, as well as rare earnestness and devotion, in the North and in the South, in city and in country, through the press, from the platform, and through the National Negro Business League. In season and out of season, often in much discomfort, and frequently against the advice of his best friends and his physician, he pleaded for his people, than whom there is no more loyal group of American citizens, loyal to the flag and all for which it stands. And they, my friends, would die for that flag if necessary.

I hope I may be forgiven if I say a few words more directly to my own people, inasmuch as they form so large a part of the audience. I hope no one will believe that I, for a moment, think I can fill Dr. Washington's place. I am earnestly and humbly aware that this is impossible. It would require the combined energy and effort of all the Negroes in America, and, in addition, the coöperation and backing of all the white people, to carry on Dr. Washington's work, and I doubt whether, even then, it would be done as effectively as he did it.

If any of us, because of weaknesses and failings within our race, or because of unfairness, injustice, and inconvenience without, or because of the color of our faces and the texture of our hair, have been hitherto lacking in appreciation of our race, or have been afraid to be unmistakably identified with the Negro race, let us, in the name of the God who made us, forever dispel any such foolish, childish, disastrous notions. Let us remember, once and for always, that no race that is ashamed of itself, no race that despises itself, that tries to get away from itself, no race that does not respect, honor, and love itself, can gain the confidence and respect of other races, or will ever be truly great and useful.

Let us remember, also, that we are not an accursed people; that races with whiter faces have, and are still going through, difficulties infinitely more trying and embarrassing than much that faces us; that we have in this country vast opportunities for growth and development, as well as for usefulness and service. We are creatures of God's most perfect handiwork, and any lack of appreciation on our part is a reflection on the great Creator. Though we Negroes are black, and though we are living under hampering difficulties and inconveniences, God meant that we should be just as honest, just as industrious, just as skillful, just as pure, just as intelligent, just as Godlike, as any human beings that walk on the face of God's earth.

I hope and I believe that because of the life that has so recently gone out from among us, we, as a people, will henceforward, as never before, unselfishly work together, not always thinking, feeling, or acting alike, but always in perfect harmony and mutual helpfulness for a great cause, for a great need, for a great race, and for a great nation. This is the most important lesson we can learn from the life and teachings of our great leader and benefactor.

At the very simple but impressive funeral service at Tuskegee, in November, more than eight thousand people—rich and poor, from city and country, educated and uneducated, from North and South, black and white—gathered to pay reverently their last tribute of respect and devotion to the man they loved. The beautiful city of Tuskegee, by special request of its honored Mayor, ceased all business during the funeral hour. Practically every white business house and organization, together with hundreds of individuals in Tuskegee and Macon County, as well as throughout the great State of Alabama (to say nothing about the colored people), sent floral offerings, and to a Negro, mind you! And this, my friends, was in the shadow, almost, of the old Confederate capitol in Montgomery. Alabama and the South loved Booker Washington; Booker Washington loved Alabama and the South, where he lived, labored, and died, and where he wanted to be buried.

The Principal of Hampton Institute, Dr. Hollis B. Frissell, a lifelong friend of Dr. Washington, and his teacher at Hampton (as well as mine), began a very beautiful and impressive prayer at the funeral service at Tuskegee with these fitting words from the Apostle Paul: "Thanks be to God, who giveth us the victory." Booker Washington's life, Booker Washington's work, Booker Washington's death, were truly victories—a victory in unselfishness, a victory in patience, a victory in simplicity, a victory in faith, a victory in a love that suffered long and was kind, was not puffed up, and rejoiced in truth and in service.

I congratulate the Negro race most heartily and earnestly, I congratulate myself, and I congratulate the nation, too, for we are all prouder, richer, happier, and better because this man lived and labored. Though he died a poor man, as far as this world's goods are concerned, he died rich in achievement and in service. As I said before, he found a most trying, embarrassing, discouraging race problem, and left us a clear, definite, hopeful, unselfish race program. Whether this program is being worked out through Edwards at Snow Hill, or Cornelia Bowen at Mount Meigs, Ala., through Long at Christiansburg, Va., through Holtzclaw at Utica, Miss., through a Jeanes School or a Rosenwald School, through Baldwin Farms or the Negro Business League, or through the lives and characters and earnest work of thousands of unnamed graduates and former students of Tuskegee Institute, it matters little. It is the same vitalizing, courageous, unselfish spirit of Booker T. Washington, in the same wise, unselfish program, working earnestly for the good of men and to the glory of God.

I believe, my friends, that you who are heirs of the opportunities, the culture, and the wealth of the ages, you who love humanity and justice, you who love our glorious country, I truly believe that you will see to it that the great institution through which Booker Washington worked, and for which he died, will be maintained and operated to its full capacity, and with the greatest possible efficiency. I believe that you will see to it that these black boys and girls, sometimes called despised and rejected children, may continue to have a chance—a chance to be trained, a chance to be educated, a chance to be efficient, a chance to be useful to their race and country, a chance to be decent, a chance to serve.

MEMORIAL ADDRESS [1]

By Emmett J. Scott [2]

Not by invitation, but by command of the First Vice-President and the Chairman of the Executive Committee of the National

[1] Delivered at the Seventeenth Annual Session of the National Negro Business League, Convention Hall, Kansas City, Missouri, Wednesday evening, August 16, 1916.

[2] Emmett J. Scott, for twenty-two years Secretary to Booker T. Washington, and of

Negro Business League, I stand here tonight to pay homage to the memory of the man who was not only the founder of our great organization, but the leader of his people in America, and one of the foremost thinkers of the world, irrespective of race, creed or color.

It is altogether sweet and beautiful that this great organization should halt its proceedings to commemorate the purposeful life of him who, on this first evening of our annual meetings, always encouraged us with a word of good cheer, sounded a vibrant note of optimism, and cordially expressed to us, and through us to the Negro people of the United States, his warmest congratulations upon the achievements of the twelve months before. Oh, how we miss him tonight!

You who knew him as man and as friend know what Kipling meant when he said:

"There is neither East nor West, Border, nor Breed nor Birth,
When two strong men stand face to face tho' they come from the
    ends of the Earth!"

He gripped men to him with hooks of steel. He loved and was loved of men.

If in my efforts to speak worthily of him, I fail to pay adequate tribute to his great and useful life, I know I shall have your forbearance, for it is only before an audience, such as this, composed of those who knew him, and loved him, and trusted him, and mourn his passing, that I could bring myself to speak of him at all.

These are days of preparedness. The world welters in an orgy of blood. Across the broad Atlantic, we hear martial strains calling men to duty, to defense of country, and to death. Our own country all but reels and rocks. There are on every side searchings of heart, admonitions, uncertainties. We know not what a day may bring forth. The military hero is the man of the hour.

The man whose name and fame we tonight celebrate, the glory

the Tuskegee Normal and Industrial Institute, was born at Houston, Texas, February 13, 1873. He was educated at Wiley University, Marshall, Texas. He was appointed a member of the American Commission to Liberia in 1909 by President William Howard Taft, was Secretary of the National Conference on the Negro held in 1912, served as Secretary of the National Negro Business League from date of its organization, functioned as Special Assistant to the Secretary of War during the World War, and became Secretary-Treasurer of the Howard University, Washington, in 1919.

of whose life we share, fought in no wars, carried upon his breast no Iron Cross, nor medal of the Legion of Honor, and yet he could have, like Heine, exclaimed: "When I die, I wish a sword placed upon my coffin, for I have been a soldier in the war for the liberation of humanity!" Our friend was indeed "a soldier in the war for the liberation of humanity!"

His Work Was Monumental

When the world's tokens of affection and respect were laid upon his bier nine months ago the outstanding tribute was that this man had spent himself for his fellows. Well did Henry Watterson, Southerner of Southerners, say: "The death of Booker Washington is a national misfortune, for his life was a national benefaction. His towering figure for more than a generation was a pillar of fire to lead his people out of the darkness of ignorance, indolence and error. He was the Negro's wisest and bravest teacher and leader. He devoted his life, every day of it, every energy of it, to bringing the Negro real freedom and to respected and self-respecting citizenship. His work, great in its purpose, great in its results, was monumental."

Fit complement of this expression from Henry Watterson was that of the Sage of Sagamore Hill, the militant, incarnate evangel of the Square Deal, Colonel Theodore Roosevelt, who, when informed of the death of his friend, said: "He was one of the distinguished citizens of the United States, a man who rendered greater service to his own race than had ever been rendered by any one else, and who in doing so also rendered great service to the whole country. I mourn his loss and feel that one of the most useful citizens of our land has gone."

My friends, it is worth while to have lived and to have deserved such encomiums as these, one from a Southern man of lineage and distinction, the other from a Northern man of birth and breeding. Notable indeed was it when this Northern white man and a company of men of great prominence, journeyed a thousand miles, to the heart of the South, to testify by their presence and their speech their appreciation of the life so beautifully and sweetly lived by our leader and friend.

He Walked Humbly with His God

I trust you will bear with me if I quote once again from Colonel Roosevelt. At the memorial exercises held at Tuskegee, Alabama, December 12, 1915, he said:

"If I were obliged to choose one sentence out of all the sentences that have ever been written in which to sum up what seems to me to be the deepest religious spirit, I should take a phrase from the prophet Micah, which says: 'What doth the Lord require of thee but to do justly and to love mercy and to walk humbly with thy God?' And Booker Washington did justice, and he loved mercy, and he walked humbly with his God. He spent his life in service, in serving the people of his own race, and in serving the people of my race just as much. He did justice to every man, and no injustice done him could swerve him from the path of justice to others; and he not only loved mercy, but he lived the love he felt for mercy; and finally, he walked humbly with his God. There was not in him a touch of the servile spirit; there was not in him a touch of unworthy abasement, but there was the genuine humility of spirit that made him eager and anxious to walk humbly and work humbly with his God for the welfare of his race, and there is not one of you here, not one of you tonight, black man or white, who does not know that every word I am speaking is the exact truth."

There have been those who have sought to read into Mr. Washington's life a spirit contrary to Colonel Roosevelt's estimate. That is why I have ventured to bring to your attention this just evaluation of the spirit which characterized his life and his work. Humility is not servility.

Let us, my friends, remember him as Guide, Philosopher, Friend, unspoiled by the great honors which came to him, for there was in him no room for personal vanity, or weakness. He was the type of leader who saw fundamentals clearly. Despite criticism and reviling, he was not ashamed to hold that each individual must acquire his own basic character, those qualities and fundamental virtues which make him a useful member of society through practical, purposeful work. Industry and thrift were the gospel which our great leader preached and practiced with a vigor that could not fail to win. Year after year he thundered from the platform of the National Negro Business League that it is only through industry and thrift that the Negro is to win his way permanently. His message fell on eager ears, and he lived to see a race stirring with hope, throbbing with ambition, stepping forth and demanding a "place in the sun," producing results, triumphing over difficulties.

Do you not recall those thrilling words at Boston last year—Boston that had reviled him, and which now rose to acclaim him when he stood on the platform of Symphony Hall this night one year ago? At that time he said:

"With our race, as it has been and always will be with all races, without economic and business foundation it is hardly possible to have educational and religious growth and political freedom. . . . An ounce of application is worth a ton of abstraction. We must not be afraid to pay the price for success—the price of sleepless nights, the price of toil when others rest, the price of planning today for tomorrow, this year for next year. If someone else endures the hardships, does the thinking, and pays the salaries, someone else will reap the harvest and enjoy the reward.

"To accomplish what I have indicated, we must have a united race, men who are big enough and broad enough to forget and overlook personal and local differences and each willing to place upon the altar all that he holds for the benefit of the race and our country. . . .

"No matter how poor you are, how black you are, or how obscure your present work and position, I want each one to remember that there is a chance for him, and the more difficulties he has to overcome, the greater will be his success."

In these words are to be found the touchstone of success, and it is to the credit of our race that it has been willing to listen and to follow his wise teachings, the advice of this man who always spoke for truth and justice; "who knew wisdom and valued not justice less; who knew justice and valued not wisdom less."

He Was a Man of Vision

Our friend was a man of vision. His life was a life of triumph, a real triumph, if you will permit me to say so, of democracy itself.

The picture of the newly-freed slave sleeping under a wooden pavement in Richmond, Virginia; a waif keeping body and soul together as best he could, with a burning thirst for education and a desire to get ahead in the world, together with the achievements of his lifetime and the triumphs of his marvelous career, prove that in truth his life was a triumph of democracy. The story of his rise from slavery reads like some stirring romance. He drank to its very lees all that poverty and servitude, with their discouraging handicaps, could offer. We may bemoan the fate which condemns a Lincoln, a Garfield, a Douglass, to penury and to struggle, and yet, as a great orator has said, "Poverty is a hard but oftentimes a loving nurse. If fortune denies the luxuries of wealth, she makes greater compensation in that greater love which they alone can ever know who have faced privations together. The child may shiver in the fury of the blast which no maternal tenderness can shield him from, but he may feel a helpless tear drop upon his cheek which will keep him warm till the snows of time have covered his hair. It is not wealth that counts in the making of the world, but character. And character is best formed amid those surroundings where every waking hour is filled with struggle, where no flag of truce is ever sent, and only darkness stays the conflict."

Thank God that this is true. Who knows but that this precious life of service and achievement might have been lost to us if he had not met and vanquished discouragement after discouragement in the grim struggle with poverty; if he had not gone on unfalteringly, with serene courage, toward the goal which must have seemed but a dim mirage at the beginning.

The secret of Mr. Washington's success in life—if indeed there were any secret about it at all—was his unfailing optimism, his dogged determination, his resolve to permit no obstacle to daunt him, and his proof on numerous occasions that he was absolutely above insult or humiliation. No disappointment could discourage him.

If it were necessary, or time permitted, examples all too numerous could be cited in proof of this statement. If the young men and women of his race everywhere could but catch some portion of his sweet spirit, his high courage, his rich optimism! For us, in every part of this country, there would dawn that new and better day for which our fathers and our fathers' fathers have worked and sung and prayed.

He Had Faith in His Race

Mr. Washington had faith in his race. He looked on every Negro home, however humble, in which dwelt industry, honesty and the domestic virtues, as a center of hope and safety for the race. It was his good fortune to live long enough to see thousands of homes founded by the men and women for whose schooling and manhood and womanhood he labored. And this great responsibility he has passed on to us, so that it is now our task to work as earnestly as did he for the establishment of more and better Negro homes, for more and better Negro schools, for more and better Negro business enterprises, for a higher level of civilization among our people.

I must not fail to speak of that large and important service rendered by him to both races in seeking to blot out sectional animosities, of interpreting one race to the other. He was the foremost missionary of our race. He sought to overcome racial misunderstandings, racial injustices, racial prejudices. Nothing could embitter him. It was his proud boast that no man could drag him down so low as to make him hate that man. He labored with divine patience, for racial coöperation and racial good will. He came to be the one beacon light of hope to men of both sections, of both races, who had been groping in a world of uncertainty and doubt. The most impressive thing, in my opinion, about Mr. Washington, was his intense earnestness in seeking to have white men understand black men, and to have black men understand white men. And I thank God that as his sense of things faded he had the deserved privilege of knowing that his labors had not been in vain; that largely through his efforts during the past twenty years there exists in our country today a better understanding between the races, a growing feeling of respect for the rights of each other, a finer spirit of mutual helpfulness.

He Loved the Southland

Booker Washington loved his native Southland. When the light of the eternal morning gilded his brow and bathed his sturdy form in its radiance, courageously he prepared for the long journey which was to bring to an end his earthly career. He wished to bear out his oft-repeated statement that he had been born in the South; had lived and labored in the South; and wished to die and be buried in the South. It could be said of him, as it was said of Abraham Lincoln: "Whether he rose or fell; whether he stood in that giant-like repose that distinguished him among his fellow-men, or exercised those unequaled powers which made him a foremost figure of the world, he always felt the tender and invisible chord that chained him to his native rock. In whatever field he stood he felt the benign and sobering influence of his early recollections. They were the rock to which he clung in storms, the anchor which kept his head to the wind, the balm which sustained him in defeat, and ennobled him in the hour of triumph."

He Loved His Race

Mr. Washington loved his race. He preached, in season and out of season, that self-help, self-discipline, self-salvation, are the only factors in the history of races or individuals that permanently count, or endure. Though his voice might sometimes chasten, it most often was heard pleading at the bar of public opinion for his race, for "fair play," for a "square deal." It was for this purpose, and in this spirit, that he stood at Atlanta; that he stood at the unveiling of Shaw's deathless monument on Boston Common; that he stood in the Chicago Auditorium before President and Cabinet and the mighty of the land at the close of the Spanish-American War; that he stood within the classic shades of old Harvard to receive the first honorary degree conferred by that institution upon one of his race. And so he stood upon an hundred, yea, a thousand platforms, throughout the country as the tribune of his race, pleading for humanity and justice, giving voice to the inarticulate educational, industrial and moral aspirations of a race.

He Was a Religious Man

Mr. Washington was a deeply religious man. He believed in, trusted, lived by the precepts of the Bible. He was not too great, and never too busy to turn to the thumb-worn copy of Holy Writ which was his invariable, comforting companion. Have you not heard him, with face aglow and faith-revealing expression, quote his two favorite passages of Scripture?

"Whatsoever things are true, whatsoever things are just, whatsoever things are pure, whatsoever things are lovely, whatsoever things are of good report; if there be any virtue, and if there be any praise, think on these things."

And that other one:

"But the fruit of the spirit is love, joy, peace, long suffering, gentleness, goodness, faith, meekness, temperance: against such there is no law."

He had the vision to see that if he could only prevail upon his race to "think on these things," no law, or laws, could prevail against them.

And now, finally, my friends, are we here simply to mourn his loss, to chronicle the details of his busy, overburdened life, to recite his splendid achievements, and the many high honors which came to him, and through him, to us? Or are we here to seek to draw some lessons from his inspiring, triumphant life?

His Self-Sacrifice, His Self-Denial, His Self-Forgetfulness

Our hearts do indeed sorrow with that brave companion who labored by his side, smoothing his pathway, relieving his life as best she could of daily fret and care. We do sorrow with the bereft children of his household who miss the joy of his presence, the tonic of his fatherly voice. We all miss him, here and everywhere. My own heart has felt its overpowering sense of loneliness, its craving for his presence. I loved him as the son loves the father in whom he sees the embodied glory of high ideals, garnered wisdom and experience. He taught me by his daily life that it is worth while to live loyally with and for one's higher self. I owe him much. I shall never cease to recall his sweet, tranquil spirit, his charm of manner, his youthful zest in the joy of work, his love for, and faith in his fellow-man. I shall never forget his self-sacrifice, his self-denial, his self-forgetfulness.

But he is gone. The lighted torch he carried now passes to our hands. The work he did was work for the nation. He was not an unprofitable servant. He gave to his race and to his country all of physical and mental vigor; he could give no more. The best, the most fruitful years of his life were spent in behalf of his fellows. His life will shine with steady radiance as the years come and go. Let us hearken to the call he sounded for brave, patriotic service; let us press forward, strong and unafraid, with patience and firm resolve, with the lessons of his devoted life ever before us, to advance the cause for which he was willing to live, for which he was willing to work, and finally, for which he was willing to die.

CHAPTER XII

OCCASIONAL ORATORY

THE Negro advocate of race rights, with no constructive program for the attainment of the things necessary to compel the recognition of his claims, lost his hold on the public during the period of trying out the optimistic program of industrial education as a means to economic efficiency. When such men had a hearing, it was usually in a sequestered sphere where they could not reach the persons they hoped to convert to their way of thinking. The majority of the white people in this country, many of whom were kindly disposed to the aspirations of the Negro, abandoned the idea of sustaining him in his claims for civic and political equality. The audience of the progressive Negro statesmen, therefore, was so reduced as to render their appeals hopelessly ineffective, except so far as moving here and there a person who might hear them as a voice crying from afar.

Negro oratory, then, passed through a transition period of inaction or reconstruction. The white man could no longer be expected to hear the story of the oppressed, and the Negroes who might thereby be moved, had, within themselves, no power to redress their own grievances. During this interlude, therefore, the Negro orator, except so far as he combated the reactionary tendencies in his own group, had little opportunity for the enunciation of a great thought, before a great audience or upon a great occasion. The most forceful expression of the plight of the race during this period came, not from the orators, but from its pamphleteers and essayists like Kelly Miller and W. E. B.

Du Bois, whose expression of advanced thought have the ring of the lamentations of a people carried away captive. Occasionally, however, there were delivered addresses of significance like these below.

"A PLEA FOR A SUSPENSION OF JUDGMENT"[1]

BY BISHOP W. T. VERNON[2]

It is a long way from the back woods of Missouri, where I was born, to a speaker's place at a Kansas Day Club banquet; and were I to use all the time allotted me in efforts to express my gratitude for the opportunity given me by President Valentine and the officers and members of this club, I still could not utter my profound appreciation for this encouragement to my people, with whom my destiny is linked forever.

This is no personal honor; but rather the expression of cheer and helpfulness to a struggling race, a faithful part of the great party represented by this great gathering tonight. I would not separate myself from my race. I am content to suffer affliction with them. Placed for a spell by His Almighty hand within this tenement of possibly less favored clay—the deathless soul which speaks through lips ofttimes derided shall not lament its presence there. The cause of my people is my cause, their struggles my struggles.

Why are we here? A destiny unseen brought the Mayflower with freedom to the western wild, cavalier to the Old Dominion and the slaver's ship to the Southland, all to people these new shores, from which admixture by devious ways, through tortuous paths, fate

[1] An address delivered before the Kansas Day Club in 1905.

[2] Bishop William T. Verson was born in Lebanon, Missouri, July 11, 1871. In his fifteenth year he entered Lincoln University at Jefferson City, Missouri, and was graduated therefrom in June 1890, as the valedictorian of his class. He taught in the public schools in the state, at Bonne Terre, and Lebanon, his birthplace. In 1896 he felt the call to the ministry and joined the Missouri Annual Conference of the African Methodist Episcopal Church in session at Springfield, Missouri. He was assigned to the Presidency of Western University, a struggling school of this denomination located at Quindaro, Kansas. It rapidly developed under his direction. He served as Register of the United States Treasury under President Theodore Roosevelt. He then went south and became the president of Campbell College, another church institution at Jackson, Mississippi. After pastoring several churches he was elected bishop at the quadrennial session of the general conference of the African Methodist Episcopal Church held at St. Louis, Missouri, in 1920, and was assigned to Africa. He is now stationed in this country.

has decreed the glorious state we call our common country. It is the way of destiny. Children of Him are we all.

The legacy of duty to the world is left with those who have opportunities; and none can sit idly by and see in vogue the law of strongest beak and sharpest claw, for truly,

> "The laws of changeless justice bind
> Oppressor with oppressed,
> And close as sin and suffered joined
> We march to fate abreast."

To wail over unfortunate conditions or bemoan what at times seems an untoward fate is to display neither manhood nor gratitude toward friends. We have just cause for hopefulness.

Remembering the sacrifice of benefactors whose memory is embalmed in history's urn, we mark the vast step from savagery of ancestor to the product of the school today. From chattering jargon and fetish adoration on native heath four centuries ago, we rung by rung have come to poets, painters, scholars of æsthetic tastes and a reverence for the Christian's God.

We, too, have heard the voice of duty, and feel a higher Providence calling us onward. We see other personalities than our own, having rights we must respect if we would in turn have ours respected, and thus do deeds that lift man up to loftier heights. We realize that every idle hand, every vicious thought, every depraved soul, every breach of law, every desire to have the shadow rather than the real, mean ignoble failure and inharmony with the divine economy of creation.

As the schools do their work we awake to obligations that bind us all and recognize responsibility to self, humanity and God.

Though at times seen and unseen foes interpose, friends in a greater degree beckon and lead us on; and if at times we stumble, fail and fall, as in the past, despairing not, we rise to progress.

We are resolved to put aside regrets for doubting, failing yesterdays, and seeing these only as warnings against future mistakes, each day essay a nobler task.

If we need examples of unconquerable courage we have but to trace your glorious career. You, too, have had your struggles.

When England, proud, victorious mistress of the seas, sought to undo that at which your ancestors for nearly two centuries wrought, England failed. And why? Your bravery and love for God and home and native land, inspired by the spirit your race always knew to know no masters, made you free. Then by your side on Boston Commons our Attucks died, at Bunker Hill was Salem, at Yorktown, when to Washington was handed the sword of Cornwallis, Negro slaves, too, stood at parade rest, believing that in some far-off day their children's children would know the freedom which that day came to you and yours.

With Perry at Lake Erie, with Jackson at New Orleans my people died. And why? In them was stuff that heroes makes, and they were led by heroes.

From American soil a spirit sprang which quickened all it touched. It swept the air even in cane brake, cotton patch and rice swamp. It made of slaves men who knew no fear if duty called.

And what more shall I say? For time would fail me to tell of Wagner, Petersburg, and of our work on sea and land from '61 to '65, when we ceased to fight as serfs, but, fighting as only free men can, proved that the Providence which sent us here had for its purpose the preserving of a nation's life as well as the giving of a higher life to us.

In peace the same devotion gave we to those whom we served. We delved in earth, we tunneled mountains, we diked and stayed the wave-dashed sea carrying all of nature's power, we felled the trees in forests primeval, we changed the course of winding river, we leveled hills and tilled the fields, we gathered stores in barn and bin, we wrought in mine and drew the load, the burden bearers we were. If aborigine or wild beast attack were threatened, we watched at day or night, and still if wanted at toil men had but to look at spreading fields, at either dawn or fading twilight, and we were there. We broke no faith; we betrayed no trust.

And since that earlier day men said, "This bondage must not be—the bondman must know freedom." And despite Fugitive Slave law, Dred Scott Decision, 'mid persecution, revilings, scourgings, yea, death, some of your race risked all, that black men might be free.

Then came the Birneys, Lovejoys, Fremonts, Beechers, Lundys, Garrisons, Phillips, Sumners, and others, the earth-born saviors of mankind, who from out the hushed past still utter forth the sentiments that baptize souls in the holy fire of martyr-like resolve; these men were God's anointed for this task.

But what of John Brown, old Osawatomie, him of Kansas whom they hanged? 'Twas then a hero slept, a martyr whose blood became the seed of the church of human liberty and freedom. He died, but dying won, for he gave impetus to the Kansas spirit and the things for which the Kansas Day Club stands. But there is still another—one standing to himself—who like his Christ, died for a race, who toiled up his Golgotha at times almost alone, whose life can be explained as being but one of the ways of an inscrutable Providence to do His work—Abraham Lincoln.

At his call a million men went south. In hedges, highways, swamp and bog they found us lost. Many of them still sleep there. They were your fathers, brothers and friends and you felt and feel the sacrifice today, and my poor feeble words can never tell you how grateful we are.

But way down there where wrong still is, where peonage, scourgings, burnings yet go on, there are black lips mute with suffering, anguished souls with outstretched arms appealing, grateful for what the past has been and praying relief from burdens that still oppress. We again look to the Republican party for relief, and I do not believe we look in vain. I know no other party, nor should my people, for through it justice will finally be ours.

When for us skies show ominous we turn with confidence to the Republican party and to Kansas. All honor to both. They stand inseparable in what for us, at least, must forever remain time's greatest drama.

With backward glance, above the smoke of battle, our eyes forever behold the gleaming sword whose upward swing preserved Kansas, and whose downward stroke freed the world from the stain of human slavery. Though veiled by battle smoke *we know what hand is at the hilt*. Through its mighty leader, Lincoln, it said, "If slavery is not wrong, nothing is wrong," and the auction block, slave pen and rattle of chains were all no more.

This party enfranchised us, and though as yet illy prepared for so vast a step, of two evils this was by far the less. For until the leaders of the Republican party legislated otherwise, the ex-masters were passing laws making our condition more intolerable than that of slavery.

Your party would not leave the Negro, who at all times had been faithful to his country, to the mercy of his oppressors who conspired to destroy the nation in peace and fought to destroy it in war. In this the Republican party was right. The contention that the Negro, no matter how intelligent or worthy, shall not vote, but must be counted and therefore represented in Congress by political opponents, is a political heresy which the Republican party, if loyal to the lofty principles which gave it birth, can never tolerate.

We have not all succeeded, many have failed as must necessarily obtain in the case of a once enslaved race, but there are many who have striven and successfully so.

The Emancipation Proclamation could not suddenly rid us of all that centuries of slavery and barbarism had left. Ours must be a growth. And by patient toil and continued effort on our part, with your sympathy and aid, this country will finally see a rightful solution of the difficulties which confront us.

Moved by enlightened self interest, laboring for country's weal, realizing the duty of man to man, the best of your race will not sit idly by and leave this task to those who care not whether that which is righteous or unrighteous shall prevail; and Kansas, as before, is prepared to lead out for that "Righteousness which exalteth a nation."

To you, our friends, I promise as a race we will not fail to respond to every ennobling call, every uplighting appeal that you may make. This problem is the problem of our whole country since the citizenship of all sections determines our national character.

We have no chiding for critics who having eyes see only our worst; who having ears hear only of our ignoble deeds; who having hearts never feel that sympathy which man should feel for fellow man. Conditions, over which the present generation had no control, gave birth to feelings, the outgrowth of ancestral days. Nor do we cherish resentment for those who harm or strive to harm us now. Omniscience alone may dare to visit the mistakes of buried sires on breathing sons or adjust accounts between the living and the dead. Time, public sentiment and God will finally reward this patient courage and make all things right. When censured and misunderstood in senate, forum or Chautauqua debate, or criticised in public press, as the weaknesses of our weakest ones are heralded abroad, we remember that these are bad because they are human rather than because they are Negroes, and though disappointed we do not despair. But to those of our critics who would forget justice I would say, forget not that each upward struggling soul, stumbling though it may, goes clinging to the skirts of the invisible God, and for your own sakes I adjure you not to cast obstacles before His face in the way of a weaker though upward struggling race.

But this is no apology for our worst elements or an upholding of the vicious. Yes; we have them in numbers far too great for their good or racial weal. They are the weights upon us, but they are ours. We will tell them of their faults and teach them that by honest labor, thrift, energy, education and by amassing realty holdings worth the name are we to rise.

Our souls are awakening, we see the light. You have indexed the way, we grow as we behold and travel it. This growth means progress, and herein is the law of the life of a race.

With education symmetrical and true, we will take the dead mass buried by slavery's hand and touch them into life. This beauteous angel which has always done its work for those of earth will roll away the stone from the tomb where is buried a race, and my people will come forth to their glory and to the amazement of the world. And you men of Kansas will welcome this.

The day this thing is done will be to your children a holy day, for they will see accomplished that for which their Kansas forbears wrought and for which many died.

Opposition spurs us onward, you pointed the way and led in the darker days, and undaunted and determined, even with torn hands, bleeding feet and anguished souls, to the heights we are going.

For nearly three hundred years we've sung the sorrow songs. We shall yet sing the songs of rejoicing and triumph. As the Danes destroyed the hearing of their war horses that they might not be affrighted in battle, so will we turn a deaf ear to all that would discourage us. In the darkest hours we hear the voice of the best of that which makes American life glorious, saying, "Onward, freedmen! Onward! Onward, struggling race, we are with you!"

And with braver hearts and firmer tread we gird ourselves for the journey and press on our way.

We realize that honest labor, whether in the lowly walks or in the higher ways of life; duty done every day, everywhere, can have but one result—sure and lasting success. Though weighted with the frailties as a necessary consequence of the past, though far from what we desire, we point to some things accomplished since freedom.

From nothing we could call our own, in forty years we own eight hundred and fifty thousand farms, nine banks, two street railways, and pay taxes on seven hundred million dollars in property.

With education for our watchword, in this same time we have reduced our illiteracy to fifty-four per cent. Thirty-seven thousand Negro teachers are training our youth, and twenty-three Negro college presidents join with many other educational leaders in striving heroically to lift the load. And our youth are going forth to attain proficiency along all the lines of true education. While this was being accomplished we had your help. You paid millions of dollars in taxes, and your philanthropists gave millions with bountiful hand, realizing that in a free country intelligent citizenship, which is guaranteed rights and which in turn gives to its country duty, patriotism, uplifting character and progressive development is best for all, whether viewed from the standpoint of self-interest or from that broader altruistic spirit, the guiding star of the preservers of the rights and liberties of mankind.

And today the wisest and best argue, and rightfully so, that he who denies education to any class of citizens, in such measure inveighs against public safety, gives us a dangerous element, places a millstone around the neck of all, and jeopardizes the welfare of our common country. True, there is race prejudice. To say that none exists is to deny the truth before our eyes; but God's justice is of loftier rank than man's prejudice. To give work to those of us who are worthy, to allow us to rise in business, trades and professions, to protect us before the law, in jury box, and courts, to allow us comforts in public places if we are decent and honorable, is justice—and is nearer God's design than any prejudice claiming God's sanction. The eternal principles of justice, whereof the Republican party is the visible utterance and expression, pertain to a realm which knows no color line. And justice will settle the problem though all else should fail.

We aspire, as do you. The loftier things of soul, the upward stress which has upborne the Aryan race to the place it so proudly holds among the people of the earth, we also feel.

Wound us and we bleed; fatally so and we die; crush our spirits, and our hearts ache and with anguished souls we suffer on. We are not strangers to natural affection. It is not as mere imitators that we also stand for a tearful interval where earth opes briefly that it may close forever above the forms of those we love. We, as do you, with anxious eyes and straining ears look and list toward the awesome mystery which lies beyond, and as do you, claim sonship with God and brotherhood with the Saviour of mankind. And with such evidence of good cheer and helpfulness before me I dare to claim for Afric's sons the loftiest destiny which anywhere waits other souls.

Finally may I say—I have more faith in the American people than ever before. I know that on this soil right will finally triumph.

Among other great principles at issue in the campaign of 1904 was this one—not by any means the least—demanding a suspension of judgment in the case of these people who have had but forty years in which to do their work. Centuries must pass before the world can decide the right of a race to live and enjoy life, liberty and the pursuit of happiness. Your mighty civilization, the product of your versatility, genius, endurance and heroic endeavor which no words can describe, is the product of a thousand years. And you stand unrivaled, alone, like a city set on a hill which cannot be hid. As a race we have been asking that the views of our enemies be not accepted; as well as that any of us guilty of vainglorious boasting, be not believed, but we ask for time in which to show the mettle in us.

And you men fought out the issue when your opponents threw down the gauntlet in the last campaign. And, as in the past, God gave us a leader. As were Washington, Jefferson and Lincoln born to hasten the fruition of Runnymede, that liberty and justice might some day come to all men regardless of color or creed, so was this man born to carry out the true American idea, the Republican party idea, the Kansas Day Club idea of fair play to all American citizens.

Men who forty years ago fought for the freedom of the black men, and their sons who fought that Cuba might be free, men, even of other parties who believe in right, followed the lead of this man of mighty purpose, mighty heart and mighty brain, whose Christ-like doctrine is not black men down and white men up, but rather no man down and all men up, and who closes the door of hope in the face of no man, and would have all rise. This man, scholar, reformer, writer, soldier, diplomat, statesman, leader of men, just, humane, best of his kind, the property of the oppressed of earth, the hope of the future, the one dreamed of by those who have died in a martyr cause, invincible because right, invulnerable because sent of God, the latter day Savior of my people for whom black heroes died in Cuba that he might live and save their race, this man—Theodore Roosevelt—spoke out, and America, indorsing Roosevelt, this organization and our party, says to the world, "We will suspend judgment and give these people time." And this was and is all we ask. And I pledge you we will not disappoint you.

In the flight of years we will be vindicators of a race and part burden bearers of a world.

The tide has turned. The nobler sons of America have said to the waves of persecution and racial strife: "Thus far and no farther."

Humanity, returning to first principles where man will be just to fellowman, at the altar of truth will bow, the sable son of earth will be called brother, and the story of how he arose to higher estate will be the theme of dreamers and of all those who write the truths that undo fiction by their strangeness.

WHENCE AND WHITHER[1]

By Bishop R. A. Carter[2]

I presume the reason I have been invited to come back to Paine College and talk to you today, after thirty years of fighting and

[1] This was the Commencement Address delivered at Paine College, Augusta, Ga., May 30, 1923.

[2] Bishop Randall Albert Carter was born at Fort Valley, Georgia, Jan. 1, 1867. He was educated at Allen University ,Columbia, South Carolina and at Paine College, Augusta, Georgia. He was fraternal delegate to the General Conference of the M. E. Church, 1900; member of the C. M. E. delegation to the Ecumenical Conference on Methodism, London, England, 1901; elected Bishop C. M. E. Church, 1914, in St. Louis, Missouri.

climbing, until I have gained some laurels and reached the top of my calling, is that you may have the privilege of reading some pages out of my book of experience. As I stand here today in this beautiful chapel I can scarcely realize that more than three decades have passed since I walked, with others, from the old remodeled horse stables, which, in those days, served as dormitories and classrooms on this campus, down to old Trinity to the commencement exercise, and dreamed great dreams as I received my diploma from the hands of the lovable, lamented George Williams Walker. I little knew then to what I was going, when I stepped forth that day, eager, happy and hopeful, into the great world to make a name for myself. If I had known what awaited me perhaps I would have shrunk back aghast. However, I can say with all modesty, I have fought bravely, I have kept the faith fairly well, and I have weathered the many storms and fierce gales of the wide sea over which I have journeyed without losing too many spars and sails. And, today I have returned to the home port, like some grizzled and weather-beaten captain, to tell you something of the hardships and dangers of the voyage which you are about to begin. I warn you that this is truly the commencement of life for you. Those years you have spent here have been merely years of training for the real battles that are now before you. So I am asking you two vital questions, *whence* and *whither?* I myself shall try to answer my question *whence?* but I cannot answer the question *whither?* I can only give you some directions, which may help you on the way, while the passing years shall give answer to that question, *whither?*

Whence?

To every thoughtful and aspiring young Negro man and woman, *whence* are we as a race? is an all-important question; for you must understand the *whence* of your race in order to know clearly *whither* you may carry it, as you journey onward.

In the beginning, let me emphasize the fact that there are many embarrassments and annoyances, but no disgrace in being a Negro. As Negroes, we may be as proud of our origin as any other race. For many years Africa, the country whence the Negro came, has been called the "dark continent," because the white world knew little or nothing of it. But it has been recently discovered that Africa is a land as rich in its ancient civilization and culture as it is in its present wealth of minerals, forests and fertile fields. It is becoming well-known that Africa had evolved and developed a culture and civilization of its own which compares favorably with the famous civilizations of ancient Asia and Europe.

Professor George Reisner of Harvard University has been conducting researches in the Sudan. He states that his researches have established that the culture of Ethiopia stood as an outpost of Egyptian civilization in middle Africa, that in the art of the Ethiopian a Greek influence obtained, and, that the invention of a script of their own was evidence that the Ethiopians were a people of genius. The glory and grandeur that was Egypt's more than three thousand years ago was disclosed recently when the tomb of King Tut-Ankh-Amen was located and opened in the Valley of the Kings' Tombs.

Since the discoveries of the former greatness of the ancient Egyptians and Ethiopians, it has suddenly been discovered that they were not Negroes. The same professor Reisner says: "The Ethiopians are not and were not African Negroes." He describes them as "dark races in which brown prevailed." I fear the learned professor would have a hard time convincing his own people that the "dark, colored races in which brown prevails" in this country are not Negroes. Happily, you cannot sponge out ethnological facts with the bitter waters of race prejudice. The Negro has been called "Sons of Ham," "African," and "Ethiopian" in scornful derision for all these years, and now it is too late to try to make him something else when it is discovered that these designations link him with the greatest civilizations of the past. As Negroes, therefore, we claim kinship with the ancient Ethiopians and Egyptians, and all colored races, and share the greatness and glory of their achievements and history.

I was looking recently at some drawings of Egyptian kings and queens. Any unprejudiced observer would decide from those drawings that they were at least Negroid; for they have the lips, noses and hair which are characteristic of the Negro. Then, King Tut-Ankh-Amen claimed Amenhotep III as his father. Dr. Alexander Francis Chamberlain of Clark University, Worcester, Massachusetts, shows that this king had a strain of Negro blood. In his book, "The Contribution of the Negro to Human Civilization," we read: "The contributions of the Negro to human civilization are innumerable and immemorial. Let us first get some glimpses of him, chiefly as an individual, in contact with the hosts of other cultures than his own. Ancient Egypt knew him, both bond and free, and his blood flowed in the veins of not a few of the mighty Pharaohs. Nefertari, the famous queen of Aahmes, the King of Egypt, who drove the Hyksos from the land and founded the Eighteenth Dynasty (ca. 1700 B.C.), was a Negress of great beauty, strong personality and remarkable administrative ability. She was for years associated in the government with her son, Amenhotep I, who succeeded his father. Queen Nefertari was highly venerated, and many monuments were erected in her honor; she was venerated as 'ancestress and founder of the Eighteenth Dynasty' and styled 'the wife of the God Ammon,' etc. Another strain of Negro blood came into the line of the Pharaohs with Mut-em-ua, wife of Thothmes IV, whose son, Amenhotep III, had a Negroid physiognomy." So the evidence is conclusive that we are kin to the planners and builders of the great palaces of Baalbec, Karnak, Luxor, ancient Memphis, the pyramids, and the Sphinx.

The question has often been asked why the Negro can so easily adapt himself to present day civilization, and can compete on terms of equality with other races in every walk of life. The answer is what scientists call atavism, which is defined as intermittent heredity, reversion to an ancestral type or trait. Atavism explains why the Negro race has produced a Coleridge-Taylor and a Harry Burleigh in music, a Pushkin, Dumas, Dunbar and DuBois in literature, a Frederick Douglass and Robert Brown Elliott in statescraft, a Booker T. Washington and Lucy Laney in education, a Price, Holsey and Turner in oratory, a Ned Gourdin, Harry West and Jack Johnson in athletics. It is a harking back of the race to the centuries of civilization and culture of its great ancestors. Atavism explains why the race in this country has made a progress which, as President Harding wrote a great convention of Negroes the other day: "has been one of the wonders of civilization's advance." It gives the reason why the Negro race has acquired, in the short space of the sixty years since its emancipation in this country, twenty-two millions of acres of land, six hundred thousand homes, forty-five thousand churches, and operates seventy-eight banks, a hundred insurance companies, besides seventy thousand other business enterprises, with a capital of one hundred and fifty million dollars.

This is the answer that history and learning give to the question of the *whence?* of the Negro race. We are justly proud.

But *whither?*

I say to you today that our past obligates us to high endeavor for the future. We, you and I, must "carry on" for the race, until we have shown to our critics that we are worthy descendants of ancient great sires. Professor Kamerer, a Viennese biologist, makes the statement that "the skill, mental and physical, acquired by men and animals during their lives can be handed down to posterity." If this statement is true, and if the demonstration offered by this Austrian student is accepted by the scientists of Cambridge University, England, then we have as a heritage all the culture and skill and civilization of all the past ages of our ancestors of Egypt and Ethiopia. This points us to the *whither* of the race. But I warn you that the race will go only as far as its individual members go. Therefore, the future of the race is in the keeping of such as you who hear me today.

Your coming to this institution, and spending years of toilsome study and privation preparing for your future activities, may be taken as indicative of your determination to help lift the race up to and beyond the heights which it once attained. I wish to mention a few of the qualities which are necessary for you in this great mission of racial renaissance.

First, you must have the God consciousness. I mean, you must realize that there is a God, and that he governs and guides you, directs, leads and protects you, in all of your ways. A constant study of the lives of men and women who have lived worthily, and have lifted the human race, convinces me that young men and women cannot accomplish much which will add to the sum total of human and racial betterment without a deep consciousness of the fact that God is with them. The stories of the lives of youthful Joseph in Egypt, and the early struggles of David, the poet-king of Israel, are gripping and instructive because of the constant emphasis laid upon the God consciousness. I cannot lay too much stress upon the thought that you cannot get along without God, and do anything of permanent value in the great world into which you are going.

I was reading recently a story of the life of Henry Ford, the automobile manufacturer, written by William L. Stidger, who knows him well. He tells of the simple faith of this great captain of industry. He believes in God and reads his Bible daily. Mr. Stidger says, when he asked Mr. Ford what part of the teachings of Jesus he liked best and thought most applicable to life, he replied, "The Sermon on the Mount." When he asked him, "Do you try to run your industry by the Sermon on the Mount?" he replied, "I do. It is our constitution. And it works." He was reminded during the interview, that Bishop Quayle had said of the late John Burroughs, the famous naturalist, and the intimate friend of Ford, "He knew the garden but never found the Gardener," he replied, "Yes. That was too bad. It doesn't seem possible that one could fail to find the Gardener, with all of these beautiful things and all of these great things about us. It is too bad that Burroughs never found the Gardener."

In the beginning of your journey in search of the *whither* in the world, God's great garden, I pray you be sure to find the Gardener first. It will simplify greatly your search, and lighten the burdens of the way.

Then, you must have thorough preparation.

You have finished a specified course of study here under the direction of teachers, but you have merely been learning how to make thorough preparation for real life. You have merely gotten the rudiments, but you have been trained to think clearly and systematically. If you are wise, you will be adding daily to your little store through all the coming years, by constant reading, and pondering, and storing the shelves of memory against the time of need. Do not get the idea that you are thoroughly prepared for the fierce conflicts which await you by what you have learned here. I recall this incident which happened some years ago at a General Conference of our church. During a sharp parliamentary battle over a question of procedure, a delegate was busily hunting up the mooted point in his parliamentary manual. The late Dr. Bonner laughingly said to him: "You haven't time to learn it now, son. You should have known it." That is the thought I am trying to impress. You must be thoroughly prepared when the time comes, by knowing the thing which you are called upon suddenly to say or do. Although I have been away from this institution more than thirty years, I read and study more now than I did while I was a student here. Unceasing acquisition of information and knowledge is the only sure path to the *whither* of wealth, or honor, or service. Do not be envious of those who excel you in ability or attainments or knowledge. Keep after them.

Also, you must have undaunted courage.

When I speak of courage I mean that "quality of mind which meets danger or opposition with intrepidity, calmness and firmness. Courage is of the intellect and will, and may be possessed in the highest degree by those who are constitutionally timid." Courage is stoutness of heart, self-reliance, red-bloodedness of spirit.

As you go forward in life you will meet with ostracism on account of your race and color. You will encounter envy on account of your mental and material possessions. You will have to grapple with the green-eyed monster, jealousy, because of your achievements and popularity. You will meet ingratitude, that meanest of all sins, from those for whom you have done most and suffered most. You will be slandered by open and secret foes. There will be many hours of deep despondency, when you will debate whether it is worth while to continue to struggle and sacrifice for others. It is then you will need unfaltering courage to nerve your arm and strengthen your soul to march onward. But remember only those of hearts of oak ever accomplish anything worth while. Some one has well said: "Everywhere and at all times, the men who have had definite convictions upon the great issues, and have courageously chosen righteousness, are the men who have directed the course of nations."

Also, you must have the ability to go the route morally.

When I say "the route," I am using a phrase used by baseball writers, meaning the ability to last through the entire game. One of the greatest assets which a young man or woman can possess on leaving school is a high moral standard—an acute sense of moral values. And this equipment must be able to stand the wear and tear of ever-changing circumstances and conditions. You must not think that you can select the Commandments which you will keep and reject those which you do not like. The moral code of mankind, crystallized into the Ten Commandments by Moses, is the result of the reasoned experience of men who lived ages before Moses. Observation and experience convinced thoughtful men long ages ago that it is harmful to the individual, as well as to the community, to lie, to steal, to kill, and to commit adultery. I wish to emphasize that it is just as immoral to steal the good name of folks whom you do not like as it is to steal their goods. It is just as immoral to destroy the reputation and hinder the progress of those whom you envy as it is to take their lives.

I have in mind some brilliant men, whose great intellects gave promise, through their young manhood, of lives of usefulness and eminence, but they could not go the route morally, and today they are wrecks along the shore, and are but sad memories to their friends. Whatever the temptation to weaken morally as the years pass, and you reach places of authority and power, resolve to play the game through without faltering. My observation is that an immoral man or woman in a position of responsibility and power and, perhaps, possessed of wealth, and the influence which wealth carries with it, is a curse to every young person with whom they come in contact. Such persons contaminate the moral atmosphere and lower the moral temperature wherever they go.

Take along with you also as you go from here a great loyalty to some high vision and for some true friendship. You go out to a race poor, despised and ostracised. Get the vision of service. Resolve to live for them, not for yourself. "In a very deep and true sense it is what a man sees that either makes or unmakes him. The effect of vision upon character and service is transforming. It elevates or debases, according to its qualities. Whether a man grovels or soars, whether he remains in the realm of animalism or rises into the spiritual, and lives in the high places of the Sons of God, is determined by his seeing." The red-haired, dreamy-eyed shepherd boy, David, became Israel's hero-king because he was possessed of such a loyalty to his vision and friendship. One can not read of the bonds which bound him to his royal-souled friend, Jonathan, and of his sublime loyalty to his vision of service to his race, without being mightily impressed with the beauty of such a nature. You can do nothing worth while in this great world unless you are a dreamer of great dreams. You will never amount to much unless you are loyal to your dreams. When I speak of loyalty to friends I do not mean partners in crime, nor associates in questionable transactions, I mean loyalty to some true, high-thinking person whom you have discovered during your school days here.

You will not mean much to aspiring young men and women as you rise in the world unless they find you loyal to your friends. The man or woman who uses friends as stepping stones on which to rise, or as tools with which to attain some purpose or desired end, and then throws them aside like a worn-out garment after the thing sought has been obtained, will reap an abundant harvest of hate and contempt as people learn of the baseness of their natures, and will die with none so poor to do them reverence.

Take with you reverence for law and authority.

Do not get the idea that you are above all authority and may break laws or disobey rules and regulations, however high you may climb in the world. Remember the man in authority who advises others to break laws or to disrespect others in authority is undermining his own authority. Only those who reverence law and authority have any business ruling over others. Only such persons can successfully rule men and women. People may fear the lawless, but will never love nor respect them. It matters not what you may think of the law or what may be your estimate of those placed over you, I counsel you to revere the law and bow to authority.

Further, let me urge you to be economical and thrifty. Do not spend every cent you lay your hands upon. If you know you are loose-fingered, tie your hands or tie your money in some way. Edison, the great electric wizard, had to do that. Recently, he told the story of taking a perfected carbon transmitter to Philadelphia in the hope of selling it for $5,000, which would just about pay his debts. The directors asked him if $100,000 would buy the transmitter. He was so astonished that he remained silent for a moment, and they inquired if they had offered enough. "The price is all right," said Edison, "yes, that's all right. But on condition that you pay me it at the rate of $7,500 a year. If you paid it to me all at once I'd probably put it into some fool invention and lose every cent of it." Take Edison's tip. Do not lose "every cent of it." Store some of your wages or salary where you can not squander them. Savings banks or real estate are safe places for money.

And now a last word about race prejudice. You will meet it at every turn and everywhere you go. Sad to say, it is growing steadily. Your color will be against you in almost every field of activity. Do not deceive yourselves into believing that anywhere in this country you will escape this curse of the age. Often it will be veiled and stealthy. Frequently, it will walk openly and unafraid, but it will be the same illogical and unreasoning thing. Learn to expect it, and face it, and conquer it. You may console yourselves, however, with the fact that the Negro race is not the only race which suffers from race prejudice. Deport yourselves in such a gentle and quiet and confident and unassuming manner that you will make those ashamed who practice it. Wherever you go, let people learn that a colored skin can cover just as much culture and refinement and decency as any other kind of skin. Also, I exhort you, try to make friends with and command the respect of those with whom you live. Do not depend upon friends who are far away. Whatever the color of the people with whom you deal daily, they will respect refinement, modesty, integrity, scrupulous honesty, industry, and money.

If you equip yourselves with the qualities which I have outlined in this talk, you will surely reach the *whither* you seek in the great world into which you are going and you will take the race with you. Some of you will aspire to climb the mountain of fame and honor and responsibility, you may succeed in doing so. Listen to the expression of the thoughts of one who has climbed to the top of that mountain, Lloyd George, perhaps the most noted Englishman of today. Speaking in the Methodist church of his boyhood home, he said: "Mr. Davies has told you that I have climbed the mountain of fame, responsibility, and honor, and in a sense that is true; but, dear friends, let me assure you that the mountain is not an ideal place for any of us. There isn't much peace there, no real rest and comfort. The higher you climb, the colder it becomes. How exposed and bleak it is! You are at the mercy of the storm and the tempest. The wind makes sport of you. On the mountain a man feels lonely. Often thick mists envelop him, and he misses his way: he can hardly see a yard ahead. What is the good of a telescope in the mist? When a person thinks he is on the right path, suddenly he comes to a part where he can go no farther, and a deep chasm opens before him. He retraces his steps and makes an effort to regain the path from which he strayed. Yes, that is the lot of the man who attempts to climb the mountain."

His experience is the experience of all of us who have climbed the mountain. Still youth will aspire to climb the mountain, and it is well that it should be thus. Else what would mankind do for leaders? Whether you are to essay climbing the mountain, or plan to serve the race in the quiet paths which lie at the base of the mountain, always bear in mind:

"Wherever's a will there's a way, my lad,
If the will have the strength to serve;
But the goal is not reached in a day, my lad,
And the winning takes patience and nerve.
It's a long, long way and a hard, hard road,
And a lifetime is hardly enough;
But you'll win if you stick
To the roadway you pick
And your heart is the right kind of stuff.

"Oh, a bit of a song will help, my lad,
And a grin will ease many a pain.
The coward goes down with a yelp, my lad,
Get up and go at them again.
It's a long, long way and a hard, hard road
To the thing that you're longing to do,
And the key to the game
Is to stick to your aim,
And the courage will carry you through.

"Aye, many a path leads out, my lad,
From the road to the thing you want,
And they're pleasant to travel, no doubt, my lad,
And it's hard to know that you can't.
It's a long, long way and a hard, hard road
And you haven't the time to rest,
So pick up your load
And stick to your road;
You will win, if you give it your best."[1]

[1] R. A. Carter, *Feeding Among the Lilies*, 272-288.

BOARDS FOR LIFE'S BUILDING[1]

By Bishop George Clinton Clement[2]

When a building is to be erected certain considerations are to be observed. The architectural design, the material to be used, the proportions and appointments, the service expected, and the cost of all. Such a building designed, completed, and occupied is first in the mind of the architect. Every detail is minutely worked out, every stone and board, every proportion and adjustment finds its position definitely determined before the pick and shovel, the saw and hammer, the trowel and plumb are lifted. A completed building is the expression of an ideal. The fears and hopes of nations, even the joys and longings of individuals, have found utterance in brick and mortar in all ages. The rock-walled abode of primitive man was meant to shield from ruthless wife-snatcher and ravenous beasts. The woven thatch and the airy awning 'neath bower and grove where eastern suns pour down their scorching rays are but echoes of the dreamy, care-free spirit of their builders. Greek art in poetry and song finds consonance with chiselled column and rejoices amid gilded dome and marbled arch. What vast expanse, what national aspiration and achievement are marked by the distance from Abram's crude sacrificial altar to Solomon's resplendent temple on Mt. Moriah! All the passion and the progress of the Hebrew people are embraced in this encycle.

The rough stone set up by the ancient Druid impersonated no less accurately the latent native force of Briton and was as prophetic of a coming race of conquerors as the matchless Westminster Abbey, the accumulative glory of England's Victorian era.

A worshipping people, devout, God-fearing, and spiritual, builds temples, their upward inspiration calling aloud from towering spire and beckoning from gilded dome. Certain it is that as temple spires

[1] This was an address delivered at the dedication of the new auditorium, Livingstone College, Salisbury, North Carolina, May, 1921.

[2] Bishop George Clinton Clement was born at Mocksville, North Carolina, December 23, 1871. He was educated at Livingstone College where he made the impression of being a thorough student and an earnest worker. He early became connected with the African Methodist Episcopal Zion Church, serving as a minister in the year 1888. He then became the Editor of the *Star of Zion*, a position which he held from 1904 until 1916, when he was elected and consecrated bishop.

have lowered or disappeared altogether, earth vision and sordid materialism have gripped the minds and hearts of the people.

The love of freedom, the rule of the populace piled high the Parthenon and the Coliseum as truly as did inordinate ambition and misguided effort contribute toward the rise and fall of Babel. The long black night of mental eclipse and moral lethargy we call the dark ages is typified in the insignificance and dearth of architectural endeavor. Just as surely did the succeeding period when learning and literature flourished bring the charming temples of the great Renaissance. India, golden bordered and dazzling with precious stones, bound her national character with jewelled chains to superstitious mosques.

World-renowned St. Peter's for Italy and the cold imposing Kremlin for Russia bear witness to the traits of two greatly dissimilar nations.

Oh! wonderful monuments of century-buried civilization away yonder in the valley of the Nile. What secret is held by you, mystic Sphinx, and what notes are those that burst from thy wind-swept throat, ancient Memnon? Whatever the answer, 'tis but an indication of what once thrilled and moved the great Afric race.

A ruling, politically minded people builds palaces, arsenals, and forts. A commercially minded people builds warehouses and markets and factories. A liberty loving people builds forums and halls and amphitheatres. Romulus and Solomon of old and Michael Angelo and Wren of later days expressed the thought and life of their times and peoples.

Today as we gather within these spacious walls and look around to determine the height and length and breadth of this building, we can but mark its plan, its material composition and its purpose. After congratulating all who have contributed to the erection of this splendid temple, may we not consider other features that are inseparable from this place and occasion—thoughts and impulses that crowd upon us?

I wish now to call your attention to a few Boards for our Life Building. These are not of fragile clay or glass, nor of perishable wood and stone, but real, living—may I suggest, eternal—timbers.

First of all, here is laid the bright and promising timber we call OPPORTUNITY. This is only another term for youth. Whatever else presses upon us for consideration, turn whither we may, we confront young and sparkling eyes, all forward-looking, anxious, and expectant. Schools are built for youth, for students, rather than for teachers. A school is the expression of a people's interest in their offspring and an augury of their future. The greatest asset of a nation is not its plains and mountains, its rivers and harbors, nor its precious metals beneath nor its glad harvest above the surface, nor its flocks and herds, nor its mansions and shops. The greatest asset of a nation is its childhood. Though poor in all else, rich is that people whose houses are filled with youth. The most vital question is not the development and conservation of forest and mine and water. The most vital question is the training and perfecting of the physical, mental, and moral life of the children. All that can be seen about us is meant for the boys and girls, the young men and young women who come upon these consecrated grounds. They hold the future of their kind within their tender grasp. Who would hinder them in any laudable enterprise? Open wide the door and bid them enter.

Comradeship

Whoever has marked the student life, especially life in a boarding school, has been impressed with the intimate personal relationships existing between students. No matter from whence they come, be it from farm or shop, crowded urban street or rural quietude, whether rich or poor, high or low in social scale, the school is to them a veritable melting pot. Differences of birth, of creed, and of class are forgotten and are eventually obliterated by the daily contact of classroom and dormitory. Farm and drawing-room go arm in arm, each eagerly learning the one from the other the fascinating story of life. If the public school is the nursery of good citizenship, then the boarding school is the garden of true democracy. Nowhere is the bane of conceit so speedily knocked from selfish heads and nowhere is respect for the opinion of others so soon manifest as in the boarding school. A comradeship which approaches nigh to that of blood ties is here developed. Upon this platform in honorable contest, when mind meets mind and fierce battles of bloodless wars are waged, crude egotism gets its death blow, and unselfish brotherhood wins the victor's crown.

Free Speech

The right to make known the promptings of the heart can be catalogued as inalienable and inherent. Freedom of speech based upon freedom of thought can scarcely be denied. By this is not meant license to misrepresent and vilify, nor the carping of malcontents and the frothings of recalcitrants, who have no respect for authority and no reverence for ancient landmarks. Honest conviction and sincere purpose must be heard. On this platform as the years come and go there should be the widest range of discussion, the sharpest criticism and the bravest defense in all fields of educational endeavor. The right of petition and protest is as old as human frailty and as limitless as human ambition. Freedom of speech is predicated upon loyalty to truth; and in all the annals of forensic effort there exists no brighter page than the one dedicated to this principle. The immortal Cicero uncovering the treacherous schemes of Catiline, the intrepid Paul making the knees of Felix to smite together, the matchless Burke demolishing the citadel of Hastings, the golden-mouthed Chrysostom, Luther the daring, Savonarola the invincible, Wesley the peerless, with Massillon and Knox, Emmett and Webster, Beecher and Phillips, Douglass and Price—who can estimate the tremendous power, the almost omnipotent influence, of the forum. May its foundations forever rest on truth and may its voice fail not to be heard.

Patriotism

No building such as we have in mind can be quite so strong and grand as we desire without somewhere in its foundation rests another timber, visible and solid. We speak of love of country—patriotism it is called. The winds that blow, the rains that fall, the sunshine and the snow, the skies that smile or frown in turn, forest and field, beach, brook, or dale, paved street or grassy sod, whatever there may be, where the eyes of infancy first open to the light, that place called HOME is the dearest spot in all the world. Rocks and surfs, jungle and desert, ice cliff and burning sand may defy us, but we rejoice to contend with them. Inequalities and injustices may trammel us, but we tear them asunder; prejudice and discrimination may confront us, we may be cast down but never overwhelmed. So the native son goes forth to fight without fear of favor, unitedly with him who says:

> "Breathes there a man with soul so dead
> Who never to himself has said
> This is my own, my native land:
> Whose heart has ne'er within him burned
> When homeward he his footsteps turned
> From wandering on a foreign strand?
> If such there be, go mark him well,
> For him no minstrel raptures swell,
> And the wretched, doubly dying, shall go down
> To the vile depth from whence he sprung,
> Unwept, unhonored and unsung."

Let us examine the walls of our building. Here are the marks of

Sacrificial Service

Youth should dream dreams and see visions, but to stop there is but to fail miserably. There is nothing wrong in building castles in the air if you have cords strong enough to bring them to the ground and to tie them there. In Athens there was a temple called Honor, built of polished marble, wide and high and noble. The floor was mirrored, the dome resplendent with gold, the whole an inspiration and a song. Every Athenian youth desired to enter this wonderful edifice, but there was but one entrance and that through another temple called Virtue. Unlike the temple of Honor, the temple Virtue was low and narrow. Whoever would enjoy the beauties and glories of honor must undergo the hardships of virtue. The lesson is plain. There is no royal road to success, although success itself is royal. The lone missionary ministering to the pitiable leper colony of the South Sea Islands, the watchful sentinel pacing his icy beat 'mid Alpine frost, the brave and weather-beaten lifeguard off death-famed Hatteras and wreck-strewn Biscay, the faithful and zealous physician pressing his way through the dark and black night to save the life of an humble peasant, alike with others in every walk of life who forget self and suffering for humanity's sake are shining examples of the truest and noblest service. Not for gold nor sounding brass, not for purple nor glittering tinsel, not for praise nor hollow flattery; but for the sake of him who so loved us that he gave his life for us, while we were yet his enemies, are we constrained to make the supreme sacrifice. Some have failed because they feared to die. Life with cowardice and compromise is to be despised, while the death of the martyr for truth and righteousness has been the dream and goal of the world's immortals.

But let us leave the dome, sun crowned and beautiful as it is, and examine that timber which is the very foundation of the building. We would liken it to the roots that hold up the cedars of Lebanon, the towering Con Con of Surinam, whose lofty head looks down upon all tropical forests, the stately palm of Africa's plain, princely and majestic. But none of these bespeak its fullest and grandest note. We have reference to

Faith in the Divine

Very recently a great man fell in death. He had sat in the councils of the wise and stood before the rulers of earth; he was counted among the foremost sociological and economic authorities of our nation, yet throughout his busy life he had no vision of God. When there came over the wires the news of his death and that strange request for his ashes to be cast from the summit of Pike's Peak to the four winds, to be blown toward a hopeless eternity, a distinct shock was felt throughout the land. Even the wife of his bosom refused to carry out the wish and declared that she deemed it a sacrilege.

How heartening it is to go back to the land of the ancient East and hear the voice of one declaring that "though he slay me yet will I trust him, for I know that my Redeemer liveth and in the latter day he shall stand upon the earth, and though after my skin worms destroy this body yet in my flesh shall I see God." Whatever of science, of fact in philosophy or literature, whatever mastery of things real or speculative we may acquire, all is vain unless they rest upon faith in the Eternal. A spiritless, Godless culture is dangerous to man and nation. The never-to-be-forgotten lesson of such culture evidenced in the World War is too recently learned to need emphasis here. Leave out Faith and this building will be a worthless shell and a constant menace. Faith binds, faith ennobles, faith makes enduring and perpetuates.

At Plymouth Rock last fall we saw the marvelous statue erected by sons of the Pilgrim Fathers and dedicated by them to Faith. The statue is crowned with a virgin, her face turned toward the rough Atlantic, her eyes searching the threatening waters and her hands outstretched to hasten the oppressed and truth seeking from over the seas. One cannot gaze long at this statue without feeling the throbbing of that faith which John Robinson preached unto the dauntless voyagers who set out on the great adventure.

Here and now may I ask that we lay this solid plank of Faith in the very foundation of our building. We must fasten it with spikes of truth and cement it around with the tears and prayers of our fathers. Here may it rest secure; to be looked upon, reverenced, and utilized until rocks to dust have crumbled and all the skies in vaporous smoke have flown, and only God himself stands out in the eternal to welcome and reward.

A KNOWLEDGE OF HISTORY CONDUCIVE TO RACIAL SOLIDARITY[1]

By C. V. Roman[2]

What consolation, then, does the Muse of History offer the troubled souls of black folks? The references in Holy Writ are sufficient to show that the Ethiopians were a people of great wealth and military power in ancient times. Simon, the African, assisting Christ to bear the Cross; the high treasurer of Candace, Queen of Ethiopians, reading the Scriptures and reaching the conclusions, under Philip's guidance, that Jesus Christ was the Son of God; and David's exuberant declaration that "Princes shall come out of Egypt; Ethiopia shall soon stretch out her hands unto God,"

[1] Delivered on several occasions by Dr. Roman.

[2] Charles Victor Roman was born at Williamsport, Pennsylvania. He was brought up in Ontario, Canada, Brant and Wentworth Counties. He belongs to the class of so-called self-made men. He taught in the public schools of Kentucky and Tennessee while studying medicine, but entered immediately upon the active practice of medicine after graduation, locating in Clarksville, Tennessee. He later practiced in Dallas, Texas, until called to Meharry Medical College, Nashville, Tennessee.

He has been president of the National Medical Association and was for ten years Editor-in-Chief of the *Journal of the National Medical Association* and is now an Associate Editor.

He was official medical lecturer to the colored troops during the World War, and has thus appeared before numerous groups in this country. Most of his important addresses thus delivered have been published in his volume entitled *The American Civilization and the Negro.*

are luminous rays from the torch of Sacred history that fall athwart the black man's troubled path; Profane history seems to have reached us as the one-sided chronicles of Aryan prejudice. In reading such history as is now available to us, one is reminded of an incident of current Texas history reported by the *Success Magazine.*

Senator Bailey was making a political speech when two unlettered sons of Ham approached the outer rim of the crowd and listened for a while; then the following conversation took place:

"Who am dat, Sam?"

"I dunno what his name am," Sam replied, "but he certainly do recommen hisself mos' highly."

The white man has written the history of the world as we now have it, and he has had no scruples about "recommending hisself." Hence the claim of sensational modern magazine writers that the Negro has made no history needs to be taken with a grain of salt, since the white man has written the history that fails to reflect any glory upon the Negro. "Only individuals immune to the teachings of evolution could imagine that a race, millenniums old, and numbering today, after centuries of more or less brutal contact with the whites, more than 150,000,000 could have existed or could continue to exist without in the slightest influencing the currents of human thought and action. It is with eyes blind to the results of the most recent investigation of the origin and the development of Negro culture in Africa, and to the achievements of the race in other parts of the globe that such people content themselves with repeating words of prejudiced origin, which have long since lost significance, and with seeing in the Negro only a beast or a half man."

Two incidents in recent times will illustrate how history is made bias: "A certain Lieutenant Colonel was at San Juan Hill—other men did the fighting—but he wrote an account of it—and did not fail to 'recommen hisself mos' highly,' and as a result honors and emoluments of office have been showered upon the historian, and not upon the soldiers that did the fighting."

The other illustrates the process from another viewpoint. Prior to the war between Russia and Japan, it was a well-attested fact that only a white nation could defeat a white nation in battle. The Abyssinians and Japanese have presented some pretty strong counter testimony; but the ethnologists have rushed to the relief of the historians and have proven the Japs white folks, to the satisfaction of everybody but the people on the Pacific coast. The case of the Abyssinians is still under advisement, the investigator having progressed only far enough to show that they are not Negroes, for Negroes have made no history. Q. E. D. The Negro and history are like success and treason:

> "Treason never succeeds. What's the reason?
> If it succeed, no one dare call it treason."

The Negro never made any history, because if anybody ever made any history he was not a Negro. Thus by circular reasoning they make their position logically invincible.

Accurate historical knowledge is one of the great needs of our leaders of today. They need it to give them that breadth of understanding and prescient optimism which alone can make leaders of sufficient intellectual procerity to command the confidence of the multitude, and bring about racial solidarity among the colored people of America.

The one great need of our race today is an intelligent, conservative leadership that can command the confidence and loyalty of the masses. I hope that the observances of these memorial days in Negro colleges may herald the dawning of a new day for Negro scholarship,—a scholarship broad enough in its sympathies to comprehend justice and fraternity; profound enough in its erudition to harmonize the different phases of human culture, from the study of Greek to the picking of cotton; accurate enough in its wisdom to discover and remedy the chromatic aberrations of the historical lenses which have shown civilization to be solidly white; strong enough in its reasoning to convince men that fitness and not race is the real test for citizenship. In other words, we need a scholarship that will give us pride of race and inspire us with a reasonable hope of final triumph and historical vindication, yea, the positive assurance of a respectable seat in the hierarchy of civilization as a distinct phyletic entity, and not as the tolerated contamination of some nobler race. Racial solidarity and not amalgamation is the desired and desirable goal of the American Negro. Phyletic triumph through racial solidarity, rather than phyletic oblivion in the Lethean waters of miscegenation, will be the teaching of that scholarship. A knowledge of history will bring this about in one of two ways.

If civilization *was* actually cradled in Africa and learning *did* originate in the Dark Continent—if the ancestors of the present Europeans *were* dark-skinned inhabitants of Asia and Africa and some of the famous characters of history *did* have Negro blood in their veins, why a verification of these facts will stimulate race pride and promote racial solidarity sufficiently to enable us to spurn as poor relations those unfortunate members of our race who are ashamed of their lineage. This is a type of Negro that is an ethnological curiosity. In contemplation of him in relation to the race, I always think of Charles Lamb's description of a poor relation:

"A poor relation is the most irrelevant thing in nature, a piece of impertinent correspondency—an odious approximation,—a haunting conscience, a preposterous shadow, lengthening in the noontide of our prosperty, an unwelcome remembrancer, a perpetually recurring mortification, a drain on your purse, a more intolerable dun upon your pride, a draw-back upon your success, a rebuke to your rising, a stain in your blood, a blot on your escutcheon, a rent in your garment, a death's head at your banquet, Agathocles' pot, a Mordecai in your gate, a Lazarus at your door, a lion in your path, a frog in your chamber, a fly in your ointment, a mote in your eye, a triumph to your enemy, an apology to your friends, the one thing not needful, the hail in harvest, the ounce of sour in the pound of sweet."

Such is the Negro who does not wish to attend a Negro church, buy from a Negro merchant, consult a Negro lawyer or doctor, deposit in a Negro bank, or live in a Negro neighborhood, or send his children to a Negro school. I do not speak of those who have not these opportunities, but of those who spurn them.

But suppose we have no historical antecedents, what then? Does this give certitude to Huxley's "Assuredly," uttered in 1865? Conceding relationship but not fraternity, he says of the American freedman: "The highest places in the hierarchy of civilization will assuredly not be within reach of our dusky cousins, though it is by no means necessary that they should be restricted to the lowest."

Let us see. If the Negro has never made any history he has certainly been in the white man's history from the beginning of that history. He has won the right to the earth by long residence if by no other right. He has been here so long that in the words of Uncle Remus, " 'Twel time has quit runnin agin him." This is sufficient answer to Ingall's lugubrious prophecy: "Destruction is Nature's final decree in equity for the black man."

As black contains by absorption all the colors of the rainbow, though it does not reflect them, so the Negro has in him all the elements of civilization and may yet reflect them as brilliantly as any of the sons of men. It is a beautiful metaphor that likens civilization to light. "The light of civilization" is a phrase as suggestive as beautiful. The similitude is apt. So let us study the action of light closely. If all the light falling upon an object pass through it, the object is transparent and invisible. Imperfect transparency indicates the reflection or absorption of some of the incident rays. Color arises the same way. If all the rays are reflected, the object is opaque and white; if all the rays are absorbed, the object is opaque and black. So really the white man has no more light than the black man, though he is more luminous. He knows no more of his origin and Nature's ultimatum for him than does the black man.

"Who in the darkness of the finite can turn over the mystic pages and read the cryptograms of the Book of Destiny?"

Light needs to strike against something to become manifest. Take a cylinder six inches long and painted black within. Have a hole in the side equi-distant from each end. Darken the room until only a single beam of light is permitted to enter. Now place the cylinder in the path of this beam of light in such a way that the beam of light will traverse the cavity of the cylinder. Look through the hole in the side, and notwithstanding the evident fact that the light is passing through this cavity, it is completely dark. No trace of the light is visible. Now introduce a pencil so as to obstruct the pathway of the beam and a ball of light will at once appear. Obstruction has made the light manifest. The American white man may be the necessary obstruction to make the Negro reflect the light of civilization.

But whatever general history, ancient or modern, may have to say of the Negro, American history cannot be truthfully written without giving the Negro some creditable roles. Fidelity, docility, good-nature, thoughtlessness, improvidence, patience, physical vigor, etc., in fact, all the slave virtues have been freely conceded us; but the virtues of freedom have been persistently ignored and denied. What we need is an historical knowledge that will paint us as we are. "Nothing extenuate, nor set down aught in malice." We want a literature of truth and inspiration that will embalm the deeds of our heroes and encourage the lives of our children. "My ear is pained and my heart is sick" when I contemplate the babbling sciolism that is parading itself as scholarship, and declaring with the fatuous egotism of nescience that "History holds nothing to the credit of the Negro."

The American Negro is *sui generis.* His condition is unique in the history of races. He is now passing through a period of adjustment—racial moving, as it were—from bondage to freedom. The freedman is becoming a FREE MAN. Losses always attend a moving. As we get settled in the house of freedom we will surround ourselves with more of the virtues and less of the vices of that condition. There are distinctive slave virtues that are not virtues in freedom. All observers see that the Negro is throwing off the former; only those associated with the best of the Negro race know that he is putting on a glorious substitute, the virtues of the free man. Slowly but surely the freedman is becoming in reality a free man.

Oh! for a Negro pen to record the lives of our great men and women! I would not circumscribe the fields of learning nor rob the white children of their pride of lineage; but I would teach Negro children the glorious deeds of Negro men and Negro women FIRST.

The story of Abram Grant from the ox-cart (where he was born) and the slave pen, to the bishopric is of more educative value to a colored youth than the story of James A. Garfield from the tow-path to the presidency. The Negro boy should know both. The lives of the founders of this school—Payne, Shorter, and Mitchell—are full of deeds that would inspire our young people. Bishop Payne was a hero of education and freedom. You cannot read his life without a thrill of admiration for the frail little body that held such a master mind. Nor is he alone; the dignitaries of our church and of all the Negro churches furnish us with many characters of light and leading, worthy of emulation and fit to inspire. But they by no means exhaust the list. From every walk in life they come. Why, down on the banks of the Cumberland river, at Nashville, Tennessee, dwells an humble fireman who has risked his life a score of times for others, and has rescued a dozen people from the clammy clutch of engulfing waters. A Negro woman crossing a mad and swollen river on floating pieces of ice, barefooted and with a child in her arms, that she might find liberty for herself and child, presents a picture of magnificent heroism, fit for song and story.

I am not preaching ethnic antagonism nor endeavoring to give a racial tinge to the facts of history, but I do wish to widen sufficiently the fields of *taught* history to include the Negroes who justly belong there. Negroes,

> "Who broke their lives from day to day,
> To pour a fragrance down the years."

A history of Methodism is as incomplete without Richard Allen as without John Wesley. A history of the American stage should include Williams and Walker as well as Booth and Jefferson; Cole and Johnson, as well as Fields and Dockstader. How could a history of stage mimicry be written without the name of Billy Kersands? The history of music would be incomplete without the Jubilee Songs and the matchless Fisk Quartette; while Sissieretta Jones and Flora Batson are names that should not be forgotten. How could the story of the adaptation of popular education to the needs of the people be told without the name of Washington; or the history of polemic protest against caste prejudice be written without mentioning Du Bois! It is a long way from a log cabin in Kentucky to the Presidency of these United States, but from the slave-pens of Maryland to the marshalship of the District of Columbia is further. While we justly honor Lincoln for the first, we should remember Douglass made the second.

> "'Make way for Liberty,' he cried;
> Made way for liberty and died,"

is as true of Crispus Attucks' rush upon the British bayonets at Boston, as of Arnold von Winkelreid's plunge upon the Austrian pikes at Sempach. Toussaint L'Ouverture is as worthy a place in the history of war as Napoleon Bonaparte. Of those turbulent and erratic souls that sacrifice themselves for the righting of others' wrongs, Nat Turner is as worthy of remembrance as John Brown. When the roll is called of great and good women whose spiritualized lives have blessed their generation, Sojourner Truth is as worthy a place as Frances E. Willard; nor should our own Frances Harper be forgotten when the singers for temperance are assembled.

When the history of American Eloquence is taught and the language of heroic souls is being transmitted to posterity, give Patrick Henry's "Give me liberty, or give me death" a high place, but in the same chapter record these words of Major Delaney:

"All the ideas I have of liberty and independence I obtained from reading the History of the Revolutionary Fathers. From them I learned a man has a right to defend his castle, even to the taking of life. My cottage is my castle; my wife and children are its inmates. If any man enter that castle to look for a fugitive slave—I care not if it be he who signed his name to that ignominious law; if he come with the Declaration of Independence flying in the air as a banner, and the Constitution of the United States upon his bosom as a breast-plate—if he enter my house to search for a fugitive slave, and I do not strike him down dead, may the grave refuse my body a resting place, and righteous heaven deny my spirit admission."

Thus spoke a black man with a knowledge of history.

A diffusion of such knowledge among the masses of our people will stimulate race pride, strengthen their consciousness of kind without lessening their patriotism, and furnish an atmosphere of mutual coöperation and helpfulness that will change the winter of our discontent into the glorious summer of racial solidarity, that magic alembic in which most of our racial difficulties will disappear.

There is an heroic race of men who are the doers of the world, the flower of their kind. They stood in the Pass of Thermopylae, and made a hundred spears deadlier than a million. They held the

Alpine Highways against the covetous Austrian hordes. They forgot arithmetic at Balaklava and transmuted four hundred Sheffield sabers into magic falchions. They lighted the torch of learning while the battle for freedom was raging and opened the Halls of Knowledge to manumitted slaves. They sped the triremes at Salamis, and redeemed a race at Fort Wagner. They lashed the sails of Drake and manned the cannon of Perry. They crawled across the Arctic ice. They cut their way through the tangles of mid-Africa. Few of their names are known and few of their graves are marked, but the glory of their courage is imperishable—a heritage for all tomorrows—a spark to heat the blood and fire the future generations with inspiration.

They are of no particular sect, nor caste, nor race. They are born alike from the loins of peasant and of peer. Their fraternity is not of breed, nor brain, nor brawn, but of truth. Duty is their mission and its fulfillment their ultimate hope.

"They wage for the ages, and not for the wages."

Like the number that John saw, they have come up through great tribulations, from every kindred and tongue and people. Who knows but this audience may furnish some? But we will not judge.

Let us close by a look to Nature for analogy and instruction and hope. Down in the sunless retreats of the ocean—way down, down, where the sunlight never penetrates and eternal night holds sway,—in this cheerless region may we find a useful and inspiring lesson. The multitudinous inhabitants of this inhospitable place may be divided into two general classes,—sedentary and migratory; the former have no eyes,—beautiful adaptation of organism to environment—Nature's economy. What use are eyes in a region of perpetual darkness? The migratory ones, however, not only have eyes, but have the power of making a light. They thus supply by their own phosphorescent energy that luminosity denied them by the sun, because of the intervening waters. It is my hope that Negro scholarship will become self-luminous with a brilliancy that will give our race correct historical perspective, and lead us to that ethnological respectability and racial solidarity which the floods of prejudice have so persistently washed beyond our grasp. In that hope let us labor earnestly, and patiently await the triumph of justice, and

"Let us pray, that come it may,
As come it will for a' that—
That truth and worth o'er a' the earth
Shall bear the gree and a' that."

CHAPTER XIII

PROGRESSIVE ORATORY

Although the white people refused to listen to the Negro orator of old, and thereby contributed to his oppression by depriving him of an audience, the case of the Negro was not hopeless, for the race was developing from within. The accumulation of wealth, the progress of education, and the development of the press among Negroes made them such a force in this country, that the whites, who had formerly ignored them, had to give their case some consideration. The conservatives were all but alarmed at the increasing number of Negroes, who during the first generation of the twentieth century, had begun to bear grievously the burden resulting from the social, economic, and political inequalities of which they had not been recently complaining. Whether the other people in the community wanted to hear the complaints of the Negroes or not, they had to give the case some consideration, for the stronger influence of the Negroes as a result of their general progress, made them a force with which the community had to reckon. In other words, the Negro of this generation began to force a large body of citizens here and there to give some attention to the appeals made by their spokesmen. Ida B. Wells-Barnett was driven from the South, but she made herself a great factor in presenting the case of the Negro to the whites in Chicago; William Monroe Trotter gave unusual impetus to the movement by his fiery oratory which he forced upon an unwilling public; William Pickens developed into such a protagonist of the forward movement, that he had to abandon teaching to devote all of his time to propaganda; James Weldon Johnson, at first a poet, easily drifted into the agitation for the enlargement of the domain of the liberty of the Negro; and numerous thinkers, influenced by the Socialist movement since the World War, have stirred the country with their radical appeal for the alignment of the Negro with the forces now desirous of reconstructing our social, economic, and political system.

THE KIND OF DEMOCRACY THE NEGRO RACE EXPECTS[1]

By William Pickens[2]

Democracy is the most used term in the world today. But some of its uses are abuses. Everybody says "Democracy"! But everybody has his own definition. By the extraordinary weight of the presidency of the United States many undemocratic people have had this word forced upon their lips but have not yet had the right ideal forced upon their hearts. I have heard of one woman who wondered with alarm whether "democracy" would mean that colored women would have the right to take any vacant seat or space on a street car, even if they had paid for it. That such a question should be asked, shows how many different meanings men may attach to the one word DEMOCRACY. This woman doubtless believes in a democracy of me-and-my-kind, which is no democracy. The most autocratic and the worst caste systems could call themselves democratic by that definition. Even the Prussian junker believes in that type of democracy: he has no doubt that he and the other junkers should be free and equal in rights and privileges.

Many have accepted the word DEMOCRACY merely as the current

[1] Delivered at various times and places by Mr. Pickens.

[2] William Pickens was born in Pendleton, Anderson County, South Carolina, January 15, 1881. At an early age he moved to Little Rock, Arkansas, where he attended high school. He began his education seriously at Talladega College. He then went to Yale where he distinguished himself by winning prizes in essay and oratorical contests. He was graduated there with high honor. He began teaching at Talladega, and served that institution for a number of years. He then became a professor at Wiley College, Marshall, Texas. From that position he was called to be dean of Morgan College. Leaving Morgan College, he entered upon the work of Field Secretary for the National Association for the Advancement of Colored People, a position which he still holds.

During his varying career, Mr. Pickens has given a large portion of his time to lectures and addresses delivered here and there throughout the United States. As a speaker, he is forceful and logical, and at the same time, enthusiastic and entertaining. In this rôle, he can be better described as *sui generis*, for as a writer and a speaker, he follows no particular models and it would be difficult for others to imitate him. His oratory is a bold defense of the Negro in the face of social proscription and terror with which the race is now afflicted.

password to respectability in political thinking. The spirit of the times is demanding democracy; it is the tune of the age; it is the song to sing. But some are like that man who belonged to one of our greater political parties: after hearing convincing arguments by the stump-speaker of the opposite party, he exclaimed: "Wa-al, that fellow has convinced my judgment, but I'll be d—d if he can CHANGE MY VOTE!"

It is in order, therefore, for the Negro to state clearly what he means by democracy and what he is fighting for.

FIRST. Democracy in Education. This is fundamental. No other democracy is practicable unless all of the people have equal right and opportunity to develop according to their individual endowments. There can be no real democracy between two natural groups, if one represents the extreme of ignorance and the other the best intelligence. The common public school and the state university should be the foundation stones of democracy. If men are artificially differentiated at the beginning, if we try to educate a "working class" and a "ruling class," forcing different race groups into different lines without regard to individual fitness, how can we ever hope for democracy in the other relations of these groups? Individuals will differ, but in democracy of education peoples living on the same soil should not be widely diverged in their training on mere racial lines. This would be illogical, since they are to be measured by the same standards of life. Of course, a group that is to live in Florida should be differently trained from a group that is to live in Alaska; but that is geography and general environment, and not color or caste.—The Negro believes in democracy of education as first and fundamental: that the distinction should be made between individual talents and not between colors and castes.

SECOND. Democracy in Industry. The right to work in any line for which the individual is best prepared, and to be paid the standard wage. This is also fundamental. In the last analysis there could be very little democracy between multi-millionaires and the abject poor. There must be a more just and fair distribution of wealth in a democracy. And certainly this is not possible unless men work at the occupations for which they are endowed and best prepared. There should be no "colored" wages and no "white" wages; no "man's" wage and no "woman's" wage. Wages should be paid for the work done, measured as much as possible by its productiveness. No door of opportunity should be closed to a man on any other ground than that of his individual unfitness. The cruelest and most undemocratic thing in the world is to require of the individual man that his whole race be fit before he can be regarded as fit for a certain privilege or responsibility. That rule, strictly applied, would exclude any man of any race from any position. For every man to serve where he is most able to serve is public economy and is to the best interest of the state. This lamentable war that was forced upon us should make that plain to the dullest of us. Suppose that, when this war broke out, our whole country had been like Mississippi (and I refer to geography uninvidiously),—suppose our whole country had been like Mississippi, where a caste system was holding the majority of the population in the triple chains of ignorance, semi-serfdom and poverty. Our nation would be now either the unwilling prey or the golden goose for the Prussian. The long-headed thing for any state is to let every man do his best all of the time. But some people are so short-sighted that they only see what is thrust against their noses. The Negro asks American labor in the name of democracy to get rid of its color caste and industrial junkerism.

THIRD. Democracy in State. A political democracy in which all are equal before the laws; where there is one standard of justice, written and unwritten; where all men and women may be citizens by the same qualifications, agreed upon and specified. We believe in this as much for South Africa as for South Carolina, and we hope that our American nation will not agree with any government, ally or enemy, that is willing to make a peace that will bind the African Negro to political slavery and exploitation.

Many other evils grow out of political inequality. Discriminating laws are the mother of the mob spirit. The political philosopher in Washington, after publishing his opinion that a Negro by the fault of being a Negro is unfit to be a member of Congress, cannot expect an ignorant white man in Tennessee to believe that the same Negro is, nevertheless, fit to have a fair and impartial trial in a Tennessee court. Ignorance is too logical for that. I disagree with the premises but I agree with the reasoning of the Tennesseean: that if being a Negro unfits a man for holding a government office for which he is otherwise fit, it unfits the same man for claiming a "white man's" chance in the courts. The first move therefore against mob violence and injustice in the petty courts is to wipe out discriminating laws and practices in the higher circles of government. The ignorant man in Tennessee will not rise in ideal above the intelligent man in Washington.

FOURTH. Democracy without Sex-preferment. The Negro cannot consistently oppose color discrimination and support sex discrimination in democratic government. This happened to be the opinion also of the First Man of the Negro race in America,—Frederick Douglass. The handicap is nothing more nor less than a presumption in the mind of the physically dominant element of the universal inferiority of the weaker or subject element. It is so easy to prove that the man who is down and under, deserves to be down and under. In the first place, he is down there, isn't he? And that is three-fourths of the argument to the ordinary mind; for the ordinary mind does not seek ultimate causes. The argument against the participation of colored men and of women in self-government is practically one argument. Somebody spoke to the Creator about both of these classes and learned that they were "created" for inferior rôles. Enfranchisement would spoil a good field-hand,—or a good cook. Black men were once ignorant,—women were once ignorant. Negroes had no political experience,—women had no such experience. The argument forgets that people do not get experience on the outside. But the American Negro expects a democracy that will accord the right to vote to a sensible industrious woman rather than to a male tramp.

FIFTH. Democracy in Church. The preachings and the practices of Jesus of Nazareth are perhaps the greatest influence in the production of modern democratic ideas. The Christian church is, therefore, no place for the caste spirit or for snobs. And the colored races the world over will have even more doubt in the future than they have had in the past of the real Christianity of any church which holds out to them the prospect of being united in heaven after being separated on earth.

FINALLY. The great colored races will in the future not be kinder to a sham democracy than to a "scrap-of-paper" autocracy. The private home, private right and private opinion must remain inviolate; but the commonwealth, the public places and public property must not be appropriated to the better use of any group by "Jim-Crowing" and segregating any other group. By the endowments of God and nature there are individual "spheres"; but there are no such widely different racial "spheres." Jesus' estimate of the individual soul is the taproot of democracy, and any system which discourages the men of any race from individual achievement, is no democracy. To fix the status of a human soul on earth according to the physical group in which it was born, is the gang spirit of the savage which protects its own members and outlaws all others.

For real democracy the American Negro will live and die. His loyalty is always above suspicion, but his extraordinary spirit in the present war is born of his faith that on the side of his country and her allies is the best hope for such democracy. And he welcomes, too, the opportunity to lift the "Negro question" out of the narrow confines of the Southern United States and make it a world question. Like many other questions our domestic race question, instead of being settled by Mississippi and South Carolina, will now seek its settlement largely on the battlefields of Europe.

THE FAITH OF THE AMERICAN NEGRO[1]

By Mordecai Wyatt Johnson[2]

Since their emancipation from slavery the masses of American Negroes have lived by the strength of a simple but deeply moving faith. They have believed in the love and providence of a just and holy God; they have believed in the principles of democracy and in the righteous purpose of the Federal Government; and they

[1] An address delivered as one of the three Commencement parts at Harvard University Commencement, June 22, 1922.

[2] Mordecai Wyatt Johnson, son of the Reverend Wyatt Johnson and Caroline Freeman Johnson; born at Paris, Tennessee, January 12, 1890. Educated in the public grade school of Paris, Tennessee, the academies of Roger Williams University, Nashville, Tennessee, of Howe Institute, Memphis, Tennessee, and of Atlanta Baptist College, Atlanta, Georgia; A.B., Morehouse College, 1911; A.B., University of Chicago, 1913; B.D., Rochester Theological Seminary, 1920; S.T.M., Harvard University, 1922; D.D., Howard University, 1923. Commencement speaker at Morehouse College, 1911. Commencement speaker Rochester Theological Seminary, Rochester, New York, 1916. Commencement part at Harvard University, Cambridge, Massachusetts, 1922. 1911-12, Professor of English at Morehouse College. 1912-13, Professor of the Social Sciences at Morehouse College. 1916-17, Secretary, Student Department of the International Committee of Young Men's Christian Associations. 1917-23, Pastor of the First Baptist Church, Charleston, West Virginia.

have believed in the disposition of the American people as a whole and in the long run to be fair in all their dealings.

In spite of disfranchisement and peonage, mob violence and public contempt, they have kept this faith and have allowed themselves to hope with the optimism of Booker T. Washington that in proportion as they grew in intelligence, wealth, and self-respect they should win the confidence and esteem of their fellow white Americans, and should gradually acquire the responsibilities and privileges of full American citizenship.

In recent years, and especially since the Great War, this simple faith has suffered a widespread disintegration. When the United States Government set forth its war aims, called upon Negro soldiers to stand by the colors and Negro civilians, men, women, and children, to devote their labor and earnings to the cause, and when the war shortage of labor permitted a quarter million Negroes to leave the former slave States for the better conditions of the North, the entire Negro people experienced a profound sense of spiritual release. For the first time since emancipation they found themselves comparatively free to sell their labor on the open market for a living wage, found themselves launched on a great world enterprise with a chance to vote in a real and decisive way, and, best of all, in the heat of the struggle they found themselves bound with other Americans in the spiritual fellowship of a common cause.

When they stood on the height of this exalted experience and looked down on their pre-war poverty, impotence, and spiritual isolation, they realized as never before the depth of the harm they had suffered, and there arose in them a mighty hope that in some way the war would work a change in their situation. For a time indeed it seemed that their hope would be realized. For when the former slave States saw their labor leaving for the North, they began to reflect upon the treatment they had been accustomed to give the Negro, and they decided that it was radically wrong. Newspapers and public orators everywhere expressed this change of sentiment, set forth the wrongs in detail, and urged immediate improvement. And immediate improvement came. Better educational facilities were provided here and there, words of appreciation for the worth and spirit of the Negro as a citizen began to be uttered, and public committees arose to inquire into his grievances and to lay out programs for setting these grievances right. The colored people in these States had never experienced such collective good-will, and many of them were so grateful and happy that they actually prayed for the prolongation of the war.

At the close of the war, however, the Negro's hopes were suddenly dashed to the ground. Southern newspapers began at once to tell the Negro soldiers that the war was over and the sooner they forgot it the better. "Pull off your uniform," they said, "find the place you had before the war, and stay in it." "Act like a Negro should act," said one newspaper, "work like a Negro should work, talk like a Negro should talk, study like a Negro should study. Dismiss all ideas of independency or of being lifted up to the plane of the white man. Understand the necessity of keeping a Negro's place." In connection with such admonitions there came the great collective attacks on Negro life and property in Washington, Chicago, Omaha, Elaine, and Tulsa. There came also the increasing boldness of lynchers who advertised their purposes in advance and had their photographs taken around the burning bodies of their victims. There came vain appeals by the colored people to the President of the United States and to the houses of Congress. And finally there came the reorganization and rapid growth of the Ku Klux Klan.

The swift succession and frank brutality of all this was more than the Negro people could bear. Their simple faith and hope broke down. Multitudes took weapons in their hands and fought back violence with bloody resistance. "If we must die," they said, "it is well that we die fighting." And the Negro American world, looking on their deed with no light of hope to see by, said: "It is self-defense; it is the law of nature, of man, and of God; and it is well."

From those terrible days until this day the Negro's faith in the righteous purpose of the Federal Government has sagged. Some have laid the blame on the parties in power. Some have laid it elsewhere. But all the colored people, in every section of the United States, believe that there is something wrong, and not accidentally wrong, at the very heart of the Government.

Some of our young men are giving up the Christian religion, thinking that their fathers were fools to have believed it so long. One group among us repudiates entirely the simple faith of former days. It would put no trust in God, no trust in democracy, and would entertain no hope for betterment under the present form of government. It believes that the United States Government is through and through controlled by selfish capitalists who have no fundamental good-will for Negroes or for any sort of laborers whatever. In their publications and on the platform the members of this group urge the colored man to seek his salvation by alliance with the revolutionary labor movement of America and the world.

Another and larger group among us believes in religion and believes in the principles of democracy, but not in the white man's religion and not in the white man's democracy. It believes that the creed of the former slave States is the tacit creed of the whole nation, and that the Negro may never expect to acquire economic, political, and spiritual liberty in America. This group has held congresses with representatives from the entire Negro world, to lay the foundations of a black empire, a black religion, and a black culture; it has organized the provisional Republic of Africa, set going a multitude of economic enterprises, instituted branches of its organization wherever Negroes are to be found, and binds them together with a newspaper ably edited in two languages.

Whatever one may think of these radical movements and their destiny, one thing is certain: they are home-grown fruits, with roots deep sprung in a world of black American suffering. Their power lies in the appeal which they make to the Negro to find a way out of his trouble by new and self-reliant paths. The larger masses of the colored people do not belong to these more radical movements. They retain their belief in the Christian God, they love their country, and hope to work out their salvation within its bounds. But they are completely disillusioned. They see themselves surrounded on every hand by a sentiment of antagonism which does not intend to be fair. They see themselves partly reduced to peonage, shut out from labor unions, forced to an inferior status before the courts, made subjects of public contempt, lynched and mobbed with impunity, and deprived of the ballot, their only means of social defense. They see this antagonistic sentiment consolidated in the places of power in the former slave States and growing by leaps and bounds in the North and West. They know that it is gradually reducing them to an economic, political, and social caste. And they are now no longer able to believe with Dr. Booker T. Washington, or with any other man, that their own efforts after intelligence, wealth, and self-respect can in any wise avail to deliver them from these conditions unless they have the protection of a just and beneficent public policy in keeping with American ideals. With one voice, therefore, from pulpit and from press, and from the humblest walks of life, they are sending up a cry of pain and petition such as is heard today among the citizens of no other civilized nation in the world. They are asking for the protection of life, for the security of property, for the liberation of their peons, for the freedom to sell their labor on the open market, for a human being's chance in the courts, for a better system of public education, and for the boon of the ballot. They ask, in short, for public equality under the protection of the Federal Government.

Their request is sustained by every sentiment of humanity and by every holy ideal for which this nation stands. The time has come when the elemental justice called for in this petition should be embodied in a public policy initiated by the Federal Government and continuously supervised by a commission of that Government representing the faith and will of the whole American people.

The Negro people of America have been with us here for three hundred years. They have cut our forests, tilled our fields, built our railroads, fought our battles, and in all of their trials until now they have manifested a simple faith, a grateful heart, a cheerful spirit, and an undivided loyalty to the nation that has been a thing of beauty to behold. Now they have come to the place where their faith can no longer feed on the bread of repression and violence. They ask for the bread of liberty, of public equality, and public responsibility. It must not be denied them.

We are now sufficiently far removed from the Civil War and its animosities to see that such elemental justice may be given to the Negro with entire good-will and helpfulness toward the former slave States. We have already had one long attempt to build a wealth and culture on the backs of slaves. We found that it was a costly experiment, paid for at last with the blood of our best sons. There are some among our citizens who would turn their backs on history and repeat that experiment, and to their terrible heresy they would convert our entire great community. By every sacred bond of love for them we must not yield, and we must no longer leave them alone with their experiment. The faith of our whole nation must be brought to their support until such time as it is clear to them that their former slaves can be made both fully free and yet their faithful friends.

Across the seas the darker peoples of the earth are rising from their long sleep and are searching this Western world for light. Our Christian missionaries are among them. They are asking these missionaries: Can the Christian religion bind this multi-colored world in bonds of brotherhood? We of all nations are best prepared to answer that question, and to be their moral inspiration and their friend. For we have the world's problem of race relationships here in crucible, and by strength of our American faith we have made some encouraging progress in its solution. If the fires of this faith are kept burning around that crucible, what comes out of it is able to place these United States in the spiritual leadership of all humanity. When the Negro cries with pain from his deep hurt and lays his petition for elemental justice before the nation, he is calling upon the American people to kindle anew about the crucible of race relationships the fires of American faith.[1]

OUR DEMOCRACY AND THE BALLOT[2]

By James Weldon Johnson[3]

Ladies and Gentlemen:

For some time since I have had growing apprehensions about any subject—especially the subject of a speech—that contained the word "democracy." The word "democracy" carries so many awe-inspiring implications. As the key-word of the subject of an address it may be the presage of an outpour of altitudinous and

[1] *Nation*, July 19, 1922.

[2] This address was delivered at a dinner to Congressman F. H. LaGuardia at the Hotel Pennsylvania, New York City, March 10, 1923.

[3] James Weldon Johnson was born in Jacksonville, Florida, in 1871. He was educated at Atlanta and Columbia Universities. After distinguishing himself somewhat in the field of letters, he served the United States Government as consul in Venezuela and Nicaragua. Returning to this country, he further distinguished himself in letters as attested by such works as *Fifty Years*, and other poems, and such sonnets as *Mother Night*.

During recent years, Mr. Johnson has been engaged in the movement for the betterment of the Negro through the National Association for the Advancement of Colored People. He has served this organization as Field Secretary and as Secretary for a number of years. In this position, he has become widely known as an honest and fearless leader qualified to present intelligently the case of the Negro at court. His addresses in this field have attracted nation-wide attention and are considered some of the most eloquent utterances of the day.

platitudinous expressions regarding "the most free and glorious government of the most free and glorious people that the world has ever seen." On the other hand, it may hold up its sleeve, if you will permit such a figure, a display of abstruse and recondite theorizations or hypotheses of democracy as a system of government. In choosing between either of these evils it is difficult to decide which is the lesser.

Indeed, the wording of my subject gave me somewhat more concern than the speech. I am not sure that it contains the slightest idea of what I shall attempt to say; but if the wording of my subject is loose it only places upon me greater reason for being more specific and definite in what I shall say. This I shall endeavor to do; at the same time, however, without being so confident or so cocksure as an old preacher I used to listen to on sundry Sundays when I taught school one summer down in the backwoods of Georgia, sometimes to my edification and often to my amazement.

On one particular Sunday, after taking a rather cryptic text, he took off his spectacles and laid them on the pulpit, closed the Bible with a bang, and said, "Brothers and sisters, this morning I intend to explain the inexplainable, to find out the indefinable, to ponder over the imponderable, and to unscrew the inscrutable."

Our Democracy and the Ballot

It is one of the commonplaces of American thought that we have a democracy based upon the free will of the governed. The popular idea of the strength of this democracy is that it is founded upon the fact that every American citizen, through the ballot, is a ruler in his own right; that every citizen of age and outside of jail or the insane asylum has the undisputed right to determine through his vote by what laws he shall be governed and by whom these laws shall be enforced.

I could be cynical or flippant and illustrate in how many ways this popular idea is a fiction, but it is not my purpose to deal in *cleverisms.* I wish to bring to your attention seriously a situation, a condition, which not only runs counter to the popular conception of democracy in America but which runs counter to the fundamental law upon which that democracy rests and which, in addition, is a negation of our principles of government and a menace to our institutions.

Without any waste of words, I come directly to a condition which exists in that section of our country which we call "the South," where millions of American citizens are denied both the right to vote and the privilege of qualifying themselves to vote. I refer to the wholesale disfranchisement of Negro citizens. There is no need at this time of going minutely into the methods employed to bring about this condition or into the reasons given as justification for those methods. Neither am I called upon to give proof of my general statement that millions of Negro citizens in the South are disfranchised. It is no secret. There are the published records of state constitutional conventions in which the whole subject is set forth with brutal frankness. The purpose of these state constitutional conventions is stated over and over again, that purpose being to exclude from the right of franchise the Negro, however literate, and to include the white man, however illiterate.

The press of the South, public men in public utterances, and representatives of those states in Congress, have not only admitted these facts but have boasted of them. And so we have it as an admitted and undisputed fact that there are upwards of four million Negroes in the South who are denied the right to vote but who in any of the great northern, mid-western or western states would be allowed to vote or would at least have the privilege of qualifying themselves to vote.

Now, nothing is further from me than the intention to discuss this question either from an anti-South point of view or from a pro-Negro point of view. It is my intention to put it before you purely as an American question, a question in which is involved the political life of the whole country.

Let us first consider this situation as a violation, not merely a violation but a defiance, of the Constitution of the United States. The Fourteenth and Fifteenth Amendments to the Constitution taken together express so plainly that a grammar school boy can understand it that the Negro is created a citizen of the United States and that as such he is entitled to all the rights of every other citizen and that those rights, specifically among them the right to vote, shall not be denied or abridged by the United States or by any state. This is the expressed meaning of these amendments in spite of all the sophistry and fallacious pretense which have been invoked by the courts to overcome it.

There are some, perhaps even here, who feel that it is no more serious a matter to violate or defy one amendment to the constitution than another. Such persons will have in mind the Eighteenth Amendment. This is true in a strictly legal sense, but any sort of analysis will show that violation of the two Civil War Amendments strikes deeper. As important as the Eighteenth Amendment may be, it is not fundamental; it contains no grant of rights to the citizen nor any requirement of service from him. It is rather a sort of welfare regulation for his personal conduct and for his general moral uplift.

But the two Civil War Amendments are grants of citizenship rights and a guarantee of protection in those rights, and therefore their observation is fundamental and vital not only to the citizen but to the integrity of the government.

We may next consider it as a question of political franchise equality between the states. We need not here go into a list of figures. A few examples will strike the difference:

In the elections of 1920 it took 82,492 votes in Mississippi to elect two senators and eight representatives. In Kansas it took 570,220 votes to elect exactly the same representation. Another illustration from the statistics of the same election shows that one vote in Louisiana has fifteen times the political power of one vote in Kansas.

In the Congressional elections of 1918 the total vote for the ten representatives from the State of Alabama was 62,345, while the total vote for ten representatives in Congress from Minnesota was 299,127, and the total vote in Iowa, which has ten representatives, was 316,377.

In the Presidential election of 1916 the states of Alabama, Arkansas, Georgia, Louisiana, Mississippi, North Carolina, South Carolina, Tennessee, Texas and Virginia cast a total vote for the Presidential candidates of 1,870,209. In Congress these states have a total of 104 representatives and 126 votes in the electoral college. The State of New York alone cast a total vote for Presidential candidates of 1,706,354, a vote within 170,000 of all the votes cast by the above states, and yet New York has only 43 representatives and 45 votes in the electoral college.

What becomes of our democracy when such conditions of inequality as these can be brought about through chicanery, the open violation of the law and defiance of the Constitution?

But the question naturally arises, What if there is violation of certain clauses of the Constitution; what if there is an inequality of political power among the states? All this may be justified by necessity.

In fact, the justification is constantly offered. The justification goes back and makes a long story. It is grounded in memories of the Reconstruction period. Although most of those who were actors during that period have long since died, and although there is a new South and a new Negro, the argument is still made that the Negro is ignorant, the Negro is illiterate, the Negro is venal, the Negro is inferior; and, therefore, for the preservation of civilized government in the South, he must be debarred from the polls. This argument does not take into account the fact that the restrictions are not against ignorance, illiteracy and venality, because by the very practices by which intelligent, decent Negroes are debarred, ignorant and illiterate white men are included.

Is this pronounced desire on the part of the South for an enlightened franchise sincere, and what has been the result of these practices during the past forty years? What has been the effect socially, intellectually and politically, on the South? In all three of these vital phases of life the South is, of all sections of the country, at the bottom. Socially, it is that section of the country where public opinion allows it to remain the only spot in the civilized world—no, more than that, we may count in the blackest spots of Africa and the most unfrequented islands of the sea—it is a section where public opinion allows it to remain the only spot on the earth where a human being may be publicly burned at the stake.

And what about its intellectual and political life? As to intellectual life I can do nothing better than quote from Mr. H. L. Mencken, himself a Southerner. In speaking of the intellectual life of the South, Mr. Mencken says:

"It is, indeed, amazing to contemplate so vast a vacuity. One thinks of the interstellar spaces, of the colossal reaches of the now mythical ether. One could throw into the South France, Germany and Italy, and still have room for the British Isles. And yet, for all its size and all its wealth and all the 'progress' it babbles of, it is almost as sterile, artistically, intellectually, culturally, as the Sahara Desert. . . . If the whole of the late Confederacy were to be engulfed by a tidal wave tomorrow, the effect on the civilized minority of men in the world would be but little greater than that of a flood on the Yang-tse-kiang. It would be impossible in all history to match so complete a drying-up of a civilization. In all that section there is not a single poet, not a serious historian, not a creditable composer, not a critic good or bad, not a dramatist dead or alive."

In a word, it may be said that this whole section where, at the cost of the defiance of the Constitution, the perversion of law, the stultification of men's consciousness, injustice and violence upon a weaker group, the "purity" of the ballot has been preserved and the right to vote restricted to only lineal survivors of Lothrop Stoddard's mystical Nordic supermen—that intellectually it is dead and politically it is rotten.

If this experiment in super-democracy had resulted in one one-hundredth of what was promised, there might be justification for it, but the result has been to make the South a section not only in which Negroes are denied the right to vote, but one in which white men dare not express their honest political opinions. Talk about political corruption through the buying of votes, here is political corruption which makes a white man fear to express a divergent political opinion. The actual and total result of this practice has been not only the disfranchisement of the Negro but the disfranchisement of the white man. The figures which I quoted a few moments ago prove that not only Negroes are denied the right to vote but that white men fail to exercise it; and the latter condition is directly dependent upon the former.

The whole condition is intolerable and should be abolished. It has failed to justify itself even upon the grounds which it is claimed made it necessary. Its results and its tendencies make it more dangerous and more damaging than anything which might result from an ignorant and illiterate electorate. How this iniquity might be abolished is, however, another story.

I said that I did not intend to present this subject either as anti-South or pro-Negro, and I repeat that I have not wished to speak with anything that approached bitterness toward the South.

Indeed, I consider the condition of the South unfortunate, more than unfortunate. The South is in a state of superstition which makes it see ghosts and bogymen, ghosts which are the creation of its own mental processes.

With a free vote in the South the specter of Negro domination would vanish into thin air. There would naturally follow a breaking up of the South into two parties. There would be political light, political discussion, the right to differences of opinion, and the Negro vote would naturally divide itself. No other procedure would be probable. The idea of a solid party, a minority party at that, is inconceivable.

But perhaps the South will not see the light. Then, I believe, in the interest of the whole country, steps should be taken to compel compliance with the Constitution, and that should be done through the enforcement of the Fourteenth Amendment, which calls for a reduction in representation in proportion to the number of citizens in any state denied the right to vote.

And now I cannot sit down after all without saying one word for the group of which I am a member.

The Negro in the matter of the ballot demands only that he should be given the right as an American citizen to vote under the identical qualifications required of other citizens. He cares not how high those qualifications are made—whether they include the ability to read and write, or the possession of five hundred dollars, or a knowledge of the Einstein Theory—just so long as these qualifications are impartially demanded of white men and black men.

In this controversy over which have been waged battles of words and battles of blood, where does the Negro himself stand?

The Negro in the matter of the ballot demands only that he be given his right as an American citizen. He is justified in making this demand because of his undoubted Americanism, an Americanism which began when he first set foot on the shores of this country more than three hundred years ago, antedating even the Pilgrim Fathers; an Americanism which has woven him into the woof and warp of the country and which has impelled him to play his part in every war in which the country has been engaged, from the Revolution down to the late World War.

Through his whole history in this country he has worked with patience, and in spite of discouragement he has never turned his back on the light. Whatever may be his shortcomings, however slow may have been his progress, however disappointing may have been his achievements, he has never consciously sought the backward path. He has always kept his face to the light and continued to struggle forward and upward in spite of obstacles, making his humble contributions to the common prosperity and glory of our land. And it is his land. With conscious pride the Negro can say:

> "This land is ours by right of birth,
> This land is ours by right of toil;
> We helped to turn its virgin earth,
> Our sweat is in its fruitful soil.
>
> "Where once the tangled forest stood,—
> Where flourished once rank weed and thorn,—
> Behold the path-traced, peaceful wood,
> The cotton white, the yellow corn.
>
> "To gain these fruits that have been earned,
> To hold these fields that have been won,
> Our arms have strained, our backs have burned
> Bent bare beneath a ruthless sun.
>
> "That banner which is now the type
> Of victory on field and flood—
> Remember, its first crimson stripe
> Was dyed by Attucks' willing blood.
>
> "And never yet has come the cry—
> When that fair flag has been assailed—
> For men to do, for men to die,
> That we have faltered or have failed."

The Negro stands as the supreme test of the civilization, the Christianity and the common decency of the American people. It is upon the answer demanded of America today by the Negro that there depends the fulfillment or the failure of democracy in America. I believe that that answer will be the right and just answer. I believe that the spirit in which American democracy was founded, though often turned aside and often thwarted, can never be defeated or destroyed but that ultimately it will triumph.

If American democracy cannot stand the test of giving to any citizen who measures up to the qualifications required of others the full rights and privileges of American citizenship, then we had just as well abandon that democracy in name as in deed. If the Constitution of the United States cannot extend the arm of protection around the weakest and humblest of American citizens as around the strongest and proudest, then it is not worth the paper it is written on.

THE SHAME OF AMERICA, OR THE NEGRO'S CASE AGAINST THE REPUBLIC[1]

By Archibald Grimké[2]

The author of the Declaration of Independence said once that he trembled for his country when he remembered that God was just. And he did well to do so. But while he was about it he might have quaked a little for himself. For he was certainly guilty of the same crime against humanity, which had aroused in his philosophic and patriotic mind such lively sensations of anxiety and alarm in respect to the Nation. Said Jefferson on paper: "We hold these truths to be self-evident, that all men are created equal; that they are endowed by their Creator with certain unalienable rights; that among these are life, liberty and the pursuit of happiness," while on his plantation he was holding some men as slaves, and continued to hold them as such for fifty years thereafter, and died at the end of a long and brilliant life, a Virginia slaveholder.

[1] Delivered on various occasions by Mr. Grimké.

[2] Archibald H. Grimké was born in South Carolina in 1849. Like his brother, he found his way north after the Civil War when he was seeking an education. At Lincoln University, where he received his first systematic training, he made an honorable record. He then studied law at Harvard University. He entered upon the practice of his profession and also participated in politics. Differing from most Negro leaders, however, he voted independently, endeavoring to support the man rather than the party. He served for some years as Consul in Haiti. The recent years of his life he has spent in Washington, largely advocating the rights of the Negro as championed by the National Association for the Advancement of Colored People. As the President of the local branch of this organization, he has rendered valuable service in snatching many a Negro from the hand of the oppressor, and in forcefully presenting the case of the race to a prejudiced world.

And yet Thomas Jefferson was sincere, or fancied that he was, when he uttered those sublime sentiments about the rights of man, and when he declared that he trembled for his country when he remembered that God was just. This inconsistency between the man's magnificence in profession and his smallness in practice, between the grandeur of what he promised and the meanness of what he performed, taken in conjunction with his cool unconsciousness of the discrepancy, is essentially and emphatically an American trait, a national idiosyncrasy. For it has appeared during the last one hundred and forty-four years with singular boldness and continuity in the social, political, and religious life of the American people and their leaders. I do not recall in all history such another example of a nation appearing so well in its written words regarding human rights, and so badly when it comes to translating those fine words into corresponding action, as this Republic has uniformly exhibited from its foundation, wherever the Negro has been concerned.

Look at its conduct in the War of the Revolution, which it began with the high sounding sentiments of the Declaration of Independence. The American colonists rose in arms because they were taxed by England without their consent, a species of tyranny which bore no sort of comparison to the slavery which they themselves were imposing on the Negro. But with such inconsistency of conduct the men of the Revolution bothered not their heads for a simple, and to them, a sufficient reason. They were white and the Negro was black and was their property. Since they were fighting for a political principle in order the better to protect their pockets, they were not disposed to give up their property rights in anything, not even in human beings. They were contending for the sacred right of loosening their own purse strings, not for the sacred privilege of loosening the bonds of their slaves. Not at all. Millions they were willing to spend in defense of the former, but not a cent to effect the latter, their loud talk in the Declaration of Independence to the contrary, notwithstanding.

Their subsequent conduct in respect to the Negro was of a piece with this characteristic beginning. First they accepted the services of the blacks, both bond and free, as soldiers, and then they debated the expediency and justice of their action, not from the point of view of the slaves but from that of the masters, and later decided upon a policy of exclusion of the slaves from the Continental army. With the adoption of such a policy the chattel rights of masters in those poor men would be better conserved. Hence the policy of exclusion. But when the British evinced a disposition to enlist the slaves as soldiers, a change passed quickly over the leaders of the Revolution, with Washington at their head. The danger to the master of a policy of inclusion was overriden readily enough in the greater danger to the cause of one of exclusion. Without a thought for the slave, he was put on the military chessboard, withdrawn, then put back in response to purely selfish considerations and needs.

Thus it happened that black men fought in that war shoulder to shoulder with white men for American Independence. In every colony from Massachusetts to Georgia, they were found faithful among the faithless, and brave as the bravest during those long and bitter years, fighting and dying with incomparable devotion and valor, by the side of Warren at Bunker Hill, and of Pulaski at Savannah.

The voluntary surrender of life for country has been justly held by all ages to be an act of supreme virtue. It is in the power of any man to give less; it is in the power of none, however exalted in station, to give more. For to lay down one's life at the call of Duty is to lay down one's all. And this all of the general weighs no more than the all of a common soldier. Weighed in the scales of truth this supreme gift of the beggar on foot balances exactly that of the prince on horseback. When prince or beggar, master or slave, has given his life to a cause, he has given his utmost. Beyond that absolute measure of devotion neither can add one jot or tittle to the value of his gift. Thank God there is no color line in acts of heroism and self-sacrifice, save the royal one of their blood-tinted humanity. Such was the priceless contribution which the poor, oppressed Negro made to American Independence.

What was his guerdon? In the hour of their triumph did the patriot fathers call to mind such supreme service to reward it? In the freedom which they had won by the aid of their enslaved countrymen, did they bethink them of lightening the yoke of those miserable men? History answers, no! Truth answers, no! The descendants of those black heroes answer, no! What then? What did such bright, such blazing beacons of liberty, the Washingtons,

Hamiltons, Madisons and Franklins, the Rufus Kings, Roger Shermans, and Robert Morrises? They founded the Republic on slavery, rested one end of its stately arch on the prostrate neck of the Negro. They constructed a national Constitution which safeguarded the property of man in man, introducing into it for that purpose its three-fifths slave representation provision, its fugitive slave clause, and an agreement by which the African slave trade was legalized for nineteen years after the adoption of that instrument. That was the reward which the founders of the Republic meted out with one accord to a race which had shed freely its blood to make that Republic a reality among the nations of the earth. Instead of loosening and lifting his heavy yoke of oppression, they strengthened and tightened it afresh on the loyal and long suffering neck of the Negro. Notwithstanding this shameful fact, the founders of the Republic were either so coolly unconscious of its moral enormity or else so indifferent to the amazing contradiction between what they said and what they did, as to write over the gateway of the new Constitution this sonorous preamble: "We, the people of the United States, in order to form a more perfect union, establish justice, insure domestic tranquillity, provide for the common defense, promote the general welfare, and secure the blessings of liberty to ourselves and our posterity, do ordain and establish this Constitution for the United States of America."

"We the people!" From the standpoint of the Negro, what grim irony; "establish justice"! What exquisitely cruel mockery; "to insure domestic tranquillity"! What height and breadth and depth of political duplicity; "to provide for the common defense"! What cunning paltering with words in a double sense; "to promote the general welfare"! What studied ignoring of an ugly fact; "and secure the blessings of liberty to ourselves and posterity"! What masterly abuse of noble words to mask an equivocal meaning, to throw over a great national transgression an air of virtue, so subtle and illusive as to deceive the framers themselves into believing in their own sincerity. You may ransack the libraries of the world, and turn over all the documents of recorded time to match that Preamble of the Constitution as a piece of consummate political dissimulation and mental reservation, as an example of how men juggle deliberately and successfully with their moral sense, how they raise above themselves huge fabrics of false-

hood, and go willingly to live and die in a make-believe world of lies. The muse of history, dipping her iron pen in the generous blood of the Negro, has written large across the page of that Preamble, and the face of the Declaration of Independence, the words, "sham, hypocrisy."

It is the rage now to sing the praises of the fathers of the Republic as a generation of singularly liberty-loving men. They were so, indeed, if judged by their fine words alone. But they were, in reality, by no means superior to their sons in this respect, if we judge them by their acts, which somehow speak louder, more convincingly to us than their words, albeit those words proceed out of the Declaration of Independence, and the Preamble of the Constitution. If the children's teeth today are set on edge on the Negro question, it is because the fathers ate the sour grapes of race-wrong, ate those miserable grapes during their whole life, and, dying, transmitted their taste for oppression, as a bitter inheritance to their children, and children's children, for God knows how many black years to come.

Take the case of Washington as an example. He was rated an abolitionist by his contemporaries. And so he was if mere words could have made him one. On paper he was one person, but on his plantation quite another. And as far as I know his history, he never made any effectual attempt to bring this second self of his into actual accord with the first. In theory he favored emancipation, while in practice he was one of the biggest, if not the biggest slaveholder in the country, who enriched himself and his family out of the unpaid toil of more than two hundred slaves. The father of his country did not manumit them during his lifetime, or of that of his wife. Not until his death, not until the death of his widow, did he, as a matter of fact, release his hold upon the labor of those people, did they escape from his dead hands. As first President, moreover, he signed the first fugitive slave law and was not ashamed to avail himself of its hateful provisions for the reclamation of one of his runaway slave-women. And yet Washington, and Jefferson also, are the two bright, particular stars of our American democracy. They had very fine words for liberty, no two men ever had finer, but when it came to translating them into action, into churning them into butter for the poor Negro's parsnips, no atom of butter did they yield, or will ever yield, churn them ever so long. *Ex pede Herculem.*

Naturally enough under the circumstances of its origin and antecedents, American democracy has never cared a fig in practice for the fine sentiments of its Declaration of Independence, or for the high sounding ones of the Preamble to its Constitution, wherever and whenever the Negro has been concerned. It used him to fight the battles for its independent political existence, and rewarded his blood and bravery with fresh stripes and heavier chains.

History repeats itself. In America, on the Negro question, it has been a series of shameful repetitions of itself. The Negro's history in the first war with England was repeated exactly in the second. In this conflict no more loyal and daring hearts bled and broke for the country than were those of its colored soldiers and sailors. On land and water in that war the Negro died as he fought, among the most faithful and heroic defenders of the American cause. But to praise him is to condemn the country, which in this instance I will leave to no less an American than General Jackson. Out of his mouth shall this condemnation be spoken. Said Jackson three weeks before the battle of New Orleans to the black soldiers who had rallied at his summons to repel a formidable invasion of our national domain by a powerful foreign enemy:

"From the shores of Mobile I called you to arms. I invited you to share in the perils and divide the glory of your white countrymen. I expected much from you, for I was not uninformed of those qualities which must render you so formidable to an invading foe. I knew you could endure hunger and thirst, and all the hardships of war. I knew that you loved the land of your nativity, and that, like ourselves, you had to defend all that is most dear to men. But you surpass my hopes. I have found in you, united to those qualities, that noble enthusiasm that impels to great deeds.

"Soldiers: The President of the United States shall be informed of your conduct on the present occasion, and the voice of the representatives of the American nation shall applaud your valor, as your General now praises your ardor. The enemy is near. His sails cover the lakes, but the brave are united. and if he finds us contending among ourselves, it will be for the prize of valor, and fame its noblest reward.''

Jackson's black troops proved themselves in the actions of Mobile Bay and New Orleans entitled to every mouthful of the ringing applause which Old Hickory gave them without stint. They got fair enough words as long as the enemy was in sight and his navy covered the waters of the country. But as soon as the peril had passed those fair words were succeeded by the foulest ingratitude. On every hand Colorphobia reared its cursed head, and struck its cruel fangs into those brave breasts which had just received the swords and the bullets of a foreign foe. They were legislated against everywhere, proscribed by atrocious laws everywhere. They had given the nation in its dire need, blood and life, and measureless love, and had received as reward black codes, an unrelenting race prejudice, and bondage bitterer than death.

Strange irony of fate which reserved to Andrew Jackson, whose mouth overflowed with praise in 1814 for his black soldiers and with fair promises of what he intended to do for them—strange irony of fate, I say, which reserved to that man, as President in 1836, the elevation of Roger B. Taney to the Chief-Justiceship of the United States, of Taney, the infamous slave Judge who wrote the Dred Scott Decision, which argued that black men had no rights in America which white men were bound to respect. The downright brutality of that opinion was extremely shocking to some sensitive Americans, but it was no more so than was the downright brutality of the facts, which it reflected with brutal accuracy. The fell apparition of American inhumanity, which those words conjured up from the depths of an abominable past and from that of a no less abominable present, was indeed black, but it was no blacker than the truth. The dark soul of the nation was embodied in them, all of its savage selfishness, greed and iniquity. There they glared, large and lifelike, a devil's face among the nations, seamed and intersected with the sinister lines of a century of cruelty and race hatred and oppression. Of course the fair idealism of the Declaration of Independence was wanting in the photographic naturalism of the picture, and so was the fictive beauty of the Preamble of the Constitution, because they were wanting in the terrible original, in the malignant, merciless, and murderous spirit of a democracy which the dark words of the dark judge had limned to the life.

God has made iniquitous power ultimately self-destructive. Into every combination of evil He puts the seed of division and strife. Without this effective check wickedness would conquer and permanently possess the earth. The law of the brute would rule it forever. Where today are the empires of might and wrong, which men reared in their pride and strength, on the Nile, the Tigris, and the Euphrates, on the Tiber, the Bosporus, and the Mediterranean? They flourished for a season and seasons, and spread themselves like green bay trees. But behold they are gone, perished, burnt up by the fires of evil passions, by the evil power which consumed them to ashes. Centuries have flown over their graves, and the places once cursed by their violence, and crushed by their oppressions, shall know them and their vulture laws and trampling armies no more forever.

So it happened in the case of the American people when in order "to form a more perfect union," they ordained and established their Constitution. Within the "more perfect union" was enfolded a fruitful germ of division and discord. No bigger at first than the smallest of seeds, the germ grew apace with the growth of the new nation, drawing abundant nourishment from the dark underworld of the slave. Slender sapling in 1815, it was a fast growing tree in 1820, bearing even then its bitter apples of Gomorrah. Where its bitter fruit fell, there fell also on the spirit of the people mutual distrust, and incipient sectional hate. And no wonder, for when the North clasped hands with her Southern sister in "a more perfect union," she did so the better to conserve a set of interests and institutions peculiar to herself and inherently hostile to those of the South, and vice versa with respect to the action of the latter in the premises. The "more perfect union" had, thank God, effected a conjunction, under a single political system, of two sets of mutually invasive and destructive social ideas and industrial forces. Differences presently sprang up between the partisans of each set, and discontent, and wide-spreading fear and contention. National legislation which oxidized and enriched the blood of the North, not only impoverished but actually poisoned that of the South. And so it came to pass that the compromise Constitution which was designed "to form a more perfect union," failed of its purpose, because with human slavery at the core of it, it brought face to face two warring social systems, whose unappeasable strife it had not the secret or the strength to subdue.

As in Egypt more than three thousand years ago, the Eternal spoke to the master-race at divers times and with divers signs, saying, "let my people go," so he spoke to the master-race in this land through divers omens and events, saying likewise, "let my people go." Those with ears to hear might have heard that divine voice in the Hartford Convention and the causes which led to its call; in the successive sectional conflicts over Missouri, the Tariff, and Texas; in the storm winds of the Mexican war, as in the wild uproar which followed the annexation of new national territory at its close; in the political rage and explosions of 1850 and 1854, and in the fierce patter of blood-drops over Kansas. They might have surely heard that commanding voice from the anointed lips of holy men and prophets, from the mouths of Garrison and Sumner, and Phillips, and Douglass, from the sacred gallows where John Brown heard and repeated it while his soul went marching on from city to city, and State to State, over mountain and river, across a continent, and from the Lakes to the Gulf with rising accent saying, "let my people go." Alas! the nation hearkened not to the voice of justice, but continued to harden its heart, until thunder-like that voice broke in the deep boom of Civil War.

When masters fall out a way oftentimes opens for the escape of their slaves. In the death grapple of the sections for political supremacy, the dead weight of two centuries of oppression lifted from the neck of the Negro. The people and their leaders of both sections despised him to such a degree that neither would in the beginning enlist his aid against the other. "We the people" of the glorious union of 1789 had quarrelled like two bloody scoundrels over their ill-gotten gains, and had come to murderous blows. Yet in spite of their deadly hatred of each other, they said in their mad race-pride and prejudice, the North to the South, and the South to the North, "go to, shall we not settle our differences without the aid of him who is our slave? Shall not we white men fight our duel to a finish; shall either of us appeal for help to that miserable being who by our laws, written and unwritten, has never possessed any rights among us which we have ever respected?" They chose to forget how in two wars this faithful man had for their sakes, received into his sad but brave breast the swords and the bullets of a foreign enemy, and all unmindful of self had helped them to achieve and maintain their liberty and independence. And thus choosing to forget his past services and to remember only their bitter race-prejudice against him, they fought on with deadly malice and violence, the one side against the other, rending their dear Union with fraternal strife, and drenching it with fraternal blood.

Perceiving the unlimited capacity of mankind for all sorts of folly, no wonder Puck exclaimed, "What fools these mortals be!" Yes, what fools, but of all the fools who have crawled to dusty death the most stupendous and bedeviled lot are those who strut their fools' feet and toss their fools' heads across their little stage of life, thanking their fools' selves that God made them different from other men—superior to other men—to rule over other men. Puffed up with their stupid race-pride and prejudice, inflated to the bursting point with their high and mighty notions, and *noli me tangere* airs, the North and the South went on for nearly two years goring and tearing each other like two infuriated bulls of nearly equal strength, before either would call on the Negro for assistance. Not until bleeding at every pore, sickened at the loss of its sordid dollar, and in despair at the threatened destruction of that to which it ascribed, as to the Almighty, all of its sectional progress, prosperity and power, viz.: the dear Union, did the North turn for help to the Negro, whom it had despised and wronged, and whom it even then, in its heart of hearts, despised and intended, upon occasion, to wrong anew.

Think of the incredible folly and selfishness of a people fighting for existence and yet begrudging freedom to an enslaved race, whom it had called upon to help defend that existence; doling out to its faithful black allies, with miserly meanness, its blood-money and its boasted democratic equality and fair play; denying to its colored soldiers equal pay and promotion with its white ones, albeit many of those white ones were mercenary aliens from Europe. Nevertheless, of such bottomless depths of folly and meanness was the National Government certainly guilty. The Fifty-fourth and the Fifty-fifth Massachusetts regiments enlisted to fight the battles of the country, with the understanding that there would be no discrimination against them on account of their color. Yet the government violated its understood pledge, and proceeded to pay, or tried to pay those men ten dollars a month where it was paying other men, because they were white, thirteen dollars a month for the same service. All honor to Massachusetts for objecting to this shameful act, and for offering to make up to her colored regiments the three dollars out of which the National government was endeavoring to cheat them. Three times three cheers for the brave and true men who had the sagacity, and the courage, and the self-respect, to resist the injustice of the government, and to refuse firmly to compromise by a cent their right to equality of pay in the army.

Take another instance of the meanness of the government's conduct toward its colored defenders. In January of 1864, Henry Wilson embodied, in a bill to promote enlistments, a clause which provided that when "any man or boy of African descent, in service or labor in any State under its laws, should be mustered into the military or naval service of the United States, he and his mother, wife and children, shall be forever free." Now will you believe that this just and moderate measure took thirteen long months before its friends could get Congress to enact it into law? "Future generations," exclaimed Charles Sumner in closing his remarks on the subject, "future generations will read with amazement, that a great people when national life was assailed, hesitated to exercise a power so simple and beneficient; and this amazement will know no bounds, as they learn that Congress higgled for months on a question, whether the wives and children of our colored soldiers should be admitted to freedom."

Need I repeat in this presence the old, grand story, how in numbers nearly two hundred thousand strong our colored boys in blue, left their blood and their bones in every State from Virginia to Louisiana? How, like heroes, they fought and died for the Union at Port Hudson, and Fort Wagner, and Petersburg, and Honey Hill, and Olustee, and Milliken's Bend? How in winter and summer, in cold and heat, in valley and on hilltop, on horse and on foot, over rivers and swamps, through woods and brakes, they rushed to meet the foe? How leaving behind them fields strown thick with their dead and wounded, they mounted the blazing sides of grim fortresses, climbing on great deeds and self-sacrifices through storms of shot and shell, to death and a place among the stars?

No, no, it is not required of me on this occasion to read afresh that glorious record. Sufficient then this: The Northern army, reinforced by the strength which it drew from that of the Negro, broke in time the back of the Rebellion, and saved the Union, so that in 1865 the flag of the nation floated again over an undivided country, and the Republic, strong and great beneath that flag, launched anew to meet the years, and to reach her fair ideals of liberty and equality which were flashing like beacon lights upon her way.

Amid widespread rejoicing on the return of peace and the restoration of the Union, the Negro rejoiced among the gladdest, for his slave fetters were broken, he was no longer a chattel. He imagined in his simple heart, in his ignorance and poverty, that he had not only won freedom, but the lasting affection and gratitude of the powerful people for whom he had entered hell to quench for them its raging fires with his blood. Yes, although black and despised, he, the slave, the hated one, had risen above his centuries of wrongs, above their bitter memories and bitterer sufferings to the love of enemies, to the forgiveness of those who had despitefully used him, ay, to those moral heights where heroes are throned and martyrs crowned. Surely, surely, he, who had been so unmindful of self in the service of country, would not be left by that country at the mercy of those who hated him then with the most terrible hatred for that very cause. He who had been mighty to save others would surely, now in his need, be saved by those whom he had saved. "Oh! Justice, thou has fled to brutish beasts, and men have lost their gratitude."

I would gladly seal forever the dark chapter of our history, which followed the close of the war. Gladly would I forget that record of national shame and selfishness. But as it is better to turn on light than to shut it off, I will, with your forbearance, turn it on for our illumination and guidance, in the lowering present.

The chapter opened with an introductoin of characteristic indifference on the part of the country in respect to the fate of the Negro. With his shackles lying close beside him, he was left in the hands of his old master who, seizing the opportunity, proceeded straightway to refit them on the disenthralled limbs of the former slave. State after State did so with such promptitude and to such effect that within a few months a formidable system of Negro-serfdom had actually been constructed, and cunningly substituted in place of the system of Negro slavery, which the war had destroyed. An African serf-power, Phoenix-like, was rising out of the ashes of the old slave power into national politics. At sight of this truly appalling apparition, the apparition of a returning slave power in thin disguise, all the old sectional fear and hatred which had existed against it in the free States before the Rebellion, awoke suddenly and hotly in the breast of the North. Thinking mainly, if not wholly of its own safety in the emergency which confronted it, and how best to avert the fresh perils which impended in consequence over its ascendency, the North prepared to make, and did in fact make, for the time being, short shrift of this boldly retroactive scheme of the South to recover within the Union all that it had lost by its defeated attempt to land itself outside of the Union.

Having tested to its entire satisfaction the Negro's value as a soldier in its war for the preservation of the Union, the North determined at this juncture to enlist his aid as a citizen in its further conflicts with the South, for the preservation of its sectional domination in the newly restored Union. To this end the Fourteenth and the Fifteenth Amendments to the Constitution were, in the progress of events, incorporated into that instrument. By these two great acts, the North had secured itself against the danger of an immediate return of the South to anything like political equality with it in the Republic. Between its supremacy and the attacks of its old rival, it had erected a solid wall of Negro votes. But immensely important as was the ballot to its black contingent, it was not enough to meet all of his tremendous needs. Nevertheless, as the North was considering mainly its own and not the Negro's necessities at this crisis, and as the elective franchise in his hands was deemed by it adequate to satisfy its own pressing needs, it gave the peculiar wants of the Negro beyond that of the ballot but scant attention.

Homeless, landless, illiterate, just emerging from the blackness of two centuries of slavery, this simple and faithful folk had surely other sacred claims on the North and the National Government than this right to the ballot. They had in truth a strong claim to unselfish friendship and statesmanship, to unfaltering care and guardianship, during the whole of their transition from slavery to citizenship. They needed the organized hands, the wise heads, the warm hearts, the piled-up wealth, the sleepless eyes, the faith, hope, and charity of a Christian people and a Christian government to teach them to walk and to save them from industrial exploitation by their old masters, as well as to vote. Did they receive from the Republic what the Republic owed them by every consideration of justice, gratitude and humanity, as of enlightened self-interest? Alas? not a tithe of this immense debt has the Republic ever undertaken to pay to those who should have been, under all circumstances, its sacredly preferred creditors. On the contrary they were left to themselves by the government in the outer darkness of that social state which had been their sad lot for more than two centuries. They were left in that darkest night of moral and civil anarchy to fight not alone their own terrible battle with poverty, ignorance, and untutored appetites and passions, but also the unequal, the cruel battle for the preservation of Northern political domination in the Union. For ten awful years they fought that battle for the North, for the Republican party, in the face of persecutions and oppressions, terrors and atrocities, at the glare of which the country and the civilized world shrank aghast.

Aghast shrank the North, but not for the poor Negro, faithful unto death to it. For itself rather it shrank from the threatening shadows which such a carnival of horrors was casting athwart its vast and spreading network of trade and production. The clamor of all its million-wheeled industry and prosperity was for peace. "Let us have peace," said Grant, and "let us have peace" blew forthwith and in deafening unison, all the big and little whistles of all the big and little factories and locomotives, and steamships from Maine to California. Every pen of merchant and editor scratched paper to the same mad tune. The pulpit and the platform of the land cooed their Cuckoo-song in honor of those piping times of peace. The loud noise of chinking coin pouring into vaults like coal into bins, drowned the agonized cry of the forgotten and long-suffering Negro. Deserting him in 1876, the North, stretching across the bloody chasm its two greedy, commercial hands, grasped the ensanguined ones of the South, and repeated, "let us have peace." Little did the Northern people and the government reck then or now that at the bottom of that bloody chasm lay their faithful black friends. Little did they care that the blood on those Southern hands had been wrung drop by drop from the loyal heart of the Negro. But enough.

Years of struggle and oppression follow and we come to another chapter of American history; namely, the Spanish-American War. In the Spanish-American War the Negro attracted the attention of the world by his dashing valor. He attracted the attention of his country also. His fighting quality was of the highest, unsurpassed, and perhaps unequalled in brilliancy by the rest of the American army that invaded Cuba. He elicited applause and grudging justice from his countrymen, dashed with envy and race prejudice. Still it seemed for a brief time that his conspicuous service had given his case against the Republic a little better standing in Court—a little better chance for a fair hearing at the Bar of Public Opinion. But our characteristic national emotionalism was too shallow and insincere to last. In fact, it died aborning. The national habit of a century and a half reasserted itself. There was no attempt made to square national profession and national practice, national promise and national performance. The Negro again had given his all to his country and had got in return at the hands of that country wrong and injustice. Southern propaganda presently renewed all of its vicious and relentless activity against the Negro. He was different, he was alien, he was unassimilable, he was inferior, and he must be kept so, and in the scheme of things he must be made forever subordinate to the white race. In this scheme of things white domination could best be preserved by the establishment of a caste system based on race and color. And so following the Spanish-American War the North and the South put their heads together to complete their caste system. Everywhere throughout the Republic race prejudice, color proscription grew apace. One by one rights and privileges which the Negroes had enjoyed for a brief space were withdrawn and the wall of caste rose higher and higher. He was slowly and surely being shut out from all the things which white men enjoyed by virtue of their citizenship, and shut within narrowing limits of freedom. Everywhere within his prison house he read in large and sinister letters, "Thus far and no farther." He was trapped, and about to be caged. In spite of the Emancipation Proclamation and the Three War Amendments he found that white men were becoming bolder in ignoring or violating his freedom and citizenship under them. The walls of the new bondage were closing about his right to life, liberty and the pursuit of happiness in this boasted Land of the Free and Christian Home of Democratic Hypocrisy and Cruelty.

Then Mr. Taft appeared upon the scene and became famous or infamous as a builder on the walls of the Temple of the New American Jerusalem, where profession is High Priest to the God of Broken Promises. He proved himself a master workman in following the lines of caste, in putting into place a new stone in the edifice when he announced as his policy at the beginning of his administration that he would not appoint any colored man to office in the South where the whites objected. Caste had won and the Negro's status was fixed, as far as this bourgeois apostle of American Democracy was able to fix it. His adds but another illustrious name to the long list of those architects of national dishonor who sought to build the Temple of American Liberty upon a basis of caste.

Then in the fullness of time came Woodrow Wilson, the ripe, consummate fruit of all this national contradiction between profession and practice, promise and performance. He can give Messrs. Washington, Jefferson, Jackson and Company odds and beat them in the subtle art of saying sonorously, grandiosely, what in action he does not hesitate to flout and spurn. When seeking the Negro's vote in 1912 he was the most profuse and generous in eloquent profession, in iridescent promises, but when he was elected he forgot straightway those fair professions and promises and began within a week after he entered the White House to put into office men filled with colorphobia, the better to finish the work of undoing in the government the citizenship of the Negro, to whom he had promised not grudging justice but the highly sympathetic article, heaping up and running over. Mr. Taft had established the principle that no Negro was to be appointed to office in the South where the whites objected—Mr. Wilson carried the principle logically one step farther, namely, no Negro was to be put to work in any department of the Government with white men and women if these white men and women objected to his presence. Segregation along the color line in Federal employment became forthwith the fixed policy of the Wilson administration.

There sprang up under the malign influence of this false prophet of the New Freedom all sorts of movements in the District of Columbia and in the Federal Government hostile to the Negro—movements to exclude him from all positions under the Civil Service above that of laborer and messenger and charwoman, to jim-crow him on the street cars, to prohibit him from intermarrying with the whites, to establish for him a residential pale in the District; in short, to fix forever his status as a permanently inferior caste in the land for which he had toiled in peace and bled and died in war. The evil influence of this false apostle of freedom spread far and wide and spurred the enemies of the Negro to unwonted activity. The movement of residential segregation and for rural segregation grew in volume and momentum in widely separated parts of the country until it was finally checked by the decision of the Supreme Court in 1917.

The condition of the Negro was at its worst and his outlook in America at its darkest when the Government declared war against Germany. Then was revived the Republic's program of false promises and hypocritical professions in order to bring this black man with his brawn and brains, with his horny hands and lion heart, with his unquenchable loyalty and enthusiasm to its aid. No class of its citizens surpassed him in the swiftness and self-forgetfulness of his response to the call of country. What he had to give he brought to the altar and laid it there—labor and wealth, wounds and death, with unsurpassed devotion and patriotism. But what he received in return was the same old treatment, evil for his good, ingratitude and treachery for his loyalty and service. He was discriminated against everywhere—was used and abused, shut out from equal recognition and promotion with white men and women. Then when he went overseas he found American colorphobia more deadly than the gun and poison gas of the Germans. In the American army there was operated a ceaseless propaganda of meanness and malice, of jealousy and detraction against him. If our Expeditionary Force had given itself with a tithe of the zeal and industry to fighting the Germans, which a large section of it devoted to fighting the black soldier, it would have come out of the war with more honor and credit, and left behind in France a keener sense of gratitude and regard than exists for them in that country today. But, alas, thousands of them were more interested in watching the Negro and his reception by the French, in concocting villainous plots to degrade him in the eyes of that people, in segregating him from all social contact with them, and in keeping him in his place, within the hard and fast lines of caste which they had laid for him in America.

But the Negro went and saw—saw the incredible meanness and malice of his own country by the side of the immense genius for Liberty and Brotherhood of France. There he found himself a man and brother regardless of his race and color. But if he has seen these things in France he has also conquered certain other things in himself, and has come back not as he went but a New Negro. He has come back to challenge injustice in his own land and to fight wrong with a courage that will not fail him in the bitter and perhaps bloody years to come. For he knows now as he has never known before that he is an American citizen with the title deeds of his citizenship written in a century and a half of labor and suffering and blood. From his brave black lips I hear the ringing challenge, "This is my right and by the Eternal I have come back to claim all that belongs to me of industrial and political equality and liberty." And let us answer his high resolve with a courage and will to match his own, and so help to redeem our country from its shame of a century and a half of broken promises and dishonored ideals.

But be not deceived, friends. Let us, like brave men and women, face the stern reality of our situation. We are where we are. We are in the midst of a bitter and hitherto an invincible race-prejudice, which beats down into the dust all of our rights, all of our attainments, all of our aspirations after freedom and excellence. The North and the South are in substantial accord in respect to us and in respect to the position which we are to occupy in this land. We are to be forever exploited, forever treated as an alien race, allowed to live here in strict subordination and subjection to the white race. We are to hew for it wood, draw for it water, till for it the earth, drive for it coaches, wait for it at tables, black for it boots, run for it errands, receive from it crumbs and kicks, to be for it, in short, social mudsills on which shall rest the foundations of the vast fabric of its industrial democracy and civilization.

No one can save us from such a fate but God, but ourselves. You think, I know, that the North is more friendly to you than the South, that the Republican party does more for the solution of this problem than the Democratic. Friends, you are mistaken. A white man is a white man on this question, whether he lives in the North or in the South. Of course, there are splendid exceptions. Scratch the skin of Republican or Democrat, of Northern white men or Southern white men, and you will find close to the surface race prejudice, American colorphobia. The difference, did you but know it, is not even epidermal, is not skin-deep. The hair is Democratic Esau's, and the voice is Republican Jacob's. That is all. Make no mistake here, for a true understanding of our actual position at this point is vital.

On Boston Commons stands a masterpiece in bronze, erected to commemorate the heroism and patriotism of Col. Robert Gould Shaw and his black regiment. There day and night, through summer and winter, storm and shine, are to march forever those brave men by the side of their valiant young leader. Into the unknown they are hurrying to front and to fight their enemies and the enemies of their country. They are not afraid. A high courage looks from their faces, lives in the martial motion of their bodies, flashes from the barrels of their guns. On and yet ever on they are marching, grim bolts of war, across the Commons, through State Street, past the old State House, over ground consecrated by the martyr's blood of Crispus Attucks, and the martyr's feet of William Lloyd Garrison. Farther and farther they are pressing forward into the unknown, into the South, to Wagner and immortal deeds, to death and an immortal crown.

Friends, we too are marching through a living and lowering present into the unknown, through an enemy's land, at the summons of duty. We are to face great labors, great dangers, to fight like men our passions and American caste-prejudice and oppression, and God helping us, to conquer them.[1]

[1] Grimké, *The Shame of America, or the Negro's Case Against the Republic.*

VICTORY FOR THE ALLIES AND THE UNITED STATES A GROUND OF REJOICING, OF THANKSGIVING[1]

BY REV. FRANCIS J. GRIMKÉ[2]

O Clap your hands, all ye peoples; Shout unto God with the voice of Triumph.

At this time, there are many reasons why we should rejoice:

(1) At last this bloody war, the most frightful, the most devastating and widespread that has ever occurred, involving practically all the nations of the world, has come to an end. I wonder if we fully realize what that means? It means that no longer the deadly submarine will be sinking merchant and other vessels in mid-ocean; it means that no longer airships will be showering down explosive bombs on cities, killing innocent women and children; it means the end of trench life, with its almost intolerable conditions; it means that no longer great armies will be pitted against each other in deadly conflict with thousands of dead and dying men following in their train; it means that no longer there shall be hospital ships and hospital trains bringing day by day from the battlefields thousands of shattered, wounded, mutilated men to be cared for and to go down life's way maimed; it means the end of the anxiety of the fathers and mothers as they scan the casualty lists as they are published from time to time; it means the end of all the awful things that have been happening during the last four years, as the result of this conflict.

Some time ago, I read a little volume entitled, "The Challenge of the Present Crisis," by Harry Emerson Fosdick, and was particularly impressed with the ghastly, hideous, awful aspect of war as he there sets it forth. Here is what he says:

[1] Delivered at the Fifteenth Street Presbyterian Church, Washington, D. C., December 24, 1918.

[2] Francis J. Grimké was born a slave in Charleston, South Carolina, November 4, 1850. At the close of the War, he went north to be educated. After some difficulties in finding such an opportunity, he entered Lincoln University in Chester County, Pennsylvania. There he took high rank as a student and was graduated in 1870. He then studied law there and served the institution as Financial Agent. Directing his attention then to theology, he entered Princeton Theological Seminary from which he was graduated in 1878. He immediately went to Washington, D. C., to take charge of the Fifteenth Street Presbyterian Church. Since then, he has distinguished himself, not only as a scholarly and influential minister, but as an outspoken defender of the rights of the Negro.

"One who knows what really is happening on European battlefields today and calls war glorious is morally unsound. Says an eye-witness: 'Last night, at an officers' mess, there was great laughter at the story of one of our men who had spent his last cartridge in defending an attack. "Hand me down your spade, Mike," he said; and, as six Germans came one by one 'round the end of a traverse, he split each man's skull open with a deadly blow.' That is war. Says a Young Men's Christian Association secretary: 'Many times these fingers have reached through the skulls of wounded men and felt their throbbing brains.' That is war. An officer's letter from the front reads:

" 'An enemy mine exploded here a few days ago and buried our brigade. Many of the men were killed, but some were not much hurt; so we dug them out and used them over again.'

"Sons of God and brothers of Jesus Christ—'dug them out and used them over again'! That is war. Said a group of German prisoners, as they bared their gashed forearms, 'We were dying with thirst—we had our choice of doing what some men do in such a case—drink the blood of an enemy or else drink our own blood. We are Christians; so we cut our own arms to get drink.' That is war. War is not the gay color, the rhythmic movement, the thrilling music of the military parade. War is not even killing gallantly as the knights of old once did, matched evenly in armor and in steed and fighting by the rules of chivalry. War now is dropping bombs from aeroplanes and killing women and children in their beds; it is shooting, by telephonic orders, at an unseen place miles away and slaughtering invisible men; it is murdering innocent travellers on merchant ships with torpedoes from unknown submarines; it is launching clouds of poison gas and slaying men with their own breath. War means lying days and nights wounded and alone in No-Man's Land; it means men with jaws gone, eyes gone, limbs gone, minds gone; it means countless bodies of boys tossed into the incinerators that follow in the train of every battle; it means untended wounds and gangrene and the long time it takes to die; it means mothers who look for letters they will never see and wives who wait for voices they will never hear, and children who listen for footsteps that will never come. That is war—'Its heroisms are but the glancing sunlight on a sea of blood and tears.' And through all these physical horrors runs a horror more appalling still, the persistent debauching and brutalizing of men's souls. One who uses his knowledge and his imagination to perceive in its abominations what war really is, while he might never dream of using Walt Whitman's language, finds it hard to be sorry that the language has been used. 'Wars,' he said, 'are hellish business—all wars. Any honest man says so—hates war, fighting, blood-letting. I was in the midst of it all—saw war where war was worst—not in the battlefields, no—in the hospitals; there war is worst; there I mixed with it, and now I say God damn the wars—all wars; God damn every war; God damn 'em! God damn 'em!' "

These are the words of a man who knows what wars are, not from hearsay, but from actual experience. And his language is not too strong. It is justified by the facts.

All wars are terrible, are detestable, but there has been no such war in its barbarity and naked brutality in all the history of the world, as the one through which we have just passed. Within the short space of a little over four years, just 1,556 days, millions of men have been slaughtered in battle, millions have been wounded, thousands upon thousands have been permanently disabled, millions of others have perished, leaving behind millions of widows and orphans. A conservative estimate places the number of soldiers and civilians who have been killed, wounded, disabled, or affected seriously in other ways, at between forty and fifty millions. We can't begin, as yet, to realize fully what a terrible, awful tragedy of blood, of suffering, of sorrow and woe, through which the world has been passing within the past quadrennium! And now, at last, the whole horrible business is over, and over, we trust, never again to be repeated until time shall be no more. One such war is enough for all the generations that are to come. Thank God, it is over; and it is meet and proper that we should rejoice, as we have been doing. On the afternoon and evening of the day when the announcement was officially made by the President to both houses of Congress, what a note of gladness ran all through the city. In every possible way the people sought to express their joy—white and black, rich and poor, high and low—all classes, conditions, races, colors, had a part in the jubilation. For once there was no division or separation, but all seemed to be moved by one common sentiment, as all ought to be, in all matters of public interest.

We are all American citizens, and have an equal interest in the closing of this bloody conflict.

(2) Another reason why we should be glad, should be grateful to God, is because this bloody conflict has ended in victory for the Allies and the United States of America. In making this a ground of rejoicing, it is not because I think that the skirts of the Allies and of the United States are clean; for they are not. These Allied nations of Europe have all of them been oppressors, have all of them been taking advantage of the darker and weaker races, exploiting them for their own selfish interest. They have all of them, for centuries, in their dealings with darker and weaker races, been acting on the principle of might instead of right. They have all of them been a unit in their purpose and determination to keep the world safe for white supremacy. They have all looked with disfavor upon any attempt on the part of any race, not embraced within their peculiar circle of affiliated races, to advance, to go forward, to assert itself, to demand for itself proper recognition and respect. This is why they look askance at Japan; why they are jealous of her; why they would hamper her more than they do, if they dared to.

So far as making the world safe for white supremacy, there is no difference, or very little, between the Central Powers and the Allies. And this war would never have been brought on had Germany been content with the status quo—with the supremacy of the white races over all the darker and weaker race. But Germany got into her head the idea of a super-man, and of a super-nation, and the super-man and -nation, the military caste in Germany, felt itself to be the German nation; and, that it was the prerogative, the divinely appointed prerogative, of this nation of super-men not only to be supreme over all darker and weaker races, but also over all the other white races as well. And there is where the rub came, where the trouble began, and that is why the war came on. The other white races, while perfectly willing to join Germany in keeping the world safe for white supremacy, were not willing to keep it safe for German supremacy—were not willing themselves to come under the German yoke. And so the war began; and so it has been fought out. And the thing that has been settled by it definitely is that Germany is not to be supreme over the other white races. That much has certainly been definitely settled. No one white race or nation is to be supreme over all other white races and nations. Though there is no objection, there certainly was not up to four years ago, to the white races holding together to keep down all the darker races.

In the treatment of weaker and darker races, there was no difference, I said, between the Central Powers and the Allies. Nor is there any difference between the Central Powers and the United States of America in this regard. In our rejoicings that victory, in this great conflict, is on the side on which the United States has been fighting, doesn't mean that we believe that its skirts are clean, that it is all that it ought to be in its appreciation of, and respect for, the rights of man; for it is not; its skirts are far from being clean.

I am well aware of the fact that we would like to get the credit for being greatly interested in democratic institutions—in making the world safe for democracy. But the simple fact is we feel no interest whatever in the reign of true democracy, which recognizes the right of every man, of whatever race or color, to have a part, and an equal part, in the government under which he lives. Lincoln had the right idea of what it meant, when he spoke of "Government of the people, by the people, for the people, shall not perish from the earth"; the framers of the great war amendments to the Constitution had the right idea when they wrote into the Fourteenth Amendment the words, "All persons born or naturalized in the United States, and subject to the jurisdiction thereof, are citizens of the United States and of the State wherein they reside. . . . Nor shall any State make or enforce any law which shall abridge the privileges or immunities of citizens of the United States; nor shall any State deprive any person of life, liberty, or property, without due process of law, nor deny any person within its jurisdiction the equal protection of the laws." And also into the Fifteenth Amendment, the words, "The right of citizens of the United States to vote shall not be denied or abridged by the United States, or by any State, on account of race, color, or previous condition of servitude."

That is not the idea of democracy, however, that is entertained by the Democratic party in this country, especially by the southern wing of it. Their idea of democracy, and it is the idea of the Administration, takes in only white men, only their rights are to be considered; only their rights are to be respected, are to be held sacred, inviolate. Men of darker hue have no rights which white men are bound to respect. And it is this narrow, contracted, contemptible, undemocratic idea of democracy that we have been fighting to make the world safe for, if we have been fighting to make it safe for democracy at all. We certainly have not been fighting to make it safe for true democracy—for democracy in any adequate or worthy sense of the term. How could we be fighting to make the world safe for democracy, except in pretense, with conditions existing as they are within our own borders, and with no desire or effort to remedy them? How could we, except in pretense, be fighting to make the world safe for democracy, and at the same time give ourselves no concern about safeguarding it at home? How can we, with any degree of honesty, of sincerity, claim to be fighting to make the world safe for democracy, when we are trampling upon the sacred, God-given, and constitutional rights of twelve millions of colored American citizens within our borders? Are the discriminations, the mean, contemptible, unworthy, and debasing discriminations that are practiced even in the departments of the government itself, and with the sanction of the Chief Executive of the Nation, who acclaims himself as the great champion of world-democracy, consistent with true democratic ideas and ideals—with the kind of democracy that is likely to be a blessing to the world? Are Jim Crow cars, insecurity of life and property, the most flagrant violations of the simplest principles of right, of justice, of humanity, and the brutal lynchings that go on, month after month, year after year—lynchings that are unsurpassed in sheer, cold-blooded, wanton cruelty by the worst atrocities of the Germans, consistent with true democratic ideas and ideals? The very men who are responsible for these outrages, who allow them to go on without any effort to remedy them, know that they are not. And yet we expect people on the other side of the water, who know conditions here, to believe that we are so tremendously interested in the fate of democracy throughout the world, that we are willing to lay our all upon the altar of sacrifice in its defense. On the face of it, it is nothing but sheer hypocrisy.

Two things I feel perfectly sure of in my own mind:

(1) That, as a Nation, we have little or no interest in true democracy—in the rights of man as man. We have not yet de-

veloped sufficiently along moral and spiritual lines to an appreciation of the dignity of man, of the true worth of man as man, created in the image of God; we are still blinded by our narrow racial prejudice; we are still so contemptibly little in our moral ideas and ideals that the color of a man's skin is to us of more value, of more importance than anything else in determining the kind of treatment that shall be accorded to him. Mr. Vardaman once said in the United States Senate, or, in an interview which someone had with him over the appointment of a colored man as Register of the Treasury, that the race question was paramount to all other issues—greater than the currency, greater than the tariff or anything else. And the fact that it is paramount, in the estimation of such a large proportion of white Americans, shows what kind of democracy is represented in this country, what kind of democracy we stand for—a democracy that counts for nothing among decent, self-respecting, right-thinking, liberty-loving men the world over. We are interested in democracy, yes, but not in true democracy—democracy that is color-blind, that rests upon the brotherhood of man, and the sacredness of the rights of all men, as men.

(2) I feel perfectly sure of another thing, our entrance into the war was not from any disinterested motive, it was from purely selfish considerations. We did not enter it as a matter of fact, until it seemed that the Central Powers were likely to be victorious; then it was that we stepped into the breach. Why, then, and not before? Because we knew perfectly well, from our knowledge of the German character and of the aim of the Kaiser for world empire, that as soon as the Allies were conquered, that our turn would come next, and, therefore, unless we joined with them before it was too late, there was no possible escape for us from the same fate. And this, I believe, notwithstanding our pretended interest in making the world safe for democracy, was the reason that took us into the war. It was in self-defense; it was in order to keep from off our own neck the yoke of German military despotism. It was all right, of course, in entering, as we did to save ourselves; and in so doing we have helped also to save the Allied nations, and to save the world from the heel of the oppressor. And for that, we deserve credit, and will receive credit; but we should receive credit only for what we are justly entitled to. We ought not to want credit for what we are not entitled to—to have ascribed to

us motives which did not actuate us, or, if they did at all, only in a minor or secondary way. We did not go into the war from any real interest in democracy. If we did, we would have long since brought forth fruits meet for repentance—we would be treating our twelve million colored citizens better than we are. And, while we are rejoicing that victory has crowned our efforts in conjunction with the Allies, we are not insensible, and ought not to be, of how far short as a Nation we come when measured by the ideals of true democracy, and the great eternal principles of right and brotherhood.

(3) There is another reason why we should be glad. It is because with the end of this war there has come the end of autocratic government throughout the world—the end of the one-man power to determine the destiny of a people or nation; the end of the arrogant assumption of the divine right to rule regardless of the will of the people. There are to be no more kaisers; no more czars; no more emperors with autocratic powers. The reign of the people has come—the reign of the common people. It is wonderful when you think of it! Four years ago, autocracy seemed never more firmly entrenched in the world than then. There was Russia, that great despotism, with a system of espionage that ramified throughout the whole empire; with its prisons filled with political offenders, and its Siberia of horrors, with thousands and thousands of innocent men and women torn from their homes, from their friends and relatives, sent there to die in want and misery, simply because they dared to think for themselves. Where is the Russian Empire today? Gone. Where is the despot who sat upon the throne? In his grave, murdered, and other members of his family also lying in dishonored graves. Where is the empire of Austria-Hungary—where is it? Gone. Where is the proud house of the Hapsburgs, that for hundreds of years sat upon the throne? Gone. The old Emperor Joseph, who was on the throne when the war began, died from old age, and of a broken heart, and the man who succeeded him, where is he? A fugitive now in Switzerland. And last of all, there was Germany, proud Germany, with a man at the head who never would admit, who spurned the idea of getting his right to rule from the people, who proclaimed himself ruler by divine right, and who held himself responsible to God only, and not to the people;

a man who, inflated with pride, felt that his mailed fist could bring the whole world to his feet.

Where is the German Empire today? Gone—a thing of the past. Where is the man who aspired to universal dominion, who shot defiance at the whole world? Where is he? Gone. No longer on his throne—forced by the very people whom he affected to ignore, to renounce his throne, and is now away from his home and his country seeking hospitality from a little kingdom, one of the smallest in Europe, stripped of all power. How wonderful it all seems, and all within the short space of four years. Lowell in his "Ode to France," describing the effect of the French Revolution, wrote these words:

"O Broker King, is this thy wisdom's fruit?
A dynasty plucked out as 't were a weed
Grown rankly in a night, that leaves no seed!
Could eighteen years strike down no deeper root?
But now thy vulture eye was turned on Spain—
A shout from Paris, and thy crown falls off,
Thy race has ceased to reign,
And thou become a fugitive and scoff;
Slippery the feet that mount by stairs of gold,
And weakest of all fences one of steel;
Go and keep school again like him of old,
The Syracusan tyrant—thou mayest feel
Royal amid a birch-swayed commonweal!

"Not long can he be ruler who allows
His time to run before him; thou wast naught
Soon as the strip of gold about thy brows
Was no more emblem of the People's thought;
Vain were thy bayonets against the foe
Thou hadst to cope with; thou didst wage
War not with Frenchmen merely—no,
Thy strife was with the Spirit of the Age,
The invisible Spirit whose first breath divine
Scattered thy frail endeavor,
And, like poor last year's leaves, whirled thee and thine
Into the dark forever!"

How striking is the language, and how accurately it describes the fate of the great autocracies that existed four years ago. Yes, "Like poor last year's leaves," they have been "whirled into the dark forever."

It is a ground of rejoicing, of thanksgiving, I say, that such governments no longer exist to curse the world. And the reason why the destruction of such governments becomes a ground for rejoicing is because all such governments rest upon the idea of might instead of right—rest upon the will of the one or the few instead of the will of the many. Whether that will be right or wrong, if there is power to enforce it, it is enforced. The issue between might and right has been clearly drawn during this conflict and fought out on a broad, world-wide arena. The issue has been in the thought of all the peoples of the earth as never before. The attempt on the part of Germany to accomplish by might what it had no right to attempt to do, has been brought home to the other nations and brought home to them in a way that they can never forget. All the blood that has been spilt, the lives that have been sacrificed, the billions of treasures that have been poured out, and all the wretchedness and misery that have grown out of this war, might have been avoided if the principle of right had been followed instead of might. The nations of the earth know now as they have never known before the evil of acting on the principle of might instead of right.

After these four years of unparalleled suffering there is every reason to believe that there is going to be a great change in the policy of nations toward each other. In their relations, one with the other, the principle of right, instead of might, is going to have a larger place than it has ever had before. The nations, in their relations with each other, will come, more and more, to realize, that even as a matter of policy, if not of principle, it is always better to follow the lead of right instead of might. And when that principle has been accepted, has firmly rooted itself in the consciousness of the nations of the earth as the course to be followed in their dealing with each other, then we may expect another thing to follow, another thing that must follow, that will inevitably follow, each nation within its own limits will come to feel that the same principles must govern. If right and not might is to determine the course to be pursued between nations in their dealings and relations with each other; then right and not might ought also to determine what goes on in their internal management as well. In this great world contest that has just closed, might as the great determining principle between nations has been driven to the wall. And, although there is no longer the boom of cannon, the roar of musketry, the battle will still go on, in each nation, until the same great principle triumphs within as well as without. A nation cannot consistently insist upon the principle of right in its dealings with other nations, and in the dealings of other nations with it, and permit the opposite principle to prevail in the management of its internal affairs. Right must prevail within as well as without. And until it does, there must be and will be constant agitation; the war for the triumph of right must go steadily on. And it will go on. And this is why the overthrow of the great autocracies or despotisms of the world, as the result of the war, becomes a ground of thanksgiving, of rejoicing. It is a step forward in the overthrow, ultimately, of the doctrine, which has so long dominated the world, that might makes right. This war, in its results, is going to make it easier to fight that pernicious principle as it shows itself in social and political injustice and oppression within nations as well as without.

The overthrow of the great autocracies in Europe, and the assertion of the right of the people to rule, as has been most emphatically done during these four bloody years, is going to make it easier for us as a people in this country to achieve what we have been contending for for years, and will go on contending for, our rights—our full rights as American citizens. We are not going to be satisfied; and, we have greater reasons now than ever before for not being satisfied. The air everywhere is filled now as never before with the thought of the rights of man. Liberty is in the air today as it has never been before in all the world's history—never before on so wide a scale. And, in addition to this, we have had a part in this world-wide contest; we have made sacrifices, we have shed our blood, we have given of our treasures; thousands of our boys are on the other side of the water, and have done their part in bringing about the great result. And when these boys get back, having sniffed the free, invigorating, liberty-loving air of France, that knows no man by the color of his skin, but makes all men of all races and complexions equally welcome, there has got to be a change here. These boys will bring back that spirit with them, and it will have to be reckoned with. They know now what it is to be a man, and to be treated as a man. And that spirit will remain with them. It cannot be quenched. It will rather be sure to communicate itself to others. They will not be satisfied, nor will we be satisfied, until segregation in these departments is done away with; until the men and women of our race are no longer discriminated against, but are accorded the same consideration as white men and women are accorded. They are not going to be satisfied, nor will we be, until Jim Crow cars are no more, until the men and women of our race are allowed to travel in decency, and to find equal accommodations in hotels, restaurants, and in places of amusement. The war over there is over; but the war over here for our manhood and citizenship rights is not over; and will not be over until they are all accorded to us as to other citizens of the Republic. So that while we are rejoicing here today, and we have good reasons to rejoice—the war is over; victory is on the side of the Allies and the United States; the great autocracies of the world have been destroyed; and might, as between nations, at least, instead of right has been struck a death blow—at the same time, we must not lose sight of the fact that victory over there does not necessarily mean victory over here; that the staggering blow that has been struck to might over there, doesn't necessarily mean that it will be felt equally over here; that here it is going to be any less insistent. So far as we are concerned, that old enemy, might, is still strongly entrenched. Why are we discriminated against in the departments? Why are we shut out of West Point? Out of Annapolis? Why are we not allowed to vote in the South? Why are we forced into Jim Crow cars? Why are we unjustly treated in the courts? Why are we brutally lynched? Is it because it is right? No, the right is all on our side—it is simply because they have the power. If right were allowed to come in, and control, all these evils would be remedied at once. So that, while we are rejoicing, as I said, let us see to it that we do not allow the advantages that have accrued to us, as the result of this war, to be lost. Instead of abating our efforts, lessening our endeavors, we should be more insistent than ever—more determined than ever to press the advantages that we have gained.

There are some members of our race, unfortunately, who have

been foolish enough to talk about letting up for a little while, as if our enemies ever let up, as if our enemies ever allow to pass a single opportunity of humiliating us, of forcing upon us conditions which are intended to impress upon us their view of us as inferiors. Should we be less insistent, less persistent, less determined, less alive, wide awake to the things that pertain to our rights, than the people who are sleeplessly vigilant in their efforts and determination to filch them from us to keep us in, what they call, our proper place, as if the proper place for any rational, responsible being is to be determined by anything except his character, efficiency, capability? It is astounding, almost incredible, that any colored man, even to the stupidest of them, should be led into such utter folly as to counsel the cessation of the struggle for our rights, even for a moment, when nothing is ever accomplished except by struggle, by earnest, persistent effort. The colored man, if he has an ounce of brains in his head, will have but one policy in regard to his rights, and that is the policy of being always on the job. Eternal vigilance is the price of liberty, and unless we are willing to pay the price, unless we are eternally vigilant, we will never get it. Let us hear no more of this nonsense, never mind from whom it comes, about letting up for a season. Not less activity, but more activity; not less agitation, but more agitation; not less plain speaking, but more plain speaking.

In an article which I wrote to the editor of the "Cleveland Advocate," these words occur: "I am writing to express my very great satisfaction at reading the two editorials in your issue of August 24th, entitled, 'Grave and Weighty,' and 'Riot of Oppression.' I was greatly delighted with them. They both have the right ring—the only kind of ring that ought ever to be heard from colored Americans—from intelligent, self-respecting colored Americans. This is no time for shilly-shallying, but for plain speaking, for a straightforward, manly presentation of our wrongs, made all the more flagrant in view of the tremendous sacrifices which we are now being called upon to make and which we are willingly making. These outrageous, damnable discriminations that are being made against us in the departments here and elsewhere all over the country, call for loud, persistent, unceasing protest. We ought not to be satisfied as long as they continue; and the time to voice our dissatisfaction is now while the war is going on; while we are going across the sea to lay our lives down in order to make the world safe for democracy. From every Negro newspaper in the country, from every city, town and hamlet, from all kinds of Negro organizations, there should be coming up to Washington a word of solemn and emphatic protest. The fight that you are making, the stand which you are taking on the race issue at this time is the one that ought to be taken, is the fight that ought to be made not only by you, but by every intelligent, right-thinking, self-respecting colored American.''

In the August 21st issue of the *Outlook,* these lines occur:

> ''We are on the march! How long shall we be marching?
> Until the roads of east and west are free;
> Until beneath the four winds of the world
> Freedom is possible for all mankind;
> Until we reach the end of the long journey;
> Until time brings the fulness of the years.
> A faith in arms is marching to the future;
> Its flags are consecrated to the dawn.''

And we, colored men and women in this country, if I sense aright the sentiment of our hearts, are on the march for our rights, and we will not stop until ''we reach the end of the long journey.'' The war that we are waging here, while our brothers are fighting on the other side, will help to hasten the dawn. That is what I wrote some three months ago; and that is the way I feel today; and is the way we all ought to feel, and must feel, if we are to hasten the dawn of better things for ourselves, and for our children.

(4) There is still another ground for thanksgiving and rejoicing, as the result of victory for the Allies and for the United States, but which I will have time simply to mention without stopping to dwell upon. As the result of this great struggle, through which we have been passing, I believe, it is going to be better for all the darker and weaker races of the world. It is going to be better for them because in the dominant nations a higher sense of justice, of right, of fair play, is going to be developed; better for them because I believe there is going to be developed a higher type of Christianity than at present prevails—than the miserable apology that now goes under that name. Things are as they are today in

these great nations of the world, and it has fared with these weaker and darker races and nations as it has, because the so-called Church of God has been recreant to its high trust; has been dominated by such a cowardly and worldly spirit that it has always been willing to listen to the voice of man instead of the voice of God—dominated by such a cowardly and worldly spirit that it has surrendered the most sacred principles of the holy religion of Jesus Christ, at the behest of the powers that be—at the bidding of wealth, social prestige and a debased public sentiment.

Look at Germany, during this terrible world-struggle through which we have been passing, and see the character of the Christianity represented there. Back of this bloody war, started by the Emperor of Germany and his military staff in sheer, wanton lust of power, and prosecuted with the utmost brutality, has been the Christian church of Germany—the men in the pews—the men in the sacred desk—the men in the chairs of theology in the great universities—the spiritual leaders of the nation—all, with rare exceptions, justified this atrocious war and threw the weight of their influence in support of the monster who sat on the throne, in his efforts to carry out his nefarious schemes of conquest and aggrandizement.

Look at the church in this country, forty millions strong! and yet, think of the awful conditions that exist here—of the injustices, and oppressions, and discriminations that go on unchecked, and no effort made to check them, to improve conditions. The very men who are back of these oppressions, injustices, discriminations, are, in many cases, not only professing Christians, but occupying high places in the church—ministers, elders, deacons, Sunday-school teachers, class leaders. These abominable conditions have sprung up, still exist, and are steadily growing worse in the midst of forty millions of Christians. Strange as it may seem, while the membership of these so-called Christian churches is increasing by the millions, race prejudice, with all the evils that grow out of it, is also steadily on the increase. In this city of Washington, the capital city of the nation, with scores of churches, representing all the great denominations, with services going on every Sunday and during the week in them all, where the Bible is supposed to be taught, and the noble and beautiful spirit of Christ, the spirit of meekness, of gentleness, of brotherly kindness, of self-sacrificing love, inculcated, in this Christian city, presided over by Commissioners, members of Christian churches—where the President of the United States and his Cabinet, the members of the Senate and the House of Representatives, and the Judges of the Supreme Court, and of the lesser courts are domiciled—all of whom, or nearly all of whom are members of Christian churches—in this city where Christianity has back of it so much respectability, so much official dignity and power—a colored man, if he were down on Pennsylvania Avenue, never mind how hungry he might be, couldn't find a restaurant in which he could get a cup of tea, or a sandwich and a glass of milk; or however tired he might be, is there a rest room into which he could go and be received, and simply because of the color of his skin, because of his race identity! That condition of things exists, has existed, and continues to exist, not against the protest of the Christian church, but with its sanction. A Christianity that allows such a condition of things to exist without throwing the weight of its great influence against it, is a spurious Christianity, is a disgrace to the holy and sacred name of Christ.

Out of this awful baptism of blood that has deluged the earth, I can't help feeling that God is getting ready for some great spiritual awakening—that He is getting ready to shake himself loose from this miserable semblance of Christianity that exists, and to set up in the earth a type of religion that will truly represent the spirit and teachings of Jesus Christ, a type of religion that will be as the inspired penman conceived it,

"Fair as the moon,
Clear as the sun,
Terrible as an army
with banners."

It is because I believe a better type of Christianity is to appear, and appear speedily, and that under its banner the world is to be conquered for Christ, and, in that conquest all the nations of the earth are to be blessed, that there is ground for thanksgiving, for rejoicing. Whether we realize it or not, God is on the throne; and, sooner or later, He will make even the wrath of man to praise Him. "The heathen may rage; the people imagine a vain thing;

the kings of the earth set themselves, and the rulers take counsel together against the Lord and against His anointed." Yet, the declaration is, "I have set my king upon my holy hill of Zion." "I will give thee the heathen for thine inheritance, and the uttermost part of the earth for thy possession." And again, "He shall have dominion from sea to sea, and from the river to the ends of the earth." So that there is bound to be, sooner or later, the triumph of right, of justice; there is bound to be, under the dominating influence of the spirit of Jesus Christ, under the development of a better type of Christianity, the establishment of better conditions throughout the whole world, for all the races of mankind. The whole plane of life is going to be lifted. There is going to be a new earth. Old things are going to pass away. Tennyson's dream is going to be realized. Certain things are to be rung in, and certain things rung out.

* * * * *

"Ring out the false, ring in the true.

* * * * *

Ring out the feud of rich and poor,
Ring in redress for all mankind.

"Ring out a slowly dying cause,
And ancient forms of party strife;
Ring in the nobler modes of life,
With sweeter manners, purer laws.

"Ring out the want, the care, the sin,
The faithless coldness of the times;
Ring out, ring out my mournful rhymes,
But bring the fuller minstrel in.

"Ring out false pride in place and blood,
The civic slander and the spite;
Ring in the love of truth and right,
Ring in the common love of good.

"Ring out old shapes of foul disease,
Ring out the narrowing lust of gold;
Ring out the thousand wars of old,
Ring in the thousand years of peace.

"Ring in the valiant man and free,
The larger heart, the kindlier hand;
Ring out the darkness of the land,
Ring in the Christ that is to be."

* * * * *

The super-man of the future is not to be of the German type, nor of the contemptible little type that we find here in America, assuming and acting upon the theory that under a white skin only is to be found anything worthy of respect; but of the Christ-type—

"The valiant man and free,
The larger heart, the kindlier hand."

The super-nation of the future is not to be the German nation, nor any of the existing nations, but the Commonwealth of Israel—the Church of the living God, purified, cleansed, Spirit-filled, God-centered, meek and lowly, girded with strength, and arrayed in beautiful garments of righteousness.

The close of this bloody war is the beginning, I believe, of the realization of this vision of better things which Tennyson saw, and which the prophets of old foresaw, and which I believe some day is going to be realized in the actual life of the world. And, it is going to be realized as the poet indicates, and, in no other way, by ringing Christ in—into our hearts—into our homes—into our churches, into our pulpits—into our colleges and universities—into our courts—into our halls of legislation—into our executive mansions—into our marts of commerce and places of business. The ringing in of Jesus Christ holds the solution of all our problems, racial or otherwise. The only cheering outlook for humanity—for the individual—for races—for nations in their internal management, as well as in their relations to each other, is to be found in accepting, and in honestly and courageously living out the principles and the spirit of Jesus Christ. And, this war has helped us, as, perhaps, nothing else has ever done in the history of the world, to realize that no mere culture, no amount of mere brain power, no advancement in science, in philosophy, in scholarship, in the accumulation of knowledge, however great, can lay the basis for lasting peace and happiness; can weld men together in one great brotherhood in which each will be interested in the well-being of the other—into a brotherhood that will be proof against the assaults of selfishness, and pride, and all the other debasing elements that are ever at work to set men against each other. Something more is needed—a new force or power of a spiritual nature must come in. And such a power or force we have in the personality of Jesus Christ. It is through him that all the families of the earth are to be blessed; it is through him that order is to come out of these conflicting passions and desires that tear men apart and keep them apart; that make them brutes instead of human beings. And, because this war, in showing the utter futility of all human devices in bringing peace to a troubled world, is driving us back to Jesus Christ—back to Christian principles and ideals, we rejoice—rejoice—we lift up our hearts in praise and gratitude to God.

"O clasp your hands all ye peoples;
Shout unto God with the voice of triumph."

INDEX